D1511115

Purdue Faculty Papers in Economic History, 1956-1966

HERMAN C. KRANNERT GRADUATE SCHOOL OF INDUSTRIAL ADMINISTRATION, PURDUE UNIVERSITY MONOGRAPH SERIES

Purdue Faculty Papers in Economic History 1956-1966

 1967
RICHARD D. IRWIN, INC.
Homewood, Illinois

First Printing, October, 1967

Library of Congress Catalog Card No. 67–17043

Printed in the United States of America

Introduction

THESE PAPERS require little in the way of introduction. They were written by members of the Purdue Economics faculty in the decade from 1956 to 1966 and published in the learned journals. In that period the new Economics Department at Purdue developed from infancy to a robust adulthood. Believing that, to some extent, history is the laboratory of economics, the faculty developed a Ph.D. program in quantitative economics which was unique in its emphasis upon the role of economic history in the training of the professional economist. Economic history advanced hand in hand with applied mathematics in the general development of modern economics on our campus.

The faculty practiced what it preached, and in these papers sparked a revolution in the study of economics using empirical materials drawn from history. Out of the faculty's interest in these matters grew the Purdue Seminar, which has drawn distinguished scholars to the campus from many lands for sessions of intensive discussion and study. This seminar, which we at Purdue jocularly named the Purdue Cliometrics Society, has become an ongoing vehicle for the continuation of quantitative work in Economic History.

The Krannert School, in deciding to make the Purdue faculty papers more generally available in this collection, hopes that continuing interest in the uses of our economic past will be encouraged.

> E. T. WEILER, Dean
> The Herman C. Krannert Graduate School
> of Industrial Adminsitration
> Purdue University

208376

Purdue University Economic History Conferences 1961-1966

1961 Meetings   (held December 1960)

J. H. McRandle and J. P. Quirk, "An Econometric Study of Strategic Decisions with Respect to the Anglo-German Naval Armaments Race, 1900–1914"

Robert Fogel, "The Social Savings Attributable to American Railroads in the Inter-regional Distribution of Agricultural Products in 1890: An Application of Mathematical Models to a Problem of History"

William Parker, "A Statistical Framework for Agricultural History"

G. W. Bertram, "The Process of Canadian Industrialization, 1870–1900"

George G. S. Murphy, "The Simple Structure of Some Historical Methods"

John W. Snyder, "Ancient Sumerian Economic Documents"

1962 Meetings   (held December 1961)

L. Davis, J. Quirk, and R. Saposnik, "A Simulation Model of the Northern World"

Richard Easterlin, "North on the Antebellum American Economy"

M. Simon and H. Segal, "A Simulation Model of British Economic Relationships with the Underdeveloped World of the 19th Century"

Paul David, "British Domestic Investment of the 1860's"

William Parker, "Output of the Farm Sector, 1840–1890"

Robert Gallman, "National Output in the 19th Century"

Dorothy Brady, "Some Aspects of the Effect of Technological Change on the Price Structure"

1963 Meetings

Robert Fogel, "The Position of Rails in the Market for American Iron, 1840–1860: A Palaeontological Reconstruction"

Eugene Genovese, "Food Costs of Slaves and Profitability of Slavery in the Antebellum South"

John Dales, "Industrialization as a Force Toward Retardation in the Rate of Canadian Economic Growth"

Dorothy Brady, "The Prices of Consumer Durable Goods"

Douglass North, "Trends in Ocean Freight Rates"

Charles Levin, "A Theory of Regional Economic Growth"

1964 Meetings

William Parker and Robert Gallman, "Civil War Southern Agriculture"

Roger Ransom, "Returns on the Ohio Canals: 1836–1860"

Peter Temin, "The Costs of Blast Furnace Operation in 1890"

Richard Easterlin, "Interrelations between Long Swings in Demographic and Economic Growth, U.S., 1820–1960"

Gordon Marker, "Internal Migration and Economic Opportunity: France, 1872–1911"

Rondo Cameron, "Banking in the Early Stages of Industrialization"

Harold Williamson, "Mass Production, Mass Consumption, and American Industrial Development"

Richard DuBoff, "Electrification and Capital Output-Ratios in American Manufacturing, 1880–1954: Some Preliminary Findings"

Eugene Smolensky, "A Model of Urban Growth: San Diego Case Study"

1965 Meetings

Heywood Fleisig, "The Costs of Mechanical Cotton Harvesting in the 19th Century"

Mancur Olsen, "Some Alleged 'Shortages of Money' in Medieval Europe"

John Bowman, "The Embattled Farmer Revisited"

Paul David, "The Mechanization of Grain Harvesting in the Antebellum Midwest"

R. Fogel and Stanley Engerman, "The U.S. Iron Industry in the 19th Century"

Marvin McInnis, "Regional Income Differentials in Canada"

William Whitney, "The Structure of the American Economy in the Late Nineteenth Century: An Exercise in Historical Input-Output Analysis"

Thomas Orsagh, "Trends in the Location of the German Smelting Industry, 1870–1914"

Robert Gallman and Edward Howle, "Capital Stock Estimates, 1840–1860"

Allen C. Kelley, "International Migration and Economic Growth: Australia, 1865–1935"

Robert Basmann, "The Role of the Economic Historian in the Predictive Testing of Proferred Economic Laws"

1966 Meetings

John Bowman, "The Embattled Farmer Revisited and Revisited Again"

William Parker, "This Little Pig Went to Market"

Richard Easterlin, "Economic-Demographic Interactions and Long Swings in Economic Growth"

Irwin Feller, "The Diffusion of the Draper Loom"

J. Fred Bateman, "The Evolution of the Dairy Industry"

Matthew Simon and David Novak, "European Imports as a Source of American Supply: 1870–1914"

Sam Bass Warner, "Industrial Location and City Growth: The Food Processing Industry"

Hal Williamson and N. Nadiri, "The Behavior of the General Price Level in the U.S., 1869–1914"

Table of Contents

PART IV

PART V

INDEX

PART I

1. Aspects of Quantitative Research in Economic History[*]

Lance E. Davis, Jonathan R. T. Hughes, and Stanley Reiter

Purdue University

I

IF WE ARE successfully to relate our work to the main body of economic history, we must be able to show the fundamental relationship between quantitative analysis and more conventional methods of economic historians. The historian reconstructs events of the past, and with them attempts to understand the institutions and modes of behavior associated with those events. He seeks to construct a consistent story revealing the fundamental nature and meaning to us of the past, thus creating insight into the past and understanding of it—something considerably beyond a mere account of what probably happened. However, this story must be based upon, and be consistent with, the reconstructed events of the past, "what probably happened."

This view of historical study is a familiar one and, in fact, almost any working historian would accept it as a definition of his activities. What has this view to do with quantitative methods in economic history, and how does quantitative economic history differ from nonquantitative writing in economic history? The answer lies partly in the nature of the materials from which the reconstruction is to be made, and partly in the technique employed to analyze these materials. We may distinguish two broad classes of materials. First, each society generates its own accounts of, and commentaries upon, contemporary affairs, as well as its own histories of the past. This class of materials can be more or less explicitly labeled historical writings. Second, in the course of its characteristic processes each society generates a body of artifacts, debris left behind in time. The processes of economic life, for example, produce masses of

* Reprinted from the *Journal of Economic History*, Vol. XX, No. 4 (December, 1960), pp. 539–47.

receipts, books of account, legal documents, tax returns, and various kinds of rolls, lists, and records; and these materials can be used to reconstruct the past. Such a reconstruction is analogous to the process frequently employed by archaeologists who utilize the surviving debris of an ancient city to provide materials for understanding the civilization that built it and lived there. Characteristically, this material consists of a mass of individual items, each of which contains a relatively insignificant piece of information. This collection, originally generated for purposes other than historical study, usually requires reorganization and analysis to enable the information contained to be brought to a form useful to the historian. That is, the information must be organized on some principle and made the basis of inferences about the past, a task familiar to the historian, but one that also contains the essential elements of a statistical problem.

If we had at hand every item of the kind under consideration (for example, every warehouse receipt issued in New York State between 1870–1900), we would face the task of formulating meaningful questions with which to confront these data, and of organizing the data to bear on these questions. Thus we might be interested in the geographical distribution of warehouses, in the time-shape of business activities, in the commodity composition of consumption, or in the profitability of warehousing, and each question would require a different method of systemization and analysis. We must, therefore, first formulate a statistical-historical model in terms of which historical meaning can be given to the observations. Having formulated such a model, we are still confronted with a large collection of observations that must be statistically summarized and described. We shall have more to say later about the problems of data processing.

In fact, however, since we generally do not have the complete collection of all observations of a given land, but rather only a sample of the surviving ones, the study of the historical process is even more complicated. For in addition to the question of analysis and systemization, we must also decide, on the basis of the observations at hand, what the whole collection would reveal if we had access to complete information. This last is the problem of statistical inference.

In brief, the logical structure necessary to make historical reconstructions from the surviving debris of past economic life essentially involves ideas of history, economics, and statistics. The offspring of such an act of interdisciplinary miscegenation calls for a name worthy of it; at Purdue the resulting discipline has been labeled "Cliometrics."

II

Your chairman has on occasion jocularly referred to us as the authors of *La Loi Lafayette* because of the frequent appearance of the tools of statistics and data processing in our work; however, this classification gives us too much credit. An examination of the literature of economic history indicates that, while the qualitative stream in the discipline has usually been the larger, there has been from earliest times a significant and respectable flow of quantitative work. The political arithmeticians —Graunt, King, and the like—as early as the 17th century were trying to infer from data an explanation of some aspects of economic history.[1] In 1851 William Newmarch produced his pathbreaking study on the circulation of bills of exchange—a study that, in statistical sophistication (given the knowledge of the time), is the equal of anything produced more recently.[2] At yet a later date, F. W. Taussig's *History of the Tariff*, and still later, the work of Arthur Cole (as represented both by his work on the evolution of the American foreign exchange market and with W. B. Smith, *Fluctuations in American Business 1790–1860*), were attempts to infer the state of the world of the past from quantitative information.[3] The National Bureau of Economic Research, although not much given to interpretation, has produced a vast amount of quantitative information that others could use, and the works of some of their authors (Kuznets, for example) certainly fall within the category of quantitative economic history.[4] More recently excellent work combining economic theory and quantitative methods can be found in R. C. O. Matthews' *A Study in Trade Cycle History* and in what is perhaps the most notable recent study of this kind, the paper by Conrad and Meyer on slavery in the antebellum South.[5]

---

[1] See, for example, Charles D'Avenant, *An Essay Upon the Probable Method of Making a People Gainers in the Balance of Trade* (London, 1699); John Graunt, *Natural and Political Observations Mentioned in a Following Index and Made Upon the Bills of Mortality* (London, 1662); Gregory King, *Natural and Political Observations and Conclusions Upon the State and Condition of England 1696* (London, 1810); Charles H. Hull (ed.), *The Economic Writings of Sir William Petty* (Cambridge, Mass., 1899).

[2] William Newmarch, "An Attempt to Ascertain the Magnitude and Fluctuations of the Amount of Bills of Exchange (Inland and Foreign) in Circulation at One Time in Great Britain, in England, in Scotland, in Lancashire, and in Cheshire, Respectively, During Each of the Twenty Years 1828–1847, Both Inclusive; and Also Embracing in the Inquiry Bills Drawn Upon Foreign Countries," *Journal of the Statistical Society of London*, Vol. XIV (1851), pp. 143–92.

[3] Frank W. Taussig, *The Tariff History of the United States* (New York and London. G. P. Putnam's Sons, 1888); Walter B. Smith and Arthur H. Cole, *Fluctuations in American Business 1790–1860* (Cambridge, Mass.: Harvard University Press, 1935); Arthur H. Cole, "Seasonal Variation in Sterling Exchange," *Journal of Economic and Business History*, Vol. II (November, 1929) pp. 203–318; Arthur H. Cole, "Evolution of the Foreign Exchange Market of the United States," *Journal of Economic and Business History*, Vol. I (1928), pp. 384–421.

[4] See, for example, Simon Kuznets, *National Product Since 1869* (New York: National Bureau of Economic Research, 1946); or Simon Kuznets, *Secular Movements in Production and Prices; Their Nature and Bearing Upon Cyclical Fluctuations* (Boston and New York: Houghton Mifflin, 1930); or "Long-Term Changes in the National Income of the United States Since 1870," *Income and Wealth of the United States Trends and Structure*, Series II, pp. 10–246.

[5] R. C. O. Matthews, *A Study in Trade Cycle History; Economic Fluctuations in Great Britain, 1833–1842* (Cambridge, Eng.: University Press, 1954); Alfred H. Conrad and John R. Meyer, "The Economics of Slavery in the Ante Bellum South," *Journal of Political Economy*, Vol. LXVI (April, 1958), pp. 95–130.

Nonetheless, the total amount of work in the field is small. Why? Is it because quantitative work is unrewarding? We think not. The dearth of quantitative economic history can probably be traced to two factors: first, the extraordinary effort that has been necessary in the past to sift and classify quantitative information; and second, the relatively recent development of statistical theory and techniques capable of handling these problems. Let us examine each of these problems in turn.

III

Recently developed computing equipment has opened to economic historians the possibility of performing prodigies of data processing and statistical calculation. Where the archaeologist can dig with spade and hard labor into the mounds of the past to unearth artifacts, the economic historian needs power shovels and bulldozers to move the mountains of paper records. The power shovels and bulldozers are now available to economic historians, but these developments in the analysis of data by machine processing methods have scarcely been applied to the more significant questions of economic history. We need to recognize that data processing at last provides us an opportunity to study the kinds of problems that, because of the unwieldiness of the purely mechanical processes of computation, have long been cast aside.

There is nothing novel or revolutionary in the problems themselves. There have always been problems in which masses of data had to be "processed" by one means or another; the early work on index numbers by Jevons and Sauerbeck are well-known examples of such large-scale computations. Another, and better, example of early data processing is to be found in the work of one of our most illustrious predecessors, William Newmarch. His work is a particularly germane example of the nature of data processing problems.

Newmarch's celebrated survey of the circulation of bills of exchange in Great Britain, one of the most brilliant contributions of the British monetary-policy debate of the mid-19th century (although not one which noticeably affected policy, interestingly enough), and subsequently, one of the pieces of historical evidence most often used in the study of 19th-century monetary phenomena, appeared in 1851.[6] Anyone who has processed data will experience a distinct "shock of recognition" when he first reads Newmarch's paper. Newmarch obtained a sample "at hazard" of the total bill circulation. The sample size was 4,367 inland and foreign bills with a nominal value of £1,216,974. From each bill he took three pieces of information, or a total of 13,101 separate pieces of numerical information. On the basis of these data and the stamp-tax returns on bills of exchange for Great Britain and certain subdivisions Newmarch

---

[6] Newmarch, "Circulation."

was able to compute an estimate of the total bill circulation. In his computation only three arithmetic operations were required once the initial classification and organization of the data had been done. Such a study by present-day computing standards would not be cumbersome. In "The First 1,945 British Steamships," for example, there were 13 initial observations per ship, or 25,285 separate pieces of numerical information on 1,945 punch cards.[7] Once on the cards, the actual computing (far more extensive than was Newmarch's) of tonnages, estimated speeds, and the index of transport capacity was not a particularly tiresome job. But in Newmarch's case, 100 years ago, 13,101 separate pieces of information to be classified, summed, averaged, and the results used to convert stamp-tax yields into aggregate value figures was an enormous undertaking. After explaining his ingenious methods to his audience, Newmarch noted that the final operations were:

. . . clearly a mere matter of calculation; but I confess that, if I had foreseen, before I undertook the task, the extent and severity of the labour it would impose, I am not at all certain that I should have ventured upon the inquiry.[8]

That data processing on this scale was done so long ago with quill pens instead of electronic computers underscores our main point. It is only the absence of machinery which is novel in the Newmarch story, not the presence of a data processing problem. Some kinds of historical problems are by nature data processing problems. In the past they have too often (but perhaps understandably) been neglected simply because too much labor was involved. Today, with the purely mechanical computational problems much reduced, economic historians have the means to study these questions. In particular these new techniques will permit the opening of new sources that, while always in existence, have heretofore been largely closed to research because of the magnitude of the task involved. First, business records that hold many of the answers to questions concerning early 19th-century American development can be made available to the study of broader questions than the history of a single business. While corporate letters, minutes, and like documents have long been utilized in business history, the labor involved in organizing sales slips, time cards, and the like has frequently prevented their use in producing data on prices, output, investment, and employment that would be more useful to the economic historian. Second, largely unorganized government data existing in committee and bureau reports could be brought together in manageable shape. And third, even correspondence, long a bugaboo of historians, could, perhaps, be better analyzed by data processing techniques together with some form of content analysis. Both economics and economic history stand to gain enormously if this work is done and done wisely.

---

[7] Jonathan R. T. Hughes and Stanley Reiter, "The First 1,945 British Steamships," *Journal of the American Statistical Association*, Vol. LIII (June, 1958), pp. 360–81.

[8] Newmarch, "Circulation," p. 149.

Our work at Purdue along these lines is, we hope, only the beginning of extensive data processing work in economic history. Since 1957 five data processing studies in economic history have been produced at Purdue. In all of our studies we have developed entirely new statistical series which are now readily available as "building blocks" for other economic historians to use in their studies. Our main results from these five papers may be briefly summarized.

In "Sources of Industrial Finance: The American Textile Industry, A Case Study," 175 observations on each of eight financial variables were brought together in a multiple regression model. The analysis of this data indicated that heretofore economic historians had tended to overstate the role of retained earnings in 19th-century American corporate finance and understate the role of borrowed capital. In addition, the analysis indicated, as might be suspected, that the importance of loans grew concomitantly with the development of the capital markets and that a firm's capital structure was responsive to short-term changes in the capital markets, output, and employment.[9]

In "Stock Ownership in the Early New England Textile Industry," data processing techniques were used to systematize some 3,782 separate stock accounts (representing the equity holdings of at least 854 individuals and firms in 11 textile mills) to uncover the trends in stock ownership over the period 1829 to 1859. The analysis indicates, first, that while mercantile capital represented a large proportion of the investment, the transfer from mercantile to industrial capital appears to have been slower than has been generally assumed. Second, that there was a considerable degree of backward integration with textile merchants and mercantile firms contributing a significant block of capital. Third, that financial intermediaries made a substantial contribution to the finance of new industry. And fourth, that out-of-state and foreign investors made no significant investments.[10]

In "The First 1,945 British Steamships," the growth of the British steam merchant marine up to 1860 was chronicled and measured in detail, by type of propulsion and build. It was shown that not only was this development more rapid than had previously been thought, but that the transport capacity of the fleet grew more rapidly than did the tonnages to the extent that it could have played the powerful role in overseas earnings which had been assigned to it by contemporaries, and which had been heavily discounted by modern scholars.[11]

In "The New England Textile Mills and the Capital Markets: A Study of Industrial Borrowing 1840–1860," 2,385 industrial loans were systematized by machine techniques in order to provide some new information

---

[9] Lance E. Davis, "Sources of Industrial Finance: The American Textile Industry, A Case Study," *Explorations in Entrepreneurial History*, Vol. IX (April, 1957), pp. 789–203.

[10] Lance E. Davis, "Stock Ownership in the Early New England Textile Industry," *Business History Review*, Vol. XXXII (Summer, 1958), pp. 204–22.

[11] Hughes and Reiter, "1,945 Steamships."

about the antebellum capital markets. The analysis produced a new series of interest rates independent of the frequently cited Bigelow estimates. It seemed to indicate that a theory of a sectored money market better explains the term structure of rates than does the more classical Lutz-Hicks expectation theory, and it presents some new data of the relative importance of various types of lenders in the markets and the cyclic and secular changes in the composition of this lender group.[12]

Finally, in "A Dollar Sterling Exchange 1803–1895," data processing techniques permitted us to organize 2,789 bills of exchange and, from the bill prices, to deduce a series of pure exchange rates. In addition to this new series, the analysis indicates that exchange rate stability did not always characterize "the gold standard"; instead, it is only after 1875, when transportation, communications, and the money markets had evolved into near-modern form, that exchange stability became common. Finally, the paper casts further light on the development of the foreign exchange market and the rise of the major foreign exchange houses—a subject previously explored by Arthur Cole.[13]

IV

We now turn our attention briefly to statistical inference. Broadly speaking, statistical inference refers to a body of techniques that permit the user to garner with some confidence a knowledge of certain characteristics of populations on the basis of observations from these populations. For example, Newmarch's estimate of the average value of all bills based on the average of the sample drawn is a statistical inference. In that case the unknown quantity (called a parameter) is the average of all bills. In the Hughes and Reiter paper on the first 1,945 steamships a more elaborate, but essentially similar, technique was employed to estimate the speed and carrying capacity of the ships from a knowledge of other related facts about them.

In other cases the unknown quantity of interest might be, for example, a measure of dispersion, or the largest observation in the population. Inference of this kind can achieve remarkable accuracy, more accuracy sometimes than that yielded by an attempt to count an entire population. This was the case in World War II when Allied estimates, based on the serial numbers of samples of German military equipment observed in battle, proved to be more accurate than the information supplied to the German government from production records, and, in addition, were available much sooner than the data derived from the latter source.[14]

---

[12] Lance E. Davis, "The New England Textile Mills and the Capital Markets: A Study of Industrial Borrowing, 1840–1860," *Journal of Economic History*, Vol. XX (March, 1960), pp. 1–30.

[13] Lance E. Davis and Jonathan R. T. Hughes, "A Dollar Sterling Exchange 1803–1895," *Economic History Review* (August, 1960).

[14] W. Allen Wallis and Harry V. Roberts, *Statistics, A New Approach* (Glencoe, Ill.: The Free Press, 1956), p. 20.

Further, there are techniques, for the study of relationships among various observable quantities, ranging from simple regression analysis to highly elaborate statistical schemes for detecting the presence of association between one pair of variables in the presence of many other associations or influences. A simple multivariable regression model, for example, was used in the study of textile financing previously cited to sort out the effects on corporate finance of firm age and historic time.

Before closing this desperately brief discussion of statistical inference, we should point out that one ought not to have too narrow a concept of the phenomena subject to quantitative analysis. It is, of course, obvious that observations, given in the form of numerical quantities such as money amounts or physical units of output, are subject to quantitative analysis. However, the possibilities of quantification go much further than this. Any phenomenon whose occurrence may be noted or counted is quantifiable, and, in addition, coding sometimes permits apparently nonquantitative phenomena to be quantified. Thus attitudes, opinions, and perceptions are studied with the aid of quantitative techniques by psychologists. Content analysis of written material provides another example of the usefulness of an extended notion of quantification. In our study of 19th-century exchange rates we coded proper names, origins, and points of payment of the bills. Thus "quantified," the mass of information could be handled and yielded us important evidence of the development of specialization in the exchange market.

V

We are not suggesting in this paper that there is to be a "new" economic history which will render nonquantitative economic historians technologically unemployed. It should be obvious that we regard ideas from statistics and data processing as natural aspects of problems of historical study. It should also be obvious that the historian's special knowledge and viewpoint is essential to the useful employment of quantitative methods. Our main point is that modern statistical techniques and computing equipment make possible the intensive exploitation of a vein of historical materials that was perforce only little worked in the past; and that if even a few economic historians would take the time to learn even a little of these new techniques, the 1960's could easily prove the most productive years in the history of the discipline. On the other hand, if the discipline chooses to remain completely in the literary tradition, we can see small hope for anything but a continual rehashing of the already existing sources and a continuation of the century-long cleavage between economics and economic history—a cleavage that should soon disappear if the economic historian is able to provide the economists with new data and new interpretations of the process of economic life.

2. The Role of the Economic Historian in Predictive Testing of Proffered "Economic Laws"*

R. L. Basmann†

Purdue University

> To express my faith I have to say many things which are common-
> place. I do not try in the least to be original, but to state as simply as
> possible things which I deem important. I wish they were even more
> commonplace than they are.
>
> —GEORGE SARTON

1. The Doctrine of Co-responsibility

IN A RECENT monograph I suggested that econometricians—*if* they wish
to *test* economic theories—must cope with the economic historian as peer
in respect of criticism and assistance (Basmann, 1964, pp. 19-20). If an
econometrician announces a statistical test as conclusive, i.e., if he pro-
nounces a given "economic law" to have been disconfirmed by relevant
"facts," his pronouncement might be discredited, not only on the ground
that his methods of statistical inference are (say) inappropriate or mis-
interpreted, but also on the ground that the essential *historical investigation* of initial and background conditions is inadequate. I stressed the

* Reprinted from *Explorations in Entrepreneurial History / Second Series* (Spring /
Summer, 1965, Vol. 2, No. 1). Copyright 1965 by Earlham College, Richmond, Ind.
Paper originally presented at Cliometrics meeting, February 4, 1965, at Purdue University.
† I am indebted to Jonathan R. T. Hughes for the many pleasant hours we have
spent together discussing history, economic history, and economic science. This paper
has been composed at his suggestion. Edward Ames, C. Lloyd, E. J. Mosbaek, and
D. H. Richardson and S. Williamson have offered helpful comments. I am indebted
also to James A. Papke and E. T. Weiler for helpful comments relating to the role
of econometrics in policy making.
The views expressed in this paper are my own, however, and I take sole responsibility for their inadequacies.

11

indispensibility of making clear statements of initial and background conditions for the predictive testing of explanatory economic models, and the necessity for suspending judgment, in the event derived prediction statements are falsified, until a really competent job of warranting the statement of initial conditions has been completed. Implicitly, at least, my remarks suggested that the job of establishing the background and initial conditions for predictive testing of proffered economic laws requires professional handling—that is, by historians.

The foregoing remark has excited some comment by economic historians, perhaps because it is regarded as a novel admission on the part of one who is reputed to be an econometrician. Therefore I take for granted that there is some interest in this point of view and I propose to amplify in this paper some of my previous remarks.

Although frequent reference is made to topics belonging to philosophy of science and philosophy of history, this paper is not supposed to be a contribution to those disciplines. Nor, of course, can it be considered as a contribution to "hard" economic history. It is concerned, rather, with some practical difficulties that stem from the legitimate demand for specialization in research. In particular, this paper is concerned with the fact that there is a more or less hypostatized boundary separating two important fields of specialization, i.e., econometrics and economic history, which *cuts straight through the heart of a natural unit of scientific activity, namely, predictive testing of proffered economic laws.* Of course, no one ever intended this unnatural cleft to occur, not to mention intending its becoming fixed to the degree it has. The founders of the Econometric Society announced it as their purpose to promote the empirical testing of economic theorems[1] (cf., Tintner, 1952, p. 3); certainly they would assent to the use of any kind of rational procedure that contributes to the goal of testing proffered economic laws. Yet even Tintner, whose depth and breadth of view on matters of method in economic inquiry are unexcelled, in warning that econometrics cannot claim to be the only method of economic research (Tintner, 1952, pp. 13–14), fails to stress the essential unity of the testing procedure and to emphasize that econometrics alone cannot suffice even where data are abundant. In Tintner's account econometrics and historical research seem to be competing rather than complementary in predictive testing: historical research is said to be more suitable than econometrics in certain subject matter branches of economics; econometrics can, for instance, throw very little light on

---

[1] According to this ancient conception of scientific explanation one is supposed to argue from well-known and established premises to hitherto unknown facts, the latter being supposed established by deduction. In econometric studies it is common to find statistical estimates labeled "reasonable" on the basis of their agreement with a priori theory, a procedure reminiscent of that of the surveyor who, having laid out a small right triangle on Earth's surface, checks the accuracy of the figure by adding his measurements of the acute angles and comparing their sum with 90°00′. The surveyor's confidence in Euclid has long ago been justified by experience, of course.

the problems of economic development; here historical method is much more fruitful (Tintner, 1952, p. 13).

A historical explanation for the unnatural split of the predictive testing activity in economics is beyond the scope of this paper. Root causes must be sought in a period antedating the founding of the Econometric Society. A more immediate cause may be briefly indicated. To begin with, many pioneering econometricians have been eager to get results that would gain the attention of policy-makers (by being of practical use to them, of course). Corollaries of that severe practical orientation are the emphasis on statistical *estimation* of economic relationships, as distinct from *hypothesis testing*, and the controversies that stemmed from the introduction of statistical methods of data reduction more suitably adapted to the form of models which economists already had been formulating for some time. The tendency of policy-oriented econometricians has been to formulate models, to argue in a more or less Aristotelian fashion for the plausibility of the underlying assumptions,[1a] and to trust to the efficacy of asymptotically efficient (viz., large-sample) methods of statistical estimation to bring them somewhere near knowing the true values of economic parameters. Gerhard Seiler dates from about 1939 the emergence of the tendency to regard statistically estimated econometric models as sufficiently reliable and effective tools for the making of definite economic policies (Seiler, 1959, p. 8); that is to say, this confidence in reliability of model formulation antedates the development of asymptotically efficient methods of econometric estimation (1940's).

The strong policy-making orientation of prominent econometricians and the emphasis on efficient *estimation* which derives from it; the relatively great prestige that most mathematically untrained economists have been willing to accord to the "invention" of "new and even better" methods of estimation,[2] together with the abundant inventory of methods and results that can readily be borrowed from the previous work of statisticians and applied with little modification to econometric problems, have undoubtedly lured many young econometricians away from investigation of the deeper problems of econometric model building and predictive testing, even though the latter afford much greater opportunities to find one's own limits in (say) applied mathematics and mathematical statistics, and, I should add, in the weighing of empirical evidence by historical methods.

[1a] See footnote 1.

[2] Rondo Cameron has commented favorably on the graduate program in economics here at Purdue, so perhaps it is not out of place for me to mention that all students are required to take a considerable number of courses in which continuous use is made of mathematical deduction, previous courses in differential and integral calculus usually being a requirement for admittance. Of course, the purpose is not to make (say) a future economic historian into an econometrician but to give him background for judging intelligently the true worth of the statistical and mathematical contributions of others.

Economic policy making is an extremely important matter, of course, and it is requisite that there be available a number of economists who, by reason of their practical knowledge of our country's economy, their perspective as reflected in awareness and acceptance of the limitations and obligations of the expert's natural role, can serve as advisers to the high dignitaries of state (cf. Sorensen, 1963, Chap. 5). To what extent the specific products of policy-oriented econometric model building are of direct service to public policy makers I am not qualified to say. Anyway, it is not the purpose of this paper to judge the technological value of econometric model building, nor to criticize any econometrician's personal decision to specialize in forecasting (see Section 2). Immediate concern is with the fact that a natural unit of scientific economic inquiry is cleft by specialization, and that this cleavage is sustained by the natural consequences of a widespread preoccupation with econometrics as the handmaid of economic policy. Alfred Marshall, you will recall, pointed out the impracticability of seeking in the immediate needs of policy making the chief stimulus for the pursuit of scientific knowledge (Marshall, 1948, Book I, Chaps. 1–4). Here it seems appropriate to add this passage from Morris Cohen's *Reason and Nature*:

> To subordinate the pursuit of truth to practical considerations is to leave us helpless against bigoted partisans and fanatical propagandists who are more eager to make their policies prevail than to inquire whether or not they are right. The pursuit of pure science may not completely prevent our initial assumptions from being biased by practical vital preferences. But this is not to deny the aloofness involved in the pursuit of pure science is the condition of that liberality which makes men civilized. (Cohen, 1959, p. 350.)

For the time being let us take it for granted that a considerable part of the work involved in subjecting proffered economic laws to predictive test belongs to the métier of the historian. What would motivate the historian and economist to cooperate in predictive testing? What are the obstacles to such cooperation? The rest of this section attempts to answer in part these questions.

To begin with, it must be admitted that the views to be expressed here are colored by a specific interest, namely, to subject economic theory, as embodied in a variety of specific explanatory models, to the hazards of predictive test. The motives that lead economists to make predictive tests of explanatory economic models differ in kind and intensity; and the point of view economists adopt toward economic history and its role in predictive testing varies with those motives. For present purposes I should like to stress one kind of motive, namely, the *aesthetic*, which is almost never mentioned except in connection with pure mathematical economics. Historians in particular should be able to appreciate that the aesthetic value of economic theory is not confined to the elegance of style with which it may be expressed in literary or mathematical symbols.

Trevelyan is supposed to have said that the poetry of history consists in its truth. Teggart emphasizes the same point: the aesthetic interest of historical narrative depends on its supposed accuracy and the factual character of the events it portrays; the aesthetic value of accuracy is sufficient to justify critical historical inference (Teggart, 1960, pp. 35–39). "The documentary scholar is thus justified in his endeavors. Through his efforts assurance is given to the public that the statements embodied in the most recent history are really true" (*Ibid.*, p. 36). All great historians from Niebuhr and Ranke to Pieter Geyl have stressed the force of this motive.

Likewise the aesthetic value of an explanatory economic model consists in its truth or, rather, in the warranted supposition of its truth; and (what is intimately bound up with the significance of its supposed truth) in its logical inability to be in agreement with any but a very narrow range of potential facts. In this connection refer to the remarks about equation (3) which appears in Section 2. I mention the aesthetic motive, not merely to argue that the aesthetic value of explanatory economic models justifies the painstaking efforts at thorough deductive exploration and statistical testing of the derived prediction statements, but rather to suggest that, in common with the aesthetic interest of historical narrative, it justifies undertaking the processes of critical historical inference when they are to be applied to the establishment of the factual character of the background and initial conditions, the fulfillment of which is necessary to render any given predictive test valid.

While I think that the aesthetic parallel between historical narrative and predictive testing of explanatory economic models warrants mention in its own right, there are other practical reasons for laying stress on it. If, as has been claimed, the task of establishing warranted background conditions for predictive testing of explanatory economic models is complicated enough to call for treatment by professional historians, then the habit of continuous close and effective cooperation between historians and test-oriented economists has to be developed. Great obstacles to such cooperation are rooted in divergences of background and training. However, the common aesthetic interest, e.g., that which motivates efforts to secure logical completeness in explanatory economic models, relevance of statistical tests, and factual accuracy in historical narrative and explanation has a strong tendency to draw those who share it into effective cooperation.

The view that holds historical criticism as important as statistical inference in predictive testing of economic models is colored also by a definite philosophical "bias," which may be broadly stated as follows: every explanatory model that rests on a set of logically consistent economic premises and allows the derivation of prediction statements whose state of agreement with relevant economic observations is not perceptually obvious, deserves to be subjected to predictive test repeatedly. That is to say, imagination should be free to construct explanatory hypotheses in any form whatsoever, subject only to those restraints that are necessary to secure intersubjective testability and economic relevance. A more or less transparent corollary is that hypothesis formulation must be free of those artificial taboos that appear in the form of methodological prescripts or legislation and choke off rational discussion (it does not matter whether that is the intended effect or not). For the most part, methodological prescriptions in the social sciences are designed to perform in lieu of efforts to disconfirm hypotheses by predictive tests.

I cheerfully admit that the *antilimitationist* bias of the foregoing policy is strong, and that it might appear extreme to some readers. For all that, I think a strong case can be made for accepting the risks inherent in following a vigorous antilimitationist policy as preferable to the dangers inherent in a "neutral" policy of allowing limitationist prescriptions to go unchallenged. Actually, the one big risk involved in holding to an antilimitation policy is largely personal, viz., a risk to the individual only. For it is widely considered by economists to be in bad taste to deliver a riposte to a limitationist sally—or at least quixotic;[3] and neutrals seem rarely to distinguish between the pronouncement of a methodological edict, on the one hand, and a simple denial of the existence of any intellectually compelling reason to heed it.[4] Another risk—though perhaps not really a risk

---

[3] Syncretists often suppose that the response of the outspoken skeptic is intended to convert the partisan of methodological legislation. Such an aim is almost never the skeptic's intention, it being so very unlikely to succeed. What the skeptic is usually trying to do is persuade the bystanders, particularly the inexperienced, not to give up their methodological freedom. Partisanship on behalf of methodological legislation is not a *crimen laesae majestatis divinae*, and the skeptic has, therefore, little motivation to save the partisan from himself, charitable as that might seem to be; rather it is the prospect that a new "school" will be formed, with its clients generating a lot of dull studies in accordance with a rigid formula and phrased in colorless in-group slang, that motivates open criticism and a pointing-out of specific dangers (cf. Boring, 1963, p. 252).

[4] It is unfortunate that many economists fail to distinguish between philosophy of science and methodology—between philosophical clarification, on the one hand, and methodological legislation, on the other. The ability to make such distinctions is a real asset in econometricians and historians who seek to cooperate effectively. For there are encountered in economics and history many real questions which, not being susceptible of answer by logical demonstration or by reference to empirical facts, yet call for systematic *clarification*. To be sure, many such perplexities are muddles that have been produced by earlier attempts to legislate method for the conduct of scientific inquiry, and generally by economists seeking short cuts to the achievement of success in research, cf. Nagel, 1954, p. 47. Attempts to clear up such muddles are not themselves efforts to introduce competing methodological prescriptions, although they are frequently taken for such. In a recent paper (Basmann, 1963) I pointed out that the Principle of Causality cannot be adduced in support of the claim made by H. Wold and R. H. Strotz (Strotz-Wold, 1960) that "causal chain" models are in some relevant sense better paradigms for causal explanation in economics than "interdependent" models. Some readers have taken my arguments as a prescription *against* the formulation of causal chain models in economics. Of course, I did not say that causal chain models are in any way inferior to interdependent models as potentially accurate representations of economic mechanisms. What I did claim (primarily for the benefit of graduate students in search of a methodology) was that the

at all—is that an antilimitationist policy tends to provide no easily traced guidelines for decision making, e.g., in respect of financial support for economic research, whereas methodological prescriptions might seem to do that very well. But if I have not gathered a totally erroneous impression from the *history of science* then it is not too inaccurate to say that the effect of a priori methodological limitations on the formulation of scientific hypotheses has been ineffective at best, or at worst, ultimately crippling. (Recall the passage quoted from Cohen above.)

Clear recognition of methodological prescriptions, of their defensive purpose in many instances, is an important initial step in establishing effective cooperation between the historian and the economist. To the extent each one can subject to scrutiny the methodological biases he has absorbed in his own training, and can recognize the absence of any compelling reason to cling to such biases in each and every case, the easier it is for both to concentrate attention on the problems of "hard" economic science. If both the historian and economist have adopted what might be termed an antilimitation bias to begin with, so much the better; effective cooperation is then much easier to achieve.

Less readily overcome are obstacles to cooperation inherent in attempts to satisfy the real need for broad *directive principles* for the guidance of inquiry. These are, in part, broad definitions of the subject matter of given branches of science or, rather, expressions of a consensus in respect of what the subject matter of a given branch of science ought to be. In part, they are heuristic *maxims* for the practical conduct of inquiry, e.g., the Principle of Causality in modern philosophy of science. Directive principles wisely used are not allowed to impose restrictions on the detailed form of scientific hypotheses, nor to entail the employment of specific techniques of investigation. Such principles are not themselves scientific hypotheses; they cannot be logically proved (or disproved), nor can they be disconfirmed by observation.

Historical methods of research are employed in the study of a wide range of very different kinds of phenomena, of course, and it seems only natural that directive principles are used to mark the boundaries between different applications of historical research. Some branches of inquiry are more "historical" than others, e.g., geology and paleontology are certainly more historical than (say) physics in the sense that recourse to historical method to establish facts and to explain infrequently recurring phenomena is more prominent in the literature of those sciences. In the same sense, most social sciences, including economics, are more historical than many branches of natural science. But the directive principles just referred to only mark off branches of scientific inquiry; they do not sepa-

---

Principle of Causality in no way singles out the causal chain model as an *ideal form* of causal explanation to which we economists ought to strive to make our explanatory models approximate as closely as possible, cf. Nagel, 1961, pp. 316–24. By the way, I said nothing original in that paper.

rate from them a realm of inquiry that is uniquely and specifically *history*.

The reader who is a historian should know better than I the annals of that quest for a science that is uniquely *history*: the scientism of Comte; the search for "historical laws" undertaken by Hegel and Marx (and thought by them to have been successful); history as the science of human development, not as just the handmaid of social science, viz., history as a science, no less and no more (Bury);[5] history as the kingdom of individualities, of details which are not to be repeated and which have value in themselves (Windelband);[6] history, the "ideographic" science that is to be sharply delineated from the "nomothetic" or law-giving natural sciences (Windelband and Rickert);[7] history as recapture of the meaning of the human past as understood (felt) by those who experienced it (Dilthey);[8] history as "explanation" adducing the general laws established by the special sciences (Hempel and others).[9] Although this paper is not concerned with the quest for a unique *history*, it is appropriate to mention that, with exception of the positivism of Comte and the prophetic philosophies of Hegel and Marx, each of the foregoing conceptions of *history* has influenced, in one way or another, the view put forward at the beginning of this section, namely, that the economic historian qua historian is involved in the predictive testing of proffered economic laws in a rather fundamental way. Finally, the very great influence of historical researches and humanistic ideals of George Sarton ought to be mentioned.[10]

To view the economic historian as solely, or even just chiefly, a "user of economic theory," as a scout in the search for examples to illustrate the economic laws formulated, and sometimes thought warranted by the intuitions of theoretical economists, is precedented, no doubt, but mistaken, for reasons I shall mention in Section 3. Equally mistaken is the

[5] Bury's inaugural address is reprinted in Stern, 1956, pp. 209–23.

[6] Possibly the most readily accessible short statement of Windelband's views of historical research, its nature and method, is given in *History of Philosophy* (1893), chap. 1, Art. 2, pp. 8–18 (Windelband, 1958).

[7] For a brief account of the epistemological theory that underlies the analysis of history by Windelband, Rickert, and their followers, and its connection with the neo-Kantian movement in philosophy, see Bochenski, 1947, pp. 101–11.

[8] See H. P. Rickman's introduction to selected passages from Dilthey's works (Rickman, 1962).

[9] Papers by Hempel, White, Nagel, Gallie, Dray, Frankel, Donegan, and Scriven on historical explanation are reprinted in Gardiner, 1959.

[10] The case for humanization of science is stated most eloquently by George Sarton in his essay, "The History of Science and the New Humanism," reprinted in Sarton, 1962, chap. III, and, of course, the idea is pervasive in all of his writings. Two additional essays of Sarton's that are especially pertinent here are "History of Science" (1956) and "Four Guiding Ideas" (1947); they are reprinted in Stimson, 1962. In the same connection, see the essays by Bronowski, 1956.

It is worthwhile noting that T. H. Huxley, in his *Progress of Science* (1887), *Science and Culture* (1880), and *On the Advisableness of Improving Natural Knowledge* (1866), in addition to explaining with great clarity the humanistic value of the pursuit of science, explains with equal clarity the relation between the technological and humanistic functions of science.

view of the economic historian as primarily a miner of facts to set before the econometrician. The whole métier of the economic historian, his intellectual participation in every stage of the testing of proffered economic laws, is required: in the formulation of such laws, in their empirical interpretation, and in the evaluation of their agreement with what actually happened in the past.

2. Historical Inference and Predictive Testing

The readers of this essay, being for the most part economic historians, will undoubtedly prefer that any remarks made about the logical structure of "historical explanation" be kept brief. I do propose, however, to discuss the logical structure of explanatory economic models in a little more detail, just to elucidate the respective tasks of the economic historian and general economist when they cooperate in the essential work of subjecting economic theory to sharp predictive test. In examining the logical structure of explanatory models we find justification for a partial division of labor between economist and historian, but, it must be stressed, for *only* a partial, not a complete division.

In order to achieve a degree of concreteness in the discussion of predictive testing I take the liberty of referring to one of the simultaneous equations models on which I have done some work.[11] That model is based on four structural relations, viz., consumption function, investment function, liquidity preference function, and supply of money function. As it is a very small model, it is not fashionably "realistic"; whether it is an accurate representation of the class of economic events it actually purports to explain is, of course, an entirely different matter, and above all, one which has to be determined by the performance of suitable predictive tests. A complete description of the class of economic events to which this model refers is beyond the scope of the present paper. A rather vague and incomplete description of the purpose for which this model has been formulated would be afforded by saying that it is to explain year-to-year changes in the endogenous variables, consumption, gross national product, long-term rate of interest, quantity of money, and gross private investment in terms of bank reserves and autonomous shifts in the *investment schedule*.[12] Of course, in putting forward such a model, we aim to discover and explain much more than just those rather crude events that can be described by year-to-year changes in the endogenous variables. The specific observations

---

11 Basmann, R. L. Lectures on Quantitative Economics, I. Purdue University, Econ. 670–71, 1964–65.

12 The shift in the investment schedule is a hypothetical construct. The investment schedule for the American economy is assumed to have shifted downward in 1939, 1942, and 1945, and upward in 1953, remaining constant between shifts. At the present juncture, the hypothesis about shifts has not been established; that is to say, the statement of timing, direction, and magnitude of the investment schedule shifts has not yet been confirmed by independent methods of historical inference.

that are employed to test the model in question were generated by the American economy during the period 1930–59. For simplicity of expression, let us say that the historical time series of observed endogenous variables describe an "event" that happened to the American economy, and let us say that the time series of exogenous variables describe (in part) the given circumstances under which that event occurred.[13]

It is convenient, however, to describe the foregoing event by a set of *sample statistics*. Sample statistics are mathematical functions of the observed endogenous variables. In certain cases we can construct a set of sample statistics fewer in number than the successive observations in the historical time series, yet containing all empirical information in the latter that happens to be relevant to the explanatory hypothesis whose truth is in question. Such a set of sample statistics is said to be *minimally sufficient* for the explanatory hypothesis and it can *replace* the immediate time-series observation in the test of the model. A minimally sufficient set of sample statistics can be constructed for the model I am referring to here.

One of the foregoing statistics is the coefficient of bank reserves in the statistical regression of gross national product on the exogenous variables, viz., bank reserves and the autonomous shift variable; let us denote this coefficient statistic by a_4. In repeated sampling under approximately constant background conditions and under initial conditions essentially the same as those described in part by the historical time series of bank reserves and autonomous shifts in the investment schedule, the statistic a_4 has a unique *probability distribution*; there is, for instance, a definite probability with which the event

$$a_4 < 0 \tag{1}$$

occurs. As it happens in the model referred to here, the probability of the foregoing event is very small:

$$Pr\ \{a_4 < 0\} \leqslant 0.000001 \tag{2}$$

less than or equal to one chance in a million.[14] Since the statistic a_4 is computed from 30 successive annual observations on the gross national product, we should expect to wait a very long time, indeed, for the American economy to produce the event (1), at least *if* the probability statement (2) is true.

If, upon computing a_4 from one of our very first samples of 30 annual observations, we find that the event (1) has occurred, we should be strongly inclined toward doubting that the probability statement (2) is true.

---

[13] In this paper we shall distinguish between *initial conditions and background conditions*. The former are represented by exogenous variables which appear explicitly in the mathematical functions of an explanatory model; the latter do not appear explicitly and might not even be measurable.

[14] That is to say, the relative frequency with which the economy is supposed to generate a sample of endogenous observations yielding $a_4 < 0$ is less than 0.000001.

Undoubtedly the reader is wondering where I got the probability statement (2) in the first place and what, if any, is the economic significance of the event described by (1). The answer is, of course, that the probability statement (2) has been derived, by mathematical reasoning from a set of *initial condition* statements with the help of a set of *economic premises,* the latter being universal statements about economic parameters, e.g., the marginal propensities to consume and spend, the *ceteris paribus* rate of decrease of desired investment with respect to interest rate, and so on.

The statistical regression equation in which a_4 appears is the unconstrained maximum-likelihood estimate of the reduced-form equation for gross national product

$$y_{t,2} = \frac{\beta_2 \gamma_3}{\Delta} z_{t,1} + \frac{\beta_4 \gamma_2}{\Delta} z_{t,2} + \frac{\beta_4 \gamma_1 + \beta_2 (\gamma_4 - \gamma_5)}{\Delta}$$

$$+ \frac{\beta_4 (u_t + v_t) + \beta_2 (x_t - w_t)}{\Delta} \quad (3)$$

where

$$\Delta = \beta_4 (1 - \beta_1 - \beta_6) + \beta_2 \beta_3$$

$y_{t,2}$ denotes gross national product, $z_{t,1}$ denotes bank reserves, $z_{t,2}$ denotes the autonomous shift variable in the investment schedule, and u_t, v_t, w_t, x_t denote random disturbances in the underlying structural relations. $\beta_1, \ldots,$ $\beta_6, \gamma_1, \ldots, \gamma_5$ denote coefficients in the structural relations. The statistic a_4 is an unbiased normally distributed estimator of the coefficient of $z_{t,1}$ in equation (3). Given the specified initial conditions, the coefficient of $z_{t,1}$ in (3) is at least 6.23 times as large as the standard deviation of its estimator a_4. From our sharpest formulation of economic premises we can deduce that

$$6 \leqslant \frac{\beta_2 \gamma_3}{\Delta} \leqslant 12.5$$

Thus the economic premises of our model are incapable of being in good agreement with any but a very narrow range of values of the sample statistic a_4.

Statement (2) is called a *prediction statement.* To show that statement (2) is a prediction statement one must display the premises of the model in question. Those premises include statements about the coefficients in the consumption function, investment function, liquidity preference function, and supply of money function, and statements about the statistical distribution of the random disturbances in those structural equations.[15] In

---

[15] For instance β_1, β_2, and β_3 are coefficients of gross national product in the consumption function, investment function, and liquidity preference function respectively. Among the economic premises that underlie the explanatory model in question are the following inequalities: (*footnote continued on next page*)

addition, the linkages among those functions would have to be displayed; moreover, the definite time sequence of exogenous variables would have to be displayed as part of the statement of *initial conditions*. Finally, the form of a_4 as a mathematical function of potential sample observations would have to be described. All of the foregoing is only preliminary to mathematical derivation, of course. That derivation would have to show that the negation of statement (2), viz., the statement

$$Pr \{a_4 < 0\} > .000001 \qquad (4)$$

contradicts at least one of the economic premises, *given the statement of initial conditions.*

Since the probability statement (2) is a logical consequence of initial conditions conjoined with economic premises, i.e., since the conjunction of the statement of initial conditions and the economic premises implies that the probablity of the event described by (1) is extremely small, the actual occurrence of that event is charged with economic significance. For, *if the statement of background and initial conditions is warranted,* then the actual occurrence of the event described by (1) disconfirms one or more (but perhaps only one!)[16] of the economic premises from which the

$$(a) \quad \begin{cases} 0.75 \leqslant \beta_1 \leqslant 0.85, \\ 1.0 \ \ < \beta_1 + \beta_6 \leqslant 1.03, \\ 0 \ \ \ \ < 2\beta_6 \leqslant \beta_3 \leqslant 0.5 \end{cases}$$

These inequalities, together with other premises, are actually employed in the derivation of the probability statement (2).

The economic premises state also that the structural disturbances u_t, v_t, w_t, x_t are independently normally distributed with zero means and very small variances; viz.,

$$(b) \quad \begin{cases} 1 \leqslant \omega_{u^2} \leqslant 2, \\ 1 \leqslant \omega_{v^2} \leqslant 2, \\ 1 \leqslant \omega_{w^2} \leqslant 2, \\ 1 \leqslant \omega_{x^2} \leqslant 2 \end{cases}$$

Nonetheless the variance σ_{22} of random disturbance in the gross national product reduced-form equation (3) shown above is not small; for, with the help of all economic premises we derive the statement

$$(c) \qquad 296 \leqslant \sigma_{22} \leqslant 40{,}494$$

From the foregoing restriction (c) we learn that our original economic premises fail to make a very definite claim in respect of the average magnitude of the random variation in gross national product. Consequently I have undertaken to sharpen the economic premises to the extent that one can derive the more precise statement

$$(d) \qquad 296 \leqslant \sigma_{22} \leqslant 925$$

[16] An important goal sought in deductive exploration of explanatory economic models is—as far as possible—to prepare to single out just those economic premises that are to be regarded as having been disconfirmed by a given predictive test. Poor agreement between a prediction statement and observations disconfirms a conjunction of several premises. In logic a conjunction is false if one or more of its constituent

prediction statement (2) is derived. It should be noticed, however, that the argument for disconfirmation is enthymematic; appeal is tacitly made to a statistical convention termed by Emile Borel *la loi unique du hasard*: *extremely improbable events do not occur* (Borel, 1950, pp. 100–101). If the event (1) actually occurs, then we agree to act as if the probability of its occurrence is greater than one chance in a million (decision rule); that is to say, we act to modify one or more of the premises from which the prediction statement has been derived.

Here a parenthesis is in order. I am often asked by students and econometricians why I regard certain kinds of event, e.g., the occurrence of (1), as "economically significant." Frequently inquirers refer to certain passages in the econometric literature in which authors seem to claim that events like that described by (1) have no significance, e.g., that even if the estimate a_4 of a given reduced-form coefficient in a simultaneous equations model turns out to have the wrong sign, it is of no consequence.[17] Such passages must be read in context, however, and in many cases close scrutiny reveals that the authors have formulated a *forecasting problem* rather than a predictive test. Clearly, any definite event, the occurrence of which can be regarded as disconfirming a probability statement that is actually derived with help of a set of economic premises, is an economically significant event. Of course, if one explicitly disclaims the intention of making a predictive test of the economic premises in question, then one is justified in referring to disconfirming events as "uninteresting," perhaps, but never in referring to such an event as "economically nonsignificant."

However, it is appropriate to mention that leading predictivists in the economics profession do not agree with me in considering events like (1) as economically significant, nor would they regard the foregoing procedure of examining the state of agreement between observations and statements as (2), which are derived with help of the economic premises, as constituting a predictive test of the latter (cf., Christ, 1952, p. 67; Friedman, 1952, p. 108). For present purposes it will be enough, perhaps, to say explicitly that the conception of predictive testing that is under discussion here has nothing essential in common with that crude form of predictivism vigorously touted by Professor Friedman and the Chicago School.[18]

---

statements is false. In many cases it will be possible to account for the poor agreement between a prediction statement and relevant observations by attributing the poor agreement to the falsity of just one or two specified economic premises. It would be very inefficient procedure to scrap the entire model in the face of a predictive test that disconfirms the *conjunction* of economic premises. It is equally inefficient to try to find the disconfirmed premises by trial and error experimentation with alternative premises.

For econometric models that contain many equations and many parameters, however, thorough deductive exploration appears to be infeasible; at least, no one seems to attempt it.

17 For an illuminating case see the paper by Stojkovic, 1964, p. 404.

18 For a general critique of predictivism see Toulmin, 1963.

(*footnote continued on next page*)

It is worthwhile, however, to contrast the *forecasting use* of statistical estimates with their use in a predictive test of an explanatory economic model. The contrast should not appear invidious, as the forecaster and testing economist are trying to accomplish two rather different things. Consider once more the statistical regression of gross national product on bank reserves and the shift variable, cf., equation (3). Suppose that the sample from which the foregoing statistical regression is computed happens to yield a large value for the multiple correlation coefficient R^2 and a small value for the estimate of the variance σ_{22} of the disturbance in equation (3); e.g., suppose that $\hat{\sigma}_{22} < 140$. The forecaster might argue rationally that (for some given purpose he has in mind) it would be sound practice to forecast the next several annual values of gross national product y_{t2}, with help of the statistical regression equation, from auxiliary forecasts of bank reserves z_{t1} and of the autonomous investment function shift z_{t2} and the assumption that the random disturbances are equal to zero.

Agreeing that the forecaster's use of the statistical regression equation is sound for the purpose announced, the economist who employs the same regression estimate in making a predictive test of the economic premise from which the reduced-form equation (3) has been derived, would mention that one or more of those premises seems to be in very poor agreement with the observations; for if the appropriate background conditions are fulfilled, then it follows from the economic premises that the probability of the event

$$\hat{\sigma}_{22} < 140 \tag{5}$$

is very small, since one of the derived prediction statements is

$$Pr\,\{\hat{\sigma}_{22} < 140\} < 0.025 \tag{6}$$

The appropriateness of the foregoing statistical regression as an instrument of forecasting does not rest on its being in good agreement with the

---

According to predictivists, the procedures followed by the testing economist, the close examination of economic observations and test statistics to determine whether there has occurred one or more theoretically very improbable events like (1) and (5), are "essentially tests of internal consistency" and "perhaps should not be called tests at all" (cf. Christ, 1952, p. 67). Predictivists do not ordinarily *derive* probability statements like (2) and (6); instead the calculated disturbances from equations like (3) or the statistical estimate $\hat{\sigma}_{22}$ are to be "examined to see whether they are very large according to some intuitive standard of how large they are expected to be" (cf. Christ, 1952, p. 67). (Just whose intuition is to be received as more cogent than mathematical derivation is not specified.) Thus predictivists seem to be content to remain ignorant of all but the most transparent testable consequences of the economic premises in their models and sometimes rationalize this content by methodological prescriptions that depreciate the employment of mathematics as an instrument of exploration of theoretical economic premises. Unfortunately the offhandedness and obscurity with which the predictivist doctrine has been retailed makes it exceptionally difficult to clarify the nature of arguments that might have been brought forward on its behalf.

premises of some explanatory economic model or other. Moreover, the accuracy with which the mathematical equations appearing in an explanatory economic model represent economic structures is not dependent on the practical suitability of those equations as instruments of forecasting. It might well be that under appropriate background conditions for the explanatory model referred to here, the reduced-form equation for gross national product (3) would not be suitable as a forecasting equation. For the variance σ_{22} of the random disturbance in that equation cannot be smaller than 296 if the model is an accurate representation of the economic mechanism it purports to describe, and might therefore not allow a sufficient degree of precision in forecasts of gross national product computed with help of the *ad hoc* assumption that random disturbances tend to be negligible. (Such an assumption, however, is transparently *not* one of the premises of the model in question.) One means of overcoming this difficulty in forecasting might be to forecast the next few disturbances with help of some additional variables not appearing in the explanatory model but which have been found to be highly correlated with a few immediately previous estimates of the random disturbance in the reduced-form equation. (The rationality of the foregoing *ad hoc* procedure cannot be overthrown merely by averring that the correlation is without theoretical significance, only temporary, and spurious in the long run.)

I repeat: the contrast drawn between the forecasting use of statistical estimates and their use in predictive testing of explanatory economic models has been stressed here solely for purposes of clarification. A few readers of my earlier monograph have interpreted the criticism of predictivism put forward there as an attack on economic forecasting (cf. Basmann, 1964, pp. 4–5, pp. 55–62). Such an interpretation rests on alien assumptions that have been read into the context of that monograph, and is completely mistaken.

Let us return to our illustration. The conjunction of the statements[19]

(a) *background and initial conditions were fulfilled during the given historical period in question;*

(b) *the event* (1), *viz.,*

$$a_4 < 0,$$

occurred in the period mentioned in (a);

is called the *falsifier* of the *conjunction* of those economic premises actually employed in the derivation of the probability statement (2) (cf. Popper, 1959, Chap. III). Notice that both (a) and (b) are *singular statements*;[20] both are potential facts.

---

[19] For more detailed accounts of the logic of scientific explanation see the paper by Hempel and Oppenheim, 1948, and the book by Nagel, 1961, chap. 2 and 3.

[20] A *singular statement* asserts that a specified event has occurred at a given time and place.

A universal statement is of the form: *For every* x, x *has the property* P. Some universal statements can be verified by exhaustive enumeration of a finite class of individuals, viz., as a conjunction of a finite number of singular statements. For ex-

Any claim that a statistical disconfirmation of one or more of the pre-diction statements derived with help of an explanatory economic model is decisive against one or more of the premises must, if it is to be valid, adduce warrant for the appropriate initial and background conditions. The specific historical problem in predictive testing occurs in connection with the conceptualizing of relevant *background conditions* and in deter-mining whether the statement alleging their fulfillment is warranted.

As in the case of "natural laws," we do not expect that proffered eco-nomic laws, even if they are true, will manifest themselves to observation under all conceivable background conditions. Pure water does not always freeze whenever its temperature falls below 0° C., even under carefully controlled laboratory conditions; no geophysicist, intending to collect observations for the testing of some proffered laws of earthquakes, would locate his seismograph in the switching yard of a rail terminal. By the same token, if there is warrant for the statement that government controls distorted the functioning of the American economy during World War II, then there is excellent reason for regarding a forecasting test (for the years 1946–47) of L. R. Klein's early dynamical model as logically invalid (cf. Basmann, 1964, p. 59).

To every explanatory economic model there corresponds a set of more or less definite background or external conditions that must be fulfilled in a given period of economic history if observations recorded for that period are to be deemed appropriate for predictive testing of that model. Those conditions, which must remain approximately constant over the period in question, are suggested in part by the structure of the model (cf. Basmann, 1964, Sec. 2.4). But the conceptualization of relevant back-ground conditions is a task for which the economic historian qua historian is equipped by training, experience, and general point of view, at least potentially. The ability to conceive of events not represented by opera-tionally interpreted symbols in a given mathematical economic model, yet which, if they occur, invalidate a proposed empirical test thereof, is not adequately cultivated by the training, formal and informal, that mathe-matical economists and econometricians normally undergo. The ability to conceptualize relevant background conditions for the predictive test of a given explanatory economic model is not to be confused with mere

---

ample: *For every* x, *if* x *is the infinitive of a currently used regular French verb, then* x *forms the future tense by adding -ai, -as, -a, -ons, -ez, -ont.*

Ideally, however, scientific laws are supposed to be strictly universal statements; such statements are not expressible as conjunctions of a finite number of singular statements and cannot be verified by exhaustive enumeration. For example: *For every* x, *if* x *is a demand function with positive own-price elasticity, then* x *has negative income elasticity.* We do not know a priori that the class of all demand functions with negative own-price elasticities is finite (cf. Hempel-Oppenheim, 1948, pp. 338–41).

Prediction statements, which are singular statements, cannot be derived from uni-versal statements (economic premises) alone, but with the help of other singular statements (initial and background conditions).

ingenuity in imagining and naming "factors" that *might* interfere with the normal functioning of the economic mechanisms the model is supposed to represent. The conceptual ability of which I speak is professional; in that respect it is like that of the mathematician in formulating problems for which there is a good chance of solution and yet which are nontrivial and worthy of attention. The conceptualization of background conditions requires the simultaneous operation of the imagination and critical foresight of the practical steps that must be taken in order to give them substance and verify their presence or absence, as the case may be. This conceptualization also requires the touch of the true artist; as the creator of Sherlock Holmes has put it, the knowledge of when to stop. For it is possible, of course, to go on indefinitely specifying background conditions that are to be fulfilled if a given test of a given explanatory model is to be considered valid. Hence the conceptualization process is open to abuse; economic theories can be "saved" by inventing background conditions, on an *ad hoc* basis, which, not being fulfilled, can be supposed to invalidate any predictive test that has even been performed.

Discouraging as it might seem to be, the economist can no more expect his statistical tests of hypotheses to be valid predictive tests unless he provides adequate warrant for initial background conditions than can (say) the physicist. In this connection it is appropriate to mention that theoretical physicists are quite dependent on the specialized knowledge of laboratory physicists and the experience of the latter with scientific equipment; even if the experimental physicist is not consulted in the formulation of the proffered law that is to be tested, he is almost always called in to interpret the documentary record of experiments performed some time back; frequently he is expected to correct that documentary record, to infer from it what actually happened in a past sequence of experiments that might be too expensive to repeat without especially good reason. No doubt the technology that the laboratory physicist commands usually permits him to control the background conditions to a sufficient degree of approximation; but

> To tell the truth, there are times when this or any kind of work seems dull, exhausting even fruitless. When after days of trying you still can't find the leak in the vacuum system, or when, after you patiently have fitted an elaborate piece of apparatus together an oscilloscope suddenly picks up a lot of meaningless "noise" from some unknown source . . . then of course the work is unattractive. This is no different from the difficulties and frustrations to be expected in any serious undertaking. (Bitter, 1963, pp. 26–27.)

For all that there is a grain of truth in the excuse frequently advanced by social scientists, namely, that natural scientists have it easy with their technological control of background conditions and the rapidity with which their experiments can be repeated; but it should not be forgotten that this is first and foremost an excuse. The extended time scale in accordance with which the unplanned "experiments" on a real economic mechanism can take place, and the various ethical restraints which prohibit economists from experimenting where they can, are serious obstacles to be sure. But it is only the exceptional difficulty of surmounting the problem of background conditions, not the problem itself, that seems to be peculiar to the social sciences and economics.

The practical skills by means of which the presence (or absence) of changes in conceptualized background conditions are detected (or verified) belong to the métier of the historian. (If the requisite ability to conceptualize background conditions is not adequately cultivated by the training the mathematical economist or econometric statistician normally undergoes, it is true a fortiori that neither his training nor experience provide him with adequate command over the tools of historical inference.) In the first place, the time of the occurrence of such perturbations of background conditions has to be conjectured, viz., a hypothesis about timing has to be formulated, and tested by reference to a documentary record and the weighing of evidence that can be gleaned therefrom. While the presence of background perturbations will often be suggested by the failure of prediction statements, which are derived with help of the explanatory model, to be in good agreement with observations (Basmann, 1964, p. 19), this failure cannot be viewed as cogent evidence for the occurrence of such a perturbation. Other data, logically independent of the endogenous observations from which test statistics are computed, have to be found, interpreted, and shown to warrant the statement that the given perturbation actually has (or has not) occurred.

It is worthwhile to illustrate briefly the sort of conceptualization and subsequent historical inference I have in mind, and for that purpose it is appropriate to mention the paper "English Pre-Industrial Population Trends" by G. L. S. Tucker (1963). Suppose that a break in the long-run trend of English population growth is conceived of as a relevant change in the background conditions for some economic hypothesis, in the formulation of which population does not itself enter explicitly as a variable. Suppose, too, that the hypothesis is to be subjected to predictive test, the sample statistics having to be computed from 18th-century observations (say) because we have already used up all subsequent observations without succeeding in disconfirming the hypothesis in question. Tucker's investigation, his test of the generally accepted hypothesis that such a sustained break occurred about 1750 against the alternative hypothesis that no break occurred about 1750 but one did much later in the century; his *explanation* of the appearance of the Griffith and Brownlee population time series (Tucker, p. 207) with help of a model local epidemic that moves from place to place over a period of decades; then illustrates the sort of investigation of background conditions I have in mind. Of course, Tucker was not seeking to validate background conditions for some definite explanatory model, and reference to his paper is made here for illustrative purposes only.

Historical studies of a more general nature are contributions to the work of conceptualizing, and finding warrant for, background conditions for predictive tests of specific explanatory models. For instance, Schlote (1952) and Imlah (1958) not only provide valuable new quantitative data, but also valuable reference material for conceptualization of background conditions, the latter in the form of narratives of significant and more or less unique events such as changes in government economic policy. This kind of contribution is, however, traditional and well understood; it will be sufficient just to mention it.

Let us consider sample statistics again. Recall that a_4, defined at the beginning of this section, is a function of observations. I said that the event described by (1) had economic significance because its actual occurrence, in conjunction with warranted historical statements of background conditions and initial conditions, constitutes a "falsifier" of one or more of the underlying economic premises of a given explanatory model. There is another sense in which the event (1) can be said to possess or lack economic significance, which, for lack of a more definite terminology, I shall refer to as its *economic interpretation*. From a purely logical point of view the symbols for observations in an economic model are completely arbitrary, of course, and some decision in respect of what they are to stand for has to be made. The significance of the event (1) is only that it disconfirms, under appropriate conditions, one or more of the underlying premises as statements about whatever it is that happens to be measured by the observations from which the sample statistic a_4 is to be computed.

Thus, (to take a different example) on the basis of one given operational definition of exchange rate, a given theory or model purporting to predict the gold points[21] might appear to be disconfirmed by observations. On the basis of a different operational definition of exchange rate, however, the same theory might be in good agreement with observation. The critical evaluation of Morgenstern's calculations of the gold points (1875–1914), and some of his conclusions about the empirical truth of exchange rate theory, which has been offered by Davis and Hughes (1960, cf. pp. 62–64), illustrates the participation of economic historians in the formulation of operational definitions of the symbols that appear in pure economic theory and explanatory economic models. But such participation is more or less informal and, from the point of view of its close connection with the formulation of definite theories and models, very infrequent. (In this regard I do not mean to undervalue the achievements of economists working on the national accounts.) The formulation of operational defini-

---

[21] The gold points are theoretical constructs, of course, and not directly observable. Hence any decision in respect of their operational definition is central to the formulation of a model of exchange rates.

tions of economic variables is, however, part and parcel of theory and model formulation. It is an essential part of theory formulation for which economic historians are by training and knowledge particularly well suited. While it cannot be separated from the formulation of economic premises and their deductive elucidation into theorems that can serve as prediction statements, it is equally true that the formulation of operational definitions of economic observables cannot be separated from the conceptualization of background conditions.

I do not mean to suggest by the foregoing remarks that economic historians will be able to cooperate effectively in predictive testing of proffered economic laws without reflecting deeply on the nature of scientific prediction and explanation in general. The economic historian has to bring to this enterprise more than a mere kit of tools.

3. Some Concluding Remarks

In contending that the determination of what of significance actually happened in economic history is a task equally as fundamental in predictive testing of proffered economic laws as the derivation of prediction statements (mathematical economics) and the manipulation of statistical computations (econometric statistics), I have not overlooked the fact that traditional historiography offers other uses for the facts that become warranted by *historical inference*. For one thing, historians offer explanations —by doing so they present modern philosophy with one of its most perplexing problems (Gardiner, 1955)—that are in many respects found to be original when viewed against the background of accepted opinion in their own time.

Much of the value of historical explanations resides in the fact that they are not always derived entirely from "that vague amalgam of currently recognized generalities, derived from common experience and more or less confirmed by our own" (Walsh, 1960, p. 66), or deduced solely from the sociology, psychology, and the economics that theorists in those fields claim to "know." I have the impression that the competent historian is not so content with the existing degree of empirical confirmation of proffered economic laws that he will hesitate to offer generalizations and hypotheses of his own making if the latter seem better to account for the facts at his disposal. In this attitude toward economic theory the historian is right. To be sure, he risks that supposedly devastating charge of "not knowing much economics," which the general historian, at least, knows that he can safely ignore. At any rate, historians immersed in facts produced by historical inference often frame explanations that might contradict some proffered economic laws or other. I plan to say more about that possibility later. For the time being I should like just to say that, from the point of view of one involved in the predictive testing of such proffered economic laws, new alternative hypotheses that really contradict old ones, are always welcome from every quarter.

It should be recognized, however, that most explanations offered by historians are not explanatory hypotheses, at least not in the sense that a well-articulated and deductively rich explanatory economic model is. I do not intend this comparison to be invidious. Hempel has coined the term "explanation sketch" to describe the explanations commonly put forward by historians (Hempel, 1942, p. 351); he reminds us of the fact that most explanations offered in history involve only tacit reference to the general laws or regularities those explanations presuppose. (See also Gardiner, 1955, pp. 96–108.) Very often the generalizations tacitly referred to in historical explanation are those of common sense, as we have already noted. But very often those underlying generalizations are potential universal hypotheses which, in their newness, are not sufficiently precise to support strict derivation of feasibly testable prediction statements. By way of illustration, I should like to mention a recent article by Nathan Rosenberg, "Technological Change in the Machine Tool Industry" (Rosenberg, 1963). The explanatory intent and pattern is clear and prominent in Rosenberg's paper. The *explicandum*, the objective of explanation, is a historical sequence of economically significant innovations. Most of the general premises are explicitly indicated; they are mechanical, thermodynamical, and chemical laws as well as general economic principles. Moreover, Rosenberg contributes an original concept of "technological convergence" and the elements of a theory to account for it. Finally, the pattern of reasoning is tightly woven. Rosenberg's explanation sketch, while certainly not a deductive explanation of the kind described in Section 2, is richer in argued conclusions and, in that sense, "better testable" than a great many policy-oriented econometric models, and, therefore, of great value, at least to economic science. In this connection it is worthy of mention that Rosenberg does not make much use of explicit economic laws.

In suggesting that historians can do much for economic science by continuing to offer their own explanation sketches, I am not departing from an attitude of strong skepticism regarding the existence of *purely historical* laws.

Economic historians are often exhorted to make greater use of economic theory and econometric technique, and they are almost as frequently condemned for failing to do so. Whether it is appropriate to raise against a piece of research in economic history the criticism that it does not make use of economic theory depends in part on the purpose of that research, but, more importantly, just what piece of economic theory the critic has in mind that the historian has failed to use. If the historical research is an explanation sketch, it will hardly be clear that it contradicts any given piece of economic theory except, perhaps, when it specifically does so at the level of announced premises. But even if a contradiction of that sort can be found, it will always be appropriate to point out to the critic that premises are logically remote from the empirical evidence that might tend to disconfirm them, and to ask the critic at least to supply reports on the predictive tests the allegedly superior premises have survived. Of course, it would hardly do for the critic to reply that most economists, or, at least, some prominent economists, believe that the theory in question is approximately true, or that an acquaintance at the "Fed" or National Bureau of Economic Research has some classified data that confirm it. The only really sound argument against a piece of research in economic history is of the same nature as a cogent argument against an explanatory economic model, namely, that at some point or other its assumptions or conclusions are at variance with publicly available independently warranted statements of fact (or, of course, that it is internally self-contradictory).

It is a fact, however, that economic historians—at least those carrying on in the "new economic history"—*do* make considerable use of economic theory and models and thereby involve themselves in the matter of predictive testing of the strictly universal economic premises they employ. Whenever economic premises are invoked to explain an event or sequence of events that occurred in the past, or are adduced as an argument for the claim that such-and-such an event "must have occurred," two questions have to be answered in the affirmative before the proposed explanation or claim can be considered as cogent:

1. Has at least one stringent predictive test of the adduced economic premises already been carried out, and have those premises survived all of the predictive tests that have been made up to now?
2. Were the background and initial conditions allegedly appropriate for application of the foregoing economic premises actually fulfilled for the time period during which the fact to be explained or inferred is supposed to have occurred?

The scientific value of research in economic history depends on the extent to which the economic premises borrowed or invented by the economic historian for explanatory purposes have withstood fairly rigorous predictive tests; it also depends on the quality of the historical investigation of the background conditions under which the economic historian proposes to employ those economic premises.

The critical appraisal of econometric practices, which appears in Section 2, is meant primarily for the economic historian who regards himself as chiefly a user of, and not responsible for, economic theory invented and established by others; as a producer of research in economic history, he cannot afford to be indifferent to the suitability and quality of the inputs he employs. For if his proffered explanations of the economic past come to naught, and his work collapses, because he had borrowed uncritically from the great catalog of inadequately tested economic models, he, and no one else, will be blamed. It has been suggested in this paper, however, that economic historians can do a great service to economic history and to economic science generally by taking a closer and better informed interest in the formulation and predictive testing of explanatory economic models, contributing their own special skills at all levels of that enterprise.

References

BASMANN, R. L. 1963, "The Causal Interpretation of Non-Triangular Systems of Economic Relations," *Econometrica*, Vol. 31 (July, 1963), pp. 439–48, 451–53.

————. 1964, *On Predictive Testing of a Simultaneous Equations Model: The Retail Market for Food in the U.S.* Institute for Quantitative Research in Economics and Management, No. 78. Purdue University.

————. 1964-65, *Lectures on Quantitative Economics*, I. Purdue University, Department of Economics.

BITTER, FRANCIS. 1963, *Mathematical Aspects of Physics.* Garden City, N.Y.

BOCHENSKI, I. M. 1947, *Europäische Philosophie der Gegenwart.* 2te Aufl., Bern.

BOREL, EMILE. 1950, *Elements de la Theorie des Probabilités.* Paris.

BORING, EDWIN G. 1963, *History, Psychology, and Science: Selected Papers* (eds. ROBERT I. WATSON, and DONALD T. CAMPBELL). New York.

BRONOWSKI, J. 1959, *Science and Human Values.* New York.

CHRIST, CARL. 1952, *A Test of an Econometric Model for the United States 1921-1947.* Cowles Commission Papers, New Series, No. 49. Chicago.

COHEN, MORRIS R. 1959, *Reason and Nature.* 2d ed. Glencoe, Ill.

DAVIS, LANCE E., AND HUGHES, JONATHAN R. T. 1960, "A Dollar-Sterling Exchange. 1803-1895," *Economic History Review*, 2d Ser., Vol. 13 (August 1960), pp. 52–78.

FEIGL, HERBERT, AND BRODBECK, MAY (eds.). 1953, *Readings in the Philosophy of Science.* New York.

FRIEDMAN, MILTON. 1952, "Comment" (See CHRIST, CARL, 1952, pp. 107–14).

GARDINER, PATRICK. 1955, *The Nature of Historical Explanation.* London.

————. 1959, *Theories of History.* Glencoe, Ill.

HEMPEL, CARL G. 1942, "The Function of General Laws in History" (Reprinted in GARDINER, *Theories of History;* pp. 344–56).

HEMPEL, CARL G., AND OPPENHEIM, PAUL. 1948, "The Logic of Explanation" (Reprinted in FEIGL AND BRODBECK; pp. 319–52).

HUXLEY, THOMAS H. 1893, *Method and Results: Essays.* New York.

IMLAH, ALBERT H. 1958, *Economic Elements in the Pax Britannica.* Cambridge, Mass.

MARSHALL, ALFRED. 1948, *Principles of Economics.* 8th ed. New York.

MULLER, HERBERT J. 1953, *The Uses of the Past.* New York.

NAGEL, ERNEST. 1954, *Sovereign Reason.* Glencoe, Ill.

————. 1961, *The Structure of Science.* New York.

POPPER, K. R. 1959, *Logic of Scientific Discovery.* New York.

RICKMAN, H. P. 1962, *Wilhelm Dilthey: Pattern and Meaning in History.* New York.

ROSENBERG, NATHAN. 1963, "Technological Change in the Machine Tool Industry," *Journal of Economic History,* Vol. 23, pp. 414–43.

SARTON, GEORGE. 1962, *The History of Science and the New Humanism.* Bloomington, Ind.

SEILER, GERHARD. 1959, *Ökonometrische Konjunkturmodelle.* Stuttgart.

SCHLOTE, WERNER. 1952, *British Overseas Trade from 1700 to the 1930's.* Oxford.

SORENSEN, THEODORE C. 1963, *Decision-Making in the White House* (Foreword by John F. Kennedy). New York.

STERN, FRITZ (ed.). 1956, *The Varieties of History.* New York.

STIMSON, DOROTHY (ed.). 1962, *Sarton on the History of Science.* Cambridge, Mass.

STOJKOVIC, GEORGE. "Market Models for Agricultural Products," (in WOLD; pp. 386–418).

STROTZ, R. H., AND WOLD, H. O. A. 1960, "Recursive *vs.* Non-Recursive Systems: An Attempt at Synthesis," *Econometrica,* Vol. 28, (April, 1960), pp. 417–27.

TEGGART, FREDERICK J. 1960, *Theory of History.* Berkeley, Calif.

TINTNER, G. 1952, *Econometrics.* New York.

TOULMIN, STEPHEN. 1963, *Foresight and Understanding.* New York.

TUCKER, G. S. L. 1963, "English Pre-Industrial Population Trends," *Economic History Review,* second series, Vol. 16 (December, 1963), pp. 205–18.

WALSH, W. H. 1960, *Philosophy of History.* New York.

WINDELBAND, WILHELM. 1958, *A History of Philosophy.* 2 vols. New York.

WOLD, HERMAN (ed.). 1964, *Econometric Model-Building: Essays on the Causal Chain Approach.* Amsterdam.

3. Fact and Theory in Economic History[*]

Jonathan R. T. Hughes[†]

Purdue University

I don't see that anyone save a sap-head can now think that he knows any history until he understands economics.

—EZRA POUND

I

IT IS CUSTOMARY that the audience stand up during the "Hallelujah Chorus" when Handel's *Messiah* is performed. This "social fact" may be observed and data can be collected each year on the recurrence of this phenomenon. Like the recurrence of industrial investment, changes in prices, unemployment, and the like, the annual rise of the concert-hall audience must be explicable by analysis of some kind. What kind? Theoretical, historical, both, or neither?

A historical analysis would soon enough produce the interesting tradition that Good King George II stood up in the London performance of 1743 in order to see the source of the great sounds onstage.[1] The rules of decorum then prevailing required that all lower ranks stand up when His Majesty did. The tradition was continued. Why? The theorist, employing the general principles of dynamic-social-decision making (or some such), could produce a suitable explanation why, when one man stands at the beginning of the chorus, the rest join. Perhaps also the dynamic principles of social decision making could explain, with the aid of difference equations, the year-by-year recurrence of the phenomenon. But such analysis would not unearth the actions of King George, since his actions were a singular phenomenon not derivable from general principles.

So to know why people stand during the "Hallelujah Chorus" we need both historical and logical methods. Neither by itself will suffice. However,

---

[*] Reprint from *Explorations in Entrepreneurial History*, Second Series, Vol. 3, No. 2. © Graduate Program in Economic History, University of Wisconsin, 1966.

[†] I am indebted to my colleague R. L. Basmann for two years of fascinating discussions regarding the logic and methods of history and science. Although much of what follows has withstood the weight of his criticisms, I assume responsibility for errors of fact or logic.

[1] Herbert Weinstock, *Handel* (2d ed.; New York, 1959), p. 253.

the *fact* that King George stood up and so did the audience can be discovered without reference to any general principles whatever, and the tendency for the audience to stand each year can doubtless be suitably explained without reference to King George. (Certainly the average highbrow, struggling suddenly to his feet as his neighbor rises, is unaware of his royal patrimony.)

Similar problems surround the study of economic phenomena that have actually occurred in the history of economic life. For, as in cultural history, not all knowledge generated in economic history needs a springboard in general principles[2] or "theory." The statements, "George II stood up in 1743," and "The crisis of 1857 had non-monetary origins," are both singular statements based upon observed factual evidence. On the other hand, any explanation of why the "real origins" of the 1857 crisis existed, and were important determinants of that crisis, involve the scholar in some resort to general principles since the facts, by themselves, explain nothing. How much theory and how much fact—both, neither, or either—ought there to be in that part of empirical economics we call economic history?

Around this question a great deal of discussion is currently centered. It has recently been argued by Robert Fogel that the separation between theoretical and factual intellectual enterprise in economic history dates from the rise of the German Historical School.[3] Doubtless the rise of that school gave a name and a certain respectability to studies in economics not rooted in received theory. But economics itself, like any science, has both a theoretical and an empirical base, and the duality of scholarly enterprise, I think, owes more to the peculiar problems of economic studies, the historical character of the evidence, the lack of laboratory technique and data, than to any particular school of thought within the discipline.[3a]

The profession has long been beset by the same problems. Schmoller and the German Historical School are the most famous revolt against theoretical economics, but partly because they acquired a label. They weren't the first nor even the most important case of alienation between "fact" and "theory" people in economics.

Most of the classic controversies over the British currency were be-

---

[2] Professor Douglass North seems to be calling for such universal reliance upon economic theory as the springbroad to empirical research. *American Economic Review*, Papers and Proceedings, 55 (No. 2): *passim.* (May, 1965).

[3] *Ibid.*, esp. pp. 94–95.

[3a] One notes with interest the lack of such problems in the current work of Vernon Smith on experimental economics. Freed from time and history, Smith, generating his own data in controlled laboratory situations, experiences virtually no problems of "theory and history." He confronts theory immediately with tests and the resulting data are used to further refine the logical structure he works with. V. L. Smith, "An Experimental Study of Competitive Market Behavior," *Journal of Political Economy*, Vol. LXX, April, 1962; "Effects of Market Organization on Competitive Equilibrium," *Quarterly Journal of Economics*, Vol. LXXVIII, May, 1964; "Experimental Auction Markets and the Walrasian Hypothesis," *Journal of Political Economy*, Vol. LXXIV, August, 1965.

tween fact and theory men, beginning with the Bank of England's suspension of specie payments (1797–1821). Henry Thornton, a most wise man and, for his time, no mean monetary theorist, attempted to amend, in *The Paper Credit* (1802), certain views concerning the internal circulation of money—views which descended through Hume and Smith to Ricardo.[4] On the basis of observation, experience, and hunch, he wanted to reject the narrow view that the nation's money supply was simply a function of the balance of payments, and that *ad libitum* issues of paper money would merely drive an equal amount of specie out of the country, and, moreover, that therefore Bank policy should be limited to issuing paper money "as if metallic"—pound for pound (sterling) of gold deposited. He noted especially that credit was usually endangered by panic and internal drain. This could be best avoided if the Bank did not necessarily contract its issues of notes during an external drain.[5] The easy axioms of the narrow view, however, were picked up and refined by Ricardo in his writings, in his Pamphlet of 1810, and finally in his plan for a national bank.[6] Ricardo had a way with the logic of economics, and so *The High Price of Bullion* triumphed over *The Paper Credit* even though the latter is incomparably the more adequate piece of analysis. Knowledge of facts separated Thornton from Ricardo fundamentally, as it would their intellectual descendants. The differences were seemingly irreconcilable, not because Thornton knew no theory, but because he knew "how things worked," whereas Ricardo and his friends cared naught for facts and were extraordinarily persuasive. As Keynes noted, Ricardo had similarly bested Malthus over the possibility of deficient effective demand ". . . and Ricardo conquered England as completely as the Holy Inquisition conquered Spain." Bank policy based upon Ricardo's theories was a catalog of needless disaster until the Germans caused the Bank Act of 1844 to be "suspended" for the last time in 1914. But we anticipate.

---

[4] A concise treatment of this classical literature is found in two essays by J. K. Horsefield, "The Duties of a Banker, I, The Eighteenth Century View," and "The Duties of a Banker, II, The Effects of Inconvertibility," printed in T. S. Ashton and R. S. Sayers (ed.), *Papers in English Monetary History*, (Oxford, 1953). The early descent of the doctrine of automatic adjustment of paper currency under gold payments is traced from Hume onward. Pp. 4–7.

[5] *An Enquiry into the Nature and Effects of the Paper Credit of Great Britain* (New York, 1939), pp. 123–28. Also Horsefield, *op. cit.*, II, pp. 23–29, on Thornton.

[6] Ricardo published three letters to the *Morning Chronicle* in 1810 as a pamphlet, *The High Price of Bullion a Proof of the Depreciation of Bank Notes*, in 1810 developing his view, in accord with Smith and earlier writers (above), that notes merely displace coin, and in his *Plan For the Establishment of a National Bank* (1824, posthumous) his view appeared in its boldest form.

The Bank of England performs two operations of banking, which are quite distinct, and have no necessary connection with each other: it issues a paper currency as a substitute for a metallic one; and it advances money in the way of loan, to merchants and others. That these two operations of banking have no necessary connection, will appear obvious from this,—that they might be carried on by two separate bodies, without the slightest loss of advantage, either to the country or to merchants who receive accommodation from such loans. [p. 1.]

The Bank's policy need not exist, apart from exchanging notes for gold, and otherwise acting as an ordinary commercial bank, restricting its loans if its own resources declined through a bullion drain.

The issue of the bullion debates came up again in aggravated form following the crises of 1825 and 1836–37. These issues were again resolved in favor of the narrow view, this time on a long-term basis in the paragraphs of the Bank of England Act of 1844. Ricardo's posthumous army, led by Field Marshal Lord Overstone, overwhelmed Tooke and the undermanned legions of the Banking School.[7] Again it was "automatic" adjustment against "plain facts." Overstone, almost in Ricardo's words, argued that if the Bank of England's action contracted the money supply and raised interest rates, prices would fall, and the balance of payments would be aided in readjusting toward its "normal" equilibrium. In fact, the laws of the currency were as true as natural law in physical science.

The great laws which determine the monetary equilibrium of the commercial world assign to this country a certain amount of money. No internal arrangements to which we may resort can alter or suspend the law . . . the monetary arrangements of this, as of every other country, must be subordinate to the great principles which regulate the monetary equilibrium of the world. Any attempt to resist or modify the result of these principles can result only in confusion and embarrassment.[8]

Thus Lord Overstone. Tooke, a long-time student of facts, a merchant (than which, in Ricardo's view, nothing could be more contemptible), could not swallow the dose in its purity. Like Lyndon Johnson, Tooke believed that, for the most part, interest rates were part of the cost of production, and attempts by the Bank of England to choke off economic activity by tightening up its credit would only raise prices so long as "other" factors made continued production profitable. Tooke (and later his friend Newmarch joined in the effort) insisted that interest rates and prices generally move in the same direction. Newmarch, like Thornton before him, argued that Bank-rate policy of the Ricardian kind only made commercial crises worse than they otherwise have been.[9] Such arguments were ignored, and have largely been ignored to the present time. Tight money policy by central banks in times of crisis became holy writ.

By mid-19th century the split between fact and theory men was put on a regular basis, from M'culloch to Palgrave, but with some exceptions. In J. S. Mill's *Principles* some factual materials were used. Jevons was an indefatigable worker on facts. So was Marshall, and it was from his theoretic hands that Sir John Clapham received his apostolic blessing as an economic historian. Yet no synthesis was achieved in England, and to

---

[7] See J. K. Horsefield, "The Origin of the Bank Charter Act of 1844," reprinted in Ashton and Sayers, *op. cit.;* also my own treatment in *Fluctuations in Trade, Industry and Finance* (Oxford, 1960), pp. 228–36 and the sources cited there.

[8] *Ibid.,* p. 231.

[9] Sir Albert Feavearyear, *The Pound Sterling* (2d ed.; Oxford, 1963), p. 266. Newmarch's view was put forward on the basis of the facts of changes in prices, interest rates, and the volume of bills of exchange in his well-known paper "The Magnitude and Fluctuations of the Amount of Bills of Exchange," *Journal of the Statistical Society,* Vol. XIV, 1851.

this day, like the Bank of England under the Act of 1844, the discipline of economics is divided into two departments. In English universities economic history tends to exist in a world apart, as if advances in the logic of economics had no relevance at all for the study of factual evidence designated economic history. (While I shall argue below for the importance of "nontheoretical" factual studies, the English extreme, separate departments of economic history, is not what I have in mind.)

The American Economic Association was not immune from the fact-theory split. As A. W. Coats has recently shown us, the problem appeared early in the history of the A.E.A. in the various forms of regionalism, social reform, institutionalism, and empiricism opposed to the orthodoxy of the "eastern" economics departments.[10]

A curious variation was based upon the belief that by careful observation of the facts, theory itself could somehow become more directly reflective of observed facts: for example, Veblen, whose identification as an economist is usually questioned these days. The business cycle seems to have been especially productive of professional disaster for those trying directly to link up fact and theory. Jevons, for all his virtuosity both in theoretical and empirical work, was led to his ultimate ruination by his addiction to his interpretation of the facts. Professor H. L. Moore's elaborate statistical studies of the weather and its effects on business conditions may also be cited. It almost seems to have been safer to stick with clean, if irrelevant, theory, and well-documented, if unedifying, fact.[11]

In the long, long run the work of the men who concentrated on discovering and establishing facts has come out well indeed compared to the theory men even if, in the short run, the theory men usually had their day. One hears little of Overstone today, but Tooke's empirical work is still in use.[12] Porter's *Progress of the Nation* is still in use, but how many read his contemporary, James Mill, anymore? Jevons's prices are still used, but how many economists today actually know his theoretical work firsthand? Recent experience is similar. When *Measuring Business Cycles* was first published, the theorists came out in full cry and Burns and Mitchell were much maligned for selecting, recording, and measuring the relevant statistical magnitudes without the explicit imposition of any given business cycle theory (in fact, it is puzzling to imagine what, with the theory of the

---

10 A. W. Coats, "The First Two Decades of the American Economic Association," *American Economic Review,* Vol. 50 (September, 1960), pp. 555–74; "The Political Economy Club," *ibid.,* Vol. 51 (September, 1961), pp. 624–37; "The American Economic Association, 1904–29," *ibid.,* Vol. 54 (June, 1964), pp. 261–84.

11 To the reader used to modern empirical work, Moore's early efforts show striking care and method. The oblivion into which that work has fallen might be a somber prospect for the empirical worker.

12 His price series were used by Jevons in the construction of his first index. The factual materials in the volumes of *The History of Prices* underpinned Clapham's narrative up to the year 1856, and thus much of modern historiography. See Clapham's tribute, *An Economic History of Modern Britain* (Cambridge, Eng., 1932), Vol. II, p. 366, n. 3.

time, Burns and Mitchell might have done).[13] The National Bureau of Economic Research still remains, and so do its theoryless techniques of business cycle measurement. But whatever happened to "business cycle theory," anyhow? Is it in fact, like the dodo, extinct? Schumpeter's great work, imposing theory upon history and statistics, now gathers dust in the corner with Montaigne's *Essays*.

This background is provided to emphasize that the present upheaval[14] regarding the "new" economic history is a further incarnation of a fundamental and long-lasting conflict in the general field of economics. It seems to me that the modern fact-theory problems, so far as they involve economic history directly, may be traced to the Keynesian Revolution and the later development of "modern" microeconomics using mathematical techniques. We find, among others, that Taussig,[15] the early Viner,[16] H. D. White,[17] and Seymour Harris[18] seriously worked with both theoretical and historical materials in their efforts to understand economic phenomena. In our own time Milton Friedman,[19] Charles Kindleberger,[20] and others are still working occasionally with serious historical problems, but the effort among theoretically minded economists is rare now. In the late 1930's, just about at the maturity of the present senior economic historians (those recently retired or now near retirement), economic

---

[13] For example, Tjalling Koopmans, "Measurement Without Theory," *Review of Economic Statistics*, Vol. 29 (August, 1947), pp. 162. ". . . utilization of the concepts and hypotheses of economic theory . . . as a part of the *process of observation and measurement* promises to be a shorter road, perhaps even the only possible road, to an understanding of cyclical fluctuations." (His italics.) Koopmans can be interpreted as favoring the limitation of relevant data by the line of theory used, only Ptolemaic data for Ptolemaic astronomers and Copernican data for Copernican astronomers. Obviously he can't have meant such an interpretation, but authors have no control over the uses of their printed views. So far, the road suggested, as a *combination* of the Kepler and Newton "stages" of research into celestial mechanics applied to economics, has apparently been no road at all.

[14] A great deal indeed has now appeared regarding the new economic history. For example: Lance E. Davis, Jonathan R. T. Hughes, and Stanley Reiter, "Aspects of Quantitative Research in Economic History," *Journal of Economic History*, Vol. 20 (December, 1960), pp. 539–47; Douglass North, "Quantitative Research in American Economic History," *American Economic Review*, Vol. 53 (March, 1963), pp. 128–30; G. C. S. Murphy, "The 'New' History," *Explorations in Entrepreneurial History*, 2d Series, Vol. 2 (Winter, 1965), pp. 132–46; the entire Discussion and Papers "Economic History: Its Contribution to Economic Education, Research, and Policy," *American Economic Review*, Papers and Proceedings, Vol. 55 (May, 1965), pp. 86–118.

[15] F. W. Taussig, *The Tariff History of the United States* (New York, 1888).

[16] Jacob Viner, *Canada's Balance of International Indebtedness* (Cambridge, Mass., 1924).

[17] H. D. White, *The French International Accounts, 1880–1913* (Cambridge, Mass., 1933).

[18] Seymour Harris, *The Assignats* (Cambridge, Mass., 1930).

[19] His students appear as men with historical interests. See *Studies in the Quantity Theory of Money* (Chicago, 1956). Friedman has recently made his entry as an economic historian with Anna J. Schwartz in *A Monetary History of the United States* (New York, 1963).

[20] In spite of his disclaimers, one is bound to consider his *Economic Growth in France and Britain 1851–1950* (Cambridge, Mass., 1964) as economic history.

theory moved dramatically ahead as an intellectual exercise. First, the problem of swallowing Keynes and his interpreters made theoretical work terribly exciting—even, for a time, at the expense of the eternal verities derived from the works of Smith, Ricardo, Mill, and Marshall. Theory suddenly had a point; it was a threat to the establishment in the university chairs—men who had trouble learning "the new economics"—and at the same time seemed to open vista after vista of profound new understanding of the real world. Then after the World War II hiatus, in the counter-reformation, Keynesian macroeconomic theory was overshadowed by the tremendous strides of new-style microeconomics, mathematical economics, activity analysis, operations research, etc. Throughout this period the generation of economic historians contemporaneous with the older, pre-Keynesian theorists continued their work with ever-dwindling numbers of recruits from economics departments. The pre-Keynesian theorists were themselves largely ignored or swept aside.

By the early 1950's the profession of economic history was largely being recruited from the ranks of graduate students in "straight" history. The small number of ranking economic historians trained as economists age 45 to 65 is dramatic evidence of this history. By 1950 the major textbook used in undergraduate courses remained largely unchanged since 1924. The revolutionary changes in the logic of economic analysis had passed American economic history by.

But when the change came to economic history it seemed terribly radical because of the long hiatus. Young men who came to economic history from economics in the 1950's and early 1960's to look for the economist's equivalent of "laws of nature" in the historical record had their primary training in the new and the "new-old" economics. They seemed to understand little of the methods and motives of the old-time fact men in economic history, and went to work rewriting economic history, revising much of the older interpretation, but also pushing the old framework aside altogether and producing entirely new information by new methods, statistical techniques, and data processing. The senior economic historians, even if they had known some old-time economic theory, seemed to comprehend little of the extensive "engineering" side of modern training in economics. As a result, entirely conservative "mainstream" methods of statistical analysis and data processing were viewed with apprehension and distrust by the older generation. A primary consequence of this was a shift in the balance of power within the economic history profession and some bad feeling at conventions.[21]

This brings us up to date. The new economic historians speak the

---

[21] The subjective character of these observations ought to be obvious to the reader. They are based upon my own observations and experiences after a decade as an economist and economic historian, reading, teaching, observing the annual convention jousting, and talking with survivors. Clearly I can claim no irrefutable authority or logic for these views. If the reader disagrees with me, I ask his indulgence since this personal interlude is, I think, important as a preliminary to what follows.

language, not of the old economic historians primarily, but of the new and the new-old economics. Their dream of the ideal economic historian is a cross between Koopmans and Kuznets. Their evaluation of a man like Clapham is, at its kindest, that he is incomprehensible.

The internal arguments of members of this Young (and Not-So-Young) Turk movement, and their assault upon their elders and upon nonquantitative practitioners, is largely what the present uproar is all about. Will these economic historians, the intellectual children of modern economics, remain "true to the facts" and still succeed in "integrating fact and theory" —as the slogan goes? Many certainly think so, but the complaint is heard that progress is slow. My point is, that against this historical background, one can easily see that progress might be slow, and also might not even take place. But it is not because of Schmoller and the German Historical School. The problem is economics itself.

II

After these preliminaries, I want to raise the temperature a bit. Not only do I think that the new economic history might not succeed in integrating fact and theory in all aspects of historical studies, but I really don't think that any general case can be made of such a procedure. It does not follow that good and useful quantitative work can only be done if it is narrowly directed by theory. If I see a two-toed horse, need I have an explanation of it based upon theory for my observation to be of use to biology? In fact, look at biology and geology. Taxonomy alone made powerful contributions to those sciences and if Carl Linnaeus anticipated Darwin, he failed to inform posterity of this momentous fact. Important measuring work was done on the physical aspects of Stonehenge without theory of even practical hypothesis—measurements which, in the event, made it easy for a man with a hunch to find a hypothesis and a believable explanation of the purposes of the monument. It was both admirable and the better part of wisdom for R. J. C. Atkinson to concede as late as 1960 regarding "why" Stonehenge was built: "We do not know, and we shall probably never know."[22] In 1964 G. S. Hawkins demonstrated in *Nature*, after employing computer techniques, that Stonehenge is a kind of neolithic computer.[23]

Measurement without theory. The *Gegenschein* has been under careful observation for two centuries without the slightest notion of what it is; but the careful work of observation made it possible for a satellite's pass through a "neutral zone" to produce a hypothesis.[24] We know a good deal from measurement about the Zodiacal light, but we await the hy-

[22] R. J. C. Atkinson, *Stonehenge* (London, 1960, Pelican edition), p. 168.

[23] Walter Sullivan, "Stonehenge Study," *New York Times,* June 21, 1964, sec. IV, p. 7; Gerald S. Hawkins, "Stonehenge: A Neolithic Computer," *Nature,* Vol. 202 (June 27, 1964), pp. 1258–61.

[24] *New York Times,* December 16, 1964.

pothesis to explain its causes and effects—if any. Kepler had no convincing idea why Mars moved about the sun in an ellipse. He favored the hypothesis based upon circular movements—the Copernican view. But Kepler's careful measurements contributed to a great hypothesis in Newton's mind.[25] Economics, too, is full of great work not based upon theory; look at Imlah and Schlote.

The measurement and study of phenomena is a root of science, as well as theoretical speculation. The same must be true of economics if it is to progress. Both kinds of activity are required. It is the wedding of fact and theory that produce understanding, but facts chosen specifically to fit the theory to be tested—the "imposition" of the theory—will yield no falsifiable, testable results. The "hard" facts of economic life, which have been measured and duly recorded by economic historians, constitute a great achievement. If those facts are not in a form convenient for tests of theory, that is unfortunate but not surprising, *since phenomena occur without reference to theoretical speculation.* There has always, obviously, been the stellar parallax, but both observation and hypothesis were necessary in our own solar system before men began the centuries-long search which finally led W. Struve in 1837 to find parallactic motion (swinging motion) in observations of the giant star Vega.[26] Theory helps us understand phenomena, not the other way around.

If the object of science, including economics, is to discover nature's laws, then the rules of the game should not include strictures about the origins of inquiry. If "science is measurement," then the springboard of measurement surely ought not to be restricted to "economic theory only." It is the good fortune of economics that research workers have always been motivated by the full spectrum of human curiosity. I have stressed theoryless measurement here a moment in order, initially, to loosen up our frame of reference. Let us now consider the uses of theory as part of the process of deduction.

III

The use of theory to illuminate fact and explain it in economics is more difficult than one might suppose at first sight. The major problems

---

[25] Stephen Toulmin, *Foresight and Understanding* (New York, 1961), pp. 18–43. Koopmans, *loc. cit.,* who states clearly the irrelevance of Kepler's Copernican hypotheses to his great discovery of the ellipse of Mars, and the importance of that unadorned set of facts to Newton, nevertheless urges that economists speed up the advance of economic science by merging Keplerian fact-finding stage with Newtonian theorizing stage. Yet Kepler was attempting to merge his own stage with that of Nicolaus Copernicus, and the advance Kepler made was not due to the aid of his hypothesis, but rather in spite of it. To Kepler the ellipse of Mars was "just one more cartload of dung" which was needed to make sense of his own ideas. Toulmin, *op. cit.,* p. 33.

[26] Sir James Jeans, *The Universe Around Us* (Cambridge, 1960), p. 27. Actually F. W. Bessel is credited with first *successfully* measuring the parallax in 61 Cygni in 1838. Struve's calculations using Vega were considered to be excessively inaccurate.

are terribly messy. I consider there to be four major problems involved. The first two problems are (1) *colligation* and (2) *the discovery of initial conditions.*

1. Colligation

Except for work such as that now being done by Smith and others in experimental economics, empirical economics is necessarily, and therefore should consciously be, caught up in the historian's eternal dilemma —colligation—the necessity of viewing a given economic event as one in a temporal sequence, not convincingly understandable except when that event is considered along with its temporal antecedents.[27] Partial equilibrium analysis, at a given moment of time, tells us a good deal about the contemporary forces producing a given phenomenon, but not how that phenomenon came to exist from some previous coalescence of economic forces, or whether the phenomenon might be expected to recur. Unless a fact is a random one, in economics there is a tendency for facts, data, to be produced by the real world *as parts of economic processes.* If price B is 101, that is a fact, and we assume that our logic of price formation will inform us why price B is what it is just now. But if Price A was 100, then the price has risen and the question "Why is B what it is?" has as part of its answer the observation that B exists because the conditions which produced A no longer exist, but have changed so as to produce B. There was a market analysis which explained A, and one or more of the assumptions, postulates, statements of initial conditions, etc., must be changed to explain B. When the economist does this, he has become a historian, whether he likes it or not.

The careful historian usually handles the colligation problem by some introductory statement setting the "tone" of the initial point of enquiry with a reference to what has gone before, wherever in time he begins his account. A masterful example of this art is found in Gibbon, such that after only six paragraphs we read:

Such was the state of the Roman frontiers, and such the maxims of Imperial policy, from the death of Augustus to Trajan.[28]

Clapham faced his colligation problem with essentially a 380-page introduction.[29] Mantoux took 190 pages to warm to his subject.[30]

On themes more modest than the rise and fall of empires and whole economic systems, less space may be needed for the problem. Yet it must always be faced, and there are really no fixed rules for deciding where

---

[27] W. H. Walsh, *Philosophy of History* (New York, 1960), pp. 59–64.

[28] Edward Gibbon, *The Decline and Fall of the Roman Empire* (New York, Modern Library edition), Vol. 1, p. 5.

[29] *Op. cit.,* Vol. 1, the first eight chapters.

[30] Paul Mantoux, *The Industrial Revolution in the Eighteenth Century* (London, 1928), all of Part I.

to begin. Here judgment based upon background learning is simply required. Thomas Wilson, writing of the "farm problem" in the 1930's,[31]
realized that the problem had antecedents and went back to the great
collapse of farm prices in 1919 for his initial "cut-in" point. Yet the problem of insufficient internal demand relative to American farm capacity
does not begin there, nor is that even a particularly important point in
time. It is amusing to see J. K. Galbraith,[32] in spite of his great surgical
skills, but possibly because of his deep knowledge of the problem, simply
throwing up his hands and going back to the early 17th century—to "the
beginning." A writer facing the question of Churchill's 1925 exchange-
rate decision might ponder whether, as Sir Albert Feavearyear suggested,[33] the reign of King Offa of Mercia really is the logical place to
trace the remote origin of "the ancient right standard of England."

Since there is no general rule, it is vitally important that the empirical
worker be intelligent about his colligation problem. If theory helps in this
effort, fine, but other considerations as simple as the death of a king, could
be key factors in choosing a cut-in point, or a cut-out point. Econometric
models involving time, like historical narratives, have a double problem,
the justification of the initial starting point, and then the internal sequence
of repercussions as changes in any of the variables produce all-around
adjustments in the other variables of a system of simultaneous equations. "Colligation" here is a set of constants and functional relationships.
Yet at the end, the final adjustment has essentially been produced by a
sequence of "events," just as surely as the peace treaty following a war,
or a great corporate amalgamation represent outcomes of historical linkages. After all, the Interstate Commerce Commission has meaning *only*
in the light of its history, and a noncolligated account of the operations
of the ICC would be a fairly mysterious narrative.

All this is doubtless a great bother to the economist anxious to get on
with his analysis, yet adequate information requires that in work using
data which have actually been generated by the economy, the colligation
problem be met, just as the log of experiments in laboratory work is part
of the information which guides current research underway. There is
always a relevant history and a beginning point in empirical work which
need careful delineation. The results depend upon it. Had Professor
Morgenstern discovered the slowly developing "stability" of the gold
points in the genesis of the 19th century gold standard, he would not have
been so alarmed at the wide variance of actual rates away from his mean
gold points. He also might not have calculated his gold points the way
he did.[34]

---

[31] *Fluctuations in Income and Employment* (3rd ed., New York, 1949), p. 160.

[32] *American Capitalism, The Concept of Countervailing Power* (Boston, 1952),
chap. xi.

[33] *Op. cit.*, p. 7.

[34] This episode is treated in Lance E. Davis and Jonathan R. T. Hughes. "A
Dollar-Sterling Exchange 1803–1895," *Economic History Review*, Second Series, Vol.
13 (August, 1960), pp. 52–78.

2. *The Discovery of Initial Conditions*

Closely associated with the problem of colligation is that of the discovery and statement of initial conditions. It is sometimes cynically said that "History is what the historian says it is." It is true that the historian chooses his facts, his unit of history, on the basis of instinct, plan or theory, and ignores the rest. Whether he is a good historian or not determines the quality of the act of selection. Second, the historian, understanding his colligation problem, must decide at which point in the stream of causation his "history" begins; whether in events $a \ldots n$, the study of event k might better begin at h or even g than merely at i. The economist is involved in precisely the same sorts of operations. When he decides, as he must, which variables he will ignore, he is "choosing his facts," and when he states his "given" circumstances in his statement of initial conditions, he is creating his "world." In an analysis of prices, he may have as an axiom that all utility surfaces are convex, and that is a "theoretic term."[35] But if he assumes that perfect competition exists for firms in his market, he is stating, as his initial conditions, that there are no barriers to entry and exit, that perfect knowledge exists, that no single firm can influence price, and so forth. By placing the relevant world of study in the universe of time and circumstance by act of exclusion (i.e., excluding both time and events around the few events in the given period of time in which events are thought to have occurred), the economist completes the historian's role.

This is more like history than it is like physical science. To the physicist many of the initial conditions of the experimental work are known from previous experiments, from knowledge of the role of the technology, the importance of the temperature of the laboratory, the character of the equipment, the fineness of the chemicals used, etc. The economist, on the other hand, "creates" these things. He chooses them for himself. His initial conditions are not given but must be actively discovered, since his laboratory is the economic world and that reality contains his initial conditions. His view of that reality largely determines how he will choose his set of initial conditions. When, for example, an economist begins an empirical analysis of the American automobile industry, with the statement that it is best considered to be a case of "perfect" competition, the statement has been informed by observation, faulty or not.

As an aside, the economist who believes that he is "free" from the historian's dilemma because history is irrelevant to economic analysis is not only reckless as an empiricist, but as a theorist as well—at least if

---

[35] The usefulness and place of theoretic terms is discussed by Ernest Nagel in his adventure into the world of economists. "Assumptions in Economic Theory," *American Economic Review*, Papers and Proceedings, Vol. LII, No. 2 (May, 1963), pp. 212–13.

his theory is supposed to be about something, since "observation includes thinking and relies on background knowledge."[36]

Schumpeter's long introduction to *Business Cycles* is certainly one of the most knowledgeable and sophisticated disquisitions in the literature concerning the fine art of discovery and statement of assumptions about reality—initial and background conditions—anterior to the use of theory and knowledge about that reality in order to understand "phenomena." It is thrice unfortunate that *Business Cycles* is now in oblivion: (1) the work is a mine of information about the history of modern capitalism; (2) Schumpeter's great culture and erudition ought to be a model for the student; (3) Schumpeter understood that scientific work, especially in economics, is usually difficult, that theories lead to "understanding" only through extensive falsifications of predictions.

Consider Schumpeter's defense of the use of the perfectly competitive equilibrium model:

The importance of the case does not, of course, rest with the frequency of its occurrence in actual life. A system satisfying its conditions in all its parts has probably never existed.[37]

But such a set of simplifying assumptions about the economy

. . . however abstract or remote from real life it may be, yet renders indispensible service in clearing ground for rigorous analysis.[38]

Schumpeter clearly saw his twofold problem, clearing the ground (by his statement of initial conditions), and rigorous analysis using theoretic notions on that cleared ground.

It is interesting to observe, time and again, Schumpeter's painstaking efforts to justify his simplifying assumptions about the real world. He was aware both that abstraction must be made *and* that the resulting assumptions should not be irrelevant to the world about which they are supposed to make *some* statement that is not meaningless. His effort to justify his classification of various economic realities, changes in tastes, population growth, money supply, etc., as endogenous and exogenous variables is a model of its kind.[39] Here again it is knowledge of reality and not just logic itself which dictates the proceedings.[40]

---

[36] C. F. Pressley, "Laws and Theories in the Physical Sciences," *Philosophy of Science* (New York, 1960), p. 207. The quote is from Mackie.

[37] *Business Cycles, A Theoretical, Historical and Statistical Analysis of the Capitalist Process* (New York, 1939), Vol. I, p. 46, n. 2.

[38] *Ibid.*, I, p. 68.

[39] *Ibid.*, I, pp. 72–129.

[40] Schumpeter was the picture of lucid methodological organization compared to the disarray into which the economics profession has fallen since Milton Friedman's initial foray into "predictivism" and the subsequent discussion. Samuelson describes Ernest Nagel's "defense" of Friedman as "an attempt to save Friedman from himself." The discussion thus generated continues and generates at least as much heat as light. Nagel, *loc. cit.*, *passim*, and Samuelson's discussion, pp. 231–36; followed by Fritz Machlup, "Professor Samuelson on Theory and Realism," and Samuelson's

Once all this is done Schumpeter proceeds to the application of his purely theoretic assumptions. The result was supposed to have been his great masterpiece and a monument to the powers of economic analysis: its surprising failure resulted from the weakness of a theoretical structure that was unequal to the task. Economists were not convinced that the logic of the three-cycle scheme together with the simplifying assumptions "explained" business cycles.[41]

For all its failure, *Business Cycles* is a singular work. Schumpeter did not choose his reality on the basis of theory. There was a phenomenon to be explained, the business cycle; there was the set of hypotheses about its development, the three-cycle scheme; and there was the relationship of history to the theory in the long statement and justification of the simplifying assumptions which enabled a great deal of "price theory" to be useful as information inputs along with crude fact. The method Schumpeter followed leads us to our further questions regarding economic history and theory: (3) *the falsification of the protasis* and (4) *treatment of externalities.*

3. Falsification of the Protasis

The process of deduction has two parts, the protasis and the apodosis. The apodosis is the consequence of the conjunction of statements which is the protasis. In empirical economics the protasis includes that statement of initial conditions, b, conjoined with the set of assumptions, axioms, etc., which comprise the theoretical knowledge employed, Θ. It is asserted that the conjunction of b and Θ will make it possible to derive s, the final conditions, apodosis, outcome, or predicted result.[42]

The statement b of initial conditions contains (as we have seen in Schumpeter) the premises relating to matters of fact; e.g., if we say that

---

"Reply," *American Economic Review,* Vol. 54 (September, 1964), pp. 733–39. Some of the central issues in this discussion are given a full airing in Jack Melitz, "Friedman and Machlup on the Significance of Testing Economic Assumptions," *Journal of Political Economy,* Vol. 73 (February, 1965), pp. 37–60. For the economic historian much of this entire discussion will seem sterile since economic historians actually do work with data *and other* historical materials regularly and the issue is not purely academic. My own preferences regarding the problems of separating simplifying and theoretical assumptions are given in footnote 42 below. If one is studying, say, the growth of a steel industry and associated economic phenomena, and one "assumes" the presence of coalfields, the existence or nonexistence of such fields is of some importance. If one assumes that the industry is monopolistic, whether this be in fact so is important.

[41] The exception is perhaps Rendigs Fels, *American Business Cycles* (Chapel Hill, N.C., 1959).

[42] Pressley, *op. cit., passim.* R. L. Basmann, *On Predictive Testing of a Simultaneous Equations Model: The Retail Market for Food in the U.S.* (Institute for Quantitative Research in Economics and Management, No. 78, Purdue University), pp. 1–22. Basmann also touches on this matter in "The Role of the Economic Historian in the Predictive Testing of Preferred 'Economic Laws'," *Explorations in Entrepreneurial History,* Second Series, Vol. 2 (Spring-Summer, 1965), pp. 159–86.

an assumption of the argument is that perfect competition exists, we are asserting that as our view of the world for the purposes of producing s, our prediction. Some of our assumptions might be entirely theoretic terms, necessary in the logical structure for its completion, but bearing no directly observable characteristics at all—for example, that all utility surfaces of our consumers are convex, or that the marginal utility of money declines for each. Our assumptions are mixed as between reality and unreality, no particular virtue attaches to either state of the assumptions *except in the context of producing* s.

This combination of assumptions about the world *we choose* (i.e., the statement b of initial conditions), together with the theoretical assumptions and statements Θ we use to produce our final conditions, s, encompasses the problems we discussed above in a particular way. Since laws of nature are hard to establish in economics, they are not commonly part of economic analysis, and in economic analysis theoretical constructions take the place of natural law in the protasis as it is usually formed in physical science.[43]

Thus neither part of the protasis, neither b nor Θ, can be taken from authority, but in economics both are chosen by the investigator himself. Hence the statement of initial conditions b must be both "realistic" enough to be relevant to the world which produced the data under examination, and yet be "abstract" or generalized enough to be amenable to combination with the set of theoretical assumptions and statements which comprise Θ. If the prediction s fails to find suitable agreement with real world data, then the *entire protasis,* and not just Θ, the theory, has been falsified, and the entire protasis must be reexamined to see whether it was a defective statement of relevant initial conditions, or a misstep in the structure of the theory, or both to which the falsification of the predicted result can be attributed. In any case, the *entire protasis* has been falsified, and we cannot say which parts without examination. After all, a perfectly good theory might fail to predict if combined with inappropriate initial conditions (theory of monopoly behavior together with relevant initial conditions tested against data from a perfectly competitive industry).

The existence of production at prices below variable costs, long noted as a practice in steel production during cyclical downswings,[44] does not

---

43 Pressley, *op. cit.,* p. 210.

44 Duncan Burn, *The Economic History of Steelmaking 1867–1939* (Cambridge, 1961), pp. 35–36. Also: Hughes, *op. cit.,* pp. 180–81; R. H. Campbell, "Fluctuations in Stocks," *Oxford Economic Papers,* New Series, Vol. 9 (February, 1957), pp. 50–55, for Scottish practice; D. H. Robertson, *A Study of Industrial Fluctuations* (London, 1948 reprint), p. 33. In the instances cited the existence of time in the "real world," ability to produce for inventories, excessive cost of rebuilding furnaces if output stops even though average revenue is less than average variable cost, the relative financial strength of the firms involved, together with financial barriers to entry into the industry, all serve to destroy the usefulness of usual stated initial condition of perfect competition in the iron and steel industries in the cyclical downswing.

mean that something is "wrong" with the theory of the firm. It does mean that a protasis which includes an assumption of perfect competition in the statement of initial conditions has been falsified. Clearly entry and exit are not "perfect."

A different notion of the protasis is found several times in Oskar Morgenstern's monumental *International Financial Transactions and Business Cycles.*[45] This vast study is an attempt to measure evidences of the international transmission of cyclical impulses through transactions of a primarily financial nature. To do this, Morgenstern had to know "what to look at" in the way of data. If one chooses to ignore trade and payments connected with goods and services (as Morgenstern explicitly did), then the relevant points at which data arise are at adjustment points which are *assumed to exist* in the basic theoretical model of the international economy.

Such points are essentially arbitrage points. (1) If country A's payments with country B run to such a deficit that bills on B purchased in country A rise to a sufficient premium, *then* a point is reached where, given the costs of shipment, it pays to buy gold and export it to B. That effective rate of exchange is the *gold export point* and marks the extreme limit of depreciation of A's exchange against B so long as gold movements are free and mint pars exist. (2) In a perfect market, one and only one price prevails. Given the costs of transferring funds, there should be no extensive or long-term interest differentials between members of the international market. In both cases, interest and exchange arbitrage, the adjustment mechanism is assumed to work in the absence of government interference and imperfections in the market. These conditions, in which such adjustments *could take place,* were widely believed to exist before 1914.[46]

Morgenstern's problem was initially to (1) mark off the gold points, within which cyclical variations of exchange rates could be traced and (2) find comparable interest rates whose variations against each other reflected basic cyclical forces. The actual data Morgenstern produced would leave in a state of near-shock an economist well versed in the painless axioms of the classical theory. Even so experienced a practitioner as Morgenstern was seemingly ill-prepared for the barbaric imperfections of the "real" 19th-century world.

In short-term interest rates gaps between countries were surprisingly great and long-lasting:

The persistence of wide gaps is a phenomenon that will occupy us still further, when the question will be raised whether they are compatible with the gold standard and the implicit close interaction of the various countries. The reader

---

[45] Princeton University Press, for the National Bureau of Economic Research, 1959.

[46] Paul Einzig, *The History of Foreign Exchange* (London, 1962), chap. 15, esp. pp. 172–73 on this point.

will notice that there are almost always very considerable differences and that this hardly conforms with the expectations one might obtain from the literature.[47]

From our viewpoint this world is upside down. We are not surprised that our protasis must be reworked after a prediction has been proven false. That indeed is how we understand the world. But we raise neither doubts about "the gold standard" nor theory alone. The gaps Morgenstern describes *did exist during what has been called the gold standard period.*

Wide fluctuations of exchange rates beyond presumed gold points were found to be even more shocking, were indeed "violations."

A further study of violations, including the incredible phenomenon of exchange rates often and persistently beyond the gold points, enabled us to isolate periods of international financial tension.[48]

There is a problem of definition here. No exchange rate can go beyond the gold points by definition, the extremities of the rates *are* the gold points. It is assumed for convenience's sake in model building that there are stable gold points but this is no reason at all for the empirical researcher to make the same assumption about data generated from real world transactions. It is a stated initial condition in the protasis that makes the gold points stable, not any condition in the world. The assumption that gold-point stability in the real world was a narrowly confined set of exchange-rate fluctuations has introduced a great deal of muddle into discussions of the gold standard.[49] Our point here is that a part of the protasis was an assumption of stability in the general factor-price equalization model. The absence of gold-point stability does not imply anything wrong with international trade theory or anything mysterious in the real world.

Long-term interest rates also scarcely fit any model which assumes a solidarity in international financial markets. Morgenstern again finds the difference "remarkable."[50] It is wholly unexpected. But *everything* is unexpected to a priori argument only. Only in conjunction with a statement of simplifying assumptions are the facts interesting and amenable to analysis and understanding. *Both* parts of the protasis provide our prediction. Morgenstern thus is mystified by interest differentials that don't disappear.

. . . capital movements never closed the permanent gaps where they existed. This indicates a lack of response quite out of keeping *with traditional theory* [my italics], and we must therefore look for such reasonable arguments as will help to enlighten us about these permanent margins.[51]

---

[47] Morgenstern, *op. cit.*, p. 157.
[48] *Ibid.*, p. 276.
[49] Davis and Hughes, *op. cit.*, pp. 60–64.
[50] Morgenstern, *op. cit.*, p. 470.
[51] *Ibid.*, p. 161.

This indeed is what ought to occur when the protasis is shown to be inadequate. But it is not the theory alone which fails to account for reality. It is theory *plus* the simplifying assumptions about that reality which have failed. Morgenstern finds that risk differences account for the differential. Studies of the background conditions, however, lead one far into a study of productivity differentials[52] wherein an explanation probably lies that is warranted by the evidence. It is not news, by the way, to the economic historian that permanent interest differentials existed, nor that gold-point stability was only a convenient simplifying assumption.[53]

There are of course many examples in the literature in which the entire protasis is viewed as theory and statements regarding theory are made directly from evidence, or about the world from theory alone. An example is Macesich's effort to impose the Ricardian price-specie flow model, in all its purity, upon the American economy of the 1830's.[54] As might be expected, he was soon in trouble. The large American current-account deficit of the period is difficult to reconcile with evidence of *net specie imports*. An appeal was made to the evidence of "exchange rates" (he used bill prices, we will return to this shortly), and except for 1837 these indicate an *excess supply* of sterling. Sales of American securities abroad were assumed to have produced the gold inflow in spite of the current-account deficit (which, *ceteris paribus,* might be associated with a gold outflow.) We were then told that "changes in exchange rates conform to theoretical expectations."[55] Again, after explaining a specie out-flow in 1839 in conjunction with a large current-account deficit and *no significant movement of "exchange rates,"* we were told that: "In general, specie movements conform with theoretical expectations."[56]

As it happens, the simplifying assumptions Macesich used are not sufficiently in concordance with the reality of the 1830's. The basic assumptions he made are: (1) stable bank reserves; (2) bimetallism works just like the gold standard; (3) stable gold points could be maintained with the existing communications (sailboats) system; (4) communications between markets on both sides of the ocean could support solidarity in the

[52] A recent attempt to explain long-term productivity differentials between the United States and the United Kingdom by an economic historian is H. J. Habakkuk, *American and British Technology in the 19th Century* (Cambridge, 1962). A penetrating critique of this work is David Landes, "Factor Costs and Demand; Determinants of Economic Growth," *Business History,* Vol. VII, No. 1, January, 1965.

[53] A straightforward discussion of gold-point stability as a slowly developing characteristic of the pre-1914 financial system may be found in Margaret G. Myers, *The New York Money Market* (New York, 1931), pp. 341–44. The long-lasting interest differential was part of the understood conditions of 19th-century finance. See tables in Sidney Homer, *A History of Interest Rates* (New Brunswick, N.J., 1963), chaps. xiii and xvi, comparable years and maturities.

[54] George Macesich, "Sources of Monetary Disturbances in the United States 1834–1845," *Journal of Economic History,* Vol. 20 (September, 1960), pp. 407–26.

[55] *Ibid.,* p. 416.

[56] *Ibid.,* p. 417.

price relationships of the "transatlantic market." These initial conditions are not in accord with the reality of the period.

But apart from that, a closer study of the "background conditions" would illuminate enough of current practices to indicate that prices of bills of exchange do not constitute exchange rates, since bill prices include a discount for interest charges, and bill prices thus tend to vary *inversely* with interest-rate movements.[57] In point of fact, throughout the period under discussion pure exchange rates—interest discount removed—show sterling at a strong premium in America (excess *demand* for sterling), something one would expect, given the balance-of-payments situation.[58] The sterling premium disappeared in the early 1840's when an American export surplus developed and sterling was in excess supply.

Hence, the conformity of Macesich's reality to his "theoretical expectations" is odd considering that he's got his facts upside down. Given the structure of the protasis, if the theory is internally consistent, his initial conditions would have to be exactly wrong.

Why there should have been a net inflow of coin and bullion from 1834 to 1838, when sterling was at a premium, remains a mystery. Perhaps foreign investment is part of the answer. The entire protasis put together by Macesich is disconfirmed and, as a result, needs to be thought out again. As for "'theoretical expectation"—that, in our view, does not exist apart from the stated initial conditions. Theory must be "about something." Obviously the bullion and exchange-rate movements of the 1830's can be explained, but by 1835 Ricardo had been dead a decade, and anyway, he knew nothing of American conditions. Fresh work is needed.

In neither of the last two cases we have used by way of illustration is the falsification of the protasis ground for not accepting theory, as a narrow predictivist might urge us to do. Instead, a more diligent search for relevant initial conditions is called for.

Finally, let it be noted again that falsification increases our knowledge. The Morgenstern findings are especially suggestive of this. Perfect confirmation of the protasis might merely indicate coincidence, or that the protasis is too general, and can be used to predict too wide a range of events to be meaningful. We gain knowledge by knowing the specific circumstances under which our apodosis is not in agreement with warranted fact. Morgenstern's gold-point violations constituted new information of the first rank when so many economists believed in perfect gold-point stability. We noted earlier a similar example of the importance of falsification in evidence that iron and steel firms continued to work in depressions when their variable costs were *not* covered (borrowing from

---

[57] Davis and Hughes, *op. cit.*, pp. 53–56 for a discussion of the adjustments that are necessary to correct the bill prices in order to "free" them of the interest discount and other anomalies, and extract from them a pure rate of exchange.

[58] *Ibid.*, p. 72, Table A–2. Compare with the chart given by Macesich in the relevant period, *op. cit.*, p. 415.

banks to pay wages). An enquiry into the components of the simplifying assumption of perfect competition and its nonconcordance with reality yielded vital new information, especially about the trade cycle.[59]

To do any work of this kind correctly calls for information which comes not from "integrating theory and history," as some "new" economic historians urge us to do, but rather from critically analyzing factual information derived from historical research *and* from understanding the nature of simplifying assumptions. I think this is *not* what some of the new economic historians are encouraging, and that it is unfortunate, both for economics and economic history. Only from rigorously constructed work of this kind will we understand both the annual rise of the *Messiah* audience *and* its royal origins. Economic history deserves no less an attempt to find the truth than does cultural history.

4. The Problem of Externalities

Finally, attempts to find uniformities in economic behavior over time are continually sandbagged by autonomous or "external" occurrences. These externalities—whether they be obvious and easily identified, like wars and harvest failures, or are more difficult to uncover—are nonsystematic disruptions of normal economic life; nevertheless, they are felt and must somehow be handled in colligated analyses like economic histories and econometric models. As Pirenne put it:

An unforeseen event is always followed by a catastrophe in proportion to its importance. It flings itself, so to speak, across the current of historic life, interrupting the series of causes and effects of which this current is constituted, damming them up . . . and by the unexpected repercussions overturning the natural order of things.[60]

Returning to Part 1 of this section, if A moved to B because of a Presidential order activated by some state agency, and none of the "technical" relationships changed initially, the order and its consequences become a part of the empirical economist's "bag of tools" if he still wants to discuss the real world relevantly. Both the historian and the empirical economist handle the problem by suitable adjustments. They must do so in order to weave the Presidential order in period B into their thinking—the results of the Presidential order will already be in the data—so that the handling of the colligation problem will not be accidentally exclusive of relevant fact. In a future period, C, the results of the Presidential order, an externality when it first appeared, might be hardened into a fact of economic life to be treated in the statement of initial conditions. Hence there is

---

[59] See footnote 44 above.

[60] Henri Pirenne, *A History of Europe from the Invasions to the XVI Century* (New York, 1956), p. 50. Pirenne is here referring to the long-term impact of the Moslem invasions upon the course of European history.

much more to the construction of the protasis than a merely a priori formulation of theoretic assumptions.

The problem, therefore, if one wants to understand the sequence of actual phenomena over time, is further complicated by an additional issue which *does not* depend for its solution upon integrating theory and history, but rather upon very carefully worked out historical inference.

However trivially obvious this would be to a historian, its importance is not always recognized in economics.[61] Also, Schumpeter's defense of the usual procedure in economic analysis is interesting.

Hence we arrive at the very important concept of factors acting from without (let us call them External Factors), which it stands to reason we must try to abstract from when working out an explanation of the causation of economic fluctuations properly so called, that is, of those economic changes which are inherent in the working of the economic organism itself.[62]

Taken at face value, Schumpeter's position is illogical since, as any economic historian should know, and as Pirenne emphasized, there *are* reactions which set permanent change in the stream of economic life due to external causes (Schumpeter agreed that his assumption would limit him somewhat to the surface of things).[63] Evidence of the changing slope of the consumption function after World War II is surely a measure of changing attitudes toward spending and saving due to an externally produced period of high earnings and liquidity which somehow came to be accepted as normal.[64] In the current jargon of economics there was a "ratchet effect" of wartime prosperity which was reinforced in the postwar period by high-level spending from wealth and earned income. The failure to recognize such factors caused an earlier generation of American economists enormous embarassment when the depression of 1946–47 failed to materialize.

Yet Schumpeter, too, has a valid point, in that, as he emphasizes, there are regularities which theory can help to elucidate, and these regularities cannot be understood unless they are studied mainly in isolation from all external events. The "Principle of Causality"[65] surely ought to stimulate economists, as well as other scientists, to try to discover isolated systems of events whose initial conditions are repeatable.

This is a great problem yet to be solved in economics. For the historian,

---

[61] See Basmann, "On Predictive Testing," *op. cit.*, pp. 57–59, for comment on current practice, and in particular, the well-known test by Carl Christ of L. R. Klein's econometric model of the United States. The model was based upon 1921–47, but the test used only the two years 1946–47 for data, as if World War II and its aftermath would have no important effects upon the structure of the economy.

[62] *Op. cit.*, Vol. I, p. 7.

[63] *Ibid.*, p. 7, n. 2.

[64] See the data and summary of the discussion in R. A. Gordon, *Business Fluctuations* (2d ed.; New York, 1961), pp. 98–105. The Korean War also had at least short-run effects upon the community's consumption habits.

[65] Philipp Frank, *Philosophy of Science* (Englewood Cliffs, N.J., 1962), chap. 12, esp. pp. 284–85.

using the marvelously flexible techniques of a verbal language, the problem is not a barrier to understanding. Economists, however, utilizing the more formal equipment of mathematics, have a problem here. I cannot believe that a new economic historian, *looking for facts on the basis of existing economic theory,* can conceivably be of much assistance here. In fact, the economic historian's contribution to the solution of the general problem of externalities will increase as he establishes, without reference to theory, the specific effects of external economic disturbances.

Concluding Remarks

In this essay I have *not* said that theory is of no use in economic history. I have said that historical investigation should not be strictly limited by theoretical information. The distinction is not a very subtle one, and I hope it does not cause misunderstanding. I agree wholeheartedly that theory helps us to understand and explain economic phenomena. But I also believe that we advance knowledge not by theory alone. There is a big difference between research which is stimulated by theoretical questions and research that is limited by them.

Much has been done in recent years to aid the understanding of economic processes by empirical research in economic history which utilizes recent advances in the training of economists. Much could be lost, however, if the new economic historian failed to mind the dictum that, in the end, the historian must remain true to the facts. This is not an excuse for unimaginative work in economic history, work which is not at all informed by theoretical insight. But it is a constraint placed by expectations of non-historians upon historians that they, like others, should try to pursue truth for its own sake. "No holds barred" as a rule of technique is a good rule in the pursuit of truth. Clio is unkind to those who confuse ends and means in the pursuit of historical understanding.

PART II

1. Measuring British Economic Growth[*]

Jonathan R. T. Hughes
Purdue University

AMERICAN ECONOMISTS are aware of the venerable British tradition of inquiry and deduction which has given rise to so much of modern economic theory and which has studded the science with the names of great theorists from Hume to Hicks. A less celebrated, but in many ways no less imposing, British tradition has been the hard core of fact gatherers, measurers, and informed observers. The tradition began with Sir William Petty and Gregory King at the end of the 17th century, was continued by Arthur Young in the 18th and by Patrick Colquhoun at the beginning of the 19th century.[1] That century witnessed a rich flowering of quantitative study. Britain was once again, as during Petty's time, deep in the throes of widely pervasive social change, this time because of the penetration of the industrial economy into the fabric of everyday life. A long sequence

---

[*] Reprinted from the *Journal of Economic History,* Vol. XXIV, No. 1 (March, 1964), pp. 60–82.

A review of two recent publications: (1) *British Economic Growth, 1688–1959: Trends and Structure,* by Phyllis Deane and W. A. Cole (New York: Cambridge University Press, 1962), pp. xvi, 348, and (2) *Abstract of British Historical Statistics,* by B. R. Mitchell with the collaboration of Phyllis Deane (New York: Cambridge University Press, 1962), pp. xiv, 513.

[1] Petty was the author of a considerable volume of work relating to economic questions. His *Political Arithmetic* was written in 1671, during the reign of Charles II, but was published posthumously in 1690. A year later, the equally well-known *The Political Arithmetic of Ireland* appeared. Both works were attempts to estimate income and wealth magnitudes. Petty's work was rudimentary compared to Gregory King's *Natural and Political Observations . . .* which was published in 1696.

Arthur Young's many writings included tracts on agriculture, husbandry, money, commercial policy, and national and international affairs. He is, of course, best known for his accounts of his travels in England, Ireland, and France. In 1774, he brought out his own *Political Arithmetic,* a volume in which an attempt was made to ascertain aggregate economic magnitudes.

Patrick Colquhoun, a London police magistrate and Lord Provost of Glasgow, is perhaps best known for his *Treatise on the Population, Wealth, Power and Resources of the British Empire,* published in 1814. *His Treatise on Indigence,* 1806, contained a more detailed breakdown of aggregates than King attempted more than a century earlier; but Sir Robert Giffen thought that many of Colquhoun's details were "fanciful": *Growth of Capital* (London, 1890), p. 101.

of mainly quantitative inquiries followed in the wake of industrialization.

The great 19th century quantitative studies were motivated again and again by policy disputes and doctrinal controversies. In brief, the tradition rested on a handful of major efforts. J. R. M'Culloch's *Dictionary of Commerce* appeared in 1832, and his *Statistical Account of the British Empire* in 1837. Thomas Tooke published two volumes of *The History of Prices* in 1838. Both M'Culloch and Tooke liberally mixed commentary with their statistical illustrations. W. F. Spackman's *Statistical Tables* followed (1843), and Tooke brought out another volume in 1840 and Volume IV in 1848. In 1849, a landmark in measurement of economic magnitudes appeared: G. R. Porter's *Progress of the Nation*. In 1852, came Braithwaite Pool's *Statistics of Commerce*. Volumes V and VI of Tooke's *History* appeared in 1857 in collaboration with William Newmarch, the rising young statistician. Newmarch published papers in 1859–61 in the *Journal of the Statistical Society* utilizing price indices (he could have seen this device used in at least two earlier works),[2] and W. S. Jevons, acknowledging his debt to Newmarch, followed with his celebrated tract, "A Permanent Fall in the Value of Gold Ascertained" (1863), in which the Jevons price index first saw light. This was to be followed in 1886 by the more extensive price index of Augustus Sauerbeck (which is still printed monthly by *The Statist*, or at least was, as of September, 1963). Meanwhile, in 1860, a new quantitative history followed a rising literature on specific industries: James Mann's *The Cotton Trade of Great Britain*. A year later, in the M'Culloch tradition came Andrew Ure's *Dictionary of Arts, Manufactures and Mines*. James Jeans' *Notes on Northern Industry* (1879) included a heavy use of quantitative information among informed observations. In 1880, came Leon Levi's massive *History of British Commerce*—a work which still has a distinctly "modern" ring—and in 1866, Thomas Ellison's *The Cotton Trade of Great Britain*, with its huge foldout tables of time series. In 1884, J. E. Thorold Rogers' *Six Centuries of Work and Wages* brought a unique viewpoint to the study of quantitative materials. In the late 1890's, A. L. Bowley's indices of 19th century wages began to appear, soon to be followed by others in collaboration with G. H. Wood. The final three works in the fact-gathering *genre* were M. G. Mulhall's *Dictionary of Statistics* (1886, 2d edition); R. H. Inglis Palgrave's *Dictionary of Political Economy* (1894), which was virtually an encyclopedia but also contained useful statistical materials; and William Page's *Commerce and Industry* (1919), which was really the end of the 19th-century tradition.

The search for data on economic growth and change was by then becoming more specialized. Progress in British economic affairs seemed to be less automatic than in the Victorian Era, and great quantitative collec-

---

[2] G. R. Porter and Joseph Lowe, as cited by T. E. Gregory in his introduction to the Adelphi Press reprint (London: P. S. King and Son Ltd., 1928) of Tooke's *History of Prices*, p. 14.

tions tended to be increasingly analytical and specific in focus. Following Bowley's work, Lord Stamp's classic, *British Incomes and Property* (1916), reopened a route started by Petty and King, and the road led through Colin Clark (1932)[3] and others to modern income accounting in Britain, then to A. R. Prest's first historical series (1948),[4] pushing the income approach backward to 1870, and then to Phyllis Deane's 1956 and 1957[5] work on very early estimates, which went literally back to the "founders" and especially to Gregory King. The index number approach was carried over to British industrial production statistics by the German scholar, Walther Hoffmann (1934),[6] and into trade by another German, Werner Schlote (1938).[7] Albert Imlah's monumental work[8] on British trade and payments data (1948 and 1952), together with Alexander Cairncross's foreign investment figures, carried the quantitative studies of Britain's overseas commerce to fruition.

There were, of course, others of prime importance: N. A. Tolles and Paul Douglas (1930) on industrial production; Paul Douglas on capital formation (1930); Lord Beveridge's prodigious researches into early price movements (beginning in the 1920's); Norman Silberling (1923);[9] H. A. Shannon 's brick index (1934);[10] R. S. Tucker's wage indices (1936);[11]

---

[3] Clark, *The National Income, 1924–31* (London: Macmillan, 1932).

[4] Prest, "National Income of the United Kingdom, 1870–1946," *Economic Journal,* Vol. LVIII, No. 229 (March, 1948), pp. 31–62.

[5] Deane, "Contemporary Estimates of the National Income in the First Half of the Nineteenth Century," *Economic History Review,* Second Series, Vol. VIII (April, 1956), pp. 339–54. "Contemporary Estimates of the National Income in the Second Half of the Nineteenth Century," *ibid.,* Vol. IX (April, 1957), pp. 451–61. Also, her "The Implications of Early National Income Estimates," *Economic Development and Cultural Change,* Vol. IV (November, 1955), pp. 3–38, and "The Industrial Revolution and Economic Growth," *ibid.,* Vol. V (January, 1957), pp. 159–74.

[6] Hoffmann's index appeared first in *Weltwirtschaftliches Archiv,* Vol. II (1934). The book analyzing the index came out a few years later, *Wachstum und Wachstumsformen der englischen Wirtschaft von 1700 bis zur Gegenwart* (Jena, 1940). A revision of this appeared as *British Industry 1700–1950,* translated by W. O. Henderson and W. H. Chaloner (New York: Kelley, 1955).

[7] Schlote, original title, *Entwicklung und Strukturwandlungen des englischen Aussenhandels von 1700 bis zur Gegenwart* (Jena, 1938), and translated by W. O. Henderson and W. H. Chaloner as *British Overseas Trade from 1700 to the 1930's* (New York: Macmillan Co. 1952).

[8] First published as three articles, as follows: Albert H. Imlah, "Real Values in British Foreign Trade, 1798–1853," *Journal of Economic History,* Vol. VIII (November, 1948), pp. 133–52: "The Terms of Trade of the United Kingdom, 1798–1913," *ibid.,* Vol. X (November, 1950), pp. 170–94; and "The British Balance of Payments and Export of Capital, 1816–1913," *Economic History Review,* Second Series, Vol. V, No. 2 (1952), pp. 208–39. All of these were brought together in *Economic Elements in the Pax Britannica,* (Cambridge, Mass.: Harvard University Press, 1958).

[9] Silberling, "British Prices and Business Cycles, 1779–1850," *Review of Economic Statistics,* Vol. V (October, 1923), pp. 219–62.

[10] Shannon, "Bricks—A Trade Index, 1785–1849," *Economica,* New Series, Vol. I (August, 1934), pp. 300–18.

[11] Tucker, "Real Wages of Artisans in London, 1729–1935," *Journal of the American Statistical Association,* Vol. XXXI (March, 1936), pp. 73–84.

Elizabeth Gilboy (1936);[12] Mrs. E. B. Schumpeter (1938);[13] and a host of others, including the important work of J. R. N. Stone.

Since space does not permit a full-scale assault upon the 20th-century literature of quantitative studies of the British economy—or on the 19th century, for that matter—the survey above is of desperate brevity. But perhaps the point is made that an illustrious quantitative tradition exists in British scholarship relating to historical studies of economic questions. One part descends from Petty and King and focuses upon the cross-sectional aggregative magnitudes of British economic life. One part, the collection and study of time series representing selected aspects of British industry, commerce, and finance, descends mainly from Tooke, M'Culloch, and Porter. One part, the conversion of unwieldy raw data into manageable statistical constructs, descends from Newmarch,[14] Jevons, Sauerbeck, and Bowley. The entire tradition has given to economics and economic history some of their most brilliant quantitative contributions, work that has been liberally applied to such special problems as growth, trade cycles, changes in productivity, monetary and commercial policy, fiscal policy, and economic planning and forecasting.

I

Now, in the single year 1962, the tradition has yielded two major contributions, works which actually flow out of the historiography, building explicitly upon the past, all the way back to the beginnings: B. R. Mitchell, with the collaboration of Phyllis Deane, *Abstract of British Historical Statistics*, and Phyllis Deane and W. A. Cole, *British Economic Growth 1688–1959*. Both volumes have diligent and informed authors; both originate in the Department of Applied Economics at Cambridge University, bear the imprimatur of the Cambridge University Press, and have benefited from the support, advice, and guidance of distinguished scholars and organizations. The volumes are described as "companion" volumes to each other and are probably most useful as a set, although in fact each is self contained.

---

[12] Gilboy, "The Cost of Living and Real Wages in Eighteenth Century England," *Review of Economic Statistics*, Vol. XVIII (August, 1936), pp. 134–43.

[13] Schumpeter, "English Prices and Public Finance, 1660–1822," *Review of Economic Statistics*, Vol. XX (February, 1938), pp. 21–37.

The late Mrs. Schumpeter's work on early trade data has now been published in a volume with a lengthy technical introduction by T. S. Ashton and a personal memoir by Elizabeth Gilboy: *English Overseas Trade Statistics, 1697–1808* (Oxford: The Clarendon Press, 1960).

[14] William Newmarch, "An Attempt to Ascertain the Magnitude and Fluctuations of the Amount of Bills of Exchange in Circulation at One Time in Great Britain," *Journal of the Statistical Society*, Vol. XIV (1851). In this remarkable paper, the author sampled 4,367 foreign and domestic bills and, utilizing stamp-tax returns, made the first systematic estimates of movements over the trade cycle of this form of commercial credit; the data are quarterly from 1830 to 1853; the extension of the data from the 1851 publication was made in *History of Prices*, Vol. VI (see n. 37 following for full citation).

The Mitchell and Deane volume is a major collection of data similar to our own *Historical Statistics of the United States,* while the Deane and Cole volume is an analysis of British economic growth centered around the construction of historical national-product and capital-formation estimates. It need scarcely be emphasized that these two volumes comprise a landmark in the study of the British economy or that their authority will be felt for at least a generation. Such is bound to be the case. The volumes rest upon the accumulated work of great scholarship, and most of the famous time series are included, along with official data from such sources as the *Statistical Abstracts,* the *Memoirs of the Geological Survey,* special parliamentary papers, and occasional departmental returns. Many of the series are linked up with earlier or later data to lengthen them. The omissions are few enough in the collection, and students of the British economy (especially, perhaps, Americans far from the British Museum) long used to the rigors of assembling primary data for themselves are now served up a glorious statistical repast.

The collection in the *Abstract* is mainly annual time series stretching back to the year 1199, when a time series on the output of white tin begins (it has a few gaps in the earlier years); its solitude is broken in 1316 when it is joined by Sir William Beveridge's wheat prices at Exeter, then, in 1585 by coal prices at Westminister, in 1594 by a wheat-price series from Eton College, in 1617 by patents "sealed," and in 1630 by wheat prices at Winchester College. At the end of the 17th century, a host of other time series joins in, so that by 1700 some 28 tables of annual time series are available. There are, in all, 249[15] tables of time series covering 16 divisions of economic information. Of the major tables (not including those given in separate notes as alternatives), an even 100 begin before 1800, and 20 end before that date; 66 tables end before 1850; 85 tables run between 1840 and 1939; 27 begin after 1890; only 26 reach beyond 1939; 10 beyond 1951. There are plenty of long series: the white-tin series is 739 years long and the yield on consols is an even 200 years—1756 to 1956 (it is the longest unbroken annual series). In all, I count 101 tables reaching 100 years or more. The divisions of the tables are: population, labor, agriculture, coal, iron and steel, tin, copper and lead, textiles, transport, building, miscellaneous production, trade, wages, national income, public finance, banking and insurance, and prices. Each division is preceded by a scholarly essay describing the field covered and is followed by a short bibliography "indicating appropriate sources of further comment or detail." Sources for the data are given in the caption heads of each table.

The Mitchell and Deane volume is easily the most extensive collection of British economic statistics ever assembled in a single volume and, as such, is a worthy legatee of the great tradition in British statistical collections.

---

[15] My count. The authors do not number the tables sequentially. Individual series are not numbered as in the *Historical Statistics of the United States;* nor have I counted them.

It is also the only collection of British data at all comparable to our own *Historical Statistics of the United States*. The comparison is an unfair one, however, since it is between the work of two scholars and their associates with limited resources, on the one hand, and—on the other—the work of American government departments supported by the organized expertise of a host of scholarly advisers and organizations and with relatively extensive resources available.

These considerations account for three main areas in which the British collection is not comparable to the American one: recent data, general coverage, and short or incomplete series. Mitchell and Deane defend their inclusion of few data more recent than 1939 on the simple ground of finances. One cannot criticize them for this. Yet it is a pity that their effort should have been so constrained, since 1939 was a generation ago. The second world war, austerity, and the events of the 1950's contained problems of great interest to economists and historians, and the expressed hope that the British *Annual Abstract of Statistics* is "easily accessible" is not, alas, the case for many scholars on this side of the Atlantic. Mitchell and Deane cover, perforce, a narrow range of economic activity, compared to the American collection. In particular, data are mainly (sometimes wholly) lacking on business organization in Britain, on education, power, distribution, communications, fisheries, geographical and climatic conditions. In addition, many interesting and useful shorter British time series are not included and remain in fairly inaccessible sources (unknown to the nonspecialist) or isolated in various parliamentary papers.

As I have indicated, these are criticisms aimed at no one except perhaps the cosmos. A shortage of money in scholarly enterprise can be an insurmountable obstacle. It is proper that reasonable criticisms be made in a review, and I think that, for all the industry, patience, and ingenuity the *Abstract* represents, it is open to some specific criticisms. Indeed it would be surprising if such were not the case. These may be treated summarily.

The agricultural-yield series (Agriculture 7) beginning in 1884 could have been pushed back more than three decades using James Caird's index.[16] Employment in coal mines (Coal 4) beginning in 1864 could have been pushed back another decade and a half using officially published data.[17] Employment in iron and steel is not even spotted earlier than 1920, yet scattered estimates exist for much earlier periods,[18] and even though continuous data might not be available, the scholar would be given considerable aid here even if only the decennial census data were used (in textiles, the authors were not so particular [Textiles 9], and do give detailed employment data at irregular intervals). The sources listed at the

---

[16] Caird, *The Landed Interest* (London, 1878), p. 160. This is an index of English wheat-harvest yields.

[17] Accounts and Papers, 1884, Vol. XIX (C. 4078), p. x.

[18] For example, *Memoirs of the Geological Survey of Great Britain and the Museum of Practical Geology*, Return of 1854, p. 85, for the year 1854.

end of the chapter on "Tin, Copper and Lead," do not include Walter Minchinton's definitive study.[19] Among the long series on cotton reprinted from Ellison's tables,[20] data on inventories (stocks) are not included.[21] This is an unfortunate omission, since the series is long and consistent and may well be the longest series extant on inventories in an industry where production is known.

Hoffman's two summary indices are included (Miscellaneous Production, 15) and the reader is forewarned in a footnote (p. 245) of some of the heavy criticisms that have been made of Hoffman's figures. Such information should include John R. Meyer's methodological criticisms,[22] because his comments bear directly upon the use of the aggregative Hoffman indices for long-run conclusions, as opposed to criticisms of specific components of the index made by others. The shipping data do not include the long and useful series (published in the *Statistical Abstracts*) on ships entered and cleared, with cargoes or in ballast, British and foreign. These are of use to scholars interested in movements of shipping earnings in the British balance of payments, both short- and long-run. Critical reference is made to the nature of the steamship data developed in recent work,[23] and this is no place to comment on it; but it is regrettable that the new Index of Transport Capacity of the British steam-merchant fleet was not included, since the Mitchell and Deane criticisms of the coverage of the raw data, even if they were thought to be well taken, do not invalidate the significance of the Transport Capacity Index, and that would be useful to scholars.

Banking and Insurance, Table 1, takes the gold and silver coinage figures back to 1662, and therefore the bibliographical suggestions ought to, but do not, include J. K. Horsefield's recent book,[24] a work of prodigious scholarship which brings to life the circumstances surrounding these early silver and gold coinages. Readily available British data on private banking are notoriously inadequate, and the deficiencies are scarcely made up in this volume. Data are given (Banking and Insurance 3) on bank deposits back to 1877 only, based upon René P. Higonnet's

---

[19] Minchinton, *The British Tinplate Industry* (Oxford: The Clarendon Press, 1957).

[20] Thomas Ellison, *The Cotton Trade of Great Britain* (London, 1886), Table 1.

[21] Deane and Cole say that before 1914 there is "no basis at all for estimates of stock variations . . ." (p. 264). In addition to Ellison's figures for cotton stocks, *The Times* published annually reports on stocks of Scottish pig iron for the mid-century period. I do not know how long this practice continued. But stocks for Scottish pig iron are available from other sources for 1845–73. See R. H. Campbell, "Fluctuations in Stocks," *Oxford Economic Papers*, New Series, Vol. IX (February, 1957), pp. 41–55.

[22] Meyer, "Review of British Industry, 1700–1950," *Explorations in Entrepreneurial History*, Vol. VIII (February, 1956), pp. 172–76.

[23] Jonathan R. T. Hughes and Stanley Reiter, "The First 1,945 British Steamships," *Journal of the American Statistical Association*, Vol. LIII (June, 1958), pp. 360–81.

[24] Horsefield, *British Monetary Experiments, 1650–1710* (Cambridge, Mass.: Harvard University Press, 1960).

survey of the relevant data.[25] The data are, as Higonnet emphasizes, most incomplete in the early years. But, if the data that exist are reliable, as far as they go, then some data are better than none. Series for deposits of eight London joint stock banks exist for the period 1834–57. The source, as such matters go, is reliable.[26] It is a pity these series were not included. It is said that "exchange rates" are mainly of interest to the specialist only (p. 438) and that, anyhow, they are readily available, and suitable references are given. Before cable transfers, regularly available quotations (for example, *The Economist*) were usually *bill prices* and not exchange rates. The difference is significant.

The paucity of data on business enterprise is an important defect in the Mitchell and Deane collection. It is therefore to be regretted that at least the data on joint stock company formation produced by Leon Levi[27] and H. A. Shannon[28] were not used. Finally, there is the problem of "What prices?" in the early British price series. The main problem of British price indices in the 19th century concerns manufactured goods. The "prices current," *Gazette* wheat prices, and other sources concentrate upon imported raw materials, foods, British coal, bar iron, and so forth. What is needed is some measure of wholesale prices, or retail prices of hats, boots, shoes, manufactured textiles, haberdashery, and so forth. Mitchell and Deane include the Gayer, Rostow, Schwartz price index for 1790–1850 (Prices 2), which has a domestic component, but the series in that component do not cover British manufactured items beyond iron bars and pigs, tin plates, soap, and the like. There are a few series in print for prices of manufactured goods—cloth, for example.[29] But in general the problem has not been solved for the 19th century by the prices included. An alternative is to be found in Adolf Soetbeer's figures for prices of 14 British-manufactured commodities sold in Hamburg from 1851 to the mid-1880's.[30] Beyond that, the construction of a British price index for manufactured goods for the 19th century remains a challenge to the industry of scholarship.

Criticisms such as these can doubtless be made of other data included in Mitchell and Deane by those with knowledge in fields different from my own. Budget considerations presumably accounted for most omissions.

---

[25] Higonnet, "Bank Deposits in the United Kingdom, 1870–1914," *Quarterly Journal of Economics,* Vol. LXXI (August, 1957), pp. 329–67.

[26] *Select Committee on the Bank Acts, Minutes of Evidence, Accounts and Papers, 1857–8,* Vol. V, p. 381. Evidence of David Salomons, Director of the London and Westminster Bank, Q. 1134, table.

[27] Levi, "On Joint Stock Companies," *Journal of the Statistical Society,* Vol. XXXIII (1870).

[28] Shannon, "The First Five Thousand Limited Companies and Their Duration," *Economic History* (Supplement to the *Economic Journal*), Vol. II (January, 1932), pp. 290–316.

[29] Ellison, *Cotton Trade,* Table 2.

[30] *R. C. on Precious Metals, Accounts and Papers,* 1888, Vol. XLV (C. 5512–1), Appendix xvi.

As I noted above, it is lamentable that many good short series are excluded. However, I doubt if there will be many complaints about this fine volume. In general, one who finds the Mitchell and Deane collection unpalatable is guilty of "not liking fried chicken."

II

The Deane and Cole volume is an attempt to trace and measure the path of British economic growth from the late seventeenth century to modern times. There is no other study like it for Britain. It is full of diligent, sometimes ingenious, and indeed sometimes staggering work, and will no doubt be the standard authority for a long time. Virtually the whole field of available data is covered, and new series for income and capital formation are generated. They form the centerpiece of the work. There is an introductory chapter, "The Long View," and a chapter at the end mainly summarizing the principal conclusions, followed by appendices on 18th-century trade statistics, on incomes during the Napoleonic Wars, and on national income estimates from 1855, and by a bibliography.

It will be most useful to go immediately to the heart of the work which is contained in seven chapters (ii through viii). In each chapter, a clear thesis is usually developed, and these theses can be stated directly. We will then examine them in some detail. In Chapter II, Deane and Cole produce evidence and arguments to support one of their primary theses, to which they return again and again throughout the study, that the point of upward inflection in British economic growth falls somewhere in the period 1745–60, and not later, in the last two or three decades of the 18th century, when the great surge connected with the industrial revolution came.[31] Moreover, the upward movement in productivity not only came before the classical innovations of the industrial revolution; it was independent of foreign trade or agricultural improvements and came simply from redoubled (harder, more intensive) efforts of labor; whereas the investment expansion of the industrial revolution came only later as a secondary response to growth. It was the pressure of population itself that led to growth in output per head of population.

Chapters III and IV treat population growth and the changing occupational distribution of the labor force over the long period covered. The essay on population is a prodigious piece. Data are broken down by county and region. Compared to the rest of England, the great growth of population in what was destined to become the home of the industrial revolution, the counties of the English Midlands, the North and Northwest, was due *not* to the effects of internal migration but rather to "the greater fecundity of their population" (p. 117). Only the London area was a net

---

[31] A brief survey is given, p. 40, of the many attempts to try to locate *the* industrial revolution in British history.

gainer in population from migration before 1780. At this point there is some confusion about cause and effect, since the evidence is used to support the 1745–60 inflection point. I must take the following statements out of context to quote them at all, but they say the same things in context: ". . . the Industrial Revolution was itself a response, in part at least, to the challenge afforded by a rising population" (p. 98). ". . . the process of industrialization was itself a potent factor in the growth of population" (p. 117). Both lines of thought continue throughout, and I cannot understand, in spite of their intricate arguments, exactly where the final judgment is supposed to fall. Can it fall both ways? It might, of course, but Deane and Cole do not really say that either. They say (at the end of Chapter II, p. 97) that at first, before 1745, there was a labor shortage and an advance in labor-saving inventions; then, population increase induced a search for labor-using innovations which conserved scarce nonlabor factors, and then ". . . the great labour-saving inventions of the eighteenth century laid the basis for the revolution in the textile industries and the introduction of the factory system." But does this really get Deane and Cole off the hook? Is it to be suggested that a labor shortage developed again after 1760? Apparently so. But is it true? The question need not be put this way unless one insists that population pressures, one way or the other, were primary forces inducing invention and innovation. But Deane and Cole insist. They also say, incidentally, that no such labor shortage existed after 1760 (p. 93).

The changing occupational structure of the labor force over time of course involves the relative decline of agricultural labor (not the numbers of farmers, as is emphasized), the virtual extinction by the end of the period (post 1945) of domestic service, and the decline of the rentier sector in the face of rising proportions of gainfully employed in industry, services, transport and communications, and in the public sector (government). This is generally a descriptive essay with no single strong thesis, but the collected data presented will repay close study.

The next essay (Chapter V) covers the changing structure of national product over time. The authors divide the history into a four-part sequence: (1), until 1710 or 1780, the agricultural share of national product held its ground;[32] (2), up to the 1830's, the main change was the rise of the industrial share; (3), from the 1830's and 1840's until 1914, the rising shares comprised transport and international trade, sharply cutting down the share of agriculture;[33] and (4), a period after 1920, is the present stage, disrupted by depression and war, which ". . . may well be characterized by relative expansion in the other service industries, excluding domestic service (which has virtually disappeared) but domi-

---

[32] This finding cannot easily be construed to support the 1745–60 thesis, especially below, when they find that the great changeover to wage incomes came before 1766.

[33] Table 37, p. 166, shows income from foreign investments alone greater than agricultural income by 1901.

nated by the services which are generally included in the government sector in this country" (p. 181).

It is suggested (p. 180) that the fourth stage (the Bureaucratic Revolution?) may well turn out to be comparable to the industrial transformation of the early 19th century.

The growth of the staple industries includes the first suggestion of a growth pattern later supported by aggregative data. It is found that the most rapid *rate of growth* in cotton textiles came in the 1820's and 1830's, trailing off in the 1840's. Dean and Cole go further than mere percentage rates of growth here and make a really powerful (and questionable, see below) assertion: "In the 1820's, 1830's and 1840's, when its net output accounted for rather more than 5 per cent of the British total . . . this was the period of the most complete industrial revolution in the cotton industry . . ." (p. 192).

In this section, Table 42 (p. 185) is an example of the really admirable and even heroic efforts that have gone into the collection and reconciliation of data in this work. The discussion (pp. 198–99) relating to the value of output in the woolen industry is perhaps the best example in the book (and that is saying rather a lot) of the use of clever reasoning in place of quantitative evidence to attempt to find numbers when they don't really exist. Such procedures are necessary in a study like this one and are also instructive. Generally, Deane and Cole conclude that textiles grew most rapidly in the 1830's and 1840's, while the iron industry expanded most rapidly in the third quarter (1850–75).

From estimates of long-run changes in the factor composition of national income four major conclusions emerge: (1), generally, there has been a shift toward wages and salaries and away from profits, dividends, and so forth; (2), the great shift in that direction began before 1760 (again supporting the 1745–60 thesis, although it is not stated why this should have occurred before the existence of a factory system which might explain the shift); (3) from about 1800 to 1914, the wage proportion of income was roughly constant; rising (4) only after 1920, and especially since 1945. The evidence here to support the 1745–60 thesis is thin indeed. They note that Gregory King in estimates for 1688 (p. 252) did not "unambiguously" classify salaries and wages of clerks, shopmen, wage earners, etc., but that in 1806 Colquhoun did so. It is presumed that the reason King ignored those categories is that they were of little importance. It is also presumed that Colquhoun's data were reasonably accurate. Adam Smith was aware of these classes of income earners in 1776, and a letter from Hume to Turgot in 1766 is cited as evidence that they existed then, or at least an abundance of small capitalists existed, so a fundamental shift *must have* occurred between 1688 and 1766. Even in 1760, Joseph Massie could make a finer distinction than King did in 1688. But perhaps King simply was not interested. There is no lack of evidence of such people in abundance long before 1760, or even before 1688 for that matter.[34] However, Deane and Cole estimate (p. 252) that only 25 to 39 percent of the persons in King's categories had incomes solely from employment in 1688. So a great change *must have* come later, but not later than 1760.

Trends in capital formation occupy the final essay before the summary of conclusions. Here the plausible view is advanced (again based upon massive quantitative research) that British capital formation grew only slowly in the 18th century, picking up some during the final 20 years, into the age of the classical Industrial Revolution. The 10 percent rate posited by W. W. Rostow for the Industrial Revolution "takeoff" is not to be found until the 1840's. The rate is 5 to 6 percent circa 1776 and rises to 7 percent by 1800. The rate slowly accelerates until the 1870's, when it is 12 percent, and then slows down, yielding to foreign investment cyclically (no footnote here to Brinley Thomas, curiously, although his thesis is stated p. 267). In the early 20th century, the rate was extraordinarily low. It is noted that in the 20th century the government has increasingly been a major source of capital formation.

Paradoxically, Deane and Cole do not pull another rug from underneath Rostow, as they think. In fact they seem to have given him the best empirical support he has found. It is true that he rashly assumed that the rate of capital formation during the Industrial Revolution takeoff was 10 percent, and they have found only 5–7 percent (pp. 260–63). But such a measure is meaningless anyway as a measure of growth (per capita) and its poten-

---

[34] It might be noted that Hume's letter scarcely refers to receivers of wages and salaries. Much of Deane's and Cole's point depends upon (1) how accurate King was about people regarded as receivers of earned incomes from employment (as opposed to rents and profits) and (2), how seriously one ought to take Colquhoun's estimates (see above, n. 1, for Sir Robert Giffin's informed opinion). One might well be especially skeptical of estimates of labor income in years before census returns existed, simply because there was so little interest in people of "the poorer sort," as Hume referred to those who worked for persons "who employ their stocks in commerce." Modern studies of 17th-century Britain reveal no particular lack of reference to small capitalists, artisans, manufacturers, and tradesmen at the time of the Puritan Revolution, long before King's study.

It is difficult to imagine these classes not supported by a sufficiency of wage earners. For example, see: Maurice Dobb, *Studies in the Development of Capitalism* (New York: Routledge, 1947), chaps. iii–vi; E. Lipson, *A Planned Economy or Free Enterprise* (Toronto: Macmillan, 1944), chap. iii; R. H. Tawney, *Religion and the Rise of Capitalism* (London: Penguin, 1938), chap. iv; Christopher Hill, *Puritanism and Revolution* (London: Secker and Warburg, 1959), chap. vi on the Earl of Clarendon's *History of the Rebellion*. In the composition of the parliamentary armies and their supporters, one sees a significantly large portion of the population in commerce, manufactures, and trades, all of which are *usually* found in association with wage and salary earners. One cannot be certain of the numbers or proportions, of course, but it seems to me that procedures such as these are less strained than the deductions of Deane and Cole from the evidence they present, which scarcely supports a position that, somewhere between 1688 or so and 1760, there was a dramatic shift in British society that led to the rise of the wage earner. All of this, of course, is based upon guessing about possible transformations of literary evidence into numbers. It is a risky business but not, perhaps, more risky than Deane and Cole attempt in translating no evidence at all—the silence of King—into numbers.

tial, without some notion of the capital-output ratio together with population increase. Deane and Cole find (p. 275) that possibly 3:1[35] or even less applied in the early 19th century, and, one presumes, a few decades earlier. If this were so (3:1) then a rate of net capital formation of 6 percent would, *ceteris paribus,* support a population growth rate of 2 percent per annum compound and would provide net growth for a smaller population increase. The population growth rates given for the relevant period (Table 26, p. 115) are much below that (half, 9.8 per 1,000 per annum for England and Wales in 1781-1800). As it stands, Rostow seems to have his takeoff with room to spare, although not with a 10 percent rate of net capital formation. There is, of course a question remaining: were the conditions for net growth achieved in the compressed time period 1783–1802 as Rostow suggests?

The summary and conclusions restate many of the central theses but, curiously, do not always really agree with what has gone before (below). In the summary chapter, the real product estimates are used (Table 73) to further support the thesis started in "Cotton," and continued later with the Hoffman index of industrial production (Table 77) that the British economy's per capita rate of growth in the 19th century was U-shaped, high until mid-century, declining slightly until the last part, when it picked up again. The precise dates are not clear except (much to my surprise, I confess) the center of the mid-century slump is 1851–61. This apparently surprised the authors too, and they suggest that perhaps the impact of the Irish famine accounts for it.

III

These then, are the main conclusions which scholars will face for a long time. And it must be confessed that they form quite a solid mass. Are they supportable? To some extent the authors' comment on Cairncross (p. 264) aptly describes their own happy position. "The Cairncross series have stood the test of time because they embody the results of much original and careful research and because to improve substantially upon them would involve a considerably larger project of research than the original." The Deane and Cole volume will doubtless stimulate further studies, but one cannot really hope for another effort of this magnitude for a long time. That does not, of course, mean that the findings in this volume will remain free from critical appraisal as more work is done. On the basis of their own work, I think Deane and Cole are open to criticism on three different levels: method, theory, and internal consistency. In addition, a number of minor criticisms can be made.

What is the economic significance of percentage rates of growth of a

---

[35] The authors are bothered by the low estimate yielded by their data for the capital-output ratio in the late 18th and early 19th centuries, but they advance plausible arguments to show that such might indeed have been the case (pp. 275–77).

time series between any two points? I think the answer must virtually be "nothing" unless one is informed by other evidence or a theoretical viewpoint. Suppose there are two time periods, A and B, and a time series moves in A from point a to b and in B from point b to c. The two time periods are of equal length. The time series moves in A from 1 to 2, and in B from 2 to 3.5. The percentage rate of growth in A is 100, and in B, 75. The average growth is 1 unit in A and 1.5 units in B. The series accelerated faster in A and grew more rapidly in B, per unit of time. Is the economic analysis of growth more concerned with A or with B? It all depends upon what is meant by "growth," and this is a bothersome thing in Deane and Cole.

The "period of maximum growth" in the cotton industry is given as the 1820's, 1830's, and 1840's (p. 189). Indeed this, as noted previously, is found to be the time of the most complete industrial revolution in cotton. Using "raw cotton imports as an index of the volume of output" as they do (p. 187, Table 43), we have the following situation: in 1899–1901, imports were 1,510 million pounds, in 1819–21, the figure was less than .10 of that, 141 million pounds. The increase, by more than a factor of 10, came somewhere in between. Where? In 1844–46, the number is 560 million pounds; just under one third of the distance has been covered, an increase of 419 million pounds, and in 25 years. In 1859–61, only 15 years later and just before the cotton famine, the number has reached 1,050 million—an increase of 490 million pounds or more than one third of the distance; it took another 50 years to climb the last 460 million pounds to the end-of-century figure. In the mere 10-year period from 1849–51 to 1859–61, the increase, 429 million pounds, was greater than the increase achieved in the whole 25 years from 1819–21 to 1844–46. Now, even if the industry accelerated most rapidly before 1849–51, it certainly grew the *most per year* in the next 10 years, and by a wide margin. This makes me suspect that the "industrial revolution" in cotton in the 1820's, 1830's, and 1840's must have been fairly anemic compared to the next decade or so. Investment indicators support this. One finds an increase of 140,001 power looms installed in the 15 years 1835–1850, and 150,365 in the next 10 years. One finds that total steam horsepower in the industry was a mere 71,005 by 1850 and 281,663 10 years later. One finds 20.98 million spindles by 1850 after 70-odd years of factory production and 30.39 million, nearly a 50 percent increase, just a decade later.[36] Moreover, as James Nasmyth and others pointed out, with speeded-up machinery the spindles of the 1850's

---

[36] For power looms in 1835: James Mann, *The Cotton Trade of Great Britain* (London: 1860), p. 32. Other data from: Parliamentary Papers, *Factory Returns, Accounts and Papers,* 1847, Vol. XLVI, p. 294; 1850, Vol. XLII, p. 745; 1857 (sess. 1), Vol. XIV, p. 7; 1862, Vol. LV, p. 23. Oddly enough, the 1850, 1857, and 1862 Parliamentary Papers cited here were used by Deane and Cole in their research on woolens—p. 200, n. 3, But they apparently overlooked the implications for their growth-rate thesis in cotton textiles of the data included in these returns.

did a lot more work than did the earlier ones.[37] In what sense was growth in the cotton industry greater in the 1820's to 1840's than in the 1850's? Percentagewise: just as it is a 100 percent increase from 1 to 2 and only 75 percent from 2 to 3.5. The notion that growth is defined as a percentage of a base number is dangerously misleading. A baby grows fastest in the prenatal period—from zero to any weight is infinite. Once the fact of birth is accepted, the most, and most meaningful, growth comes later on, although exactly when depends upon what interests the observer.

Walther Hoffmann's index is used to show that growth slowed down at mid-19th century. Like so many aggregative measures used, a lot depends upon how the data are grouped. The Hoffmann index is 5.7 (actually 5.65) in 1800 and 77.1 in 1900,[38] or an increase of 71.4 index points in the century. By quarter-century intervals, the increase took place as follows: first quarter 5.1 index points, second quarter 12.5, third quarter 26.0, fourth quarter 27.8. The reader might be surprised to learn that 26 points per 25 years is thought to be slower than 12.5 per 25 years, but on a percentage basis it is a slower rate of growth. Is "growth" acceleration, "fastest," or what? To Deane and Cole it is "acceleration." But this will nearly always mean, in economic time series, somewhere near the initial *accouchement*. To an economic historian, a more relevant date will depend upon other things, such as the extent of change in the economy engendered by the rise in output. To others it may be "more," "most," "fastest per year," or some relatively *qualitative* notion like "most pervasive." Finally, growth of time series can be exponential, and no attempt has been made by Deane and Cole to see if their data are not better described by an exponential function than by the straight percentage increases they use. If an exponential were to be found a good fit, it could, as in the United States case, imply a fundamental change in interpretation.[39]

A study of this magnitude necessitates the grouping of data over succeeding time periods. But overlapping 10-year averages mask all meaningful short-run variations in growth. Those who view economic growth as a process of change and variation over succeeding short periods will get short shrift here. It is as if no work had ever been done upon British economic development in which the long run is viewed as the sum of short-run experience.[40] The result is a view of British growth that is like

[37] Nasmyth's conclusions are reported in Parliamentary Papers, *Reports of Factory Inspectors, Accounts and Papers*, 1852–53, Vol. XI, pp. 23–27. See also Thomas Tooke and William Newmarch, *History of Prices*, Vol. VI (London, 1857), pp. 536–37.

[38] *British Industry 1700–1950* (cited in n. 6), Table 54, parts A and B, shows total industrial production excluding building.

[39] Edward Ames, "Trends, Cycles and Stagnation in U.S. Manufacturing Since 1860," *Oxford Economic Papers*, New Series, Vol. XI (October, 1959), pp. 270–81.

[40] Not only those concerned with the path of growth determined by business-cycle experience are ignored (Gayer, Rostow, and Schwartz are cited, but not concerning their cycle scheme), but the relatively new "long-cycle" studies are also not men-

a stick doll, able to bend only at a few hinges. The rich detail of experience is blotted out, and something called the "growth process" replaces it.

Thus when a century-long series like "Blast Furnaces Built," is taken as an investment series (pp. 227–29, 263) without adjustment for qualitative changes, the result is most misleading. According to Lowthian Bell,[41] the typical blast furnace in 1835 was 40 to 50 feet high, had a cubic capacity of 5,000 feet, had a cold blast, and made 70 tons of pig a week. In 1865, the typical blast furnace was 80 feet high, had cubic capacity of 20,000 feet, the blast temperature was 1,000 degrees F., and 450 to 550 tons of pig was the weekly make. As the escaping gases were utilized to raise the heat of the blast, these furnaces were increasingly expensive by virtue, not only of size, but of equipment too. The same sort of objection can be raised about other physical increases used to estimate physical magnitudes measured in monetary terms (investment, income, capital formation). For instance, the increase in spindles installed in the cotton industry is taken as a measure of capital equipment installed. It is assumed that each spindle represented a like amount of complementary investment throughout. This was clearly not the case; changes in prime movers, speed of equipment, and so forth meant that a given spindle in 1831 might represent less (or more?) investment in 1831 than in 1860, or 1880, or 1914. Similarly, changes in organization (integration of spinning and weaving at mid-century, for example) meant a change in total investment represented by a given spindle as internal economies were utilized. Deane and Cole have answers to such objections. They are explicitly aware of the limitations of the data they use. These reservations concern the concept of "growth" used, the massive groupings and aggregations of data used, and the inflexibility of some of the indicators employed. Users of the long estimates in these chapters should be careful to find out precisely what Deane and Cole mean by their indicators and their estimates before using them extensively.

One of the main theses of the study states that the real beginning of movement into the industrial economy began in the 1740's. This theme is the most recurrent one in the whole book, by my count. It is stated with varying strength, and emphasis, and meaning, throughout. All of the arguments in its favor are given full play, although they are not always consistent with each other (below). In the final chapter, the thesis is restated in what one must assume is the authors' definitive view (p. 285).

The beginning of sustained economic growth can be traced to the middle of the 18th century [before the classical Industrial Revolution is usually dated] . . . at this stage however, the expansion of the economy was apparently

---

tioned. Not relevant to the study of growth? Was economic growth something other than the sum of experience, the sum of expansions and contractions in economic activity over time?

[41] I. L. Bell, *Principles of the Manufacture of Iron and Steel* (London, 1884), p. 24.

swamped by the growth of population which also dates from slightly before mid-century. There is little evidence of an appreciable acceleration in the long-term rate of growth of real incomes per head until the last two decades of the eighteenth century.

More decisive statements of this thesis are found throughout: for example, referring to import statistics (p. 47): ". . . it is clear that the period of rapid growth starts, not in the 1780's, but in the mid-forties, and the expansion at the end of the century [the Industrial Revolution] represents *little more than a return to a movement initiated a generation before*" [my italics; J. R. T. H.].

That this early period of rapid growth antedates any stated organizational or technological reasons for it is apparently no problem to Deane and Cole. Indeed, it is argued generally (see especially p. 58) that technological change was primarily a response to growth, and growth was due to more intensive human effort with a given technology. It is a take-off without technology, or agriculture, or trade; and—in fact—without any perceptible increase in per capita output. The beginning of growth is seen as a sort of quickening of all the indicators; it is not growth as is ordinarily imagined, where capital formation leads to a change in output per head greater than zero.

The Deane and Cole thesis on 1745–60 may be briefly put. There were signs, primarily in data for the volume of imports, that in about 1745–60 the economy began to grow impressively (although *not* per capita, as noted above). What were the sources of this acceleration? Not in technology; not in 1745–60, which was before the great inventions. Even though the export industries seemed to grow most rapidly (p. 83), exports are eliminated generally as a stimulus in the 18th century by assuming (1) that British trade and payments were strictly bilateral with each partner, with *only* Britain containing sources of rising productivity; hence (p. 83): "We shall argue here that the expansion of the British export trade was limited by the purchasing power of Britain's customers, and this in turn was limited by what they could earn in exports to Britain."

Then, (2), it is noted that the gross barter terms of trade consistently turned against the United Kingdom during expansions and in favor of the United Kingdom during contractions. From this, another major conclusion is reached (p. 85).

In the light of this evidence, it is difficult to see the expansion of trade as a largely exogenous factor which quickened the pace of industrial growth. . . . It seems that the explanation of the higher average rate of growth in the second half of the century should be sought at home rather than abroad.

Did the acceleration stem from agricultural advances? No. Of the estimated 25 percent increase in per capita agricultural output in the 18th century, virtually all came before 1750 (p. 75). A long argument against Keynes, Ashton,[42] and others is developed showing that (1), the marginal propensity to consume was no lower in the agricultural sector than in industry; (2), demand was price inelastic for agricultural products; but (3), demand was also price inelastic for industrial products (pp. 89–90). High authorities are cited to support these assumptions. Hence, good harvests would reduce agricultural incomes and would not raise real incomes in the industrial sector appreciably; and poor harvests would lower real income in the industrial sector and do little good for the agricultural sector. Only when prices of all commodities rose simultaneously could rising incomes be translated into rising demand in all sectors (p. 90). There is one major loophole in the argument. Improvements in production in the nonagricultural sector were not translated into higher measurable real incomes. Here there is a gap in the analysis, since increased productivity, however small, as well as higher real income in the industrial sector due to falling food prices, had to be used up in something besides inventories and hoards. What happened to the residual rise in real income in the industrial sector from occasional good harvests and from increased productivity in the nonagricultural sector before 1740? Gin (p. 93 and, again, pp. 127, 134, 288).

Barring a managerial revolution, where could the stimulus for increased output come from? Having eliminated all other sources, we are left with the weight of the human hand, if you like: changes in the intensity of each unit of labor, as population and prices rose (p. 93).

When prices rose . . . agricultural incomes also rose and the wage-earning population as a whole had to work harder to maintain their traditional standard of life. It is not surprising, therefore, that the rise in prices after 1743 seems to have been associated with a modest rise in total output per head.

By then, the "gin mania" (p. 127) was over.

This thesis, making 1745–60 the upward inflection point in British economic growth and basing the rise upon harder work due to the pressures of expanding population, constitutes a major departure from tradition (pp. 89–90), although Deane and Cole note that recent work by economic historians supports their view. Their data do show an increase in imports in 1745–60, but there is also one in about 1712–35 (Figures 1 and 2, and Table 85, pp. 319–20) which is ignored (except where it is dismissed outright, p. 280); and neither increase compares to the massive rise after 1780 which is usually associated with the Industrial Revolution. This fact Deane and Cole state bluntly in several places, but they stick to the importance of 1745–60 and to their interpretation of that period.

That interpretation, however, is partly based upon a logical confusion.

---

[42] T. S. Ashton's conclusions are cited, p. 89, n. 4. Keynes' position on the role of good and bad harvests is found in *The General Theory of Employment, Interest and Money* (London: Macmillan and Co., Ltd., 1936), p. 330. See also, R. C. O. Matthews, *A Study in Trade-Cycle History* (Cambridge, Eng.: The University Press, 1954), pp. 99–105.

They admit (above) that export industries in the period grew faster than others. But, as we noted above, the unfavorable movements in the gross barter terms of trade during expansions lead them to dismiss exports as an exogenous force. This does not necessarily follow, on either a macro or a micro level. Only an explosive import multiplier could cause trade to be a net drag upon income expansion—*from whatever source, including a rise in exports.* It might, in certain circumstances, be a filip to income if the gross barter terms were "favorable" in expansions; but an unfavorable movement would not be necessarily a drag, any more than one would say that costs inhibit profit. There must be costs for output to exist. Moreover, the assumption of the bilateral character of British trade and of the absence of any sources of rising productivity (and hence of increased demand for exports) beyond the limits of the British Isles is one that is not apparent in existing data, nor in existing interpretations of 18th-century history.[43] Assuming that investment were some function of sales, or profits, or both, for individual enterprises, rising export sales could stimulate investment in firm *A*, even if firm *B* were being battered by rising import costs of its raw materials. The concept of gross barter terms of trade relates to a macro condition which does not translate directly into any particular micro investment-and-growth situation unless the economy has but one export, one import, and one single firm, and lives solely by foreign trade.

The agricultural argument has several curious features about it, including the glaring one that in the Deane and Cole analysis good harvests were apparently good for no one. One of the major defects of this study generally is the total lack of a monetary sector, so that changes in the money stock are left out of account altogether. The omission of money creates an odd condition in the analysis of the importance of price changes with two "real" sectors selling to each other, is it really a possibility that *all* prices might rise together? Without a monetary sector? I don't doubt that all prices rose, but why? I can find no authority, nor do they cite one, which holds that gin drinking was on such a level as to actually absorb increments in national productivity before 1740. We recall similar W.C.T.U. claims in this country long ago, and we all know our

---

[43] A rough breakdown of the direction of British overseas trade in the relevant period is given in Mitchell and Deane *Abstract*, "Overseas Trade," Table 10, pp. 310–11. The data hardly suggest bilateralism; in fact, they strikingly suggest the opposite. That British trade partners had no sources of increasing productivity of their own, or did not trade among themselves, is an odd notion. Even the North American colonies did a brisk trade outside the British Empire—a well-known case being the colonial outcry against the Sugar Act of 1764. New England merchants had ". . . been accustomed to disregarding the provisions of the Molasses Act of 1733 and importing the larger part of their molasses from the French and Spanish West Indies." S. E. Morison and H. S. Commager, *The Growth of the American Republic* (3rd ed.; New York: Oxford Press, 1942), p. 147. In the case of trade outside the Empire, the majority of British trade, there is no reason at all to presume that ability to buy from Britain was limited strictly by ability to sell to Britain.

Hogarth. But experience hardly proved the W.C.T.U. to be correct. The 18th Amendment brought no surge in labor productivity. Deane and Cole rely upon gin in several places, as noted, to solve problems. It is a shame that they give no source for their information.

If these criticisms are valid, then an increase in productivity in 1745–60, however slight could indeed have been a product of foreign trade, or of monetary factors, or of any number of sources in addition to the main-line argument that British labor became less feckless under the pressure of population growth. Little evidence is given to support this thesis, and the reader, recalling how few other societies have ever conquered population pressures by hard work alone, can perhaps be pardoned for some skepticism on this point. Deane and Cole later state flat-out that foreign trade made its contribution to growth. In their concluding chapter they say the usual things about the "engine of growth" after 1780 (pp. 281 and 312), thus contradicting their earlier argument. But in point of fact, since they place such emphasis upon the rise of imports up to 1760 as a measure of increasing internal activity, what of exports? Exports, in fact, grew more rapidly than imports up to 1755–64 (Table 14, p. 48). Deane and Cole note that exports lagged from the 1760's to the 1780's. But that is not the point. Could exports have been a stimulus to domestic activity in the crucial (for Deane and Cole) period 1745–60? Apparently so.

IV

Deane and Cole repeatedly use the logic of economics in a manner which is even more baffling than those examples already noted. For example, this sentence (p. 27) might be interpreted variously by the reader: "If we have concluded that real wages rose on the average it is only because the price data suggest strongly that the increase in the value of money outweighed the fall in real wages." But the following argument (p. 12) defies any analysis whatever: "On the other hand it is certain that there were important changes in the value of money during the latter part of the eighteenth century and these changes must have had their effects upon prices."

There is a great deal of this sort of cloudy writing adding difficulties to a narrative which is, in any case, a hard job to absorb. Comprehension is not in any way enhanced by the use of such antique phrases as "value of money," "active" and "passive" payments balances—words which never did, and do not now, convey any unambiguous meanings. We are told (p. 220) that "diminishing returns was a problem of long standing in the coal industry." Were there industries in which this was not true?[44] The following (p. 277) apparently is a claim that income did not respond to

----

[44] Under what conditions would a firm in a competitive market find its equilibrium position *before* its marginal cost reached the minimum?

investment via any known income-generating process: "It was not until the railway age and the steel age that men began to build vast capital-installations which inflated the rate of growth of capital out of all proportion to the current growth of income, so that they might reap a corresponding return at a later date." The "unearned increment" becomes a plan; investment is made on the assumption that an industrial revolution will come and bail the capitalists out (p. 277 again). "In effect it is of the essence of a pre-industrial economy that new capital formation is not necessarily productive and it is one of the features of the process of industrialization that it makes some forms of existing capital more productive than at the time of their creation."

One feature of the general approach to evidence in Deane and Cole that is endlessly frustrating is the tendency to advance a most tentative hypothesis, to go on at length about the inadequacies of the data, and then slowly to turn hypothesis into hard fact without relevant supporting evidence. On the matter of the production of a race of wage and salary earners, craftsmen, shopkeepers, and the like before 1760 (above, and pp. 251–55), Deane and Cole provide a gem of an example of how to carry your point:

Briefly, therefore, if it is possible to accept the national-income and wage-bill estimates we have been considering as reasonably reliable measures of what they purport to measure, our conclusions might be summed up as follows. The share of employees in the national income grew significantly in the period before industrialization gathered momentum on a sufficiently broad front to induce sustained economic growth. The proportion seems to have changed comparatively little in the nineteenth century and early twentieth century in spite of a structural transformation of the British economy.

Now, this is the part where it is shown that Colquhoun mentioned classes of income earners that King didn't, and Turgot received a letter from Hume saying that such persons exist "in every civilized community."[45] No quantitative evidence of this change is introduced, and note that the Industrial Revolution has simply disappeared altogether, having apparently made no significant impact upon the occupational distribution of labor. It all happened before 1760 even though, before there were factories, the industrial proletariat must have found little reason to have left the farm or whatever. One wonders what Deane and Cole find so necessary about the 1745–60 emphasis in this work, since they admit that the classical Industrial Revolution brought the first sustained increase in output per capita, and they even produce data which can be interpreted as support for Rostow's takeoff in the 1780's (above).

---

[45] Is Hume referring here specifically to England and Wales, as a matter of close observation, or is he just generalizing? It is not clear in Deane and Cole why Hume's observation is to be considered as the equivalent in numerical accuracy to King's explicitly numerical treatment. But that is partly the issue here.

V

The work is marred by a number of minor errors, misprints, vagaries, and inconsistencies. The main ones can be listed quickly. The Irish population problem has been attributed to the Irish land-tenure system as much as to the potato alone, as is stated here (p. 9).[46] The year 1847 is not considered to be a cyclical peak (p. 15, n. 2), 1845 is.[47] Clapham *did not* attribute the rise in prices in the 1850's and 1860's to the gold discoveries alone (p. 7); he included a marked increase in the use of paper money of all sorts in his increase in supplies of money.[48] The heading of Table 5 (p. 19) is unclear, no differentiation being made between a money figure and the following index numbers. How can real wages generally move less than money wages, if money wages move "in the opposite direction to prices" (p. 21)? "During the first quarter of the eighteenth century the British economy was dominated by the sudden rise of the cotton industry" (p. 30). The *last* quarter (see pp. 51–52)? The discussion, pp. 30–32, on the changing structure of British exports would have gained considerably by reference to Nurkse's work.[49] What is the evidence to support the contention that "nabob" wealth was important in financing the Industrial Revolution (p. 35)? What is meant (p. 39) by the rehabilitation of the N. B. E. R. word "congeries"? The ratios 12:1.5 and 33:21 are not necessarily "similar" as segments of logistic curves over the intervals stated, 53 years and 40 years (pp. 52–53). If population growth accelerated before there were factories, how could it be obviously true that ". . . the rise of Lancashire stimulated the growth of population in the surrounding areas . . ." (p. 116)? The reference (p. 123) to Figure 7 is a misprint; the reference should be to Figure 6. What "consensus" of opinion is it that agrees (p. 125) that ". . . the standard of life of those closest to the margin of subsistence probably fell between 1790 and 1820, and improved thereafter"? Reference is made to Hobsbawm, in the bibliography, but not to Hartwell. Can it really be shown that the "abnormally high" (p. 127) death rates of the metropolitan counties before 1750 were due to the gin mania" (also p. 134)? Since no explanation is given for the rise in the population in the Northwest (a description is not an explanation), why should we "expect" the same pattern in the Midlands (p. 132)? Surely it is not suggested by S. H. Coontz that demographic "equilibrium"

---

[46] *The Great Famine, Studies in Irish History*, 1845–25, R. D. Edwards and T. D. Williams (ed.) (New York: New York University Press, 1957), chaps. i and ii.

[47] A. D. Gayer, W. W. Rostow, A. J. Schwartz, *The Growth and Fluctuation of the British Economy, 1790–1850* (Oxford: The University Press, 1953). Vol. I, p. 304, Fig. 82.

[48] J. H. Clapham, *An Economic History of Modern England* (Cambridge, Engl.: The University Press, 1942), Vol. II, pp. 336–39.

[49] Ragnar Nurkse, "The Relations between Home Investment and the External Balance in the Light of British Experience, 1945–1955," *Review of Economics and Statistics*, Vol. XXXVIII (May, 1956), pp. 121–54.

could apply to a time period of a few decades (pp. 134–35)? "An industrial revolution characteristically entails extensive changes in the industrial distribution of the labour force" (p. 136). But it is elsewhere denied, as previously discussed here, that such a change occurred in Britain during the industrial revolution. "The process of change in the composition of the labour force slowed briefly in the second quarter of the century when the numbers (though not the proportion) occupied in agriculture grew quite strongly and manufacture merely maintained its share" (p. 144). The relevant Tables (30, p. 142, and 31, p. 143) show the opposite to have been the case.

The argument (p. 145) that domestic servants set "certain limits" to the rate of expansion of productivity before World War II is not compatible with Habakkuk's argument[50] that there was usually a labor surplus in Britain. Is there any way to know who is correct? Can both be? Table 32 (p. 146) contains a gross misspacing, column 1, line 3. Surely the sum of the figures for paupers, vagrants, and beggars given outdoor relief, occasional relief, and relief in workhouses in the year 1803 (p. 150) contains considerable double counting.[51] The importance of the cotton gin was not merely to reduce prices of raw cotton (pp. 183–84). It made possible the enormous growth of the British industry based upon American cotton. The attribution of the "mania" of 1825 to railways (p. 230) is not in agreement with other major authorities,[52] and no information is shown to support the railway as so important a factor. It is stated (p. 246) that the share of labor in the national income was long "relatively constant," until the full employment of World War II forced the share up. Yet the relevant table (65, p. 247) shows a greater percentage increase from 1905–14 to 1925–34 (26.4) than in 1930–39 to 1946–55 (15.4). While it is true that inventories (stocks) would make little difference in the capital-formation estimates, it is not the case (p. 264) that there is "no basis at all for estimates of stock variations before 1914."[53]

VI

Deane and Cole begin their volume by saying that there will be more long-term studies like theirs because of the need to test and assess theories of economic growth. Recalling similar ambitions of the last generation of economists regarding business-cycle theories and the paucity of quantitative tests of those theories, one might well wish that there would be a

---

[50] H. J. Habakkuk, *American and British Technology in the Nineteenth Century* (Cambridge, Engl.: The University Press, 1962), pp. 196–97.

[51] Can it be shown that they do not? Considering the weight of the conclusion: ". . . something like one in ten of the population was in regular receipt of poor relief," surely it is reasonable to suspect some double counting.

[52] W. T. C. King, *History of the London Discount Market* (London: Routledge, 1936), chap. ii.

[53] See prior discussion of this point.

better ground to hope for more studies like *British Economic Growth 1688–1959*. The Deane and Cole volume is a major contribution to the quantitative study of the British economy and of economic growth generally. I cannot but express unfeigned astonishment and admiration for the diligence and ingenuity in this work. It is vulnerable to criticism, but that is hardly surprising for a volume so ambitious and complex. I hope that such criticism only sharpens interest in the work. The field will never be the same again, and Deane and Cole will stand as a major landmark. By joining this with the Mitchell and Deane volume of statistics, Cambridge has made 1962 a banner year in the quantitative study of economic history. However critical he may be (and the more so, the better), the scholar will be profoundly grateful for these volumes.

2. Foreign Trade and Balanced Growth: The Historical Framework*

Jonathan R. T. Hughes
Purdue University

I

THE APPEARANCE of yet another paper on the subject of foreign trade and balanced growth would seem to call for an apology, or at least for an explanation. My excuses for entering into this particular discussion are two: I do not agree with some of the more celebrated statements concerning the benefits which trade with industrial countries "should" have brought to the primary-producing countries, and I further do not think that what we know of the economic history of the "developed" countries justifies the notion that the success of their internal responses to the stimuli of external trade was due to simultaneity in the rates of growth of their component economic sectors. It seems to me that a widening of the differences of per capita real incomes between the industrial and the primary-producing countries, partly as a consequence of trade, should not have been unexpected, and that part of this widening was due to the repeated successful creation and correction of imbalances in the economic structures of the industrial countries. These bald assertions clearly call for careful analytical support. This I will attempt to provide in what follows.

This paper focuses mainly upon the internal reactions of nations to the stimulus of international trade. An attempt is made to explain why, with the international permeation of industrial technique accompanying the growth of international trade, the inequality of per capita incomes between industrially well-developed and the poorly developed nations has widened. Growth was facilitated by specialization and trade, and, on the basis of available studies in economic history it is shown here why the notion of "balanced growth" currently employed by some economists is

* Reprinted from the *American Economic Review*, Vol. XLIX, No. 2 (May, 1959), pp. 330–37. Concerning the issues involved in this paper, the author has profited from discussions with Professors Carter Goodrich, Donald Gordon, Hrothgar Habakkuk, Ragnar Nurkse, and Stanley Reiter.

misleading. The "simultaneous" expansion of all economic sectors envisaged by some growth theorists did not characterize economic development in the advanced Western nations—and for good reason. It is argued that, paradoxically, balanced economic growth (mutually supporting lines of investment) was achieved by the Western nations because short-run imbalances were continuously created and corrected. The imbalances were the products of specialization, trade, and increased factor mobility, the necessary corollary of specialization. The correction of these imbalances was a critical part of overall growth and consisted mainly of the elimination of impediments to factor mobility—impediments which were not removed in the primary-producing countries engaged in international trade.

II

We must first clear away some theoretical timber. While it is clear, in theory, that under certain circumstances international trade is capable of bringing about factor-price equalization internationally, it is not the case, as has been asserted, that this necessarily implies an international equalization of per capita real income.[1] The two are not the same thing at all. It is a combination of natural endowment and its uses (including trade) relative to population resources which determines per capita real income, and on this subject the theory of international trade does not, by itself, tell us much. We know that trade under the classical conditions should bring maximum world output, and we know from recent theory that, barring transport and similar costs, there may develop international equality of factor prices. Unless there is knowledge about relative factor endowments, this information alone leads us to no particular expectations about the likely movement of relative per capita incomes among the trading countries. Moreover, application of other branches of economic theory leads us to expect that the distance between per capita real incomes in the developed and underdeveloped countries would tend to widen, not tend to equality, and that trade probably hastens this process.

The main conditions for rapid and sustained growth are precisely those

---

[1] Hence the best-known recent transformation of the factor-price equalization arguments into an income-equalization argument is formally incorrect. To quote Myrdal: ". . . according to the classical doctrine movements of labor and capital between countries would not be necessary to bring about a development toward an *equalization of factor prices and, consequently, incomes.*" Again: "We thus see the strange thing that in recent decades, while international economic inequalities have been growing and recently also have become a more and more pressing practical concern in international politics, the theory of international trade has developed in the direction of stressing ever more the idea that trade initiated a tendency toward a gradual *equalization of factor prices and incomes* as between different countries." Gunnar Myrdal, *Rich Lands and Poor* (New York, 1957), pp. 151–52. (My italics.) While it may be true that theory has been stressing the possibilties of factor-price equalization, it certainly has not been stressing equality of incomes. These are two different things.

which are generated by successful industrialization:[2] high levels of consumption and saving based upon rising productivity, vigorous innovating by entrepreneurs, efficient channeling of savings into investment through flexible financial institutions, and so forth. Possible gains from trade between countries which have achieved these conditions and poorly organized underdeveloped countries would doubtless be distributed in favor of the former where elements of organized human skills determine market conditions and the terms of trade. Thus the widening of per capita incomes between the developed and the underdeveloped countries after many decades of trade between them would not, *ceteris paribus*, be unexpected. But trade was, historically, a stimulus, at least initially, to expansion of output, however unequally that expansion was distributed among the trading countries. To understand more fully the conditions which generated this disparity we need to know, among other things, what determined the internal reactions of various countries to the stimulus of external trade. Here we can learn some useful lessons from an examination of certain aspects of the history of economic growth and of international trade theory.

III

The statistical fact of the great difference in per capita "incomes" between the trading countries was thrown into clear relief in *Industrialization and Foreign Trade*,[3] the pioneering work of the great Swedish foreign trade economist and statistician, Folke Hilgerdt. He demonstrated that after a century of industrialization and rapidly expanding foreign trade, per capita supplies of manufactured goods were extremely unequal as between the industrial and primary-producing countries even though trade in primary products had risen about twice as much as had trade in manufactured goods. By 1926–29, he estimated that to raise per capita supplies of manufactured goods in the primary-producing countries of the world to only one half the levels then prevailing in the industrial nations, the primary-producing countries needed to have imports equal to twice the value of all the commodities then entering into world trade. This was clearly impossible to accomplish, and on this basis Hilgerdt argued that international trade on the basis of comparative advantage would never, by itself, suffice to raise two thirds of the world's population to a standard of life anywhere near that which prevailed in the industrial countries which supported the other one third (*ibid.*, Chapter 2). By that time there had been, after all, plenty of time, mainly in favorable circumstances as regards the conditions of trade and payments, for international trade to

---

[2] A rigorous statement of these pen-worn truths will be found in Donald F. Gordon, "Obsolescence and Technological Change: Comment," *American Economic Review* (September, 1956), pp. 646–52.

[3] League of Nations, 1945, reprinted by the United Nations in 1948.

spread its benefits among the world's commercial nations. There was certainly no evident tendency for per capita incomes, as indicated by per capita supplies of manufactured goods, to tend to equality between the industrial and the primary-producing countries.

What had happened was the nightmare from which we are still trying to extricate ourselves, both in the world of affairs and in the learned journals where the debate on development and balanced economic growth rages. The rise of the great multilateral system of international trade and payments of the 19th and early 20th centuries had stimulated a broad growth of productivity together with a widening of markets only in a limited number of countries, and had left the other trading countries with isolated sectors of high productivity surrounded by relatively unchanging economic backwardness. Why had this occurred?

IV

I think that at least part of the answer to this critical question is to be found in economics; moreover, economics of the most old-fashioned and familiar kind. The approach to the answer again lies in the realm of theory.

In a recent paper[4] Mr. Myint, of Oxford, has differentiated between three separate inducements for international trade to be found in the writings of the classical theorists. He calls these: the theory of comparative costs, the vent for surplus theory, and the productivity theory.

In the "comparative cost" theory trade allows for specialization and greater efficiency of use of resources with given production-possibility functions.

The "vent for surplus" theory does not comprise the Ohlin-type isolated economy in full employment where, with the introduction of trade, the greatest (relative) advantage goes to the most plentiful factors. Instead, the "surplus" is essentially in the form of disguised unemployment. Trade brings a once-over change to productive employment once markets and the external economies of transportation, etc., are introduced. After this, growth occurs along a normal-curve path and new factor combinations do not occur. Here is a theoretical statement which roughly corresponds to the experience of many underdeveloped countries.

The "productivity" theory, however, postulates that with the widening of markets there will occur judicious assessments of new profit possibilities and new factor combinations will appear, raising productivity, and, in turn, introducing the possibilities of further change. Consequently the floodgates of rapid economic development are opened. This is no static theory of comparative costs. If I may be permitted to quote Mr. Myint:

---

[4] H. Myint, "The 'Classical Theory' of International Trade and The Underdeveloped Countries," *Economic Journal* (June, 1958), pp. 317–37.

In contrast [i.e., to comparative costs] the "productivity" doctrine looks upon international trade as a dynamic force which, by widening the extent of the market and the scope of the division of labor, raises the skill and dexterity of the workmen, encourages technical innovations, overcomes technical indivisibilities and generally enables the trading country to enjoy increasing returns and economic development. (*Ibid.*, pages 318–19.)

Now here is a statement about international trade theory and economic development which makes good sense to the economic historian, and evokes certain well-known characteristics of the economic development of the Western industrial nations.

V

In the Western countries, time and time again, the expansion of foreign trade provided the opportunity for innovation to create dramatic structural changes—changes which raised productivity and thus produced expanding output per capita. But here we reach a crucial point. These structural changes involved wholesale substitution of factors and factor mobility. Where these two processes did not take place easily, there was a harsh adjustment as in the celebrated reduction of the British handloom weavers to abject poverty. Old processes and skills were scrapped. Moreover, some of the rising export industries supported local industries, many of which subsequently developed into efficient industries capable of competing in international trade. In Professor North's terminology, the export base supported and helped to develop the residentiary industries.[5]

This process created a moving, changing complex of end products which satisfied consumer demand and the creation of which gave rise to complementary investment which generated income and supported more innovation. This process could continue so long as old factor combinations gave way to new and more efficient combinations. Here we have, in a dynamic world, mutually supporting investment in different areas of production which widened the market for expanding output. Or in other words, the end result was a close approximation to Professor Nurkse's equilibrium notion of balanced growth.[6]

It is crucial that one realize that this balanced growth was an end result produced and maintained by the ceaseless ebb and flow of innovations and changing factor combinations. It was not a phenomenon created by the simultaneous expansion of mutually supporting sectors. The mutually supporting sectors were in fact the survivors of a persistent war of attrition, the intensity of which was made possible by continued response

[5] Douglass C. North, "Location Theory and Regional Economic Growth," *Journal of Political Economy* (June, 1955), pp. 243–58.

[6] Ragnar Nurkse, "International Trade Theory and Development Policy," paper prepared for the Roundtable of the International Association, Rio de Janeiro, Aug. 19–28, 1957, I am indebted to Professor Nurkse for permission to cite this unpublished paper.

to new profit possibilities. Individual sectors or industries plunged ahead, sometimes carrying the system along, sometimes destroying important parts of the old way of doing things. The net result was an increase in per capita output, but the cost to the losers could be high indeed. Hence, while it may be clear, as Professor Lewis argues, that the logic of simultaneous growth is as ". . . unassailable as its simplicity . . . ," it is equally clear that an appeal to the history of the successful industrial nations is no place to look for empirical support for simultaneous growth as an economic policy for the underdeveloped countries.[7]

I should like to expand on this point. I have said that balance was the net product of imbalance. What precisely does imbalance refer to? I mean by this awkward term, disturbances which raised the possibility, in terms of profits and higher productivity, of disrupting the existing order of things with new factor combinations. Basically there were three ways in which the dynamic consequences of imbalances were felt, in the cases of: derived demand, complementarity, and competitive pressure. I will illustrate each with an example taken from the literature of economic history.

The derived-demand case is familiar to us in Mantoux's chapters on the great inventions of the industrial revolution; for example, the impact of power spinning on weaving. Here in a series of connected production processes, all leading to a single finished product, a single innovation raised demand for the next process in line—demand which was derived from the demand for the final product. By lowering the sum of the supply prices of other components, there was an increase in demand for the remaining component (total demand for the finished product remaining unchanged).[8] This took the form of increased profit possibilities for innovation in the area where the old process prevailed. Thus for a while after power spinning had been introduced, the handloom weavers sported £5 notes in their hatbands, but ultimately their skill was rendered superfluous by the power loom. The imbalance created by improved spinning was filled by the power loom. Growth from higher productivity was the result. Here is what Mantoux observed when he said that innovation was forced by innovation.[9]

The complementarity case is well known; for example, the impact of the internal combustion engine upon the demand for rubber and petroleum products. A full statement of this was given by Karl Marx in the

---

[7] W. A. Lewis, *The Theory of Economic Growth* (London, 1955), p. 283. Whereas the logic of balanced growth might be "unassailable," a careful scrutiny of Leonard Arrington's *Great Basin Kingdom* (Harvard, 1958) will show that even in the United States in the 19th century balanced growth could be a blueprint for near-disaster if rigorously pursued.

[8] An interesting historical example at a point of Marshall's statement of derived demand. Alfred Marshall, *Principles of Economics* (8th ed.; London, 1949), pp. 317–20.

[9] Paul Mantoux, *The Industrial Revolution in the Eighteenth Century* (London, 1949), pp. 244–51. For the earlier imbalance set up by the introduction of the flying shuttle, see pp. 211–13.

first volume of *Capital* (he also was aware of the derived-demand case). Discussing the great changes which had taken place in the British engineering industries in the mid-19th century, he notes the necessity of change in complementary industries:

> But the huge iron masses that had now to be forged, to be welded, to be cut, to be bored, and to be shaped, demanded, on their part, cyclopean machines, for the construction of which the methods of the manufacturing period were utterly inadequate . . . it was only during the decade preceding 1866, that the construction of railways and ocean steamers on a stupendous scale called into existence the cyclopean machines now employed in the construction of prime movers. (Glaisher edition, London, 1918, page 380.)

The competitive case has always been a critical one and is perhaps most familiar in two aspects. In the first, innovation killed older factor combinations—for example, the steamer and the sailing ship in ocean transportation. In the second, innovations which threatened the survival of firms employing older methods spurred the adoption of competing innovations—for example, the railway in Britain and the adoption of the iron-screw collier by the Tyneside coal owners.[10]

These processes of imbalance, when they were corrected, resulted in growth and development, rising per capita output due to the successful adaptation of technology and the adoption of new methods. One need not be a devotee of Schumpeter's system to see the virtue of it here. Either by trade or by domestic investment (or both) market demand created by imbalance was filled. But it was filled by further expanding the market— by raising productivity in new or in cognate lines of industry. Imbalance, by offering incentives, gave new enterprise a chance to strike a new balance.[11] The result was a Schumpeterian world where total output expanded rapidly with cyclical interruptions; and even these helped to speed the process by hurrying obsolete methods along to their graves.

VI

What we have finally to consider is why this desirable kind of development was so limited in the area of its permeation: why a process which characterized the development of nearly every country in northwest Europe and in the areas of European settlement overseas did not spread elsewhere, say in Southeast Asia or in Latin America.

Here we rely once again on Professor Nurkse. As we have noted, balanced growth did not mean that there were never supply shortages. But

---

[10] Jonathan R. T. Hughes and Stanley Reiter, "The First 1,945 British Steamships," *Journal of the American Statistical Association* (June, 1958), pp. 378–80.

[11] A short discussion of this concept and its applicability to American economic development was given by Professor Carter Goodrich, in an as yet unpublished paper, "Economic History and Economic Development," at the Texas Conference on Economic Development, Apr. 21, 1958. I am indebted to Professor Goodrich for permission to cite this paper.

shortages were created, then overcome, and, with cyclical interruptions, there was a rising trend of per capita output. Where the reaction to foreign trade gave rise to supply shortages, the Western countries responded by new factor combinations, the "productivity" inducement derived from trade. As Nurkse argues, international trade—Professor Robertson's "engine of growth"—could best transmit its advantages where the mobilization of new factor combinations was possible. The problem was not the allocation of given resource combinations to make a given output but, rather, that increments in output over time had to be provided by new combinations of factors. Hence the Rhineland's manufacturing industries could innovate and could maintain their growth in the international market of the 19th century after only a brief experience, while parts of Asia after centuries of trade with the West remained single-product economies so far as international trade was concerned. In too many cases, the product (or product combination) was the original one where trade on the "vent for surplus" lines had, for the most part, brought only an initial gain in terms of per capita output. Growth in these areas remained unbalanced, and indeed barely kept ahead of the growth of population.

On the basis of the analysis developed in this paper, a study of the differences in internal reactions to trade can be reduced to a study of relative impediments to factor mobility, given the factor endowments. Since so many of these impediments in the underdeveloped countries were, and are, social and cultural, policies for their elimination may well lie outside the realm of economic policy. Indeed, economic impediments were partly overcome long ago; railways, port facilities, banking systems, and so forth were introduced. Lately even state policies which impeded the development of new forms of economic activity have been in the process of reform.

But the failure of "residentiary industries" to grow up around the great export industries of the underdeveloped countries was, and is, also due to the continuation of social and cultural patterns which are hostile to factor substitution, mobility, and, indeed, even to the expansion of a domestic market.[12] When Western economists ask Asians and Africans to adopt our industrial system, or something like it, they are asking these people to "be like us" in more ways than just the adoption of the latest machines. Herein lies the ultimate barrier to the development of Western-type living standards in underdeveloped countries, I think, even if nature's parsimonious ration of natural endowments can be overcome.

Thus I arrive by a circuitous route at the most obvious and commonplace position on underdevelopment. But I think it is worth doing to show, in an organized way, that what we have experienced in economic history is not inconsistent with economic theory and involves a lot more than just economics. This I hope will be of some use to students of economic underdevelopment.

---

[12] Henry G. Aubrey, "Industrial Investment Decisions: Analysis and Comparison," *Journal of Economic History* (December, 1955), pp. 335–51.

3. Trends, Cycles, and Stagnation in U.S. Manufacturing Since 1860[*]

Edward Ames[1]
Purdue University

I. Introduction

INTUITION unaided might tell us that the trend for U.S. manufacturing output for the period 1915–55 gives a higher average rate of growth than one for the period 1915–40, but not, however, whether the 1955 level of output was as high as an extrapolation of the 1860–1914 trend.

Studies before World War II[2] spoke of a slowing down in the rate of growth of U.S. output. It is not clear whether further slowing down has occurred since then by comparison with the pre-1929 era.

Over 40 years have elapsed since World War I and it should be possible to determine whether, as some have claimed, it affected the growth of U.S. manufacturing output.

To aid in answering questions like these, a continuous index of manufacturing production for 1860–1955 (Table I) was prepared by joining together indices for shorter periods. It should be presented with some apology to those who maintain that it is nonsense to talk about an index of manufacturing output over a period so long: either it uses a single set of commodities (in which case it ignores the very important industries which have appeared or disappeared over the century); or it uses different commodities for different subperiods (in which case it is not measuring the same thing at all times). In either case, price changes are so closely asso-

---

[*] Reprinted from *Oxford Economic Papers*, Vol. XI, No. 3 (October, 1959), pp. 272–81.

[1] My thanks are due to the Purdue Computing Laboratory, and to Mr. David Jonah in particular, for assistance in programming the material in Part II.

[2] Such as Arthur Burns, *Production Trends in the United States since 1870* (New York: National Bureau of Economic Research, 1934). In the light of the discussion in this paper, one might raise the question of whether the retardation Burns found was spread evenly over the period, or whether (as his tables 16, 17, and 45 suggest) it began only about 1910.

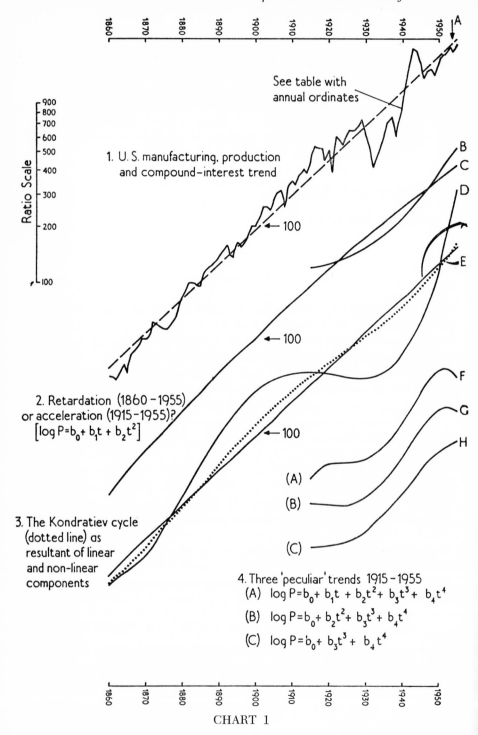

CHART 1

ciated with output changes that weight bias is necessarily a factor so important that no index is unambiguously meaningful.[3]

My approach was the latter. Suppose that the subindex for each component period shows the growth of industries which were "representative" (in a Marshallian sense) during that portion of the total period. The total index is then a step toward an index whose commodity composition would change from year to year, and which would describe the common behavior of "representative industries," in general, without regard for their specific technological or social characteristics.[4]

TABLE I

MANUFACTURING OUTPUT IN THE UNITED STATES, 1860–1955

$(1899 = 100)$

Year	Decade									
	1860	*1870*	*1880*	*1890*	*1900*	*1910*	*1920*	*1930*	*1940*	*1950*
0......	16	25	42	71	100	173	249	320	438	753
1......	16	26	46	73	111	166	199	269	584	806
2......	15	31	49	79	127	190	302	203	737	833
3......	17	30	50	70	126	204	288	234	897	906
4......	18	29	47	68	121	191	273	259	876	846
5......	17	28	47	81	140	224	306	309	744	939
6......	21	28	57	74	152	266	325	363	616	
7......	22	30	60	80	156	264	326	387	675	
8......	23	32	62	91	127	261	341	303	688	
9.....	25	36	66	100	166	228	374	384	636	

SOURCE: For 1860–1909, Frickey's Index of Production for Manufacture (Edwin Frickey, *Production in the United States, 1860–1914* [Cambridge, Mass., 1947], p. 54). For 1910–39, Fabricant's series on manufacturing output (reprinted in *Historical Statistics of the United States, 1789–1945* [Washington, D.C., 1949], col. I–13, from Solomon Fabricant, *The Output of Manufacturing Industries, 1899–1937* [New York, 1940], Table 1, p. 44; and, by the same author, *Employment in Manufacturing, 1899–1939* [New York, 1942], p. 331). This series was adjusted to give the same average index for 1910–14 as Frickey's index for this same period. For 1940–55, Federal Reserve Indices were used, the index using 1935–39 weights being used for the period 1940–46, and the index using 1947–49 weights being used for the period 1947–55. The indices were adjusted so as to yield the same averages, respectively, for the years 1935–39 and 1947–49, as the indices which they superseded.

II. Rates of Growth and Retardation

Over the period from 1860 until 1914 the rate of growth of manufacturing production was 4.7 percent per year; from 1915 through 1955 the rate of growth was 3.8 percent per year.[5] A second-degree parabola (log

---

[3] I shall follow the example of Gerschenkron, who showed that if U.S. machinery output were priced at 1899 prices, the index of machinery output in 1939 was 555 percent of 1899; if 1939 prices were used, the index in 1939 was 70 percent of 1899 (Alexander Gerschenkron, *A Dollar Index of Soviet Machinery Output, 1927–28 to 1937* [Santa Monica, Calif., 1951], p. 37). Like him, I find it interesting to see what can be done with indices.

[4] This concept of "own rate of growth" is suggested by Gregory Grossman's article on National Income in Abram Bergson (ed.), *Soviet Economic Growth* (New York, 1953).

[5] These rates are obtained from regression functions of the form $\log P = b_0 + \sum b_i t_i$ fitted to the periods in question.

$P = b_0 + b_1t + b_2t^2$) indicates a slight retardation ($b_2 = -0.0444 \times 10^{-3}$). If output growth were really slowing down, the variance about this second-degree function should be less than the variance about compound interest functions ($\log P = b_0 + b_1t$) fitted to the pre-1914 and post-1914 periods separately. Actually it is not (Table II). Moreover, a consistent retardation should certainly show up in the second part of the period, and probably in the first. A logarithmic parabola fitted to the pre-1914 period does show some retardation ($b_2 = -0.0127 \times 10^{-3}$), but since 1914 there has been acceleration in the rate of growth ($b_2 = 0.0342 \times 10^{-2}$).

These findings suggest more complicated trends in manufacturing production than some simple constant retardation factor over the entire period. There are, however, grounds for accepting a compound interest growth function without more ado.

The compound interest function ($\log P = b_0 + b_1t$) fitted for the entire period, accounts for 97.7 percent of the original variance. A fourth-degree function ($\log P = b_0 + b_1t + b_2t^2 + b_3t^3 + b_4t^4$) accounts for 98.3 percent of the original variance. But the data are perhaps not precise enough to justify this refinement; a fourth-degree function may not be intelligible enough to be of scientific use; and even if it were, a reduction of 0.6 percent in the variance is too small to warrant the adding of three more terms to the trend function.[6] It might seem that if Arthur Burns found retardation over the period 1870–1929,[7] it was only because he was studying too short a period for the basic linearity of the trend to be quite clear.

III. The Kondratief Cycle

The foregoing discussion makes sense if "trend" is a purely descriptive number, answering questions such as these: (1) What was the average rate of growth? (2) What was the average rate of retardation or acceleration? (3) How rapidly is the rate of retardation (acceleration) changing? and so on. With adjustments for changes in the number of degrees of freedom, one can also ask how much better an explanation is which includes retardation (or a steadily changing retardation, etc.) than is one which excludes the possibility.

A statistical operation such as trend fitting involves calculating trend regression coefficients and residual variances. It also requires examination

---

[6] Almost all trend functions fit well. Of the 45 trends in powers of t, only 3 fail to account for 70 percent of the original variance, and only 7 fail to account for 80 percent. The fourth-degree function fitted to the entire period leaves 1.7 percent of the variance unexplained; 8.4 percent can be explained by the function $\log P = b_0 + b_1t$ and not by a function containing only terms in t^2, t^3, and t^4; a function in terms of t^2, t^3, t^4 explains 0.6 percent of the variance not explainable by the term in t; but 89.3 percent of the variance can be explained equally well by either a compound interest function or by the function $\log P = b_0 + b_2t^2 + b_3t^3 + b_4t^4$. The principle of Occam's razor suggests the compound interest function.

[7] Burns, *op. cit.*, chap. 4.

of the individual deviations of observations about the trend line. If years known to have been prosperous are below the trend values, on some trend calculation, then there may be reason to withhold approval of the trend, however well it may fit on least square criterion.[8]

The period before 1914 shows a higher rate of growth plus retardation; the period since then a lower rate plus acceleration. Suppose that secular forces do not proceed smoothly over time, even though in a sufficiently long interval they may be summarized by a compound interest function. Then periods of rapid expansion (say 1860–1914 or 1940–55) may be followed by periods of slower growth (say 1915–40). Compound interest functions fitted to the shorter periods will naturally show differing rates of growth.

If the speeding up and slowing down of this "trend" is periodic over say 60- to 80-year intervals, we have a "Kondratief cycle" of some sort: 1860–1914 was, perhaps, a Kondratief upswing; the period since then was at first a Kondratief downswing and, more recently, a new upswing. On this assumption, line D in Chart 1 shows the shape of this "long cycle." A function of a peculiar sort ($\log P = b_0 + b_2 t^2 + b_3 t^3 + b_4 t^4$) was fitted to the entire period because it maximizes nonlinear, "cyclical" influences of a long-term sort. This particular trend, which we can reject on other grounds, has the virtue of showing this clearly marked "long cycle." When linear terms are admitted into the function ($\log P = b_0 + b_1 t + b_2 t^2 + b_3 t^3 + b_4 t^4$) the amplitude of these fluctuations, of course, is greatly reduced, although their influence is apparent.

Thus the decrease in average rates of growth accompanied by an increase in acceleration when we compare the pre-1914 with the post-1914 data is explainable either by a "fluctuating trend,"[9] or a Kondratief cycle. If the Kondratief cycle is approximated by the fourth-degree power function used here, however, it provides us with only two troughs (1867 and 1942) and one peak (1904).

IV. Stagnation in the Interwar Period

Another extremely simple hypothesis can serve to explain the curious fact that the period 1860–1955 there is an apparent retardation; whereas for the more recent period 1915–55 there is an apparent acceleration in the rate of growth.

---

[8] Thus a fourth-degree trend function fitted to the manufacturing index for 1860–1914 alters only the fourth significant figure of the coefficient of determination obtained by fitting a linear trend. However, it passes above known business cycle troughs and below known peaks in 21 out of the 28 recorded for this period by the National Bureau, whereas the latter does so in only 17 cases.

[9] B. Weber and S. J. Handfield-Jones, "Variations in the Rate of Economic Growth in the U.S.A., 1869–1939," *Oxford Economic Papers*, 1954, pp. 101 ff., agree that there was no retardation. On the other hand, they found a recurrent fluctuation in growth rates, averaging about 25 years in length (p. 107) which is not detected by the methods used here.

For the period 1860–1914 let us assume a linear trend.[10] For the period since 1914 the coefficient of determination of a linear trend is only 0.790, compared to 0.989 for a linear trend over 1860–1914. Even adding terms in t^2, t^3, and t^4 raises the coefficient only to 0.863.

Curiously enough, however, functions containing terms in t give lower coefficients of determination than those with an equal number of terms but not including t. For example, the function $\log P = b_0 + b_3 t^3 + b_4 t^4$ fits the data better than any other combination of powers up to the fourth. And all of the functions $\log P = b_0 + b_1 t + b_i t^i$ ($i = 2, 3, 4$) fit worse than functions in which the term $b_1 t$ is replaced by a term in a higher power of t.

TABLE II

RESIDUAL VARIANCE ABOUT TREND LINES BY PERIODS
UNDER VARIOUS HYPOTHESES*

		1915–55			
Hypothesis	*1860– }1914*	*Total*	*1915–}34*	*1935–}55*	*1860–}1955*
Compound interest curve, fitted to entire period	7,935	51,870	26,062	25,808	59,805
Logarithmic parabola, fitted to entire period	7,655	42,573	23,544	19,029	50,228
Two compound interest curves, fitted to pre-1914 and post-1914 periods	7,786	40,487	22,002	18,485	48,273
Kondratief hypothesis†	7,213	37,577	18,848	18,729	44,790
Hypothesis C	7,786	30,943	14,886	16,057	38,729
Hypothesis B	7,786	30,202	14,145	16,057	37,988
Hypothesis A	7,786	25,640	9,583	16,057	33,426

* These figures should be multiplied by 10^{-5}. The total variance of the logarithms is 615,574 $\times 10^{-5}$ for 1860–1914; 192,321 $\times 10^{-5}$ for 1915–55; and 2,587,359 $\times 10^{-5}$ for 1860–1955.

† The function $\log P = b_0 + b_1 t + b_2 t^2 + b_3 t^3 + b_4 t^4$ is here fitted to the entire period. Fitted just to 1860–1914, it leaves a residual variance of $6,758 \times 10^{-5}$; fitted just to 1915–55 it yields a residual variance of $26,587 \times 10^{-5}$.

Graphical analysis shows that the "peculiar trends"—those without a term in t—are level or even declining in the early period (say 1915–30), and rise very steeply thereafter. Several of these are reproduced in the chart, Part 4.

Formulated more precisely, these trends suggest that manufacturing production rose during the latter, but not the earlier, part of the period. To use traditional terminology, manufacturing industry was "stagnant" from 1915 until some time in the 1930's, and "developing" thereafter. On this hypothesis, for the first part of the second period (1915–34) the trend

---

[10] A fourth-degree function for this period does not increase the third figure of the coefficient of determination, so that less than one tenth of 1 percent of the total variance is accounted for by terms in t^2, t^3, and t^4. Moreover, the straight-line trend fitted to the entire period gives almost as good a fit for 1860–1914 as the straight-line trend fitted to the subperiod. Of the total residual variance about the straight-line trend fitted to the period 1860–1955, more than five sixths occurs in the period after 1914.

was set equal to the average level of the logarithms of the index over these years. I then averaged the logarithms of the index for 1946–55, placed this value at the centre of the period, and computed the trend forward to 1955 and backward to 1935 on the assumption that a developing industry could grow at the same rate (4.7 percent per year) as it had before World War I. This hypothesis is not only more intelligible, but it fits better than the fourth-degree function $\log Y = b_0 + b_1 t + b_2 t^2 + b_3 t^3 + b_4 t^4$; while its residual variance is only 55 percent of that about the compound interest trend fitted to the entire period (Hypothesis A, Table II).

This hypothesis, of course, has certain objectionable features. The trend value for 1914 is $\log 191 = 2.2810$, that for 1915 is $\log 272 = 2.4342$. The trend value for 1934 is $\log 272 = 2.4342$, that for 1935 is $\log 368 = 2.5661$. And the slope of the trend line for 1935–56 is not fitted by least squares methods. The hypothesis accounts for 98.7 percent of the total variance for the period 1860–1955, as compared to 98.3 percent under the Kondratief hypothesis, and 97.7 under a single compound interest trend fitted to the entire period.

As an alternative, instead of a completely stagnant trend line from 1915 to 1934 we join the 1914 and the 1935 trend values with a straight-line trend in the logarithms, so that there is one high rate of growth for 1860–1914 and for 1935–56, and one low rate for 1915–34. This hypothesis (Hypothesis B in Table II) fits better than the Kondratief hypothesis, but worse than Hypothesis A.

Finally, the period from 1915 through 1929 may have been basically a continuation of the pre-1914 period, but 1929 marked a basic discontinuity in the economy. If we extrapolate forward to 1929 the compound interest trend for 1860–1914; and extrapolate backward to 1930 the trend already used for 1935–55, we obtain results (Hypothesis C in Table II) almost as good as Hypothesis B and therefore better than the Kondratief hypothesis, but worse than Hypothesis A.[11]

V. The Logistic Trend

The logistic curve, represented by the function $P = [a + bc^t]^{-1}$ has been used by some economists to represent output trends. It is S-shaped, rising from one asymptote of zero at an increasing rate until P has the value $a^{-1}/2$; growth then retards until finally an upper asymptote of a^{-1} is reached as $t \to \infty$. The basic methods of fitting it[12] do not determine uniquely the exact position of the trend—and in this case they yield somewhat differing results. Findings must therefore be stated rather cautiously.

---

[11] Hypothesis A gives a coefficient of determination of 0.867; Hypothesis B 0.843; and Hypothesis C 0.838 over the period 1915–55. By comparison, a compound interest trend gives $R^2 = 0.790$, and a fourth-degree function 0.863.

[12] See Harold T. Davis, *The Analysis of Economic Time Series* (Bloomington, Ind., 1941), pp. 250–53.

In particular, the "coefficient of determination," measuring the percentage of the variance in the original data which has been accounted for by the trend, is not uniquely determinable in a least squares sense.

For the period 1860–1955 as a whole, the logistic curve explains about 92 percent of the variance, whereas the compound interest function explains about 98 percent of the variance of the logarithms. Since the most violent fluctuations in the manufacturing index—the 1929 depression and World War II—are concentrated at the "high end" of the series, residual variance of logarithms should be less than that of the data themselves.

TABLE III

CHARACTERISTICS OF LOGISTIC TRENDS FITTED TO VARIOUS
INTERVALS OF THE INDEX OF MANUFACTURING
PRODUCTION, 1860–1955

Mid-point of period fitted	Span of period	Indicated inflexion point* — Production level	Indicated inflexion point* — Date	Percentage of variance explained
1887	1860–1914	3,928	1987	98
1895	1860–1929	741	1951	98
1908	1860–1955	708	1946	92
1935	1915–55	499	1937	76
1942	1930–55	405	1937	79

* The production level (1899 = 100) here is half of the upper asymptote. The dates at which this point would have been reached, assuming the given trend, were in some cases obtained by extrapolation.

Table III shows that the later the midpoint of the period for which logistic curves are fitted, (a) the lower the percentage of variance explained by the trend, (b) the lower the upper asymptote, and (c) the earlier is the "critical point" at which the slowing down of the rate of growth begins.[13] Since the curve fits well until 1929, either some discontinuity occurred at about that year,[14] or else a different basic trend function underlay the data, accounting for the systematic shifts in the date and level of the inflexion points shown in Table III.

If a discontinuity in the trend occurred in 1930, a "splice" of two trends is possible. This splice explains about one third of the variance left from a fitting of a single logistic curve for the whole period 1860–1955. Thus

---

[13] The error may be in the methods of curve fitting. It was observed that the Pearl-Reed method, which weights relatively heavily the first third of the period fitted, tends to give good fits in the early period, but low trend values for later years. Davis's method, on the other hand, gives good fit in later years, but low trend values in earlier years. However, Davis warns that no method gives completely reliable results unless the data extend for a "considerable period" beyond the inflexion point. This is probably not the case here.

[14] Under the logistic hypothesis, a single discontinuity in 1915 may be excluded, since the fit for 1860–1929 is as good as that for 1860–1914; and since the fit for 1930–55 is better than that for 1915–55. Assuming a discontinuity in 1915, 92 percent of the variance can be explained, but this result is no better a fit than the fit of a single logistic curve to the entire period.

95 percent (rather than 92 percent) of the variance can be explained on the assumption that a new logistic trend "went into operation" in 1930. On the other hand, this trend has its upper limit at 810, while the production index was well above this level in 1943–44 and again in 1952–55. Moreover, on this particular hypothesis, the trend of output was "almost stagnant" after the end of World War II, and grew most rapidly in the late 1930's. This view may accord with cyclical analysis, but hardly with secular analysis.

Algebraic functions in the logarithms suggest that although output has, on the average, risen at a slower rate since 1915 than it did formerly, this rate of growth has been accelerating. The logistic trend, however, suggests that (1) growth increased at an accelerating rate through 1929; (2) there was then a discontinuous change, with a new growth pattern setting in; (3) this growth pattern, by 1955, either had actually reached its upper limit, or was only slightly below it. Algebraic functions of the logarithms will lead one to high, and the use of logistic trends to low, forecasts of output.

VI. Conclusions

1. Algebraic trend functions fitted to the logarithms in general fit the data very closely, and show that:

   (a) Over a period of almost a century, American manufacturing output has risen at an average rate of 4.4 percent per year. No strong evidence of a slowing down in the rate of growth exists; and since 1915 there is evidence of an accelerating rate of growth.

   (b) There is a little evidence of a Kondratief cycle in manufacturing output, with a trough in 1867, a peak in 1904, and a trough in 1942.

   (c) However, there is more evidence of a period of stagnation over the period 1915–35. The rest of the period since 1914 can well be summarized in terms of a compound interest rate of growth of 4.7 percent per year.

2. The logistic trend function also gives a very good fit to the production index prior to 1929. In contrast to the logarithmic trends, it suggests acceleration in the rate of growth until that time; indeed a single logistic trend fitted to 1860–1955 has the level of expansion accelerating until 1946, with a "saturation level" roughly 50 percent above the 1955 peak. The period since 1914, analyzed by logistic trend analysis, shows a new cycle of growth, discontinuous with earlier trends, which by 1955 had virtually spent itself. Thus the more recent past, on this analysis, gives less promise of future expansion than it does on the basis of other trend functions. However, logistic functions, particularly since 1929, do not seem to fit the data as closely as the algebraic functions.

3. In any case, the development of manufacturing output seems to have been interrupted in the first third of the century, and discontinuity

in the growth pattern is suggested whichever method of trend analysis is used.

Appendix

I. Computation of Regression Equations of the Form

$$\log P = b_0 + \sum_i b_i t^i$$

Appendix Table I shows the results of computing trends of the form

$$\log P = b_0 + \sum_i b_i t^i$$

A total of 15 such functions were fitted for the periods 1860–1914, 1915–55, and 1860–1955. These functions took all combinations of i for i equals 1, 2, 3, 4. In this calculation, which was performed on the digital computer of the Purdue Computing Laboratory, values of the coefficient of determination (R^2), and the residuals of the data about each trend line were computed.[1]

In addition, the following data were obtained: (1) whenever the sign of the residual about the trend changed (i.e., the data crossed the trend line), this was taken as indication of an upward or downward cyclical movement. One half the total number of sign changes then equals the number of "residual cycles." (2) The average length of residual cycles was computed.[2] (3) A "reference cycle pattern" was prepared from National Bureau timing of reference cycle peaks and troughs. In the period following a reference cycle trough up to and including a reference cycle peak, the index could be expected to be increasing; following a reference cycle peak up to and including the following trough, the index could be expected to be declining. Agreement of the signs of first differences of residuals about trend with the reference cycle pattern was measured. (4) If the entire economic process consists of a trend and of a short-term movement with the timing exhibited by the reference cycle, reference cycle peak years should be above trends, and reference cycle trough years should be below. For each trend calculation, the number of cases in which production in reference cycle peak and trough years "straddled" the trend lines in this way.

II. The Length of the Business Cycle as a Criterion in Trend Fitting

Some economists distinguish cyclical from secular influences and there has been discussion of whether there are several orders of cycle. If the secular movement of production is relatively smooth, and if there is a

---

[1] A tabulation of the regression coefficients for these functions is available from the writer on request. So also are the constants obtained from fitting the logistic curve under the various assumptions as to discontinuity described in the text.

[2] E. M. Frickey, *Economic Fluctuation in the United States, 1860–1914* (Cambridge, Mass., 1942, pp. 44–45), shows the effect of changing the function fitted upon the length of residual cycles in pig iron production.

APPENDIX TABLE I
Results from Fitting of Algebraic Trend Functions to Production Index

Function number	Function fitted: log P equals	A. Coefficient of determination			B. Number of residual cycles*			C. Average length of residual cycles (year)†			D. Turning-point straddling‡		
		1860–1914	1915–55	1860–1955	1860–1914	1915–55	1860–1955	1860–1914	1915–55	1860–1955	1860–1914	1915–55	1860–1955
I	$b_0 + b_1t + b_2t^2 + b_3t^3 + b_4t^4$	0.989	0.863	0.983	8.5	5.0	12.5	6.5	8.2	7.7	50	47	45
II	$b_0 + b_2t^2 + b_3t^3 + b_4t^4$	0.986	0.854	0.899	8.0	4.5	4.5	6.9	10.3	21.3	36	37	11
III	$b_0 + b_1t + b_3t^3 + b_4t^4$	0.989	0.851	0.980	8.5	4.0	11.5	6.5	10.3	8.3	36	47	45
IV	$b_0 + b_1t + b_2t^2 + b_4t^4$	0.989	0.844	0.981	8.5	4.0	13.0	6.5	10.3	7.4	50	47	53
V	$b_0 + b_1t + b_2t^2 + b_3t^3$	0.989	0.840	0.981	8.5	4.5	14.0	6.5	9.1	6.9	50	47	49
VI	$b_0 + b_1t + b_2t^2$	0.989	0.830	0.981	8.5	2.5	14.0	6.5	16.4	6.9	50	26	49
VII	$b_0 + b_1t + b_3t^3$	0.989	0.822	0.980	8.5	3.5	10.5	6.5	11.4	9.1	50	37	34
VIII	$b_0 + b_1t + b_4t^4$	0.989	0.814	0.980	8.5	5.5	13.0	6.5	7.5	7.4	50	47	36
IX	$b_0 + b_2t^2 + b_3t^3$	0.980	0.832	0.834	5.0	4.5	2.5	11.0	9.1	38.4	21	37	2
X	$b_0 + b_2t^2 + b_4t^4$	0.973	0.835	0.329	5.0	5.5	1.0	11.0	7.5	96.0	14	47	2
XI	$b_0 + b_3t^3 + b_4t^4$	0.950	0.848	0.866	5.0	5.0	1.5	11.0	8.2	64.0	29	58	6
XII	$b_0 + b_1t$	0.989	0.790	0.977	8.5	5.0	8.0	6.5	8.2	12.0	21	47	23
XIII	$b_0 + b_2t^2$	0.929	0.828	0.261	2.0	3.0	3.5	28.0	13.7	27.4	7	5	15
XIV	$b_0 + b_3t^3$	0.834	0.786	0.819	1.0	5.0	1.0	55.0	8.2	96.0	0	26	2
XV	$b_0 + b_4t^4$	0.745	0.721	0.322	1.0	5.0	2.0	55.0	8.2	48.0	0	26	6

* One residual cycle has been counted for every two sign changes in the residuals.

† The number of years in the period divided by the number of residual cycles.

‡ The number of cases in which the observations were *above* trend in years of reference cycle peaks and *below* trend in years of reference cycle troughs. There were 28 reference cycle turning points in 1860–1914; 19 in 1915–55; a total of 47. These figures, computed from the formula $s - f/s$, where s = number of cases counted by the above rule, t = total number of turning points, $f = t - s$, measures in National Bureau usage, the extent to which the results differ from the results which would be obtained by chance. Complete straddling would result in a coefficient of 100 (every peak would be above, and every trough would be below, the trend); while complete absence of straddling would result in a coefficient of 0.

single cycle in the economy, business-cycle peaks would in general be *above* and troughs *below* trend values. Moreover, if a correct method of trend fitting has been used, the index should cross the trend line twice in every full cycle. If neither of these expectations is fulfilled, either the concept of a "smooth" secular trend over a long period should be abandoned, or the concept of higher order cycles should be accepted.

The method of counting cycles described above may overestimate the number (underestimate the length) of residual cycles, since every minor bobble about the trend line is treated as a cycle. It will not, however, underestimate the number (overestimate the length). For none of the logarithmic trends fitted does the average length of these cycles fall below six and one half years; in contrast, the average length of the National Bureau's reference cycle is less than three years.[3]

Secondly, a test comparable to those made by Mitchell and by Burns and Mitchell was made: the number of reference cycle turning points straddling the trend line[4] minus those not straddling the trend was expressed as a percentage of all turning points in the period. This percentage would be taken as the probability that chance factors alone could have accounted for the failure of all turning points to straddle. This probability is not strong. The failure to straddle may equally well be ascribed to nonchance factors, including in particular the hypotheses (which may well be equivalent) that the true trend is not as smooth as has here been assumed or that there is a cycle of longer duration than the reference cycle.

---

[3] The variations in the length of the residual cycles are consistent with Frickey's findings in the pig iron case. In the extreme examples, where less than two cycles appear over the period under study, it is not hard to reach the conclusion that a "bad trend" is being used.

[4] A reference cycle peak which is above the trend, or a reference cycle trough which is below the trend, straddles the trend in this argument.

4. Immigration into Canada, 1851-1920*

Duncan M. McDougall

Purdue University

The purpose of the paper is to provide more firmly based estimates of some aspects of Canadian population growth. In Part I estimates are derived of the natural increase in the Canadian population by decades from 1851 to 1931 based on survival rates derived from life tables. The figures on natural increase then permit the derivation of net migration estimates. In Part II new estimates of immigration are developed that, together with the net migration figures of Part I, yield estimates of emigration by decades. Part III tests some of the results by an examination of the limited information available on other aspects of Canada's economic development in the period.

I

THE LIFE TABLE is a basic tool of population study. The most recent application of the life table to the problem of the reconstruction of Canadian population growth was made by Nathan Keyfitz.[1] While the same method is used here, we feel that we have made more realistic assumptions in deriving a life table designed to represent the mortality characteristics of early Canadian populations.

A life table reflects the course of mortality in a population. It is constructed from enumerated characteristics of a population—age, sex, deaths and, if possible, births. From these data it is possible to derive estimates of the probability of survival of a population by age and sex. For purposes of estimation it is convenient to derive a single survival rate by using the enumerated age-sex distribution for any census population.[2]

---

* Reprinted from *Canadian Journal of Economics and Political Science*, Vol. 27, pp. 162–75. The author wishes to acknowledge the financial support of the Purdue Research Foundation. The Foundation does not, of course, share in any way the responsibility for the views or conclusions of the paper.

[1] "The Growth of Canadian Population," *Population Studies*, Vol. IV (June, 1950), 47–63.

[2] The mechanics of life table construction are laid out in simple form in Louis I. Dublin and Alfred J. Lotka, *Length of Life* (New York, 1936), chaps. I. and XIV. Our single survival rate was calculated from quinquennial survival rates based on the stationary population column with a correction factor applied to the 0–1 age group.

By use of the calculated survival rate for any decade and with knowledge of the population of Canada as enumerated at a census, it becomes possible to estimate an expected population at the next census. For example, by applying to the population of Canada in 1901 the survival rate calculated from a life table constructed to represent the mortality of the Canadian population between 1901 and 1911, an estimate is derived of the population 10 years of age and over for 1911. The difference between this estimated population for 1911 and the actual population of 1901 gives an estimate of the natural increase in the decade 1901–11 from within the population at the beginning of the decade. The difference between the estimated population for 1911 and the actual population for 1911 gives a measure of the net migration of those aged 10 years and older during the decade.[3] The net migration figure is thus a residual in two senses. First, it is an arithmetic residual in the sense of a balancing item on the population balance sheet. Second, it is a residual because it estimates only that part of the gross flows that remains at the end of the decade to be counted in the census.

The life table clearly plays a crucial role in the analysis. Unfortunately, no dependable life table exists for the Canadian population prior to 1931 nor are there any mortality and population figures sufficiently accurate to construct tables. Life tables for Canada can only be approximated by using the mortality experiences of other countries. Keyfitz's solution was to use English life tables as a means of extrapolating back to 1851 the Canadian life tables of 1931 and 1941.

There are only three sets of mortality estimates available covering the latter half of the 19th century. They are the Massachusetts mortality data, the Swedish mortality data, and the English life tables.[4] The Massachusetts figures are not very reliable in themselves, and they suffer from the more serious disadvantage that they refer only to a limited geographic area. To use them as a measure of the mortality of the Canadian population would require that they be weighted by some index expressing the differences between the characteristics and environment of the populations of Massachusetts and Canada.

The Swedish figures, while reliable and consistent, refer to a population differing in important characteristics from the Canadian population. In particular the urbanization of the Swedish population was less rapid than the Canadian. By 1900 only 22 percent of the Swedish population resided in towns and cities in contrast to the 37 percent of the Canadian population listed as urban in 1900. The differences in the mortality of rural and urban populations preclude the direct use of the Swedish data to the Canadian population.

---

[3] Children born within the decade and children immigrating to Canada who are less than 10 years old at the next census cannot be distinguished by this method. Thus the net migration figure derived refers to those 10 years of age and over.

[4] On this point see the note by Dorothy S. Thomas in Simon Kuznets and Ernest Rubin, *Immigration and the Foreign Born* (New York, 1954), pp. 66–68.

The English life tables are reliable and consistent, and they extend back to the early 19th century. Furthermore, Dublin and Lotka have asserted that it would be "a fair presumption that the earlier English life tables would also represent approximately the conditions of mortality in the United States at the corresponding epoch."[5] The use of the earlier English life tables as a basis for estimating the mortality of the Canadian population in the 19th century can be made with some confidence on the grounds that Canadian mortality in that period was similar to that in the United States.[6]

While the English tables[7] are used as a basis for estimating survival rates for the Canadian population in the latter half of the 19th century, we did not feel that the Canadian tables[8] of 1931 and 1941 could be used as a means of modifying the early English tables to conform to the Canadian experience. As Dublin and Lotka have indicated in the passage quoted above, a bench mark closer to the 19th century is needed because of errors that would result had the trend in mortality in Canada and Great Britain been different in the 20th century. Such a bench mark is available in the United States life table prepared by J. W. Glover[9] for the white population of the original death registration states during the decade 1901–10. The fact that the Glover table includes only a limited number of states is providential from our point of view. The mortality of the white population in the selected states was probably closer to the mortality in Canada than, for example, the mortality in the United States as a whole. The ratio of United States to English survival rates for the decade 1901–10 was then used to modify the English survival rates back to 1851–60.

The next problem was to estimate the survival rates for the Canadian population in the 20th century. To solve this problem we compared the survival rates for the American and British populations in the decade 1901–10 and the Canadian and British populations for the period 1930–32 by age and sex. The rates for the North American countries and for Great Britain showed improvements over the period except for the upper end of the age distribution. In the decade 1901–10 the survival rates for American males were slightly below those of British males up to the age group

---

[5] Dublin and Lotka, *Length of Life*, p. 45.

[6] The age, sex and, given the inevitable differences in definition, the rural-urban distributions were quite similar in the two countries in the latter half of the 19th century.

[7] *The Registrar General's Decennial Supplement, England and Wales, 1931* (Her Majesty's Stationery Office, 1952), Part III, pp. 27–30.

[8] Canada, Dominion Bureau of Statistics, *Life Tables for Canada and Regions, 1941 and 1931* (Ottawa, 1947).

[9] U.S. Department of Commerce, Bureau of the Census, *United States Life Tables, 1890, 1901, 1910, and 1901–1910* (Washington, D.C., 1921), pp. 66–67 and 72–73. The included states are Maine, New Hampshire, Vermont, Massachusetts, Rhode Island, Connecticut, New York, New Jersey, Indiana, Michigan, and the District of Columbia.

40–44, and slightly above for older age groups. In 1930–32 the survival rates for Canadian and British males were roughly equal up to the age group 25–29, but for older age groups the rates for Canadian males were above those for British males. Moreover, the differences in the older age groups were greater than they had been between the American and British males in the earlier decade. Roughly the same picture was shown for females although the differences in each period between the North American and British survival rates were smaller than for males. Thus, while the mortality rates in both North America and Great Britain improved in the 20th century, a relatively greater improvement was shown for North America.

The existence of a trend in the differences between the survival rates of the populations of Great Britain and North America in the 20th century, while precluding the use of the English life tables after 1900, raises again the question of the suitability of the English life tables as a basis for estimating Canadian mortality in the 19th century. To use the English tables is to assume that the differences in trend noted above are a phenomenon entirely of the 20th century. It might be argued that the trend should also be extrapolated back to 1851. There is almost no evidence to support a choice between the two methods. If it could be shown, for example, that the relative improvement in the North American survival rates was due to the institution of medical improvements previously implemented in Great Britain, a trend would have to be built into the extrapolation to derive estimates of Canadian survival rates. An attempt to answer the question by examining records of causes of death failed because of the lack of consistency in the categories used in the different countries over the period and a lack of data for the North American population extending back into the 19th century.

On the basis of the foregoing analysis we made the decision that the best estimate of Canadian mortality over the whole period would be to use the United States life table as a basis for extrapolating the English tables from 1900 back to 1851; to use the United States table for the decade 1901–10; and to use a linear interpolation of the United States table for 1901–10 to the Canadian table for 1930–32 as a measure of the survival rate for the period 1910–30.

The differences between the methods used in this paper to calculate the survival rates for the Canadian population and the methods used by Keyfitz lead to different estimates of natural increase and net migration. Our survival rates lie below those developed by Keyfitz for every age-sex group for every decade because of our use of the American table for 1901–10. The result is that our estimates of natural increase are smaller and therefore our estimates of net migration are larger if positive, and smaller (in absolute value) if negative, for each decade than those derived by Keyfitz. The relevant figures are given in Table III.

II

Given the net migration figures in Table III, it is an easy step, using the Dominion Bureau of Statistics figures of immigration, to arrive at decade totals of emigration from Canada. The disadvantage of this procedure is that the immigration figures are subject to doubt. For example, no immigration into Canada from the United States is recorded between 1892 and 1896 while in the previous five-year period immigration of over 51,000 per year is recorded. Also, there is evidence that the immigration series, at least in some periods, would be more aptly entitled arrivals rather than immigrants.[10] Finally, the immigration total of 903,000 recorded for the decade 1880–90 appears to be too large when compared with the total of 1,074,000 recorded for the 40-year period 1851–80 plus 1891–1900. This part of the paper is devoted to constructing independent estimates of immigrant flows into Canada.

True immigration figures are impossible to estimate. An immigrant would be defined ideally as a person landing in a country with the intention of taking up permanent residence, who, in fact, realizes his intention. We have no way of measuring intentions or realizations, but, from an economic point of view, it would be relevant to distinguish between transients and persons remaining for, say, a minimum of one year. A certain amount of income is generated by the activity of transporting transients, but that activity is not likely, even given the apparent volume of immigrants passing through Canada, to make a lasting contribution to economic development. In fact, if plans are made on the expectation of the settlement of persons who are in reality transients, serious misallocations of resources may result.

There are two sources of information on the volume of the migration of persons by sea to Canada: the emigration records of European countries and the Canadian records of arrivals. If both emigration and immigration (or departures and arrivals) were zealously counted it would be a simple matter, taking into account time lags and deaths at sea, to check one series against the other. We have already indicated, however, that we do not feel that the Canadian records are completely reliable.

In the estimating procedures used in this part of the paper, frequent use is made of the American immigration series. These figures are used because they are not as subject to the problem of transient, as opposed to passenger, movements as are the Canadian statistics, and because they

---

10 We hold this in spite of the fact that the Canadian authorities are quoted by Ferenczi to the effect that from 1866 on the Canadian immigration figures include as far as possible only immigrants proper. According to the definition "immigrants are those who have never been in Canada before and who declare their intention to reside there permanently." Imre Ferenczi, *International Migrations,* Vol. I (New York, 1929), pp. 357–59.

give in greater detail the immigrants' country of origin, needed in the following calculations. Up to 1867, the American immigration series relate to alien passengers derived from passenger lists deposited with the various collectors of customs. From 1867 to 1903 they refer to alien immigrants, that is, persons intending permanent residence, but include only persons traveling third class. After 1903 an effort was made to count all immigrants. From 1903 until as late as 1912 there are indications that the attempt to include cabin passengers in the total was inadequate, but there is uncertainty about the effect of this on the series.[11]

Our estimates of immigration into Canada are based on the available data relating to emigration from other countries. First we estimated emigration from continental Europe, next from the British Isles, and finally from the United States.

The following basic assumption was used to derive estimates of emigration from Europe (excluding the British Isles) to Canada. During the period 1850 to 1920 the movement of people from Europe to Canada occurred as part of the wavelike movement of population to North America.[12] The proportion of this movement that Canada received was determined by relative economic conditions in Canada, but Canada did not exercise any attraction independent of the attractive force of North America in general.

There is a fairly complete series of passenger movements from some European countries and ports, notably in Britain and Germany, to Canada, but there are only fragmentary records for most other countries. Ferenczi's estimates of emigration from Europe to British North America, derived by adding together all the available national estimates of emigration, suffer from the incompleteness of the national figures.[13] An attempt was made to fill in the gaps in the national data by extrapolation, using the available continuous series, but the totals showed far too large an emigration from Europe, primarily as a result of double counting. When a Norwegian emigrated he was counted in the Norwegian totals, but he was probably counted again if he shipped from, say, London or Rotterdam.

While the series listing the absolute number of emigrants from Europe to British North America are too fragmentary to use, the records taken by some European countries and port officials on the intended destination of emigrants are useful as samples of the intentions of the total emigrant flow. From these records quinquennial averages of the emigration to British North America from European regions were calculated as a per-

---

[11] Marian Rubin Davis, "Critique of Official United States Immigration Statistics," in Walter F. Willcox (ed.), *International Migrations*, Vol. II (New York, 1931), pp. 645–58. Kuznets and Rubin, *Immigration and the Foreign Born*, begin their series of immigration with the year 1908. See also Brinley Thomas, *Migration and Economic Growth* (Cambridge, 1954), chap. IV.

[12] See Thomas, *Migration and Economic Growth*, chap. VII.

[13] Ferenczi, *Migrations*, Part II, Table II, pp. 241–50.

centage of the emigration from the same regions to the United States. These percentages were then applied to quinquennial totals of the number of immigrants from the same European regions arriving in the United States.[14] No attempt was made to separate the passengers from the immigrants. The evidence in Ferenczi suggests that, excluding the British Isles, there was relatively little net passenger movement in any decade from Europe to the United States before 1920.[15]

This estimating procedure was not used after 1920. During the quinquennium 1920–24 the percentage of persons emigrating to North America and giving Canada as their destination jumped sharply. It is clear that the effective immigration barrier erected by the United States in 1921 makes the method of estimation used up to that time completely unreliable.

The estimates of emigration from Europe (excluding the British Isles) to Canada are presented in Table I, along with quinquennial totals of immigrant arrivals by sea into Canada from countries other than the British Isles given in part by the Dominion Bureau of Statistics and in part by a series showing immigration by sea through Quebec and Montreal supplied by the Dominion Bureau of Statistics and published by Ferenczi.[16] For six of the nine quinquennia between 1851 and 1895 our estimates agree quite closely with those of the Dominion Bureau of Statistics. Disagreement occurs in 1851–55, 1866–70, and 1881–85. In the first two periods our estimates are based on the emigration of German citizens through the Port of Hamburg only (see n. 14 above). On the other hand, the Dominion Bureau of Statistics series shows some unaccountable gaps. For example, it shows an annual average immigration by sea between 1851 and 1870 of only 39 persons from all countries except the British Isles, Germany, and Norway; disagreement between the series is therefore not unexpected. We feel, however, that the difference for the period 1881–85 is a significant one. More will be said about this difference in Part III. We take the agreement in the earlier period as support for the

---

[14] The immigration from regions of Europe into the United States is given in U.S. Department of Commerce, *Historical Statistics of the United States, 1789–1945* (Washington, D.C., 1949), Series B308–316, pp. 33–34. We distinguished four regions, (1) Scandinavia, (2) Germany and Poland, (3) Southern Europe, (4) Other Northwest, Other Central, and Eastern Europe. The percentages representing emigration to British North America as a percentage of emigration to the United States were derived from the following sources: for region (1) emigration from Sweden and Denmark, Ferenczi *Migrations,* Table IV, p. 752, and Table III, p. 670; for region (2) 1850–70, emigration of German citizens through Hamburg, *ibid.,* Table IIIa, p. 695, and 1871–1924, emigration of German citizens, *ibid.,* Table VIII, pp. 700–701; for region (3) emigration of Italian citizens, *ibid.,* Table XI, pp. 828–31; and for region (4) from alien emigration through German ports, *ibid.,* Table XII, pp. 706–707.

[15] Ferenczi, *Migrations,* Text table, 7, p. 195.

[16] For the period before 1881 and for the period 1900–1908 see *ibid.,* Table I, p. 360, and Table VI, pp. 364–65. For 1881–99 see Canada, Dominion Bureau of Statistics, *Canada Year Book, 1936,* p. 186, and for 1908–21 see *Canada Year Book, 1942,* p. 153.

TABLE I

Quinquennial Totals of Emigration from Europe to Canada, 1871–1920
(Thousands of Persons)

	Scandi- navia	Ger- many and Poland	South- ern Europe	Other North- west, Other Central, and Eastern Europe	Total	DBS "Other"
1851–55..........	0	113	0	0	113	36
1856–60..........	0	37	0	0	37	28
1861–65..........	0	30	0	0	30	35
1866–70..........	0	31	0	0	31	66
1871–75..........	°	1	0.8	11	13	15
1876–80..........	°	3	0.9	3	7	3
1881–85..........	°	4	2	13	19	41
1886–90..........	3	2	8	30	43	38
1891–95..........	5	15	4	12	36	34
1896–1900........	2	2	4	35	43	65
1901–05..........	16	1	24	59	100	222
1906–10..........	15	3	44	39	101	199
1911–15..........	16	5	61	127	209	384
1916–20..........	4	3	10	8	25	47

° Less than 0.5 thousand.
NOTE: Detail may not add to total due to rounding.
SOURCE: See text and n. 16.

estimating procedure used here and for our assertion that there was relatively little passenger movement from Europe to Canada. The agreement also leads to the conclusion that transient flows were minor between 1850 and 1895.

The differences in the four quinquennia between 1896 and 1915 are substantial. Part of the difference after 1895 may be due to the fact that, after the American legislation of the 1890's and 1900's which barred contract laborers and physically, mentally, or politically undesirable groups, some immigrants used Canada as a "back door" to the United States. Given the laxness in enforcing these laws, however, this reason is unlikely to account for much of the difference. Some more of the difference may be explained by the possibility that Europeans took advantage of inducements offered to immigrants by Canada but had no intention of staying and, in fact, recorded the United States as their destination when they left Europe. A major part of the difference may be a result of the counting of transients by overzealous Canadian officials, perhaps for political reasons.

Emigration from the British Isles to Canada would at first glance appear to be the easiest series to estimate. The movement of people out of the British Isles has been recorded in a lengthy and relatively complete series.[17] The difficulty is that the data record total passenger movements up to 1912 rather than the movement of migrants. Again, the American data were resorted to as a means of estimating the flow of migrants.

The records of passengers from the British Isles destined for the United States were compared with the American records of immigration from the British Isles.[18] It was then assumed that in any five-year period the differences between the two series represent an estimate of passenger, as opposed to emigrant, movement.[19] To quote again from Ferenczi, the differences between the two series "are largely accounted for by the fact that the British statistics are of passengers and the United States statistics, after 1869, are of immigrants."[20]

The percentage of passengers in the outflow from the British Isles to the United States was then assumed to be equal to the percentage of passengers in the outflow from the British Isles to Canada. Up to the period 1871–75 the passenger component of the flow to the United States was essentially zero.[21] From that period to 1896–1900 the proportion of passengers increased to a high of roughly 50 percent. The proportion decreased in each quinquennium thereafter until by 1916–20 it was again essentially zero.[22]

Our estimates of the flow from the British Isles to Canada are presented in Table II. The differences between our series and the one published by the Dominion Bureau of Statistics[23] stem not only from the apparent inclusion of passengers in the latter series but also from the fact that our series includes only emigration of residents of the British Isles. The Dominion Bureau of Statistics series may well include all persons shipping from the British Isles, including transmigrants from continental Europe. Such persons would be included as immigrants from Europe under our method.

The estimate of the inward movement across the land boundary of Canada from the United States was the most difficult of all movements to

---

17 N. H. Carrier and J. R. Jeffery, *External Migration, 1815–1950* (Her Majesty's Stationery Office, 1953), Table D/F/G(1), pp. 95–96.

18 U.S. Department of Commerce, *Historical Statistics, 1789–1945*, Series B306–307, pp. 33–34.

19 The problems of time lags and deaths at sea were ignored.

20 *Migrations*, p. 196.

21 This is substantiated by Carrier and Jeffery who quote the United Kingdom Board of Trade statement in H.C. 112 of 1887 that "the passenger movement . . . dealt with has always been spoken of as emigration; but during the last 20 years especially it has become obvious that many passengers are dealt with who do not go away from the United Kingdom to settle abroad." Carrier and Jeffery, *External Migration*, 140.

22 On April 1, 1912, the United Kingdom Board of Trade made adjustments to the manifests used in counting persons leaving by sea that permitted the authorities to identify permanent emigrants, persons leaving to take up residence abroad for at least a year. *Ibid.*, p. 140. There is general agreement also that by 1912 the American authorities were counting immigrants only. Davis, "Critique," p. 651.

23 See n. 16 for sources of this series.

estimate. Before 1908 the figures are quite unreliable. While Canada does have records of immigration from the United States, there are gaps in the data and there is evidence of double counting and incomplete counting.[24] The estimates from American sources are just as poor.[25]

The United States, with the cooperation of the Canadian authorities, began to count population movements across her land borders in the fiscal year 1908.[26] From that date on, annual series list emigrant aliens departed by countries of intended future permanent residence.[27] Beginning in 1918

TABLE II

QUINQUENNIAL TOTALS OF IMMIGRATION INTO CANADA FROM EUROPE, THE BRITISH ISLES, AND THE UNITED STATES, 1851–1920
(Thousands of Persons)

	From British Isles (1)	From Europe (2)	From United States (3)	Total (4)	Immigrant Arrivals DBS (5)
1851–55	159 (155)	113	107 (n/a)	379	151
1856–60	40 (58)	37	30 (n/a)	107	81
1861–65	48 (67)	30	30 (n/a)	108	97
1866–70	83 (115)	31	44 (n/a)	158	82
1871–75	102 (134)	13	45 (n/a)	160	181
1876–80	60 (69)	7	26 (n/a)	93	162
1881–85	134 (154)	19	67 (282)	220	477
1886–90	121 (127)	43	64 (245)	228	409
1891–95	59 (96)	36	37 (53)*	133	182
1896–1900	41 (57)	43	33 (248)*	117	157
1901–05	173 (224)	100	106 (192)	380	556
1906–10	426 (320)	101	205 (299)	732	1,088
1911–15	538 (506)	209	292 (404)	1,039	1,295
1916–20	216 (149)	25	94 (222)	334	417

* No immigration from the United States is recorded for the years 1892–96 inclusive.
NOTE: Detail may not add to total due to rounding.
SOURCE: Col. (5), for 1852–93, *Canada Year Book*, 1942, Table I, p. 153 (total for year 1851 added by extrapolation); 1894–1908, *ibid.*, 1948–49, Table I, p. 175; 1909–31, *ibid.*, 1955, Table I, p. 167.
Figures in brackets are official estimates. For 1851–80, Ferenczi, *Migration*, Table I, p. 360; 1881–1920, see n. 16. Official estimates of immigration from Europe are given in Table I above.

figures also exist for American citizens departed by countries of intended future permanent residence.[28]

The calculation of estimates of the flow of persons from the United States to Canada had to be made by extrapolating back the known figures for the recent period. The basis of the extrapolation was the assumption

[24] Ferenczi, *Migrations*, pp. 357–59.
[25] Davis, "Critique," pp. 652–56. See also Thomas, *Migration and Economic Growth*, pp. 42–50.
[26] Earlier attempts beginning in 1892 by the new United States Bureau of Immigration with the cooperation of steamship lines serving Canada and the Canadian railways were not successful. Davis, "Critique," pp. 652–53. See also Kuznets and Rubin, *Immigration and the Foreign Born*, pp. 55–60.
[27] U.S. Department of Labor, *Annual Report of the Commissioner General of Immigration, 1930* (Washington, D.C., 1930), Table 84, pp. 208–11, gives the series for 1908–30.
[28] *Ibid.*, 1931, Table 80, p. 215.

that in any five-year period the immigration from the United States to Canada bore the same relationship to the movement of immigrants to Canada from the British Isles and Europe as existed between 1909 and 1914. Or, what amounts to the same thing, the percentage changes between quinquennia in the absolute flows of immigrants from the United States to Canada were the same as the percentage changes in the flows from the British Isles and Europe to Canada. This assumption has its basis in the belief that international migration before 1920 was motivated predominantly by economic forces. If the flow of transatlantic migrants to Canada increased in any period, then the economic forces that caused the increase would be likely to induce a similar increase in the number of immigrants from the United States.

Because the records of the movement of American citizens to Canada begin in 1918, the flow of American citizens to Canada between 1909 and 1914 had to be estimated before the calculation could be made. This was done by assuming that the annual average American citizen movement for the period 1909–14 was the same as the annual average for the period 1918–21. This estimate, plus the recorded alien flow from the United States to Canada in the period 1909–14 was 39.0 percent of the immigrant flow from the British Isles and Europe to Canada in the same period.[29] The results of the calculation are shown in Table II.

Given the immigration figures of Table II and the net migration figures of Table I, it is possible to make up a balance sheet of Canadian population growth by decades from 1851–1921. Such a balance sheet is presented in Table III. It should be kept in mind that the emigration figures are residuals, and therefore include the residual errors of the primary series. In addition, the emigration estimates include more than the outflow of people. An immigrant who comes to Canada and dies before the next census will be included by the above method amongst the emigrants of the decade. Finally, it must be remembered that the method by which the figures of net migration were calculated could not take any account of the 0–10 age group. The immigration figures, however, include all age groups.[30]

III

The estimates of immigration into Canada developed in this paper differ in every decade to a greater or lesser degree from the series published by the Dominion Bureau of Statistics. The only way of checking the data presented in Table III as they now stand is on the basis of the reasonableness of the methods used in deriving them. In this part of the paper some subsidiary information is considered as a means of assessing

---

[29] The American figures were for fiscal years ended June 30 while the figures for transatlantic migrations were calendar years. No adjustment was made for the difference.

[30] We have made no attempt to estimate immigration from any country outside Europe, the British Isles, and the United States.

some part of the estimates. An alternative would be to proceed further to derive independent estimates of emigration that could then be checked against the residual emigration figures of Table III. Unfortunately the available data are too scanty to permit such a procedure. In fact, the scarcity of information severely limits the extent to which an independent check of the estimates is possible. For that reason the analysis of this section is limited to the three decades 1851–60, 1881–90, and 1901–10 in which the estimates derived in this paper differ sharply from the Dominion Bureau of Statistics estimates.

There appears to be a general consensus among Canadian economic historians that Canada experienced three periods of economic expansion in the period covered in this paper: the first in the 1850's, the second centered around 1870, and the third beginning in the late 1890's and continuing into the 20th century. Thus two of the decades in which the immigration estimates differ sharply coincide with periods of prosperity for Canada. In the decade 1851–60 the estimates of this paper indicate that the official figures understate, and in the decade 1901–10 that they overstate, the flow of immigrants. There is no sharp difference associated with the prosperity centered around 1870 because the estimates of this paper are tied to census year bench marks.

In the absence of statistical information the staple model of Canadian development can be used to assess the meaning and validity of the differences noted. Although the model is not very discriminating because it is not subject to quantification and there is therefore no basis for judging quantitative differences in the variables, it remains the most widely accepted tool for examining Canadian economic history.

A model of the role of the staple product in Canadian economic development can be formulated in the following way. We begin with an exogenous increase in the demand for a Canadian export and some available excess capacity in the export sector of the economy. This increased demand for a Canadian export leads to increased incomes and, after a lag, to increased investment in the export sector. Through the multiplier, incomes are increased in the home production sector also. Increasing incomes lead to increased importations of goods and, in turn, to an increase in customs and excise revenues. The increased tax revenues encourage the federal government to embark on long-awaited development schemes. The deflationary effects of a continuing merchandise deficit are offset, or more than offset, by the inflationary effects of capital borrowing on the basis of the optimism engendered by the rising demand for exports and the rising tax revenues.[31]

How does the international flow of people fit into this model? We assumed an initial elasticity in the factor supplies of the export sector

---

[31] Canada, *Report of the Royal Commission on Dominion-Provincial Relations* (Ottawa, 1940), Book I, pp. 61–62. Richard E. Caves and Richard H. Holton, *The Canadian Economy* (Cambridge, Mass., 1959), pp. 30–47.

TABLE III
POPULATION BALANCE SHEET FOR CANADA, BY DECADES, 1851–1921
(Thousands of Persons, Ten Years of Age and Over)

	Total Population Start of Decade	Natural Increase during Decade	Net Migration during Decade	Total Population End of Decade	Immigration during Decade	Emigration during Decade
1851–61........	1,639	464 (495)	+154 (+123)	2,258	486 (209)	332 (86)
1861–71........	2,258	543 (563)	−170 (−191)	2,630	266 (186)	436 (376)
1871–81........	2,630	575 (619)	− 40 (− 85)	3,164	253 (353)	293 (438)
1881–91........	3,164	617 (669)	−154 (−205)	3,628	448 (903)	602 (1,108)
1891–1900......	3,628	595 (654)	−115 (−181)	4,107 (4,101)	249 (326)	364 (507)
1901–11........	4,107 (4,101)	631 (711)	+794 (+715)	5,532 (5,528)	1,111 (1,782)	317 (1,066)
1911–21........	5,532 (5,528)	841* (916) *	+306 (+233)	6,679 (6,677)	1,373 (1,592)	1,067 (1,360)
1921–31........	6,679 (6,677)	1,348 (1,389)	+142 (+103)	8,169	— (1,198)	— (1,095)

* Includes 120,000 additional deaths due to World War I.

NOTE: Figures in brackets are from Keyfitz, "Canadian Population," Table 4, p. 51. The differences in the total population figures result from the fact that for the years 1901–31 we used the figures in 1951 *Census*, I, Table 19, while Keyfitz used 1941 *Census*, II, Table 41.

of the economy, but when the large-scale development projects are undertaken and expansion begins in the export sector additional quantities of labor are required. The question is how much labor? Presumably a good that qualifies as a staple must have a production function consistent with the resources available for its exploitation. In the case of Canada one would assume this to mean that relatively little labor would be required. On the other hand there are increases in the ancillary activities, such as transportation and distribution, connected with the development of a new product or area as well as increases in those activities stimulated by rising incomes. Such activities do require substantial quantities of labor that could come from either immigration or reduced emigration. The problem is complicated by the existence of the United States which affected the growth of the Canadian labor force in two ways. First, as has been argued in Part II, Canada did not exert an independent attractive pull on immigrants. She competed with the United States for immigrants and shared in the total transatlantic migration only in so far as immigrants believed economic conditions in Canada were more attractive than in the United States (ignoring the politically oriented part of the migration flow). Second, the American economy exerted at various periods an attractive force on the labor force Canada did acquire.

Both the decades 1851–60 and 1901–10 were periods of prosperity based primarily on exports but because of the uncertainties implicit in the model we do not see that it offers any basis for making a choice between the Dominion Bureau of Statistics estimates and the ones developed here. Therefore, even though we feel the differences are real and significant, we are willing to let our estimates of the migration for these two decades stand supported only by the arguments of Part II that the differences result from counting errors.

The real problem comes in the decade 1881–90 primarily because it is part of the period 1873–96 during which evidence of prosperity combines with evidence of a "great depression." Those who use the staple model generally skip the period 1873–96 for good reason. In truth there is little evidence in the trade statistics, federal revenues, or price records to provide a clear picture of the Canadian economy in that period.

That there is uncertainty about the period is shown by the fact that Caves and Holton, to quote one of the most recent works, say "the wave of Europeans in the 1880's . . . by-passed Canada to populate the Great Plains of the United States. . . ."[32] In the same chapter they reproduced Keyfitz's table that shows for the period 1881–90, using the Dominion Bureau of Statistics series, an immigration total of 903,000 and an emigration total of 1,108,000 (mid-1881 to mid-1890). Our estimates show an immigration total of 448,000 and an emigration total of 602,000. It should also be noted that the Dominion Bureau of Statistics records an

---

[32] Caves and Holton, *The Canadian Economy*, p. 35.

immigrant inflow from the United States of 527,000 persons for the decade 1881–90. The census of 1891 shows the total population of Canada to be not quite 500,000 greater than in 1881 and the American-born population to be only 3,000 greater.[33] While this is entirely possible, given the definition of an immigrant as one who changes residence for a minimum of one year, it marks the decade as one clearly worth examining.

It is certainly not clear how a satellite economy such as Canada in the 19th century could show periods of very rapid, large-scale development without the stimulus of a rising demand for her exports. On the other hand, as Buckley has convincingly argued, to study Canadian economic development solely in terms of staple commodities ignores far too much of the total economic process that was quite as essential to the development of the Canadian economy.[34]

We feel, following Buckley, that the use of the staple model has caused historians to overlook the evidence in favor of counting the decade 1881–90, or at least some part of it, among the relatively prosperous periods of the last half of the 19th century. The evidence presented by Buckley on gross investment in railways and in his index of urban building indicates that there was considerable activity in Canada during the decade. We would suggest that the activity grew out of two factors: railroad construction financed by the federal government related to an expected rather than a current export demand; and interregional shifts of resources associated with changes in Canada's industrial structure.

It has been said that Canada at Confederation was no more than a group of scattered, debt-ridden ex-colonies. It is pertinent then to ask how she could absorb successfully the tremendous inflow of resources that we know came in between 1900 and 1913 if the intervening period was largely one of depression. The only answer is that the period was not one of great depression. The last quarter of the 19th century must have witnessed quite marked changes in Canada's economic structure.

The estimates developed in this paper indicate that the decade of the 1880's, when more emigrants came to Canada than in any decade between 1860 and 1900, was the period when much of this change was accomplished. However, we know that the United States was experiencing a substantial prosperity during the same period.[35] Thus even though Canada

---

[33] See also comments by Kuznets and Rubin, *Immigration and the Foreign Born*, p. 59, on this same point.

[34] Kenneth Buckley, "The Role of Staple Industries in Canada's Economic Development," *Journal of Economic History*, Vol. XVII (December, 1958), pp. 439–50. John H. Young, "Comparative Economic Development: Canada and the United States," *American Economic Review*, Vol. XLV (May, 1955), Supplement, pp. 80–93, also expresses doubts about the gloominess of the period 1873–96.

[35] Simon Kuznets, "Long-Term Changes in the National Income of the United States since 1870" in *idem*, ed., *Income and Wealth of the United States*, International Association for Research in Income and Wealth (Cambridge, 1952), Table 3, p. 50, shows a rate of growth of net national products for the period 1874–83 to 1879–88 of 30.7 percent. See also the evidence in Thomas, *Migration and Economic Growth*, pp. 109–13.

was developing, the United States probably attracted the major part of transatlantic immigration and at the same time attracted some part of the Canadian labor force. On the basis of this evidence we would argue that an immigration total of 448,000 and an emigration of 602,000 are figures closer to reality than those presented by Keyfitz and the Dominion Bureau of Statistics.

5. The Investment Market, 1870–1914: The Evolution of a National Market*

Lance E. Davis
Purdue University

I

IT IS NECESSARY not only that capital be accumulated, but also that it be mobilized for productive use, if an economy is to benefit from an increase in capital per person.[1] The classical model of resource allocation assumes that within any economy capital is perfectly mobile. It implies, therefore, that once allowance is made for uncertainty and risk, returns on investment are equal in all industries in all regions. Such a model, while logically consistent, is not very useful for analyzing the process of economic growth. In the early stages of development, because the uncertainty discounts are high, capital is not very mobile. As a result, rates of return vary widely between industries and between regions; and growth in high-interest regions is retarded. Development, in part then, takes the form of a reduction in uncertainty discounts—a reduction that makes it possible for capital to move more freely between regions and industries.

In a Robinson Crusoe economy, where the saver is also the investor, capital mobilization presents no problem. The more complex the economy, however, the more difficult it is to tranfser the command over resources gained by nonconsumption from the savers to those who wish to use these resources—that is, the investors. In the case of the United Kingdom, as Postan has shown, each of several personal fortunes could have financed the entire industrial revolution. Despite these personal accumulations, the new industries were unable to acquire funds even at interest rates in excess of 20 percent. At the same time, the land-connected industries (agriculture, brewing, milling, and mining) were able to

---

* Reprinted from the *Journal of Economic History*, Vol. XXV, No. 3 (September, 1965), pp. 355–99.
[1] M. M. Postan, in an unpublished series of lectures given in the graduate economic history seminar at Johns Hopkins University during the academic year 1954–55.

command large quantities of capital, although rates of return were near zero (and sometimes, perhaps, negative).[2] In the case of the United States, the mobilization problem was even more complex. Not only did capital have to move from old to new industries, but mobilization frequently involved geographic movement as well. In general, most of the savings accrued in the developed areas (that is, in the Northeast), but the demand for capital moved steadily toward the South and West. At the same time as comparative advantage shifted, early accumulations in foreign trade and shipping had to be transferred into textiles and other light industry during the first half of the 19th century. In the second half, funds had to be mobilized for heavy industry; and in the present century petroleum, chemicals, and electronics have become great demanders of new capital.

Although Douglass North has argued that barriers to capital mobility were not important in the United States,[3] many students of the 19th century have felt they were. Moreover, a fund of qualitative information suggests that the economy encountered substantial problems in its attempts to mobilize capital across regional and industrial boundaries.[4] The purpose of this paper is to provide some quantitative measures of the barriers to interregional mobility and to suggest that certain institutional innovations in the period 1870–1914 acted to reduce these barriers.

For simplicity, the United States has been divided into six geographic regions—regions originally defined by the Comptroller of the Currency. Because of the timing of American development, only two of the six lie entirely west of the Mississippi River. East of the Mississippi, New England has been separated from the Middle Atlantic states, but the remainder of the divisions quite closely follow those laid down by North. Region I is New England; Region II, the Middle Atlantic states; Region III, the South; Region IV, the Old Northwest Territory plus the first-settled states of the West North Central region; Region V includes the Great Plains and part of the Mountain states; and Region VI, the Pacific and the remainder of the Mountain states.[5]

---

[2] Postan.

[3] North, "Capital Formation and the Industrialization of the United States," a paper delivered before the Second International Economic History Conference, Aix-en-Provence, France, 1962.

[4] See Lance E. Davis, "Capital Formation and the Industrialization of the United States: Comment," a paper delivered before the Second International Economic History Conference, Aix-en-Provence, 1962, and "Capital Immobilities and Finance Capitalism: A Study of Economic Evolution in the United States 1820–1920," *Explorations in Entrepreneurial History,* Second Series, Vol. I, No. 1 (Fall, 1963), pp. 88–105.

[5] Region   I: Maine, Vermont, New Hampshire, Massachusetts, Connecticut, and Rhode Island.

   Region   II: New York, New Jersey, Pennsylvania, Delaware, Maryland, and the District of Columbia.

   Region III: Virginia, West Virginia, North Carolina, South Carolina, Georgia, Florida, Alabama, Mississippi, Louisiana, Texas, Arkansas, Kentucky, and Tennessee.

II

The major quantitative series for the analysis of the short-term market have been derived from the annual reports of the Comptroller of the Currency. These reports include state-by-state balance sheets for both reserve-city and nonreserve-city national banks at two or three dates per year. These balance sheets are reported in sufficient detail to permit earning assets to be separated from nonearning assets. In addition, for the years 1888 to 1914 the reports include gross earnings of the same banks on a state-by-state basis; and for the years 1869 to 1914 they report net earnings (gross earnings less losses and bank operating expenses). The gross rates of return on earning assets (gross earning divided by earning assets) appear to be a good approximation of the average rate of interest earned by the national banks. Moreover, since operating expenses tended to be relatively constant between regions and years and since losses are a short-run phenomenon, the net rates of return are a fairly good proxy for long-term movements in the average interest rates earned.

Because reserve-city banks had different reserve requirements than did nonreserve-city banks, and because the assets of the former might differ significantly from those of the latter, the two are reported separately in the following analysis. (Otherwise, an apparent rate differential might reflect only differences in the mix of reserve-city and nonreserve-city banks in a region.) For the same reason, the city of New York is reported separately.[6]

Interregional interest differentials were a well-known phenomenon in the 19th century; and contemporaries generally assumed that they were the result of certain capital immobilities.[7] The term "disinclination of capital to migrate" was used to explain the phenomenon, and it was estimated that an interest differential of 2 percent was necessary to overcome

Region IV:　Ohio, Indiana, Illinois, Michigan, Wisconsin, Minnesota, Iowa, and Missouri.

Region　V:　North Dakota, South Dakota, Nebraska, Kansas, Montana, Wyoming, Colorado, New Mexico, and Oklahoma.

Region VI:　Washington, Oregon, California, Idaho, Utah, Nevada, and Arizona.

Region　O:　New York City.

[6] Because of the difficulties induced by changing definitions, Chicago and St. Louis are included in their respective regions. The law required 25 percent reserves (all in lawful money) in central reserve-city banks; 25 percent (but up to one half could be in the form of bank deposits) in reserve-city banks; and 15 percent (up to three fifths in deposits) in nonreserve-city banks.

[7] It is, of course, true that other factors aside from uncertainty may have engendered (and probably did engender) a part of the differential. It is likely that in the early period eastern lenders may have felt western loans were more risky. In addition, since the average loan size in the West was smaller, these loans may have entailed a higher percentage of administrative costs. These reasons, on the other hand, cannot be used to explain away the entire differential. Since substantial differentials were also apparent in the net rates of return (after losses had been deducted) it must have become obvious that western loans were not "all that much" riskier, but the differentials persist for some decades. Moreover, the differentials continued after the size differentials between eastern and western loans began to diminish.

this barrier.[8] Table 1 displays Breckenridge's estimates of intercity rate differentials in the mid-1890's, and these differentials correspond fairly closely to the estimates based on the Comptroller of the Currency's reports.

Since it was 1913 before national banks were permitted to invest in mortgages, bank loans tended to be short term; and the regional differentials in the rate of return tend to reflect differentials in the interest rate of short-term commercial paper. Tables 2, 3, 4, and 5 display the gross and net rates of return to national banks in the period 1869–1914. For each region, column 1 shows unweighted average rates and column 2 an average weighted by the earning assets of the banks in each region. Because these returns were subject to sharp short-term fluctuations (particularly in years when only a few banks were operating in a region), Charts I through IV display three-year moving averages of the weighted rate series. Chart I displays gross earnings for nonreserve-city banks and Chart II, gross earnings for reserve-city banks. Charts III and IV show net earnings for nonreserve-city and reserve-city banks respectively. The New York City rate is displayed separately in each chart. Since it represents the rate of return in the nation's financial center, it is a useful referent.

In general, the unweighted bank data show differences in the mid-1890's that are comparable to those reported by Breckenridge; whereas the weighted average, dominated by the largest cities, shows less variation between regions. The two series are, however, not strictly comparable, since Breckenridge includes both reserve-city and nonreserve-city banks in his enumeration. City for city, Breckenridge's rates are slightly above those derived from bank earnings, and this difference undoubtably reflects the "nominally lower yielding" government bonds in the banks' portfolios.

All four charts indicate that differentials were higher in the earlier years than they were in the later. This pattern suggests that there was a gradual movement toward a national short-term capital market during the period. Other evidence also appears to bear out this conclusion. The rates in the eastern regions tended to close before those in the West and South. Moreover, the differentials between banks in reserve cities tend to narrow before the differentials between the nonreserve-city banks.

Charts II and IV indicate that, with the exception of the Pacific region, there appears to have been a marked decrease in the interest differentials between the reserve cities sometime in the late 1890's. In the early 1870's, with few exceptions, the New York City rate represented a lower boundary for the regional rates. In the latter years of that decade, however, the differentials between New York and Regions I and II largely disappeared. During the early 1890's, the rate in Region IV tends to close on the eastern

---

[8] R. M. Breckenridge, "Discount Rates in the United States," *Political Science Quarterly*, Vol. XIII (1898), p. 129.

TABLE 1

THE AVERAGE WEEKLY RATE OF DISCOUNT, 1893–97
(In 43 Cities of the United States, Arranged According to the
Geographical Divisions in Which They Lie)

	Percentage			*Percentage*	
New England			*Middle states*		
Boston	3.832		Cincinnati	5.012	
Hartford	4.602		Chicago	5.742	
Providence	4.982		Pittsburgh	5.838	
Portland	6.000		St. Louis	5.903	
			Milwaukee	6.276	
Average		4.854	Indianapolis	6.369	
			Cleveland	6.376	
Eastern states			Detroit	6.415	
New York	4.412		St. Paul	6.607	
Baltimore	4.567		Minneapolis	6.903	
Philadelphia	4.642		Kansas City	6.911	
Buffalo	6.007		St. Joseph	6.969	
			Duluth	7.253	
Average		4.907			
			Average		6.352
Southern states					
New Orleans	5.853		*Western states*		
Richmond	6.000		Omaha	7.980	
Memphis	6.103		Denver	10.000	
Nashville	6.673		Average		8.990
Louisville	6.826				
Charleston	7.026		*Pacific states*		
Galveston	7.311		San		
Mobile	7.957		Francisco	6.216	
Savannah	7.992		Los Angeles	7.057	
Atlanta	8.000		Portland	8.000	
Birmingham	8.000		Salt Lake		
Houston	8.000		City	8.000	
Little Rock	8.015		Tacoma	9.273	
Dallas	8.342		Seattle	9.969	
Average		7.293	Average		8.583

SOURCE: Breckenridge, *Political Science Quarterly*, Vol. III, p. 126.

rates; and, in the second half of that decade, the gap between rates in the East and those in Region VI narrows substantially. Although the differentials diminish between the Plains regions and those in the East, the rates in Region V remain above those in the East throughout the period. In the South, the rates show much less of a tendency to close than in any other region. Thus, although the rates in Region III compare favorably in the 1870's with those in the East, by 1914 they are among the highest in the country.

These rates are, of course, weighted by total earning assets, and therefore they tend to be dominated by the rates prevailing in the largest cities in each region. An examination of the unweighted rates (see Table 3) indicates that the evolution toward a national market was more gradual.

TABLE 2

GROSS RETURNS RESERVE-CITY BANKS BY REGIONS, 1888–1914

Year	NYC	I (1)*	I (2)†	II (1)*	II (2)†	III (1)*	III (2)†	IV (1)*	IV (2)†	V (1)*	V (2)†	VI (1)*	VI (2)†
1888	5.78	5.32	5.32	5.92	5.48	6.24	6.33	6.69	6.65	6.97	6.97	6.90	6.90
1889	4.99	5.30	5.30	5.77	5.33	6.28	6.40	7.16	6.59	7.90	7.90	7.80	7.80
1890	5.90	4.91	4.91	6.00	5.49	6.47	6.55	6.29	6.34	7.46	7.46	7.75	7.75
1891	6.01	5.17	5.17	5.94	5.54	6.95	7.11	6.64	6.84	8.38	8.38	7.63	7.63
1892	4.57	4.45	4.45	5.64	5.41	7.18	7.29	9.18	6.61	7.87	7.87	8.60	8.60
1893	5.36	4.72	4.72	5.60	5.38	6.19	6.35	5.78	5.77	5.56	6.71	7.69	7.69
1894	4.63	4.80	4.80	5.62	5.36	8.84	8.74	6.74	6.31	5.72	7.80	7.22	7.22
1895	4.02	3.87	3.87	4.92	4.52	6.96	6.98	5.78	5.31	11.46	6.94	7.54	7.54
1896	4.70	4.48	4.48	5.48	5.52	6.23	6.51	5.46	5.47	5.74	6.28	7.37	7.37
1897	4.43	4.33	4.33	5.48	5.11	9.01	9.22	5.99	5.51	13.66	8.39	6.62	6.62
1898	4.10	4.14	4.14	5.39	5.04	7.52	7.34	5.35	5.32	10.25	9.05	4.99	5.00
1899	3.18	3.19	3.19	5.27	4.79	7.41	6.47	4.62	4.50	21.43	9.86	5.85	6.18
1900	4.47	4.48	4.48	5.33	4.89	7.10	6.38	5.09	5.44	5.50	4.49	4.35	5.22
1901	3.51	3.67	3.67	4.79	4.48	7.07	6.21	3.83	3.82	3.54	3.22	5.40	5.75
1902	5.40	3.71	3.71	4.77	4.52	5.86	5.73	5.41	4.99	10.34	9.01	5.55	5.64
1903	4.72	4.30	4.30	4.91	4.96	6.65	6.22	4.38	4.46	4.76	3.76	4.35	4.48
1904	4.74	4.48	4.48	5.08	5.12	6.61	6.00	5.06	4.70	5.92	5.55	5.65	5.20
1905	2.40	3.62	3.61	3.67	2.87	7.05	6.23	4.55	4.34	6.55	4.94	6.11	5.07
1906	4.64	4.66	4.66	4.86	4.88	5.80	5.53	4.94	4.62	5.66	5.36	5.38	4.67
1907	5.09	5.13	5.13	4.96	5.00	5.39	5.25	4.68	4.51	6.43	6.85	4.95	4.57
1908	4.86	5.59	5.59	4.96	5.07	6.46	6.19	5.18	5.20	5.91	5.78	6.07	5.45
1909	4.47	4.81	4.81	5.11	4.77	6.27	6.12	4.99	4.85	5.96	5.90	5.39	5.13
1910	5.50	5.99	5.99	5.22	4.99	6.78	6.60	5.36	5.23	6.64	6.50	6.12	5.17
1911	5.04	5.37	5.37	5.24	5.06	6.75	6.74	5.94	6.13	8.26	6.34	6.30	5.70
1912	5.21	5.35	5.35	5.25	5.29	7.54	6.72	5.75	5.39	7.31	7.01	5.30	6.19
1913	5.76	6.73	6.73	5.43	5.57	6.73	6.72	6.00	5.90	7.30	7.16	6.10	6.27
1914	5.09	6.15	6.15	5.60	5.92	7.93	7.52	6.27	6.10	8.32	8.21	6.14	6.32

* Unweighted.
† Weighted.
SOURCE: *Annual Report of the Comptroller of the Currency.*

TABLE 3

Gross Returns Nonreserve-City Banks by Regions, 1888–1914

Year	I (1)*	I (2)†	II (1)*	II (2)†	III (1)*	III (2)†	IV (1)*	IV (2)†	V (1)*	V (2)†	VI (1)*	VI (2)†
1888	5.99	5.96	5.80	5.86	8.57	8.35	7.24	7.07	9.83	10.42	10.71	8.83
1889	6.31	6.16	6.00	6.22	8.84	8.52	7.29	7.18	9.60	9.81	10.13	8.81
1890	6.33	6.62	6.19	6.15	8.61	8.22	6.97	6.93	9.55	9.61	9.53	8.85
1891	6.20	6.11	6.08	5.99	8.51	8.48	7.16	7.08	9.83	9.19	10.33	9.30
1892	5.64	5.48	5.94	5.82	8.37	8.21	6.86	6.76	9.63	9.01	9.26	8.59
1893	5.53	5.45	5.21	5.63	7.72	7.84	6.42	6.31	13.50	9.72	9.02	7.88
1894	5.38	5.34	5.58	5.54	7.80	7.85	6.77	6.65	8.58	7.42	8.99	8.12
1895	5.16	4.96	5.46	5.44	8.21	8.29	6.35	6.32	8.90	8.06	8.52	7.87
1896	5.27	5.16	5.48	5.48	7.68	7.87	6.47	6.33	10.40	8.60	9.87	8.67
1897	5.17	5.12	5.58	5.50	7.81	7.71	6.71	6.53	9.29	8.65	8.37	7.44
1898	5.24	5.30	5.18	4.94	7.82	7.97	6.11	5.97	9.26	8.72	8.39	8.52
1899	5.32	5.33	5.53	5.54	7.71	7.70	6.03	5.89	9.24	8.56	8.31	7.91
1900	6.57	6.24	6.34	6.02	7.79	7.64	6.26	6.21	9.24	8.95	7.78	7.61
1901	5.36	5.22	5.20	5.19	6.91	7.12	4.37	4.41	6.72	6.36	7.17	7.15
1902	5.01	4.97	4.69	4.39	6.78	7.00	5.20	5.00	7.57	6.66	7.62	6.52
1903	4.86	4.92	5.22	5.09	6.76	6.83	5.28	5.13	8.55	8.15	8.33	7.44
1904	4.90	4.90	5.17	5.11	6.67	6.82	5.51	5.31	8.67	8.17	7.60	7.57
1905	4.32	3.62	3.04	2.59	6.55	6.61	5.32	5.13	7.99	7.63	7.34	7.06
1906	4.56	4.16	4.82	4.80	6.44	6.63	4.90	4.50	7.94	7.64	8.79	7.51
1907	4.87	4.93	4.70	4.68	6.20	6.25	4.94	4.85	7.80	7.51	7.75	6.67
1908	6.26	5.82	4.83	4.97	6.28	6.35	5.40	5.28	7.64	7.37	8.93	5.14
1909	4.80	4.85	5.00	5.09	6.28	6.50	5.16	5.16	7.98	7.80	8.27	6.98
1910	5.06	5.10	5.11	5.33	6.56	6.64	5.63	5.54	8.17	7.92	9.83	7.11
1911	5.16	5.20	5.20	5.37	6.98	7.03	5.94	5.83	8.88	8.61	8.87	7.41
1912	4.98	4.96	5.21	5.32	6.83	6.83	6.02	5.92	8.76	8.66	9.76	7.12
1913	5.34	5.35	5.37	5.56	6.96	7.01	6.17	6.06	8.78	8.68	9.11	7.23
1914	5.57	5.63	5.61	5.69	7.12	7.14	6.32	6.21	8.63	8.65	8.84	7.39

* Unweighted.
† Weighted.
SOURCE: *Annual Report of the Comptroller of the Currency.*

TABLE 4
Net Returns Reserve-City Banks by Regions, 1869–1914

Year	NYC	I (1)*	I (2)†	II (1)*	II (2)†	III (1)*	III (2)†	IV (1)*	IV (2)†	V (1)*	V (2)†	VI (1)*	VI (2)†
1869	3.83	5.37	5.37	4.60	4.64	5.67	5.77	5.07	5.18				
1870	3.25	5.29	5.29	4.10	4.18	8.72	8.31	3.82	3.88				
1871	3.09	4.70	4.70	4.37	4.51	5.59	5.38	4.03	3.59			7.32	7.32
1872	3.36	4.62	4.62	4.05	4.14	4.69	4.74	4.10	3.35			7.59	7.59
1873	3.56	4.86	4.86	4.16	3.92	4.50	4.04	4.69	4.80			8.51	8.51
1874	3.12	4.23	4.23	4.04	3.87	4.31	3.96	4.10	3.99			6.20	6.20
1875	2.62	3.51	3.51	3.72	3.42	3.36	3.34	4.30	4.56			6.92	6.92
1876	0.37	2.32	2.32	3.17	2.96	4.85	4.81	3.97	4.21			5.47	5.47
1877	1.00	1.57	1.57	2.81	2.81	3.12	3.13	2.57	2.23			4.32	4.32
1878	1.30	0.98	0.98	1.91	2.20	3.39	3.50	2.11	2.08			5.16	5.16
1879	0.91	0.89	0.99	2.09	2.48	1.72	1.73	2.57	2.80			4.58	4.58
1880	3.10	2.29	2.29	2.27	2.54	3.21	3.21	3.11	3.30			5.31	5.31
1881	2.84	2.45	2.45	2.57	2.86	4.29	4.29	3.30	3.32			6.74	6.74
1882	2.47	2.38	2.38	2.24	2.48	3.33	3.34	4.03	3.87			4.78	4.78
1883	2.32	2.24	2.25	2.61	2.66	3.62	2.68	2.36	2.77			5.31	5.31
1884	1.39	2.06	2.06	2.86	2.88	3.32	3.35	2.86	2.89			5.24	5.24
1885	1.57	1.27	1.27	2.26	2.32	2.25	2.26	2.49	2.39			3.69	3.69
1886	2.20	2.25	2.25	2.24	2.38	1.69	1.56	3.11	3.00			4.37	4.37
1887	2.74	2.19	2.19	2.98	2.85	2.73	2.76	3.08	3.38			3.25	3.25
1888	2.59	2.73	2.73	2.95	3.14	1.94	1.90	2.75	3.12	1.91	1.91	4.80	4.80
1889	2.30	2.69	2.69	2.95	2.81	3.05	3.07	3.30	3.22	3.08	3.08	6.06	6.06
1890	2.53	1.78	1.78	2.72	2.80	3.19	3.16	2.96	3.12	2.41	2.41	5.45	5.45
1891	2.83	2.72	2.72	2.75	2.85	2.41	2.44	2.95	3.27	2.72	2.72	5.48	5.48
1892	1.91	1.69	1.69	2.57	2.52	1.95	1.96	2.62	2.78	0.74	0.74	6.07	6.07
1893	2.29	2.25	2.25	2.75	2.71	2.63	2.66	2.24	2.33	1.29	1.26	5.33	5.33
1894	1.26	1.51	1.51	2.23	2.31	0.96	1.13	0.48	1.01	−0.11	0.01	4.20	4.20
1895	1.14	1.26	1.26	2.24	2.13	1.58	1.81	1.48	1.67	0.52	0.44	4.42	4.42

TABLE 4 (*Continued*)

		I		II		III		IV		V		VI	
Year	NYC	(1)*	(2)†	(1)*	(2)†	(1)*	(2)†	(1)*	(2)†	(1)*	(2)†	(1)*	(2)†
1896........	1.45	1.81	1.81	2.21	2.17	2.49	2.00	1.55	1.45	1.96	1.51	4.19	4.19
1897........	1.37	1.82	1.82	2.16	2.10	2.85	2.27	0.93	1.22	—1.39	—0.41	3.60	3.60
1898........	1.40	1.36	1.36	2.26	1.98	2.60	2.37	1.53	1.80	0.68	0.79	2.91	2.91
1899........	1.03	0.80	0.80	1.89	1.57	1.97	1.49	1.22	1.44	2.22	1.50	3.30	2.98
1900........	1.94	2.06	2.05	2.47	2.54	2.90	2.55	2.20	2.38	1.37	0.91	2.53	3.13
1901........	1.48	1.41	1.41	1.95	1.89	3.43	2.82	3.21	3.04	3.45	2.98	2.55	3.03
1902........	3.15	1.56	1.56	2.85	2.31	3.00	3.02	2.37	2.35	3.80	5.10	2.90	3.06
1903........	2.46	2.01	2.01	2.08	2.28	2.93	2.67	1.85	1.93	1.16	0.78	2.22	2.37
1904........	2.72	1.80	1.80	1.77	1.92	3.17	1.77	1.92	1.89	2.00	1.39	2.44	2.59
1905........	1.07	1.16	1.16	1.56	1.22	3.90	3.74	1.59	1.62	3.83	2.09	2.65	2.46
1906........	2.50	1.88	1.88	2.03	2.10	2.63	2.48	1.93	1.79	2.11	1.86	2.19	2.30
1907........	3.01	2.34	2.34	2.37	2.26	2.74	2.60	1.90	1.88	2.96	3.42	4.28	3.23
1908........	2.16	1.91	1.91	1.13	1.57	2.72	2.40	1.53	1.71	1.75	1.69	2.46	2.38
1909........	1.94	1.33	1.33	1.98	1.63	2.47	2.15	1.55	1.47	2.10	1.84	1.85	2.12
1910........	2.48	2.22	2.22	1.84	2.16	2.79	2.49	1.66	1.63	2.27	2.33	2.45	2.30
1911........	2.00	1.75	1.75	1.51	1.41	2.18	1.92	2.06	2.44	2.28	1.62	2.18	2.46
1912........	2.01	1.37	1.37	1.57	1.51	3.15	2.50	1.43	1.33	1.97	2.01	1.79	1.94
1913........	2.26	2.03	2.03	1.53	1.55	2.51	2.35	1.59	1.38	1.81	1.67	1.98	2.07
1914........	1.58	1.68	1.67	1.63	1.81	2.32	2.12	1.62	1.72	1.62	1.57	1.73	1.75

* Unweighted.
† Weighted.
SOURCE: *Annual Report of the Comptroller of the Currency.*

TABLE 5

Net Returns Nonreserve-City Banks by Regions, 1869–1914

| | Region | | | | | | | | | | | |
| | I | | II | | III | | IV | | V | | VI | |
Year	(1)*	(2)†	(1)*	(2)†	(1)*	(2)†	(1)*	(2)†	(1)*	(2)†	(1)*	(2)†
1869	6.32	6.36	5.10	4.93	5.56	5.46	6.44	6.28	4.29	3.79	12.52	11.64
1870	5.78	5.77	4.65	4.35	5.63	5.17	6.01	5.80	4.08	3.77	8.81	7.38
1871	5.36	5.44	4.60	4.78	5.45	5.34	5.79	5.61	7.41	5.24	18.62	14.21
1872	5.33	5.42	3.90	4.16	4.99	4.96	5.32	5.20	5.19	4.21	15.24	12.81
1873	5.50	5.75	4.46	4.33	5.59	5.38	5.39	5.24	6.55	6.29	7.40	6.42
1874	5.41	5.34	4.12	3.84	4.69	4.57	4.96	5.08	5.64	5.23	9.17	6.68
1875	4.91	4.87	3.80	3.67	4.53	4.84	4.93	4.96	5.65	5.12	10.25	7.56
1876	3.87	3.88	3.81	3.14	4.33	4.59	4.70	4.62	5.27	4.24	8.36	7.31
1877	3.29	2.94	3.51	2.89	3.45	3.62	3.76	3.66	3.99	2.99	8.55	6.81
1878	3.03	2.83	2.83	2.35	2.39	2.42	3.53	3.46	2.57	2.26	5.92	5.42
1879	2.84	2.51	2.84	2.32	2.58	2.70	3.21	3.07	4.67	3.05	7.48	6.34
1880	3.51	3.34	3.06	2.85	2.99	3.09	3.67	3.38	4.88	3.79	6.90	4.94
1881	3.70	3.70	3.26	3.15	4.60	4.34	4.02	4.00	6.32	5.38	8.53	5.72
1882	3.37	3.34	2.92	2.94	4.16	3.92	4.15	3.94	5.47	5.24	6.84	5.16
1883	3.10	3.04	3.04	2.90	3.76	3.69	3.98	3.63	4.33	3.72	5.14	3.31
1884	2.85	2.81	2.87	2.82	4.63	4.55	4.36	3.95	5.22	5.19	6.46	5.22
1885	2.60	2.43	2.73	2.44	4.07	4.08	4.18	3.79	4.74	4.88	6.11	5.44
1886	3.29	3.02	3.00	2.87	4.13	4.41	3.62	3.58	4.59	4.74	5.30	4.51
1887	3.47	3.34	3.16	3.19	4.35	4.21	4.50	3.97	4.56	4.77	4.19	3.96
1888	3.44	3.13	3.11	3.02	4.42	4.40	3.73	3.60	4.84	5.57	7.08	5.75
1889	3.61	3.37	3.34	3.35	4.61	4.59	3.76	3.73	4.18	4.51	6.55	5.37
1890	3.63	3.40	3.36	3.32	5.17	4.59	3.66	3.62	4.29	4.35	5.30	5.03
1891	3.48	3.32	3.24	3.08	4.49	4.49	3.81	3.79	4.18	3.90	5.95	5.24
1892	2.86	2.72	3.04	2.87	3.72	3.63	3.36	3.35	4.03	3.39	4.86	4.22
1893	2.82	2.82	2.52	2.75	3.19	3.33	2.99	3.01	5.63	3.60	4.53	3.50
1894	2.34	2.28	2.59	2.37	2.14	2.45	2.17	2.17	1.65	0.42	2.14	0.41
1895	2.15	2.06	2.49	2.17	2.88	3.02	2.38	2.43	1.98	1.17	1.83	1.52

TABLE 5 (Continued)

Year	I (1)*	I (2)†	II (1)*	II (2)†	III (1)*	III (2)†	IV (1)*	IV (2)†	V (1)*	V (2)†	VI (1)*	VI (2)†
1896	2.38	2.36	2.49	2.36	2.98	3.14	2.25	2.41	2.68	1.13	4.18	2.08
1897	2.23	2.14	2.20	2.02	2.58	2.70	1.84	1.97	1.79	1.25	1.00	0.64
1898	2.09	2.04	2.02	1.99	2.95	2.97	1.94	2.03	2.93	2.29	2.65	2.11
1899	2.71	2.10	2.44	2.24	2.94	3.05	2.15	2.17	2.87	2.45	2.81	2.88
1900	2.95	2.72	3.40	2.81	3.66	3.61	2.47	2.49	3.67	3.11	3.09	3.25
1901	2.44	2.19	2.51	2.32	3.35	3.49	3.90	3.88	4.00	3.47	3.59	3.32
1902	2.23	2.06	2.66	2.81	3.38	3.47	2.63	2.71	3.42	3.03	5.18	3.38
1903	2.27	2.24	2.78	2.54	3.20	3.32	2.46	2.43	3.93	3.61	3.87	3.49
1904	2.12	1.96	2.55	2.41	3.16	3.17	2.42	2.32	3.74	3.43	3.29	3.18
1905	1.95	1.48	1.46	1.21	3.05	3.10	2.19	2.08	3.29	3.13	3.52	3.21
1906	2.31	2.03	2.29	2.30	3.08	3.19	2.07	1.90	3.41	3.15	3.56	3.58
1907	2.52	2.40	2.13	2.25	3.05	3.19	2.14	2.11	3.67	3.50	3.19	3.14
1908	2.80	2.50	1.93	1.92	2.76	2.83	2.13	2.11	3.34	3.18	3.53	2.12
1909	1.90	1.87	1.98	1.90	2.55	2.76	1.86	1.86	3.43	3.29	2.91	2.90
1910	2.12	2.17	2.04	2.08	2.64	2.77	1.91	1.86	3.03	2.95	3.62	2.99
1911	2.12	2.08	2.05	1.93	2.67	2.84	1.97	1.93	3.17	3.09	3.01	2.71
1912	1.90	1.87	1.96	1.84	2.48	2.58	1.92	1.89	2.83	2.82	1.90	2.46
1913	1.90	1.89	1.98	1.82	2.47	2.62	1.91	1.89	2.65	2.72	3.02	2.56
1914	1.38	1.38	1.21	1.22	2.43	2.53	1.72	1.74	2.22	2.36	2.31	2.08

* Unweighted.
† Weighted.
SOURCE: *Annual Report of the Comptroller of the Currency.*

As Charts I and III indicate, the nonreserve-city rates display the same tendencies that were visible in the city figures; however, in this case the rate of closure was much more gradual. In the late 1870's the rates in Regions I and II come together, but they are still well above the New York rate. In fact, it is the beginning of the 20th century before the differential between rates in these two regions and Region IV and those in

CHART I

THREE-YEAR MOVING AVERAGE GROSS RETURNS
Nonreserve-City Bank

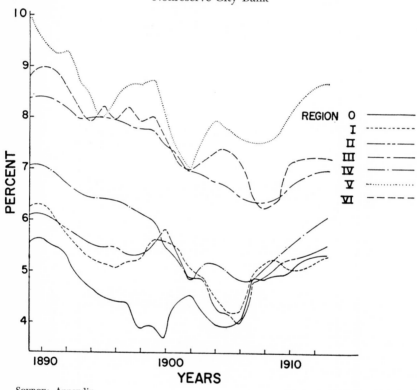

SOURCE: Appendix.

New York City largely disappear. From that point on, however, it is difficult to select the New York rate from among the four.

Although the variance is much reduced, as late as 1914 the rates prevailing in the South, the Great Plains, and the Pacific Coast states are still substantially above those in the more eastern regions. With the nonreserve-city, as with the reserve-city banks, the South appears to be a case apart. Southern rates were not abnormally high at the beginning of the period, while rates in Regions V and VI stood far above those prevailing in the East. However, while western rates were declining fairly rapidly, those in the South were moving much more slowly. By 1914, rates in Region III appear more typical of western than of eastern rates.

The movements in the unweighted nonreserve-city rates follow the pattern set by the weighted series; but once again the trends are more gradual. Overall then, the picture seems clear. Between 1870 and 1914, a national short-term capital market gradually evolved. The movement

CHART II
THREE-YEAR MOVING AVERAGE GROSS RETURNS
Reserve-City Bank

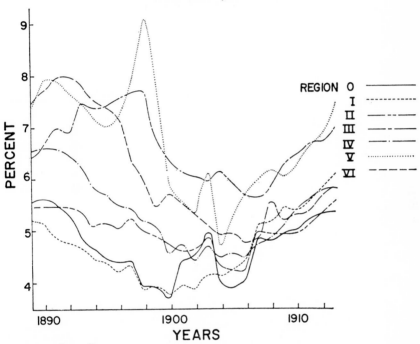

SOURCE: Appendix.

started in the major eastern cities and moved first to the large cities in the other regions. From that point the market grew to encompass those smaller city and country areas with the best banking facilities and finally those areas with the least developed banking structures.[9]

When, in 1890, Breckenridge examined the interregional interest differentials, he concluded that they were permanent and attributed them to the legal barriers that prohibited national branch banking in the United

---

[9] It is interesting to note that the movements of the regional rates seem to display a sequence of long swings. It appears that there was a long swing with a trough in 1878, a peak in 1887 or 1888, and a trough in 1895. A second long swing appears to date from the 1894 trough. The peak was apparently in 1901 and the final trough somewhere around 1914. With the exception of the first trough, these movements conform quite closely to the long swings in commodity output found by Robert E. Gallman.

States.[10] With the omniscience of hindsight, it is obvious that these differentials have been reduced and were, in fact, declining during the 1890's. Moreover, the reductions did not result from the passage of new laws permitting interstate branching. Instead, a series of new financial institutions capable of surmounting the barriers raised by distance and by the lack of adequate branch-banking legislation was innovated. In the

CHART III
THREE-YEAR MOVING AVERAGE NET RETURNS
Nonreserve-City Bank

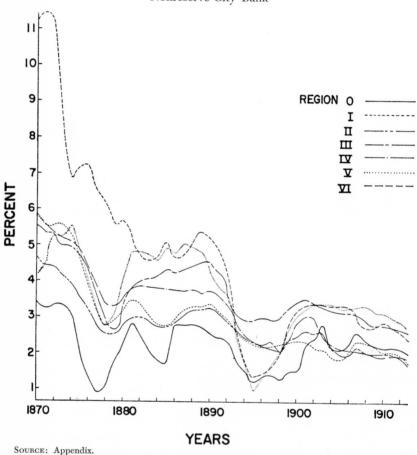

SOURCE: Appendix.

period from 1870 to 1914, barriers to short-term mobility were overcome (or at least reduced) by direct solicitation of interregional funds, by commercial bank rediscounting, and most important, by the evolution of a national market for commercial paper.

In regions with high interest rates, commercial banks had an incentive

---

[10] Breckenridge, *Political Science Quarterly,* Vol. XIII, p. 129.

to solicit additional funds. In regions with low rates, both banks and private investors were given a powerful incentive to seek more lucrative alternatives, particularly if distant investments could be made more certain. As a result, it was not long before western banks began to issue certificates of deposit to surplus savings units in the East. Since these certificates were insured by national banks, they must have appeared "more certain" to eastern investors. The volume of these transactions was never large, but it might have become significant if the Comptroller of

CHART IV
THREE-YEAR MOVING AVERAGE NET RETURNS
Reserve-City Bank

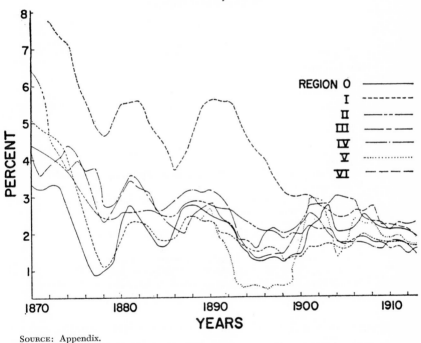

SOURCE: Appendix.

the Currency had not moved to stop these flows. In his report of 1890 the Comptroller, E. S. Sacey, reported:

The items reported as deposits, which most frequently invite the criticism of this office, arise out of transactions like these:

(1) A bank with business in a locality where rates of interest rule high negotiates with persons living at distant points, where loanable funds are more abundant, and secures certain sums for a fixed period and at a rate of interest current for loans at the place where the lender resides, issuing certificates of deposit therefor.

(2) A bank similarly situated issues its certificates of deposit payable at

a future date, drawing interest, and in some cases accompanied by collaterals, and places these certificates with a broker for sale.[11]

One may wonder what notions of banking policy might have dictated these words, but there is little question that the result was yet another legal barrier to inhibit the flow of funds between regions.

It was also possible for banks in high-interest regions to increase their free reserves by rediscounting commercial paper in banks located in lower interest areas. Table 6 suggests that banks in the later 19th century did

TABLE 6

VOLUME OF NATIONAL BANK REDISCOUNTING 1892–97

(Figures Are the Proportion of Rediscounted Loans
to All Loans and Discount)

Region	Proportion Discounted (Percentage)	
	Slack Period	Peak Period
New England[1]	1.13	1.50
Eastern States[2]	.42	.53
Southern States[3]	2.69	8.00
Middle States[4]	1.25	1.50
Western States[5]	3.00	3.38
Pacific States[6]	2.00	2.45

[1] Maine, New Hampshire, Vermont, Massachusetts, Rhode Island, Connecticut.
[2] New York, New Jersey, Pennsylvania, Delaware, Maryland, Washington, D.C.
[3] Virginia, West Virginia, North Carolina, South Carolina, Georgia, Florida, Alabama, Mississippi, Louisiana, Texas, Arkansas, Kentucky, Tennessee.
[4] Ohio, Indiana, Illinois, Michigan, Wisconsin, Minnesota, Iowa, Missouri.
[5] North Dakota, South Dakota, Nebraska, Kansas, Montana, Wyoming, Colorado, New Mexico, Oklahoma, Indian territory.
[6] Washington, Oregon, California, Idaho, Utah, Nevada, Arizona.

SOURCE: Breckenridge, *Political Science Quarterly*, Vol. XIII.

rediscount to some extent, but that the volume of rediscounting was relatively small. During the five-year period covered by Breckenridge's survey, rediscounts average only about 1½ percent of total loans and discounts, and the figure exceeded 3 percent in only one month. In general, banks appear to have used rediscount only to meet seasonal and panic demands. However, banks in regions with the high interest rates tended to discount more than banks in low-rate areas; and the South seems to have engaged in significantly more rediscounting than any other region.[12] Whatever the reasons, however, rediscounting which could have provided the mechanism for interregional capital transfers did not do so.

Given the Comptroller of the Currency's views on direct solicitation

---

[11] *Report of the Comptroller of the Currency, 1890,* Vol. I, p. 14.
[12] Breckenridge, *Political Science Quarterly,* Vol. XIII, pp. 136–37.

and the bankers' views on rediscounting, it is doubtful that the volume of funds moved by these techniques would even have been sufficient to arbitrage out the regional differentials. More important was the evolution of a national market for commercial paper.

In the United States there has always been a widely held view among lawmakers that local banks should serve the local communities. In the antebellum decades, a number of states actually passed laws prohibiting bank loans to persons living in other states.[13] Despite these restrictions, banks in low-interest areas began to seek more lucrative investment opportunities than those available at home; as a result, even before the Civil War the foundations for an active commercial-paper market in the East had been laid.

Since the market was centered in the large eastern cities, it was the rates in these areas that were first affected; however, the market began to spread into the Midwest in the two decades after the end of the war. There are records of commercial-paper dealers operating in Indianapolis in 1871. By 1880 commercial paper was being traded in Milwaukee, Chicago, and Minneapolis; and by the turn of the century nine or ten houses were operating in each of the latter two cities. The expansion of the market continued across the Plains and on to the Pacific Coast. By the early 1880's Kansas City had been integrated into the market; and by 1910 further growth had encompassed Wichita and Dallas. On the Pacific Coast, brokers' offices were opened in San Francisco, Seattle, and Los Angeles about the turn of the century.

"By 1913 it could be said that the commercial paper houses had branches or representatives 'in all the large cities' in the United States."[14] More important from the viewpoint of this study, in each case the timing of the expansion of the commercial-paper market conforms fairly closely to the closing of the interregional rate differentials.

The profits earned by the commercial-paper houses induced additional entry, and increased competition forced the brokers to extend the area of their operations in search of prime paper and good customers. As late as the 1890's a typical brokerage firm maintained a single office, and bankers who wanted to buy bills called there. Thereafter, however, the note firms began to employ salesmen to call on prospective customers, and by the first decade of the 20th century some brokers employed "several score" salesmen. The brokers competed more actively for bills as well. In order to penetrate areas not previously served, the firms began to open

---

13 Albert Greef, *The Commercial Paper House in the United States* (Cambridge, Mass.: Harvard University Press, 1938), p. 18. Nor is this view completely dead today. In a recent book, a respected historian has suggested that the failure of Rhode Island to pass such legislation was a major defect of its political system; P. J. Coleman, *The Transformation of Rhode Island* (Providence, R.I.: Brown University Press, 1963), p. 199.

14 Greef, pp. 39–40.

branches in some cities and to establish correspondent relations in areas that could not support a branch.[15]

The added competition also began to infringe on long-established monopolies. Among the first groups to feel the squeeze were the western bankers who had been accustomed to high returns on their investments. In 1892 an Iowa banker said:

> Until recently, western bankers were able to maintain their loaning rates regardless of the depression of the eastern markets, but now there has arisen an element that wages constant war on the established rates. It is the festive note broker, who with his eastern capital, steps in to disturb the harmonious relations between banker and borrower, and just at the time there seems to be an opportunity to dispose of idle funds at a profitable rate, the banker is confronted with the alternative of cutting his rates or seeing his loans going to outside dealers.[16]

The press of competition also had its effects on the note houses. In the 1870's commission rates ranged as high as $\frac{1}{2}$ percent, but by the 1880's a $\frac{1}{4}$ percent rate appears to have been common. By the middle of that decade brokers in the largest cities had reduced their rates to $\frac{1}{8}$ percent, and 20 years later there are reports of some transactions with no commission charge.[17]

More important, however, because of the increased activity in the commercial-paper market, many small cities and towns were integrated into the national capital market; capital moved more easily across regional boundaries; and interest rates in the high-interest areas began to decline.

III

The data on long-term interest rates are not as good as those from the "short end" of the market. The Comptroller of the Currency, while publishing balance-sheet information on savings banks, private banks, and loan and trust companies (institutions that operated in the long-term market), did not report the earnings of these intermediaries. As a result, the evidence presented in this section is quite fragmentary. What evidence there is, however, strongly suggests that: (1) interregional interest differentials did exist, (2) there was a tendency for these differentials to decline over the period, and (3) the movement toward a national long-term capital market did not proceed as far or as fast as the movement toward the short-term market.

The best data on long-term interest rates probably lie in the offices of the county recorders, where every mortgage was made a matter of public record. These recorded mortgage rates are not always reliable (partic-

---

[15] *Ibid.*, pp. 64–65.

[16] J. K. Deming, "Modern Methods of Soliciting Business," *Proceedings,* Iowa Bankers' Association, 1892, p. 21.

[17] Greef, pp. 107–8.

ularly in the South and West), but they do provide a fair index of inter-regional differentials. The task of collecting these rates from every county (or even a sample of counties) would be, at lest, heroic; however, the Census Bureau has surveyed records for the years 1880–90.[18] In addition, two studies of the records of single Midwest counties are available for the period 1865–80; and a sampling of mortgage rates in several western states provides some further information.[19] Finally, a study of farm mortgages in 1914–15 provides some data on regional rates at the end of the period.[20] These rates are reproduced in Tables 7, 8, and 9.

Table 7 indicates that marked regional differentials in mortgage rates existed during the 1880's. Over the period, rates averaged 5.9 percent in Region I, 5.8 percent in Region II, 7.9 percent in Region III, 7.3 percent in Region IV, 9.8 percent in Region V, and 10.7 percent in Region VI. (The farm mortgage rates displayed in the second half of the table show similar differentials.) Over the period, however, there appears to have been a movement toward greater equality. In 1880 the coefficient of variation for the six regional rates was 28 percent (26 percent for the farm mortgage rates), but by 1889 this figure had declined to 21 percent (20 percent for farm mortgages).

Although there appears to have been substantial movement toward a national market in the years before 1890, there is some question about the period 1890–1914. Some evidence suggests that improvements in the market were quite substantial, and other evidence indicates that they were less so. Over the whole period 1869–1914, however, it appears that some progress toward a national market was made, but the pace appears to have been slower than it had been in the case of the short-term market.

A comparison of the farm mortgage rates from the 1890 census with those from the Department of Agriculture survey of 1914–1915 suggests that progress toward a national market may not have been too great over the period 1890–1914. The coefficient of variation for the 1914 figures is definitely less than that for the year 1880 (21 as compared with 26 percent), but it is slightly higher than the figure for 1889. The two series are not, however, strictly comparable. Certainly the years after 1914 saw substantial progress. The next regional mortgage rates come from the 1930 census (the figures from the 1920 census do not include commission charges), and by that later date interregional differences have largely disappeared (the coefficient of variation is less than 2 percent).

---

[18] C. K. Holmes and J. S. Lord, "Report of Real Estate Mortgages in the United States," in *Eleventh Census of the United States*, Vol. XII (Washington, D.C., 1895), pp. 4–5.

[19] R. F. Severson, "The Sources of Mortgage Credit for Champaign County, 1865–1880," *Agricultural History*, Vol. XXXVI (July, 1962); J. Ladin, "The Sources of Mortgage Credit for Tippecanoe County, 1865–1886" (unpublished); Allan Bogue, *Money at Interest* (Ithaca, N.Y.: Cornell University Press, 1955).

[20] U.S. Department of Agriculture, Bulletin 384, *Costs and Sources of Farm Mortgages in the United States* (Washington, D.C.: U.S. Government Printing Office, 1916).

TABLE 7
MORTGAGE INTEREST RATES BY REGION, 1880–89

	All Mortgages* Region					
Year	I	II	III	IV	V	VI
1880......	6.04	6.06	7.97	7.72	10.89	12.48
1881......	5.90	5.80	7.96	7.39	11.28	11.40
1882......	5.88	5.85	7.91	7.23	10.30	10.70
1883......	5.87	5.83	7.87	7.25	9.94	10.77
1884......	5.88	5.84	8.02	7.29	9.58	10.65
1885......	5.83	5.79	8.08	7.31	10.09	10.88
1886......	5.75	5.70	8.03	7.18	9.75	10.14
1887......	5.69	5.69	7.86	7.10	9.57	9.49
1888......	5.82	5.66	7.91	7.10	7.24	10.43
1889......	5.78	5.66	7.80	6.90	9.00	9.95

	Farm Mortgages† Region					
Year	I	II	III	IV	V	VI
1880......	6.03	6.11	8.02	7.81	10.51	11.94
1881......	5.98	6.01	8.02	7.48	10.75	11.11
1882......	5.93	5.90	7.93	7.34	9.65	10.52
1883......	5.95	5.83	7.90	7.34	9.21	10.71
1884......	5.95	5.79	8.05	7.40	9.03	10.10
1885......	5.90	5.78	8.13	7.46	9.57	10.63
1886......	5.86	5.76	8.02	7.32	9.60	9.84
1887......	5.82	5.75	7.88	7.19	9.42	9.07
1888......	5.88	5.70	7.90	7.22	9.09	10.19
1889......	5.87	5.74	7.82	7.14	8.96	9.85
1914*.....	5.7	5.6	7.6	5.9	7.6	8.2
1914†.....	5.7	5.8	8.3	6.3	8.7	8.6
1930......	6.1	6.0	6.8	5.9	6.5	6.9

* Without charge.
† With charge.
SOURCE: *Eleventh Census*, Vol. XII, and U.S. Department of Agriculture, Bulletin 384.

Other evidence also indicates that there were substantial regional interest differentials and suggests that some progress toward a national market was made in the period under consideration. Table 8 compares average interest rates in one Indiana county with rates in one Illinois county. Although both are in Region IV, Tippecanoe County began to develop before Champaign County. Table 8 indicates that interest rates in Tippecanoe County were continually below those prevailing in Champaign County, but that the differential declined over the period (by 1880 the difference is negligible). Moreover, Champaign County drew on eastern investors for about 40 percent of its long-term mortgage funds after 1870, but the peak eastern investment in Tippecanoe County was only half that amount, and the average was less than one fourth.[21] In the case of Tippecanoe County, it appears that, in the early years, when local sources could have been usefully supplemented by eastern capital, effec-

[21] Ladin, p. 8; Severson, p. 3.

TABLE 8
AVERAGE MORTGAGE INTEREST RATE, TIPPECANOE COUNTY, INDIANA,
AND CHAMPAIGN COUNTY, ILLINOIS—1865–80

Year	Tippecanoe	Champaign	Champaign-Tippecanoe Difference
1865	7.0	8.5	+1.5
1866	7.3	8.8	+1.5
1867	8.5	9.1	+ .6
1868	8.3	9.3	+1.0
1869	8.5	9.5	+1.0
1870	8.3	9.7	+1.4
1871	8.1	9.8	+1.7
1872	8.6	9.8	+1.2
1873	8.6	9.6	+1.0
1874	8.5	9.6	+1.1
1875	8.3	9.4	+1.1
1876	8.7	9.4	+ .7
1877	8.6	9.0	+ .4
1878	8.6	8.6	0
1879	7.9	8.0	+ .1
1880	7.1	7.2	+ .1

SOURCE: Ladin and Severson.

tive interregional markets did not exist. Later, when Champaign County began to develop, improvements in the interregional capital markets permitted the mobilization of eastern capital.

Similar trends appear to mark the modal interest series presented in Table 9. Again, since those taken from Bogue almost certainly do not represent a complete enumeration of all mortgages and the Severson and Ladin figures are drawn from only two counties, the evidence is only suggestive. It does, however, appear that the rates in Region IV were significantly below those in Region V, that all rates fell after 1878, that rate differentials between eastern and western states tended to narrow, and that this latter trend continued after 1890.

Additional evidence in found in the annual report of the Comptroller of the Currency. Although earnings are not reported, the balance sheets of private banks, savings banks, and loan and trust companies are included. Since the loan and trust companies were almost all located in the East, they provide little interregional information. If, however, one is willing to accept two perhaps not-too-unreasonable assumptions, some interesting conclusions can be adduced from the balance sheets of the savings and private banks.

Let us assume that (1) if a banker is faced by two investment alternatives of equal risk, he will choose the one that yields the highest returns; and (2) the securities market for any bank is broader than the loan market for that same bank.[22] Given these two assumptions, it follows that a bank in a high-interest area will tend to put a larger portion of

---

[22] This characteristic is certainly true of financial markets today and was probably more true in the earlier period.

TABLE 9
PREVAILING MORTGAGE INTEREST RATES, SELECTED STATES, 1868–1903

Year	Indiana	Illinois (A)	Illinois (B)	Iowa	Dakotas	Kansas	Nebraska
1868	10.0	10.0	10.0	10.0		12.0	
1869	10.0	10.0	10.0	10.0		12.0	
1870	10.0	10.0	10.0	10.0		12.0	
1871	10.0	10.0	10.0	10.0		12.0	12.0
1872	10.0	10.0	10.0	10.0		12.0	12.0
1873	10.0	10.0	10.0	10.0		12.0	12.0
1874	10.0	10.0	10.0	10.0		12.0	12.0
1875	10.0	10.0	10.0	10.0		12.0	12.0
1876	10.0	10.0	10.0	10.0		12.0	12.0
1877	10.0	9.0	10.0	10.0		12.0	12.0
1878	10.0	8.0	10.0	10.0	10.0	12.0	12.0
1879	8.0	8.0	8.0	10.0	10.0	10.0	10.0
1880	8.0	7.0	8.0	10.0	10.0	10.0	10.0
1881			7.0			8.0	10.0
1882			7.0			10.0	10.0
1883			7.0			8.0	9.0
1884			7.0			7.0	9.0
1885			7.0			8.0	10.0
1886			7.0				9.0
1887			7.0				9.0
1888			7.0			8.0	10.0
1889			7.0			8.0	10.0
1890			6.0			7.0	8.0
1891			6.5				8.0
1892			6.5				8.0
1893			6.5				7.0
1894			6.5				7.0
1895			6.5			7.0	6.0
1896						7.0	6.0
1897							6.5
1898							6.0
1899							5.0
1900							5.0
1901						6.0	
1902			6.0				
1903						5.0	

SOURCE: Indiana, Ladin; Illinois (A), R. Severson; Illinois (B), Iowa, Dakotas, Kansas, and Nebraska, Bogue, pp. 13, 29, 47, 61.

its assets in loans (as opposed to securities), while a bank in a low-interest area will behave in the opposite manner. Thus the ratio of

$$\frac{\text{Loans}}{\text{Loans} + \text{Securities}}$$ is a fair index of the rate of interest on loans in any area.[23]

If each state year is taken as an observation, and if states are divided

---

[23] Legal restrictions on investment policy can affect portfolio composition, but since there were no restrictions on lending at home these legal restrictions would tend to increase the sensitivity of the ratios. Moreover, while state-to-state differences in legal regulation certainly did exist, these differences would tend to "wash out" between regions.

into regions and years into eras, the problem can then be formulated as an exercise in the analysis of variance where the rows are regions and the columns are time periods.[24] If there were no regional differences in rates, there should be no significant row effects; if there were no variations between time periods, there should be no significant column effects; and if there were no interactions between the interregional rate differentials and the passage of time, the interaction term should not be significant.

The results of three separate analyses of variance tests are displayed in Table 10. In the case of private banks, no banks in Region I reported

TABLE 10

ANALYSIS OF VARIANCE OF $\dfrac{\text{LOANS}}{\text{LOANS} + \text{SECURITIES}}$

FOR SAVINGS AND PRIVATE BANKS BY TIME PERIOD
AND REGION OF LOCATION

TEST NO. 1
SAVINGS BANKS 1870–1914 WITHOUT REGION V

	Degrees of Freedom	F Ratio	Significance Level
Years	7	7.46	.001
Regions	4	104.07	.001
Interaction	28	1.95	.001

TEST NO. 2
SAVINGS BANKS 1885–1914 ALL REGIONS

	Degrees of Freedom	F Ratio	Significance Level
Years	5	7.45	.001
Regions	5	80.33	.001
Interaction	25	1.27	.2

TEST NO. 3
PRIVATE BANKS 1855–1914 WITHOUT REGION I

	Degrees of Freedom	F Ratio	Significance Level
Years	7	3.74	.001
Regions	3	21.59	.001
Interaction	21	1.33	.2

SOURCE: *Annual Report of the Comptroller of the Currency* (1899, 1900, and 1910 are not included).

after 1890, and the analysis was limited to the other five regions. Moreover, there were no reports from several regions before 1885, and therefore the time period was truncated to the period 1885–1914. In the case of the savings banks, reports went back into the 1870's for all regions except V, and the first reports from institutions in that area date from the quin-

---

[24] Analysis of variance assumes that taken all together the observations are normally distributed and that they are homogeneous within each cell. In this case the normalcy assumption was not fulfilled with the raw data, but an arc sin transformation produced a distribution that met the two assumptions.

quennium 1885–89. As a result, savings-bank test No. 1 covers the time period 1870–1914 for all regions except V; and test No. 2 includes all six regions for the period 1885–1914.

These tests seem to substantiate the theses advanced earlier. There is no question but that there were significant differences between the ratios in the various regions and various time periods. Moreover, it appears likely that the differences arising from location may have diminished over time. In every test, the F ratio for both columns and rows was significant at the .001 level. The interaction term in test No. 1 is also significant at the .001 level. In tests No. 2 and 3, however, that same term is significant at only the .2 level. At the same time, the exclusion of Region V from tests 2 and 3 causes an even further drop in the significance of the interaction term. Moreover, the decrease in the interaction term between test No. 1 and a test run on savings banks for the period 1885–1914 without Region V is significant at the .01 level. Thus the data suggest that substantial progress toward a national market was made in the period 1870–85 but that thereafter progress was slower. It does not, however, indicate that there was no progress after that date (the interaction term is greater than one and is significant at the .2 level), nor does it indicate that the slowdown was a function of changing circumstances rather than merely of past progress (the more improvement has occurred in the past, the less room there is for improvement in the future). These questions are still open.

A national long-term market appears to have begun to develop during the period under consideration, although its progress may not have been steady. In the short end of the market, it was the commercial-paper houses that provided the institutional framework for a national market. In the case of the long-term market, no single institutional development was so important; however, the growth of life insurance companies, the development of the mortgage banking business, and the evolution of a national securities market all appear to have made some contribution.

The period after the Civil War saw life insurance companies emerge as the nation's most important nonbank intermediaries. In the years from 1869 to 1914, the assets of the nation's life insurance companies increased more than twentyfold.[25] This growth, as North has shown, is associated with the innovation of new types of life insurance policies (particularly industrial and tontine).[26] These companies would not have played such an important role in the process of capital mobilization had it not been for the concomitant evolution of their investment policies. Within the companies, professional management developed, and one aspect of this development was a widening of investment horizons. Externally, and perhaps

---

[25] *Historical Statistics of the United States* (Washington, D.C.: U.S. Government Printing Office, 1961), pp. 675–76.

[26] D. North, "Capital Accumulation in Life Insurance between the Civil War and the Investigation of 1905–06," in W. Miller (ed.), *Men in Business* (Cambridge, Mass.: Harvard University Press, 1952).

more important, the period was marked by a gradual easing of the legal regulations that had restricted the investment policy of many of the largest companies.

While legal restrictions may have been more important than managerial timidity, the evolution of professional management did contribute to a widening of the list of feasible investment alternatives.[27] Harold F. Williamson's study of the Northwestern Mutual Life Insurance Company shows clearly the impact of widening sales and investment horizons on that firm's portfolio. In his own words:

> From 1858 until 1865 the Company sold insurance and made its investments almost exclusively in the state of Wisconsin. . . . Beginning about 1866 and ending around 1880 Northwestern supplied the same investment functions for Wisconsin and its neighboring states . . . . The third phase of Northwestern's evolution as an investment institution began about 1881 and extended into the 1890's. By the early 1880's Northwestern was firmly established as a national marketer . . . .[28]

In general, these conclusions appear to be borne out by the investment record of the Northwestern. Table 11 indicates a gradual widening of that firm's investment horizons, but it appears that Northwestern did not really become a national investor until the 20th century. Of course, since the firm collected funds wherever policies were sold, it was not necessary for it to become a national investor to successfully mobilize funds across regional boundaries.

Zartman has argued that it was changes in investment regulations that were most important in restructuring the investment portfolios of the large insurance firms and that the period was marked by substantial reductions in legal limitations.[29] As originally written, laws governing the investments of mutual life insurance companies tended to emphasize safety and to demand that funds be invested close to home. In the late 1860's only four states permitted investment in corporate securities; and most states had some restrictions on investment policy. During the last third of the century, however, many of these laws were altered to provide a wider range of legal investments. In New York, for example, the original law prohibited investments in out-of-state mortgages. An 1868 amendment permitted insurance companies to invest in mortgages anywhere within 50 miles of New York; in 1875 the legal boundaries were extended to include every adjacent state; and in the 1880's the New York mutuals were granted the right to invest in mortgages anywhere. By 1905, only Georgia, Nebraska, Pennsylvania, and Texas retained laws prohibiting investment

---

27 Lester Zartman, *Investments of Life Insurance Companies* (New York: H. Holt, 1906). Insurance companies in Connecticut and Massachusetts, subject to less severe restrictions, did invest more widely than did firms with home offices in New York.

28 H. F. Williamson and O. A. Smalley, *Northwestern Mutual Life: A Century of Trusteeship* (Evanston, Ill.: Northwestern University Press, 1957), pp. 127–28.

29 Zartman, p. 243.

TABLE 11

Percentage of Distribution of the Northwest Mutual Life Insurance Company's Mortgage Loans, by Region, 1872–1907

Year	Middle Atlantic	South Atlantic	E-S Central	E-N Central	W-N Central	Mountains	Pacific	W-S Central
1872	0	.9	2.3	72.1	24.1	.6	0	0
1875	—	1.6	2.1	68.4	27.1	.8	0	0
1880	—	.8	.4	73.0	25.1	.6	0	0
1887	0	—	—	63.2	35.4	1.2	0	0
1892	0	—	2.8	55.2	31.2	9.2	0	0
1897	—	—	4.1	61.8	26.8	6.7	.5	—
1902	1.6	.6	3.1	61.8	26.6	4.7	1.6	0
1907	1.4	1.3	2.6	44.0	44.2	2.7	3.8	.1

— indicates less than .1 percent.
SOURCE: Williamson and Smalley, pp. 64, 78, 122.

in out-of-state mortgages. Similarly, by 1905, California, Colorado, Utah, Connecticut, New Jersey, Pennsylvania, Illinois, and Wisconsin had all begun to permit some investment in corporate securities.[30]

Given professional management and an absence of legal restrictions, there were still substantial technical problems in handling distant investments. Therefore, it might have taken longer for the insurance companies to become important forces in interregional mobilization had it not been for the parallel development of brokerage institutions designed to service their portfolios. The New York Life, for example, depended upon Vermilyea and Company to handle their securities account, and other firms appear to have employed similar agents.[31] For mortgages, the mutuals frequently turned to western agents. A. L. Ward, for example, a Minneapolis mortgage broker and later an important midwestern banker, acted as the resident mortgage agent for a number of insurance companies.[32]

Table 12 displays the interest rates earned on mortgages by insurance companies located in various regions. These series show the impact of the institutional development in management and regulation. While large differentials are characteristic of the early years, they tend to decline over the period. For example, a projection based on a linear regression through the mortgage rates earned by companies in Regions II and VI for the years 1878–89 suggests that (if the trend had continued) the differentials would have disappeared in 1905 (as in fact they did). This result contrasts markedly with a parallel projection posed on regression through the mortgage census data for the years 1880–89. In the latter case, rates would not have closed until 1921. Although these projections are very rough, they are quite suggestive. It does not appear unreasonable to conclude that the insurance companies, freed of their managerial and legal restrictions, were willing to move funds across regional boundaries before most private investors were willing to take this step. Moreover, the data suggest that the companies were not large enough to arbitrage out the market.

For a short two-decade period in the 1870's and 1880's, the mortgage company played a very significant role in the interregional mobilization of capital. At first the companies merely acted as middlemen. They made mortgage loans in the West and sold these mortgages in the East. As long as they performed the brokerage function, they did little to reduce the uncertainty discounts of the eastern investors, although they did make western investment easier. As competition increased, however, they began to guarantee the mortgages they sold; and from a guarantee it was an easy step to a general debenture issued against a portfolio of mortgages. The first mortgage companies were organized about 1870, but it was the

[30] *Ibid.*, pp. 150–70.

[31] M. James, *The Metropolitan Life, A Study in Business Growth* (New York: Viking Press, 1947), p. 105.

[32] C. S. Popple, *Development of Two Bank Groups in the Central Midwest* (Cambridge, Mass.: Harvard University Press, 1944), pp. 37–38.

TABLE 12

RATE OF EARNINGS ON MORTGAGES HELD BY LIFE INSURANCE
COMPANIES, BY REGION OF LOCATION, 1868–1904

Year	I	II	IV	VI
1868	7.4	8.1	7.2	
1869	8.1	6.7	8.1	
1870	9.5	7.6	8.5	
1871	8.2	7.2	9.0	
1872	9.0	7.4	8.1	
1873	8.5	7.5	9.9	
1874	8.5	7.2	9.5	
1875	7.8	6.7	7.7	
1876	8.2	7.0	9.3	
1877	6.8	6.9	8.7	13.3
1878	6.6	6.4	8.6	9.4
1879	6.4	6.5	9.5	11.8
1880	6.8	6.3	9.2	5.2
1881	6.7	6.1	8.3	8.5
1882	6.7	5.8	7.8	9.2
1883	6.6	5.8	7.3	8.2
1884	6.7	5.7	7.3	8.5
1885	5.8	5.8	7.1	9.3
1886	6.6	5.9	7.0	9.0
1887	6.4	6.4	7.1	9.1
1888	6.3	6.4	7.3	9.6
1889	6.4	6.1	7.0	9.0
1890	6.5	6.1	6.9	7.8
1891	6.3	5.9	6.5	8.4
1892	6.2	5.6	6.7	9.7
1893	6.2	5.5	6.7	7.9
1894	6.0	5.6	6.6	8.3
1895	6.0	5.5	6.5	7.0
1896	5.8	5.4	6.4	6.8
1897	5.1	5.4	6.6	6.6
1898	5.6	5.4	6.3	6.0
1899	5.4	5.2	6.1	5.5
1900	5.4	5.1	5.9	5.4
1901	5.1	5.1	5.7	5.4
1902	5.1	5.1	5.6	6.0
1903	5.0	4.9	5.5	5.2
1904	5.1	5.1	5.6	5.3

SOURCE: Zartman, pp. 89–91.

middle 1880's before they began to issue bonds.[33] At the height of their popularity (about 1890) there were at least 167 companies operating in the United States.[34]

The history of the mortgage company has yet to be written, but Allan Bogue has provided an excellent study of a single company (the J. B. Watkins Land Mortgage Company of Lawrence, Kansas). Moreover, examination of contemporary chronicles suggest that the Watkins firm was probably fairly typical of the larger mortgage companies. The firm was

[33] D. M. Frederiksen, "Mortgage Banking in the United States," *Journal of Political Economy*, Vol. II (March, 1894).

[34] *Ibid.*, p. 213.

organized in 1870; began as a middleman but shifted into guaranteed mortgages and later into debentures; enjoyed 20 years of profitable existence; and went bankrupt in the early 1890's.

To succeed, it was necessary for Watkins to sell his mortgages (and later his bonds) quickly. To accomplish this end, he had by 1877 a branch office in New York City and sales agents in Buffalo, Albion, Batavia, Rochester, Syracuse, Rome, and Johnstown, New York; in Wilmington, Delaware; in Boston, Massachusetts; in Warner, New Hampshire; and in Ferrisburg, Vermont. In 1878, in search of still more investors, he opened a second branch in London, England.[35]

An analysis of Watkins' customers provides considerable evidence about the sources of the eastern capital that flowed into western farmlands. Less than 1 percent of Watkins' customers were institutional investors. About equal numbers of men and women appear on his roster of customers; and, of the men, about 15 percent were ministers, teachers, and doctors. Over a quarter of his customers were English, and most of the rest lived in New England or in the Middle Atlantic states.

In the early 1890's, in the face of agricultural depression, the J. B. Watkins Company, like most mortgage companies, collapsed. Many of those that managed to remain solvent turned to other lines of endeavor. The management of Wells Dicky, for example—one of the oldest and largest mortgage companies in the upper plains—withdrew entirely from the mortgage business and shifted the company's resources to other financial activities. The industry's collapse was in part a function of the tenuous financial structure on which it had been built; contributing factors were the narrow margin of profitability of farms west of the 98th meridian, the failure of eastern investors to understand the nature of agriculture in this semiarid land, and of course the general price decline. In the 1870's, many of the mortgages had been on farms in Iowa, Minnesota, or the eastern parts of the Great Plains states. After 1880, however, an increasing proportion of the new mortgages were located in the western counties of the Plains states; and in the mid 1880's, this area was subject to a prolonged drought. Drought meant falling incomes, and deflation meant rising debt burdens; as a result, many mortgages went into default. The mortgage companies were not strong enough financially to carry the burden of the foreclosed land, and they too were unable to meet their obligations.[36] For two decades thereafter it was difficult to lure eastern capital into western mortgages.

Although they operated for only a short period, the mortgage companies played a significant role in the movement of funds from Regions I and II into Regions IV and V. Moreover, if progress toward a national long-term market did slow down after 1890, the failure of the mortgage companies may well have been a contributory factor.

---

[35] Bogue, pp. 86–88.
[36] *Ibid.*, p. 267.

Throughout much of the 19th century, the formal securities markets had aided interregional mobilization of funds for the public sector and for the growing transportation industries. They had, however, made little direct contribution to western or southern manufacturing. By the end of the century, however, some changes were evident. In 1885 the New York Stock Exchange organized a department of unlisted securities, and this department became the route by which a number of distant manufacturing companies reached the "big board." More important, J. P. Morgan turned his attention to manufacturing, and his success convinced many investors that paper investments in manufacturing were safe and profitable. International Harvester, for example, was a combine of Midwest firms. Most had been locally owned, but after the merger it was eastern capital that poured in and released the local capital for other activities. Thereafter, imitation was easier. As investors became convinced of the profitability of paper securities, the number of brokerage houses increased. In 1900 no firm but Morgan (and perhaps Kuhn Loeb) could successfully have marketed a major industrial issue, but by the 1920's several could and did. The increased competition reduced profits and increased capital mobility.

Nor did the securities markets mobilize only eastern capital. By the 20th century, the Old Northwest Territory had become a savings surplus area, and the securities markets began to mobilize these funds as well. In 1905 a New York banker said: "The whole great Mississippi Valley gives promise that in some day distant perhaps it will be another New England for investments. There is developing a bond market there which is of constant astonishment to eastern dealers."[37]

IV

Interest differentials should induce capital to move between regions, and these movements should, in turn, reduce interest differentials. Richard A. Easterlin has estimated interregional capital flows for the period 1880–1920, and these estimates are displayed in Table 13. A comparison of these movements with changes in interest differentials is presented in Chart V. The changes in interest differentials are represented by the slope term of a linear regression passed through the weighted net returns to nonreserve-city banks over the period 1880–1914. (The results change but little if gross earning 1888–1914, or net earning of reserve-city banks, is used.)

This model is, of course, very rough and oversimplified. Changes in interest rates are a function of the demand for and supply of both foreign and domestic funds, and nothing in this model directly represents these underlying factors. Nonetheless, the results are suggestive. With the exception of Region VI (the Pacific Coast), regions importing capital

---

[37] Frank A. Vanderlip, quoted in G. Edwards, *The Evolution of Finance Capitalism* (New York: Longmans, Green, 1938), p. 185.

TABLE 13
Interregional Capital Movements, 1880–1920

Region	(Change in Nonagricultural Wealth Located) minus (Change in Nonagricultural Wealth Owned) (in millions of dollars)
I	− 4,775.1
II	−17,354.8
III	+ 8,575.9
IV	+ 9,347.5
V	+ 5,815.6
VI	− 282.1

Source: E. S. Lee, A. R. Miller, C. P. Brainerd, and R. A. Easterlin, *Population Redistribution and Economic Growth in the United States, 1870–1950* (Philadelphia: American Philosophical Society, 1957), Vol. I, pp. 729–33, Vol. II, pp. 179–81.

tended to experience the greatest reductions in interest rates while those exporting capital tended to experience the least decline. The coefficient of rank correlation for the six observations is only .5, but if the Pacific region is excluded the coefficient rises to .9.

It appears, therefore, that capital did move in response to interest differentials (at least east of the Rocky Mountains). Moreover, a state-by-state analysis of the Pacific region shows that capital did move out of the low-interest state (California) toward the remainder of the region. (If California is excluded, the other five states imported $5,863,200,000 between 1880 and 1920.) These results appear to bear out the conclusion that a national capital market was developing; however, they suggest that

CHART V
Changing Interest Differentials and Interregional Capital Flows 1880–1920

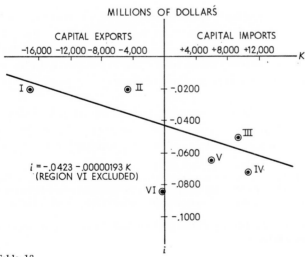

MILLIONS OF DOLLARS

CAPITAL EXPORTS   CAPITAL IMPORTS
−16,000 −12,000 −8,000 −4,000   +4,000 +8,000 +12,000   K

I ⊙   ⊙ II   −.0200

−.0400

⊙ III

−.0600   ⊙ V

$i = -.0423 - .00000193 K$
(REGION VI EXCLUDED)   ⊙ IV

−.0800
VI ⊙

−.1000

i

as late as the first decades of the 20th century the connections across the
Rockies were still tenuous.[38]

V

In the analysis of both the long- and short-term capital markets, the
South stood apart. In the case of the short-term market, interest rates
(which at the beginning of the period appeared not much different than
those prevailing in the New England and Middle Atlantic area) stood
by the end of the period considerably above the rates from these regions
and almost as high as rates charged in the Plains and Pacific regions. An
examination of the South's financial institutions suggests some reasons for
this pattern. Of all six regions, the South almost certainly had the poorest
commercial banking facilities. The region was slow to adopt free banking,
and what banks there were (dominated by the political and social elite)
were not very competitive. Nor did the region receive much help from the
National Banking Act. Since the region was almost unrepresented in Congress when the Act was passed, the law was not well suited for the region's
needs. In particular, both the minimum capital requirements (too high for
small agricultural banks) and the distribution of bank-note quotas discriminated against the region. Thus in 1870, when there were 1600 national banks, fewer than 100 were in the South. There were none at all in
Mississippi and Florida and only 27 in all Arkansas, Texas, Louisiana,
Georgia, North Carolina, and South Carolina.[39] Nor were even these
banks very aggressive. Designed to service the commercial community,
they frowned on industry and did little to help agriculture. Throughout
the latter half of the century, for example, the managers of the growing
textile mills were continually complaining that local banks would not
discount their paper.[40]

Although the southern banks did attempt to increase their lending
power through a fairly extensive use of rediscounting, the commercial-
paper market (so important to the evolution of a short-term credit market
elsewhere in the country) failed to develop in the South. At the turn of the
century, when the purchase and sale of single-name paper had become the
standard method of moving funds between regions, a leading southern
banker included among his rules for "sound" banking the following warning: "Lend your money to your regular customers, and do not make a rule
of buying commercial paper . . . . Do not permit any loans to be made on

---

[38] In this light, it is interesting to note that if analysis of variance Test No. 1 is
repeated without the Pacific region, the f ratio for the interaction term rises to over 2.

[39] P. Trescott, *Financing American Enterprise* (New York: Harper and Row,
1963), pp. 58–59.

[40] B. Mitchell, *The Rise of Cotton Textile Mills in the South* (Baltimore: Johns
Hopkins Press, 1921).

single name paper, unless otherwise secured, no matter what the commercial rating may be."[41] Nor did southern reluctance to utilize the commercial-paper market appear to have decreased over the next decade and a half (in the nation as a whole, the volume of commercial-paper transactions almost tripled between 1907 and 1914).[42] In 1908 a New York banker reported that the South was the only section of the country not buying commercial paper to any great extent; and in 1911 the Minnesota Superintendent of Banks reported that "the market for commercial paper extends over the length and breadth of this land, excepting some portions of the southern states.[43]

A similar lack of development is seen in the long-term market. The 1890 census of mortgages indicates that rates in the South, while higher than those in New England and the Middle Atlantic states, were not significantly above those in Region IV and were well below those prevailing in Regions V or VI. By 1914, however, while rates in every other region had declined substantially, those in the South were higher than they had been in 1880. Moreover, they were now substantially above the rates in Regions I, II, and IV, and only slightly below those in Regions V and VI. (By 1930 only Region VI had higher rates.) Again it appears that the South stood apart.

In the long- (as in the short-) term market, institutional development was retarded in the South. Mutual savings banks (the most important nonbank intermediaries in the early years) were never important, and even stock savings banks were slow to start.[44] Moreover, the mortgage companies that had aided the transfer of funds into Regions IV and V had little impact upon the South. Of the 167 mortgage companies enumerated by the New York report of 1891, only 6 were located in the 13 southern states (3 in Texas, 2 in Florida, and 1 in Georgia). By comparison there were seven in Colorado alone.[45] Nor did life insurance companies develop to fill the gap. The 1890 census enumeration of Class A life insurance companies indicates that only six southern companies operated during the decade 1880–90, and by 1890 three of these had gone out of existence.[46]

The failure to mobilize long-term capital through normal market

---

[41] A speech by W. S. Witham appearing in the *Proceedings* of the American Bankers' Association, 1898, p. 128 and p. 130, quoted in M. Myers (ed.), *New York Money Market,* Vol. I (New York: Columbia University Press, 1931).

[42] Greef, p. 59.

[43] *Ibid.,* p. 50.

[44] In the years 1870–85, there were only five state-year observations on savings banks among the 13 southern states. This compares with 62 in Region I, 53 in II, 18 in IV, and 12 in VI. If comparison is made in terms of number of banks, the results are even more skewed.

[45] Frederiksen, *Journal of Political Economy,* Vol. II, p. 213.

[46] *Eleventh Census of the United States,* Vol. XI, "Report of Insurance Business in the United States," Part II, "Life Insurance" (Washington, D.C., 1895).

channels is also reflected in the experience of capital users in the South. The complicated arrangements entered into by Nathaniel Davis in his attempts to get credit for his Alabama cotton plantation were probably typical of planters in the South, and they certainly do not reflect a well-developed capital market.[47] In the case of the textile industry, development frequently took the form of direct investment by northern firms. To take advantage of labor and transport cost differentials, such firms frequently opened branches in the South and at times even moved their entire plants into the area.[48] Since these latter movements bypassed the capital markets, they had little impact on interest differentials. An examination of Chart V suggests, for example, that southern differentials declined much less rapidly than the size of capital movements would lead one to expect—a reflection, perhaps, of the relative volume of direct investment.

The evidence strongly suggests that the institutional developments that speeded the flow of capital across geographic boundaries in other regions lagged in the South. The question of why it lagged is still open; and on that question, further research would almost certainly be most rewarding. Some tentative hypotheses do, however, suggest themselves. The Civil War undoubtedly played some role. The fact that the southern states were not represented in Congress when the National Banking Act was passed accounts in part for the failure of the act's authors to take account of that region's needs. Moreover, the war destroyed a number of financial connections between that region and the North, and these had to be completely replaced. The sons of Hugh Davis, for example, were unable to depend upon northern factors for finance (as their father had done) and were forced to turn to local informal markets.[49]

The close connection between agricultural investment and political and social prestige may well have hindered the movement of local capital from agriculture to manufacturing and, in addition, may have engendered an economic environment that resisted the penetration of "foreign" finance. At the same time, the resulting political structure produced laws designed to prevent competition, and the lack of competition in southern banking was certainly apparent.

Finally, it may be that conservative southern attitudes did not lend themselves well to innovation; and financial innovations were needed. These suggestions are, of course, mere speculations. There is, however, little question that the South represents an interesting counter example to the thesis that the economy moved gradually toward a national capital market in the period 1870–1914.

---

[47] W. T. Jordan, *Hugh Davis and His Alabama Plantation* (Tuscaloosa: University of Alabama Press, 1948).

[48] J. Keslensky, "Financing Southern Industry, 1865–1915" (unpublished); and Mitchell.

[49] Jordan.

VI

It appears that interregional interest differentials did exist in the 19th century. Moreover, in the case of short-term rates, the differentials had been substantially reduced by World War I, and this reduction appears to have been the result of the growth of a national short-term capital market. In particular, the commercial-paper market appears to have made substantial contributions to this process. In the case of the long-term capital market, institutional developments appear to have reduced interest differentials, but some (particularly in the South and the Pacific region) continued to exist. Although the evidence strongly suggests that the nation moved toward a national long-term market in the period, the speed of this movement may have been retarded after 1890. No single institutional development appears to have played a dominant role in the growth of the nation's market, but several developments may have made substantial contributions. The expanded investment activities of the life insurance companies were important, as was the development of the formal securities market. The growth of mortgage banking in the 1870's and 1880's aided movements of capital into Regions IV and V; and the failure of these companies in the 1890's may have contributed to the retardation in development of a national long-term market. Finally, the South appears to have been less affected by these new financial institutions than any other region; however, the explanation of the failure of this region to develop an adequate set of financial institutions requires still further work.

APPENDIX TABLE 1

THREE-YEAR MOVING AVERAGE OF GROSS RATE OF RETURN TO RESERVE-CITY NATIONAL BANKS

Year	NYC	I (1)*	I (2)†	II (1)*	II (2)†	III (1)*	III (2)†	IV (1)*	IV (2)†	V (1)*	V (2)†	VI (1)*	VI (2)†
1889	5.56	5.18	5.18	5.90	5.43	6.33	6.43	6.72	6.52	7.44	7.44	7.48	7.48
1890	5.64	5.13	5.13	5.90	5.45	6.57	6.68	6.70	6.59	7.92	7.92	7.73	7.73
1891	5.50	4.84	4.84	5.86	5.48	6.87	6.98	7.37	6.59	7.91	7.91	7.99	7.99
1892	5.32	4.78	4.78	5.73	5.45	6.78	6.92	7.20	6.41	7.27	7.66	7.97	7.97
1893	4.86	4.66	4.66	5.62	5.38	7.41	7.46	7.24	6.23	7.05	7.46	7.84	7.84
1894	4.67	4.46	4.46	5.38	5.09	7.33	7.36	6.10	5.80	8.25	7.15	7.48	7.48
1895	4.45	4.39	4.39	5.34	5.14	7.35	7.41	5.99	5.70	8.31	7.01	7.37	7.37
1896	4.38	4.23	4.23	5.30	5.05	7.40	7.57	5.74	5.43	10.28	7.20	7.18	7.18
1897	4.41	4.32	4.32	5.45	5.22	7.59	7.69	5.60	5.43	9.88	7.91	6.33	6.33
1898	3.90	3.89	3.89	5.38	4.98	7.98	7.68	5.32	5.11	15.11	9.10	5.82	5.93
1899	3.92	3.94	3.94	5.33	4.91	7.34	6.73	5.02	5.09	12.39	7.80	5.06	5.47
1900	3.72	3.78	3.78	5.13	4.72	7.19	6.35	4.51	4.59	10.16	5.86	5.20	5.72
1901	4.46	3.95	3.95	4.96	4.63	6.67	6.10	4.78	4.75	6.47	5.58	5.10	5.54
1902	4.54	3.89	3.89	4.82	4.65	6.52	6.05	4.54	4.42	6.22	5.33	5.10	5.29
1903	4.95	4.16	4.16	4.92	4.87	6.37	5.98	4.95	4.71	7.01	6.11	5.19	5.10
1904	3.95	4.13	4.13	4.55	4.32	6.77	6.15	4.66	4.50	5.75	4.75	5.37	4.92
1905	3.93	4.25	4.25	4.54	4.29	6.48	5.92	4.85	4.55	6.05	5.28	5.72	4.98
1906	4.04	4.47	4.47	4.50	4.25	6.08	5.67	4.72	4.49	6.22	5.72	5.48	4.77
1907	4.86	5.13	5.13	4.93	4.98	5.88	5.66	4.93	4.78	6.00	6.00	5.47	4.90
1908	4.81	5.18	5.18	5.01	4.95	6.04	5.85	4.95	4.85	6.10	6.17	5.47	5.05
1909	4.94	5.46	5.46	5.10	4.94	6.50	6.30	5.18	5.09	6.17	6.06	5.86	5.23
1910	5.00	5.39	5.39	5.19	4.94	6.60	6.49	5.43	5.40	6.95	6.25	5.94	5.32
1911	5.25	5.57	5.57	5.24	5.11	7.02	6.69	5.68	5.58	7.40	6.62	6.21	5.37
1912	5.34	5.82	5.82	5.30	5.31	7.01	6.73	5.89	5.80	7.62	6.84	6.25	5.70
1913	5.35	6.08	6.08	5.43	5.59	7.40	6.99	6.01	5.79	7.64	7.46	6.26	5.85

* Unweighted.
† Weighted.
SOURCE: Table 4.

APPENDIX TABLE 2

THREE-YEAR MOVING AVERAGE OF GROSS RATE OF RETURN TO NONRESERVE-CITY NATIONAL BANKS

Year	NYC	Region I (1)*	I (2)†	II (1)*	II (2)†	III (1)*	III (2)†	IV (1)*	IV (2)†	V (1)*	V (2)†	VI (1)*	VI (2)†
1889	5.56	6.21	6.25	6.00	6.08	8.67	8.36	7.17	7.06	9.66	9.95	10.12	8.83
1890	5.64	6.28	6.30	6.09	6.12	8.65	8.40	7.14	7.06	9.66	9.54	10.00	8.99
1891	5.50	6.06	6.07	6.07	5.99	8.50	8.30	7.00	6.92	9.67	9.27	9.71	8.91
1892	5.32	5.79	5.68	5.75	5.81	8.20	8.18	6.82	6.72	10.99	9.31	9.54	8.59
1893	4.86	5.52	5.42	5.58	5.66	7.97	7.97	6.68	6.57	10.57	8.72	9.09	8.20
1894	4.67	5.36	5.25	5.42	5.53	7.91	8.00	6.51	6.43	10.32	8.40	8.85	7.96
1895	4.45	5.27	5.15	5.51	5.49	7.90	8.00	6.53	6.43	9.29	8.03	9.13	8.22
1896	4.38	5.20	5.08	5.51	5.47	7.90	7.96	6.51	6.39	9.53	8.43	8.92	7.99
1897	4.41	5.22	5.19	5.41	5.31	7.77	7.85	6.43	6.28	9.65	8.66	8.88	8.21
1898	3.90	5.24	5.25	5.43	5.32	7.78	7.79	6.28	6.13	9.27	8.64	8.36	7.95
1899	3.92	5.71	5.62	5.69	5.50	7.77	7.77	6.14	6.02	9.25	8.74	8.16	8.01
1900	3.72	5.75	5.60	5.69	5.58	7.47	7.49	5.55	5.50	8.40	7.96	7.75	7.56
1901	4.46	5.65	5.48	5.41	5.20	7.16	7.25	5.28	5.21	7.84	7.32	7.52	7.09
1902	4.54	5.08	5.04	5.04	4.89	6.82	6.98	4.95	4.85	7.61	7.06	7.71	7.04
1903	4.95	4.92	4.93	5.03	4.86	6.74	6.89	5.33	5.15	8.26	7.66	7.85	7.18
1904	3.95	4.69	4.48	4.48	4.26	6.66	6.75	5.37	5.19	8.40	7.98	7.76	7.36
1905	3.93	4.59	4.23	4.34	4.17	6.55	6.69	5.24	4.98	8.20	7.81	7.91	7.38
1906	4.04	4.58	4.24	4.19	4.02	6.40	6.50	5.05	4.83	7.91	7.59	7.96	7.08
1907	4.86	5.23	4.97	4.78	4.82	6.30	6.41	5.08	4.88	7.79	7.51	8.49	6.44
1908	4.81	5.31	5.20	4.84	4.91	6.25	6.35	5.17	5.10	7.81	7.56	8.32	6.26
1909	4.94	5.37	5.26	4.98	5.13	6.37	6.48	5.39	5.33	7.93	7.70	9.01	6.41
1910	5.00	5.01	5.05	5.10	5.26	6.61	6.71	5.58	5.51	8.35	8.11	8.99	7.17
1911	5.25	5.07	5.09	5.17	5.34	6.79	6.83	5.86	5.76	8.60	8.40	9.49	7.21
1912	5.34	5.16	5.17	5.26	5.42	6.92	6.96	6.05	5.94	8.81	8.65	9.25	7.25
1913	5.35	5.30	5.31	5.40	5.52	6.97	6.99	6.17	6.06	8.72	8.66	9.23	7.25

* Unweighted.
† Weighted.
SOURCE: Table 3.

APPENDIX TABLE 3

THREE-YEAR MOVING AVERAGE OF NET RATE OF RETURN TO NONRESERVE-CITY NATIONAL BANKS

Year	NYC	I		II		III		IV		V		VI	
		(1)*	(2)†	(1)*	(2)†	(1)*	(2)†	(1)*	(2)†	(1)*	(2)†	(1)*	(2)†
1870	3.39	5.12	5.12	4.37	4.44	6.66	6.49	4.31	4.21				
1871	3.23	4.87	4.87	4.17	4.28	6.33	6.15	3.99	3.60				
1872	3.34	4.73	4.73	4.19	4.19	4.93	4.72	4.28	3.91			7.81	7.81
1873	3.35	4.57	4.57	4.08	3.98	4.50	4.24	4.30	4.05			7.43	7.43
1874	3.10	4.20	4.20	3.97	3.74	4.05	3.78	4.36	4.45			7.21	7.21
1875	2.04	3.35	3.35	3.64	3.42	4.17	4.04	4.12	4.25			6.20	6.20
1876	1.33	2.47	2.47	3.23	3.06	3.78	3.76	3.61	3.66			5.57	5.57
1877	.89	1.62	1.62	2.63	2.65	3.79	3.81	2.88	2.84			4.99	4.99
1878	1.07	1.15	1.15	2.27	2.50	2.74	2.78	2.42	2.37			4.69	4.69
1879	1.77	1.39	1.39	2.09	2.41	2.77	2.81	2.60	2.73			5.02	5.02
1880	2.28	1.88	1.88	2.31	2.63	3.07	3.07	2.99	3.14			5.54	5.54
1881	2.80	2.37	2.37	2.36	2.63	3.61	3.61	3.48	3.50			5.61	5.61
1882	2.54	2.36	2.36	2.47	2.67	3.75	3.44	3.23	3.32			5.61	5.61
1883	2.06	2.23	2.23	2.57	2.67	3.42	3.13	3.08	3.18			5.11	5.11
1884	1.76	1.86	1.86	2.58	2.62	3.06	2.76	2.57	2.68			4.75	4.75
1885	1.72	1.86	1.86	2.45	2.53	2.42	2.39	2.82	2.76			4.43	4.43
1886	2.17	1.90	1.90	2.49	2.52	2.23	2.19	2.89	2.92			3.77	3.77
1887	2.77	2.39	2.39	2.72	2.79	2.12	2.08	2.98	3.17			4.14	4.14
1888	2.81	2.54	2.54	2.96	2.93	2.58	2.58	3.04	3.24	2.47	2.47	4.70	4.70
1889	2.71	2.40	2.40	2.88	2.92	2.73	2.71	3.00	3.16	2.74	2.74	5.44	5.44
1890	2.56	2.40	2.40	2.81	2.82	2.88	2.89	3.07	3.24	1.96	1.96	5.66	5.66
1891	2.42	2.07	2.07	2.68	2.72	2.52	2.52	2.84	3.06	1.58	1.57	5.66	5.66
1892	2.34	2.22	2.22	2.69	2.69	2.33	2.35	2.60	2.79	.64	.67	5.63	5.63
1893	1.82	1.82	1.82	2.52	2.51	1.85	1.92	1.78	2.04	.57	.57	5.20	5.20
1894	1.57	1.67	1.67	2.41	2.39	1.72	1.87	1.40	1.67	.79	.57	4.65	4.65
1895	1.29	1.53	1.53	2.23	2.21	1.68	1.65	1.17	1.38	.37	.66	4.27	4.27
1896	1.32	1.63	1.63	2.20	2.14	2.31	2.03	1.32	1.45		.51	4.07	4.07

APPENDIX TABLE 3 (*Continued*)

						Region							
		I		II		III		IV		V		VI	
Year	NYC	(1)*	(2)†	(1)*	(2)†	(1)*	(2)†	(1)*	(2)†	(1)*	(2)†	(1)*	(2)†
1897......	1.41	1.67	1.67	2.21	2.08	2.65	2.21	1.34	1.49	.42	.63	3.57	3.57
1898......	1.27	1.33	1.33	2.10	1.88	2.47	2.04	1.23	1.49	.50	.63	3.27	3.16
1899......	1.46	1.41	1.41	2.21	2.03	2.49	2.14	1.65	1.87	1.42	1.07	2.92	3.01
1900......	1.48	1.42	1.42	2.10	2.00	2.77	2.29	2.21	2.29	2.35	1.80	2.80	3.05
1901......	2.19	1.67	1.67	2.42	2.25	3.11	2.80	2.59	2.59	2.87	3.00	2.66	3.07
1902......	2.36	1.66	1.66	2.29	2.16	3.12	2.84	2.48	2.44	2.80	2.95	2.56	2.82
1903......	2.78	1.79	1.79	2.23	2.17	3.03	2.82	2.05	2.06	2.32	2.43	2.52	2.67
1904......	2.08	1.66	1.66	1.80	1.81	3.33	3.06	1.79	1.81	2.33	1.42	2.43	2.47
1905......	2.10	1.61	1.61	1.79	1.75	3.23	3.00	1.81	1.77	2.65	1.78	2.43	2.45
1906......	2.19	1.80	1.80	1.99	1.86	3.09	2.94	1.81	1.76	2.97	2.46	3.04	2.66
1907......	2.56	2.05	2.05	1.84	1.98	2.70	2.49	1.79	1.79	2.27	2.32	2.98	2.64
1908......	2.37	1.86	1.86	1.83	1.82	2.64	2.38	1.66	1.69	2.27	2.32	2.86	2.58
1909......	2.20	1.82	1.82	1.32	1.78	2.66	2.35	1.58	1.61	2.04	1.95	2.25	2.27
1910......	2.14	1.77	1.77	1.78	1.73	2.48	2.18	1.76	1.85	2.21	1.93	2.16	2.30
1911......	2.17	1.78	1.78	1.64	1.69	2.71	2.30	1.72	1.80	2.17	1.99	2.14	2.23
1912......	2.09	1.72	1.72	1.54	1.49	2.61	2.26	1.69	1.72	2.02	1.77	1.98	2.16
1913......	1.95	1.69	1.69	1.58	1.62	2.66	2.33	1.55	1.48	1.80	1.75	1.83	1.92

* Unweighted.
† Weighted.
SOURCE: Table 4.

THREE-YEAR MOVING AVERAGE OF NET RATE OF RETURN TO NONRESERVE-CITY NATIONAL BANKS

		Region												
		I		II		III		IV		V		VI	
Year	NYC	(1)*	(2)†	(1)*	(2)†	(1)*	(2)†	(1)*	(2)†	(1)*	(2)†	(1)*	(2)†
1870......	3.39	5.82	5.86	4.78	4.69	5.55	5.32	6.08	5.90	5.26	4.27	13.32	11.08
1871......	3.23	5.49	5.55	4.38	4.43	5.36	5.16	5.71	5.54	5.56	4.41	14.22	11.47
1872......	3.34	5.40	5.54	4.32	4.43	5.33	5.23	5.50	5.35	6.38	5.25	13.75	11.15
1873......	3.35	5.41	5.50	4.16	4.11	5.08	4.97	5.22	5.17	5.79	5.24	10.60	8.64
1874......	3.10	5.27	5.32	4.13	3.95	4.92	4.93	5.09	5.09	5.95	5.55	8.94	6.89
1875......	2.04	4.73	4.69	3.91	3.55	4.52	4.67	4.86	4.89	5.52	4.86	9.26	7.18
1876......	1.33	4.02	3.90	3.71	3.23	4.10	4.35	4.46	4.41	4.97	4.12	9.05	7.22
1877......	.89	3.40	3.22	3.39	2.79	3.39	3.55	4.00	3.91	3.93	3.16	7.61	6.51
1878......	1.07	3.05	2.76	3.06	2.52	2.81	2.92	3.50	3.39	3.73	2.76	7.32	6.19
1879......	1.77	3.13	2.90	2.91	2.51	2.65	2.74	3.47	3.30	4.03	3.03	6.77	5.56
1880......	2.28	3.35	3.19	3.05	2.77	3.39	3.38	3.63	3.48	5.29	4.07	7.64	5.67
1881......	2.80	3.53	3.46	3.08	2.98	3.91	3.78	3.94	3.77	5.56	4.80	7.42	5.27
1882......	2.54	3.39	3.36	3.07	3.00	4.17	3.98	4.04	3.86	5.37	4.78	6.84	4.73
1883......	2.06	3.11	3.06	2.94	2.89	4.18	4.06	4.16	3.84	5.01	4.72	6.15	4.56
1884......	1.76	2.85	2.76	2.88	2.72	4.15	4.11	4.18	3.79	4.76	4.60	5.91	4.66
1885......	1.72	2.91	2.75	2.87	2.71	4.28	4.35	4.05	3.77	4.85	4.94	5.96	5.06
1886......	2.17	3.12	2.93	2.96	2.83	4.18	4.24	4.10	3.78	4.63	4.79	5.20	4.64
1887......	2.77	3.40	3.16	3.09	3.03	4.30	4.34	3.95	3.71	4.66	5.02	5.52	4.74
1888......	2.81	3.51	3.28	3.20	3.19	4.46	4.40	4.00	3.77	4.52	4.95	5.94	5.03
1889......	2.71	3.56	3.30	3.27	3.23	4.74	4.53	3.71	3.65	4.43	4.81	6.31	5.38
1890......	2.56	3.57	3.36	3.31	3.25	4.76	4.56	3.74	3.71	4.21	4.25	5.93	5.21
1891......	2.42	3.32	3.15	3.21	3.09	4.46	4.24	3.61	3.59	4.17	3.88	5.37	4.83
1892......	2.34	3.05	2.95	2.93	2.90	3.80	3.82	3.39	3.38	4.61	3.63	5.11	4.32
1893......	1.82	2.68	2.60	2.72	2.66	3.02	3.14	2.84	2.84	3.77	2.47	3.85	2.71
1894......	1.57	2.44	2.38	2.54	2.43	2.72	2.93	2.51	2.54	3.08	1.73	2.84	1.81
1895......	1.29	2.29	2.23	2.53	2.30	2.65	2.87	2.27	2.34	2.10	.98	2.72	1.34

APPENDIX TABLE 4 (Continued)

Year	NYC	I (1)*	I (2)†	II (1)*	II (2)†	III (1)*	III (2)†	IV (1)*	IV (2)†	V (1)*	V (2)†	VI (1)*	VI (2)†
1896.	1.32	2.25	2.19	2.39	2.18	2.79	2.95	2.16	2.27	2.15	1.26	2.34	1.41
1897.	1.41	2.24	2.18	2.24	2.12	2.83	2.94	2.01	2.14	2.46	1.63	2.61	1.61
1898.	1.27	2.35	2.10	2.22	2.08	2.82	2.91	1.97	2.06	2.53	2.00	2.15	1.88
1899.	1.46	2.59	2.29	2.62	2.35	3.18	3.21	2.19	2.23	3.15	2.62	2.85	2.75
1900.	1.48	2.70	2.34	2.79	2.46	3.32	3.38	2.84	2.85	3.51	3.01	3.17	3.15
1901.	2.19	2.54	2.33	2.86	2.65	3.46	3.52	3.00	3.03	3.70	3.20	3.96	3.32
1902.	2.36	2.32	2.16	2.65	2.56	3.31	3.43	3.00	3.01	3.78	3.37	4.22	3.40
1903.	2.78	2.21	2.09	2.66	2.59	3.24	3.32	2.50	2.49	3.69	3.36	4.11	3.35
1904.	2.08	2.12	1.90	2.26	2.05	3.13	3.19	2.36	2.28	3.65	3.39	3.56	3.29
1905.	2.10	2.13	1.83	2.10	1.97	3.10	3.15	2.23	2.10	3.48	3.24	3.46	3.32
1906.	2.19	2.26	1.97	1.96	1.92	3.06	3.16	2.13	2.03	3.46	3.26	3.43	3.31
1907.	2.56	2.55	2.31	2.12	2.16	2.97	3.07	2.12	2.04	3.47	3.28	3.43	2.94
1908.	2.37	2.41	2.26	2.01	2.02	2.79	2.93	2.05	2.03	3.48	3.33	3.21	2.72
1909.	2.20	2.27	2.18	1.98	1.97	2.65	2.79	1.97	1.94	3.27	3.14	3.35	2.67
1910.	2.14	2.05	2.04	2.02	1.97	2.62	2.79	1.92	1.88	3.21	3.11	3.18	2.87
1911.	2.17	2.05	2.04	2.02	1.95	2.60	2.73	1.93	1.90	3.01	2.96	2.84	2.72
1912.	2.09	1.98	1.95	2.00	1.86	2.54	2.68	1.94	1.91	2.89	2.88	2.64	2.57
1913.	1.95	1.73	1.71	1.72	1.62	2.46	2.58	1.85	1.84	2.57	2.63	2.41	2.36

* Unweighted.
† Weighted.
SOURCE: Table 5.

PART III

1. The Sterling Crisis of 1337-39 *

Edward Ames

Purdue University

THE STERLING CRISIS of 1337–39 is interesting for two reasons. First, it seems to be the earliest such crisis for which detailed analysis is possible. Second, the details of this crisis, when compared to those pertaining to the 1340's, offer what might be called a "textbook example" of the differences between nonconvertible and convertible foreign exchange systems.

The basic series to be analyzed is given in Table 1.[1] It consists of a chronological arrangement of the transactions recorded by the Peruzzi.[2] Most of these are taken from statements of the form "x pounds sterling were paid by (or to) so-and-so, and the account was charged y pounds Florentine." The transactions represented by these quotations mainly represent expenses incurred by the main office of the firm in Florence and by its customers. They are not transactions of the London office of the firm. Most Peruzzi dealings in sterling were presumably transactions of the London office, which was both a lender to the English king and the papal fiscal representative in England. The London office accounts are missing, and the transactions by the Florence office are mainly for relatively small sums. Many are for what we should now call "expense accounts" by members of the firm traveling in northern Europe for periods of months, or even fiscal years (which seemed to begin July 1). It has been assumed that on a transaction described as covering expenses between two given times the reported exchange rate was that which prevailed at the midpoint of the interval. Where more than one transaction took place (or centered in) a given month, the quotations were averaged, equal

---

* Reprinted from the *Journal of Economic History*, Vol. XXV, No. 4 (December, 1965), pp. 496–522. This research was in part supported by a grant from the Rockefeller Foundation.

1 Unless otherwise specified, all exchange rate quotations are taken from A. Sapori (ed.), *I Libri di Commercio dei Peruzzi*, Milan: Publicazioni . . . "Studi medievali," Vol. I, cxxvii plus 571 pp. Other medieval account books edited by Sapori (e.g., the Alberti and Gianfigliazzi accounts) or by De Roover (e.g., the Guillaume Ruyelle accounts) do not have much information on exchange rates.

2 The table omits several transactions (pp. 131, 134–36, 359, 365) in which the Florence office credited the London branch for purchases of Flemish currency with sterling. These allowed the London office to reduce slightly its debts on the Continent. As "capital transactions" they were not important, and as exchange rate quotations they were complicated.

TABLE 1

The Exchange Rate of the Pound, as Recorded in the Peruzzi Accounts, 1334–45

(Price of One Pound Sterling, in Florentine Silver Currency) [*]

Date[a]	Quotation	Page Reference
October 1334..........	10/10/0	58
July 1335.............	10/12/6[b]	7, 223
January 1336..........	9/10/0	352
May 1336.............	10/10/0	223
August 1336..........	10/10/0	158
October 1336.........	10/ 8/0	194
November 1336.......	10/ 0/0	150-52
January 1337..........	9/10/0[c]	85, 91-92, 136, 346
February 1337........	9/ 0/0	57
May 1337.............	9/ 4/0	195
June 1337............	9/ 0/0	255
November 1337.......	9/ 5/0	124, 134
January 1338..........	9/ 2/6[d]	91-92, 370
March 1338...........	9/12/6[e]	136, 352
May 1338.............	9/ 4/8	365
June 1338............	9/10/0	128
August 1338..........	9/15/0[f]	150, 158
January 1339..........	10/ 0/0[g]	62, 80, 91-92, 124, 134, 365, 370
February 1339........	9/10/0	261
March 1339...........	10/14/0	113
April 1339............	9/10/0	93
June 1339............	9/10/0	151
July 1339.............	10/13/2[h]	62, 261
September 1339.......	10/10/0	129
October 1339.........	10/ 7/6[i]	131, 359
November 1339.......	10/ 5/0[j]	93
February 1340........	10/ 5/0[j]	123
July 1340.............	10/ 5/0	62, 80
September 1340.......	10/ 0/0	269
January 1341.........	10/ 5/0[k]	122, 124, 128, 140, 142, 143, 360
February 1341........	10/ 5/0	269
March 1341...........	10/ 8/4[l]	93, 107, 137
September 1341.......	11/ 3/4[m]	124, 140, 143, 269, 360
November 1345.......	10/17/4	156

[*] Throughout this paper, we shall write x/y/z for £x *ys. zd.* and y/z for *ys. zd.* All currencies were of the Carolingian type, although the names for "libra," "solidus," and "denarius" varied from country to country.

[a] Most transactions are over intervals centering in given month.
[b] One transaction at 10/15/0, one at 10/10/0.
[c] Two transactions at this rate.
[d] One transaction at 9/5/0, one at 9/0/0.
[e] One transaction at 10/5/0, one at 9/0/0.
[f] One transaction at 10/0/0, one at 9/10/0.
[g] Two transactions at 10/10/0, one at 10/4/0, one at 9/10/0, three at 9/5/0.
[h] One transaction at 10/16/3, one at 10/10/0.
[i] One transaction at 10/10/0, one at 10/5/0.
[j] For the year ending June 30, 1340, which centers between these two dates, rates are quoted as follows: 10/10/0, three; 10/5/0, ten; 10/4/0, one (pp. 91–92, 122, 124, 127, 128, 134, 140–44, 269, 360, 365, 370).
[k] In addition, for the year ending June 30, 1341, centering at this month, quotations of 11/2/0 (p. 370), 10/10/0 (p. 144), 10/4/0 (p. 269), 10/0/0 (p. 140).
[l] Two transactions at 10/10/0, one at 10/5/0.
[m] Two transactions at 11/10/0; one at 10/10/0.

weights being assigned to each transaction regardless of the size of the individual transactions.[3]

The price of sterling ranged from 9 to over 11 pounds Florentine. It is a familiar assertion that if two countries are on metallic coinage, the exchange rates will vary within the limits governed by the cost of shipping and insurance. It is natural to inquire whether fluctuations of this magnitude are apt to have exceeded these "silver points."

For the six years 1330–35 the price of wine in England averaged 54 *d.* per dozen gallons, according to Thorold Rogers.[4] Thus, it was possible to make and transport French wine to England at a delivered price of about .45 *d.* per pound avoirdupois. Transportation alone would therefore have been less than .45 *d.* per pound avdp. One Tower pound of silver at this time could be made into £ 1 3*d.* of coin, so that one pound avdp. of silver

TABLE 2
NUMBER OF TRANSACTIONS BY PRICE OF POUND STERLING

Period	At Least 10 Pounds Florentine	Below 10 Pounds Florentine	Total
January 1337–June 1339	6	22	28
Other	54	3	57
Total	60	25	85

would have made £ 1 6*s.* 3*d.* If the cost of transporting (and especially insuring) silver[5] were 10 times as great as that on wine, it would have amounted to roughly 1.4 percent of the value of the shipment. If the par value of sterling was of the order of 10 pounds Florentine, the silver import and export points would have been in the order of three shillings Florentine above and below par. The actual fluctuations are far in excess of this range.

Table 1 suggests that the exchange rate of sterling, in terms of Florentine currency, was lower between January, 1337 and June, 1339 than at other periods. Table 2 presents the evidence pertaining to the generalization: The price of sterling was below 10/0/0 from January, 1337, through June, 1339, and above 10/0/0 the rest of the time. This table suggests that there was a significant difference in the probability that a Peruzzi sterling transaction would occur at a lower rate in this period of 1337–39 than at other periods in the interval observed.

Statements of this sort are dealt with in the theory of contingency

[3] An attempt was made to determine whether the market was "thin," by investigating whether large transactions were conducted at rates differing from those on small transactions. There seems to have been no systematic difference between the two.

[4] *A History of Agriculture and Prices* (7 vols.; Oxford, 1866–1902). This wine was presumably of relatively low quality, since (as James has shown) the king's butler paid substantially higher prices than this.

[5] Presumably most of the insurance was self-insurance, but shippers would have to cover the risk somehow.

tables. They are typically of the form: Is event A more likely to occur in samples of Type I than in samples of Type II? That is, are the two samples likely to have been drawn from the same population? The theory permits of formulating significance tests[6] which state how likely it is that differences in the proportion of occurrence of event A would be as great as those actually observed, in pairs of samples drawn from a single popula- tion, at random. If the Peruzzi data may be considered as random draw- ings from a single population, there is less than 1 chance in 100 that results as different as these would have been obtained for the two periods.

This sort of test, used with economic data, is apt to be overoptimistic, in the sense that too many hypotheses will be retained and too few rejected.[7] Significance test criteria in this paper eliminate the least ac- ceptable hypotheses. A conclusion which passes a test is considered ac- ceptable, pending the development of more relevant tests.[8]

The data in Table 1 might reflect either (1) a low point in English exchange rates in 1337-39 or (2) a high point in Florentine rates in that period. If the first possibility is correct, the pattern shown in Table 2 would not be repeated if exchange rates were computed between Floren- tine currency and other North European currencies. If the latter is correct, the 1337-39 dip should be found for other North European currencies.[9]

Tables 3–5 summarize Peruzzi transactions in the Low Countries (actually Bruges and Ghent) and in France (Paris) over this period. In both cases, the transactions involved both gold and silver coin, so that separate calculations are needed. The Peruzzi recorded transactions in Paris and in Avignon. The latter is disregarded, as being a part of the Mediterranean rather than of the northern economy. The French silver coinage was of two types, *tournois* and *parisis*. In addition, the French coinage was being depreciated over the period, so that the adjectives *good* and *current* appear in the Peruzzi books. It would appear that the *tournois*

---

[6] We used *Tables for Testing Significance in a 2 x 2 Contingency Table*, compiled by D. J. Finney, R. Latscha, B. M. Bennett, and P. Hsu (Cambridge, Eng.: The University Press, 1963).

[7] Correlations performed on randomly selected economic time series are, on the average, higher than those to be expected on the basis of ordinary significance tests. See Edward Ames and Stanley Reiter, "Empirical Distributions of Correlation and Autocorrelation Coefficients in Economic Time Series," *Journal American Statistical Association*, Vol. LVI (1961).

[8] The main reason for caution in the use of statistical significance tests involving time series data is that economic data change only gradually Consequently the suc- cessive observations in a time series are not independent of each other in the manner assumed by significance tests.

[9] The restriction to northern Europe made in the preceding paragraph seems to be important. At the time under study, the Florentines were the principal Mediter- ranean power to trade in northern Europe; but the economic affairs of northern Europe were largely independent of those of Mediterranean Europe, because of the difficulties in communication. Our conclusion will be that Florentine currency was a "key currency," or roughly the equivalent of "gold and dollars"; and we assume that the market for this currency in northern Europe was largely independent of the market for this currency in the South.

TABLE 3

THE EXCHANGE RATE OF FLANDERS-BRABANT CURRENCY IN TRANSACTIONS
RECORDED IN PERUZZI ACCOUNTS, 1329–39
(Price of One Pound Flanders-Brabant Currency, in Pounds
of Florentine Silver Currency)

| | Quotations on Flemish[a] | | |
| | Silver | Gold | Page |
Date[b]	Currency	Currency	Reference
March 1329......	26/15/10		164, 275
July 1335.......	30/ 0/ 0		7
January 1338....	29/15/ 0		86
March 1338.....	29/13/ 4		269
November 1338..	31/ 0/ 0		86
January 1339.....	30/ 0/ 0	2/ 2/ 3[c]	106, 114, 121, 359, 366
February 1339...	30/ 0/ 0	2/ 2/ 0	106
April 1339.......	[28/10/ 0]	2/ 4/ 0	93
May 1339.......	30/ 0/ 0		131
June 1339.......	29/11/ 8		134
July 1339........	26/16/ 3	1/18/ 0	260
August 1339.....	[28/ 7/ 6][d]	1/18/10	135, 137
October 1339....	[26/18/10][e]	1/18/ 0[e]	113, 135, 359
January 1340.....	[26/ 9/ 5][f]	1/17/ 6	106, 107, 140, 269
February 1340...	[25/15/ 0]	1/17/ 0	123
September 1340..	[23/15/ 0][g]	1/17/ 0	107, 140, 141, 269, 366
July 1341........	[23/ 4/ 0]	1/17/ 0	145

[a] Quotations in brackets are derived from gold currency quotations, at rates of conversion given in the source.

[b] Virtually all transactions are on intervals centering on given month.

[c] One transaction at 2/2/6 and one at 2/2/0.

[d] One transaction at 26/15/0 silver and 1/17/11 gold; one transaction at 30/0/0 silver (no gold price listed).

[e] One transaction at 26/16/3 silver and 1/18/0 gold; one transaction at 27/11/4 silver (no gold price listed). In connection with the latter, it was observed that "good" *gros tournois* were worth 30/0/0 a *fior.*

[f] In addition, for the year ending June 30, 1340, centering on this month, rates of 26/16/10 (p. 141), 26/4/8 (p. 141, 365) were quoted.

[g] One transaction at 24/9/3 (p. 107); one at 23/9/3 (pp. 140, 269); one at 23/1/9 (pp. 141, 366).

quotations could be treated as constant about 2/10/0 over 1335–38, while the *parisis* transactions were stable at about 2/16/0 until mid-1337 and then dropped to about 2/10/0 in 1338.

Table 6 presents contingency tables for French and Flemish exchange rates which are comparable to Table 2. Flemish currency tended to be *higher* in 1337–39 than at other times. This result is not significant in the case of silver coin, but it is significant at the .01 level for gold coin. Neither silver nor gold French coin was significantly different in 1337–39 than at other periods.

Given only the sterling transactions, we would be unable to decide whether sterling fell or Florentine currency rose in 1337. Given sterling and Flemish quotations, we could conclude that sterling fell relative to Florentine currency, and that Florentine currency fell relative to Flemish. But the observation that there was no significant change in Florentine currency relative to Flemish silver, to French gold, or to French silver currency suggests that Florentine currency was stable in this period.

TABLE 4

EXCHANGE RATES FOR GOLD CURRENCY IN PARIS

(Price of French Currency, a *fior*)

Date	Quotation	Page Reference
March 1335..............	1/10/3	29, 111, 192
July 1335...............	1/ 9/0	109
August 1335............	1/10/6	110
July 1337...............	1/ 9/7	30
August 1337............	1/10/6	323
September 1337.........	1/10/8	120
January 1338............	1/10/6	123
April 1338..............	1/10/9	151
July 1338...............	1/11/0	151
August 1338............	1/11/0	151
March 1339..............	1/10/0	123

TABLE 5

THE PRICE OF FRENCH SILVER CURRENCY IN PARIS

(in Florentine Silver Currency)

Date	Quotation	Description of French coin	Page Reference
January 1330......	2/ 7/8	good *gros tournois*	30
February 1331.....	2/ 5/0	good *gros tournois*	30
March 1335.......	2/19/4	*parisis*	29, 111
	2/10/1	good *tournois*	192
April 1335.........	2/16/10	good *tournois parisis*	191-92
September 1335....	2/12/1	good *tournois parisis*	7, 192
June 1337.........	2/17/6	*parisis*	30
May 1338.........	2/11/7	current *parisis*	151
	2/ 9/2	good *parisis*	151
July 1338.........	2/12/0	current *parisis*	151
	2/ 9/7	good *tournois*	151
August 1338.......	2/12/0	*parisis*	153
	2/ 9/7	current *parisis*	151

These results are a sort of paradox. During the entire period 1335–45, the metal content of both English and Flemish silver coin was unchanged,[10] yet the exchange rates of these currencies fluctuated outside the silver import and export points. The metal content of French silver and gold coin was steadily reduced.[11] The French exchange rates recorded by the Peruzzi, however, show stability.

Half of the apparent paradox may be resolved simply. The Peruzzi accounts are careful to specify the kinds of French coin purchased. Indeed, in France a variety of coins circulated side by side, so that any-

[10] Sir John Craig, *The Mint: A History of the London Mint from AD 287 to 1948* (Cambridge, Eng.: The University Press, 1953). W. A. Shaw, *The History of Currency, 1252 to 1894* (London, n.d. [1895?]).

[11] Shaw lists the following French mint buying prices for one mark of silver: February, 1336, 3/12/6; November, 1338, 4/12/0; January, 1339, 5/0/0; August, 1340, 7/0/0; December, 1340, 7/10/0; January, 1341, 9/4/0; June, 1342, 12/10/0. For gold, the buying price, per mark, was: January, 1331, 39/0/0; February, 1336, 50/0/0; November, 1338, 58/0/0; May, 1339, 61/10/0; August, 1339, 69/0/0.

TABLE 6

DISTRIBUTION OF MONTHLY FLEMISH AND FRENCH QUOTATIONS IN
JANUARY 1337–JUNE 1339 AS COMPARED TO OTHER PERIODS

	Number of Transactions in Which Price of Flemish Silver Coin, in Terms of Florentine Silver Currency, Was:		
	At Least 29/0/0	*Below* 29/0/0	*Total*
January 1337–June 1339	5	4	9
Other	3	18	21
Total	8	22	30

	Flemish Gold Coin, in Terms of Florentine Silver Currency, Was:		
	At Least 2/0/0	*Below* 2/0/0	*Total*
January 1337–June 1339	4	0	4
Other	0	7	7
Total	4	7	11

	French Silver Coin, in Terms of Florentine Silver Currency, Was:		
	At Least 2/11/0	*Below* 2/11/0	*Total*
January 1337–June 1339	1	3	4
Other	3	2	5
Total	4	5	9

	French Gold Coin, in Terms of Florentine Silver Currency, Was:		
	At Least 1/10/6	*Below* 1/10/6	*Total*
January 1337–June 1339	6	2	8
Other	1	2	3
Total	7	4	11

one equipped with a scale was able to reduce the coinage to some common denominator of weight.

The remainder of the paradox will occupy the rest of this paper. It would appear that during the 1330's, at least, sterling had a fluctuating exchange rate. It is natural to inquire whether there is any independent evidence to support this assertion. Table 7, therefore, presents a number of sterling quotations for the period 1342–1429. From this table, one would conclude that over much of the 14th century sterling was a fluctuating currency. This conclusion does not depend on the existence of a downward trend, since this would be consistent with the increase in the English mint prices of silver which are known to have occurred. Rather it depends upon short-term ups and downs in the quotations.[12]

---

[12] *The Calendar of Entries in the Papal Registers* lists 54 different months over the period 1372–1489 in which one Florentine gold florin was worth 12 silver *gros tournois*. Thus not all exchange rates in the *Calendar* fluctuate, and not all are stable.

(*footnote continued on next page*)

TABLE 7
PRICE OF ONE POUND STERLING, IN (GOLD) PAPAL FLORINS,
MISCELLANEOUS DATES 1342–1429

Date	Price	Page Reference	Implied Price of Sterling in Florentine Silver	
April 1342.............	7.2	616	10/ 8/9*	10/ 1/7†
June 1343.............	7.5	1	10/17/4	10/10/0
August 1344..........	7.2	14	10/ 8/9	10/ 1/7
December 1344........	7.2	13	10/ 8/9	10/ 1/7
June 1345.............	7.4	18	10/14/7	10/ 8/7
June 1346.............	7.5	26	10/17/4	10/10/0
March 1347...........	7.5	31	10/17/4	10/10/0
September 1348........	7.2	38	10/ 8/9	10/ 1/7
May 1356.............	7.5	634	10/17/4	10/10/0
July 1356.............	6.7	620	9/14/3	9/ 5/10
January 1357..........	6.5	634	9/ 8/6	9/ 2/0
(no month) 1357......	6.7	624–25	9/14/3	9/ 5/10
September 1359........	7.2	633	10/ 8/9	10/ 1/7
March 1380...........	6.1	262	8/16/10	8/ 9/5
February 1392.........	5.6	281	8/ 2/5	7/16/10
March 1392...........	6.4	282	9/ 5/7	9/ 0/7
December 1392........	6.7	451	9/14/3	9/ 5/10
March 1414...........	6.0	134	8/14/0	8/ 8/0
September 1421........	6.0	193	8/14/0	8/ 8/0
October 1428..........	6.0	50	8/14/0	8/ 8/0
December 1429........	6.0	171	8/14/0	8/ 8/0

* This column was calculated on the assumption that the mean of the rates quoted for June 1345 and June 1346 in this table (7.45) corresponds to the rate quoted for November 1345 in Table 1 (10/17/4).

† This column was calculated on the assumption that the rates of 7.5 quoted in this table correspond to a "normal prewar" rate of 10/10/0 found in Table 1.

SOURCE: *Calendar of Entries in the Papal Registers Relating to Great Britain and Ireland* (London, 1897).

Is it reasonable to speak of 1337–39 as a crisis? Table 7, taken in conjunction with Table 1, suggests that it is. During the 1340's, it would appear that sterling quotation varied over the range 7.2 to 7.5, or less than 5 percent.[13] By this standard, the year 1337 was marked by an unusual drop in sterling. Was this drop so great as to suggest that the "crisis" occurred only in the Peruzzi accounting division? Table 8 shows that a decline of 14 percent in sterling rates occurred from May, 1356 to January, 1357, and that a 20 percent increase in sterling took place in 1392. We conclude that in 1337 a crisis occurred but that this crisis is not unparalleled in magnitude in the 14th century.[14]

This fact lends credence to the assertion that the quotations in the calendars represent rates which may actually have existed in the markets, rather than in bookkeeping conventions or aberrations.

[13] Compare this range with the range of about 3 percent suggested by the calculations of silver import and export points given above.

[14] The long-run changes in sterling rates implied by Table 7 are roughly what one would expect from the changes in the metal content of sterling coin. In 1342 one Tower pound of silver made 243 *d.* of coin and in 1412–65 it made 360 *d.* In 1344 one Tower pound of gold made 15/0/0 in coin, and after 1412 it made 16/13/4. If the (apparently fixed) sterling rate of 6.0 prevailing after 1412 is computed back-

The crisis of 1337–39 obviously had something to do with the beginning of the Hundred Years' War, the abortive campaign in Flanders, and the various schemes by which the king sought to pay for the war by operations in the wool market. We shall consider how these various political and fiscal factors entered into the balance of payments.

A number of statements can be made with some assurance. These will be based on contingency tables, and accompanied by parenthetical numbers to denote the significance of the statement. For any such statement, the reader will be able to construct, from the tables presented, contingency tables of the following form:

	The Number of Years in Which Series X Was:	
In the Period	*Above Mean Value*[15]	*Below Mean Value*
1333–36 (or 1330–36)	4 (or 7)	0
1337–43	1 (or 2)	6 (or 5)

If these tables have the frequencies indicated, or if there is a zero in the lower left box, the statements may be taken as significant. Given two significant statements, we prefer those which relate to four rather than seven prewar years, on the grounds that (1) the test is sharper and (2) it covers a smaller variety of possible peacetime conditions and thus more closely approximates "prewar." Where we make negative statements, we have in mind that there is not a significant difference between prewar and wartime conditions.

For instance, if we consider the balance of trade, our problem is to compare the import of wine with the export of wool. It is stated in the literature that there are the most important items of trade. Import data (Table 8) are incomplete. However, wartime imports, while a little higher during the war than before (3,634 tons compared to 3,452 for alien imports; 113 ships compared to 91 ships for non-London denizens) are not significantly different. Price data are incomplete. For this period, prices were not increasing; at some later date they doubled, but it is not possible to say now when this increase took place. So we conclude that the value of imports did not change much.

The value of exports, however, fell (table 9). Domestic prices averaged a little less during the war years than before, but not significantly. Despite a considerable increase in export duties (customs and subsidy) the estimated sum (Table 9, col. 2) of domestic prices plus export duties rose insignificantly during the war years. The volume of exports was significantly lower during the war (.005). Consequently, the value of exports at the farm (col. 4) dropped significantly (.05). The drop in foreign exchange

---

ward we would therefore estimate the silver rate at 8.00 and the gold rate at 6.67 in 1344; these bracket the actual quotations for the 1340's.

[15] Means are calculated for the entire period 1333–43 (or 1330–43).

earnings (col. 6) is not significant for the war years as a whole. But the very sharp drop in earnings in 1337 coincides with the decline in sterling in Table 1; and the sharp increase in 1339 coincides with the rise in sterling in Table 1. The details of the wool trade during the period are com-

TABLE 8

ENGLISH WINE PRICES AND IMPORTS, 1333–43

Year, Ending Michaelmas	Price of Wine*	Imports of Wine	
		By Aliens†	By Non-London Denizens‡
1333..............	48	1586	
1334..............	54	6166	126
1335..............	51	3190	77
1336..............	57		94
1337..............		2146	43
1338..............	54		
1339..............		4648§	83
1340..............		2022	235
1341..............		4258	114
1342..............		3411	106
1343..............		3829	101

* Pence per dozen gallons. Thorold Rogers. (His figures are universally criticized, but seldom improved upon.)
† In tons. M. K. James, "The Fluctuations of the Anglo-Gascon Wine Trade during the Fourteenth Century," *Economic History Review*, Second Series, Vol. IV (1951).
‡ Ships from which the king's prise was taken; *ibid.*
§ February to Michaelmas rate.

TABLE 9

ENGLISH WOOL PRICES AND EXPORTS, 1333–43
(Fiscal Year Ending Michaelmas)

Year, Ending Michaelmas	English Wool Prices		Wool Export‡ (Thousand Sacks)	Value of Exported Wool	
	Domestic Prices* (Pence per Clove)	Domestic Price Plus Duty†		At Farm§	At Frontier‖
				(1333–1343 mean = 100)	
1333.......	24.0	26.0	28.3	159	127
1334.......	17.5	19.5	34.6	142	116
1335.......	21.2	19.5	34.1	170	115
1336.......	25.0	28.0	21.8	127	105
1337.......	24.8	27.8	4.3	20	20
1338.......	17.8	23.8	19.5	81	81
1339.......	20.2	26.2	41.8	99	189
1340.......	18.0	24.0	20.3	43	84
1341.......	18.0	26.0	19.6	71	88
1342.......	22.0	28.0	21.8	112	105
1343.......	19.5	25.5	15.8	72	70

* Rogers.
† Duties may be somewhat unsatisfactorily estimated from data in Sir James H. Ramsay, *The Genesis of Lancaster* (Oxford: Clarendon Press, 1913), Vol. I, p. 182; Vol. II, pp. 88–90; and from the papers by F. R. Barnes and by G. Unwin in G. Unwin (ed.), *Finance and Trade under Edward III* (Manchester: The University Press, 1918).
‡ E. M. Carus-Wilson and Olive Coleman, *England's Export Trade, 1275–1547* (Oxford: University Press, 1963). It has been necessary to adjust data for some ports to place them on a 12-month basis.
§ An index of the products of columns (1) and (3).
‖ An index of the products of columns (2) and (3).

plicated and need not detain us here. We may generalize about the war period as a whole only if we can say that the large exports of 1339 represent a working off of stocks accumulated in England but not exported during the period of the monopoly.[16] We then would obtain (by averaging 1337–39) a significant (.05) decline in exports. We are reluctant to juggle numbers to obtain a statistically significant table, but we find some force in the argument.

The data on commodity trade therefore associate the crisis of 1337–39 with the decline in wool exports and consequently with the political and economic maneuvers involving royal trading in wool.

Data on government revenue and spending for this period have never been disentangled. However, it is possible to give average monthly data for 10 subperiods of the period 1329–44 (Table 10) for the Wardrobe, which was the most important single source of spending. A large part of the revenue of the Exchequer (the Receipt) was at this time turned over to the Wardrobe. In particular, the Wardrobe carried out most of the spending in which the king was personally interested, such as wars, the wool schemes, and so forth. Wardrobe began to increase its expenditures some time before the beginning of the Flemish campaign; and the period of greatest Wardrobe spending began late in 1338 (that is, about the time sterling began to rise). The timing of changes in Wardrobe spending do not, therefore, coincide with the changes in sterling reported in Table 1.

In modern times, the outbreak of a major war is apt to lead to increases in the price level because (to oversimplify) governments never raise enough taxes to cover military expenses, and they increase the supply of money at a time when (owing to military procurements) they are reducing the supply of consumer goods. Modern readers will be interested in the significant (.01) drop in prices following the beginning of the Hundred Years' War (Table 11). There is again an oversimplified explanation of this drop. Comparatively speaking, the 14th-century army was labor-intensive, and the modern army is capital-intensive. A 14th-century army fighting on foreign soil (as the English army was in the Hundred Years' War) cost money mainly because it had to buy food and fodder it could not plunder. Such military expenses were a direct reduction of the domestic money supply, since paper money could not yet be used. In contrast, preparations for war (raising troops at home) should not have monetary repercussions, since the taxpayers' money was transferred to the troops, who spent it for food and fodder. Except for imports of horses or armor no foreign repercussions need occur.

We have not found the date at which English troops began to land on the Continent; but when the king arrived in Flanders in late 1337, he found his army there. The year 1338 was marked by the peak in English military force in Flanders (so far as we can tell), and everyone seems to

---

16 It is known, of course, that the king had great difficulties in actually laying his hands on wool while the monopoly existed.

TABLE 10
WARDROBE ACCOUNTS, MONTHLY RATES*

| | Receipts | | | | Expenditures | | | | |
| | Exchequer of | | | | | | | | |
	Receipt	Account	Other	Total	Household	Other	Total	Expenses	Advances
Sept. 29, 1329–Oct. 15, 1331....	1,101		371	1,473	845	757	1,603	1,519	84
Oct. 16, 1331–Sept. 29, 1332....	640		181	821	746	228	974		
Sept. 29, 1332–Sept. 29, 1333....	1,856		198	2,053	769	1,156	1,924	1,874	50
Sept. 29, 1333–July 30, 1334....	786		490	1,276	824	571	1,395	1,323	72
July 31, 1334–Aug. 31, 1337....	3,290	137	130	3,557	886	2,754	3,640	3,562	78
Aug. 31, 1337–July 11, 1338....	2,049	111	464	2,624	858	2,396	3,253	2,952	301
July 12, 1338–May 27, 1340....	5,842	983	6,902	13,728	1,060	13,988	15,048	9,828	5,221
May 27, 1340–Nov. 25, 1341....	1,232	208	948	2,388	793	2,759	3,552	2,897	655
Nov. 25, 1341–Apr. 11, 1344....	2,130		274	2,404	897	2,180	3,077	3,039	38
Apr. 11, 1344–Nov. 24, 1347....	5,168		194	5,362	1,071	4,695	5,766	5,441	325

* T. F. Tout, Chapters in the Administrative History of Medieval England (Manchester: The University Press, 1920), Vol. VI, Appendix II. (Details may not add to total because of rounding.)

TABLE 11

THE "PRICE OF COMPOSITE UNIT OF CONSUMABLES," 1329–43

(1451–75 = 100)

1329	119
1330	120
1331	134
1332	131
1333	111
1334	99
1335	96
1336	106
1337	85
1338	79
1339	96
1340	86
1341	85
1342	84
1343	97

SOURCE: E. H. Phelps Brown and Sheila V. Hopkins, "Seven Centuries of the Price of Consumables, Compared with Builders' Wage-Rates," *Economica*, Vol. XXIII (1956).

have gone home in 1339, when exports began to pick up again. The chronology of the military operation (expensive, although abortive) coincides roughly, therefore, with the sterling crisis under discussion.

The data on travel between England and the Continent serve to cast some better light upon the probable timing of military expenditures, since there is probably a connection between the size of the English military establishment on the Continent and the movement of government officials to the Continent.

Movement of people into and out of England was controlled at least as early as the 1230's. Travelers to the Continent were usually required to leave through the Cinque Ports, and were sometimes restricted to Dover. Several categories of traveler were recognized: pilgrims, members of religious orders in England with headquarters on the Continent, merchants, persons traveling on the king's business, and so on.

It would be most interesting, of course, to obtain data on the travel of merchants, although such data are difficult to evaluate, since documents sometimes pertain to entire firms and sometimes to individuals; moreover, it sometimes seems to be the case that some members of a given firm are considered residents of England, while other members are considered aliens because they work in foreign (Florentine or Flemish) main offices. But travel restrictions do provide information which gives clues about foreign spending by English. As early as 1258, exit permits distinguish between persons allowed to take coin out of the country and persons not allowed to.[17] Beginning in the 1290's it is possible to obtain fairly con-

---

[17] *Calendar of Close Rolls*, 12 Hen. III, pp. 31, 317; 43 Hen. III, p. 351. Thus Feaveryear is incorrect in stating that the Statute of Stepney in 1299 is the first prohibition on the export of coin (*The Pound Sterling* [Oxford: Clarendon Press, 1931], p. 3). See also *CCR*, 7 Edw. I (1280), p. 519.

The following abbreviations are used in citations in the remainder of this paper:

tinuous series which separate exit permits into those permitting, and those prohibiting, the carrying of travel expenses, in coin, out of the country (Table 12).

Permits of this sort are not an exact count of the number of persons traveling, for the permit includes attendants accompanying a person of rank. But permits will be an indicator of the amount of travel.

TABLE 12

PERMITS TO LEAVE ENGLAND THROUGH DOVER, 1294–1326*

Calendar Year	Taking Silver or Coin for Expenses	Taking No Silver or Coin	Page References
1294........	1		367
1296........	2		511
1299........	3‡	1	265, 328; *CCW*, 103
1300........	3‡	2	349, 355, 369, 379, 416, 445
1301........		1	465
1302........		2	550
1303........	1	4	137, 513, 539, 550, 566
1304........		2	69, 169, 209
1305........	1	1	236†
1306........		2	375, 473
1307........	8		482, 483, 505, 508, 510, 8, 9, 12
1308........	2		24, 122
1309........	2		165, 185
1310........	2		203, 277
1311........	6		310, 316, 451, 372, 430
1313........	1		69
1317........	4		43, 564
1321........		1	499
1326........	1		554

* Years in which no permits were reported have been omitted from this table.
‡ In these years, one person was given permit to depart without search.
† See also *Records of the Parliament Holden at Westminster on the twenty-eighth Day of February in the thirty-third Year of the Reign of King Edward the First* (A.D. 1305), F. M. Maitland (ed.), (London, 1893), p. 95.
SOURCE: *CCR*, except as noted. This table was prepared using the index to the *Calendar*. To the extent that permissions or prohibitions were issued but not addressed to officials of Dover or to Wardens of the Cinque Ports, or that the index is incomplete, this table is in error.

It is natural for an economist to inquire whether these permits and prohibitions reflect economic and political conditions, or whether they depend solely on the nature and rank of the individual seeking to travel.

CCR—*Calendar of Close Rolls;* CCW—*Calendar of Chancery Warrants, 1244–1326;* CFR—*Calendar of Fine Rolls;* CLB—*Calendar of Letter Books Preserved among the Archives of the Corporation of the City of London* (the letter following "CLB" designates the book cited, e.g., CLB-C is Book C); CMI—*Calendar of Inquisitions, Miscellaneous.* (All these series are publications of the Historical Manuscripts Commission.) Rotuli—*Rotuli Parliamentorum, ut et Petitiones et Placita in Parliamento, Anno 6 Edward I—Anno 19 Henry VII* (London, 1832); Ruding—Rogers Ruding, *Annals of the Coinage of Great Britain and Its Dependencies* (3rd ed., London, 1840); Ruffhead—*The Statutes at Large, from Magna Charta to the Twenty-Fifth Year of the Reign of King George the Third, Inclusive,* Owen Ruffhead (ed.), (London, 1786).

In the first case, there would be few years in which permits and prohibitions on the export of coin would be simultaneously issued. Actually, the combinations logically possible[18] occur almost exactly as if there were independent probabilities of .42 that at least one permit would be issued and of .27 that at least one prohibition would be issued. For the period covered by Table 12, there is therefore no evidence of a "travel-permit policy" in this sense, but we shall later relate these permits to the system of foreign exchange controls.

TABLE 13

LICENSES FOR MEMBERS OF THE CLERGY TO LEAVE ENGLAND
THROUGH DOVER (OR THE CINQUE PORTS) CARRYING
EXPENSE MONEY BUT NO *Apportum*, 1324–49*

Calendar Year	Number of Licenses	Page Reference‡
1324........	1	211
1327........	9	108, 198, 207, 210, 217, 224
1328........	1	400
1329........	9	494, 564–67, 571
1330........	1	145
1331........	11	319, 323, 331, 332, 333, 335, 419
1332........	4	547, 580, 586, 597
1333........	3	119, 121–22
1334........	5	246, 294, 305, 324, 330
1335........	10	483–84, 488, 506, 518–21, 523, 525
1336........	10	555, 648–49, 657, 666, 671, 676, 698, 731
1337........	1	118
1338........	1	414
1341........	2	124, 276
1343†......	1	118
1344†......	5	293, 361, 453, 465, 477
1345†......	5	554, 557, 561, 567, 581
1346†......	1	143
1348†......	1	523
1349†.......	3	148, 75, 90

* This table was attained through the use of the indexes to the several volumes. It may be in error where the indexes are incomplete. Years in which no licenses were reported have been omitted from this table.

‡ All page references refer to appropriate volumes of the *CCR.*

† With two exceptions in 1345 and one in 1349, the licenses specify that only gold coin is to be exported.

Beginning in 1324, the *Close Rolls* data come to refer solely to the members of monastic orders and occasionally to other clergy. They use the formula: "X may take with him expense money (either a stated sum or a "reasonable amount") but no *apportum*." The *apportum* was a contribution by an English order to its foreign headquarters.[19]

18 Permits only; prohibitions only; both; neither.

19 In 1304–7, the monasteries were required to make such payments in coin, in contrast to the papal nuncios, who were required to transfer money to Rome by letter of exchange (*CPR*, 35 Edw. I. p. 514; *Rotuli*, I, 222, and II, 217; Ruffhead, I, 161). Evidently some change was later made, for the Peruzzi made payments which were evidently *apportum* (Sapori, p. 195, gives an example).

The period 1324–39 is covered in Table 13. In each of five years during the first half (1324–36), six or more travel permits were issued; in no year of the second half (1337–49) were more than five permits issued. The number of monks allowed to take their expenses out of the country was thus significantly less (.025) during the Hundred Years War than it had been before.

Two varying interpretations of this difference may be made. The monks may have wished to stay in England because of wartime disturbances. Or the king may have kept them from leaving, either because he did not wish them to take information abroad, or because he did not wish them to take money abroad. We may observe (1) that the permits issued began to drop in 1337, when the price of sterling had begun to fall but before hostilities became important and (2) that when travel revived slightly in the 1340's, the permits specified that only gold coins might be taken out of England. This latter restriction was in accord with monetary policy generally, and we shall return to it later. There is therefore some basis for believing that the restrictions on monastic travel had something to do with foreign exchange policy.

Persons not traveling for monastic orders frequently obtained "protections" from the king, as well as powers of attorney for persons representing them in their absence. These documents were issued to people traveling to Wales, Scotland, and Ireland as well as "beyond the seas," but it is specified what their destination may be. It is also specified whether their travel is "on the King's business" or their own. Persons traveling "on the King's service" were civilian rather than military.[20] Table 14 tabulates the number of travelers "beyond the seas." In this table, travel to Gascony and Aquitaine is listed separately, because such travel presumably did not have the same foreign exchange consequences.[21]

The number of pilgrims going abroad dropped significantly (.02) in wartime. For other nonofficials there was no such drop, but the years 1337–40 were unusually low. This low period either may reflect a genuine drop in travel during the period of the sterling crisis, or it may be the beginning of a true wartime decline which is concealed by an increasing tendency of merchants going to Flanders in 1341–43 to obtain protections. We suspect the latter possibility may be the case.

The greatest numerical variations in the number of persons leaving England take place in the category "on the King's service." These were highest in consequence of the (presumably diplomatic) missions of 1331–32 or of the king's expedition to Flanders in 1337. It is possible to

---

[20] One may compare the 334 persons who traveled abroad in 1337 on the king's service, and mostly "with the King" in Flanders, with the over 1,200 persons pardoned for crimes from murder on up as reward for military service overseas in 1338–39. Moreover, presumably not all the troops were felons.

[21] Moreover, the large number of protections going to nonofficials traveling in Gascony and Aquitaine in 1337–38 seems to have been associated with naval convoys of ships going in those years (and only in those years) to these destinations.

TABLE 14

PROTECTIONS AND POWERS OF ATTORNEY ISSUED BY LETTERS PATENT FOR PERSONS GOING "BEYOND THE SEA," 1330–45

Calendar Year	Not on King's Service			Gascony and Aquitaine	On King's Service			
					Going Abroad		Staying Abroad	
	On Pilgrimages	Going Abroad	Staying Abroad		G + A	Other	G + A	Other
1330........	10	21	14		19	17	2	1
1331........	23	21	40	2	50	104	4	2
1332........	23	32	13	1	2	121	2	3
1333........	8	13	9		5	27	2	3
1334........	5	15	19	1	4	37	3	
1335........	3	15	6		9	23		2
1336........		17	9	6		31	5	
1337........	1	10	7	15	3	334	1	4
1338........		14	7	11		38		24
1339........		1	1	2		3		2
1340........	1	1	2		5	8		
1341........		16	7			6		
1342........		27	5			2		
1343........	14	19	4			5		
1344........	3	9	2			10		1
1345........	3		1			1		

SOURCE: *CPR*. Unlike Table 13, this represents a count taken page by page. It is probably subject to some double counting. Persons receiving protections usually obtained at the same time power of attorney for their representatives in England; where the two documents were obtained at different dates, single individuals may have been counted twice.

associate such journeys at least roughly with foreign expenditures on official accounts, as they would be called in modern usage, since they correspond in the first instance to official expenditures on the acquisition of allies or in the second to actual military expenses abroad.

The crisis of 1337–39 was followed by a period in which the price of sterling was at prewar levels, coincident with the recovery in wool exports in 1339. But in 1343–44 there was a new crisis, in the course of which sterling was devalued[22] and gold coinage introduced for the first time since 1279. This second crisis has provoked more discussion in the litera- ture than has the one we have discussed, probably because bimetallism has long interested economists. Some comparison of the two crises is instructive.

There was a 30 percent drop in wool exports in 1343, with no evidence of a decline in the import of wine. There was an increase in private travel reported, but some of this increase may be illusory (in that merchants seem to have been more inclined than formerly to obtain royal protec- tion). Official foreign travel was low, and of course the Crecy campaign had not yet begun. An explanation in short-run terms would stress the decline in exports in 1343. In longer run terms, it would be stated that the level of exports had been low for the entire period since 1336, while imports had not fallen.

Table 1, unfortunately, gives no impression of the period 1342–44. It merely indicates that in 1345 the price of sterling was at the prewar level —which might seem odd, since its metal content had been reduced 10 percent. Table 8 indicates that the range between high and low prices of sterling was about 4 percent of par value. This range is notably less than the 15 percent variation in the preceding crisis. The general assess- ment of the literature, however, is that the second crisis was the more severe, or at least the more interesting, of the two.

Why did sterling fluctuate more widely in 1337–39 than in 1342–45? The simple-minded explanation would be this: in 1343 wool exports de- clined, but in 1337 they declined more than in 1343; also, there were important royal expenditures abroad in connection with the campaign in Flanders. Therefore, we should expect sterling to have declined more in 1337–39 than in 1343. However, this explanation raises a difficulty: if the crisis of 1337–39 was really the more serious of the two, why did devalu- ation occur in 1343–44, the "lesser" of the two crises?

The answer to this question is to be found in the foreign exchange controls of the period. Table 15 gives a history of the regulations govern- ing the export of precious metals from 1279–1346. The early part of the period is not under discussion, but it serves to establish basic policies and certain long-run tendencies. The regulations are ordinarily quite explicit; and where no specification is made, it is reasonable to conclude

---

[22] That is, the number of pennies made from a Tower pound of silver was in- creased from 243 to 270—about 10 percent.

TABLE 15

REGULATIONS ON THE EXPORT OF PRECIOUS METALS FROM ENGLAND, 1279–1346*

Calendar Year	Silver		Gold		Source
	Coin	Bullion	Coin	Bullion	
1279	F	n.s.[a]	n.s.[a]	n.s.[a]	Red Book of the Exchequer, pp 181–82
1299	L	L	N	n.s.[a]	Ruffhead, pp. 137–38
1300	L	L	N	L	CCR 18 Edw. I, p. 390
1307	L	L	N	L	CCR 35 Edw. I, p. 522; 1 Edw. II, p. 44
1324	r.e.[b]	F	N	F	CCR 17 Edw. II, p. 156
1326	F	F	F[e]	F	Ruding, I, 209
1331	F	F	N	F	CFR 5 Edw. III, pp. 251–52
1333	L	L	N	n.s.[a]	CFR 7 Edw. III, p. 347
1335	L[d]	L	N[d]	L	Ruffhead, pp. 215–17
1342	F[e]	F	N[e]	F	CCR 16 Edw. III, p. 685
1343	F	F[f]	N	n.s.[a]	Rotuli, II, 137–38
1344	L[g]	L	P	L	CCR 17 Edw. III, p. 263
1345	L	L	P	L	CCR 19 Edw. III, p. 587
1346	L	L	P	L	CCR 20 Edw. III, pp. 144, 150

* P = permitted; L = license required; F = forbidden; N = no England gold coin at this date.

[a] Not specified.

[b] "Reasonable expenses" were allowed travelers.

[c] Ruding's discussion seems questionable to me on this point.

[d] Coin for export was to be brought at the Tables of Exchange in Dover and elsewhere. CCR 9 Edw. III, pp. 514, 529.

[e] The coin of other countries, gold or silver, could be exported without license.

[f] Nobility was allowed to take out vessels of silver.

[g] Licenses were issued for new coin only. CCR 18 Edw. III, p. 457.

that no restriction existed on exports. In some cases exports are specifically allowed, and these cases have been so designated in the table. Table 16 shows a gradual extension of foreign exchange controls after 1279. At first only silver coin could not be exported, but after 1299 silver and gold bullion were also restricted. In 1324, restrictions on silver coin were briefly eased, but apparently[23] there was a complete prohibition on the export of precious metals until 1333. The 1324 regulation was apparently the occasion for the licenses recorded in Table 13. At any rate, during 1333–35 there was a brief relaxation in controls over the export of gold bullion. Licensing of gold bullion exports was in force from 1335 to 1343 but was then lifted. Export of foreign gold coin was allowed in 1342. The following year, when English gold coin was minted, the export of English gold coin (but not bullion) without license was authorized. Throughout this period, the export of silver in any form was either licensed or prohibited.

It is a commonplace of foreign exchange theory that foreign exchange rates will fluctuate if there is no convertibility. The textbook example usually given is that of countries on an inconvertible paper standard. The theory would equally well apply to countries which were on a metallic-coin standard internally, but which did not allow the import or export of precious metals. If controls are imperfectly enforced, or if some licenses are issued, movements of exchange rates will be smaller than if controls are complete.

Consequently, if we observe that the movement of gold out of England was permitted after 1343, we should predict what actually happened: that fluctuations in the sterling exchange rate would occur with smaller range than they had in the 1337–39 crisis when the export of all precious metals was licensed.

The defense of this hypothesis requires evidence on the movement, legal or illegal, of precious metals in crisis and noncrisis years. The first source of information is the *Calendar of Fine Rolls*, which contains royal injunctions to local officials that they should take appropriate action against currency violators.[24] There is a record of such royal actions over the period 1333–48.[25] In only one year of the period 1333–36 were royal

---

[23] The word "apparently" is used advisedly. In other years the qualification "except by license" appears in the calendars, and, as Table 13 shows, licenses to take coin abroad for travel expenses were certainly issued. Either the phrase escaped the notice of the editors of the Calendars, or else it was taken for granted by royal officials.

[24] The violations include illegal exports of precious metals and also failures to deliver "false" and clipped coin to the Exchange for minting. (False coin was non-English coin which resembled the penny but contained less silver. In the 1340's it was described as Lussheborne—Luxemburg—and at other dates it had other designations.)

[25] The page references for given years are: 1333, p. 347; 1337, pp. 6, 56, 60, 61; 1338, pp. 81–82; 1339, pp. 113, 135; 1341, pp. 216, 252; 1342, p. 309; 1343, pp. 318–19; 1344, pp. 357, 365; 1345, pp. 415, 443, 448; 1346, pp. 467, 474, 485; 1347, pp. 17, 18, 29, 30; 1348, pp. 67, 68.

actions taken, and in only one year of the period 1337–48 was no action taken. The king was more likely (.03) to be concerned about foreign exchange violations in wartime than in peacetime, in the sense of telling his officials to stop them. The only wartime year he took no action was 1340, which by our records was a relatively good year for wool exports.

In every crisis year (1337–39 and 1343–45) at least two royal actions were taken, while in six of the ten noncrisis years fewer than two actions were taken. Thus, the king was more likely to take two or more actions in crisis years than in noncrisis years (.05).[26]

Unfortunately, the *Calendar of Fine Rolls* entries all tell officials to stop both illegal exports and illegal imports of coin. If there were any entries which enjoined only one illegal action, we could be sure that only one illegal action was taking place. If all entries enjoin both, we cannot be sure that the document is not using a conventional legal expression.

To investigate this question, we present Table 16, which lists the reports of exchange control violations other than those reported in the *Calendar of Fine Rolls*. According to these records, illegal imports of false coin were not more likely to occur in years when there were illegal exports of sterling than in other years. If we take the entries from the *Calendar of Fine Rolls* as evidence of the simultaneous violation of both export and import regulations, and alter Table 16 accordingly, we will conclude that the two violations are more likely to occur together than separately (.01). I believe that the discrepancies between the *Calendar of Fine Rolls* and the other records point to the formula used in the *Calendar* having been a mere legalism.[27]

Table 16 shows that there is a tendency for one or the other of the two offenses to prevail in certain periods. Thus, in 1310–20 imports of false money predominated; from 1334 to 1342 illegal exports of sterling predominated; from 1345 to 1348 imports of false money predominated. In only 3 years of the 50 did the two offenses occur simultaneously, and 2 of these 3 years were in the crisis period: 1343 and 1344.

If it is profitable to perform an action illegally, it should also be profitable to perform it legally, with the king's license.[28] Consequently, we would predict that if the records on foreign exchange licensing could be

---

26 "Two actions" means "action on two occasions," for a single action often involved instructions to several local officials.

27 There is no inherent absurdity in the proposition that the two offenses might occur simultaneously. In the 20 years since 1945, there have been many occasions when a traveler from the United States could go to Canada with one silver dollar, purchase 11 Canadian dimes with it, and return to the United States to purchase $1.10 in U.S. goods with them. The 20th-century traveler would have committed no crime, while the 14th-century traveler would have placed his body and goods at the king's pleasure. The transaction described would have been profitable whether or not Canada was adding to its reserves of gold and dollars at the time.

28 The converse is not true. It may be profitable to do something if one has a license but not profitable to take the risk of capture and punishment if the act is illegal.

TABLE 16

DATA ON VIOLATIONS OF FOREIGN EXCHANGE REGULATIONS FROM
SOURCES OTHER THAN THE *Calendar of Fine Rolls,* 1300–49[*]

Calendar Year	False Money Imports	Illegal Sterling Exports	Source
1300......	X		CLB-C, p. 83; CFR, pp. 412, 509; CCW, p. 113
1301......		X	CLB-C, p. 89; CCR, p. 480
1305......	X	X	CPR, p. 341; CCR, pp. 328, 471
1307......		X	CCR, p. 522
1310......	X		CCR, p. 329
1311......	X		CFR, p. 79
1315......	X		CCR, p. 228
1317......	X		CCR, p. 448
1319......	X		CCR, pp. 123–24
1320......	X		CCR, p. 198; CPR, p. 500; CCW, p. 512
1323......		X	CCR, p. 701
1327......	X		CCR, p. 140
1334......		X	Rotuli, II, 377
1335......	X		CPR, p. 153
1337......		X	CCR, p. 76
1341......		X	Ruding, I, 213
1342......		X	Ruding, I, 214
1343......	X	X	Rotuli, II, 137, 141; CPR, pp. 81, 100, 170
1344......	X	X	Rotuli, II, 149, 155; CPR, pp. 392, 430; CCR, p. 351
1345......	X		CPR, p. 587
1346......	X		Rotuli, II, 160
1347......	X		Rotuli, II, 167; CPR, p. 303; CCR, p. 284
1348......	X		CCR, p. 492

[*] Years in which no violations were reported are omitted from this table.

tabulated, they would reveal outflow of sterling until 1342, and an inflow of silver beginning in 1345.

The output of the English mints[29] gives us some clues about the flow of silver. In years when imports of false coin were occurring, mint output was likely to be larger (specifically, over £2,000) than in other years (.05). Such a statement cannot be made with respect to years in which there were illegal exports of coin. We can thus support (though not prove) the following argument: England in the long run imported all its silver. We can associate years of illegal imports with years of high mint output; and we can, therefore, surmise an association between illegal and legal imports of silver. If we could associate years of illegal coin exports with years of high mint output, we could associate illegal exports with reduced English demand for cash balances. Since we cannot, we must look to balance-of-payments situations for an explanation of the illegal

[29] Harry A. Miskimin, *Money, Prices and Foreign Exchange in Fourteenth Century France* (New Haven: Yale University Press, 1963), Appendix B.

exports. Owing to the lack of data on wool exports (the customs were farmed) and imports alike in the 1340's, we cannot be as sure about trade at that time as in the preceding decade.

We may make one final observation. Comparing Tables 12 and 16, we may say that in years in which there were illegal exports of coin, the king was more likely to issue two or more licenses to export coin (for travel expenses) than in years in which there were no such illegal exports. This statement might merely mean that both legal and illegal export of coin increased in years when there was more foreign travel. It might also mean something more interesting. Suppose that travelers had an option of buying a letter of exchange or of applying for a license to take out coin. Then in years when the sterling exchange rate was low, applications for licenses would be relatively large, while in years when the sterling rate was high, travelers would use the letters.

The second possibility seems to be ruled out by a comparison of Tables 13 and 16. For we know that sterling declined in 1337, and we should expect that the monastic orders would have applied for more, rather than fewer, licenses in 1337–39 than formerly.[30] But if the king used these licenses as an instrument of foreign exchange control (as he would today), then the drop in licenses would be explained by a desire of the king to reduce the outflow of coin rather than by any failure of the monastic orders to realize the desirability of using coin rather than letters of exchange.

The evidence we have discussed suggests that the appearance of illegal imports of false coin in 1343 can be explained by the devaluation of silver. They point to an excess demand for silver beginning at that time. Excess demand is a sign that prices are below equilibrium levels. Walras has shown, of course, that the sum of excess demands and supplies in an economic system must be zero. The excess demand for silver, then, would have to be accompanied by an excess supply of goods and/or gold. Our data on commodity trade suggest a trade deficit rather than a surplus, and we can conclude there must have been an excess supply of gold in the mid-1340's. That is, gold was leaving the country, because the price of gold coin in England was above equilibrium levels.

This view has been expressed before,[31] in connection with the conclusion that the price of English gold coin should have been lowered so as to keep gold coin in circulation. We suggest that the monetary policy aimed precisely at having the gold used to cover a balance-of-payments deficit without a corresponding reduction in the (silver) domestic money supply. (We are certainly not expressing the policy in 14th-century

---

[30] The only reference to the prohibition on the use of letters of exchange by the alien priories relates, as noted in an earlier footnote, to 1304–7; by the 1330's they seem to have been using letters.

[31] Craig, pp. 66–69; Ruding, Vol. I, pp. 217–19; Ramsay (cited in Table 9), Vol. I, p. 339; Hughes, Crump, and Johnson, "The Debasement of the Coinage under Edward III," *Economic Journal,* Vol. VII (1897), p. 197.

terminology.) In support of this view we cite (1) the permission to export gold coin, after 1342; (2) the provision, in 1343, that merchant importers should be paid in gold coin;[32] (3) the provision, in 1342, that wool exporters should accept payment in Flemish silver;[33] (4) the provision that wool exporters should sell imported bullion to the Exchange in proportion to their exports;[34] and (5) the general interest in parliament (on which all sources agree) in trying to confine the use of gold to mercantile transactions in international trade. The consequence of this policy was, of course, that exchange rates in the 1340's fluctuated much less than in 1337–39, and we suggest that such a reduction may have been one of the objectives of monetary policy.

In time, of course, gold came to be part of the English monetary system, but in the 1340's it may well have been considered as merely a useful means of stabilizing exchange rates without reductions in the money (silver) supply, or even as a means of increasing the money (silver) supply in a period of deflation—as we should now call it.

---

[32] *Rotuli,* Vol. II, p. 138.

[33] *CCR,* 16 Edw. III, p. 415.

[34] Ruding, p. 213, states that in 1340 two marks of silver were to be imported per sack of wool exported. I have not found any other source for this statement. In 1343, silver exports were to be one third of the value of exports (*Rotuli,* II, 138). This provision, in some form, lasted until 1348, when the Flemish instituted a similar regulation, thereby forcing the English to abandon it.

2. The United States Business Cycle before 1860: Some Problems of Interpretation*

Jonathan R. T. Hughes and Nathan Rosenberg

Purdue University

I

THIS PAPER is prompted by the dissatisfaction of the authors with the state of the economic history of business fluctuations in the U.S. up to 1860. The existing literature dealing with the historical origins of business fluctuations is, we feel, dominated by sweeping generalizations which, as they stand, are open to serious question by the student of business cycles or teacher of American economic history.[1] Even the best of the "general" explanations are largely unsupported by empirical data and can only be regarded, at best, as interesting assertions. Needless to say, a major portion of our difficulties must be attributed to the absence of detailed quantitative studies such as have illuminated much of British history in recent years, and have contributed so much to an understanding of crucial aspects of that country's economic development.[2]

The inadequacy of the available data is, of course, a serious handicap, and efforts to improve and expand them ought to be accorded the highest priority. Most of the published data for the pre-1914 period are not only

* Reprinted from the *Economic History Review,* Second Series, Vol. XV, No. 3 (1963), pp. 476–93.

[1] While it may be true that there also exists no single, empirically verified, "theory" of the business cycle, we think that the theorist has a range of freedom in the assignment of "cause" that the economic historian does not have in this matter. It is, after all, quite a different matter to say "this might happen" as the theorist does, than to say "this did happen" as the economic historian does. Thus we think the shortcomings of business-cycle theory constitute no valid excuse for the shortcomings of economic history in the matter of the history of business cycles. Business-cycle theory is only a small and eccentric part of the body of economic theory. The economic historian is not limited to business-cycle theory for his analytical tools.

[2] R. C. O. Matthews' *A Study of Trade Cycle History* (Cambridge, Eng.: Cambridge University Press, 1954) may be taken as an example of the best of the recent British literature.

annual but are so highly aggregated as to be quite unsatisfactory as a set of indicators unless supported, at the very least, by detailed study and analysis of individual economic sectors and geographic regions over shorter periods of time. It is scarcely necessary to belabor the obvious fact that business fluctuations have not occurred instantaneously at the end of calendar years, with all industrial sectors and geographic regions moving, in lockstep, from cycle phase to cycle phase. What is needed to remedy this weakness is to undertake, as extensively as possible, a dis-aggregation of the existing data with respect to time intervals, economic sectors and geographic regions. Until such information concerning the interstices of the economic process becomes available, we must either (1) develop highly "schematic" and hypothetical analyses, based upon some combination of existing theory and inadequate empirical materials, (2) remain silent, or (3) confine our analyses to what can be extracted from the existing data.

It is with the last procedure that we are primarily concerned in this paper. We have asked ourselves whether anything can be done to squeeze more information from the small supply of annual data which is now available. It is certainly possible to establish what these data do not permit us to say about the cycle, and this is primarily what we have attempted in the following pages. In order to do this, we have chosen the period from the 1820's to 1860 for study. We have made a very general, plausible hypothesis into a "null" hypothesis. We thus have new information, even though much of it is in negative form.

We began with the hypothesis that data on "internal improvements" (which comprise the main body of investment data known to us for the period) might be expected to show some cyclical characteristics, i.e., that they will either lead, or conform to, the cycle, but will not be contra-cyclical. The hypothesis was based upon the assumption that significant changes in income would be generated by these initial investment ex-penditures (multiplied by some expansion coefficient). The data are plotted on simple arithmetic scales to see if they move in conformity with the business cycle as it is known to us through the efforts of the National Bureau of Economic Research (N.B.E.R.). This method is crude in the extreme, but it is in accord with the quality of the data. Similarly, we plotted data for the balance of trade on the basis of certain assumptions (below) as to how it might be expected to behave over the course of the cycle. Finally, we performed a similar operation on the federal budget. The results are surprising and, we think, serve to underscore a serious need for a complete reappraisal of the economic history of American business fluctuations before 1860.

II

As the first step in our analysis, we will examine the existing general explanations of the pre–Civil War business cycle. For the most part, they fall into three categories which have sometimes been mixed together: (1) overspeculation, (2) reckless or excessive financial expansions, (3) the cycles were imported. We will treat each of these briefly.

1. The cloudy phrase "overspeculation" doubtless entered into the literature of business-cycle history because of the dutiful attention paid by historians to the on-the-spot analyses of cause and effect given by financial journalists. Nineteenth-century journalists were fond of this phrase, and it evidently was intended to mean that there was something illegitimate about the credit transactions in any expansion which could not be honored in the subsequent business contraction. Moreover, it was speculation which pushed expansions and the unsoundness of that speculation which made it impossible for the expansions to be maintained. Retrospectively, "speculators" were simply former "businessmen" who could not meet their obligations. This view of the expansion phase of the cycle may be illustrated by the treatment of 1837 in a recent textbook, and of 1857 by the concluding remarks of a monograph on the crisis of 1857. On 1837:

. . . rapidly rising prices of the new land being opened up in the United States unleashed a wild speculative boom. When the panic of 1837 arrived, the collapse affected not only private speculators, but many of the states. . . .[3]

On 1857:

The changes that were brought about because of the overexpansion in railroads and other enterprises and the halting of this expansion because of the panic helped to bring about a self-correction.[4]

Such phraseology need not be applied to each expansion and crisis separately; here they are simply lumped together:

Both panics followed periods of widespread speculation, much unsound banking, general overtrading, and the promotion of numerous large and costly undertakings such as new canals and railroads.[5]

Similarly:

As in 1837, so in 1857, overproduction, too great speculation, too much tying up of capital in fixed improvements or investments led to a financial crisis.[6]

In a noted recent work it would almost appear that all commercial activity was unethical and self-destructive in the 1830's:

Besides overtrading in government lands, 'speculations in unimproved town lots, mines, and every description of rash undertakings increased at the same

---

[3] George Soule and Vincent P. Carosso, *American Economic History* (New York: Dryden Press, 1957), p. 97.

[4] G. W. Van Vleck, *The Panic of 1857* (New York: Columbia Press, 1943), p. 107.

[5] Leonard P. Ayres, *Turning Points in Business Cycles* (New York: Macmillan Co., 1939), p. 18.

[6] Blanche E. Hazard, *The Organization of the Boot and Shoe Industry in Massachusetts Before 1875* (Cambridge, Mass.: Harvard University Press, 1921), p. 103.

rate'. The Jacksonian democracy was everywhere absorbed in schemes to make money hand over fist. The whole economy was in a fever of excitement and expansion, stimulated by streams of immigrants and capital goods pouring in from Europe.[7]

Now precisely what do such statements tell us about the analysis of expansion and contraction of economic activity?

Two points may be made here. (1) Since effective demand in a recession was less than effective demand at the peak of the previous expansion, all businesses whose markets were not invariant with respect to current income encountered difficulties in realizing credits which had been based upon the rising levels of income which prevailed during the expansionary phase of the cycle. This was so regardless of how "sound" such transactions were at the time they were made. The future was misjudged. It was not simply the marginal speculators, or the worst offenders of a Schumpeterian "secondary wave," who were caught. For only the strongest liquidity positions could possibly enable merchants to pay for, and carry, their unsold stocks at a time when bank credit was drastically reduced. (2) In any case, it cannot be seriously entertained that a rise in investment, by itself, caused income to fall, and "speculation," even if it meant only commodity speculation, was investment. (Only if there was nothing but juggling of inventories at inflated prices, and only if these inventories were withheld from production, and could not be replaced, would speculation cause output to fall.) However, if a great part of all credit purchases which had been based upon expectations of a rise in demand

---

[7] Bray Hammond, *Banks and Politics in America* (Princeton, 1957), p. 453. Our survey of the literature on the uses of one variant or the other of "over" with regard to the level of real or monetary transactions in the cycle cannot be given completely in this place. Following is a short bibliography ranging from monographs, old and new, to textbooks, old and new, with the relevant pages listed for the period 1820–60. Both general "over" activity and "over" banking are here included. J. S. Gibbons, *The Banks of New York and the Panic of 1857* (New York, 1858), pp. 369–70; William G. Sumner, *A History of the American Currency* (New York: Henry Holt and Co., 1874), pp. 79–80, 84, 90, 118, 124, 132–43, 152, 185–86; A. Barton Hepburn, *History of Coinage and Currency in the United States* (New York, 1903), pp. 122, 163, 166, 170; Ira Ryner, "On the Crises of 1837, 1847, and 1857," *University of Nebraska Studies*, 1905, Vol. V., esp. p. 143; F. W. Taussig, *Tariff History of the United States* (New York, 1914), p. 117; Charles J. Bullock, John H. Williams, and Rufus Tucker, "The Balance of Trade of the United States," *Review of Economic Statistics*, 1919, Vol. I, p. 218; Margaret G. Myers, *The New York Money Market*, Vol. I (New York: Columbia University Press, 1931), pp. 30, 53, 54, 201–02; Leland H. Jenks, *The Migration of British Capital to 1875* (New York: Knopf, 1938), pp. 87–88, 118; Ayres, *loc. cit.* and pp. 9, 15; H. U. Faulkner, *American Economic History* (6th ed.; New York: Harper & Bros., 1949), pp. 167–68; G. R. Taylor, *The Transportation Revolution* (New York: Rinehart, 1951), pp. 340–50; Harold Somers in H. F. Williamson (ed.), *The Growth of the American Economy* (New York: Prentice-Hall, 1955), pp. 319–24; H. E. Krooss, *American Economic Development* (New York: Prentice-Hall, 1955), pp. 31–33; Soule and Carosso, *loc. cit.* and p. 162. Among those who have not accepted the overspeculation (monetary or real) aphorisms without critical and qualifying comment, one may cite; Thomas S. Berry, *Western Prices Before 1861* (Harvard, 1943), esp. pp. 469, 517–26.

actually found no market, the absence of such a market could scarcely be attributed to the previous *rise* in expenditures. Something real must have declined, offsetting the rise in so-called speculative expenditures, in order for the market to contract. That "something," whether it be investment, consumption, exports, or the government sector, was necessarily independent of the rise in speculative expenditures. Hence, "excessive speculation" by itself tells us nothing except that expenditures rose during the expansion phase. Unless we know why such transactions were not profitable in the end, we know nothing about the causes of the downturn which followed the speculation.

2. Loose financial methods, "reckless overbanking," "monetary over-investment," and so forth, were also great favorites of 19th-century journalists. These too have been absorbed uncritically into the literature as if they were actually explanations of the causes of business fluctuations. One of the better and more widely used textbooks reads as follows on the crisis of 1837:

The crisis of 1837 represents another instance of monetary over-investment coupled with unfavourable exogenous developments.[8]

On 1857 the same book says:

The crisis of 1857 again was dominated by monetary over-investment with both domestic and foreign exogenous factors operating.[9]

A noted classic attributes the expansion of the 1830's and the crisis of 1837 to speculation of all sorts, a "paper money mania" and, on the 1857 crisis, states that the currency was "recognized as the root of the trouble."[10] Those works specializing in monetary history mostly emphasize banking difficulties to the virtual exclusion of industry, trade, commerce, and agriculture. Even where the scope is broadened it usually is ambiguous. A peculiar circumstance of this sort in the literature relates to the role of the movement of specie in 1836–37 when the federal surplus was distributed among the states. It is agreed that this factor had disturbing effects. But what and how? While one author says gold flowed from the eastern cities to rural areas,[11] thus draining the eastern monetary cities of funds, another author has it that the gold moved from the West to the eastern cities causing a monetary contraction in the rural areas.[12] Can they both be correct? Did the gold move both ways? A third eminent authority simply says that the gold moved about and the effects were disturbing.[13] However, these are side issues. In both the 1830's and the

---

[8] Somers in Williamson (ed.), *op. cit.*, p. 319.

[9] *Ibid.*, p. 322.

[10] Sumner, *op. cit.*, pp. 320–21.

[11] Taylor, *op. cit.*, p. 342.

[12] Somers in Williamson (ed.), *op. cit.*, pp. 320–21.

[13] Hammond, *op. cit.*, pp. 453–57.

1850's the expansions and crises were, to the monetary people, mainly due to overbanking, excessive credit and so forth.[14]

But what do such phrases mean? Consider two variants, (*a*) monetary overinvestment and (*b*) all other excessive credit extensions. Monetary overinvestment either means simply that the banking system put so much money into circulation that, for some reason, the economy floundered in a sea of banknotes, or, alternatively, that there was a rapid growth of real investment supported by bank credit which, again for "some reason," could not be maintained. But what precisely was this "some reason"? The argument seems to be based upon a sort of gravitational law of banking, that expansions supported by a banking system necessarily breed their own contractions. Perhaps this is so, but it is not immediately obvious, and it can scarcely be said to constitute an explanation of the cyclical downturn until the specific intermediate steps in the causal chain are carefully spelled out. Clearly, further growth, monetary overinvestment, is not itself the terminating agent. With respect to *what* is the investment over or excessive?[15] What is the "over" in overinvestment? Tedious though it may be, it is useful to recall that the banking system *as a whole* is not liquid, that *any* expansion of the monetary system will be found excessive if that expansion occurs within the framework of a fractional-reserve banking system and if holders of debt obligations press for payment in sufficiently large numbers.

The more general and even less useful variant of the "financial excesses" explanation implies simply that bankers and merchants were fools and/or incompetents, and that therefore their credit activities were doomed to fail and to bring the sound part of the economy down with them. These foolish or ill-conceived activities could be either purely domestic in scope or they could involve (gullible) foreigners. But if credit ventures turned out to be so foolish, why exactly was this so? The proposition that men are fallible (and some more so than others), while scarcely open to dispute, is not very helpful in accounting for a particular cyclical downturn.

3. There are, finally, explanations which argue that the cycle was

---

[14] Schumpeter attributes the *violence* of the 1836–39 crisis, as well as its aftermath, to "wildcat banking." Joseph A. Schumpeter, *Business Cycles* (New York: McGraw-Hill, 1939), Vol. I, pp. 295, 299–300. Within Schumpeter's larger analytical schema, however, such factors as wildcat banking and overspeculation are mere epiphenomena, superimposed upon the more fundamental rhythms of economic activity resulting from innovation. "On the surface, it was not the effects of the innovations on the economic structure that caused the trouble—and, in fact, they did not cause the *crisis*—but simply over-commitments, inconvenient calls on shares, failure of expected returns to materialize, unfavourable gold movements incident to foreign financing, and so on. Hence, it is perfectly understandable that students who look mainly to the mechanism of crises, should develop a propensity for monetary explanations, for quite naturally the mechanism of money and credit will be the first thing to reflect all this and to be affected by it" (p. 300).

[15] For a challenging definition of overspeculation see Sumner, *op. cit.,* p. 124.

imported.[16] Such analyses, however, must contend with similar statements that foreign countries imported their cycles from the U.S.A. Nevertheless, this position has the single virtue that it is plausible. Moreover, it does more than merely shift the blame elsewhere. For example, if before 1860 the volume of investment in the U.S.A. was critically dependent upon the availability of credit in the London capital market, and that in turn, via Britain's balance of payments, was partly determined by Britain's terms of trade, then the relative abundance of raw materials would, through the price-cost relationship, provide a remote source of fluctuations which could be subjected to empirical investigation. At the present time there is no serious analysis along these lines of the internal relationships within the Anglo-American economy.[17] We possess only conflicting and inconclusive statements regarding the source of origin and direction of transmission of business cycles. These problems warrant much further investigation but cannot, unfortunately, be pursued here.

Forms (1) and (2) of the general analyses of expansion and crisis in the American economy are frequently found together and, so conjoined, may be restated briefly. Prosperity was generally characterized by periods of feverish optimism (*why* such optimism prevailed when it did is usually not explained) during which time the country's permissive credit mechanism underpinned a rapid expansion of speculative investment in western lands, canal and railroad construction, etc. These periods were generally terminated by a failure of the credit mechanism to continue the expansion, leading to a "collapse of the speculative bubble," "prostration of the economy," etc. Now it is clearly integral to these discussions that prosperity periods were characterized by a rapid growth of real investment, and that upper turning points and recession phases were characterized by a sudden decline in real investment. Indeed, without such variations, at least by implication, the overspeculation and monetary overinvestment theses would be devoid of any substantive economic content whatever.

---

[16] The most noted one of these perhaps is that of W. B. Smith and A. H. Cole, *Fluctuations in American Business, 1790–1860* (Harvard, 1935). They also employ variations of the phrases noted above. But they do offer evidence that the foreign element was a source of cyclical disturbances in this early period when U.S. foreign trade was larger in proportion to national income than it was in later years. For example: ". . . viewing the whole period, 1820–45, one is impressed with the frequency with which the course of domestic commodity values manifested response—more or less belated—to movements abroad" (p. 67). This pioneering work might well have been the origin of a revolution in the study of the economic history of business cycles in the United States had it been followed up by similar studies.

[17] Cf., however, George Macesich, "Sources of Monetary Disturbances in the U.S., 1834–1845," *Journal of Economic History* (September, 1960), pp. 407–426. Macesich argued that American bimetallism acted precisely like a pure gold standard in a country whose banks maintained stable, uniform bank reserves. For exchange-rate data to support this argument the *prices* of bills of exchange were used, unadjusted for interest-rate discounts. There is no source given for the bank-reserve data and the evidence given and the conclusions drawn are widely at variance. We can do no more here than refer to Rondo Cameron's comments on the article in *Economic History Review*, April, 1962, p. 601.

We propose to show, among other things, that even the meanings we have attributed here to the overspeculation and monetary overinvestment theses are not borne out by the investment data available to us.

We do not want to be misunderstood as arguing that monetary factors and, especially, the peculiarities of the credit system, were of no significance in the pre–Civil War years. Rather, we are insisting (1) that there has been an excessive and rather naïve preoccupation with value judgments about the profit motive and with purely monetary phenomena, (2) that, as a corollary of (1), the relationships between monetary and real factors have been insufficiently explored, and (3) that, as will be demonstrated below, the available data on the behavior of real investment are of such a nature as to justify a complete rejection of existing analyses, at least in their present forms.

A final word might be said regarding the received literature. As it stands it is probably a gross distortion of American economic history. The economic historian seems to have become stuck at a stage which marked the beginning of investigation into business-cycle theory. Early business-cycle theory concentrated upon finding a suitable explanation of the periodic crisis. Later, of course, as the study of business cycles became concerned with the properties of the whole range of the cycle, trough to trough (peak to peak), the phenomenon of the crisis was no longer the center of focus. Economic historians however, when they do comment on the business cycle, still limit themselves almost exclusively to the great crises and ignore the intervening fluctuations. Thus in American economic historiography leading up to 1860 there are many accounts of the expansions leading up to the crises of 1837 and 1857, but the expansions preceding the peaks of 1839, 1845, 1847, 1853, and 1860 are scarcely given any analytical treatment whatever. A necessary result of this concentration on the two great crises of the antebellum period is a warped and unrealistic view of American economic development in the period, a view which nearly uniformly holds that expansions, whether monetary or real, were dangerous, reckless, criminal, and wasteful. All one needs, on logical grounds, to abandon virtually the whole of this literature is a view that fluctuations in economic activity are the consequences of justifiable (i.e., initially profitable) expansions blocked by structural maladjustments—not unlike the events of 1957–58. Where were the reckless speculators, etc. five years ago? Or is it assumed to be the case that only modern cyclical variations have been economic phenomena, whereas the earlier cycles were primarily moral problems?

III

We turn now to an examination of the data for internal improvements and the hypothesis that these contributed to cyclical fluctuations. We compare movements of these data with the statistics of net railway mileage, the federal government's budget, the foreign balance of trade, and the pattern of reference-cycle dates established by the National Bureau of Economic Research.[18]

An additional question involves the role of government in initiating the cyclical pattern. Most of the great internal improvements in this period—roads, canals, and railways—were dependent, either wholly or in part, upon government (federal, state, or local) financial assistance of some sort. Important detailed studies of state and local governments done by economic historians in recent years point unmistakably to the conclusion that governments played a crucial role in American development in the antebellum period through their assistance to the financing of the country's major "social overhead" investments.[19] Can it be inferred then, that "government," through the variations in expenditures on development projects, was also partly responsible for the pattern of the business cycle? This question, as well as the more general one concerning the role in business fluctuations of expenditures on internal improvements before 1860, can be answered provisionally on the basis of available data.

The sources for the data we have examined in this study include old and modern secondary works, official statistics and some unpublished manuscript materials.[20] It should be noted that the data which we have used are not complete. We have examined the major areas of the national economy for which data are readily available in the years 1820–60. Perhaps some day it will be possible to compute "total" figures for the

---

[18] A. F. Burns and W. C. Mitchell, *Measuring Business Cycles* (New York, 1946), pp. 78–79 and chaps. 2–4.

[19] This is not meant to imply that a uniform pattern of governmental assistance and responsibility existed throughout the country. On the contrary, one of the most interesting aspects of these antebellum studies is the complete demolition of all dogmatic generalizations which were formerly the stock-in-trade of historians in describing the relationship between government and private enterprise in the United States. There appear to have been very few preconceptions or rigid definitions concerning the proper role of government in economic affairs; least of all, it appears from these studies, was there any massive public commitment to the ideal of laissez-faire. Rather, it seems everywhere to have been taken for granted that public institutions bore a major responsibility, through assistance and even direct participation where necessary, for the growth and vigorous development of the economy. The precise form which such assistance took was subject to enormous variation, and state and local governments showed a remarkable flexibility in adapting themselves to local conditions and special needs.

The literature on this subject is now very extensive, and in order to save space the reader is referred to the works cited by Carter Goodrich in "Recent Contributions to Economic History: The United States, 1789–1860," *Journal of Economic History,* March, 1959, especially pp. 25–30. In addition to these recent works, the early article by Callender, may still be cited as perhaps the best introduction to the period. G. S. Callender, "The Early Transportation and Banking Enterprises of the States in Relation to the Growth of Corporations," *Quarterly Journal of Economics,* Vol. XVII (November, 1902), pp. 111–62.

[20] We are especially indebted to Dr. Harvey Segal for permission to use materials from his unpublished dissertation: *Canal Cycles, 1834–1861: Public Construction Experience in New York, Pennsylvania and Ohio,* deposited in the Butler Library at Columbia University.

investment and expenditure sectors we are examining. However, the fact that such totals do not now exist is hardly sufficient reason to abstain from using the data for our purposes—with the necessary qualifications.

Our main conclusion may be stated briefly: except for railway construction, knowledge of movements in expenditures for internal improvements do not contribute to our understanding of the *origins* of fluctuations before 1860. Nor do government expenditures in general contribute to this. If students of the business cycle are ever to tell us the origins of the U.S. business cycle before 1860, our conclusions, by reducing the number of possible sources of cyclical variations in expenditures, may at least be helpful in indicating to such students where they ought *not* to look.

IV

During the years 1820–60 fluctuations in the path of American economic growth manifested themselves in considerable variations in internal activity as well as in changes in the external balance.[21] Not all of the fluctuations were of equal importance in this regard, and the path of American internal growth determined which of these fluctuations, or groups of them, had the strongest income effects abroad.

The evidence indicates that, in broad terms, the American development between 1820 and 1860 was most rapid during the 1830's and 1850's. In both of these periods investment in internal improvements—in canals, roads, and, finally, in railways—played a dominant role in accelerating the rate of economic growth. Most important from a shorter run point of view, investment in these sectors generated incomes and helped to induce further investments on a broader scale. Since the U.S.A. was in this period something of an underdeveloped country, and was undergoing an acceleration in its industrial growth, an increased tempo in domestic activity was accompanied by sharp expansions in the importation of goods from abroad. Under these circumstances, we would expect the U.S. balance of payments to perform in the conventional manner for an underdeveloped country, with current-account deficits piling up during the periods of most rapid growth, and smaller deficits or even surpluses (especially the latter in view of the drastic secular increase in primary product exports—particularly cotton[22]—to Britain and the rest of Europe) accumulating during periods of relative quiescence on the American scene.

We find that this is, in fact, a useful first approximation.[23] However,

---

[21] Smith and Cole, *op. cit.* secs. II and III; *Historical Statistics of the U.S.* (Washington, D.C.: U.S. Government Printing Office, 1949), Series M42–55.

[22] For the period 1815–60 raw cotton alone accounted for over one half the value of total American domestic exports. Taylor, *op. cit.*, Appendix A, Table 11.

[23] Professor Douglass North's recent revised estimates of the U.S. balance of payments to 1860 show general results similar to those in the text above. In North's estimates strong current-account deficits develop in the 1830's and 1850's (taking gold shipments into account). Douglass C. North, "The U.S. Balance of Payments,

in the 1850's the U.S.A. became a major gold producer and exporter,[24] and, counting gold as a commodity, the current account, even if absolutely dependable data were available, would not be expected to fluctuate in so uniform a manner. This difficulty (in addition to the problems connected with the use of various current estimates) disappears if we apply the same logic to the U.S. balance of merchandise trade. Net U.S. earnings on "invisibles" were evidently not of major significance since the pattern described above did in fact obtain with reasonable uniformity until the 1870's, by which time the growth of American capacity to supply its own capital goods removed this indicator of economic growth.

CHART I

U.S. BALANCE OF MERCHANDISE TRADE

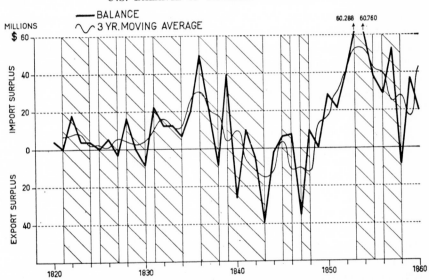

SOURCE: *Historical Statistics of U.S., 1789–1945*, Washington, D.C.: (U.S. G.P.O., 1949).

In Chart I the trade balance is plotted and "smoothed." On the basis of the discussion above, Chart I,* and the "Reference Cycle" dates established by the N.B.E.R. (below) we hypothesize that the most important investment booms of the period centered upon the import peaks of 1836–39 and 1853–56, with the necessary leads and lags taken into account. Furthermore, it is apparent that the international income effects of variations in American economic activity were strongly felt in Great

---

1790–1860," in *Studies in Income and Wealth*, Vol. 24, *Trends in the American Economy in the Nineteenth Century* (Princeton, N.J.: Princeton University Press, 1960), pp. 573–627.

[24] *Historical Statistics of U.S., op. cit.*, Series U 4–6.

* Shaded areas in the charts are the years of cyclical contractions; 1834–60 from the National Bureau of Economic Research; dates from 1820 to 1833 are our own estimates.

Britain on the expansion side in the mid-1830's and 1850's (in the latter case actually from 1844 onward) and on the contraction or stagnation side in the early 1840's.

V

Against this general background we will now examine certain major areas of expenditures in the domestic economy. Here we need more specific dates and we fall back upon convenient authority—the National Bureau of Economic Research. We find initially a distinct contracyclical pattern in the federal budget. In the later sections we find: (1) variations in railway construction and road building tended to support the expansion of the 1830's, the mid-1840's and the 1850's and to contribute to the stagnation of the early 1840's, (2) the pattern of expenditures on canals and other internal improvements was such as to intensify the expansion of the 1830's and 1850's, and to contribute to the contraction of the early 1840's. The turning points for these processes, concerning which we maintain a strict agnosticism, would be in the general neighborhoods of the reference-cycle dates of the N.B.E.R.[25]

Peaks	*Troughs*
1836	1834
1839	1838
1845	1843
1847	1846
1853	1848
1856	1855
1860	1858

In examining the role of federal government expenditures, we deal first with expenditures from this source which were devoted to the construction of roads and canals. These expenditures were small by comparison with expenditures for similar purposes by state governments (below). Federal expenditures on roads and canals appear to have conformed rather closely to fluctuations in general business activity. To judge the cyclical and contracyclical effects of these data we are interested in first-order differences (plotted, Chart II).

Chart II is to be interpreted in two ways. First, all points above the zero line represent increases in expenditures, and all points below the zero line represent decreases. Second, the vertical distances between points on either side of the zero line represent, *ceteris paribus,* changes in the extent of expansionary or contractionary effects compared to earlier points on the same side of the zero line. For example, in 1839 government expenditures in this area were still declining, but the effects were less contractionary than they had been in 1838. Hence, all upward movements below the zero line represent tendencies for the government's expendi-

---

[25] *Measuring Business Cycles, op. cit.,* pp. 78–79.

CHART II
CHANGES IN FEDERAL EXPENDITURES ON ROADS AND CANALS (in dollars)

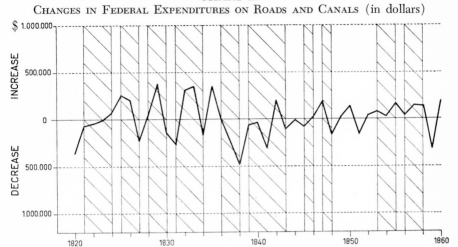

SOURCE: *Historical Statistics of U.S., op. cit.*

tures to be less contractionary than before, etc. We find here that the government expanded its outlays on roads and canals in 9 out of the 18 years of business expansion, and reduced the amount of the decrease in expenditures in 3 years. In the 22 years of business contraction, the government reduced its expenditures on roads and canals in 11 years and cut the amount of the increase in 2 years. Slightly more than half of the time, then, the government's expenditures on roads and canals conformed to cyclical movements. In the boom of the mid-1830's and in the downturns of 1837–38 and 1840–43 there is a clear tendency for these expenditures to move in cyclical fashion.

When we turn to an examination of the gross federal budget we are confronted with a drastically altered situation. Although, as we have just seen, federal expenditures on roads and canals tended to be cyclical, such tendencies were completely swamped by the impact of the overall federal budget whose effects were, to a striking extent, contracyclical.

The federal budget will be judged to have an expansionary effect on the economy when, *ceteris paribus,* (1) it runs to deficits, (2) the deficits are enlarged or not reduced, and (3) the surpluses are reduced. The budget will be judged to have a contractionary effect when, *ceteris paribus,* (1) it runs to surpluses, (2) the surpluses are enlarged or not reduced, and (3) the deficits are reduced. The budget results are plotted in Chart III.

Certain interesting facts emerge clearly from an examination of Chart III. It is immediately apparent that the federal budget was, on balance, decidedly contracyclical in its impact on the economy.[26] With the excep-

---

[26] For reasons noted above this conclusion is doubtlessly less strong on the surplus side in the mid-1830's than would appear from movements in the raw data.

CHART III
Total Federal Receipts and Expenditures

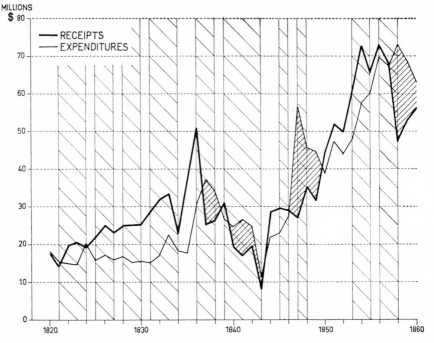

tion of the years 1847–49, when deficits were incurred in financing the Mexican War, the periods of significant government deficits occurred in the depressed years following the cyclical peaks of 1836, 1839, and 1856, i.e., in the years 1837–38, 1840–43, and 1857–60. On the other hand, during the two great periods of business expansion which culminated in the years 1836 and 1856 we find continuous surpluses in the budget of the federal government (in point of fact, the federal budget maintained a surplus throughout the years 1825–36 and 1850–57).

The reasons for what might, retrospectively, be regarded as most commendable behavior on the part of the federal budget, are easily elucidated. Basically, the explanation is that the major revenue sources of the federal government were extremely sensitive to fluctuations in business activity, rising sharply during business expansions and declining precipitously during contractions. Federal expenditures, on the other hand, were less sensitive to such variations, in most cases following with a lag and within a narrower range the direction of movement in federal revenues.[27] These revenues were derived overwhelmingly from customs

---

[27] During the periods when the federal budget was running a constant surplus, it seems to have been the growing volume of government receipts which provided the inducement to increase expenditures—in an effort to eliminate the surplus. This point

duties. Revenue from the sale of public lands was next in order of importance but of a far smaller order of magnitude.[28]

Because federal revenues were derived almost entirely from customs duties and land sales, and because revenue from these sources, as is to be expected, moved in close conformity with the business cycle, large surpluses were built up in the years preceding 1837[29] and 1857, and were rapidly converted into substantial deficits as revenues began to decline. Thus, federal revenues jumped from $21,800,000 to $35,400,000 and then to $50,800,000 in the years 1834, 1835, and 1836, respectively, and then plummeted to $25,000,000 in 1837. Since at the same time expenditures rose to a peak in 1837, the federal surplus of almost $20,000,000 in 1836 was converted into a deficit of $12,300,000 in 1837.

The pattern just described is not, of course, uniformly observable in each of the smaller cycles which have been identified during the 1820–60 period. However, the federal budget was clearly contractionary during the great swings of capital formation in the 1830's and 1850's and generally expansionary during the relatively depressed periods of the late 1830's, early 1840's, and late 1850's. During these periods, therefore, it may be regarded as a factor which limited the severity of the depressions and may have played an important role in inducing the subsequent recoveries. On the other hand, with respect to the more intensive periods of capital formation already cited, the evidence is plain that such periods were not stimulated by an expansionary federal budget. Beyond such general observations, the absence of any reliable GNP data unfortunately makes it impossible to evaluate the role of the federal budget in these matters with any pretense at quantitative precision.

VI

On the level of state and local government expenditures and for total railroad building we have a number of representative, and highly significant, series. Two of these, railway mileage in operation and miles of surfaced roads, "represent" investment outlays, the units being miles.

---

has been made, in rather partisan fashion, as follows: "By prodigality in all fields except that of internal improvements, by the elevation of extravagance and political graft to the status of open government policy, the Jackson administration lifted the total of Federal expenditure, despite the disappearance of a $3,000,000 interest item, from $16,000,000 to $37,000,000 between 1828 and 1837. Still, these expenditures could not catch up with the income that bloated the federal Treasury." W. J. Schultz and M. R. Caine, *Financial Development of the United States* (New York: Prentice-Hall, 1937), p. 217.

[28] The year 1836, when the phenomenal volume of public land sales boosted revenue from this source to an amount slightly in excess of customs receipts, was quite exceptional.

[29] The budgetary surpluses accumulated in the years after 1825 were, of course, intimately connected with the notorious episode of tariff revision associated with the period. See Taussig, *op. cit.*, esp. pp. 68–108.

Changes in these represent annual additions to mileage,[30] but since these are cumulative time series (i.e., they rise in every year) we are interested in the second-order differences in evaluating the cyclical effects of investment in these sectors. The annual data are plotted in Chart IV.

CHART IV

RAILWAY MILEAGE AND MILES OF SURFACED ROADS ADDED

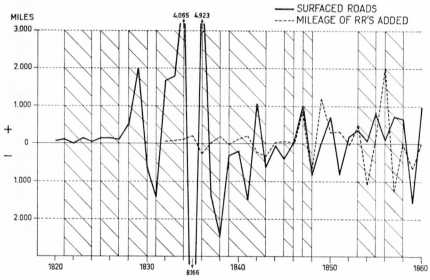

SOURCE: *Historical Statistics of U.S., op. cit.*

Chart IV is interpreted in generally the same manner as Chart II. From 1831 to 1836 the building of surfaced roads increased at an increasing rate in every year except 1835 when a sharp decline in the rate of growth occurred. Railway mileage rose steadily from 1832 to 1836. The cyclical slump of 1837 is strongly evident in new miles added in both series, whereas the 1839 recovery is evident only slightly in a reduced rate of decline in surfaced road building. Both series reflect the depression of the early 1840's with road building generally depressed all the way to 1846 with the exception of the single year 1842. Both series rise in the 1847 expansion, decline in 1848, and then rise generally (except for a decline in road building in 1848 and another slight fall in 1853). Railways decline in 1854 and then both roads and railways contribute to the 1855–56 expansion, with railways declining in 1857 and 1859 and rising slightly in 1858. Both these major series, then, conform quite well

---

[30] The authors are aware of the hazards involved in using mileage-added figures as a measurement of the annual volume of railway investment. In particular, such data tend to overstate the volume of construction for the year in which a section of track was opened, and to understate the volume during the years of actual construction. However, it is likely that, if the tracks were laid down in relatively small "doses," a substantial part of the error may have cancelled out.

to the cycle, and it is argued that income effects from investment in these areas contributed to the cyclical pattern of fluctuations in general business activity.

Once again the quantitative significance of our conclusion cannot be

CHART V

EXPENDITURES ON CANALS AND INTERNATIONAL IMPROVEMENTS

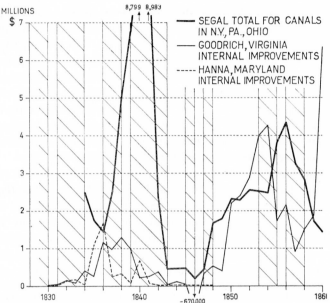

SOURCE: H. S. Hanna, "A Financial History of Maryland, 1789–1848," *Johns Hopkins University Studies in Historical and Political Science,* Vol. XXV (1907); H. Segal, *Canal Cycles, op. cit.;* C. Goodrich, "The Virginia System of Mixed Enterprise," *Political Science Quarterly,* Vol. LXIV, 1949. Virginia figures represent net investment from the Virginia Fund for Internal Improvements. The negative figure for the year 1846 represents an accounting procedure, i.e., the writing off or writing down of certain assets.

exactly assessed in the absence of reliable money estimates, in this case for outlays on roads and railways and for aggregate investment outlays.[31]

---

[31] It is apparent that no reliable series exist showing the yearly outlays on early railway construction. Even if the annual mileage-added data could be corrected to satisfy most of the criticisms which have been made of them, the job of applying adequate cost coefficients to these data might well be simply insurmountable. See, for example, Harold Pollins, "Aspects of Railway Accounting Before 1868," *Studies in the History of Accounting,* pp. 332–35 for such a conclusion in the case of the British railways. Other devices might be employed (e.g., see Matthews, *op. cit.,* pp. 120–26) to prorate hypothetical expenditures on the basis of assumptions about lags in railway construction for the purpose of deducing the possible cyclical effects of railway expenditures. For our purposes, assuming that the data for mileage added are of the proper general order of magnitude, and that the *turning points* in the data are accurate on an annual basis, what is required is a cost coefficient which is reasonable. Costs of factors changed from year to year, however, and there could be no real pretense of accuracy, even if the coefficients were changed yearly to take into account changes in prices. The computation of a cost coefficient would involve initially some figure for annual average cost per mile. What might such a figure be? There are

Nevertheless, in view of the obviously immense magnitudes of the investment projects under consideration, it may be asserted with some confidence that L. H. Jenks[32] is substantially correct so far as our present knowledge goes and that we have here a factor which contributed to the intensity of cyclical fluctuations in the antebellum period.

It might be regarded as plausible to expect other data for internal improvements to move in the same manner. Although such a hypothesis is attractive out of a fondness for symmetry as well as one the grounds of theoretical expectations, the facts as we now have them are rather intractable. We find, in fact, that the hypothesis is only weakly supported. Existing time series for state expenditures on internal improvements do not conform well to the cyclical turning points, although they do support the broad direction of movements in economic activity. Dr. Harvey Segal has compiled a series for total canal expenditures in the states of New York, Pennsylvania, and Ohio. Since the aggregate figures for these three states comprised a very large percentage of total canal expenditures for the entire country, they are of considerable significance.

Dr. Segal's data (Chart V) clearly show that the expansions in 1839, 1849–50, and 1856 were aided by canal investment, and that the slump years of 1842–43 and 1857–58 were intensified by declining canal expenditures. The cycle is thus illuminated to some extent. However, his data also show that canal expenditures continued to mount during the slump

---

many possible starting figures. The roughest one would be simply average total capitalization per mile of track taken from the *Historical Statistics.* In 1850 this figure is roughly $35,000 per mile; for mileage added from 1850–55 it is about $42,000 and in 1855–60 it is about $38,000. Estimates for "cost of construction" including Ringwalt's and the Eighth U.S. Census for 1850, and Poor's for the New England and Middle Atlantic's States in 1859, run from about $18,000 per mile in the Gulf States in 1850 to $49,000 in New England and the Middle Atlantic States in 1859. Ringwalt's average for the entire U.S. in 1850 is roughly $43,000 per mile. Thomas Tooke, on the other hand, used $29,202 (£6,000 converted at £1 = $4.867) per mile as his figure for average cost of construction of U.S. railways which existed in 1854. If one took any reasonable minimal figure for a cost coefficient from these, say only $30,000 per mile, it is clear that certainly in the railway boom of the 1850's, and in some cases earlier, changes in railway-construction outlays, which were cyclical, could have largely offset changes in other major components of aggregate spending which moved contracyclically. However, not much more can be said with any confidence on the basis of existing figures. For data on which the figures in this footnote are based see *Historical Statistics, op. cit.,* Series K 18–27, p. 201; H. V. Poor, *History of the Railroads and Canals of the United States of America* (New York, 1860) for "cost of road" in New England and the Middle Atlantic states; J. L. Ringwalt, *Development of Transportation Systems in the United States* (Philadelphia, 1888), pp. 116–17 and *Preliminary Report of the Eighth Census,* pp. 230–31 for mileage by region; Thomas Tooke and William Newmarch, *A History of Prices and the State of the Circulation during the Nine Years 1848–1856* (London, 1857), (Vols. V and VI of Tooke's *History of Prices*), p. 380. The authors are indebted to Professor Lance E. Davis for suggesting the "total capitalization" approach to an average cost figure.

[32] L. H. Jenks, "Railroads as an Economic Force in American Development," *Journal of Economic History,* 1944, Vol. IV, pp. 1–20. Reprinted in *Enterprise and Secular Change* (Homewood, Ill.: Richard D. Irwin, Inc., 1953), pp. 161–80. Jenks also notes other studies of railway construction and the business cycle.

years 1840–41, and actually reached their all-time peak in the latter year. Moreover, it is apparent from Dr. Segal's data that the cyclical expansion of the mid-1840's, with two peaks in the years 1845 and 1847, were not directly related to canal expenditures. Professor Goodrich's data for expenditures by the state of Virginia on internal improvements show that they contributed to expansions in 1836, 1849–53, 1856, and 1859–60. The Virginia series are also low generally in 1840–43 and 1846 and show drastic decreases in 1855 and 1857. Finally, Hanna's data for Maryland may be briefly cited (Chart V). Expenditures on internal improvements in Maryland appear to have been concentrated on 1835–36, thus contributing to the expansion of those two years. These expenditures then declined to insignificant amounts during the depression of the early 1840's.

Thus we can say that if these series are in any sense a valid sample of the total for similar expenditures (or if contrary movements of expenditures of other states did not offset them, which is most unlikely in view of the fact that the data cited were from states where, collectively, most of the internal improvements took place),[33] then, except for the business expansion of the mid-1840's, these expenditures generally supported the broad movements of business activity. They were high in the 1839 expansion, declining in the depression years of the early 1840's (sharply after the peak in 1841), they rose strongly in the great expansion of the 1850's, and declined in 1857–58. However, it is clear also that these series do not account for turning points and that the great boom years of the 1830's could not have been mainly the result of either canal building or other kinds of internal improvements.

VII

From this mixed bag we conclude that the main expansions of the 1830's and 1850's were underpinned by construction of railways and roads, and that declines in expenditures for such purposes also contributed to the depression of the early 1840's and the slump after 1856. These data conform to the cycle, although they do not lead it and hence cannot have caused the turning points. Also the same can be said roughly for canals and internal improvements in the states for which we have presented data, with the major reservations that the 1835–36 expansion could hardly have been a result of increased expenditures on canal building, and canal building, furthermore, did not fall off in the 1840–43 depression until 1842. Again it is clear that these data could not have contributed to the turning points. Set against these conclusions we have the federal budget, mainly

[33] The following qualification, however, is in order. Since our data on canal building are primarily for eastern states, and since, during the 1850's, a higher percentage of total canal building took place outside this region as compared with the 1830's and 1840's, it is possible that our sample is not as representative for the 1850's as it is for the previous two decades.

contracyclical in its variations, which could have offset the income effects of large parts of these expenditures on social overheads which did happen to conform to the cycle. This was not by any means always the case, however; for example, in 1841–42 a huge decline in canal expenditures was recorded for Pennsylvania, New York, and Ohio, amounting in total to $6,500,000. The decline in canal expenditures was partly offset by a federal budgetary deficit in 1842 of $5,200,000, but this represented a decline in the deficit of more than $4,000,000 compared to 1841.

The American business cycle was strong and pervasive in its effects from 1830 to 1860, so pervasive that at least in the 1830's and 1850's it has been argued (elsewhere) that variations in American demand for British goods provided the main dynamic (and unstable) elements in British overseas trade,[34] and therefore were important determinants of the pattern of the international cycle. But where, precisely, did the variations in aggregate demand originate in the American economy? Where were the origins of the American cycle? The answer remains clouded in obscurity. If the arguments in this paper are at least approximately correct, this obscurity is largely due to an unwarranted retention of explanations which, in their theoretical frailties, constitute a somewhat doubtful inheritance from earlier generations, and which are seriously at variance with the crude and fragmentary data which are currently available. A totally fresh assault upon the problem seems overdue.

---

[34] Matthews, *Study in Trade Cycle History*, pp. 43–44; Jonathan R. T. Hughes, *Fluctuations in Trade, Industry and Finance* (Oxford: Clarendon Press, 1960), p. 40.

3. The Commercial Crisis of 1857[*]

Jonathan R. T. Hughes

Purdue University

1. Introduction

THE COMMERCIAL CRISIS of 1857 has been considered by economic historians as an example par excellence of a "financial crisis" where domestic credit abuses and international financial manipulations brought trade and industry to grief. The principal purpose of this paper is to show that serious industrial difficulties existed in Britain which *preceded* the monetary crisis.[1] It is also shown that the character of the trade cycle in the 1850's differed significantly from that of the period 1790–1850, and that some modern theoretical tools are useful in explaining the 1857 crisis. Finally, it is hoped that this paper, in a brief space, will serve to draw attention to the magnitude of Britain's economic expansion during the 1850's.

The crisis of 1857 has been called the first worldwide commercial crisis in the history of modern capitalism.[2] This accolade is not entirely accurate since earlier cyclical fluctuations in Britain had important repercussions on incomes and trade in the countries supplying raw materials;[3] but with the development of more rapid communications (steam navigation on the transatlantic trade routes and the telegraph in Europe and Britain) the speed at which the 1857 catastrophe spread was unprecedented. Within weeks of the initial American crisis which culminated in New York in October, 1857, the major industrial and commercial centers of the world were paralyzed. By October 12, 62 of New York City's 63 commercial

* Reprinted from *Oxford Economic Papers* (New Series), Vol. 8, No. 2, June, 1956.

1 The author is indebted to Messrs. H. J. Habakkuk and C. N. Ward-Perkins of Oxford University for their helpful criticisms.

2 M. von Tugan Baranowsky, *Studien zur Theorie und Geschichte der Handelskrisen in England*, Jena, 1901, p. 124; J. H. Clapham, *The Bank of England*, 1944, Vol. II, p. 226; Hans Rosenberg, *Die Weltwirtschaftskrisis von 1857–1859*, Berlin, 1934, p. 8.

3 R. C. O. Matthews, *A Study in Trade Cycle History*, 1954, pp. 75–78.

4 *Economist*, November 14, 1857.

banks had suspended payments. A month later, after a series of bank and
mercantile failures, demands on the Bank of England for assistance so
reduced the Bank's reserve of notes that the government was obliged to
intervene and the Bank Act of 1844 was suspended for the second time
since its enactment. On the Paris Bourse the British government's action
detonated a financial panic which was likened to the days immediately
following the 1848 revolution,[4] and other Continental centers were shaken
from Vienna to Stockholm. Within eight days of the British government's
action, banks and commercial houses in northern Europe (mainly centered in the old Hanse trading area) were closing their doors, and state
intervention was required in all the major capitals of northern Europe to
keep financial and trading channels open. Thus, in the period from October 12 to the middle of December, 1857, the crisis spread over half the
world and finance, trade, and industry floundered in depression.

Contemporary investigators of the crisis declared that it was due to
excessive speculation and abuse of credit."[5] But the investigating committee was already sitting on the question of the 1844 Bank Act and their
investigation had an overwhelming monetary bias. The *Report* of the
committee was based almost entirely upon the opinions of two public
accountants and of a host of bankers.[6] The industrial side of the crisis
was ignored; and the majority opinion was mainly in opposition to the
testimony of the few witnesses who represented the commercial world.[7]

There had, in fact, been no speculation of the kind known in 1839 or in
1847; credit abuses existed, as in all the early 19th-century crises, but the
abuses had no more been responsible for the violent monetary and commercial collapse in the 1857 crisis than for the great boom periods of the
fifties. Sir John Clapham rightly concluded that:

. . . the Committee of 1858 sat too early, and was not provided with facts
enough, to explain the world-wide crisis of 1857 or to comment on it intelligently.[8]

There were important real factors involved in the 1857 crisis. The condition of the various sectors of the British economy in 1857 was related to
a combination of external and internal factors. The main external factors
were: (1) the 1853 boom (related primarily to the effects of the Australian
and Californian gold discoveries), (2) the Crimean War, and (3) the
1856–57 export boom. The main internal factors were: (1) the availability
of industrial raw materials, (2) the home market's ability to absorb the
products of industry, (3) import demand, (4) the growth of banking and
commercial credit, and (5) the effects upon the money market of losses of

---

[5] *Report of the Select Committee on the Bank Acts and the Recent Commercial Distress, Accts., Papers,* 1857–58, Vol. V (381) (hereinafter called *S.C. of 1858*), sec. 82.

[6] *Ibid.,* secs. 60–61.

[7] *Ibid.,* evidence, QQ. 2117–20, 2369–73, 2887, 5006–12.

[8] *The Bank of England,* 1944, Vol. II, p. 238.

gold by the Bank of England. Any assessment of the relative importance of these factors is complicated by their interdependence.

2. The Background of Economic Expansion

The 12 years between the depression and political conflicts of 1848 and the beginnings of the American Civil War in 1860 witnessed a revolution in British trade and industry. Vast economic growth abroad, a more than doubling of the volume of British overseas trade, new raw material sources for industry both at home and abroad, rapid expansion of industrial capacity, high farming, the successful introduction of the iron-screw steamship into commercial ocean navigation, the spread of railways, half the world linked together by telegraph and plans laid for the other half— all these were important factors in the economic expansion of the 1850's. Indeed, with the rapid increase in gold production, low interest rates at the beginning of the period, and extensive international lending and increasing international trade, Colin Clark's three conditions for a long period of rising prices prevailed.[9]

The gold production following the development of the Californian mines in 1848–49 and the Australian discoveries in 1851 was quickly felt in the commercial world, and in the nine years following 1848 the world's supply of precious metals rose by an estimated 30 percent.[10] The minimum Bank of England rate of discount was 3 percent or less for 239 weeks from November, 1848, to June, 1853;[11] and in 1852, when bank rate fell to 2 percent, the market rate was so low that London discount houses refused 1½ percent for deposits.[12] British foreign investment was extensive: railways in India, the United States, Canada, France, Germany, Belgium, Spain, Italy, Russia, and elsewhere. Textile factories and iron and locomotive shops were being set up abroad with British capital.[13] The expansion of trade was unprecedented: from 1815 to 1845 the value of British exports had increased only from £51.6 to £60.1 million; by 1848 it had fallen to £52.8 million. In the following nine years the value of exports more than doubled: it stood at £122 million in 1857, an increase of nearly £70 million. In the 1858 depression the value of exports was still £115.8 million and by 1860 had reached £136 million, an increase of about £20 million, or twice the increase which had occurred in the 20 years from 1815 to 1845.[14]

[9] *The Conditions of Economic Progress*, 1940, p. 467.

[10] Thomas Tooke and William Newmarch, *A History of Prices*, 1857, Vol. VI, p. 158 (Newmarch).

[11] R. G. Hawtrey, *A Century of Bank Rate*, 1938, Appendix 1, p. 281. All references to the level of bank rate hereafter refer to this source unless otherwise specified.

[12] *Circular to Bankers*, June 19, 1852.

[13] L. H. Jenks, *The Migration of British Capital*, 1938, chaps. vi and viii and Appendix A; J. H. Clapham, *The Economic Development of France and Germany* (4th ed.; 1951), chap. vii.

[14] *Statistical Abstract for the United Kingdom.*

The increase in trade is to some extent a measure of the growth of British industrial capacity; and production data emphasize this growth. Production of pig iron from British ores increased from about 2,249,000 tons in 1850 to 3,827,000 tons in 1860.[15] In the same period, coal raised in the U.K. increased from about 51,000,000 tons to 84,043,000 tons;[16] imports of cotton increased from 1.7 to 3.4 million bales;[17] consumption of cotton (indicating actual production) increased from 1.5 million bales to 2.5 million bales;[18] the installed horsepower of the British cotton industry rose from 82,005 to 294,130; and employment in the industry increased from 190,287 to 231,646.[19] Railway mileage opened in the U.K. nearly doubled, rising from 6,621 in 1850 to 10,443 in 1860.[20] The tonnage of ships built and registered in the U.K. increased from 133,695 in 1850 to 323,200 in 1855,[20] and was still 211,968 in the year 1860 following a prolonged shipbuilding depression (below).

In many respects the British economy had prepared itself in the 1840's for the economic expansion represented by these data. The great increase in British population during the first 50 years of the 19th century made possible the waves of emigrants who peopled developing areas from America to Australia and enhanced the growth of British trade. Moreover, the growth of population provided a reservoir of labor in Britain which could be drawn upon. In the years 1845–50 some 1.3 million people emigrated from the U.K. in the wake of agricultural and industrial distress,[20] while the migration of agricultural workers into the towns threw Britain's existing unemployment into sharper relief. This sort of internal migration reached its peak for the 19th century during the 1840's. Manchester and Liverpool gained more population from this source than ever "before or after."[21] Whatever the growth of population and its movement into the manufacturing towns meant in terms of social problems, in the cold calculus of labor supply for industry, labor emigration, and internal migration during the "hungry forties" must be considered a boon, and perhaps a precondition, of the development of the "prosperous fifties."

Economic historians have customarily taken the year 1850 as an arbitrary dividing line in the history of the 19th-century British economy; this procedure has a certain legitimacy as well as convenience. The intellectual climate of the fifties was favorable to the expansion of industry; "free trade" had already permeated the press and politics, and in the Crystal Palace Exhibition in 1851, Britain's eyes were turned outward to world

---

[15] A. D. Gayer, W. W. Rostow, A. J. Schwartz, *The Growth and Fluctuation of the British Economy 1790–1850*, 1953, Vol. I, p. 320 n.; *Mineral Statistics*.

[16] *Report on Coal Supply 1871, Accts, Papers*, xviii (c. 435–ii), Vol. 3, p. 886.

[17] *Statistical Abstract*.

[18] Thomas Ellison, *The Cotton Trade of Great Britain*, 1886, Table 3.

[19] *Factory Returns, Accts, Papers*, 1850, Vol. XLII (745); 1862, Vol. LV (23).

[20] *Statistical Abstract*.

[21] A. K. Cairncross, "Internal Migration in Victorian England," *Manchester School*, 1949, Vol. XVII, p. 70; also J. H. Clapham, *An Economic History of Modern England*, 1942 ed., Vol. II, pp. 536–37 on urbanization.

trade and enterprise. At home the ill effects of 1847 had mostly passed away, and the London capital market was prepared for new investment both at home and abroad. By 1850 the railways had finished making their calls;[22] the new trunk lines conceived in the 1845–46 railway mania were mostly completed (and legislation made it possible for the hangover of unprofitable schemes to be abandoned).[23] The secular growth of population and demand had brought about the utilization of the excess capacity existing after 1847. On the land, scientific farming with drainage, deep ploughing, new fertilizers, improved stockbreeding, steam threshing, etc., had put British agriculture on a more competitive basis (although at the same time, the dependence upon the external food supply had continued to grow and even in the best harvest years Britain could no longer feed herself). Britain was preparing for further economic expansion by accident, necessity, and indeed, by design: for not only were other conditions especially propitious for growth, but also, there was abundant leadership at hand. In the 1850–53 boom the great foreign demand for British commodities came to the Britain of Chapman, Stephenson, Brunel, Nasmyth, Brassey, Vaughan, Bessemer, Salt, and the host of other financial, industrial, engineering, and commercial geniuses of the age these names represent.

Early in the fifties Britain invested heavily in textiles, iron, coal, engineering, manufacturing, and shipping as home and foreign demand recovered. The new situation was illuminated early in 1853 when the National Association for the Protection of British Industry voted to dissolve itself.

. . . the present state of political affairs has rendered its exertions no longer necessary, and . . . the objects for which the Association was first established have, by a concurrence of unforeseen circumstances, been completely changed. . . .[24]

A period of stagnation had given way to one of intense activity; and halfway through the fifties old Thomas Tooke looked back with wonder to the earlier decade.

For myself, I confess that, after pursuing for a long period, with all the patience and industry I could command, the various kinds of statistical and general evidence connected with the state of Great Britain since 1840, the impression which has been most strongly produced on my mind is one of unfeigned astonishment at the solidity and vastness of the amelioration which has been accomplished.[25]

The growth of industry and commerce was not smooth, but the trade cycle in the years 1848–60 occurred against a secular background of eco-

---

[22] *History of Prices,* Vol. V, p. 389 (Tooke).
[23] 13 & 14 Vict., c. 83.
[24] *Circular to Bankers,* February 12, 1853.
[25] *History of Prices,* Vol. V, p. 448.

nomic expansion—even in the depths of the 1858 depression the value of British exports was higher than it had ever been before 1857.

3. The Trade Cycle and the Monetary System

The trade cycle in the fifties falls roughly into five periods: (1) 1850–53; upswing and boom, (2) 1854–55, Crimean War, (3) 1856–57, export boom, (4) 1858, depression, and (5) 1859–60 recovery. But these periods are meant only to be generally descriptive; and the trade fluctuations specifically do not indicate the pattern or magnitudes of fluctuations in investment and home income.

Exports reached peaks in 1853, 1857, and 1860, while import peaks came in 1854, 1857, and 1860 (Chart 1). Troughs were uniform for both exports and imports in 1855, 1858, and in 1861 (the first year of the American Civil War which witnessed the beginning of a sharp decline in British exports to that country). The general trade recovery in 1850–52 became a boom in 1853 when exports to Australia and the U.S.A. rose strongly. By late 1853 the Australian market was oversupplied, exports declined, and stringency developed in the London money market, where the bank rate rose from 2½ to 5 percent between January and September. The outbreak of war with Russia brought prosperity to certain sectors of the economy, but it also cut off the Russian market and caused a shipping shortage, which further limited exports. Imports continued to rise in 1854; the harvest failure of 1853 necessitated extraordinary corn imports from America in American ships, in addition to the 1853 Ukrainian supply which was got out of Odessa before the port was blockaded.[26] Moreover British importers purchased large supplies of timber, flax, and other Russian source raw materials from the Baltic countries in anticipation of war shortages. The decline in both imports and exports in 1855 was small and represented no considerable hardships to British industry. During the period 1850–55 the main fluctuations in exports were related to the Australian and American trades, without which no cycle appears in the data (Chart 1). This was partly due to the steady rise in exports to the Continent, as indicated in Chart 1 by the curve for reexports (most of which were to the Continent), as well as by exports to areas other than U.S.A. and Australia. When the war ended in 1856 an extensive export boom developed; it was related mainly to a mild American import increase as well as to an increase in exports to the Continent. But the 1856–57 export boom was as short-lived as it was violent. Following the 1858 depression exports again rose, in this case the India and China trades provided the initial stimulus, while the American trade recovered in 1859; exports to the Continent were still less than 1857 by 1860.

---

[26] J. E. T. Rogers, *The Economic Interpretation of History*, 1888, p. 293.

Since Britain had an expanding industrial economy and imported raw materials while exporting finished products, the difference between the rates of increase (slopes of the curves in Chart 1) of the value of imports and exports in boom periods, provides an instructive illustration of one of the major problems of the trade cycle in this period. In each of the boom periods 1850–53, 1856–57, and 1859–60 the increase in imports was con-

CHART 1

THE COMMERCIAL CRISIS OF 1857

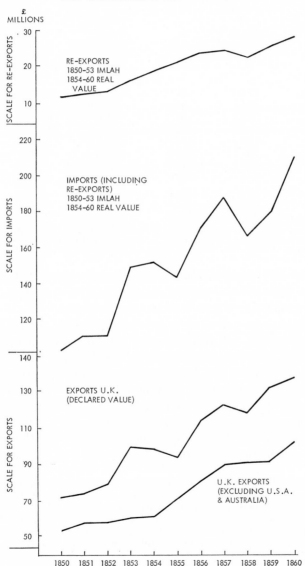

siderably in excess of exports. Imports tended to be anticyclical;[27] their increases helped to widen the adverse balance of payments and typically led to high rates of interest and to pressure in the money market.

Some aspects of this process over the cycle from 1850 to 1858 can be seen in Table I.

TABLE I
BRITISH OVERSEAS TRADE, TERMS OF TRADE, EXPORTS OF BULLION
AND SPECIE 1850–60

	Exports of Home Products	Net Imports	Visible Trade Balance	Net Barter Terms of Trade	Visible Bullion and Specie Exports
	(£ mlns.)			(1880 = 100)	(£ mlns.)
1850........	71.4	91.0	−19.6	111.1	6.9
1851........	74.4	97.0	−22.6	110.0	9.1
1852........	78.0	97.0	−19.0	104.9	10.3
1853........	98.9	131.7	−32.8	100.8	18.9
1854........	97.2	133.8	−36.6	94.6	22.6
1855........	95.7	122.5	−26.8	89.4	18.8
1856........	115.8	149.1	−33.3	91.6	24.8
1857........	122.1	163.7	−41.6	87.1	33.6
1858........	116.6	141.4	−24.8	98.0	19.6
1859........	130.4	153.9	−23.5	98.2	35.7
1860........	135.8	181.9	−46.0	94.9	25.7

SOURCE: Exports 1850–60, imports 1854–60, visible bullion exports 1850–60, *Statistical Abstract*; imports 1850–53, A. H. Imlah, "Real Values in British Foreign Trade 1798–1853," *Journal of Economic History*, 1948, Vol. viii, p. 149; net barter terms of trade, Imlah, see above.

In 1852–53 and 1856–57 as the increase of imports exceeded exports and the adverse trade balance widened, there was a rise in bullion exports.[28] In each case the terms of trade[29] turned against Britain.

The adverse turning of the terms of trade associated with these import increases was caused in part by raw material shortages which will be discussed in some detail in a later section, but which may be treated briefly at this stage of the discussion. Since the raw materials for principal British industries were foreign and/or agricultural in origin, rapid increases in British demand to maintain raw material supplies for export industries during boom periods resulted in rising prices of such raw materials as cotton, wool, silk, etc. The transportation lag as well as the natural lag involved in increasing the supply of these raw raterials while export

---

[27] This usage of the term anticyclical follows R. C. O. Matthews, *op. cit.*, pp. 95–97. High incomes in the boom encouraged imports and discouraged exports; there thus tended to be an outflow of bullion in the booms.

[28] The period 1858–60 was a special case related to bullion shipments to India following the India Mutiny. This will not be discussed in the present paper; British readers are referred to pp. 463–65 of the author's unpublished thesis in the Bodleian library.

[29] The author is indebted to Professor A. H. Imlah for permission to use his unpublished calculations of the net barter terms of trade.

industries raised production and competed for foreign markets, resulted in
a turning of the terms of trade against Britain. As Britain increased her
foreign payments to cover the increasing external imbalance the domestic
supply of gold and bank notes decreased. This factor was of critical importance in the development of the 1857 crisis since the 1856–57 export
boom was associated with an increase in visible bullion exports of from
£24.8 to £33.6 million and marked monetary stringency. The long period
effects of the bullion drain on the Bank of England's position are seen in
Chart 2.

CHART 2

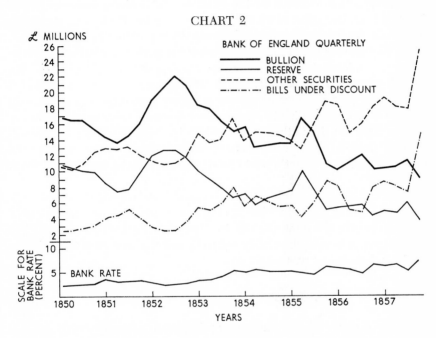

The great bullion drain of the 1850's has been considered one of the
paradoxes of monetary history in the 19th century.[30] Although Britain
received annually the greater part of the new gold production, the period
1853–57 was one of an increasing shortage of gold and high interest rates.
Table I and Chart 2 together indicate the causes of this phenomenon.
Along with the increasingly adverse trade balance and the export of
bullion in 1850–57 (Table I) the Bank of England's bullion hoard (and
therefore reserve of notes declined (Chart 2). But at the same time, the
rise in trading activity meant a greater demand for money; hence the
secular rise in the Bank's holdings of bills and "other securities"[31] while the
bullion fell and interest rates increased.

As can be seen by a close scrutiny of Chart 2, the Bank, in the short run,

---

[30] Professor Hicks's "Rostow Paradox," *The Trade Cycle*, 1950, p. 154 n.

[31] I.e., holdings of securities other than government securities, mainly short-term
commercial paper.

consistently pursued the policy of raising its discount rate as commercial demand rose and the bullion and reserve fell. This was according to the received banking doctrines of the time, but as is also evident in Chart 2, the Bank was granting extended accommodation from a shrinking bullion base; and was thus increasingly getting itself into a position where it would be unable to withstand unusually heavy demands upon its reserve. During periods when the bullion increased the Bank's policy was consistent and the discount rate was reduced in order to encourage discounting. This was conspicuous in both the summers of 1855[32] and 1857.

Greater accommodation by the Bank for the business community was justified from one point of view, however, since the Bank was attempting to provide for the legitimate needs of rapidly expanding business transactions. The secular growth of trade during the period is illustrated by the sharp rise in joint stock bank deposits; the deposits of eight London joint stock banks rose from £12 million in 1850 to over £40 million in 1857.[33] At the same time, the average volume of bills of exchange in circulation increased from £66 million to an estimated £180 to £200 million.[34] Moreover, neither the rise in the volume of bills in circulation[35] nor the growth of joint stock bank deposits was adversely affected by increases in the discount rate. Trade continued to grow, more bills were drawn, new loans and deposits created; at the same time imports rose, raw material prices increased, the Bank's gold holdings declined, and interest rates rose with the expansion of trade. In 1857 this top-heavy structure of credit toppled in the panic, the discount rate rose to 10 percent, the bullion in the Bank's issue department was drastically reduced, and the reserve of notes in the banking department was wiped out.

4. Investment and Price Instability

By the summer of 1857 there was widespread unemployment and depression in major sectors of British industry, and this contributed to the trade and monetary causes of the crisis. The external forces which had influenced the pattern of trade fluctuations naturally were also felt in industry; but the pattern of investment arising from these stimuli was not the same as the trade pattern. For example, high and rising costs (including interest rates) had adverse effects on investment in certain sectors in 1856–57, while at the same time, falling prices in other sectors dampened investment (below). High levels of production did not always mean

---

[32] The 1855 episode is discussed briefly by Clapham, *Economic History of Modern England,* Vol. II, pp. 365–66.

[33] S. C. of 1857–58, Q. 1134.

[34] *History of Prices,* Vol. VI, pp. 590–92 for Newmarch's famous estimates of the bill circulation up to 1853 and Appendix 39 of *Select Committee on the Bank Acts, Accts., Papers,* 1857, Vol. X (220).

[35] See *History of Prices,* Vol. VI, p. 588, for period up to 1853; pp. 479–512 of the author's unpublished thesis manuscript cited above for period up to 1859.

profitable production.[36] The resulting investment pattern conditioned by such factors in the fifties was roughly: 1850–53, boom in nearly all industrial sectors; 1854–55, uneven, heavy investment in iron, coal, and shipbuilding, but a decline in investment in textiles, railways, and nonwar-stimulated industries; 1856–57, stagnation in new investment in nearly all sectors; 1858, depression; 1859–60, uneven recovery, depression continuing in investment in iron, coal, shipbuilding, but an investment boom developing in most textiles.

The stagnation of investment during the postwar period 1856–57 was due to basic internal imbalances as well as to price instability; the internal imbalances followed uneven investment activity. The 1853 boom witnessed unexampled investment and expansion of production in nearly all major sectors of industry; in Lancashire, Leonard Horner, the factory inspector, commenting on the first six months of 1853 observed:

> At no period during the last seventeen years that I have been officially acquainted with the manufacturing districts of Lancashire have I known such general prosperity; the activity in every branch is extraordinary. . . . It is not to be wondered at . . . that I should hear of a great scarcity of hands, of much machinery standing idle from the want of people to work it, and of a rise in wages.[37]

The 1853 boom permeated most other sectors of the economy except agriculture.

A new source of iron ore had been opened in the Cleveland district but although new investment was proceeding rapidly there and in the other iron districts, iron prices were rising precipitously by 1853, capacity production had been reached, and many ironworks had a backlog of orders.[38] Freight rates rose by more than 100 percent in 1852–54[39] and the shipbuilding industry, under the impact first of the boom in the Australian and American trades, and later the war demand, was experiencing an unexampled expansion of production. While 1854, the first year of the Crimean War, was one of stagnation in some trades, cotton and worsteds, other industries, iron, coal, shipbuilding, and woolens, were geared for war production and by 1855 prosperity was strengthened to a considerable degree by the revival of the cotton export trade.

When peace came in 1856, the major industries were prepared to meet the increase in foreign demand with productive capacity already expanded by five years of extensive investment, three (1851–53) in which

---

[36] E.g., 1854–57 was a period of rising production of cotton goods (except 1857, when production declined some but was still high) yet is was considered by contemporaries to be a depression, i.e., with raw material costs rising more rapidly than prices of finished goods, profits were depressed. See W. O. Henderson, *The Lancashire Cotton Famine*, 1934, pp. 5, 9.

[37] *Reports of Factory Inspectors, Accts, Papers*, 1852–53, Vol. XL, six months ending June 30, 1853, p. 19.

[38] See, e.g., Harry Scrivenor, *History of the Iron Trade*, 1854, p. 300.

[39] *History of Prices*, Vol. V, p. 319.

the investment boom had been general, and two (1854–55) when certain industries, such as iron, coal, and shipbuilding, had experienced a continued rapid expansion of capacity. Thus in 1856–57, expanded production to meet the export boom was not accompanied by a renewed investment boom. Net additions to installed horsepower in the textile industry fell from 6,547 in 1853 to only 2,455 in 1856.[40] Short time and unemployment in textiles in 1857 (see below) doubtlessly was accompanied by an even more drastic reduction in new investment. The shipbuilding boom reached its peak in 1855 when 323,000 tons were built and registered in the United Kingdom; in 1857 this figure had fallen to 250,472[41] tons and was accompanied by widespread unemployment as shipyards lay idle (below). In the iron and coal industries the pattern was similar to that in shipbuilding, with new capacity coming into operation, and the war demand ended, prices fell and investment was reduced. There were about 200 new collieries opened in 1855, about 235 in 1856, and only 76 in 1857; by 1858 this number had fallen to 8.[42] Considering the time lag necessary for new construction, it is clear that the end of the Crimean War also meant a temporary end to large-scale investment in new collieries. The same investment pattern prevailed in the iron industry; there were 106 known new blast furnaces set up in the United Kingdom in the three years 1853–55 (and perhaps as many as 130) while in the three years 1856–58 this number fell to about 70.[43]

Decreased new investment during 1856–57 contributed to the inability of the domestic market to absorb its share of the rising volumes of new production and finally led to an impasse in 1857 when production could no longer be continued at full capacity profitably. But the impasse in 1857 was to be found in the supply of raw materials as well as the market situation. For those industries like coal, iron, grains, and other nonanimal agricultural products where the source of production was domestic, the end of the war demand coupled with expanded capacity meant declining prices as production increased; for those industries like textiles, the effort made to utilize expanded capacity meant rising raw material costs since the raw materials were foreign and/or agricultural in origin. The resulting price instability is illustrated in Chart 3.

Price group I represents basic items whose source of supply was domestic; price group II represents those items whose source was foreign and/or agricultural.[44] In both cases (and in the Sauerbeck general index)

[40] *Reports of Factory Inspectors, Accts., Papers,* 1854, Vol. XIX; 1852 (sess. 1), Vol. III.

[41] *Statistical Abstract.*

[42] *Mineral Statistics.*

[43] *Ibid.* The data for both coal and iron are at best only indicative of the pattern of investment, the enumeration methods used in these early numbers of *Mineral Statistics* seem rough in the extreme.

[44] Price group I is an unweighted arithmetic mean of the Sauerbeck price relatives for coal, pig iron and bar iron, and English wheat; price group II is an average of the relatives for cotton, wool, silk, and leather.

CHART 3

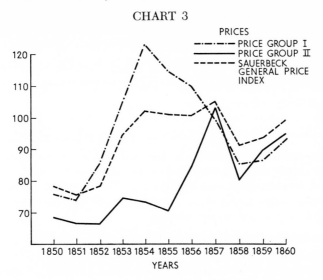

PRICES
—·—·—·— PRICE GROUP I
——————— PRICE GROUP II
— — — — — SAUERBECK
GENERAL PRICE
INDEX

the 1853 inflation is obvious; the first year of the Crimean War brought a high level of prosperity to the industries represented by price group I, but as new capacity was brought into use and production rose, prices fell steadily through 1857 to the trough in 1858. Price group II shows the depressing effects of the war,[45] but with the postwar trade boom, the great increase in productive capacity, and the inelastic supply of raw materials, the period 1856–57 was one of rapid raw material cost inflation (the relative stability of the unweighted general price index in 1854–57 thus being partly the result of compensating divergent movements of all the price relatives represented by the main two subgroups).

As each industrial group continued to press the expanded capacity into operation the industrial crisis developed; in the case of those industries in price group I, e.g., iron, it was related to falling iron prices, in the case of price group II, e.g., cotton manufacturing, it was related to rising raw material prices. In both cases the sources of raw materials, and the character of the investment pattern in 1850–55 as well as the market situation were crucial factors. We may illustrate briefly the positions of iron and cotton in the period at the beginning of the 1857 crisis.

In iron, continuing production, the slack home market (due to the dropping off of new investment noted above, as well as the immediate cessations of government war expenditures in 1856) meant falling prices and rising stocks.

At that time [1856] the effects of overmanufacturing were producing unhealthy symptoms in all branches of trade. Spasmodic efforts were made to force sales, often at ruinously low prices, while especially in the iron works

---

[45] A period, also, in which stocks of raw materials were produced. See, e.g., Ellison, *op. cit.,* Table 3 for stocks of raw cotton held in Britain in 1853–55.

of some districts, the raw materials on hand were converted into marketable value, notwithstanding the large stocks already unsold, and their rapid accumulation by those rash proceedings.[46]

In cotton, while the weak home market meant a limit on price increases of finished goods, international competition for available cotton supplies and greatly expanded capacity at home meant rising raw cotton prices. Therefore, while iron was faced with plethora and crisis from falling prices, cotton textiles were faced with famine and a raw material inflation.

. . . the distress . . . is likely to be felt, and that before long too, from the inadequate supply of the raw material which affords employment to such vast numbers of inhabitants of this district. . . . I believe that if every spindle now in work is kept employed . . . by the end of 1857 we shall not have a single bag of cotton left in the country.[47]

The conflicting elements presented by this price instability contributed to the developing industrial dilemma in the summer of 1857—a period when the anticyclical trade and monetary forces (above) progressed to a point of crisis.

The Convergence of Disequilibrating Forces

During the summer and autumn of 1857 the converging threads of the crisis drew together. As raw material imports increased to sustain industrial production, gold flowed out and pressure developed on the money market. At the same time, the public's brief enthusiasm for shares, which had followed the end of hostilities in early 1856, began to wane as industrial difficulties became more evident; share prices fell in New York, Paris, and London. The rise in raw material prices and other costs became prohibitive; production was reduced in the textile industry; the iron industry, already plagued by rising stocks and falling prices, took on an increasingly gloomy tone. Depression reigned in shipbuilding and building construction, and with increasing signs that the export expansion was at an end, Britain was poised on the edge of an economic crisis when news of the financial panic in America precipitated a general credit contraction and rush for liquidity. By the end of November, 1857, the Poor Law Guardians were besieged by masses of unemployed.

The impending crisis was evidenced early in 1857 by a prolonged depression in the stock market and by periods of monetary pressure. Early in 1857 the gold stock of the Bank fell sharply; in April the bank rate was increased from 6 to 6½ percent; five days later, ordinary loans on prime bills were limited to 30 days while loans on bills of longer usance were

---

[46] Robert Hunt writing in the Introduction to *Mineral Statistics,* number for 1860, p. xvi.

[47] Mr. J. A. Turner, President of the Manchester Commercial Association, speech quoted *Liverpool Mercury,* January 21, 1857.

CHART 4

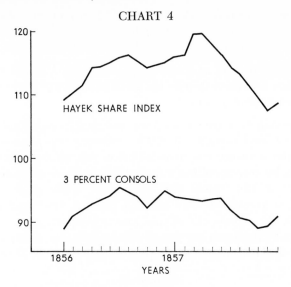

limited to 14 days. By April 11 the bullion was down to £9.1 million, the lowest point since November, 1847. A decline of share prices on the Paris Bourse had been in progress since early 1856,[48] and the depression spread to London. Share prices in London fell steadily from May to December, 1857, and consols declined from July to October (Chart 4). The state-guaranteed Imperial Russian Railway share issue was undersubscribed even though it was being marketed by a syndicate including Barings and *Crédit Mobilier;*[49] even with such glittering sponsorship there was no available risk capital. By July 8 all the capitals of the financial world were ". . . simultaneously exhibiting an unexampled and apparently incurable depression. . . ."[50] A day later with the India Mutiny receiving its initial serious notice in the press the London money market seemed on the edge of panic.

A continued depression like that now prevailing in the stock market . . . is almost unprecedented. The anxiety with regard to India overpowers all other considerations, and if any serious news were to arrive tomorrow . . . it would most probably produce a panic.[51]

The depression in shares continued without abeyance (Chart 4), market interest rates softened and hardened weekly[52] but prices continued to

---

[48] Share prices on the Bourse declined as much as 40 percent from May, 1856, to May, 1857; e.g., *Credit Mobilier* fell from 1980 to 1300; *Darmstädter Credit Bank* from 420 to 270; *Franz Joseph Orientbahn* from 180 to 60%. Max Wirth, *Geschichte der Handelskrisen* (Frankfurt-am-Main, 1858), p. 357.

[49] R. W. Hidy, *The House of Baring* (Harvard, 1949), p. 435.

[50] *The Times*, July 8, 1857.

[51] *Ibid.*, July 9, 1857.

[52] The bank rate had been reduced to 5½ percent July 16 to encourage discounting following a temporary increase in the bullion.

fall; Great Western Railway declined from 70 on January 1, 1857 to 56 by August 10.[53] By September the long boom in mining shares, one of the leading share investments of the period, had clearly ended.

> Since February last an important change has come over the spirit of our market. An epoch of great activity has given place to one of the longest and most severe depressions in years.[54]

The depression in the money market was matched by industrial difficulties.

As the increased capacity in textiles (above) was used to meet the 1856–57 export demand, raw material prices rose precipitously and were not matched by corresponding increases in the finished goods. In 1855–57 the price of raw cotton rose 47 percent while prices of finished goods rose an average of only about 4 percent; raw wool rose by 57 percent while the export price of yarn rose only 8 percent and cloth seems to have actually declined; the rise of other textile raw material costs was similar, e.g., in the same period the price of raw silk rose 50 percent.

TABLE II
TEXTILE PRICES 1855–58

	Raw Cotton	Raw Wool English	Raw Silk	Average Cotton Cloth, Printed and White	Woolen and Worsted	
					Yarns	Cloths
	(d. per lb.)				(1847–50 = 100)	
1855.....	5.62	13.0	16	3.24	97	89
1856.....	6.31	16.0	22	3.36	102	83
1857.....	7.75	20.5	24	3.49	105	83
1858.....	6.87	15.65	19	3.31	118	88

SOURCE: Raw Cotton, Wool and Silk, Sauerbeck, *op. cit*; Average cotton cloth, Ellison, *op. cit.* Prices of Woolen and worsted yarn and cloth, quoted in Hamburg, Adolf Soetbeer, "Economic Relations of Precious Metals and the Currency Question," *R.C. on Precious Metals, Accts., Papers,* 1888, Vol. XLV (c. 5512–1), Appendix xvi, pp. 236–37.

The raw cotton shortage was already acute at the end of 1856 when the available supply represented only 8 to 12 weeks' consumption.[55] Early in 1857 Lancashire manufacturers took matters into their own hands and agreed upon a "short time movement"; mills were shut down in an effort to relieve the pressure on supply. By the end of May the movement had spread throughout most of the industry.

> With regard to the short time movement it is said that in Manchester almost all the manufacturers are working short time, some of them in greater degree than the committee propose. In Salford only one firm is on full time . . . a majority at Littlebrough are in favour of the measure. . . . At Accrington, Church and Great Harwood mill owners representing three-fourths of the horse-

---

[53] *Times,* August 10, 1857.
[54] *Mining Journal,* September 12, 1857.
[55] See, e.g., Ellison, *op. cit.,* Table 3.

power have met and agreed that short time is most desirable. Several Rochdale spinners and manufacturers have been more or less at reduced hours for some time. The mill owners at Bacup went upon 40 hours per week on Monday, both in spinning and weaving; and both classes at Burnley and the neighbourhood have given notice for a resort to the same hours on the 1st of June next. Both classes at Stockport also have signed an agreement to the extent of 15–16th of the horse-power.[56]

By the first week in June when Preston and Blackburn went on short time, the movement was general, and throughout the summer the raw material shortage persisted. In addition, the wage increases won by the operatives during the war period were maintained so that unit costs remained inflated from that source.[57]

In other textiles there were also widespread reductions in output because of the cost inflation and the inability of either the home or foreign markets to absorb corresponding increases in the prices of finished goods. As early as March, 1857, short time was adopted in the Leicester[58] woolen industry and many operatives were thrown out of employment. By June worsteds were similarly affected.

During the first six months of this year, 1857, the state of trade in the worsted districts has been exceedingly unsatisfactory. Much spinning machinery has been comparatively unemployed, so high has been the price of wool compared with that of yarn . . . every branch of the manufacture is . . . depressed.[59]

By mid-June short time had become general in the Leeds district.

The manufactures continue dull, and are weekly decreasing their production; and all through the great valley district the mills are only engaged in working short time.[60]

The hosiery trade at Loughborough and Hinckley was similarly affected, and by September the tone of the silk trade was one of quiet desperation.

Another month is gone and still no business in silk, consumers restricting their purchases within the narrow limits of their daily wants, and this only when of the most pressing character—all striving to do the least possible—and this feeling, confirmed as it has been by numerous failures, and occasional forced sales on foreign account . . . it is not surprising that prices have fallen considerably.[61]

When the monetary crisis struck in the autumn unemployment in the textile industry was already widespread.

. . . the great number of factories, especially in the cotton trade, working short time, many entirely closed, the latter frequently from bankruptcy, show the

[56] *London Commercial Record*, May 29, 1857.
[57] G. H. Wood, *The History of Wages in the Cotton Trade*, 1910, p. 128.
[58] *Times*, March 2, 1857.
[59] J. James, *History of the Worsted Manufacture in England*, 1857, p. 530.
[60] *London Commercial Record*, June 12, 1857.
[61] *Economist*, October 10, 1857.

very depressed state of trade which now exists, *and which has existed in the cotton trade for a long time.*[62]

Because of the pervasiveness of the textile crisis, and the relative importance of the industry, the effects of the raw material inflation were felt in other sectors of the economy. The inflation of textile raw material prices had important *deflationary* effects: (1) it dampened induced investment, (2) it had depressing income and psychological effects within the domestic economy, and (3) it tended to increase the pressure on the money market by raising the adverse balance of payments.

The first effect is obvious; and the opinion that 1854–57, a period of rising production, was one of depression in the cotton industry (above) supports the conclusion already suggested by available figures for the decline in the new installed horsepower, that the main source of induced investment in textiles in this period was the *profitability,* and not merely the level of production, and in 1854–57 production was not considered profitable enough to continue investment on the scale of the 1853 boom. Moreover, as the raw material inflation caused investment to be cut back in new plant and equipment in textiles, the adverse income effects spread to other trades and industries, and in the end, to basic industries like iron and coal and those producing cotton manufacturing machinery.

The second (combined) effect, while important enough throughout 1854–57, was especially important in the spring and summer of 1857. There were 2.2 million workers shown in the 1861 census as employed in mining, basic industries like iron and shipbuilding, or in textiles and other manufacturing industries, and those textile industries known to have been on short time or seriously depressed by the summer of 1857 (cottons, woolens, worsteds, silk, hosiery, and lace manufactures) employed some 889,000 workers in the 1861 enumeration. From this it can be seen that the direct effects on income of the losses in wage earnings during the spring and summer of 1857 may have affected a third of the industrial labor force. Counting laborers not enumerated as working directly in textiles but who nevertheless were employed in some stage of the manufacture, including transportation and other related trades, it is easily seen that the adverse income effects of production cuts in the summer of 1857 must have been strongly felt. Also the wage losses must have been directly felt in the retail trades immediately, and, although there were many aspects of the economic situation in 1857 to destroy business confidence and enhance the financial panic when it came, the long period of depression and unemployment in the major industrial areas was surely among the most important.

Finally, the high prices of imported raw materials meant an additional drain of bullion, pressure on the money market, and higher money rates.

---

[62] Leonard Horner in *Reports of Factory Inspectors, Accts, Papers,* 1857–58, Vol. XXIV, p. 10, year ending October 31, 1857 (author's italics).

The adverse trade balance rose from £26.8 million in 1855 to £41.6 million in 1857; an increase of nearly £15 million in spite of the unprecedented growth of exports. During the same period the value of imports of textile raw materials rose from £37.2 million to £57.5 million, an increase of some £20 million. By calculating the difference between the increase in the aggregate value of textile raw material imports and hides,[63] and what their aggregate value would have been had each individual commodity import increased in value only as it increased in volume in 1855–57, we find that some £13.4 million of the £20 million increase in the value of imports of cotton, wool, silks, and hides resulted solely from rising raw material prices. By thus raising the adverse trade balance and contributing to the efflux of bullion in the period (above), the rise in raw material prices made an important contribution to the development of the monetary crisis.

Important as the textile crisis was, however, it was only one of several weak sectors in the industrial economy by 1857, and the condition of all of these sectors was a direct result of the investment pattern outlined above, as well as of the related condition of the domestic market in the post–Crimean War period.

The end of the Crimean War demand brought an immediate decline in shipbuilding, while at the same time the mastery of techniques for producing iron-hulled screw steamships made the great wooden sailing ships obsolete in the coastal, Baltic, and even in the Mediterranean routes. In 1856–57 ships were in excess supply in spite of the great increase in trade. Shipowners were aware of these difficulties at the beginning of 1857.

In estimating the prospects for the current year we cannot hide from ourselves that we have far too much tonnage afloat for the purpose of our legitimate trade.[64]

The decisive introduction of iron steamships in the Crimean War partially displaced the demand for wooden ships, while at the same time the end of war demand and the great tonnage built during the war combined to cause a depression in shipbuilding. Already in 1856 the end of the war and speculative hopes of builders had resulted in thousands of artificers being discharged; at the Woolwich Dockyard alone some 2,000 workers were summarily dismissed early in 1856 and applied for government assistance to emigrate to Canada.[65] The depression deepened in 1857 as new tonnage planned and under construction continued to fall;

---

[63] Leather was also sharply inflated in price in the period due to the introduction of sewing machinery of various sorts into boot and shoe and machine belt making and the consequent rise of leather consumption as the 1856–57 export boom progressed. The inflation of leather costs is therefore considered along with textile raw materials as part of the same process, even though no evidence exists that inflation in leather costs was predominant in causing depression in those industries using leather as the primary raw material.

[64] *Times* January 3, 1857.

[65] *Ibid.*, April 23, 1857.

in July 500 carpenters were idle in the Wear shipyards; two months earlier 1,000 hands had been discharged.[66] Tonnage built and registered in the U.K. fell from 323,200 in 1855 to only 250,472 in 1857. The Clyde ship-builders had launched 85,000 tons in 1855, and only 57,000 tons in 1857; the tonnage of ships under construction was 61,000 in 1853, and only 38,000 in 1857. The ship sellers of Liverpool sold 108 fewer ships in 1857, representing 69,000 tons, than in 1856.[67] The postwar depression in ship-building was already acute in 1857 and did not regain the 1855 tonnage again until 1863.

Another weak sector in the home economy in 1856–57 was building construction. The high level of short-term interest rates in 1856–57 made it difficult to negotiate mortgages at the relatively long-term rates while contractors themselves were loathe to borrow at higher rates.

> Persons can now realize from 5 to 6 per cent very readily upon loans, or merely by deposits at joint stock banks, and, therefore, are not to be satisfied with 4 or 5 from builders encumbered with the business of mortgages and other securities. . . .[68]

This situation was aggravated by the development of large-scale tech-niques in building construction; the large outlays involved could no longer be financed out of the private funds of individual builders, and they depended upon raising capital in the money market.[69] The depression developed steadily in 1856–57; in Birmingham 2,784 new houses had been built in 1853 and in 1856 this number was a mere 803.[70] Mass meetings of unemployed builders were held throughout London early in 1857 and by April the building trades in London alone listed 20,000 to 30,000 unem-ployed.[71]

In some areas, especially the northeast, the decline in certain agricul-tural prices in 1856–57, e.g., corn, was a further source of distress in the home economy. But more important was the critical condition of the iron industry.

The expansion of capacity in 1850–55 had already resulted in excess supply and falling prices in 1855, and by the summer of 1857 the situation had become acute. Wages had remained high from the war period[72] and

---

[66] *Mining Journal*, July 18, 1857.

[67] *Times*, January 5, 1858; January 5, 1859. A contributing factor in the depression in shipbuilding may have been the cheapness of American-built ships after the 1857 crisis had ruined many American shipowners. See Basil Lubbock, *The Colonial Clip-pers*, 1921, p. 113.

[68] *Building News*, April 3, 1857; also *ibid.*, January 23, 1857, and *Times*, January 27, 1857.

[69] *S.C. of 1857*, evidence of Edward Capps, London builder and surveyor, QQ. 5413–67.

[70] *Times*, February 9, 1857.

[71] *Building News*, April 3, 1857.

[72] E.g., ". . . pigs are 10s. per ton lower than they were but a year ago while wages have undergone no reduction whatever." *Mining Journal*, October 24, 1857. See also *Wolverhampton Chronicle*, July 8, 1857 on prices and wages.

the maintenance of full production at falling prices meant an increasingly unprofitable market. Free market prices fell steadily from the spring of 1857 when warrants for Scotch pig iron were 88s. per ton to September 21 when they had declined to 68s. As the pressure mounted warrants fell to 59s. 6d. on October 27 and by November 10 when the monetary liquidation was near its peak they declined as low as 52s. per ton.[73] The powerful ironmasters' association, which met regularly to fix the official trade price, tried to stabilize the market by agreement and in spite of falling market prices, the trade (published) prices held firm until the middle of October. During this time the market prices reflected the true situation and in spite of the agreed trade prices, individual firms sold for what they could get.

Early in July from Wolverhampton came the report

It must be confessed that there are parties who are selling lower than the . . . [trade's] . . . quotations, but the leading houses will not give way.[74]

By the middle of July manufacturers were ". . . selling below the trade quotations to a greater extent than was the case a few weeks ago."[75] At the same time the Glasgow iron trade was greatly depressed.

Since this day se'nnight our pig iron market has maintained a state of unbroken monotony. . . . Many of our foundries are slack and the bar iron trade in the district has not been so dull in many years.[76]

The iron export trade of Wales was similarly affected and exhibited the "greatest depression" in August.[77] It was hoped that the depression would be broken in midsummer by the reduction of the American iron tariff; but the newly developed iron industry in that country (which had been encouraged by the Crimean War iron price inflation) was now in operation and with a developing American economic crisis in 1857, the expected improvement did not materialize.

The great falling off within the last few months has been in the United States demand, and this has been the more felt from the fact that the reduction in the tariff has come into effect there, which was expected to have considerably increased the orders from that country.[78]

The fruits of the great expansion of capacity during the 1853 boom and the Crimean War years came into a market which could not absorb the increased production without the stimulus of the rapid new investment of previous years, or the extraordinary demand of the war period. With both the home market and the export trade depressed, and no hope of a revival of the American market, the iron industry was in the forefront of those British industries whose difficulties in 1857 led, in conjunction with the

---

73 Prices taken weekly from *North British Mail* (Glasgow).
74 *Wolverhampton Chronicle*, July 1, 1857.
75 *Mining Journal*, July 18, 1857.
76 *Times*, July 6, 1857.
77 *Mining Journal*, August 1, 1857.
78 *Ibid.*, August 8, 1857.

monetary crisis, to industrial depression.[79] Immediately upon the outbreak of the monetary crisis, furnaces and shops closed down and the roads of the iron districts were filled with unemployed workmen.

Thus, following a prolonged depression on the stock market, pressure in the money market and with the industrial economy already in a distressed state, the impact of the American monetary crisis on Britain had immediate effects. Between September 26 and October 10 the bullion reserve of the Bank was reduced more than £1 million, from £11.3 million to £10.1 million. On October 8 the discount rate was raised from 5½ to 6 percent. The *échéance* was shortened to admit only bills of 30 days or less. In the following week discounts at the Bank rose by £1.1 million. A further increase in the rate to 7 percent was ordered on October 12 and by the 17th the Bank's holdings of private securities had risen to £22.4 million, the highest ever known.[80] The bank rate was advanced by stages of 1 percent to 10 percent on November 9. By the 11th the bullion had fallen to £7.2 million and the reserve of notes was a mere £958,000. On the night of the 12th the reserve of notes had fallen to £130,630.

The Bank's discount rate weapon had not stopped the demand for accommodations; indeed, each increase in the bank rate was followed by greater discounting and in the three days from the increase in the rate of 10 percent to the suspension of the act on the 12th, the Bank discounted more than £4 million.[81] On November 12 applications for assistance from unimpeachable parties were apparently nearly as great as the remaining reserve[82] and the government suspended the Bank Act by authorizing the temporary issue of excess fiduciary notes.

There was no "magical" effect as there had been in 1847.[83] The discount panic was checked but the crisis continued and the Bank actually exceeded its fiduciary limit by some £928,000. The great demand for accommodation at the Bank had represented a general liquidation of credit. The industrial crisis was already deep; and business confidence was gone. There were no substantial "runs for gold" in England and few bank runs, but there were both in Ireland and Scotland (the only bank run of significance in England brought down the Borough Bank of Liverpool, below).

The panic in Britain had been marked by some very large failures. The Borough Bank of Liverpool closed its doors on October 27 with immediate liabilities of £1 million. This failure was followed immediately by the failure of Messrs. Dennistoun and Cross, foreign merchants and

---

[79] Indeed, it has been thought that the depression in the iron industry in 1857 was a primary cause of the 1857 crisis in Britain. M. V. Clark, *History of Manufactures* (Washington, D.C.), 1929, p. 249.

[80] *Economist*, October 17, 1857.

[81] *S.C. of 1857–58*, Appendix 4.

[82] Clapham, *The Bank of England*, Vol. II, p. 231.

[83] C. N. Ward-Perkins, "The Commercial Crisis of 1847," *Oxford Economic Papers*, New Series, Vol. II (1950), p. 78.

shareholders (unlimited) to the extent of £208,000 in the Borough Bank.[84] The liabilities of Dennistoun and Cross were in excess of £2 million when they closed their doors on November 8. This failure, which shook the City, had been preceded by the failure on November 4 of the great steelmakers Messrs. Naylor Vickers & Co. of Sheffield for about £1 million.

The panic gained in intensity from the middle of October and became a rout on November 9 with the failure of the Western Bank of Scotland which prompted the Bank of England to raise the discount rate immediately to 10 percent. The Western Bank had 101 branches, deposits of £5.3 million and liabilities of £8.9 million. This failure induced a run on other Glasgow banks, and on November 10 the City of Glasgow Bank suspended payments. The authorities in Glasgow called for troops to withstand expected rioting.

In London, meanwhile, failures were mounting and on the 11th the great discount house of Sanderson, Sandeman & Co. fell with liabilities of £5.3 million. Only the extensive accommodation offered by the Bank of England to the other discount houses saved them. Overend and Gurney alone received assistance of £1.8 million in a matter of three days, and it was feared that Alexanders' might fail.[85] In the final three months of 1857 the Bank gave loans and discounts of £35.8 million (their total for 1857 was £79.4 million), of which Scottish banks received £1.3 million, English banks £7.1 million, bill brokers and discount houses £9.4 million, and merchants and traders £18 million.[86]

Other bank failures included the Wolverhampton and Staffordshire Bank which failed on November 17 throwing the already hard-pressed Midlands into disorder, and the Northumberland and Durham District Bank which failed on November 26 with liabilities of £2.6 million. The exact toll of failures cannot be told, but known failures in Britain with liabilities at or above £5,000 numbered 267, of which 102 were in the Metropolis.[87] Estimated liabilities of houses which failed in the final three months of 1857 run from £41.5 to £50 million, at least twice the estimates for the 1847 crisis.[88]

On the Continent the crisis culminated at Hamburg in December. In that city, financial transactions were paralyzed, and only a loan of 10 million Austrian florins from the Austrian State Bank saved the situation. The loan's conditions were acceded to by the Hamburg Senate on December 12 and the crisis ended abruptly.[89]

---

[84] Their balance sheet given in D. M. Evans, *History of the Commercial Crisis,* 1859, Appendix, p. cxxxviii.

[85] See Clapham's acount of the 1857 crisis in the Bank of England, Vol. II, pp. 226–38.

[86] *S.C. of 1857–58,* Appendix 13.

[87] W. R. Callender, *The Commercial Crisis of 1857,* 1858, appendix.

[88] *Annual Register,* 1857, "Chronicle," p. 221; Callender, *op. cit.,* p. 195; Evans, *op. cit.,* p. 51.

[89] Wirth, *Geschichte der Handelskrisen,* pp. 425–31, and "The History of Banking

The pervasiveness as well as the violence of the 1857 crisis had been unique. All the major commercial centers of the world had been struck by it.

Conclusion

The analysis of the causes of the 1857 crisis developed in this paper raises questions concerning the interpretation of 19th century trade cycles in Britain which may be treated briefly in conclusion.

The evidence adduced above shows that the legacy of the 1858 Committee stating that the 1857 crisis was caused by "excessive speculation and abuse of credit" was somewhat superficial. It proved indeed to be misleading insofar as it caused subsequent writers to overlook other origins of the crisis. However, by concentrating in the main on these other aspects of the 1857 crisis in the present paper it is not meant to entirely bypass the traditional interpretation, but rather, by presenting an analysis of the complex origins of the crisis, to effect a shift in emphasis.

Contemporaries had considerable justification for fixing their eyes on certain monetary aspects of the crisis, and especially those dealing with the expansion of commercial credit. The immense development of the London discount market during the period following the enactment of the 1844 Bank Act, together with the dominance, as the principal negotiable credit instrument, of the inland bill of exchange, with all its well-known variations and abuses, were subjects worthy of close attention. But the concentration of the 1858 Committee on monetary factors led it to ignore the obvious; the rise of the London discount market and the vast growth of the bill system were related parts of the overall expansion of industry and trade. The abuses of the bill system merely aggravated the monetary crisis when it came; the abuses had not caused the expansion of the economic system. Bills and the London discount market lubricated the mechanism of the expansion of trade and industry, but the mechanism was more fouled than was the lubricant by 1857.

Secondly, the pattern of monetary and "real" crises in the 1850's does not conform to the cycle schema recently developed from research in the period 1790–1850. In that cycle schema "major" cycles, those initiated by the combination of both domestic investment and export booms, typically were terminated by monetary crises, while "minor cycles," those not characterized by the existence of booms in domestic investment, ended less violently.[90] In the fifties the major cycle boom, 1853, did not end in a violent monetary convulsion, while the 1856–57 export boom, which was not accompanied by a boom in domestic investment, ended in a monetary collapse which was most violent indeed.

---

in Germany and Austria-Hungary," printed in *A History of Banking in all the Leading Nations* (New York, 1896), pp. 1–2; S.C. of 1857–58, Appendix 20, for description of the 1857 crisis in Hamburg.

[90] Gayer, Rostow, Schwartz, *op. cit.*, Vol. II, pp. 558–63.

If the character of the trade cycle in the 1850's does not conform closely to that of earlier periods, it is not to be wondered at; the character of the trade cycle in the fifties was not more different from that of preceding periods than was its contemporary economic, social, and political environment; and trade cycle history is, after all, but a thin slice of "history" itself. The changing environment, both internal and external, must be taken into account.

The expansion of trade under the stimulus of an unprecedented increase of the commercial world's stock of monetary gold, the related growth of the monetary system and the ascendency of the London bill market,[91] the rapid growth of transportation and communication, combined with the unexampled expansion of industry within Britain, as well as overseas, made the world economy of the fifties markedly different from that of earlier periods, and indeed, even from the years immediately preceding 1848. The relatively slow, although extensive, development of the British industrial economy in the period 1790–1850 should not be expected, a priori, to perform in a cyclical fashion exactly like that of the period of the 1850's—as, indeed, it did not. Moreover, the strong autonomous external forces of the 1850's account for many developments which appear to be unique when compared to earlier periods; the Crimean War itself caused a sufficient autonomous external disturbance (which permeated the economic data all the way from railway construction to cotton exports)[92] to make similarities between the cyclical sequences of the fifties and those earlier periods largely fortuitous. More important, the changing character of the economy also differentiated the 1850's sharply from earlier periods when the industrialization of Britain was more limited.[93] In the more broadly industrialized society developed during the 1850's the repercussions of balance-of-payments difficulties, money market pressures, industrial disturbances and unemployment, and the resulting depressions in trade, were both more extensively felt and more rapidly communicated than in earlier periods.[94] The money market was vulnerable to the demands of an extensive and closely integrated system of trade and finance and could be put under strain from general pressure even without the presence of heavy demand for long-term investment funds.

Thus, although it may be true that in earlier periods violent monetary

---

[91] See W. C. T. King, *History of the London Discount Market* (1936), esp. chaps. 6 and 7.

[92] Railway construction had no important *cyclical* effects in the 1850's and indeed, its income effects tended to be contracyclical in the fifties as they had been in the forties. See chap. viii of the author's thesis cited above for the fifties and Ward-Perkins, *op. cit.*, pp. 85–87 for the forties.

[93] Clapham, *Economic History of Modern Britain*, Vol. II, p. 22. The 1851 census clearly shows that Britain was not yet very fully industrialized.

[94] E.g., during the crisis of 1839 when there was a monetary panic in London, H. W. Hobhouse stated "we knew nothing of it in the country." Quoted, Matthews, *op. cit.*, p. 184.

crises were usually associated only with trade booms which were accompanied by considerable domestic investment, it is clear that the pattern was not typical of the 1850's, and need not have been.

The spread of industrialization during the 1850's seems to make certain aspects of modern trade cycle theory more useful to economic historians in that period than in earlier periods. Although we will argue that this conclusion should hold for most modern general theories of the trade cycle, we will discuss briefly only certain aspects of one trade cycle model which are thrown into focus by the particular emphasis of the analysis developed in the present paper.

In the analysis developed above, the condition of the textile industry in the period 1854–57 suggests the emergence of a sectional resource ceiling of a somewhat modified Hicksian type. But there are considerable difficulties in applying Hicks's system to describe the 1850's without raveling the theory to a certain degree. Perhaps the principal difficulty is that the "ceiling" did not directly raise the *cost* of investment in new plant and equipment, but by raising the cost of production, and given the weakness of the market, it did dampen the incentive to invest. The basic problem is essentially the same as that encountered above in the major and minor cycle schema. The 1856–57 export boom was not a "strong boom," i.e., the acceleration factor did not drive the system to a resource ceiling;[95] new investment in textiles had fallen off considerably when the raw material shortage developed in Britain because investment made in the previous boom (and to a lesser extent in the Crimean War) was being brought into full production.

This difficulty may be overcome, however, since the textile sector was affected by both domestic and foreign investments,[96] and during the period leading up to 1857 there is evidence of a considerable growth of capacity in textile industries abroad.[97] This tended to relate the raw material shortage to a strong boom for textiles on a world scale even though in Britain new investment was generally declining in the period 1854–57.[98]

While the strong boom argument is thus of some significance in the development of the crisis in the textile sector, other important sectors of

---

[95] See *Trade Cycle,* chap. x on the real ceiling and strong and weak booms.

[96] That is, the market for wool, silk, and cotton, etc., was both foreign and domestic as was the source of the raw wool supply, while such raw materials as cotton and silk were entirely foreign in their source of supply and thus foreign competition was an important element in the availability of supplies for British industry.

[97] Hidy, *op. cit.,* p. 436, on continental production; A. L. Dunham, "The Development of the Cotton Industry in France," *Economic History Review* (1928), Vol. 1, pp. 286–88; E. J. Donnell, *Chronological and Statistical History of Cotton* (New York, 1892), p. 647, on American production; and Ellison, *op. cit.,* p. 100, on American and especially continental competition with Britain for available cotton supplies in the period 1841–60.

[98] The author is indebted to Mr. R. C. O. Matthews for the suggestion of this line of argument.

the economy developed in a weak boom fashion. There was in fact a combination of Hicks's three main lines for the ending of a boom.

... with the monetary system remaining passive, the expansion will come to an end in one or other of two ways—either it must die away through weaknesses of the accelerator, or it must be killed by hitting the real ceiling. When we allow for the monetary reaction, we have a third possible way—that the monetary system may find itself over-extended, so that it breaks the boom by monetary contraction, with the object of restoring monetary equilibrium.[99]

In the 1857 crisis all three possibilities were present together, the "real ceiling" in textiles and the dying away of induced investment in such areas as iron and shipbuilding came at the same time the bullion drain weakened the money market and hastened the monetary crisis. There were thus elements of both the Hicksian "constrained" and "free" cycles in the development of the 1857 crisis—but these elements existed concurrently and in modified forms.

These illustrations are not intended as verification or rejection of the relevant portions of the trade cycle model under discussion; but they do indicate that by the 1850's the economy was sufficiently developed to enable modern general trade cycle analysis to be invoked by the economic historian with some benefit. In the case of the investment-dampening effects of the raw material shortages in textiles, this is not, strictly speaking, the sort of real ceiling envisaged in the Hicks model, but there is a certain family resemblance. Moreover, those effects were a general cyclical force of considerable importance, and their importance in the analysis developed above are in contrast to the effects of rising raw material prices on the system in the period 1790–1850.[100]

There may be important implications suggested in this concerning the use of modern trade cycle theory in interpreting British trade cycle history. These may be stated briefly although they are admittedly tentative and require more extensive investigation. It may well be that modern trade cycle theory will be most useful to the economic historian when applied to periods after the industrialization of Britain became quite advanced. As regards earlier periods, economic historians may quite legitimately concentrate on analyses of a less general character; "manias," harvest failures, and mechanical imperfections in financial methods may be more profitably considered as causal factors. In the relatively nonindustrialized British economy of the early 19th century, sensitivity to cyclical repercussions (including fluctuations in foreign trade) was mainly limited to the more diminutive base of trade and industry—which was nevertheless highly volatile to such special disturbances.[101] The growing strength and

---

[99] *Trade Cycle*, p. 159.

[100] See R. C. O. Matthews, "The Trade Cycle in Britain 1790–1850," *Oxford Economic Papers*, New Series, Vol. 6 (1954) p. 7, on findings for investment-dampening effects of rising costs in the period 1790–1850.

[101] E.g., the deflationary effects of poor harvests in the 1830's, Matthews, *Study in*

flexibility of the industrial economy gradually reduced the dangers of general disruption by specific disturbances, but the economy became highly sensitive to general cyclical impulses. In Britain, as in the world economy, the increasing interdependence of expanding trade, industry, and finance was accompanied by the emergence of the trade cycle as a problem which plagued the entire economy. One of the "blessings" of progress, and the price of becoming increasingly involved in the world market, was the extension of the impact of cyclical fluctuations to the whole economy. Pressure in London in 1839 was not felt in the country, but in 1857 the country was deeply involved in the crisis which shook the metropolis.

Quite understandably, modern trade cycle theory developed from observations of present industrial society and financial methods might not be easily applied to an analysis of fluctuations in a largely agricultural society, where only very limited amounts of corporate shares and bonds were available, and where the "old financial system" of the inland bill and the London bill market had not yet been rendered obsolete by the giant bank amalgamations, the dominance of the foreign bill in London, the growth of branch banking and other savings institutions, and the rise of the government departments as major institutions involved in the channeling of savings into industrial investment in Britain.

In the 1850's, while the British economy was developing rapidly into the industrial society we know today, it still contained elements of the old as well as the new society. But the magnitude of industrialization in the 1850's indicates clearly enough why elements of modern theory might be more directly applicable there than in the period before 1848. During the 1850's the growth of trade and the expansion of the monetary system lessened the impact of such elements as harvest failures and manias upon the economic system, but the spread of industrialization and the increasing commercialization of every aspect of British life were welding together an interdependent system of trade, industry, and finance in which cyclical impulses, and income repercussions of either external or internal imbalances, quite rapidly permeated the entire economy.

Trade Cycle History, chap. iv. Poor harvests in the 1850's in 1853, and 1859, heavy imports of corn, and high corn prices did not have the same deflationary effects.

4. A Dollar-Sterling Exchange, 1803-95[*]

Lance E. Davis and Jonathan R. T. Hughes

Purdue University

I

THIS PAPER is an attempt to improve the understanding of 19th century exchange rates, and presents an entirely new series of quarterly data for dollar-sterling transactions. These series, covering nearly the entire 19th century, have been compiled by data processing methods from the records of a single Philadelphia business firm, and constitute a history of exchange prices derived from actual purchases of sterling bills of exchange (bills payable in Britain).[1] In addition, by adjusting for the interest discount on the trade and finance bills for the years 1831–95, a continuous estimate of the "pure" exchange rate—the first ever available to students of 19th-century monetary phenomena—has been adduced.

New light is cast on the "old financial system" that provided the mechanism of international payments before World War I, and it is shown that some revision in the interpretation of the economic history of the period is required. Also, the assumed gold-point "stability" in the 19th century actually seems to have existed, so far as the dollar-sterling exchange is concerned, only in the last 25 to 30 years of the century. Gold-point stability did not depend upon natural order, but rather it developed with the transportation and communications network and with changes in the structure of the exchange market. The actual exchange rates appear to have adjusted themselves to the pace of American economic development and to structural changes in the American balance of payments. Thus, over the long period, the rate moved from a persistent sterling premium to a value averaging close to par. The relative current

[*] Reprinted from the *Economic History Review*, Vol. XIII, No. 1 (August, 1960), pp. 52–78.
[1] For assistance, suggestions, and criticisms of this research we are greatly indebted to Professor James Angell, Professor Arthur Cole, Mr. David Dye, our colleague Professor Stanley Reiter, and to the School of Industrial Management of Purdue University for assistance in defraying the computing costs.

account positions of the United States and the sterling countries, and also the great monetary crises of the period are reflected in the data. Finally, the study suggests that a part of the exchange-rate stability after 1875 was related to specialization among foreign-exchange dealers and the consequent development of an "orderly market."

II

The data come from the records of Nathan Trotter, a Philadelphia metals importer. These records are on deposit in the Baker Library of the Graduate School of Business Administration of Harvard University.[2] During the period from 1803 to 1895 a total of 2,789 bills of exchange were purchased by the Trotter firm and remitted to England to cover British obligations.[3] These bills were mainly of the old commercial type maturing in 30, 60, or 90 days. The record of each bill includes (1) the date of purchase, (2) maturity of the bill, (3) percentage premium or discount (or price paid) for the bill, (4 and 5) the names and (6 and 7) addresses of the drawers and the acceptors (and/or payers), together with the means of conveyance (name of ship, date of sailing, etc., in the years before 1870),[4] and (8) the face amount of the bill.

These bills were mainly drawn on British (usually London) firms to cover American commercial shipments to Britain.[5] Although the bills were drawn on many firms, the acceptors gradually tended to concentrate among the famous British merchant houses specializing in the acceptance business, and as time passed such names as Baring, Brown-Shipley, and Morgan came to predominate. There is no doubt that these were mainly "first-class" bills.

The data, then, are actual dollar prices paid by an American firm for prime sterling exchange *at the relevant maturities*. Exchange rates arising from actual transactions are, in important ways, superior to averages of advertised rates in the commercial press. However, indiscriminate use of the Trotter series should be avoided since data for a single firm only may not be altogether representative. Still, the bills originated in the mainstream of the Anglo-American trade, were endorsed by the best British houses, and were continuously purchased by a successful and old-established firm. Taken together, the facts indicate that the bills were probably representative of the best of such exchange available at any given time. Confidence in these exchange-rate estimates would be improved by the addition of data from firms located in other American cities where ster-

---

2 We are indebted to Mr. Robert Lovett, Chief Archivist of the Baker Library, for generously making these materials available for this study.

3 There are also much less comprehensive figures for various American-European transactions that we have not treated in this paper.

4 We will be glad to supply, at cost, complete decks of these cards to interested scholars.

5 For a complete discussion of Trotter and his business, see Elva Tooker, *Nathan Trotter Philadelphia Merchant* (Cambridge, Mass.: Harvard University Press, 1955).

ling bills were regularly marketed, but such information is not now available.

Had Trotter not purchased time bills of exchange, he could have invested in American earning assets. Trotter was, in fact, granting credit to Americans, and thus the bill prices reflect an interest payment. Moreover, since credit was being granted in the American market, the discount on the bills was the American rate.[6] The British acceptors enhanced the status of the bills by their signatures; but this was done for a fee and in no way altered the essential fact that American discount rates affected the price Trotter paid for the bills.[7]

III

Although materials relating to dollar-sterling exchange rates have generally been considered to be among the most complete economic data available to students of the 19th century, examination of the literature indicates that these materials are fragmentary and can be misleading.[8] First, existing series are not true exchange rates, but are instead bill prices. Thus, since most 19th-century bills were time rather than sight drafts, bill prices reflected both exchange and interest charges. Second, the existing series have been drawn from contemporary newspapers; and as the controversy between Ricardo and Bosanquet emphasized long ago, there can frequently be marked differences between published and actual rates.[9] By adjusting for interest charges and by using data derived from actual transactions, we have attempted to overcome these difficulties.

To produce a comparable series of bill prices covering the 93-year period, adjustments of the original series were necessary. Before 1874, the prices paid for bills of exchange were recorded at face value plus or minus some premium or discount in percent. Thereafter, however, quotations were entered in dollars paid per pound. Adjustment (1) converts the quotations after January 1, 1874 from dollars per pound to a percentage premium or discount.

Adjustment 1.

$$\text{Percent premium or discount} = \frac{\text{Dollars per pound quotation} - \$4.8665}{\$4.8665}.$$

---

[6] This is true regardless of what Trotter's British correspondents did with the remitted bills—whether they were held until the British importer paid them at maturity, or had them discounted in Britain.

[7] The best study we know of this aspect of British merchant banking in the period is still W. T. C. King, *History of the London Discount Market* (1936).

[8] Arthur H. Cole, "Seasonal Variation in Sterling Exchange," *Journal of Economic and Business History*, Vol. II (1929–30), p. 203.

[9] Piero Sraffa (ed.), *The Works and Correspondence of David Ricardo*, Vol. III, *Pamphlets and Papers 1809–1811* (Cambridge, Eng.: Cambridge University Press, 1951), p. 159–75.

Until the resumption of specie payments in 1821 gold payments were suspended in Britain and, since gold was undervalued at the U.S. Mint, it did not circulate in America. Since there are no adequate estimates of sterling prices in this period and, with American bimetallism, there are no reliable American data, it is impossible to adjust the quotations for these depreciation factors. Thus the figures from 1803 to 1821 (Table A–4) are not even pure bill prices, but include also the additional charge necessary to convert dollars into gold less the discount realized from converting gold into sterling.

From 1822 to 1834 both the United States and England maintained convertability, but since gold remained undervalued at the U.S. Mint it seldom circulated in the United States and no true par existed. Moreover, during this period, even the nominal par was incorrect in terms of the legal gold content of the dollar and the pound.[10] Although a pure bill price cannot be estimated, it is possible to adjust for the effects of the American undervaluation of the pound. Adjustment (2) corrects all bill quotations from the years 1823 to 1834 (Table A–5) for the official valuation of the pound at $4.444.[11]

$$\textit{Adjustment 2.} \quad \text{Corrected bill price} = \frac{\text{Actual bill price}}{1.0274}.$$

In 1834 Congress established a new gold-silver purchase price with silver undervalued, gold flowed into the Mint, and the country gradually attained a *de facto* as well as a *de jure* gold standard.[12] After 1834, there-

---

[10] Arthur Cole has emphasized the problems inherent in attempting to estimate exchange rates before 1834:

"In short, there was no true par during the period before 1834. At first the relationship between American and English paper gave no firm basis; and later the comparison of silver and gold, though practically less extremely variable, was theoretically as unsure."

The reader should bear in mind this warning as regards the pre-1834 exchange estimates. "Evolution of the Foreign Exchange Market in the United States," *Journal of Economic and Business History,* Vol. I (1928–29), p. 407.

[11] The revenue act of July 31, 1789 had established an exchange value for the pound of $4.444 while in gold content the true ratio should have been $4.566. A. Barton Hepburn, *A History of Currency in the United States* (New York: Macmillan Co., 1915), p. 61.

[12] The American currency was a bimetallic one with the price of an ounce of pure gold worth 15 ounces of silver according to the Coinage Act of 1792. Since the silver price of gold in Europe was higher than 15–1, gold was undervalued at the U.S. Mint, and, in accordance with Gresham's Law, tended to leave the country. One consequence was a considerable disruption of the American currency system with foreign coins entering into circulation in the U.S.A. In 1834 an attempt was made to correct the difficulties in the United States currency system by raising the silver price of gold from 15:1 to 16.002:1 (and in 1837 a further adjustment placed the silver valuation of gold at 15.988 ounces to 1 ounce of gold), where it remained until 1873 when the United States ceased minting silver dollars. See such standard works as F. W. Taussig, *Principles of Economics* (3rd ed., 1921); or more recently, Ross M. Robertson, *History of the American Economy* (1955).

fore, bill prices no longer reflect depreciation or silver conversion charges, but instead contain only exchange and interest rates. However, the rate quotations need further adjustment since, by custom, they were quoted as percentage deviations from a $4.444 pound, even though the exchange par after 1834 was $4.8665. Adjustment (3) corrects the 1834–74 data for a quotation based upon a customary par of $4.444 rather than a true par of $4.8665.

Adjustment 3. Corrected bill price $= \dfrac{\text{Actual bill price}}{1.09456}$.

Finally, between 1862 and 1879 some bills were purchased in depreciated greenbacks, and it is necessary to adjust for this depreciation of the paper currency. Adjustment (4) corrects the greenback bills for the additional payments needed to purchase gold dollars.

Adjustment 4. Let V_S = value of the bill in pounds
  K = \$4.8865
  D = dollar price in gold of \$1 greenback[13]
  V_G = value of the bill in greenbacks
  P = total premium or discount (exchange rate + interest payment + greenback discount)
  E = premium or discount required to purchase a bill with gold

then

$$V_G = \frac{KV_S + E(KV_S)}{D}$$

and

$$P = \frac{V_G - KV_S}{KV_S}$$

substituting for V_G

$$P = \frac{\dfrac{KV_S + E(KV_S)}{D} - KV_S}{KV_S}$$

which reduces to

$$P = \frac{1 + E}{D} - 1$$

thus

$$E = D(P + 1) - 1.$$

These four adjustments provide a clear bill price series for the years 1835 to 1895 (Table A–1) and a series adjusted for the undervaluation

---

13 Greenback depreciation estimates are the daily figures of Wesley C. Mitchell and were applied, day by day, on the date of purchase. *Gold, Prices and Wages Under the Greenback Standard*, University of California Publications on Economics, I (Berkeley: California University Press, 1908), pp. 287–338.

of the pound (although not a clear bill price series) for the years 1823 to 1834 (Table A–5).

However, the data still contain an interest element. For the earlier period there are no adequate estimates of American interest rates, and so no interest adjustment is made before 1831. Even after that date there are no reliable interest series for Philadelphia; and, as a result, it is necessary to substitute other series. In the postbellum period the eastern United States possessed an integrated short-term credit market. Therefore, Macaulay's data on 60- to 90-day commercial paper rates in New York City are taken to represent an adequate approximation of similar rates in Philadelphia. For the earlier period, because of poorer communications and certain capital immobilities, no single market did exist. Therefore, two series were chosen: Bigelow's data on 60- to 90-day paper in New York and Boston (a particularly volatile series) and Davis's data on 30- to 60-day textile credit in Boston (a more stable series).[14] It appears probable that the Philadelphia rates lay somewhere between Bigelow's and Davis's estimates. If the differences between the series were large, the exchange-rate estimates based on them would be of little value; however, as the chart indicates, the range is quite small and therefore the adjusted series can be taken to present an accurate and usable exchange-rate series for the antebellum period.

Adjustment (5) corrects the bill prices for the interest component.

Adjustment 5. Let P = the price paid for the bill in dollars

$\bar{P}$ = the price paid in dollars after the discount for interest

d = the exchange premium or discount in dollars

m = \$4.8665

$\dfrac{d}{m}$ = the exchange rate

B = the face value of the bill in pounds

i = the rate of interest

$$\left(\frac{(\text{annual rate} \times \text{bill length in days})}{365} \right)$$

$$\bar{P} = (m + d)B$$

$$P = \bar{P}(1 - i)$$

---

[14] Macaulay's figures are in Frederick R. Macaulay, *The Movements of Bond Yields, Interest Rates, Stock Prices in the United States Since 1856* (New York: National Bureau of Economic Research, 1938), A142–A151. Davis's figures are in Lance E. Davis, "The Rate of Interest and Ante-Bellum Finance: Some Notes on the Capital Market 1840–1860," Appendix A–3 (forthcoming).

Bigelow's figures are in Macaulay, *op. cit.*, A248–A250.

substituting for $\bar{P}$

$$P = B(m + d)(1 - i)$$

then

$$\frac{d}{m} = \left[\frac{P}{mB(1 - i)} - 1 \right].$$

Since, in the case of a time bill, the buyer is actually lending the seller money, a positive interest rate will reduce the selling price of the bill. Therefore, adjustment (5) should increase the premium or reduce the discount.

The data (Tables A1, A2, and A5) have been corrected for the relevant adjustments.

IV

Although there are no independent checks on the adjusted figures, it is possible to compare the bill price series with Martin's independent estimates for the period 1835 to 1895.[15] As the chart indicates, there is general compatibility between the Trotter bill series and data previously derived from newspaper accounts; however, the two conflict in several periods. In part these differences simply reflect the origin of the two series, but in part they also seem to indicate underlying economic differences. Table A–1 clearly shows three periods of substantial difference between the series. First, for the unsettled years 1839 to 1841 the Trotter data average much higher and show much sharper peaks than do Martin's series. Second, opposite cycles of considerable magnitude exist during the Civil War years 1863 and 1864. Third, although the two series move together very closely after 1865, the Martin series average about .5 percent below the Trotter figures.

Of the three periods the last can be most easily explained. Both series are bill prices (not corrected for interest rates); however, while the newspaper data are for 60- to 90-day bills throughout, the Trotter figures are conditioned by the maturities of the bills actually purchased and reflect the general reduction of maturities that followed the Civil War. Thus the changed position of the Trotter figures after 1865 probably represents nothing but the difference between interest on 0 to 20-day bills and those of longer maturities.[16]

Although both series reach peaks in the fourth quarter of 1839 and again in the fourth quarter of 1841, the peaks in the Trotter series are much the sharpest (8 and 4 percent sterling premium as compared with 0 and 0 percent). Moreover, the Trotter series indicate roughly a 2.5 percent sterling premium during these years while the newspaper series

---

15 Joseph G. Martin, *One Hundred Years History of the Boston Stock Market* (Boston: privately printed, 1897), pp. 28 and 51a.a.

16 A comparison of the two series after interest adjustment shows the same conformity that characterized the antebellum period.

show about a 1 percent sterling discount. The divergence here most probably is due to actual economic differences rather than to any problems inherent in the data. Although the whole country suffered from the crisis of 1839, Philadelphia was more severely hit than other areas. The crisis of 1839–41 was touched off in Philadelphia by the initial difficulties of the Bank of the United States and culminated less than two years later with the final collapse of that institution.[17] The banks of Philadelphia had been active in the foreign-exchange market, and Pennsylvania alone of the financial and foreign-exchange centers suspended payment on her debt.[18] It is not surprising that Philadelphia received more than its share of foreign suspicion. Moreover, Philadelphia trade suffered more from the crash than did trade in other areas and those Philadelphia merchants who were still solvent were pressed for payment of their outstanding foreign debts. Thus the Philadelphia merchants, forced into the exchange market, raised the demand for bills while the depressed state of business activity reduced the supply.

The divergence that occurs during the sixties is much more difficult to explain. The Trotter series show a trough of −2.5 percent in the second quarter of 1863 and a peak of 2.5 percent in the third quarter of 1864. Conversely, Martin's series show a peak of 2 percent in the third quarter of 1863 and a trough of −3.5 percent in the second quarter of 1864. Since Union fortunes were at their nadir in 1863 and Union success was fairly well assured by 1864, logic would dictate a pattern similar to that found in the newspaper series. The divergences, then, must have been the product of conditions peculiar to Philadelphia.

V

Perhaps the most striking and original findings of this study appear in the analysis of the long-term movements of the dollar-sterling exchange rates (Table A–1). In particular two facts stand out. First, if the Civil War years are excluded, there appears to have been a gradual damping of the rate fluctuations over the period. Second, although on the average slight sterling premiums prevailed throughout, there was a steady reduction of this premium over time.

During the 1830's the rates varied from −5 to 13 percent, in the 1840's

---

[17] For a general discussion of financial difficulties during the period 1839–41 see Bray Hammond, *Banks and Politics in America from the Revolution to the Civil War* (Princeton, N.J.: Princeton University Press, 1957), pp. 500–48; also Robert C. O. Matthews, *A Study in Trade-Cycle History* (Cambridge, Eng.: Cambridge University Press, 1954), chap. v.

[18] For a description of the foreign-exchange dealings of the Second Bank of the United States, see Ralph Hidy, "The House of Baring and the Second Bank of the United States 1826–1836," *Pennsylvania Magazine*, Vol. LXVIII (1944), pp. 270–72. The suspension of state debts is best covered by Reginald C. McCrane, *Foreign Bondholders and American State Debt* (New York, 1935). Also in Leland H. Jenks, *The Migration of British Capital to 1875* (New York, 1927), pp. 99–125.

from 2.5 to 3.5 percent, in the 1850's from .5 to 2.5 percent, in the first postbellum decade from —.5 to 1 percent, and from —.5 to .5 percent during the last two decades of the study. Further evidence of this trend can be seen in the variances shown in Table 1. This progressive damping has been noted before, but scholars usually explained it by reference to

TABLE 1

VARIANCES OF EXCHANGE RATES BY DECADE

Decades	Bigelow	Variance Davis	Macaulay
	All Quarters		
1834–40	.001460		
1841–50	.000269	.000260	
1851–60	.000110	.000052	.000100*
1861–70			.000140
1871–80			.000060
1881–90			.000005
1891–95(3)			.000007
* 1857–60			
	Periods of Bank Suspension Excluded		
1834–40	.000590		
1841–50	.000181	.000094	
1851–60	.000077	.000050	.000086*
1861–70			.000088
1871–80			.000029
1881–90			.000005
1891–95			.000007
* 1857–60			

factors external to the American economy. The reduction is supposed to have been due to reduced ocean-transport costs coupled with the increased speed and reliability of transport and communications and the development of adequate ocean insurance.[19] These were important factors, but they were powerfully reinforced by fundamental changes within the U.S. economy. First, as the banking system developed greater stability, bank specie suspensions became less frequent. Because suspensions effectively revoked the "gold standard" in the areas affected, early financial crises produced extraordinarily wide fluctuations in the exchange rates.[20] Second, as communication and transportation facilities improved, the U.S. financial market became better integrated; and thus internal exchange rates disappeared and rates in any city were conditioned by rates in contiguous areas. This widening of the "extent" of the exchange market also tended to damp the amplitude of the fluctuations. Only during the Civil War was this tendency reversed—in that period the effects

19 Arthur H. Cole, "Evolution," pp. 405–6.
20 Evidence of the effects of banking improvements on the exchange rates can be garnered from a comparison of the variances of the series adjusted for bank suspensions with variances of the unadjusted series (Table 1). Over time the two figures tend to come together.

of secular improvements in the markets were more than offset by war-induced changes in expectations and in the balance of payments. Moreover, secession drastically reduced the extent of the market.

In general the reduction of the sterling premiums was due to the secular strengthening of the American current-account position. The largest sterling premiums existed during the 1830's when the United States incurred large current-account deficits, and during the 1850's when American imports increased rapidly. Conversely, the largest sterling discounts occurred during the 1840's, when American imports were sharply curtailed and the U.S. ran an actual surplus on current account.[21] Finally, after 1875 the sterling premium practically disappears, and this disappearance follows the emergence of an almost permanent current-account surplus in the U.S. balance of payments.

Table A–3 shows the secular drift in the maturities of the bills of exchange. Before 1867 the customary length was about 60 days. After 1867, however, the average length dropped to 10 days and after 1882 all bills were sight bills. Although the decline followed closely on the completion of the Atlantic Cable and manifested itself in the shift to sight drafts, the evidence indicates that it was not due to the innovation of cable transfers. Instead, the introduction of sight drafts was evidently a delayed response to the continuous improvements in the speed and reliability of ocean transport that had been in process for more than two decades.[22] The slow innovation of cable drafts is very surprising; in fact, after the initial decline, average maturities actually increased until the mid-1870's. Cable drafts were not used until 1879 and it was 1882 before time bills had disappeared from Trotter's purchases.[23] Perhaps, since the drawing of a time bill involved the granting of credit by the drawer to the payer, changes in the credit structure were necessary prerequisites for a shortening of the average maturity. Certainly it is possible that the absence of a decline in maturities before 1867 and the slow innovation of cable drafts may indicate a failure of alternative credit sources to supply funds. Such a shortening may well have awaited developments in the credit market that relieved the sellers of the necessity of supplying the buyers with credit.

VI

To what extent can a purely a priori model of exchange rate fluctuations constructed without reference to the economic history of the period

---

[21] Charles J. Bullock, John H. Williams, Rufus S. Tucker, "The Balance of Trade of the United States," *Review of Economic Statistics,* Preliminary Vol. I (1919), pp. 219–20.

[22] See Douglas C. North, "Ocean Freight Rates and Economic Development," *Journal of Economic History* (December, 1958), on the importance of such factors as improved port facilities and other external economies in speeding up ocean transport in the 19th century: Jonathan R. T. Hughes and Stanley Reiter, "The First 1,945 British Steamships," *Journal of the American Statistical Association* (June, 1958), on steamers and improved speeds in ocean transport before 1860.

[23] Cole, "Evolution," p. 415.

describe actual movements of rates in the 19th century? Although the Trotter data provide a rough descriptive answer to this question a really adequate answer can only be supplied by the application of the data to detailed short-term studies. A formal a priori analysis is easily developed under drastic simplifying assumptions.

Assume a two-country economy without interest or exchange arbitrage, and no extraordinary events which might shake financial "confidence." Assume further that, in bilateral trade, each nation's imports of goods and services (including gold) constitute the supply of each nation's currency to the other (exports, then measure reciprocal demand).[24] If, then, cycles developed inversely (a postulate of the classical price-specie flow analysis) the expanding country would have the exchanges "against" it; that is, its currency would be in excess supply. If, as was usually the case in the Anglo-American trade in the 19th century, the short-period cycles were not inverse, but rather were roughly synchronous, the same analysis applies, but the adverse exchange would be a measure of relative expansions and favorable exchange of relative contractions.[25]

Using this general model it is at times possible to judge the relative intensities of expansions and contractions—assuming fixed import propensities. However only when the simplifying assumptions are relaxed and allowance is made for the actual patterns of economic growth and change in the period can the larger portion of the movements in the exchange rates actually be understood. Fundamentally, there are three explanations for the breakdown of the simple model: (1) the narrowing of the gold points in the 1870's (the *communications effect*), (2) gold-payment suspensions during extreme monetary crises (the *crisis effect*), and (3) the secular expansion of American demand throughout the ante-bellum period (the *development effect*).

The "development effect" appears particularly marked before 1860. The United States was a large-scale capital importer and, usually, a debtor on current account. Thus the exchanges frequently reflect the impact of excess dollar demand for sterling. In the years of rapid internal expansion (the 1830's and 1850's) sterling was at a strong premium and only during the stagnation of the early and middle 1840's did the sterling premium give way to a discount for any extended period. Before 1860, then, the development effect obscures the expected results.

There were always gold points in the Anglo-American trade; that is, exchange rates so extreme that gold was shipped instead of bills. Wide

---

[24] By taking imports as given, we subsume the elasticities of demand for imports and exports which constitute the formal analysis of exchange-rate determination. For the formal analysis see Joan Robinson, *Essays in the Theory of Employment* (Oxford, 1947), "The Foreign Exchanges," pp. 134–55.

[25] We thus avoid the perilous questions raised by the existence of the "long cycle" in the Anglo-American economy treated by Brinley Thomas in his *Migration and Economic Growth* (Cambridge, Eng.: Cambridge University Press, 1954). It has been noted that, for both technical and structural reasons, the range of fluctuations of the dollar-sterling exchange narrowed drastically after the mid-1860's. Cyclical effects can, therefore, be observed only within very narrow limits after that period.

as these were in the earlier years of the century, they did impose limits on the exchange fluctuations. However, in times of bank suspension the expected cyclical effects are further obscured by total or partial suspensions of gold payments that acted to broaden the gold points. At these times the crisis effect obscures the "expected" results.

As the exchange market developed, and as both internal and external communication and transportation networks were improved, the communications effect also affected the exchanges so as to obliterate many of the expected results derived from the simple model. After 1870 the reduction of the costs of exporting gold, the more rapid communications, and the formalization of exchange arbitrage left little room for fluctuations in exchange rates.

An examination of the short-term fluctuations in the exchange rates underscores the divergence between the actual movements in rates and those expected from the simple model.

In the interest-corrected data, the a priori model first fails to make adequate predictions in the years between 1836 and 1842, a period marked by two general American bank suspensions. The first lasted from May 10, 1837, when the New York banks led the banking system into a general suspension, until 1839, when the Philadelphia banks finally resumed payments. The second general suspension began on October 10, 1839, when the Bank of the United States first closed its doors and only the banks of New York and New England maintained payments. Although resumption was attempted in Philadelphia early in 1841, final resumption was delayed until the spring of 1842.[26] In this period little scope remains for the a priori analysis to explain short movements.

Wide fluctuations recurred in the period 1846–49, but again the simple model does not adequately explain the fluctuations. The great Irish immigration to the U.S. increased the sterling supply, as did British imports of American grain that rose during the famine and after the repeal of the Corn Laws.[27] Moreover, early in 1847 the first of the two British financial crises of that year struck London; the second came in the autumn. Initially, sterling fell to a discount; but by the fall of 1847, with the restriction clause of the Bank Act "suspended," and bank rate at 8 percent, sterling again rose to a strong premium—the exchanges had been "turned."[28]

The exchange-rate phenomena of the 1850's are particularly mystifying. The sterling premium rose as the American crisis of 1857 developed, and this was followed by a sharp decline at the end of the year when a

---

[26] For discussion of this period see Hepburn, *History*, chaps. v, vi; W. G. Sumner, *A History of the American Currency* (New York, 1874), pp. 132–54.

[27] C. N. Ward-Perkins, "The Commercial Crisis of 1847," *Oxford Economic Papers*, New Series 2, No. 1 (January, 1950), pp. 80–81, on British food imports in 1845–48 from the U.S.

[28] The method of temporarily suspending the 1844 Bank Act devised in 1847 was utilized again in 1857 and in 1866. It is described by Ward-Perkins, *ibid.*, p. 78.

10 percent bank rate ruled in London, and the Bank Act of 1844 was again suspended.[29] Neither the simple formal model, nor a more complex one based upon the obvious external evidence, suffices to provide an altogether satisfactory explanation of the movement of the exchange rates in 1857—nor, for that matter, in the 1850's in general.[30]

Although short-term fluctuations in 1860–65 can be partly explained by the basic model, the outbreak of war injected other new elements that can only be analyzed in terms of a more complex scheme. In America 1860 was a prosperous year with large gold exports and a sharp reduction in the merchandise deficit. These events were accompanied by a dollar premium which lasted into 1861. This premium is an expected result. As war pressure increased, however, gold imports rose and the merchandise deficit increased sharply. A general specie suspension followed in December, 1861. The resulting sterling premium was broken only once during the war by the short-lived dollar premium of 1863 (perhaps a reflection of the Treasury's attempts to make gold payments on the debt coupled with the Treasury's strengthened position following the authorization of a $900 million 6 percent bond issue of March, 1863).[31] Although the more complicated model is needed to explain these fluctuations, the extraordinarily large merchandise deficit of 1864 ($157.6 millions, the largest yet seen in American history) was accompanied by the reappearance of the sterling premium—another expected result.

The end of hostilities was accompanied by a reduction in the amplitude of fluctuations—a manifestation of the development effect, coupled with the disappearance of the crisis effect as the banking system was stabilized. So powerful were these forces that the resumption of specie payments, the American bank suspensions of 1873 and 1893 and the "Baring Crisis" of 1890 had no extraordinary effects upon the exchanges. Apparently by the 1870's the gold-payments mechanism, both domestic and foreign, of the classical "gold standard" era had become efficient enough to wipe out the crisis effects, while the development of a quick and efficient interest and exchange arbitrage market, supported by telegraphic communications, limited expected exchange movements within the narrow range customarily associated with the gold points.

VIII

The Trotter data cast a light on the pre-1914 financial system in two areas: exchange stability (the gold points), that will be treated here, and

---

[29] Jonathan R. T. Hughes, "The Commercial Crisis of 1857," *Oxford Economic Papers*, New Series, Vol. 8, No. 2 (June, 1956), pp. 215–16.

[30] Professor Cole suggests that the peculiar exchange-rate pattern of the 1850's may be explained in terms of the adjustments to the changes in tariffs (both American and British), and thus in relative prices, that occurred during the later 1840's. Although there is no direct proof of this thesis, it does provide a logical explanation, and certainly is worthy of further exploration.

[31] On the Loan Act of 1863 authorizing the U.S. Treasury to sell bonds to make gold payments see Sumner, *American Currency*, pp. 206–8.

the perfection of the market for short-term international funds, the subject of the following section.

When gold could be freely purchased and shipped abroad, gold exports were an alternative to bills of exchange. Thus a limit, the gold points, existed to fluctuations in the exchange rate. The precise levels of the pre-1914 gold points have never been agreed upon. Indeed, few students have been bold enough even to estimate the actual exchange limits.[32] Fluctuations about the mint-par values are generally thought to have been small, with the actual amplitude determined by the costs of shipping gold.

Table A–1 indicates that the exchanges were fairly stable during the 1850's and were permanently stabilized by the mid-1870's.[33] However, the ranges of the exchange fluctuations differed markedly between the two periods. The sterling premium was, on the average, much higher during the 1850's than it was after 1870. The size of the premium in the 1850's is difficult to explain. The American economy was then expanding rapidly and imports were growing concomitantly. At the same time, however, American exports were growing and in most years Britain incurred a bilateral trade deficit with the United States. Moreover, U.S. gold exports to and capital imports from Britain were substantial.[34]

Considering these movements, and especially in view of the fact that the exchange rates were evidently more stable during the fifties than in

---

[32] See Oskar Morgenstern, *International Financial Transactions and Business Cycles* (Princeton, N.J.: Princeton University Press, 1959), pp. 176–91, for an enumeration and discussion of gold-point estimates.

For many decades *The Economist* printed what it called the gold-point "standards." But these were not meant to be *the* gold points. Indeed, the editors frequently reported rates of exchange which exceeded their own gold-point standards, and apparently did not think this inconsistency worthy of comment. If the rates were usually out of line for a known cause, e.g., the Bank of France paying premium prices for specie, some comment might be made, but usually the editors were silent.

[33] Professor Cole argues that the stability of the 1850's was a false stability, i.e., not induced by the maturity of the market but by the large supplies of gold available in the United States and the large gold exports, that characterized the period. Arthur Cole, "Seasonal Variations," p. 202.

[34] The official British figures show a bilateral trade deficit with the United States in each year from 1854 to 1860. The official American figures show a bilateral trade surplus with Britain in each year between 1856 and 1860. However, they show a bilateral trade deficit with Britain in 1850 and from 1852 to 1855. In most cases the discrepancies between these two sets of data are far too wide to be accounted for by freight charges counted into the value of imports. If it were not for the heavy U.S. gold exports and the flow of British capital to the United States, the official American data might afford some explanation of the exchange-rate movements up to 1855. However, the gold exports leave the United States with a net trade-gold surplus with Britain in every year except 1850, 1853, and 1854; and even in those years the deficits are so small that modest capital imports should have depressed the price of sterling below par. We cannot explain the exchange rates in this period from the trade data.

British data in each year are to be found in the *Statistical Abstract* for the period. The American data are to be found in U.S. Congress, *The Miscellaneous Documents of the House of Representatives*, 52d Cong., 2d sess., 1892–93 (30 Vols., Washington, D.C.: Government Printing Office, 1893), Vol. 26, pp. XLIV and LX.

any previous decade, even the fact that the fifties was a period of financial chaos and specie suspension in America hardly accounts for the continued sterling premium. We can offer no solution for this paradox. The fact that both British and American records show a heavy American export of gold to Britain during the 1850's affords additional proof that a sterling premium did exist; and our examination of British and American trade suggests the explanation must lie in the extant system of multilateral trade and payments. Evidently the international economy at mid-century offers a fruitful ground for further research.

In the 1870's and after, the smooth-working gold-payments system damped fluctuations, and, at the same time but for other reasons, the long-term sterling premium was virtually eliminated. If when one speaks of the "stable" exchanges of the gold standard one is referring to the period after 1875, the data support the assumption of stability. However, they also indicate that the stability that prevailed before 1870 was something quite different in character.

Even for the late period, however, the rates appear to have been somewhat less stable than has been generally assumed. In the most exhaustive examination of this issue in the literature, Professor Morgenstern has found numerous occasions when the exchanges fluctuated beyond the known estimates of the gold points.[35] Morgenstern calls these rates "violations" of the gold points. However, by accepting the validity of the known gold-point estimates, Professor Morgenstern has accepted a very peculiar definition of "the" gold points. If his work is accepted uncritically, it would appear that even after 1875 Trotter continually violated the gold export point. Professor Morgenstern's median New York export point is a .473 percent sterling premium while his maximum New York export point is only .678 percent.[36] As Table A–5 indicates, Trotter frequently bought sterling at premiums beyond one or both of these points.[37] Moreover, since the Trotter data are quarterly averages, it would seem that these violations were even more flagrant than Morgenstern's monthly violations.[38]

What were the gold points? The Trotter series indicate the rates at which sterling was actually purchased. Professor Morgenstern's gold points are, on the other hand, merely contemporary estimates and his median points result from splitting the difference between conflicting estimates. Moreover, since Morgenstern is perfectly aware that the gold points could differ as between individuals, it is odd that he considers his

---

[35] Morgenstern, *International Finance Transactions*, pp. 241–76.

[36] *Ibid.*, Table 33, p. 177, for New York export point (London import point); p. 172 for discussion of New York–London points.

[37] See Table A–2 below in the years 1876, 1880, 1881, 1882, 1884, 1886, 1889, 1891, and 1895.

[38] *Financial Transactions*, pp. 276–78 for Morgenstern's discussion of his exchange-rate data.

aggregated estimates to be *the* gold points.[39] His own data indicate that there was, in fact, slightly more variation in the exchange rates than his gold-point estimators thought; and the Trotter figures provide additional support for this conclusion. Thus the violations of Professor Morgenstern's gold points would hardly seem to be an "incredible phenomenon."[40] The Trotter data, of course, do not establish a new estimate of the gold export point, but they do, however, place a lower limit on the size of that figure.

What the gold points actually were is a complex question; it appears certain, both from our data and from Professor Morgenstern's violations, that students of the gold standard have given the payments mechanism that existed from 1875 to 1914 more stability than it actually had. But, compared to the previous three quarters of a century, the period was characterized by remarkable exchange-rate stability. This stability is, of course, a long way from "fixed" exchange rates. Actually the only point that separates us from Professor Morgenstern is the definition of stability. By his criteria, the exchanges were less stable than might be expected; by ours (comparison with what had gone before), the exchanges after 1875 were remarkably stable.

VIII

Was the dollar-sterling exchange market always specialized to the extent it was in 1875–1914? The analysis of Trotter's bills adds new material relating to this question, and also provides additional information on the origins of sterling bills in the U.S. market. Although Miss Tooker has attempted to analyze the sources of some of Trotter's bills, her results differ significantly from those we obtained.[41] While Miss Tooker used a sample of Trotter's bills, the analysis presented in this paper utilizes a complete enumeration. Moreover, Miss Tooker has taken as point of origin the location of the last endorser of the bill. Such a classification would be important in a study of internal trade patterns, but it is largely irrelevant to a study of international trade where the important point is the geographical distribution of the original drawers.

Table 2 indicates that the most important sources of bills were Philadelphia and the American South. During two short periods, however, significant quantities of bills also originated in British North America and the Caribbean.

The American South was an important source of sterling bills in almost every year from 1811 to 1860.[42] Such long-term dominance, although it disagrees with Miss Tooker's findings, is consistent with the generally accepted picture of American foreign trade in the antebellum period. A

---

[39] *Ibid.*, p. 167, n.l.

[40] *Ibid.*, p. 276.

[41] Elva Tooker, *Nathan Trotter*, pp. 98–102.

[42] For purposes of this study the South is defined as the area south of the Mason-Dixon line and the Ohio River and east of Mississippi (excluding Baltimore and Washington, D.C.).

study of American trade figures indicates that the South generated between 40 and 60 percent of total American exports in every decade before the Civil War; and it seems reasonable to assume that the South did not purchase an equal share of the total imports.[43] Miss Tooker, however, states that southern bills were not important in Philadelphia until after 1840. Although her conclusion appears to conflict with the facts, an examination of the data does suggest some explanations for it. First, there was an increase in the proportion of southern bills after 1840, but this was probably only a reflection of the economic disturbances in Philadelphia. Second, before 1840 many southern bills were attracted to Philadelphia by the Second Bank of the United States—an institution with important factoring connections in the South and with a predilection for dealing in the foreign exchange market.[44] Before the Bank's collapse, many southern bills bore its endorsement; but, thereafter, such bills came directly to the Philadelphia market.

Although local and southern bills usually represented the bulk of the exchange available in Philadelphia, during the last half of the 1820's and during the 1840's bills from Canadian North America and the West Indies appeared in profusion. The first influx of West Indian and Canadian bills evidently resulted from changes in Anglo-American commercial policy. In 1823 the American tariff was modified to admit products from the West Indies and Canada at much reduced duties. Although the British did not reciprocate until 1826, the American action did stimulate trade and probably accounts for the increased number of West Indian bills appearing after 1823. In January, 1826, the West Indian trade was opened to American shipping and a new surge of Caribbean bills came to the Philadelphia market. However, this liberal policy was soon reversed and beginning in January, 1827, only British North America remained open to American shipping. As a result, until 1830 the American West Indian trade was conducted through the intermediate ports in Canada and Nova Scotia. The increase in British North American bills that appeared after 1826 was almost certainly due to Canada's new role in the West Indian trade.[45]

Bills originating outside the U.S. decline in importance after 1830, and this decline apparently is due to changes in the American balance of payments. Although during the 1830's American imports grew much more rapidly than exports, there was also an increase in the flow of British capital to the U.S.; and thus the need for foreign bills payable in London was to some extent relieved.[46]

[43] George Taylor, *The Transportation Revolution* (New York, 1951), p. 451. At the outbreak of the Civil War the South represented slightly less than one third of the total population. If one assumes the propensities to import were the same in the South as in the rest of the country, the excess of southern bills should have turned up in other parts of the country to supply a part of the difference between nonsouthern exports and imports.

[44] Ralph Hidy, "Baring and the Second Bank," 270–71.

[45] Harold A. Innis, *The Cod Fisheries, The History of An International Economy* (New Haven: Yale University Press, 1940), pp. 249–60.

[46] Between 1831 and 1838 American imports exceeded exports by $150 million,

TABLE 2
Geographic Distribution of Bills by Drawer
(In Percent of Total)

Date	Phila-delphia	New York	U.S. South	U.S. North	U.S. West	British North America	Carib-bean and South America	Balti-more and Wash-ington	Europe
1803....100.00									
1804....72.11								11.95	15.94
1805....95.66									4.34
1806....97.05		2.95							
1807....98.47		1.53							
1808....89.74		10.26							
1809....95.44		4.56							
1810....42.93	53.03	4.04							
1811....	47.71	52.29							
1812....98.83	1.17								
1813....92.59		7.41							
1814....n.d.*									
1815....		55.31	44.69						
1816....18.03		.72	81.12						
1817....57.90		42.10							
1818....51.58	8.84	39.58							
1819....16.67		83.33							
1820....		83.64				16.36			
1821....22.09		74.76	3.14						
1822....77.85		22.15							
1823....92.50		4.50				3.00			
1824....59.60		22.87				1.75	15.78		
1825....26.30		43.47	2.27			27.96			
1826....47.22		7.79			13.18	28.42	3.41		
1827....40.29	18.27	3.78			32.46	.98	4.22		
1828....54.54		11.45			33.11	.90			
1829....32.70		24.04	1.61		29.09	12.55			
1830....39.35					60.65				
1831....55.94					30.37		13.68		
1832....49.21		44.24			3.68	2.87			
1833....24.08		70.61	4.40		.90				
1834....49.03		50.97							
1835....58.84		41.16							
1836....86.55		8.88				4.57			
1837....41.53		49.94		.07	1.72	6.74			
1838....22.45		77.56							
1839.... 8.78	14.41	76.82							
1840....10.00	2.57	80.77				6.34		.31	
1841.... 4.43	10.87	72.99		.44		11.25			
1842....16.77	28.07	35.19			6.37	10.46		2.38	
1843.... .91	40.55	3.65			14.14	40.75			
1844....29.10		24.48			8.32	37.48		.62	
1845....10.09		10.01			11.84	68.07			
1846....17.50	1.07	15.52			21.36	44.56		.26	
1847....60.78		12.02			2.66	19.22		5.31	
1848....54.32	5.76	27.15				12.77			
1849....68.65		25.78			.53	3.93	1.11		

TABLE 2 (*Continued*)

Date	Phila-delphia	New York	U.S. South	U.S. North	U.S. West	British North America	Carib-bean and South America	Balti-more and Wash-ington	Europe
1850	63.01		34.66			.56	1.15		.62
1851	63.22		31.13				5.32		.33
1852	75.09		13.14				11.77		
1853	74.67		25.33						
1854	61.07		32.22				6.71		
1855	81.96		18.04						
1856	74.79		25.51						
1857	79.20		20.80						
1858	75.77		24.23						
1859	78.40	1.77	15.59					4.23	
1860	65.36	18.74	13.85				2.04		
1861	94.94	5.06							
1862	92.65					5.17	2.18		
1863	96.73	3.27							
1864	100.00								
1865	100.00								
1866	100.00								
1867	100.00								
1868	100.00								
1869	100.00								
1870	100.00								
1871	100.00								
1872	100.00								
1873	100.00								
1874	100.00								
1875	100.00								
1876	100.00								
1877	100.00								
1878	96.63		3.37						
1879	100.00								
1880	100.00								
1881	100.00								
1882	100.00								
1883	100.00								
1884	100.00								
1885	100.00								
1886	100.00								
1887	100.00								
1888	100.00								
1889	14.31		85.69						
1890	73.98		26.02						
1891	100.00								
1892	100.00								
1893	100.00								
1894	100.00								
1895	100.00								

Again, in the 1840's, West Indian bills appear in significant quantities in Philadelphia. The increase of foreign bills in this case can probably be traced to three separate but not altogether unrelated factors. First, the crisis of 1837–41 reduced the supply of local bills. Second, the cessation of capital imports raised American demand for real bills. Third, the rising level of British income engendered an increase in the consumption of West Indian commodities and as a result, produced a supply of uncovered bills available for sale in the United States.[47]

Before 1860 about half of Trotter's bills were of local (Philadelphia) origin; and, of those acquired after the Civil War, almost all were originally drawn there. The antebellum concentration is not surprising. Philadelphia was important as a trading center; and, although the city's commerce grew little in the pre–Civil War period, bills were generated and appeared on the local market. Only once during the years covered by the study do Trotter's records indicate a marked reduction in the proportion of Philadelphia bills. Although local bills represented about one half of the total during the first six decades, between 1838 and 1846 they represented less than 12 percent. This sharp decline can probably be traced to the disturbed condition of the Philadelphia financial and commodity markets following the crises of 1837–39.

After 1860 the proportion of Philadelphia bills rose precipitously; and, except for three years, local bills constituted the entire market supply from 1863 to the end of the period. Moreover, as the proportion of Philadelphia bills rose, there was a steady decline in the number of drawers. By 1874 two firms, Brown and Brown, and Drexel and Company, supplied almost all the bills purchased by Trotter.[48]

A similar concentration is seen in payers of the bills purchased by Trotter. In total, Trotter's bills were "accepted" by 295 different persons or firms.[49] Apparently Trotter, to avoid compromising his own credit with protested bills, continually tried to acquire bills with the best English endorsements. Famous Anglo-American names appear among the payees of Trotter's bills from the very beginning; however, in the early days, unfamiliar names predominated. Trotter was increasingly able to buy bills bearing names of prominent London or Liverpool houses and from 1834 to

---

but during the same period borrowing in England by American governmental units alone amounted to $147 million. *Historical Statistics of the United States, 1789–1945* (Washington, D.C.: Government Printing Office, 1949), pp. 243–44; Bullock, Williams, Tucker, *op. cit.*, pp. 217–19; Leland H. Jenks, *op. cit.*, pp. 65–98.

[47] Arthur D. Gayer, W. W. Rostow, Anna J. Schwartz, *The Growth and Fluctuations of the British Economy, 1790–1850* (Oxford, 1953), Vol. I, pp. 311–12.

[48] In the years between 1864 and 1895 the two firms generated £534,705 worth of bills, 86 percent of the total purchased; and after 1873 they generated £410,450 or 97.5 percent of the total.

[49] The primary acceptors might have been either British importers or finance houses that specialized in accepting responsibility for payment of the bills on maturity. Included among the 295 Trotter acceptors are only the initial signatures on each bill—not collateral signers.

1865 about £299,000, or roughly 45 percent of the total, bore some 13 names.[50] Here is evidence of specialization, but nothing compared to what followed. From 1865 to 1895 only 10 names appear as acceptors on Trotter's bills, and from 1877 to the end, only 2, Brown-Shipley and J. S. Morgan. These two firms endorsed more than 86 percent of the £609,634 of bills bought by Trotter after the Civil War. From 1803 to 1895, of the 295 endorsers and acceptors who provided Trotter with a total of £1,454,120 worth of sterling exchange, Brown-Shipley and Morgan provided over £800,000 or about 55 percent.[51]

Thus it appears that the increase of Philadelphia bills, the reduction in the number of drawers, and the constant decline in the number of payers does not reflect any shifts in the pattern of the American export trade. Instead they appear to have been manifestations of the development of the foreign-exchange market and the growth of private banking houses specializing in international transactions. In all probability, these private houses drew against their British correspondents to pay American producers scattered over the country.[52]

This leads to further conjecture that, at least in the Anglo-American trade, the gold-payment system of the pre-1914 period achieved some of its celebrated gold-point stability because the market became highly centralized and dominated by efficient large-scale dealers in gold and foreign exchange who could ship gold with easy facility when the occasion arose.

IX

Our main conclusions may be summarized briefly. It appears that the exchange-rate stability commonly associated with the pre-1914 gold standard was a characteristic of the dollar-sterling exchange only after the early 1870's. Before that time the dollar-sterling rates varied widely; and these short fluctuations constitute (except for 1861–65) an indicator of the rate of internal U.S. expansion (or stagnation). Over the whole 19th century, the gradual decline in the sterling premium appears to have reflected the gradual movement of the United States from debtor to creditor on current account. There were of course other factors, in addition to the current-account position, to explain the gradual decline of the sterling

---

[50] Brown-Shipley, Morgan, Barings, Peabody, Rothschild, Glyn Mills, Barclay, Alexander, Dennistoun, the Bank of England, Stuart, Huth, and the Union Bank.

[51] Some bills endorsed by George Peabody are included as Morgan bills from 1854 to 1865. J. S. Morgan was a member of the Peabody firm in London and the firm became J. S. Morgan & Co. during the American Civil War when Peabody retired. F. L. Allen, *The Great Pierpont Morgan* (New York, 1956), p. 8.

Brown-Shipley had endorsed a bill purchased by Trotter in 1803, and the name of J. S. Morgan first appeared on a Trotter bill in 1850.

[52] Professor Cole also notes this growing specialization of the exchange market and the emerging dominance of Brown Brothers & Company. The Trotter data, however, seem to indicate that specialization was achieved in the early 1870's, almost a decade before Cole's estimate. Cole, "Evolution," pp. 408–10.

premium. Whereas the early instability of the exchanges was indicative of chaotic financial conditions and the slowness of ocean communications and transportation in the early 19th century, the later stability may be attributed to improvement in banking, transportation, and communications, as well as the moderating effects of increased specialization in the foreign-exchange market.

Was this pattern peculiar to the transatlantic trade? It might well have been, because of the great distances involved, and the (relative) slowness of communications before the 1870's. It would be useful to see a similar or comparable study of other exchanges, perhaps London–Paris. Although the Anglo-American trade may have been a special case, this study does raise a lingering suspicion that the payments system of the trading world before the 1870's was subject to considerably more instability than has been thought.

TABLE A–1

ANGLO–AMERICAN BILL OF EXCHANGE PRICES, TROTTER AND MARTIN SERIES,
1835–95

(By Quarter)

Year	Quarter	Premium or Discount Trotter	Premium or Discount Martin	Year	Quarter	Premium or Discount Trotter	Premium or Discount Martin
		%	%			%	%
1835	1	—2.42	—2.02	1846	1	— .68	— .87
	2	.20	— .42		2	— .91	.27
	3	— .16	— .11		3	—1.61	— .57
	4	— .43	.19		4	—2.55	—1.94
1836	1	— .56	— .19	1847	1	—3.23	—3.23
	2	—2.00	—2.02		2	—2.87	—3.01
	3	—1.69	—1.79		3	—2.73	—2.55
	4	—1.48	— .78		4	.29	.27
1837	1	— .97	— .72	1848	1	.62	.73
	2	4.56	2.17		2	.60	.80
	3	8.72	9.25		3	— .08	.12
	4	5.03	4.76		4	—1.66	.57
1838	1	— .35	— .61	1849	1	—1.56	— .80
	2	.92	—2.70		2	—2.29	—1.18
	3	.08	—1.10		3	— .40	— .04
	4	.02	.31		4	— .50	.34
1839	1	— .27	— .34	1850	1	—1.02	— .72
	2	— .65	— .23		2	.15	.04
	3	.50	— .23		3	.05	.95
	4	7.91	— .11		4	.71	.80
1840	1	3.80	—1.18	1851	1	.53	.57
	2	3.16	—1.56		2	.89	.92
	3	1.17	—2.24		3	.61	.84
	4	.82	— .80		4	.83	.92
1841	1	— .04	—1.18	1852	1	.52	.65
	2	1.94	—1.71		2	.61	.23
	3	2.24	— .72		3	1.00	.84
	4	3.79	.19		4	.57	.57
1842	1	1.21	— .95	1853	1	.16	.23
	2	—2.30	—2.02		2	.26	.04
	3	—2.73	—2.21		3	— .18	.08
	4	—3.04	—2.28		4	.23	.00
1843	1	—3.71	—3.50	1854	1	— .56	— .38
	2	—1.43	—2.09		2	— .04	— .38
	3	— .62	— .44		3	.25	— .04
	4	—1.11	— .72		4	— .40	.12
1844	1	— .78	— .72	1855	1	— .62	— .76
	2	— .56	— .95		2	.64	.46
	3	.14	— .04		3	.41	.27
	4	.09	.50		4	— .93	— .72
1845	1	.13	.42	1856	1	— .29	— .68
	2	.23	.19		2	.38	.23
	3	.21	.27		3	.41	.34
	4	—1.02	— .44		4	— .01	— .19

TABLE A–1 (*Continued*)

| | | Premium or Discount | | | | Premium or Discount | |
| | | Trotter | Martin | | | Trotter | Martin |
Year	Quarter	%	%	Year	Quarter	%	%
1857	1	— .66	— .87	1869	1	— .07	— .30
	2	.04	— .34		2	.43	— .30
	3	— .30	— .19		3	.78	— .34
	4	— .58	—3.84		4	.12	— .53
1858	1	—2.24	— .19	1870	1	— .30	— .68
	2	— .03	— .11		2	.12	— .08
	3	.32	.12		3	.93	.19
	4	.14	.14		4	.17	— .42
1859	1	.17	.12	1871	1	.50	.08
	2	.61	.46		2	1.16	.69
	3	.75	.65		3	.67	— .02
	4	.54	.50		4	.54	— .44
1860	1	— .58	— .38	1872	1	.39	— .46
	2	— .14	— .11		2	.82	— .70
	3	.40	.42		3	.19	—1.04
	4	—2.72	—1.98		4	.70	—1.81
1861	1	—3.84	—4.07	1873	1	— .31	— .11
	2	—3.46	—2.78		2	— .68	.21
	3	—1.35	—2.36		3	— .50	— .40
	4	—1.01	—1.48		4	—2.54	— .80
1862	1	.59	.82	1874	1	.05	— .65
	2	1.70	.90		2	.97	.23
	3	.67	1.02		3	.74	.07
	4	.49	.80		4	.58	— .22
1863	1	2.62	1.93	1875	1	— .52	— .56
	2	—2.38	1.01		2	.77	.07
	3	— .46	2.00		3	.77	— .26
	4	— .58	.63		4	.11	—1.01
1864	1	— .07	.43	1876	1	.29	— .11
	2	.93	.04		2	.48	.29
	3	1.05	—3.42		3	.33	.12
	4	2.45	—1.46		4	— .62	— .77
1865	1	.32	— .80	1877	1	— .32	— .52
	2	1.14	— .36		2	.46	.14
	3	— .20	— .32		3	.21	— .41
	4	.10	— .61		4	— .45	—1.04
1866	1	— .80	—1.22	1878	1	— .27	— .58
	2	.36	— .84		2	.25	— .17
	3	— .74	—1.77		3	.06	— .62
	4	.08	— .59		4	.18	—1.04
1867	1	.12	— .61	1879	1	.41	— .22
	2	.74	.25		2	.44	.14
	3	.74	.27		3	— .28	— .72
	4	1.11	— .07		4	— .80	—1.02
1868	1	.66	.29	1880	1	.05	— .56
	2	.98	.59		2	.50	— .15
	3	.72	.14		3	— .44	— .80
	4	.74	— .06		4	— .96	—1.16

TABLE A–1 (Continued)

| Year | Quarter | Premium or Discount | | Year | Quarter | Premium or Discount | |
		Trotter	Martin			Trotter	Martin
		%	%			%	%
1881	1	— .61	—1.13	1889	1	.50	— .05
	2	— .57	— .51		2	.46	.23
	3	— .36	— .90		3	.28	— .22
	4	— .55	—1.20		4	— .08	—1.02
1882	1	.72	— .36	1890	1	— .02	— .77
	2	.58	.12		2	.16	— .29
	3	.55	— .26		3	.33	— .62
	4	— .22	—1.09		4	— .09	—1.08
1883	1	— .22	— .87	1891	1	.50	— .29
	2	— .16	— .41		2	.51	— .13
	3	— .06	— .58		3	.30	— .56
	4	— .30	— .85		4	— .48	—1.02
1884	1	.68	— .05	1892	1	.00	— .27
	2	.08	— .11		2	n.d.*	.19
	3	— .37	— .68		3	.40	.14
	4	— .45	—1.06		4	.18	—. 26
1885	1	— .21	— .60	1893	1	.28	— .05
	2	.07	.00		2	.19	— .10
	3	—. 09	— .39		3	.11	— .72
	4	.20	— .48		4	— .02	— .60
1886	1	.63	.19	1894	1	.29	— .07
	2	.56	.18		2	.45	.28
	3	.10	— .48		3	.17	.09
	4	— .47	—1.08		4	.24	.14
1887	1	— .26	— .38	1895	1	.50	.39
	2	— .07	— .10		2	.70	.38
	3	— .39	— .89		3	.59	.55
	4	— .19	— .92		4	n.d.	.33
1888	1	.13	— .29				
	2	.45	.07				
	3	.44	— .18				
	4	.45	— .34				

* No data.

TABLE A–2
ANGLO-AMERICAN EXCHANGE-RATE ESTIMATES, 1835–95
(By Quarter)

Year	Quarter	Premium or Discount			Year	Quarter	Premium or Discount		
		Bigelow	Davis	Macaulay			Bigelow	Davis	Macaulay
		%	%	%			%	%	%
1835	1	—1.61			1847	1	—1.46	—2.14	
	2	.94				2	—1.53	—1.74	
	3	.66				3	—1.51	—1.71	
	4	.49				4	1.84	1.17	
1836	1	1.19			1848	1	2.74	1.48	
	2	.23				2	2.91	1.70	
	3	1.79				3	2.10	.87	
	4	2.73				4	.86	— .70	
1837	1	2.13			1849	1	.37	— .50	
	2	8.64				2	— .46	—1.31	
	3	9.96				3	.98	.60	
	4	6.09				4	1.05	.54	
1838	1	1.80			1850	1	.54	.01	
	2	2.59				2	1.43	1.19	
	3	1.12				3	1.16	1.05	
	4	1.10				4	1.98	1.76	
1839	1	1.03			1851	1	1.73	.74	
	2	.70				2	2.17	1.99	
	3	2.70				3	2.48	1.68	
	4	12.78				4	2.76	1.87	
1840	1	5.48	4.65		1852	1	1.91	1.56	
	2	4.61	3.96			2	1.60	1.74	
	3	2.18	2.23			3	1.87	1.88	
	4	1.95	1.87			4	1.60	1.62	
1841	1	.98	1.56		1853	1	1.66	1.27	
	2	2.90	2.89			2	1.85	1.38	
	3	3.32	3.37			3	1.51	.91	
	4	5.35	4.88			4	2.41	1.19	
1842	1	3.07	2.36		1854	1	.73	.56	
	2	— .98	—1.32			2	1.77	1.14	
	3	—1.60	—1.79			3	2.05	1.40	
	4	—2.00	—2.03			4	1.48	.73	
1843	1	—2.75	—2.68		1855	1	1.41	.56	
	2	— .67	— .38			2	2.02	1.76	
	3	.02	.53			3	1.50	1.52	
	4	— .54	— .37			4	.72	.26	
1844	1	— .04	n.d.*		1856	1	1.40	.84	
	2	.34	.28			2	1.62	1.51	
	3	.92	1.08			3	1.73	1.58	
	4	1.21	1.41			4	1.58	1.13	
1845	1	1.02	.88		1857	1	.93	.53	.81
	2	1.05	.93			2	1.32	1.26	1.45
	3	1.32	1.14			3	1.39	.87	1.57
	4	.06	— .20			4	3.29	.71	2.68
1846	1	.90	.38		1858	1	—1.40	—1.11	—1.36
	2	.78	.08			2	.73	.93	.68
	3	— .07	—1.07			3	1.04	1.32	.94
	4	—1.34	—1.79			4	.91	1.20	.89

TABLE A–2 (*Continued*)

		Premium or Discount					Premium or Discount		
Year	Quarter	Bigelow	Davis	Macaulay	Year	Quarter	Bigelow	Davis	Macaulay
		%	%	%			%	%	%
1859	1	1.07	1.17	1.02	1871	1			.94
	2	1.68	1.62	1.64		2			1.19
	3	1.92	1.80	1.85		3			.70
	4	1.73	1.61	1.60		4			.75
1860	1	.40	.45	.43	1872	1			.90
	2	.65	.89	.77		2			.90
	3	1.34	1.44	1.48		3			.19
	4	—1.33	—1.66	—1.15		4			.95
1861	1			—2.57	1873	1			— .13
	2			—2.31		2			— .12
	3			— .29		3			— .45
	4			.05		4			— .59
1862	1			1.58	1874	1			.40
	2			2.69		2			.96
	3			1.17		3			.74
	4			1.22		4			.61
1863	1			3.56	1875	1			.09
	2			—1.46		2			.81
	3			.24		3			.77
	4			.51		4			.14
1864	1			.94	1876	1			.88
	2			2.06		2			.93
	3			1.30		3			.92
	4			3.23		4			— .34
1865	1			1.65	1877	1			— .02
	2			1.20		2			.55
	3			1.02		3			.24
	4			1.36		4			— .32
1866	1			.27	1878	1			— .18
	2			1.26		2			.40
	3			.16		3			.14
	4			.76		4			.35
1867	1			.27	1879	1			.45
	2			.81		2			.47
	3			.83		3			— .26
	4			1.18		4			— .51
1868	1			.71	1880	1			.06
	2			1.17		2			.49
	3			.81		3			— .44
	4			.89		4			— .57
1869	1			.11	1881	1			— .61
	2			.55		2			— .11
	3			.85		3			— .35
	4			.47		4			— .33
1870	1			— .25	1882	1			.71
	2			.41		2			.57
	3			1.19		3			.54
	4			.20		4			— .22

TABLE A–2 (*Continued*)

Year	Quarter	Premium or Discount			Year	Quarter	Premium or Discount		
		Bigelow	Davis	Macaulay			Bigelow	Davis	Macaulay
		%	%	%			%	%	%
1883	1			— .22	1890	1			— .02
	2			— .16		2			.16
	3			— .06		3			.32
	4			— .31		4			— .09
1884	1			.67	1891	1			.49
	2			.08		2			.50
	3			— .37		3			.30
	4			— .46		4			— .48
1885	1			— .21	1892	1			.00
	2			.06		2			n.d.*
	3			— .09		3			.39
	4			.19		4			.17
1886	1			.62	1893	1			.27
	2			.56		2			.18
	3			.09		3			.10
	4			— .47		4			— .01
1887	1			— .26	1894	1			.28
	2			— .07		2			.44
	3			— .39		3			.16
	4			— .19		4			.32
1888	1			.12	1895	1			.49
	2			.44		2			.69
	3			.43		3			.59
	4			.44		4			n.d.
1889	1			.49					
	2			.45					
	3			.27					
	4			— .08					

* No data.

TABLE A–3
AVERAGE MATURITY OF BILLS OF EXCHANGE, 1803–95
(By Year)

Year	Average Maturity Days	Year	Average Maturity Days	Year	Average Maturity Days
1803	30.0	1834	54.0	1865	43.7
1804	54.0	1835	60.0	1866	51.6
1805	52.5	1836	58.0	1867	11.1
1806	56.8	1837	54.6	1868	11.7
1807	56.0	1838	59.4	1869	11.8
1808	51.4	1839	55.8	1870	12.4
1809	54.0	1840	54.8	1871	11.3
1810	50.0	1841	57.9	1872	16.2
1811	40.0	1842	59.3	1873	19.4
1812	45.0	1843	59.3	1874	16.2
1813	45.0	1844	65.9	1875	17.6
1814	n.d.*	1845	56.8	1876	15.9
1815	60.0	1846	62.6	1877	13.7
1816	45.0	1847	55.4	1878	9.9
1817	62.7	1848	47.8	1879	4.3
1818	54.1	1849	56.4	1880	2.3
1819	60.0	1850	57.4	1881	5.3
1820	54.0	1851	57.4	1882	0.0
1821	60.0	1852	57.3	1883	0.0
1822	60.0	1853	56.3	1884	0.0
1823	53.3	1854	56.6	1885	0.0
1824	62.0	1855	60.0	1886	0.0
1825	50.4	1856	60.0	1887	0.0
1826	48.2	1857	58.6	1888	0.0
1827	40.4	1858	60.0	1889	0.0
1828	39.1	1859	58.8	1890	0.0
1829	39.6	1860	60.0	1891	0.0
1830	42.8	1861	55.7	1892	0.0
1831	50.7	1862	48.8	1893	0.0
1832	56.5	1863	54.0	1894	0.0
1833	49.6	1864	42.0	1895	0.0

* No data.

TABLE A–4
ANGLO-AMERICAN BILL OF EXCHANGE PRICES, UNCORRECTED, 1803–34
(By Quarter)

Year	Quarter	Premium or Discount	Year	Quarter	Premium or Discount
		%			%
1803	1	— .56	1815	1	n.d.*
	2	n.d.*		2	n.d.
	3	—28.00		3	8.98
	4	n.d.		4	10.60
1804	1	—29.00	1816	1	n.d.
	2	—27.50		2	16.52
	3	—31.00		3	14.78
	4	—31.00		4	8.32
1805	1	—33.50	1817	1	2.24
	2	—36.48		2	2.03
	3	—18.73		3	2.43
	4	—33.70		4	2.78
1806	1	—37.50	1818	1	1.68
	2	—33.39		2	.76
	3	—33.33		3	.17
	4	—33.68		4	— 2.50
1807	1	—36.00	1819	1	.00
	2	—35.35		2	.00
	3	—36.00		3	n.d.
	4	—33.11		4	2.75
1808	1	—25.91	1820	1	.50
	2	—25.00		2	.00
	3	n.d.		3	n.d.
	4	—21.26		4	2.23
1809	1	n.d.	1821	1	5.74
	2	—32.23		2	8.96
	3	—30.00		3	9.00
	4	—29.78		4	10.25
1810	1	—15.10	1822	1	12.56
	2	2.70		2	10.86
	3	4.50		3	9.66
	4	—10.00		4	n.d.
1811	1	n.d.	1823	1	4.50
	2	—15.00		2	4.09
	3	—20.00		3	6.78
	4	—18.00		4	7.94
1812	1	—15.00	1824	1	8.20
	2	n.d.		2	9.00
	3	n.d.		3	9.05
	4	—18.00		4	8.45
1813	1	n.d.	1825	1	5.00
	2	—12.99		2	5.48
	3	n.d.		3	8.80
	4	—12.50		4	8.97
1814	1	n.d.	1826	1	7.39
	2	n.d.		2	9.47
	3	n.d.		3	10.73
	4	n.d.		4	10.97

* No data.

TABLE A–4 (*Continued*)

Year	Quarter	Premium or Discount %	Year	Quarter	Premium or Discount %
1827	1	10.41	1831	1	6.62
	2	10.32		2	9.04
	3	10.29		3	10.21
	4	11.20		4	10.39
1828	1	10.71	1832	1	10.21
	2	10.04		2	9.89
	3	10.49		3	7.98
	4	9.85		4	8.08
1829	1	8.65	1833	1	7.54
	2	8.97		2	8.18
	3	9.13		3	7.67
	4	9.36		4	4.53
1830	1	8.16	1834	1	— 9.15
	2	6.86		2	— 7.50
	3	6.56		3	n.d.
	4	6.50		4	— 2.24

* No data.

ANGLO-AMERICAN EXCHANGE RATE ESTIMATES BY QUARTER 1835–95

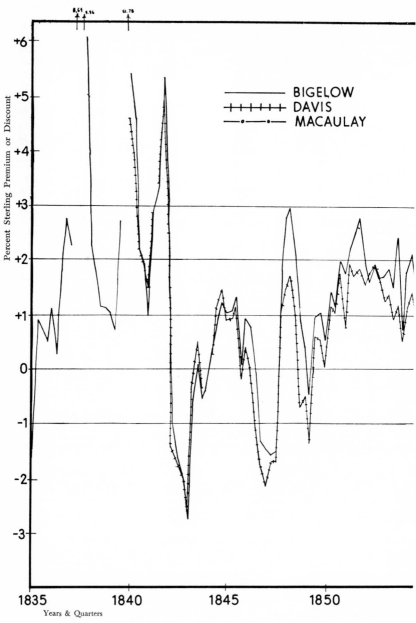

Years & Quarters

SOURCE: Appendix A–2.

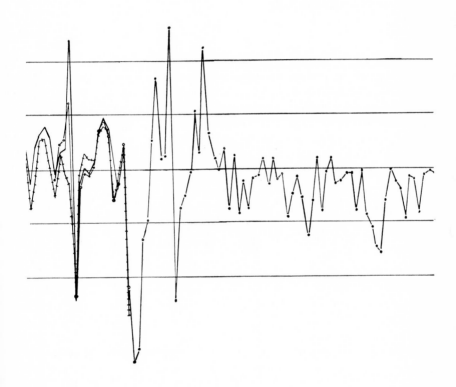

1860   1865   1870   1875

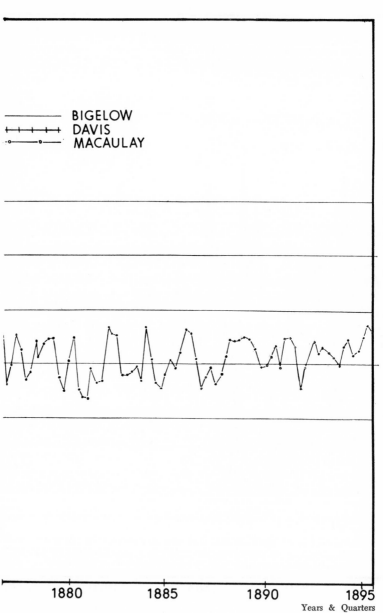

5. Effective Reserves, Credit, and Causality in the Banking System of the Thirties[*]

George Horwich
Purdue University

I. Two Hypotheses

THE MOST SERIOUS challenge to American monetary policy occurred in the 1930's when member bank excess reserves rose to astronomical levels—5 to 6 billion dollars, compared with customary holdings of less than 50 million in the preceding decade. This has been widely cited as prima facie evidence that the banking system of the thirties was in a "liquidity trap." Bankers were said to be indifferent between the holding of cash and noncash assets. This resulted in a zero marginal rate of lending and investing with respect to reserve changes. The supply of bank credit responded only to outside forces, particularly to movements in the demand for loanable funds by eligible borrowers.[1]

An alternative point of view holds that the excess reserves were the result of a low, but nevertheless positive, response of bankers to reserve increases. The excess reserves were functional, serving as a voluntary additional reserve over the legally required minimum. This was merely a reflection of the high, but not necessarily infinite, liquidity preferences characteristic of the decade. In the words of Paul Samuelson, "They [excess reserves] were felt to be necessary in a world where uncertainty

* Reprinted from D. Carson (ed.), *Banking and Monetary Studies*, Reprint Series No. 81, pp. 80–100.

This paper was begun at the Institute on Training in Monetary and Credit Policy, sponsored by the Social Science Research Council and the Board of Governors of the Federal Reserve System in the summer of 1957. A first draft was read at the meetings of the Econometric Society in December, 1957; an abstract appeared in *Econometrica* (October, 1958), pp. 602–3. The author wishes to acknowledge many helpful suggestions, particularly those of the late Edward J. Kilberg, whose tragic death in August, 1958, terminated a promising career; R. I. Robinson, R. G. Thomas, and E. T. Weiler.

1 The most consistent proponent of this view is E. A. Goldenweiser. See *Monetary Management* (New York: McGraw-Hill, 1949), pp. 57–59, and *American Monetary Policy* (New York: McGraw-Hill, 1951), chap. ix.

dictates a diversification of portfolios."[2] On this interpretation the excess reserves were not idle "surpluses," to which bank lending was unresponsive. On the contrary, when the Federal Reserve sought to remove excess reserves by doubling reserve requirements in 1936–37, member banks sold government securities as a sharp reaction to their reduced "effective" reserves position.[3]

The policy implications of each hypothesis are clear. If a liquidity trap prevails, bankers ignore reserve changes in either direction, while passively supplying loanable funds in accordance with shifts in market demand. Monetary policy, acting through the banks, is totally ineffective. We shall refer to this as the Keynesian view. On the other hand, if bank earning assets and the money supply are in any degree causally dependent upon reserves, then, barring widespread liquidity traps elsewhere in the economy, the member banks may serve as a medium for altering national income and employment. We shall call this the Wicksellian view of banks and monetary policy.

A test of which hypothesis most accurately describes the behavior of the banking system in the 1930's will be made with data obtained from member bank call reports. We shall try to establish whether reserves were causally influential in determining both the level and composition of member bank earning assets. However, in order to study these relationships, it is necessary to adjust the raw data on reserves for lack of comparability in the capacity to use them. This is done by means of an effective reserves series, which is described in the appendix to this essay. Effective reserves express any change in the legal capacity to use reserves as a change in the volume of reserves, with the capacity held constant. Thus, a lowering of the reserve requirement (r_r) appears as that increase in reserves, which, under the fixed requirement, finances the same maximum purchase of earning assets that the lowered requirement makes possible. Effective reserves, as described in the appendix, also incorporate several factors other than the reserve requirement that affect reserve availability.

The following section summarizes the author's earlier banking study of the 1950's for comparison with the thirties. Section III presents the data on total earning assets and effective reserves for 1930–39. Section IV is an initial test of the Keynesian hypothesis, using money income as a

---

[2] P. A. Samuelson, "Fiscal Policy and Income Determination," *Quarterly Journal of Economics* (August, 1942), pp. 594, n. 3, and 594–95.

[3] See L. H. Seltzer, "The Problem of Our Excessive Banking Reserves," *Journal of the American Statistical Association* (January, 1940), p. 28, n. 7; E. S. Shaw, *Money, Income, and Monetary Policy* (Homewood, Ill.: Richard D. Irwin, Inc., 1950), p. 443; Steiner, Shapiro, and Solomon, *Money and Banking* (4th ed.; New York: Holt, Rinehart & Winston, Inc., 1958), p. 596; K. Brunner, "A Case Study of U.S. Monetary Policy: Reserve Requirements and Inflationary Gold Flows in the Middle 30's," *Schweizerische Zeitschrift für Volkvirtschaft und Statistik* (March, 1958), pp. 160–201; and M. Friedman, *A Program for Monetary Stability* (New York: Fordham University Press, 1959), pp. 45–46.

proxy variable for investment demand. Sections V and VI examine the behavior of the loan and investment components, respectively, of total earning assets. Section VII discusses the impact of interest rates and possible lags in bank responses. Section VIII is a summary.

II. The Fifties[4]

Total member bank earning assets were related to effective reserves for the period December 31, 1952, to December 31, 1955. Thirty-seven monthly observations on member bank effective reserves, R'', were obtained by the method outlined in the appendix. Whereas unadjusted reserves declined during this period from $19.95 billion to $19.00 billion, R'', expressed in terms of a "standard" requirement of .1557, rose from $21.38 billion to $25.11 billion. Statistical measures gave evidence of a constant and sensitive response of total earning assets, E, to effective reserves of the same month. Out of 36 monthly increments of R'', 26 increments of E were in the same direction, and seven of those that were not were clearly a delayed reaction of one or two months to a sudden reversal of a trend in R''. Out of 35 corresponding second differences of R'' and E, 30 were of the same sign. The agreement in the signs of second differences was especially pronounced (all but one were in agreement) when the first differences of the same month were of opposite sign. This tempered the divergence of the two series by giving them the same direction of concavity (thus if R'' is rising by rising amounts, while E is falling, the agreement of second differences implies that E falls by *declining* rather than increasing amounts). The linear correlation coefficient between E and R'', $r_{ER''}$, was .95; that between their first differences, $r_{\Delta E \Delta R''}$, was .63; and between their second differences, $r_{\Delta\Delta E \Delta\Delta R''}$, .72. The equation of the least squares regression line, in billions of dollars, was $E = 10.34 + 4.86\,R''$. Whenever interest rates and business activity were rising, the observations tended to lie above the regression line. Periods of falling interest rates and activity were characterized by points below the line.

III. The Thirties: Four Phases

Figure 1 presents the time series of member bank earning assets and effective reserves on call report dates from December 31, 1929, to December 30, 1939 (see the Appendix, Table 4, for the data and the adjustments leading to effective reserves). There were three call reports in

---

[4] This section summarizes my paper, "Elements of Timing and Response in the Balance Sheet of Banking, 1953–55," *Journal of Finance* (May, 1957), pp. 238–55. The specific results reported here differ somewhat from those of the article in that they are based on the adjustments described in the Appendix, rather than in the original paper.

1932, 1933, 1936, and 1937, and four in each of the remaining six years. These furnish 37 observations on the variables at an average interval of $3\frac{1}{3}$ months. Earning assets are defined as all loans and investments, gross of valuation reserves. Reserves are deposits at the Federal Reserve plus vault cash. The standard requirement for effective reserves is .077.

Earning assets fall from \$35.39 billion in December, 1929, to \$24.79 billion in June, 1933, and rise to \$33.94 billion by December, 1939. Unadjusted reserves rise from \$2.93 billion at the beginning of the period to

FIGURE 1

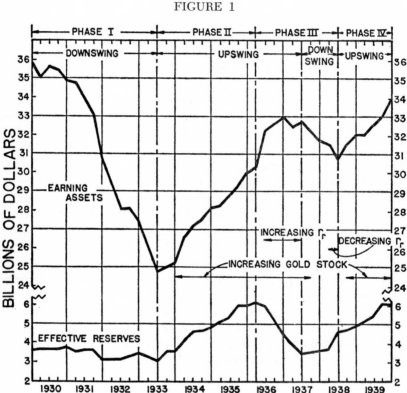

\$12.44 billion at the close. Most of this increase is due to the upward revaluation and tremendous inflow of gold that began in 1934. However, R'' is \$3.50 billion at the start, and only \$6.10 billion at the close of the decade. The substantially smaller rise in effective than in unadjusted reserves is due chiefly to the increase in the required reserve ratio from .074 to .153. Periods of gold inflow and changing reserve requirements are indicated in Figure 1 between the call report dates nearest to these events. The National Bureau's upswings and downswings of economic activity are similarly marked off at the top of the chart.

Figure 2 is the scatter diagram of corresponding values of R'' and E. Although 24 out of 36 first differences of the two time series in Figure 1 have the same sign, $r_{ER''}$ is only .04 and $r_{\Delta E \Delta R''}$ is .17. However, the data in Figure 2 seem to arrange themselves into four distinct subperiods or phases as follows:

I. From December, 1929, to June, 1933, the least squares line has a high positive slope (the "b" value) and a comparatively low vertical-axis intercept. The equation of the line is $E = -15.35 + 13.93 R''$, and $r = .85$. The observations move in zigzag fashion from the top of the line to the bottom, making this a period of considerable liquidation of earning assets and some decline in effective reserves.

II. This phase extends from June, 1933, to March, 1936. The fitted regression line has a relatively gentle positive slope, a high vertical intercept, and an extremely narrow dispersion of points about it—r is .99. The equation of the line is $E = 19.09 + 1.80 R''$. Over time the points start at the lower end of the line and rise along it monotonically to its upper reaches.

III. This phase, for which all observations are dated, begins when earning assets in the second quarter of 1936 rise sharply by almost $2 billion, while effective reserves decline $148 million. This vertical movement is located in the right central portion of the figure. The next point, that for December, 1936, lies well above the line in the upper central portion of the figure. It reflects a further increase in earning assets, coinciding with the first wave of required-reserve increases and the resulting loss of effective reserves. Reserve requirements were raised again in the first and second quarters of 1937, and the corresponding points are plotted to the left of that for December, 1936. Earning assets dipped in the first quarter of 1937, rose in the next, and then fell continuously from December, 1937, to June, 1938, even though R'' increased. Thus, during this phase the time sequence of points is from right to life above the line, and then from left to right below the line. The least squares equation is $E = 33.57 - .38R''$, and r is $-.42$.

IV. The final phase is very much like Phase II. Starting in June, 1938, the observations move up along a rising line of gentle slope and considerable intercept. The equation is $E = 24.07 + 1.56 R''$. The intercept is $5 billion greater, and the slope is .24 less than that of the line of Phase II. r, again high, is .93.[5]

The four phases are also marked off on Figure 1 above the cyclical subdivisions.

Considered independently, the lines of Phases II and IV might be interpreted to support the Wicksellian hypothesis. If, in fact, E is causally related to R'', then during these two phases the marginal response of earning assets to effective reserves was low, but uniform. Though bankers were permitted by law to invest $1/.077 - 1 = \$12$ for every dollar received under the standard requirement, they chose instead to spend less

---

[5] The agreement in signs of first differences of R'' and E, by phases, is as follows. In Phase I, 7 out of 12 pairs of first differences have the same sign; in Phase II, all 11 have the same sign; in Phase III, 1 out of 6; in Phase IV, 5 out of 6.

FIGURE 2

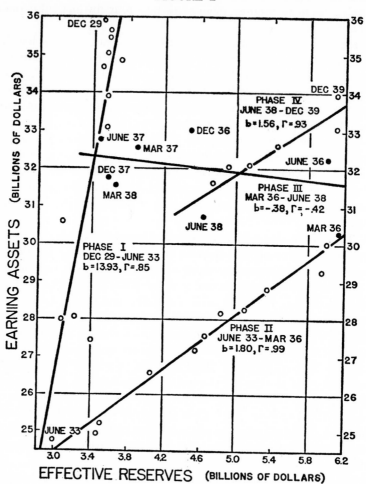

EFFECTIVE RESERVES (BILLIONS OF DOLLARS)

than $2. At the same time the high positive intercepts of the two lines indicate that the ratio of E to R'' (the "average" propensity to invest) fell as R'' increased. This is the counterpart in our model of the growing excess reserves. But is the Wicksellian view really tenable? The events of Phase I are not particularly incompatible with the Wicksellian interpretation. One would not expect any line generated by the most severe financial liquidation in American history to resemble the lines of other, more stable periods. Moreover, the slope of the line of Phase I is indeed positive; the contraction of earning assets coincided with a decline in effective reserves. But the evidence difficult to square with the Wicksellian hypothesis is this: Why did the linear relationship between E and R'' shift upward by $5 billion between Phases II and IV? (And, to a lesser extent, why did the slope of the relationship decline from 1.80 to 1.56?) This is equivalent to asking why member banks reacted as little or as belatedly to the doubling of reserve requirements during Phase III. Why, instead of backing down along the line of Phase II, did the points move up and to the left along a new line?

The answer to these questions may lie in additional variables, which, independently or jointly with R'', determined the level of earning assets. R'' and E may not in fact be causally connected; their overall correlation of .04 may measure their true relationship more accurately than do the correlations of any of the subperiods that we have conveniently selected. However, before turning to other variables, there is further evidence in the data already presented that points against the Wicksellian view. We noted in Section II that during the fifties the *second* differences of R'' and E were closely related. This relationship, more than any other, seemed to reflect the independent behavioral response of bankers to their effective reserves. It is almost totally absent from the thirties. Out of 35 second differences of R'' and E, only 15 have the same sign. This lack of agreement is as likely to occur when R'' and E are highly correlated, as in Phases II and IV, as when they are less correlated, as in Phases I and III.[6] And there is an almost total lack of agreement in second differences when first differences are of opposite sign.[7] All of this is reflected in a low correlation, $r_{\Delta\Delta E\Delta\Delta R''} = .13$. In view of these circumstances it is difficult to argue that total earning assets are an active, controlled response by bankers to their current effective reserves.

IV. Business Activity

The choice of a second variable to explain earning assets of the thirties is immediately suggested by Figure 1, where there is a close association between the series on earning assets and the National Bureau's reference dates of business activity. The long, almost uninterrupted liquidation of earning assets during Phase I ends exactly at the lower turning point in the business cycle of the second quarter, 1933. There follows a continued rise in E, coinciding with the business upswing, and not really terminating until the upper turning point of the second quarter, 1937. The decline in E, starting at the end of the second quarter, 1937, is abruptly reversed at the Bureau's lower turning point in the second quarter, 1938. The rise of E in Phase IV coincides exactly with the final business upswing of the decade.

It may be that the demand for loanable funds is closely correlated with

---

[6] The agreement in signs of R'' and E second differences, by phases, is as follows. In Phase I, 5 out of 11 pairs of second differences are in agreement; in Phase II, 7 out of 11; in Phase III, 2 out of 7; in Phase IV, 1 out of 6.

[7] When signs of first differences of R'' and E disagree, the signs of second differences are in agreement in Phase I, one out of four times; in Phase III, two out of six times; in Phase IV, none out of one time. There is no disagreement between signs of first differences in Phase II (see n. 5 above). While there are five disagreements in signs of first differences in Phase I (see n. 5), one such disagreement occurs during the initial pair of first differences of the decade; there is no information on the simultaneous second differences.

the general state of the economy, and this demand either supplements or replaces effective reserves as a critical variable determining the supply of bank credit. In order to test this possibility, member bank earning assets must be related to an index of economic activity of equal frequency. The Commerce Department's monthly series on total personal income is the most comprehensive statistic available for this purpose. Since E occurs at intervals of two to six months, a measure of the rate of flow of income was obtained by taking the mean of the monthly personal incomes prevailing during each of the call report intervals. The resulting adjusted personal income series, Y (see Appendix, Table 4, and Figure 3), was compared with the values of E occurring at the close of the interval for which Y is computed. These are the results of the statistical analysis: 33 out of 36 first differences of E and Y have the same sign; $r_{EY} = .93$ and $r_{\Delta E \Delta Y} = .61$. However, only 18 out of 35 second differences of E and Y have the same sign, and $r_{\Delta \Delta E \Delta \Delta Y} = .22$.

Apart from the second differences, to which we shall return in a moment, the agreement between E and Y is impressive. It is particularly significant that the sudden transition from the line of Phase II to that of Phase III, occurring during the second quarter of 1936, coincided with the largest increase ($3.7 billion) in the adjusted personal income series of the decade.

If Y is, indeed, a measure of the demand for loanable funds, does it explain E best in conjunction with R'', or by itself? $r_{EY} = .93$, and the multiple correlation coefficient of E on R'' and Y, $r_{E.R''Y}$, is .94 (see Table 1). But the partial correlation between E and R'' with the effects of Y

TABLE 1

CORRELATION COEFFICIENTS BETWEEN BANK-HELD EARNING ASSETS (E),
EFFECTIVE RESERVES (R''), AND AGGREGATE INCOME (Y),
1930–39 and 1953–55

Variables	1930–39*			1953–55*		
		Δ	$\Delta\Delta$		Δ	$\Delta\Delta$
ER''	.04	.17	.13	.95	.63	.72
EY	.93	.61	.22	.81	.12	.22
$E.R''Y$	.94	.63	.25	.97	.64	.72
$ER''.Y$	—.25	.22	.13	.91	.63	.71
$EY.R''$	.94	.62	.22	.66	.11	.06

* In the first column under each time period are the linear correlation coefficients for the combination of variables shown at the left. In the second and third column are the coefficients between the first and second differences, respectively, of the same variables.

removed, $r_{ER''.Y}$, is —.25. Thus, the improvement of .01 in predicting E by adding R'' to Y is due to a net *negative* relationship between E and R''. The partial correlations of first differences of E and R'' (.22) and E and Y (.62) support ΔY as the major explanatory variable, but the contribution of $\Delta R''$ to ΔE is positive. Although $r_{\Delta \Delta E \Delta \Delta Y . \Delta \Delta R''}$ is low (.22), $r_{\Delta \Delta E \Delta \Delta R'' . \Delta \Delta Y}$ is even lower (.13).

The fifties provide an interesting contrast in the relation between current economic activity and earning assets (Table 1). Taking personal income of the same month, r_{EY} is .81, but $r_{EY.R''}$ falls to .66, while $r_{ER''.Y}$ is .91 and $r_{E.R''Y}$ is .97. Both R'' and Y are apparently important in explaining E, but R'' is of greater importance, while $\Delta R''$ and $\Delta\Delta R''$ are relatively of overwhelming importance in accounting for ΔE and $\Delta\Delta E$, respectively.

The comparatively low correlation of second differences of E and Y in the thirties (.22) tends to throw doubt on the causal influence of business conditions on E. However, Y is at most an approximation to the external demand factors acting on earning assets, and it would be unreasonable to expect as high a correlation as exists, say, in the fifties between second differences of E and R'' (.72), which are almost certainly causally related. In the latter case the measurement of the relevant independent variable, R'', is direct and completely accurate.[8]

A more fruitful approach to the study of causality in the banking system at this point might be to disaggregate earning assets into loans and investments, and to study separately the influence on each of them of effective reserves and the demand for loanable funds, measuring the latter variable in the most direct possible way.

V. Loans

The correlation coefficients between bank loans (L), R'', and Y for both the thirties and the fifties are presented in Table 2. Clearly the business demand for funds, as represented by income, is the only variable that can be taken seriously as a possible determinant of bank loans. In the thirties $r_{LR''} = -.54$ and $r_{LR''.Y} = -.70$, while the correlations for the first and second differences of these combinations of variables are zero or only slightly greater. Though r_{LY} is but .49, $r_{LY.R''}$ is .68, and the correla-

---

[8] It is, of course, possible that the causality runs from bank earning assets (and the money supply) to income, rather than conversely. However, the available evidence on the time lag between money creation and the response of income (Friedman: 12–16 months; Mayer: 3–12 months; Culbertson: 3–6 months; Kareken and Solow: 3–6 months) seems to preclude this possibility in our data. As a rough approximation to the lag, I correlated the money supply with personal income, and the increments of each. This was done with quarterly data in the thirties and monthly data in the fifties. In the latter decade both correlations reached a peak at an income lag of five to six months. In the thirties, the peak, less pronounced, occurred at a lag of two quarters. It would thus seem highly improbable that our adjusted income series in the thirties, which is the mean of the monthly incomes of each quarter *preceding* the earning asset figure, is much influenced by the latter. The only conceivable exception to this rests on the possibility that earning assets respond dependently to *shifts* in the demand for loanable funds. The money so created would be immediately "active" and more likely to influence income within a very brief period. In fact this may be the case with respect to bank loans (as opposed to investments) in both decades (see Section V). But this mechanism is entirely consistent with the Keynesian view of banking in the thirties, which our correlation of income and earning assets purports to substantiate.

TABLE 2
CORRELATION COEFFICIENTS BETWEEN BANK LOANS (L),
EFFECTIVE RESERVES, AND INCOME, 1930–39 AND 1953–55

Variables	1930–39			1953–55		
		Δ	$\Delta\Delta$		Δ	$\Delta\Delta$
LR''	—.54	.00	.09	.74	—.16	—.11
LY	.49	.69	.31	.99	.70	.53
$L.R''Y$	.78	.69	.32	.99	.73	.63
$LR''.Y$	—.70	.00	.01	.50	—.28	—.21
$LY.R''$	.68	.69	.31	.98	.72	.55

tions of first and second differences of these same variables are both .69 and .31, respectively.

In Figure 3 the loan time series follows income rather closely, except for a continuing decline in loans between June, 1933, and March, 1936, while income rises. The failure of bank loans to follow the business upswing of Phase II probably represents a lag in the replacement of the defunct security loans by other types, as well as the decided structural shift in the banking portfolio toward investments. The scatter diagram of L against Y can be approximated by three lines, each of which fits the data very closely. The first, that of Phase I, slopes upward. The observations move down along the line, from right to left. The second, that of Phase II, starts at the lower terminal of the Phase I line and falls very

FIGURE 3

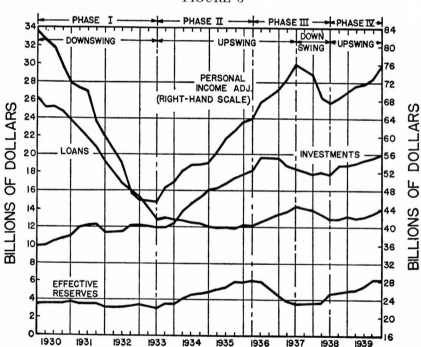

gently to the right. This is also the time sequence of the points. The final line, which combines Phases III and IV, begins at the lower right terminal of the preceding line, and rises parallel to the Phase I line. Over time the observations move up and down along this final path.

One might question the causal relation between L and Y, were it not for the fairly substantial correlation of first differences of these variables. The agreement between *signs* of first and second differences also supports a causal interpretation. Out of 36 first differences of L and Y, 24 have the same sign. Out of 34 nonzero second differences, 22 are in the same direction; but more significant is the fact that on 11 observable occasions when first differences disagree, 10 of the corresponding second differences are in agreement. By contrast, ΔL and $\Delta R''$ have the same sign only 11 out of 36 times, while $\Delta\Delta L$ and $\Delta\Delta R''$ agree but 18 out of 35 times.

The data for the fifties reveal an extremely close correlation between L and Y, reading both vertically and horizontally in Table 2. Though the simple and partial correlations between L and R'' are .74 and .50, respectively, the correlations of first and second differences are low and negative.

VI. Investments

The correlation coefficients between bank investments (I) and R'' in the thirties are as follows: $r_{IR''} = .75$, $r_{\Delta I \Delta R''} = .33$, and $r_{\Delta\Delta I \Delta\Delta R''} = .11$. In the fifties the same correlations are, in order, .75, .67, and .71. Investments in the thirties thus correlate positively with effective reserves to some extent, but not nearly as consistently as in the fifties. The scatter diagram of I against R'' in the thirties resembles that of E against R'' (Figure 2), with the exception of Phase I. The IR'' observations of Phase I are concentrated—in no particular pattern—just below the lower left terminal of the line of Phase II. During Phase I investments rose while R'' decreased (see Figure 3).

There is not much correlation between bank investments and personal income in either decade.[9] But it is possible to measure the external demand for loanable funds represented by investments more directly than by the income variable. Investment demand mediated through the securities market is in fact identically equal to the volume of new securities supplied in any interval. The Keynesian would thus expect to find a close correlation between bank holdings and the total outstanding supply of any eligible security. High correlations would tend to substantiate the Keynesian view, if we can assume that the aggregate supply is in general independent of the bank demand. The single most important investment in the banking portfolio is government securities, which were 37 percent of bank investments at the start of the thirties, and 72 percent at the close.

---

[9] In the thirties $r_{IY} = .20$, $r_{\Delta I \Delta Y} = .19$, and $r_{\Delta\Delta I \Delta\Delta Y} = .01$. For the fifties the correlations of the same variables are .20, $-.23$, and $-.01$, respectively.

Table 3 reports the correlation coefficients between member bank holdings of marketable government securities (G), the total outstanding supply (T), and effective reserves for both the thirties and the fifties.[10] While $r_{GR''}$ in the thirties is .71, r_{GT} is .99. But the correlations between first and second differences of G and T are much higher than for G and R''. Partialing out T raises the latter correlations, but not to the consistently high level of the correlations between G and T.

TABLE 3

CORRELATION COEFFICIENTS BETWEEN BANK-HELD GOVERNMENT SECURITIES (G), THE TOTAL OUTSTANDING SUPPLY (T), AND EFFECTIVE RESERVES, 1930–39 AND 1953–55

Variables	1930–39			1953–55		
		Δ	$\Delta\Delta$		Δ	$\Delta\Delta$
GR''	.71	.24	.04	.59	.68	.72
GT	.99	.71	.75	.38	.57	.70
$G.R''T$	.99	.81	.79	.76	.74	.83
$GR''.T$	.71	.55	.37	.72	.58	.58
$GT.R''$	.99	.79	.79	—.60	.41	.55

In the fifties T is much less significant in relation to G. In fact, while $r_{GT} = .38$, $r_{GT.R''}$ is —.60. The correlations of first and second differences of G and T, with R'' removed, are well below the corresponding correlations of the thirties. However, these partial correlations of increments in the fifties are far from zero, and it is probably true that changes in G were influenced by changes in T in both decades.[11] Under any circumstances a failure by the Treasury to replace, say, maturing notes, is likely to be accompanied by a reduction in note holdings of most investors, including banks. It would be surprising if banks wanted to, or were able to, maintain their notes by transfer from the existing stock. The significance of the thirties is not that particular bank investments were correlated with the total volume outstanding, but rather, the high degree of that correlation. In the fifties the banks clearly charted their own course with respect to government securities, in spite of some inevitable association between increments of G and T. Ultimately the aggregate of all earning assets was controlled by the quantity of effective reserves. In the thirties one is tempted to describe G as being *dependent* upon T. Reserves seemed to lurk in the background, perhaps occasionally conditioning, but rarely pushing bank investments above the ceiling (or below the floor) created by the aggregate supply of new issues.

---

[10] Data for the thirties on total government securities are taken from *Banking and Monetary Statistics* (Washington, D.C.: Board of Governors of the Federal Reserve System, 1943), pp. 509–10.

[11] There is, of course, an element of spuriousness in all of these correlations, since G is a component of T. But the correlations of the thirties are to be evaluated not in absolute terms but relative to those of the fifties. Moreover, while the correlations are higher in the thirties, G/T was, on the average, less than a third in that decade, and more than a third in the first half of the fifties.

In view of these findings let us examine the three intervals during which total earning assets and the adjusted personal income series moved in opposite directions (Sections IV). The first is for the quarter ending June 30, 1930, during which earning assets (mainly investments) rose $600 million, in spite of a decline in personal income and an almost negligible rise ($17 million) in effective reserves. This quarter witnessed total corporate and state-and-local-government bond issues of over $2 billion— an increase of several hundred million over the preceding quarter, and much greater than that of any subsequent quarter until 1939.[12] Thus, the bank purchases were entirely consistent with the Keynesian view; i.e., in this interval a portion of the investment demand schedule relevant to bank credit moved in a direction opposite to personal income.

In the quarter ending September 30, 1932, earning assets rose by $44 million, in spite of the largest decline ($6.6 billion) in adjusted personal income of the decade. In fact bank loans of $663 million were liquidated, but government securities, coinciding with substantial new issues, more than replaced the loans. Again a relevant segment of the investment demand schedule diverged from the income series.

The contraction of earning assets in the first quarter of 1937, while income rose, is one of the most controversial episodes relating to Federal Reserve policy of the decade. It is widely cited as a reaction to the reserve-requirement increases of 1936–37, and even regarded by some as a contributing factor in the depression of 1937–38.[13] Member banks unloaded $828 million in government securities—mostly bonds and notes, but some bills as well. However, there were offsetting increases in bank loans of $339 million, and in other securities of $14 million, making the net reduction in earning assets $475 million. The increase in loans followed the rise in income, but the decrease in government securities was accompanied by a decline in the total outstanding of only $17 million. Relative to effective reserves, the contraction of earning assets was $475/605 = .785$ of the change in R''. This fraction is half the slope of the line of Phase IV, and much less than half of that of Phase II. Moreover, the contraction of earning assets was dwarfed by the $2.7 billion increase of the preceding nine months, occurring while R'' fell $2.1 billion through earlier Federal Reserve action. The contraction was also quickly followed

---

[12] Total corporate and state-and-local-government bond issues were $1,872 million in the first quarter of 1930, and $2,058 million in the second quarter (*Banking and Monetary Statistics*, p. 489). For the decade as a whole, the correlation between year-end bank holdings of corporate bonds and the total outstanding is .88; for first differences, .64; and for second differences, .59. The data on the total outstanding, which allow for defaults, are from W. B. Hickman, *The Volume of Corporate Bond Financing since 1900* (Princeton, N.J.: Princeton University Press, 1953), p. 359.

[13] Cf. C. L. Warburton, "Bank Reserves and Business Fluctuations," *Journal of the American Statistical Association*, December, 1948, pp. 547–58; Brunner, "A Case Study," *op. cit.*, pp. 193–200; Friedman, *A Program for Monetary Stability*, p. 20; and W. W. Haines, *Money, Prices, and Policy* (New York: McGraw-Hill Book Co., Inc., 1961), pp. 577–79.

by an increase in earning assets of $214 million in the second quarter of 1937 (loans rose $586 million, but investment liquidations continued). Finally, the reduction in earning assets from mid-1937 to mid-1938 was in complete accord with the deteriorating business situation, and was not visibly affected by the lowering of reserve requirements in May, 1938.

Any attempt to link the sale of bank investments in 1937 to the loss of reserves is thus undermined by the very weak relationship between earning assets and reserves in the surrounding periods and in the decade as a whole. The total outstanding supply of investments stands as a very close correlate of bank holdings, but this general relationship does not explain the particular events of 1937. The explanation for the security liquidations of that year might accordingly lie in variables not considered by this study. My own choice is the Keynesian liquidity preference doctrine: bankers *expected* interest rates to return to the level of the 1920's, and they could no longer justify their continued holding of the low-yielding governments. 1936 was a year remarkably similar to those of the preceding decade. Numerous business indicators were at their highest levels since the late and even early twenties; prices, including the stock market, rose for the second consecutive year. It is perhaps especially significant that the decline of long-term interest rates, beginning in 1932, had been leveling out in both 1935 and 1936.

VII. Interest Rates and Lags

A. *Interest Rates*

An effort to relate bank responses in the thirties to interest rates was generally unsuccessful. Correlations between various earning assets and their yields, including combinations of first and second differences of each series, were uniformly low. This was equally true of the fifties, though as noted (Section II), the degree of reserve utilization appeared in the scatter diagram as varying directly with the movement of interest rates. No such simple pattern emerged from the data of the thirties.[14]

From the Keynesian point of view, the evidence as to a liquidity trap in the thirties clearly does not imply a rigid setting of interest rates by the banks. That is, while the supply of bank credit may have been infinitely elastic in response to external demand, it was a shifting schedule not tied to a single level of interest rates. This is self-evident in the continuing downward trend of interest after 1932. Thus, it is not surprising that bond yields were falling in approximately half of the total intervals in which member banks (on net) bought government bonds, and of those

---

[14] Since the interest rate is both a dependent and independent variable to the banking system, a simultaneous-equations approach might yield more fruitful results. But this has not yet been undertaken.

in which they sold government bonds. In the remaining periods of both purchases and sales, the yields were either rising or generally constant.[15]

B. Lags

Since the sale of government securities by banks in 1937 followed by several quarters the initial round of reserve-requirement increases, there may be a general lag between earning assets and effective reserves throughout the thirties.[16] This was tested by correlating earning assets with effective reserves of the preceding call-report interval (R''_{-1}). $r_{ER''_{-1}} = .18$, $r_{\Delta E\Delta R''_{-1}} = .34$, and $r_{\Delta\Delta E\Delta\Delta R''_{-1}} = .15$. Lagging R'' by two intervals, the results are: $r_{ER''_{-2}} = .29$, $r_{\Delta E\Delta R''_{-2}} = .20$, and $r_{\Delta\Delta E\Delta\Delta R''_{-2}} = -.23$. In the fifties, where the data are monthly, $r_{ER''_{-1}} = .92$, $r_{\Delta E\Delta R''_{-1}} = -.16$, $r_{ER''_{-2}} = .92$, and $r_{\Delta E\Delta R''_{-2}} = .08$. The correlation of first differences (which we take as the more reliable indicator of causality) of lagged responses is virtually negligible in the fifties, a decade in which the relationship is in fact primarily between nonlagged variables. In the thirties the correlation of lagged response is clearly an improvement over the nonlagged coefficients (Table 1). There may, in fact, be a weak lagged relationship between R'' and E, but this does not compete seriously with the nonlagged Keynesian interpretation of the decade.

VIII. Summary and Conclusion

Two hypotheses of banking behavior in the 1930's were tested. The first, a "Keynesian" view, holds that member banks were in a liquidity trap; bank credit responded not to reserve changes but to the external demand for loanable funds. An alternative view, the "Wicksellian" hypothesis, holds that effective reserves were the basic determinant of bank credit. The overall correlation between total bank earning assets (E) and effective reserves (R'') is extremely low. However, there are two subperiods, one extending from June, 1933, to March, 1936, and the other, from June, 1938, to December, 1939, during which E and R'' are highly correlated along rising lines of small slope and considerable intercept. But the later line has a much greater intercept than the earlier one; and the points intermediate between the lines, during which effective reserves were drastically reduced by reserve-requirement increases, are widely scattered along a line of slight downward slope. The failure of effective reserves to explain the shift of the two lines, the erratic pattern of the intervening

---

[15] For a possible relationship between interest and banking behavior in the thirties, see J. H. Kareken, "Our Knowledge of Monetary Policy," *American Economic Review* (May, 1961), pp. 41–42, who refers to statistical data of G. Morrison in "Portfolio Behavior of Banks" (Dissertation, University of Chicago, 1962).

[16] I am told that this hypothesis is tested favorably by Morrison in "Portfolio Behavior of Banks."

period, and the poor relationship between second differences of E and R'' tends to contradict the Wicksellian hypothesis.

Total earning assets correlate closely with an adjusted personal income series, which is advanced as a proxy variable for the external demand for loanable funds. The loan component of E correlates especially well with income, and not at all with effective reserves in both the thirties and the fifties. Among bank investments in the thirties, government securities are correlated somewhat with reserves, and very substantially with changes in the total outstanding supply of such securities. The latter variable is identified as a component of the aggregate investment demand schedule. In the fifties an essentially opposite pattern of relationships exists between bank-held government securities and the independent variables. No particular connection was found between interest rates and bank responses in the thirties; evidence as to a lagged relationship between E and R'' was slight.

Perhaps the most interesting finding of this study is the passive or "Keynesian" character of bank loans in both the thirties and the fifties. In the latter decade investments rounded out the portfolio, establishing a sensitive Wicksellian relationship between total earning assets and reserves. But in the thirties the total supply of investments acted as a restraint which the banks were either unwilling or unable to overcome. On net, the total supply of bank credit conformed remarkably well to the Keynesian model.

In retrospect, the action of the Reserve authorities in doubling reserve requirements in 1936–37 appears less unwarranted than it did to many observers at the time. The case for federal deficit spending, financed by borrowing from the member banks and the public, appears more compelling than ever. To this writer, it is conceivable that when the entire story of the thirties is told, there may even appear positive reasons for preventing economic expansion based upon independent action of the banks.

Appendix: Effective Reserves[*]

The adjustment for effective reserves is derived in two steps. First, an adjustment is made to render all reserve components comparable in terms of their availability to the banker. Thus, reserves, such as those arising from Federal Reserve borrowings or bank capital subscriptions, which are in the first instance entirely excess and fully spendable, are raised over components coming from primary deposits, part of which are immediately

---

[*] The following account of the adjustments for effective reserves differs in a number of important respects from the author's earlier discussion, "Elements of Timing," *op. cit.*, pp. 240–48. In particular, the adjustment for the fully available reserve component, the adjustment for earning assets, and the omission of vault cash from reserves in the earlier analysis are all superseded by the procedure described here.

held as required reserves. Second, an adjustment is made in which the capacity to spend reserves of comparable availability is held constant by the use of a fixed or standard reserve requirement.

We employ the following symbols: R is the total quantity of reserves held by all member banks; it consists of member bank deposits at the Federal Reserve plus vault cash. D is total net deposits in member banks, which are total deposits subject to reserve requirements less allowable deductions in computing the required reserve.[17] E is total earning assets (loans plus investments) gross of valuation reserves. r_r is the average required ratio of reserves to total deposits for all member banks. r_{rs} (arbitrarily selected)is the standard required ratio of reserves to deposits, relative to which the reserves of every period are to be expressed.

A. The Adjustment for Varying Availability of Reserves

If reserves enter the banking system solely through primary deposits, we have the aggregate balance sheet equality,

$$R + E = D \tag{1}$$

For a fully loaned-up banking system, $D = \dfrac{1}{r_r} R$ and

$$E = R \left(\frac{1}{r_r} - 1 \right) \tag{2}$$

However, if a portion of reserves is acquired from, say, Federal Reserve borrowings, then (1) is replaced by

$$R + E = D + d \tag{3}$$

where d, the quantity of reserves so obtained, appears on the liability side as borrowings due to the Federal Reserve. In equilibrium (i.e., excess reserves are zero) earning assets are now

$$E = R \left(\frac{1}{r_r} - 1 \right) + d \tag{4}$$

We wish to express the effect of d in raising E as an increase in the volume of reserves. That is, we want that reserve level, R', which will produce (4) by a simple equality of the form of (2). We let

---

[17] Beginning August 23, 1935, net deposits are gross deposits less demand balances due from domestic banks and all cash items in process of collection. Prior to that date the allowable deduction was demand balances due *to* (rather than *from*) banks, plus numerous other items, including U.S. government deposits, cashiers' and travelers' checks, and the difference between amounts due to, and amounts due from, banks.

$$R' = R + \left(\frac{r_r}{1 - r_r}\right) d \qquad (5)$$

The reader may verify that $E = R'\left(\frac{1}{r_r} - 1\right)$, where E is given by (4).

In general, the quantity, d, arises from reserve components backed by (a) liabilities other than net deposits and (b) capital not invested in fixed assets. The major items under (a) are Federal Reserve borrowings, loans due to other member banks (federal funds),[18] and (until 1935) reserve-free government deposits. Fortunately, it is not necessary to enumerate every possible circumstance giving rise to fully available reserves. Such reserve components are simply measured directly on the aggregate balance sheet by the observed quantity, $d = R + E - D$.[19]

B. The Adjustment for Changing Reserve Requirements

We assume that the preceding adjustment to reserves has been made, and that E is given by (2), except that $R = R'$. Suppose that a prevailing reserve requirement, r_{rs}, is replaced by a new one, r_r. This may be due to a shift of deposits between time and demand, a regional shift of deposits, or an announced change. The maximum level of E changes simultaneously from E' to E''. We want to express this movement of E as a function of reserves, holding the requirement constant at r_{rs}. That is, we want a reserve level, R'', such that

$$E'' = R''\left(\frac{1}{r_{rs}} - 1\right) \qquad (6)$$

Since $E'' = R'\left(\frac{1}{r_r} - 1\right)$, we obtain the level of "effective" reserves by taking the difference between the two equalities, and solving for R'':

$$R'' = R'\left(\frac{r_{rs}(1 - r_r)}{r_r(1 - r_{rs})}\right) \qquad (7)$$

In general, r_{rs} is the fixed or "standard" requirement in terms of which all

---

18 A loan of excess reserves between member banks provides funds to the receiving bank on the same terms granted by the Federal Reserve. The liability backing the reserves is without a reserve requirement, and is thus a component of d (borrowings due to other banks), rather than D. Meanwhile, the loan appears in the earning assets of the lending bank.

19 The value of d (see Table 4) is $5,835 million at the opening of the decade; $4,207 million at the close; $5,899 million at its maximum in March, 1930; and $3,015 million at its lowest point in mid-1935. On the other hand, the correction factor, $[r_r/(1 - r_r)] d$, rose from $423 million to $760 million over the course of the decade, reaching a high of $816 million in mid-1937, and a low of $269 million in mid-1935. In general, R' exceeds R, and rises overall by a greater amount.

reserves are expressed, and r_r is the reserve requirement of any current period.[20]

Having made the adjustments for effective reserves, can the observed figure, E, be retained for comparison to R''? That is, does the observed level of earning assets, relative to R'', express the same propensity to invest present in the unadjusted data? It does, if we define the propensity to hold earning assets as

$$\eta = \frac{E(\text{obs.})}{E(\text{max.})_{r_r}} \tag{8}$$

the ratio of the observed to the maximum level of earning assets obtainable under the current requirement. We define $E(\text{max.})_{r_{rs}}$ as the maximum level obtainable under the standard requirement. Then it follows that

$$\eta E(\text{max.})_{r_{rs}} = E(\text{obs.}) \tag{9}$$

upon substituting $R'\left(\dfrac{1}{r_r} - 1\right)$ for $E(\text{max.})_{r_r}$ in η, $R''\left(\dfrac{1}{r_{rs}} - 1\right)$ for

$E(\text{max.})_{r_{rs}}$, and (7) for R''.[21]

---

[20] It can be shown that effective reserves based on a given standard reserve requirement differ by a constant factor from those based on another standard requirement. Let R''_a be a series based on r'_{rs}, and R''_b, a series based on r''_{rs}. Then, substituting expressions of the form of (7), $R''_a/R''_b = r'_{rs}(1 - r''_{rs})/r''_{rs}(1 - r'_{rs})$, a constant.

[21] One of the underlying assumptions of this whole analysis is that E and R'' are not effectively the same variable, as they would be if the Federal Reserve bought or sold securities directly to the member banks. However, an examination of the data shows little or no evidence of such direct transactions during the periods studied.

TABLE 4
Derivation of Member Bank Effective Reserves and Series on Earning Assets and Personal Income, 1930–39 (Call Report Dates)
(Dollar Figures in Millions)

		d	r_r	μd †	R'	$\delta(r_{rs} = .077)$ ‡	R''	$\Delta R''$	$\Delta\Delta R''$	E	ΔE	$\Delta\Delta E$	Y^*	ΔY^*
	R													
1929														
12/31	2,932	5,835	.074	466	3,398	1.0439	3,547			35,934			83.3	
1930														
3/27	2,850	5,899	.072	458	3,308	1.0752	3,557	10		35,056	—878		81.1	—2.2
6/30	2,892	5,566	.072	432	3,324	1.0752	3,574	17	7	35,656	600	1,478	79.6	—1.5
9/24	2,885	5,755	.072	447	3,332	1.0752	3,583	9	8	35,472	—184	784	75.3	—4.3
12/31	3,068	5,412	.073	426	3,494	1.0593	3,701	118	109	34,860	—612	428	71.7	—3.6
1931														
3/25	2,825	5,410	.072	420	3,245	1.0752	3,489	—212	330	34,729	131	481	70.4	—1.3
6/30	2,915	4,966	.072	385	3,300	1.0752	3,548	59	271	33,923	—806	675	69.3	—1.1
9/29	2,893	5,744	.073	452	3,345	1.0593	3,543	—5	64	33,073	—850	44	63.2	—6.1
12/31	2,498	5,690	.074	455	2,953	1.0439	3,083	—460	455	30,575	—2,498	—1,648	59.8	—3.4
1932														
6/30	2,476	5,359	.073	422	2,898	1.0593	3,070	—13	447	28,001	—2,574	76	53.9	—5.9
9/30	2,642	5,459	.074	436	3,078	1.0439	3,213	143	156	28,045	44	2,618	47.3	6.6
12/31	2,934	4,660	.075	378	3,312	1.0289	3,408	195	52	27,469	—576	620	45.8	—1.5
1933														
6/30	2,640	4,289	.077	358	2,998	1.0000	2,998	—410	605	24,786	—2,683	—2,107	45.3	—0.5
10/25	3,098	4,548	.077	379	3,477	1.0000	3,477	479	889	24,953	167	2,850	48.7	3.4
12/30	3,149	4,423	.077	369	3,518	1.0000	3,518	41	438	25,220	267	100	49.9	1.2
1934														
3/5	3,634	5,183	.077	432	4,066	1.0000	4,066	548	507	26,548	1,328	1,061	52.4	2.5
6/30	4,292	4,589	.079	394	4,686	.9726	4,558	492	56	27,175	627	—701	53.6	1.2
10/17	4,526	3,855	.080	335	4,861	.9593	4,663	105	387	27,559	384	—243	53.8	0.2
12/31	4,689	4,080	.080	355	5,044	.9593	4,839	176	71	28,150	591	207	54.0	0.2
1935														
3/4	5,052	3,770	.081	332	5,384	.9465	5,096	257	81	28,271	121	470	56.2	2.2
6/29	5,470	3,015	.082	269	5,739	.9339	5,360	264	7	28,785	514	393	59.3	3.1
11/1	6,203	3,723	.084	341	6,544	.9097	5,953	593	329	29,301	516	2	61.4	2.1
12/31	6,238	3,640	.084	334	6,572	.9097	5,979	26	567	29,985	684	168	63.3	1.9

TABLE 4 (*Continued*)

		R	d	r_r	μd †	R'	$\delta(r_{rs}=.077)$ ‡	R''	$\Delta R''$	$\Delta\Delta R''$	E	ΔE	$\Delta\Delta E$	Y^*	ΔY^*
1936	3/4	6,408	3,746	.084	344	6,752	.9097	6,142	163	137	30,288	303	—381	64.0	0.7
	6/30	6,320	3,806	.085	354	6,674	.8981	5,994	—148	—311	32,259	1,971	1,668	67.7	3.7
	12/31	7,269	3,830	.127	557	7,826	.5734	4,487	—1,507	—1,359	33,000	741	—1,230	70.5	2.8
1937	3/31	7,275	3,967	.146	678	7,953	.4881	3,882	—605	902	32,525	—475	—1,216	72.7	2.2
	6/30	7,526	4,073	.167	816	8,342	.4160	3,470	—412	193	32,739	214	689	75.9	3.2
	12/31	7,594	4,084	.164	801	8,395	.4254	3,571	101	513	31,752	—987	—1,201	73.7	—2.2
1938	3/7	7,852	3,989	.165	788	8,640	.4222	3,648	77	—24	31,521	231	756	68.6	—5.1
	6/30	8,716	3,991	.145	676	9,392	.4918	4,619	971	894	30,721	—800	—569	67.4	—1.2
	9/28	8,968	4,094	.146	700	9,668	.4881	4,719	100	—871	31,627	906	1,706	68.4	1.0
	12/31	9,440	4,017	.147	692	10,132	.4842	4,906	187	87	32,070	—443	—463	69.7	1.3
1939	3/29	9,889	4,067	.147	701	10,590	.4842	5,128	222	35	32,095	—25	—418	71.2	1.5
	6/30	10,722	4,165	.149	729	11,451	.4764	5,455	327	105	32,603	508	483	71.7	0.5
	10/2	12,390	4,086	.152	732	13,122	.4654	6,107	652	325	33,075	472	—36	72.9	1.2
	12/30	12,444	4,207	.153	760	13,204	.4618	6,098	—9	661	33,941	866	394	75.6	2.7

* Billions of dollars.
† $\mu = r_r/(1 - r_r)$.
‡ $\delta = r_{rs}(1 - r_r)/$

6. The Effects of Devaluation on Exports, A Case Study: United Kingdom, 1949-54[*]

M. June Flanders

Purdue University

WHEN THE POUND STERLING was devalued in September, 1949, the rest of the Sterling Area (except for Pakistan) followed suit immediately. Within a few days, most of the countries of Western Europe had devalued their currencies also, although not all of the European devaluations were as large as the British.[1]

Whatever the reason for the devaluation (there seem, in fact, to have been several), such a realignment of the relative prices of the world's currencies might be expected to have many repercussions. The purpose of this paper is to examine some of these repercussions, specifically, the effect of the devaluation on some of the major exports of one of the devaluing countries, Great Britain.[2]

In the period dealt with, 1949–54, there were several important factors influencing the level of British exports quite independently of the devaluation.[3] The most obvious of these is the Korean War. This had the effect, in the first place, of raising the volume of world trade considerably, as the demand for "strategic materials" increased. For this reason alone, simply

---

[*] Reprinted from *Bulletin of the Oxford University Institute of Statistics*, Vol. 25, No. 3 (1963), pp. 165–98.

[1] The following countries devalued by 30.5 percent: Australia, Burma, Ceylon, Denmark, Egypt, Eire, Finland, Greece, Holland, Iceland, India, Iraq, Israel, New Zealand, Norway, South Africa, Sweden, United Kingdom. The following countries devalued by less than 30.5 percent: Belgium and Luxembourg (12.3 percent), Canada (9.3 percent), France (5.6 to 22.2 percent), Italy (8.1 percent), Portugal (13.3 percent), Siam (20.0 percent), West Germany (20.7 percent). *Economist*, October 29, 1949, p. 968, and International Monetary Fund, *Schedule of Par Values*, Ninth Issue (Washington, D.C., December 1, 1949), pp. 11–13.

[2] In view of the importance of exports to a country such as Great Britain, the question posed is interesting per se. In addition, however, it can be argued that a study of exports is preferable to one of imports. For any one country, exports are less readily subjected to the influence and control of regulating governmental agencies.

[3] *Vide* United Nations Economic Commission for Europe, *Economic Survey of Europe in 1950*, Geneva, 1951, chap. 1.

examining the value, or even the volume, of British exports would not give us any insight into the question of the effects of the devaluation.

Secondly, as a result of the increased demand for the materials required for war production and the execution of rearmament programs, there was a general rise in prices, so that values of exports changed more than did quanta. Theoretically, of course, this could be overcome by examining the quantum figures of exports, but this creates serious practical difficulties. To get an index number for quantities exported of groups of commodities, or for total exports, would be meaningful only if all prices moved more or less equiproportionately, which they did not. An alternative method of approach, which would avoid completely the problems raised by price changes, would be to examine the quantities exported by individual commodity. This would, as we have noted, eliminate the index number problem, but there are other difficulties connected with such a method. Since a few samples would be inadequate, it would be necessary to obtain data for a great many separate items and then to consolidate them, possibly into an index using predevaluation shares of total British exports as weights, for example. This could, of course, be done, but it would be a large undertaking and would still leave unsolved the first problem, that of how to separate a change in British exports due to devaluation from a change due to the increase in total worldwide demand for a large number of commodities.

A third effect of the Korean War, which we indicated above, was that not only was the level of world prices altered, but there was also a change in the pattern of relative prices. This is, of course, intimately related to the fact that there was a change in the structure of world demand. (We say that the two phenomena were related. They are not, however, identical, because even an equal upward shift in all demand curves would yield a large range of percentage changes in prices, depending on supply conditions.) If a high proportion of Britain's traditional exports consisted of commodities the demand for which increased relatively much as a result of the war this would give quite different results, if we studied either the quantity or the total value of exports, than would obtain if British exports consisted primarily of goods the demand for which did not change much as a result of the war. In neither case would this reveal anything about the effects of the devaluation. It must be noted, however (and we shall return to this point subsequently), that our method, that of examining market shares of various commodity groups, is subject to this same objection "in the small," and we have not been able to avoid this problem completely.[4]

---

[4] A hypothetical example of the kind of problem we are referring to is the following: There is a worldwide increase in the demand for sewing machines (in response to an increase in the demand for military uniforms in excess of the decline in demand for civilian clothing), but the British exports of sewing machines increase very little. It may be, in such a situation, that Britain has traditionally manufactured and exported sewing machines for private use, whereas machines for industrial use are produced primarily in, say, Switzerland. Then the figures of market shares of exports

In view of the difficulties noted above, we take the position that in studying the effects of the British devaluation of 1949 we shall find it more useful to examine the market shares of various British exports rather than the total quantities or values of exports. Analytically, this implies that we are utilizing the concept of the elasticity of substitution in demand. We make the assumption that the total worldwide level of demand for a good is given, in the sense that it does not depend on the British price or on the ratio of British prices to the prices of other exporters. But we assume the ratio of the total purchases of that good bought from the United Kingdom does depend on the ratio of the British export price to the prices charged by other exporters. The demand function implied by this is

$$Q_1/Q_2 = f(P_1/P_2R),$$

where Q_1 is the quantity (of a given good) exported from Country 1, and Q_2 is the quantity exported from Country 2. P_1 and P_2 are the respective prices, and R is the exchange rate, i.e., the number of units of Country 1's currency in a unit of Country 2's currency. By this definition of R, if Country 1 devalues, R increases. This demand function, then, states that the ratio of quantities of a given good demanded from two countries (or groups of countries) is a function of the ratio of their prices (both expressed in terms of the currency of one of them). The elasticity of this function is the percentage change in market share divided by the percentage change in the price ratio

$$\sigma_2{}^1 = \frac{d\left(\dfrac{Q_1}{Q_2}\right)}{d\left(\dfrac{P_1}{P_2R}\right)} \cdot \frac{\dfrac{P_1}{P_2R}}{\dfrac{Q_1}{Q_2}}.$$

Note that we have defined the P's and Q's as the quantities and prices of the *same goods* coming from different sources. Technically, this is fallacious. If we are speaking really of the same good, and if there is free trade, then, of course, the price must be the same, regardless of where the good originates, and the elasticity of substitution will be virtually infinite.

It is not necessary to enter at this point into the well-known controversy over the definition of a commodity. We have computed market shares of British exports for four commodity groups. In each case the groups are sufficiently homogeneous for it to make sense intuitively to talk about substitution between the products of several countries; at the same time they

would show a decline in the British share which could not be explained in terms of the devaluation. As we noted above, there is really no way in our method for avoiding this. The fact that our "commodity groups" are fairly large, however, increases the probability that such errors will cancel each other out. In other words, a bias of this type is less likely to occur if we consider all of "machinery" as a group, than if we examine the exports of only one small class of machinery.

are heterogeneous enough (and world markets in these goods imperfect enough) to make it obvious that the elasticity of substitution in demand is unlikely to be infinite.[5]

The four commodity groups studied are iron and steel, power-generating machinery, textiles, and vehicles. The first two are producers' goods exclusively, the latter two are both producers' and consumers' goods. Together they constitute about 30 percent of British exports. These groups vary with respect to the share of the United Kingdom in the world market; they vary also with respect to the homogeneity of the products and the degree of competition in the markets for them. Automobiles, for example, are relatively highly differentiated in the mind of the purchaser, whereas product differentiation is slight when one is buying 50-count mercerized thread or iron ingots.

In Table I we show summaries of the data.[6] For each commodity group, for each year, 1949 to 1955, we have computed three ratios:

1. The ratio of British exports to world exports.
2. The ratio of British exports to the exports of the other devaluing countries.
3. The ratio of British exports to the exports of nondevaluing countries.

In collecting the data, however, we have found it impossible to use either absolute quantities or indices of quantities. Absolute quantities have no

---

[5] There has been some discussion in the literature as to the usefulness and appropriateness of the concept of the elasticity of substitution, both in general and in its application to studies of demand for exports. We refer the reader specifically to Irving Morrissett, "Some Recent Uses of Elasticity of Substitution—A Survey," *Econometrica*, Vol. XXI, No. 1 (January, 1953), pp. 41–62; Jan Tinbergen, "Some Measurements of Elasticities of Substitution," *Review of Economic Statistics*, Vol. XXVIII, No. 3 (August, 1946), pp. 109–16; T. C. Chang, "A Statistical Note on World Demand for Exports," *Review of Economics and Statistics*, Vol. XXX, No. 2 (May, 1948), pp. 106–16; T. C. Chang, *Cyclical Movements in the Balance of Payments* (Cambridge, Eng.: Cambridge University Press, 1951), chap. lv, pp. 66–78; J. J. Polak, "Note on the Measurement of Elasticity of Substitution in International Trade," *Review of Economics and Statistics*, Vol. XXXII, No. 1 (February, 1950), pp. 16–20 (followed by a reply by Tinbergen, pp. 20–21); Z. M. Kubinski, "Measurements of Elasticity of Substitution in International Trade," *South African Journal of Economics*, Vol. XXII (June, 1954), pp. 210–22. In general, the objections raised to the use of the concept of the elasticity of substitution apply least to the kind of situation with which we are concerned; in fact, several of the writers refer explicitly to the type of problems we are considering as an exception to their objections.

[6] The detailed data have not been included here. They can be found in the author's unpublished doctoral dissertation, "British Export Shares, 1949–1954: A Case Study of Devaluation," University of California, Berkeley, 1960. The "raw data" consist of the dollar value of exports, annually, for each of the four commodity groups, from all the countries exporting significant quantities of each commodity. In each case, the figures are for total exports, and are not broken down by destination. Where the original data were presented in the currencies of the country of origin, they were converted to dollars at official exchange rates. Unless it is otherwise stated, all the tables and references to data in this paper are taken from the material to be found in the statistical appendices to the dissertation.

TABLE I
(Millions of United States Dollars)

		Total Value of Exports from				Percentage which United Kingdom Exports Constitute of Exports from		
		United Kingdom	All Devaluing Countries	All Nondevaluing Countries	Total World	Devaluing Countries	Nondevaluing Countries	World
Iron and steel	1949	300.12	776.25	1,163.52	1,939.77	38.6	25.8	15.5
	1950	289.10	934.74	793.45	1,728.19	31.0	36.4	16.7
	1951	291.09	1,328.79	1,500.37	2,829.16	22.0	19.4	10.3
	1952	366.37	1,493.29	1,761.35	3,254.64	24.5	20.8	11.3
	1953	378.01	1,501.41	1,269.19	2,770.59	25.2	29.8	13.6
	1954	383.23	1,497.00	1,210.87	2,707.87	25.6	31.6	14.2
Vehicles and parts	1949	992.76	1,394.03	1,296.48	2,690.51	71.2	76.6	37.0
	1950	959.50	1,280.56	1,140.91	2,421.47	74.9	84.1	39.6
	1951	1,073.38	1,635.37	1,568.08	3,203.45	65.6	68.5	33.5
	1952	851.40	2,085.90	1,536.12	3,622.01	40.8	55.4	24.0
	1953	1,042.94	2,052.54	3,073.38	5,125.92	50.8	33.9	20.0
	1954	1,126.23	2,532.42	2,764.87	5,297.29	44.4	40.7	21.0
Power-generating machinery	1949	161.37	208.69	220.96	429.65	77.3	73.0	37.6
	1950	144.44	216.85	204.30	421.15	66.6	70.7	34.3
	1951	174.69	312.51	286.56	599.07	55.9	60.9	29.2
	1952	196.01	405.62	270.92	676.54	48.3	72.3	29.0
	1953	212.61	441.55	282.29	723.84	48.2	75.3	29.4
	1954	228.42	461.77	283.49	645.26	49.5	80.6	35.4
Textiles	1949	823.35	1,638.75	907.88	2,546.63	50.2	90.7	32.3
	1950	677.12	1,620.86	955.56	2,576.42	41.8	70.9	26.3
	1951	833.14	1,881.18	1,282.33	3,163.51	44.3	65.0	26.3
	1952	633.08	1,489.76	932.02	2,421.78	42.5	67.9	26.1
	1953	614.21	1,436.38	898.86	2,335.24	42.8	68.3	26.3
	1954	591.58	1,474.26	1,014.75	2,489.01	40.1	58.3	23.8

The ratios computed here are of values not of quantities. When we defined the concept of the elasticity of substitution, the market share was expressed as Q_1/Q_2, the ratio of indices of physical exports.

conceptual meaning when we are speaking of fairly broad commodity groups and the international trade statistics do not give quantity indices for such groups. What we have used, therefore, are value shares. The percentages, then, are of British share of total (or of nondevaluing countries') exports, for each commodity group, expressed in dollar value. Since the purpose of devaluation is to increase net earnings of foreign exchange, shares of value of exports are, of course, not uninteresting. We should note, however, that the percentages we derive in this way will be, in general, biased downward, as compared with the results that would be obtained if we used quantity indices. The quantity indices would give us $d(Q_1/Q_2)$. What we actually have is $d(Q_1P_1/Q_2P_2R)$. In our problem, we expect P_1/P_2R to fall as a result of the devaluation. Therefore, we would expect the quantity shares to be higher than the value shares. That is to say, there is probably a downward bias in our figures.

It should be noted that this is not contingent upon any assumption about what happens to the terms of trade. A fall in P_1/P_2R does not imply a worsening of the terms of trade; it simply means that the sterling prices of British exports fall more (or rise less) than the sterling prices of exports of the same commodities from the nondevaluing countries. This is quite consistent with either an increase or a decrease in the prices of British exports relative to the prices of British imports.

The Actual and the Expected Results

In a rather general and crude way, one would expect the following results from the devaluation: First, the ratio between British and world exports should increase. Second, the ratio between British exports and exports from the other devaluing countries should remain the same. Third, the ratio of British exports to those from the nondevaluing countries should increase, and, in fact, should increase more than the first ratio.

These are the results that would obtain in a world in which the *ceteris paribus* assumption really was applicable and in which the substitution demand curve for British exports had a negative slope. The elasticity of that demand curve would, of course, determine the size of the change in the first and third ratios.

In point of fact, there was great diversity in the behavior of export shares in the period under review. In every year except 1951 there were some shares falling while others were rising. A few broad generalizations, however, are possible.

First, for all four commodity groups, the ratio of British exports to world exports was lower at the end of the period than at the beginning. For two of the groups, however, iron and steel and power-generating machinery, the differences were very slight: the shares in 1954 were almost as high as in 1949.

Second, the ratio of British exports to the exports of other devaluing countries was lower, for every commodity group, at the end of the period than at the beginning. Furthermore, the differences were large for all the groups, ranging from a decline of roughly 10 percent in textiles to nearly 40 percent in vehicles.

Third, the ratio of British exports to those of the nondevaluing countries was higher for two of the commodity groups and lower for the other two. The cases in which this ratio was higher were iron and steel and power-generating machinery, which, as we noted above, were the commodities for which Britain's share of the world market remained nearly constant. In these commodities, then, Britain's gains, at the expense of nondevaluing exporting countries, were about equal to her losses in market shares vis-à-vis the other devaluing countries.

Some Suggested Explanations of the Differences between the
Actual and Expected Results

There are three possible explanations of the difference between the expected effects of the devaluation on British market shares and the realized changes in the shares, which were, in fact, either rather small or negative. The first possibility is that the elasticity of substitution in demand for British exports was, in fact, very small in absolute value. In fact, since shares decreased, this would imply a positive elasticity.

The second alternative is that other events than the devaluation caused the substitution demand curve for British exports to shift in such a way as to offset the expansionary effect on export shares, which the devaluation would otherwise have had. The events we are thinking of primarily are:

1. The devaluation of other currencies.
2. The Korean War.
3. The recovery of the German and Japanese economies.
4. The existence of, and changes in, trade controls and regulations.

The third possibility is that the substitution demand curve was not shifting, and the elasticity of substitution in demand was not low, but rather that

(a) the supply of exports from the United Kingdom was inelastic, or
(b) British export prices, relative to the relevant prices elsewhere, rose by more than the devaluation, or at least did not fall enough.

It should be noted that an inelastic supply of exports might or might not result in a rise in British export prices, depending on the methods of price determination in effect in the several British industries. It should be noted also that the prices of British exports could rise relative to those of other countries, even if supply were not inelastic: a rise in the overall British price level, relative to that of other countries, would have the same effect, and this might be due to any one of a number of causes, such as an inflationary domestic monetary policy, for example. A third point to be noted here is that, in order for export shares to decline because of inelastic supply conditions, it is not necessary that supply be perfectly inelastic. If total exports are increasing, one country's share will decline if her sales increase less rapidly than the total.

We then have six "qualifying factors" which must be considered before we come to any conclusions about the elasticity of substitution of demand for exports or the "wisdom" of devaluation. These include the four factors mentioned above, which might have caused the substitution demand function for British exports to shift, as well as the two which would have operated directly on the export shares, causing them to be lower, for any given value of the elasticity of substitution, than they would otherwise be.

Unfortunately, as was noted, the effects of these factors cannot be quantified. Also they cannot in all cases be separated one from another. As an example, let us consider the impact of the Korean War. We noted previously that the major effect of this was to increase the total volume of world trade, which is precisely the sort of situation that had led us to study market shares of exports. This would be the end of it if we could assume that there would be no change in shares directly induced by this change in volume of trade. There are, however, two obvious facets to this problem, involving others of the qualifying factors mentioned above. One of these is the impact on supply elasticities. More will be said on this subject below, but we shall have to take cognizance of the fact that different countries participated to varying degrees in the hostilities and rearmament, and this implies differing influences on their elasticities of supply. (This statement holds for both the supply of exports available to foreigners and the output of exportable goods.) Secondly, along with the increase in the volume of trade went an increase in the prices of raw materials and a redistribution of world income in favor of raw material-producing countries. Apart from a number of probable effects of this redistribution on the world's marginal propensity to import certain commodities we have the additional problem of the reaction of the several governments to their increased earnings of foreign exchange in general, and of dollars in particular; specifically, there is the question of the effect of these increased earnings on import controls and exchange regulations. Thus, apart from the obvious difficulty of separating out empirically the effects of several different "causes," we have the problem that even on a purely abstract, conceptual level we have an interaction here of at least three of our qualifying factors: the conflict in Korea, differing elasticities of supply, and changes in controls and regulations. Nevertheless, it is essential that we consider these qualifying factors, and we shall deal with them individually to the extent that it is possible to do so.

(1) *The Effects of the Devaluation of Other Currencies.* In general,

we would expect the improvement in the United Kingdom's share of exports (both of total world exports and as a ratio to the exports of the nondevaluing countries) to be smaller in the case of a group devaluation than if the United Kingdom had devalued alone. The effect of the devaluation on the part of other countries, furthermore, would be greater, the more similar the export patterns of the other devaluing countries to that of Great Britain. If the United Kingdom shared equally with the other devaluing countries in the benefits of the devaluation, as far as increased export shares were concerned, then the ratio of exports from Great Britain to those of the other devaluing countries would remain constant over the period studied. If Britain got more than her "share" of the benefit, this ratio should have risen; if she got less, it should have declined.

While we can, therefore, arrive at some measure of the extent to which the various devaluing countries shared in the benefits of the devaluation, we cannot say anything about how much more the ratio of British exports to those of the nondevaluing countries would have increased if no other countries had devalued. (We refer here to the algebraic increase; the shares may have increased more or decreased less.) For the purposes of making a practical judgment about the desirability or advisability of the devaluation, however, this question is irrelevant. Whether or not a solo devaluation would have benefited the United Kingdom is not really important in the present context. What does concern us is whether or not the devaluation by a number of countries redounded to the advantage of Britain.

In Table II we show the ratios of the United Kingdom's exports to those of the other devaluing countries, excluding Germany.

TABLE II

THE RATIO OF EXPORTS FROM THE UNITED KINGDOM TO THOSE FROM THE OTHER DEVALUING COUNTRIES, EXCLUDING GERMANY

Exports	*1949*	*1950*	*1951*	*1952*	*1953*	*1954*
Textiles	52.8	43.3	47.8	46.2	46.5	44.1
Power-generating machinery	81.9	76.1	71.4	64.7	65.9	67.4
Iron and steel	43.5	39.4	30.3	33.5	32.4	33.8
Vehicles	72.9	81.9	75.7	58.4	64.3	59.2

In three of the four commodity groups studied, the ratio was higher in 1949 than at any time after the devaluation up to and including 1954. The exception was in vehicles, where the ratio rose sharply in 1950, then started to fall again, and by 1954 was very much lower than in 1949. It might be possible to seek *ad hoc* explanations for each commodity individually. Nevertheless, the impression remains that the United Kingdom benefited less from the devaluation than did the other devaluing countries as a group. These data do not permit us to estimate to what extent this was due to differences in the elasticities of substitution of demand, and to what extent it was the result of other factors, notably differences in supply elasticities and differences in price level changes between the United Kingdom on the one hand, and the other devaluing countries on the other.

There are several reasons for excluding Germany when computing the ratios presented in Table II. First, it is argued that the large changes in German exports over the period were due primarily to the economic recovery of that country, and only secondarily to the devaluation. Strictly speaking, of course, economic recovery in this context is simply a shift of the supply schedules to the right, and this should be handled as merely a special case of the phenomenon of different supply conditions in the several devaluing countries. However, we take the position that the growth of German productive capacity and exports was sufficiently rapid and dramatic to be separated from shifts in supply in other countries. Furthermore, it was exogenous (in the sense that it was not, apparently, a result of the devaluation) and unlikely to recur in comparable proportions. Also, in discussing supply differences we shall be thinking primarily (as we were in the previous section) of differences in elasticities rather than shifts in the schedules.

A second reason for excluding Germany is that she devalued by a considerably smaller percentage than did the United Kingdom and most of the other devaluing countries. Thus, there is less justification for attributing the increases in her share of exports in world markets to the devaluation than in the case of the other devaluing countries. Germany having devalued less than the other countries,[7] should then—if we assume that the gains were equally distributed—have benefited less from the devaluation than the others. This reinforces our intuitive judgment that the growth in German exports must be explained primarily on grounds other than the devaluation.

Differences existed, among the devaluing countries, in the extent of price level changes, but these do not appear adequate to explain the declining share of British exports in those of the devaluing bloc as a whole. British prices in terms of home currency rose after the devaluation, so that the index in dollar terms stood as high in 1951 as in the first nine months of 1949. The same was true, however, of most of the other European devaluing countries, although in a number of cases the increase was less than in Britain. From 1952 to 1954, the British wholesale price index was constant, however, whereas prices in most other countries were falling. Again, however, the differences between the overall price behavior in the several countries are not, it would seem, large enough to explain the shifts in export shares.[8]

---

[7] The German devaluation was 20.7 percent, the lowest of all the countries we have classified as devaluing. Others, such as Belgium, Italy, Portugal, and Canada devalued less than Germany, but these have been treated as nondevaluing countries in our analysis.

[8] See International Monetary Fund, *International Financial Statistics*, Vol. VIII, No. 12 (December, 1955), pp. 36–37, "Price Indexes Expressed in U.S. Dollars," 1950 = 100, and pp. 38–215, "Country Tables."

(2) *The Effects of the Korean War.* Of the six qualifying factors listed above, this one, the impact of the fighting in Korea, offers perhaps the least justification for consideration here. The reason for this is not that the effects of the conflict were unimportant. On the contrary, it is precisely the magnitude of its consequences, *inter alia,* that has led us to adopt the share of world markets as an empirical measure of the effects of the devaluation. But this is exactly the reason for excluding it from consideration as a qualifying factor. If, in fact, the sole effect of the conflict were to raise the volume of world trade but not to affect its distribution, then this would be completely taken care of by our use of the market-shares approach; we would not have to qualify our results as to changes in market shares by any discussion of the effects of the Korean War. If, however, the conflict and its attendant rearmament and stockpiling of materials altered the distribution as well as the size of world trade, then we should take this into account. It can be argued, however, that even in this event we should not treat it as a separate factor, on the grounds that it will affect our results only indirectly by operating on one or more of the other factors influencing market shares. If, for example, the conflict led to a differential, which would not otherwise have existed, in elasticities of supply of exports between the United Kingdom and Belgium then this should properly be included in our discussion of the effects of differences in supply conditions. Nevertheless, we feel that these indirect effects attributable to the Korean War are sufficiently important and interesting to be treated separately and we shall so treat them, despite our awareness that conceptually it involves overlapping with discussion of other factors.

The initial impact of the outbreak of the war was a wave of "scare" buying, particularly on the part of the United States, and a sharp increase in prices of raw materials.[9] This would be expected to affect the British terms of trade and hence, eventually, domestic costs in the manufacturing industries. However, there is no a priori reason for this to have had a greater effect on costs in British industries than on those in the same industries in other countries. In fact by the end of 1950 the terms of trade had turned sharply against the United Kingdom, but they had moved to an almost equal degree against other devaluing European countries (and even more unfavorably against Germany) except for the Scandinavian countries, which typically import a higher proportion of manufactured goods than the United Kingdom.[10] In her position as an international financial center and as banker for the Sterling Area, the United Kingdom was, of course, peculiarly affected by the large increase in the volume traded and in the prices of raw materials, since these affected the dollar earnings of the Sterling Area as a whole. These issues, however, while

---

[9] See United Nations Economic Commission for Europe, *Economic Survey of Europe in 1950,* Geneva, 1951, p. 8.
[10] *Ibid.,* p. 93.

relevant to a broader study of the effects of devaluation, are outside the scope of our investigation.[11]

During 1951 and especially during the latter half of the year, the speculative boom, particularly in raw materials markets, subsided somewhat, but demand for the products of heavy industry remained high.[12] This might be expected to raise the value of British exports but not necessarily the market shares. In fact, most market shares fell, as can be seen in Table III.

TABLE III

BRITISH EXPORT SHARES—1950 AND 1951

Percentage Supplied by the United Kingdom	Vehicles and Parts	Power-Generating Machinery	Iron and Steel	Textiles
World exports—1950	40	34	17	26
1951	34	29	10	26
Exports of all devaluing countries—1950	75	67	31	42
1951	66	56	22	44
Exports of nondevaluing countries—1950	84	71	36	71
1951	69	61	19	65
Australian imports—1949–50	85	53	45	77
1950–51	80	53	39	68
1951–52	78	51	25	65
Canadian imports—1950	30	—	15	47
1951	13	—	14	42
Norwegian imports—1950	31	28*	22	—
1951	50	23*	12	—
Ratio of United Kingdom to U.S.A. exports to South America (percent)—1950	40	—	—	—
1951	21	—	—	—

* These figures are based on imports of "nonelectrical machinery."

At this period the decline in market shares seems to be attributable quite largely to inelasticity of the supply of exports. Here one can see the combined effect of a number of factors influencing the supply of exports: inelastic supply of output of exportables, increased domestic absorption leading to a rise in domestic demand for the export goods, and what might be called a feedback from an "input-output" effect. (To the extent that one export good (for example, steel) is used in the output of another export good (for example, automobiles), an increase in the output of the latter necessarily implies an increase in the domestic demand for the former.) The availability of exports had a particularly restrictive influence in iron and steel, with defense needs preempting supplies of both exports and domestic goods.[13] The elasticity of supply of output appears to have

---

[11] *Vide* United Nations Economic Commission for Europe, *Economic Survey of Europe in 1951*, Geneva, 1952, p. 12.

[12] *Ibid.*, p. 3.

[13] *Economist*, January 13, 1951, p. 92; February 3, 1951, p. 281.

been very small, with total domestic production, in physical volume, rising somewhat in 1950 and falling back in 1951 to a level only slightly higher than the 1949 output. With home demand increasing, the elasticity of supply of available exports was negative, and exports were less in 1951 than in 1950.[14] These decreases in market shares occurred in the face of a very large increase in the dollar value of world exports; the 1951 figure was approximately two-thirds higher than the 1950 amount. It is true that these figures incorporate price as well as quantity changes, but the increase in the dollar value of British iron and steel exports during 1951 was negligible, rising only from $289 million in 1950 to $291 million in 1951.

CHART 1

RATIO OF UNITED KINGDOM EXPORTS TO WORLD EXPORTS; VALUE

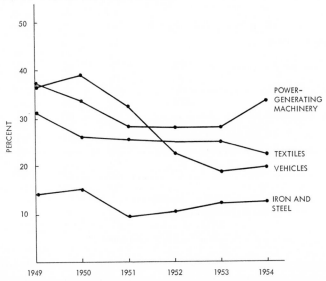

The input-output effect of the "steel shortage" was felt in other industries such as vehicles.[15] Here the elasticity of supply of output was negative, apparently owing primarily to the difficulty in obtaining steel; production and the volume of exports both declined sharply by about the same absolute amount.

Other devaluing countries fared better with respect to exports and export shares. Thus, while the ratio of British exports of iron and steel to those from the nondevaluing countries fell sharply in 1951, with only a slight increase in the total value of those exports, French and German

---

[14] For a detailed statement of British output, exports, and domestic consumption for each of the four commodity groups and the changes from year to year in each of these magnitudes and in the ratios of exports to production, see Appendix II in June Flanders, *op. cit.*

[15] See *Economist*, pages quoted above.

exports rose in value by 60 percent and 80 percent respectively and exports from Belgium-Luxembourg more than doubled. These divergences between the British and continental experiences can be attributed, at least in part, to the greater extent of the defense effort in the United Kingdom and its effect on the availability of exports. The Belgium-Luxembourg exports and market shares are shown in Table IV. These figures indicate clearly the increases in 1951 and 1952 and the subsequent return to prewar ratios.

TABLE IV

EXPORTS OF IRON AND STEEL FROM BELGIUM-LUXEMBOURG

	1948	*1949*	*1950*	*1951*	*1952*	*1953*	*1954*
Value (millions of U.S. dollars).....	—	452	294	661	715	498	480
Percent of world exports...........	—	23	17	23	22	18	18
Percent of Australian imports supplied by Belgium-Luxembourg*........	—	1.5	6	9	15	5	2
Percent of Canadian imports supplied by Belgium-Luxembourg.........	1.7	2.4	4	8	7	4	2.5
Percent of Norwegian imports supplied by Belgium-Luxembourg.........	27	28	13	39	34	17	19

* Australian figures give imports from Benelux, not from Belgium-Luxembourg. Years are not calendar years; the figure for 1948 is for 1947–48, that for 1949 is for 1948–49, etc.

TABLE V

EXPORTS OF TEXTILES—1949, 1950, 1951
(Millions of United States Dollars)

	1949	*1950*	*1951*
Belgium-Luxembourg	180	219	221
France	360	368	449
Germany	80	58	138
India	180	281	112
Italy	183	182	300
Japan	152	228	226
United Kingdom	823	677	833
United States	301	217	378

In textiles, the worldwide boom did not occur until the latter part of 1950, when there was a great deal of scare and speculative buying; the results of this tended to appear in the 1951 figures. The value of British exports rose sharply; German exports, though initially small, more than doubled within a year; but exports from the United States and Italy rose even more than from the United Kingdom, and the ratio of British exports to those from the nondevaluing countries fell. Through the first part of 1951, demand continued high but raw materials were scarce. This was particularly the case in wool, where the United States was preempting much of the supply for use in uniforms.[16] (See Table V.)

One would expect that as the war progressed there would be a decline

---

[16] *Economist,* November 4, 1950, p. 706.

in the strength of Britain's competitive position vis-à-vis the United States and other "Dollar Bloc" countries. The heavy spendings of the United States in its war and armaments activities was increasing the dollar earnings of many countries, and the recipients were anxious to spend these on American goods. They could implement this desire by the loosening of controls, enlarging of quotas, and similar "easing" policy measures. Since the dollar was freely convertible into any other currency, this implies that the devaluation did not in itself succeed in moving existing trade patterns into conformity with market demands. Many countries were still probably importing less from the United States than they would have liked, as suggested, at least, by the fact that they did increase their relative shares of purchases in the United States when they could. (See Table VI.)

TABLE VI

RATIOS OF UNITED KINGDOM TO UNITED STATES EXPORTS

	1950	1951	1952
Imports of textiles into Canada.....................	121	107	76
Imports of power-generating machinery into Australia*..	152	162	137
Imports of vehicles into South America..............	40	21	25

* Not calendar years; see note, Table IV.

In raw material exporting countries, this effect is observable quite early in the war and shows up in the 1951 figures. It is probably responsible, at least in part, for the shift in imports of vehicles into South America in favor of the United States. Similarly, in the fiscal year 1951–52, imports of power-generating machinery into Australia from the United Kingdom fell relative to imports from the United States. There was actually a large increase in imports from the United States, which was probably a reflection of the large dollar earnings of the previous year.

The pattern of American exports and imports (in dollar totals) seems to support the analysis above, as can be seen in Table VII. In interpreting these figures we assume that, at least in the period in question, individuals in the countries importing from the United States were always willing and ready to spend more dollars than they were able to obtain. The changes from one year to another in American exports of goods and services (apart from military grants) are thus treated as depending upon changes in the willingness of governments to permit dollar spending. United States imports increased sharply between 1949 and 1950, by over 2 billion dollars. They rose again in 1951, by over 3 billion dollars. Exports, however, fell in 1950 and did not increase until 1951. We can regard the rise in exports in 1951 as a delayed response to the previous year's increase in imports, as recipients of dollar credits spent their earnings. However, this increase does not appear to be simply a reflection of a one-year lag in imports behind exports in the importing countries, since United States exports in 1951 rose above the 1950 level by much more than the increase

CHART 2
RATIO OF UNITED KINGDOM EXPORTS TO EXPORTS OF THE
DEVALUING COUNTRIES; VALUE

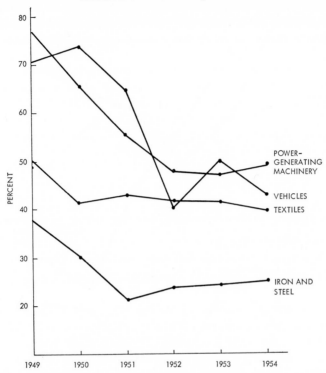

in imports in 1950 exceeded the 1949 values. (This is true both in the aggregate, and, with only a few minor exceptions, for the individual regions shown in Table VII.) This suggests that the countries experiencing increased dollar earnings in 1950 hesitated to spend them. (In addition, there may have been a lag between the relaxation of quantitative and exchange controls and an increase in the level of commercial orders.) As the increase continued in 1951, there was a greater willingness to spend both accumulated and current supplies of dollar credits. In 1952, although imports continued to rise, albeit less sharply than in the previous two years, exports from the United States decreased. Countries earning dollar credits were using these credits to build up their reserves of gold and dollars. This is further borne out by the movement of gold and short-term dollar holdings, which increased in the case of almost every country and region in the world and which rose, in the aggregate, by over 1 billion dollars during 1952.[17]

This explanation of the time pattern of the effects of the Korean War is consistent with our figures of export shares. In the case of every com-

---

[17] U.S. Department of Commerce, Office of Business Economics, *Balance of Payments: Statistical Supplement* (Washington, D.C., 1958), pp. 190–91.

CHART 3

RATIO OF UNITED KINGDOM EXPORTS TO EXPORTS OF THE
NONDEVALUING COUNTRIES; VALUE

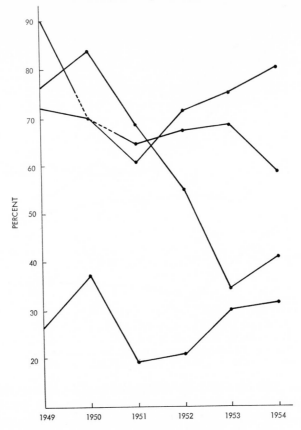

modity group except textiles, the ratio of British exports to those of the
nondevaluing countries reached a trough in 1951, the year in which the
ability and willingness of other countries to spend dollars was at its
peak.[18] This does not prove that the causal explanation we have offered
above of the variations in American exports and imports is correct. It does,
however, add credibility and strength to the explanation we have provided. Further support comes from the fact that the ratio of British
exports to those of the group of the devaluing countries does *not* show
the same pattern, which implies that there was a shift from devaluing
to nondevaluing countries (especially the United States) as sources of
imports. Only in the case of iron and steel was the ratio of British exports
to those of the devaluing countries at a minimum in 1951. (In that case,
as we have argued above, the elasticity of supply of output was an
important factor, since the United Kingdom appears to have been more

---

[18] See Chart 1.

TABLE VII
CHANGES IN UNITED STATES EXPORTS* AND IMPORTS BY AREA
(Millions of Dollars)†

	Total	United Kingdom	Continental Europe O.E.E.C.	British Dependencies	Other European Dependencies	Other Europe	Canada	Latin-American Republics	All Other Sterling	All Other Non-sterling
Change in imports, 1950....	2,396	66	321	231	−70	44	418	616	176	579
Change in exports, 1951....	4,962	540	863	8	75	141	702	1,302	634	724
Change in imports, 1951....	3,044	193	675	186	60	16	358	579	274	692
Change in exports, 1952....	−758	−234	−333	28	39	−309	391	−262	−78	1

* Exports exclude military supplies and services transferred under grants.
† These figures have been computed from those given in the *Balance of Payments: Statistical Supplement*, loc. cit., pp. 12–84.

unfavorably affected in this regard by the Korean War than were some of the other devaluing steel-producing countries.) In textiles, the ratio of British exports to those of the other devaluing countries rose in 1951, while in vehicles and power-generating machinery the ratio continued to fall until 1952 and 1953, respectively.

In short, we are stating the not surprising conclusion that the heavy imports into the United States in 1950 and 1951 led to an increase in America's share of world exports. This means that

1. Not all the dollars earned by this increase in United States imports were "hoarded" by the receiving countries.
2. Not all the United States exports, engendered by the spending of these dollars by their recipients, constituted a net addition to world trade, but that at least some of this spending involved a substitution of American goods for those of other countries.

(3) *The Effects of the Economic Recovery of Germany and Japan.* The effects of the rapid expansion of the German economy, from the low level of activity which prevailed at the end of World War II, can be seen in the case of all the commodity groups we have studied. The recovery of Japan is evident primarily in iron and steel and also in textiles.

In iron and steel, the shares of Germany and Japan in total world exports rose sharply in 1950 and 1951 respectively, as is shown in Table VIII.

TABLE VIII
GERMAN AND JAPANESE SHARES IN WORLD IRON AND STEEL EXPORTS*

Exports from	1949	1950	1951	1952	1953	1954
United Kingdom	300	289	291	366	378	383
Germany	86	201	367	400	335	364
Japan	34	26	205	263	140	167
World	1,940	1,728	2,829	3,255	2,771	2,708
Ratio of German to world exports (percent)	4	12	13	12	12	13
Ratio of Japanese to world exports (percent)	2	1.5	7	8	5	6
Ratio of United Kingdom to world exports (percent)	16	17	10	11	14	14

* Figures are in millions of United States dollars.

After 1951 the German share stayed at approximately the same level, but the Japanese share declined somewhat. In terms of absolute values of exports, both countries reached their peak in 1952, and for Japan that was also the peak year with respect to her share in the world market. The British share, meanwhile, was at a very low trough in 1951 and 1952. These diverse movements serve to support the contention that what happened in this period was that importers sought temporary sources for needed supplies which they could not obtain from traditional sources.

Australian imports provide an excellent example of this, as can be seen in Table IX.

TABLE IX
AUSTRALIAN IMPORTS OF IRON AND STEEL*

Source	1949–50	1950–51	1951–52
United Kingdom	12,515	15,941	17,239
Germany	1,818	2,215	5,184
Japan	3,873	8,503	21,793

* Figures are in millions of Australian pounds.

Similar developments took place in Canadian imports, shown in Table X, but here it is interesting to note that while imports from both Japan and Germany fell in 1953 as compared with 1951 and 1952, they did not return to their 1950 level. This is particularly true of imports from Japan.

TABLE X
CANADIAN IMPORTS OF IRON AND STEEL*

Source	1950	1951	1952	1953
United Kingdom	22,398	34,808	28,932	29,109
Germany	1,250	7,896	2,103	1,612
Japan	193	1,667	3,432	1,065

* Figures are in millions of Canadian dollars.

Having found a place, in an emergency situation, in the Canadian market, the Japanese products maintained a considerable portion of the initial gain.

In textiles, the rapid growth in both Germany and Japan can also be seen. (This is shown in Table XI.) The picture is one of a declining industry; in 1954 the dollar value of world trade in textiles was appreciably lower than in 1949. This affected the exports of Great Britain, Belgium-Luxembourg, Italy, and the United States. German exports, however, rose

TABLE XI
GERMAN AND JAPANESE SHARES IN WORLD TEXTILE EXPORTS*

Exports from	1949	1950	1951	1952	1953	1954
United Kingdom	823	677	833	633	614	591
Belgium-Luxembourg	180	219	221	160	173	188
Italy	183	182	300	136	120	115
United States	302	217	378	291	251	241
Germany	80	58	138	120	115	133
Japan	152	228	226	229	238	353
World	2,547	2,576	3,164	2,422	2,335	2,489
Ratio of German to world exports (percent)	3	2	4	5	5	5
Ratio of Japanese to world exports (percent)	6	9	7	9	10	14
Ratio of United Kingdom to world exports (percent)	32	26	26	26	26	24

* Figures are in millions of United States dollars.

sharply, hit a peak in 1951, and then declined in 1952. After that, they rose again and by 1954 had almost regained the 1951 level. Japanese exports rose in every year except 1951. Note that the increase in the Japanese share of world exports between 1949 and 1954 is exactly equal to the decrease in that of the United Kingdom.

German exports of power-generating machinery rose tremendously in the period under review. (See Table XII.) In 1949 there were two major exporters, the United Kingdom and the United States; Germany exported one fifteenth as much as the United Kingdom. In 1954 there were three large exporters, Germany having taken third place, with fourth-place Switzerland very far behind. In this period German exports increased more than tenfold and were more than half as large as those of the United Kingdom by 1954. British exports improved substantially, both in absolute value and in relation to the exports of the nondevaluing countries, chiefly the United States. Presumably, however, they would have improved still more if it had not been for the renewed German competition.

TABLE XII

THE GERMAN SHARE OF EXPORTS OF POWER-GENERATING MACHINERY[*]

Exports from	1949	1950	1951	1952	1953	1954
United Kingdom	161	144	175	196	213	229
United States	148	121	185	184	186	169
Germany	12	27	68	103	119	123
World	430	421	599	677	724	645
Ratio of United Kingdom to world exports (percent)	38	34	29	29	29	35
Ratio of German to world exports (percent)	3	6	11	15	16	19
Ratio of United Kingdom to devaluing countries' exports (percent)	77	67	56	48	48	50
Ratio of German to devaluing countries' exports (percent) ..	6	12	22	25	27	27
Ratio of devaluing countries' exports to world exports (percent)	49	52	52	60	61	72

[*] Value figures are in millions of United States dollars.

In the market for vehicles, the competition from Germany became increasingly apparent during the period. By the middle of 1951, though export supplies were still lagging behind demand in the British motor industry, there was already a growing awareness of the inroads that German cars were making into European markets.[19] This competition was undoubtedly enhanced by the fact that, from the consumer point of view, British and German automobiles are closer substitutes than are British and American cars. The value of British exports of vehicles was only slightly higher in 1954 than in 1949, while German exports rose from

---

[19] *Economist*, July 21, 1951, p. 171: August 4, 1951, p. 307.

one thirtieth to more than one half the value of the United Kingdom's exports. That this rise is attributable primarily to the recovery of German industry, rather than to the fact that Germany also participated in the devaluation, is evidenced by the much smaller increases in the exports of the other devaluing countries.

As was noted above, the major impact of German competition in vehicles was in European markets. In exports to Australia and Canada, the German share rose considerably over the period, but by 1954 it was still very small. In Norway, however, imports from Germany rose every year except 1950, more than doubled between 1952 and 1953, and by 1954 were two-thirds as great in value as the British.

(4) *The Effects of Controls and Regulations.* The effect of quantitative restrictions and direct controls on imports is, from the point of view of the exporting country, to place constraints on the demand for exports. The kind of demand curve actually facing the exporting country will depend, *inter alia,* on whether the authorities in the importing country fix the quantity of the good which will be allowed to enter or whether they allocate a fixed amount of foreign currency which may be spent on the commodity.

In terms of absolute quantities, the amount imported at any given price cannot be greater than that which would be demanded in a free market situation. But in terms of market shares, the proportion imported from a given country may exceed the desired, free market ratio. Consider three countries, A (the United Kingdom), N (any nondevaluing country), and M (any country which imports from both A and N). It may be that, because of restrictions on imports from N, Country M is importing a higher proportion of a given commodity from A, and a lower proportion from N, than she would like to. (This may be the case regardless of whether or not imports from A are also restricted.) The situation would be that depicted in Figure 1. Starting from A, any decline in P_a/P_nR will bring the actual position closer to the free market situation. When we get below B, the effect depends on whether or not imports from A are restricted. If they are, the ratio Q_a/Q_n remains the same and we begin to diverge again from the free market situation. If, however, imports from A are not restricted, there will be a movement along the curve DD and an increase in Q_a/Q_n.

A movement from A toward B would have no effect on Country A's earnings of foreign exchange if the price remained constant in terms of M's currency; the only effect would be that the relative amount being imported from A as compared with N would be closer to the desired proportions. If price in terms of M's currency fell, the initial effect would be to reduce A's earnings of foreign exchange. However, the fall in the domestic price in M might have an income effect on the total demand curve for that commodity and shift the demand upward. The quantity purchased from N could not increase, since there were restrictions. If

FIGURE 1

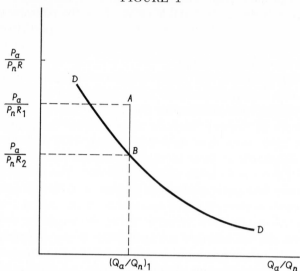

imports from A were not restricted, they would increase, and Q_a/Q_n would increase. If imports from A were restricted, buyers in M would bid up the domestic prices of imports from both A and N. A's share of the market would not increase, but her earnings of foreign exchange might be higher than they would be in the absence of this secondary effect.

Whether or not changes in foreign prices or in exchange rates have any effect upon the domestic prices of imports in M depends primarily on the structure of the world market for the commodity in question. If there is a competitive world market for the good and a single world price, then there will be no relationship between changes in the world price and changes in domestic prices. The domestic price in the importing country will be determined by the intersection of a given demand curve with a perfectly inelastic supply curve, and there is no reason for the price thus obtained to bear any relationship to the world price. The commodities with which we are dealing are not, however, characterized by competitive markets with single prices.

Where there is not a single world price, the effect of a change in the exchange rate on the domestic prices of imports depends on the relative bargaining strength of the importer as compared to that of the exporter. At one extreme, a devaluation by A would leave the domestic prices of A's goods in M unchanged with all the profit going to the exporters in A. At the other extreme, the price in terms of A's currency would remain the same and the importing firms in M would receive a monopoly profit, or the domestic price to buyers in A would fall. In that case, or in the more likely intermediate case in which the profit is divided between the two countries, there will be an incentive for importers in M to switch to A as a source of supply whenever possible. This will not be possible if controls are specific as to country of origin, but it will be possible if they are regional. In the case of Australia, for example, which will be discussed below, there seems to have been a shift, within the group of soft-currency imports, in favor of those from the countries which devalued and away from those originating in nondevaluing countries. Obviously, the less specific the quotas as to the origin of imports, the more scope there is for the play of market forces. In the extreme case in which restrictions are global, limiting only the total quantity of imports of any given commodity and leaving buyers free to obtain these from any source, the quotas will have no effect on market shares (except insofar as the marginal propensities to import a certain good from the several exporting countries differ from the average).

Difficult as it is to assess the effects of the *existence* of regulations, we encounter further difficulty when we inquire about the effect of a *change* in controls and regulations. Changes occur in the willingness of exchange control and import licensing authorities to permit certain imports by administrative fiat, and these do not necessarily appear in published statements about the controls. Further, the question is closely connected with the effects of the Korean War, since, as has already been noted, the strictness with which the controls were administered often varied with the foreign exchange reserve position of the several countries, and this was directly affected by changes in American foreign spending.

A careful study of the pattern of quantitative controls in all the countries importing from the United Kingdom, and of changes in these controls, even those changes which are published and about which information is obtainable, clearly involves a major investigation in and of itself, and we shall not attempt it here. We shall, however, summarize the developments in the pattern of restrictions in one major importing country, Australia, partly because these developments are themselves of importance and interest, and partly because they serve to illustrate the complexity of the problem, and the difficulty involved in showing clearly the connection between changes in controls and changes in the structure of imports.

In the spring of 1952, Australia found herself faced with a large balance-of-payments deficit. The heavy buying of wool, particularly on the part of the United States, following the outbreak of the Korean War, had inflated wool prices, leading to an increase in Australian foreign exchange earnings and in Australian domestic money incomes. This, in turn, had led to a sharp increase in Australian imports. When the boom in the world markets for wool subsided, export earnings fell quickly, but the demand for imports remained high, since the domestic price and cost structure had been adjusted upward in response to the increase in the price of wool. Australia was forced to curtail imports, either by domestic deflation or by controls on imports directly, and she chose the latter course. In March, severe cuts were announced in imports, primarily in consumption goods, which were to be reduced by 80 percent below the level obtained in 1950–51. These cuts were supposed to be nondiscriminatory, but it was felt in Britain, at the time, that the United Kingdom would be the hardest hit, since it was primarily in consumption goods that she had hoped for a strong demand for her exports in the coming year.[20]

A few months later, in May, dollar imports were cut by 20 percent, but this was not a discriminatory move as far as the United Kingdom was concerned, inasmuch as it did not directly benefit British exporters; the cuts were applied to imports of commodities in which the United Kingdom exports were not competing.[21]

Shortly after the restrictions were imposed, the authorities in Australia began to permit the sale of unused quotas of consumption goods from nondollar countries. These quotas were transferable not only with respect to country, excluding dollar countries, but also with respect to commodity, provided the commodity actually imported was also in Category B (the consumption good group). Thus, for example, when this arrangement first went into effect, holders of quotas for textiles were selling unused quotas, and would-be importers of nondollar tobacco were heavy buyers.[22] It is possible that this trading of quotas is sufficient to explain the fact[23] that, in textile imports in the year 1952–53, Australia shifted to devaluing countries as a source for her greatly reduced imports. Imports of textiles from the United Kingdom as a proportion of total textile imports rose slightly, while the ratio of British imports to those from the nondevaluing countries rose significantly. Part of this may have been due to an administrative tightening up on dollar licenses but at least some of this shift occurred without reference to the "hardness" of the currencies. Imports from Italy, for example, which we have classified as a nondevaluing "soft-currency" country, were cut the most in that year.

From the end of 1952 until October, 1954, there was periodic easing of import restrictions and raising of the quotas applied in 1952. These concessions applied primarily to nondollar, non-Japanese imports, although in the latter part of the period Australia began to raise Japanese quotas, out of fear of retaliation, and in the spring of 1954 the restrictions against Japan were lifted. The longer the restrictions remained in force, the more difficult it became for the Australian government to remove them, since from the point of view of domestic producers of import substitutes they had the same effect as very high tariff walls. In fact, as the quotas became

---

[20] *Economist*, March 15, 1952, pp. 634, 670; March 22, 1952, p. 744, ff., p. 747; March 7, 1953, p. 691.

[21] *Economist*, May 17, 1952, p. 473.

[22] *Ibid*.

[23] See Appendix V, June Flanders, *op. cit.*

larger there was growing pressure at home to replace the quantitative controls with tariffs and thus continue the protection of Australian industry.[24]

In the fall of 1954, in response to a loss of reserves brought on by the increase in imports in the past year, and in response also to pressure from Australian industry for renewed protection, controls on nondollar imports were again tightened.[25]

Clearly, the effects of such erratic movements in the restrictions of even one country are difficult to assess. Furthermore, a decline in total imports of any one commodity from the United Kingdom is perfectly consistent with an increase in Great Britain's share of that market. This is exactly what we observed, for example, in the case of textiles, discussed above. It was also the case in power-generating machinery. In iron and steel, the value of imports from the United Kingdom rose slightly in 1952–53 and fell sharply in 1953–54, but the share of the total accounted for by Britain rose tremendously, since imports from the United States and the Benelux countries were cut drastically.

As we stated earlier, a detailed study of the regulations and controls in every country is outside the scope of this project, but this is precisely what is required in order to make an exact evaluation of the effects of restrictions and changes therein. The behavior of various countries differed so much that even the question as to whether restrictions increased or decreased over any given period cannot be answered by a simple generalization.[26] And even if we were able to state, in general, whether countries had tightened up or loosened their restrictions overall, we would still not be able to state with certainty what effect this had on the structure of trade. Some countries tightened their restrictions across the board, maintaining the already existing structure; others tightened nondollar quotas and left dollar restrictions the same, thus lessening the degree of discrimination against the dollar. Frequently, in such cases, subsequent relaxation of restrictions involved a reversal of this movement, and an increase in antidollar discrimination. Thus, in 1954 South Africa adopted an announced policy on admitting imports on a nondiscriminatory basis, whereas New Zealand liberalized nondollar imports to a greater extent than imports from the dollar area.[27]

Despite such difficulties, one might hazard the opinion that in general the controls and regulations did not vitiate the effects of the devaluation. Where they discriminated against dollar goods, of course, they tended to

---

[24] *Economist,* November 22, 1952, p. 564; February 7, 1953, pp. 372–73; February 21, 1953, p. 504; July 11, 1953, pp. 122–23; September 19, 1953, pp. 805–6; March 13, 1954, p. 785; May 8, 1954, pp. 463–64.

[25] *Economist,* October 9, 1954, pp. 152–53.

[26] *Vide,* e.g., International Monetary Fund, *Fourth Annual Report on Exchange Restrictions* (Washington, D.C., 1953), p. 40 ff., and *Fifth Annual Report on Exchange Restrictions* (Washington, D.C., 1954), p. 3 ff.

[27] *Ibid.,* esp. *Fifth Annual Report,* p. 10.

reinforce, rather than counteract, the effects of the devaluation. Where they were, by decree or in fact, regional, importers were still free to choose between a limited range of supplying countries, so that a partly free market obtained. Again, the fact that we are concerned with market shares rather than with totals frees us from some of the difficulties arising from the fact of quantitative restrictions. Thus, as we saw above, Australia could cut sharply her imports of certain goods from all sources and yet direct the distribution of her purchases among different countries, more or less in accordance with market considerations.

(5) *The Supply of Exports.* The supply of exports depends, manifestly, both on the supply of output of exportables and on the domestic demand for the export goods. The relative importance of these two in any particular situation is extremely difficult to assess. In the particular case at hand, the matter is further complicated by departures from a free-market allocating mechanism. On the one hand, governmental action was instrumental in allocating the output of a number of industries between exports and domestic consumption, so that changes in domestic consumption did not accurately reflect changes in quantities desired by domestic purchases. On the other hand, market forces were not entirely absent, since the government agencies responsible for these decisions, such as the Ministry of Supply, were affected both by the strength of the pressure of domestic demand and by the ease with which additional supplies available for export could be marketed abroad.

Examination of the data of production, exports, and domestic consumption cannot, in the nature of the case, yield any conclusive proofs about the direction of causality. It does, however, provide a basis for informed "guessing." If the major obstacle to an expansion of exports were, in fact, limitations on output, we would expect to see, with increasing output, a rising ratio of exports to production. If, alternatively, it were primarily the pressure of domestic demand which limited the level of exports, we would be inclined to expect a close, and perhaps an increasing, relationship between changes in production and changes in domestic consumption; that is, a decreasing proportion of exports to production. In fact, what we observe[28] is a fairly stable, but generally increasing, ratio between exports and total production. While this, as was indicated, in no sense constitutes a proof, it is, nevertheless, consistent with the hypothesis that domestic absorption was not a major obstacle to an increase in exports. An important exception, discussed above, was the domestic demand for iron and steel during the Korean War.

In an economy characterized by perfectly flexible prices, the relative (domestic) price of export goods would rise whenever the elasticity of supply was less than infinite. At the other extreme, in an economy in which all prices were administered, we would expect, at least temporarily, to find shortages and gluts in individual markets. Since neither the order

---

[28] See Appendix II, June Flanders, *op. cit.*

books of businessmen nor price data by relevant commodity groups (of a type which would permit us to separate out the effects of an overall price level increase) are available to us, we have had to rely on informed public and private information, to be found in such sources as *The Economist* and *The Board of Trade Journal.* The consensus of opinion presented in these is that, in the year immediately following devaluation, there were shortages, on the supply side, in the heavy manufacturing metals industries, but not in textiles. An exception here is the above-mentioned shortage of raw wool that developed during the Korean War, leading to difficulties in the woolen textile industry.[29]

In heavy industry the major bottleneck in production was in steel. This shortage was felt both in the availability of iron and steel as export items and in the production of other exports, such as automobiles and engineering products. The Korean War, with its attendant rearmament spending, appears to have been the major factor leading to these shortages. Before the war, steel supplies were apparently readily available to all users except automobile manufacturers.[30] In vehicles, steel shortage led to a continuation of excess demand for exports,[31] but as early as the first quarter of 1950 there was concern and skepticism regarding the future buoyancy of foreign markets, at least for certain types of commercial vehicles,[32] and by the end of 1951, Germany was becoming an increasingly worrisome competitor in continental automobile markets.[33] Throughout the period, however, there was a two-way relationship between exports of vehicles and steel allocations to the automobile industry. On the one hand, steel allocations were used, at least in part, as a "weapon to influence the division of the output of the motor industry between home and export markets,"[34] and on the other hand allocations were determined, both for the industry as a whole and for individual producers, by exports, and particularly by exports outside the Sterling Area.[35]

By 1953, and certainly by 1954, the pressures brought on by the war effort had eased, and supply conditions seemed to be no longer a seriously limiting factor in any of the industries with which we are concerned. Thus, for example, in describing the experiences of 1953, *The Board of Trade Journal* commented that in the engineering industries the rate of output was faster than the rate of new orders, and that this was still true early in 1954.[36]

On balance, availability seems to have been a significant factor in

---

[29] *Vide,* e.g., *Economist,* February 4, 1950, p. 286; August 12, 1950, p. 329; November 4, 1950, p. 706; May 19, 1951, pp. 1186, 1192.

[30] *Economist,* March 4, 1950, p. 496.

[31] *Economist,* August 4, 1951, p. 307.

[32] *Economist,* March 25, 1950, p. 671.

[33] *Economist,* July 21, 1951, p. 171.

[34] *Economist,* March 4, 1950, p. 496.

[35] *Economist,* June 7, 1952, p. 671.

[36] *Board of Trade Journal,* Vol. CLXVI, No. 2988 (March 27, 1954), pp. 626–32.

limiting British exports of automobiles before the Korean War, and of all products of heavy industry during the war. In the two years after the end of hostilities, availability of exports had not, apparently, been of major consequence in determining the level of exports or the British share in world markets. Two qualifications to this statement are necessary, however.

First, we cannot say definitely that the shortages in British industry caused by the war effort did not lead to a loss of previously established, traditional markets, which was not fully made up after the war. Thus, as was stated earlier, we have reason to believe that such was the case, at least to some extent, in the Canadian purchases of steel.

Second, we have been referring here only to observed shortages. As was pointed out above, if all prices were perfectly flexible there would be no shortages at all, and the effect of supply inelasticity would be felt on the domestic prices of the export goods rather than on the length of the firms' order books. To the extent, then, that relative prices were flexible in the United Kingdom in the period under review, we cannot say that the absence of observed shortages implies that the elasticity of supply was very high. We could make an "informed guess" about the degree of inelasticity of supply that manifested itself in this way if we had the data for price movement by industry in relation to overall price level changes, preferably for several countries. Such information is not, unfortunately, readily available.

However, while we do not have domestic prices for the export commodity groups we are considering, we do have export prices.[37] The increase in the unit value of exports for the four groups, from 1950 to 1954, were as follows: cotton, 5 percent; woolen and worsted yarns and manufactures, 26 percent; iron and steel, 24 percent; machinery, 33 percent; vehicles, 20 percent. The wholesale price index in 1954 was 25 percent higher than in 1950. Thus only in the case of machinery did the export price rise significantly more than the general wholesale price index. This result, however, is interesting. There is hardly any question of shortages and lack of availability of textiles for the period we are considering, and the observed shortages, at various times during the period, in iron and steel and in vehicles production, have been mentioned before. We have found little in the literature to suggest the existence of observed shortages and very long order books in machinery production, however, and the large increase in its relative price suggests that this may be precisely such a case of inelastic supply and flexible prices that we discussed above. This is possible, but in this case unlikely. In the first place, British exports did better in this commodity group than in any of the others we have studied. In fact, the British share rose between 1953 and 1954, at the same time that the total value of world exports was actually falling. Previously to that, however, the total value of world exports was increasing

---

[37] See Appendix VI, and also Table III, June Flanders, *op. cit.*

steadily, which suggests that the relative price rise in this industry was caused primarily by overall worldwide expansion in trade and in demand. Secondly, the fact that United States machinery prices also rose very substantially, and more than the American wholesale price index, tends to support this argument, indicating that world demand was inelastic, or else was shifting upward, or both.

(6) *The Movement of Prices.* With respect to prices, there are several possibilities, a priori, as to both the causes and effects of changes. If British prices were, without devaluation, rising faster than prices in the rest of the world, then the devaluation might be expected, at best, to prevent a weakening of the United Kingdom's competitive position. Thus, granting the inflationary tendency, devaluation would have constituted, in effect, an improvement as compared with not devaluing, even with no resulting increase in market shares. If, on the other hand, prices rose in Britain more than elsewhere because of the increased prices of imported raw materials in the United Kingdom resulting from the devaluation, then this would have to be considered an inevitable result of the devaluation. In such a case one might argue that a country with a very high import content of exports could not hope and should not attempt to cure her export problem by devaluation.

If we examine the data on comparative movements of British and American prices of the commodity groups we are studying, and[38] examine also the data in Table XIII, we find that British prices rose more than American prices, but by less than the extent of the devaluation. The price rise, then, offset but did not completely eliminate the differential caused by the devaluation, except in the case of wool products (British woolen

TABLE XIII

RATIOS OF PRICE INDEXES IN 1954 TO 1948 INDEXES, UNITED STATES
AND GREAT BRITAIN

United States		*Great Britain*	
Cotton products	84.8	Cotton yarns and manufactures	116.0
Wool products	104.5	Woolen and worsted yarns and	
Iron and steel	127.4	manufactures	154.4
Miscellaneous machinery	124.1	Iron and steel	128.3
Internal combustion engines	128.9	Machinery and parts thereof	144.1
Generators, engine driven	159.5		
Generators, turbine driven	144.8		
Generators, steam driven	129.1	Vehicles (including locomotives,	
Motor vehicles	118.4	ships, and aircraft)	126.9

prices rose by 54 percent compared with an American increase of only 4.5 percent). This may help to explain the sharp decline in Britain's share in world textile markets, especially since some of the other determinants of trading quantities and patterns discussed above, such as lack of avail-

---

[38] *Ibid.*

ability of supply, operate less strongly in this commodity group than in some of the others.

The results are less precise when we compare the movement of British import and export prices and terms of trade with those of the other devaluing European countries.[39] In the immediate postdevaluation period, British price behavior seems to have been about average; the fall in export prices, in dollar terms, in 1950, was neither highest nor lowest in the group of devaluing European countries, and the same was true of the rise in export prices in 1951. But after the Korean War the price behavior began to diverge. The export prices of all the European devaluing countries fell, but those of the United Kingdom fell less than those of most of the other countries. It might be argued that this was due to the high import content of British exports, but the fact is that the British terms of trade improved considerably between 1952 and 1954, while those of the other European countries deteriorated or, at best, improved only slightly, as in the case of Denmark. On the other hand, the German terms of trade improved far more than the British, a clear indication that terms of trade alone are not an adequate measure of a country's competitive position in world markets. We use these figures merely to suggest that the behavior of British prices cannot be attributed entirely to the higher costs of imports nor can it be considered to be completely an inevitable result of the devaluation.[40]

The Import Patterns of Individual Countries

Our analysis of market shares has been based on the implicit assumption that the world consists of one unified market. Suppose, however, that this is not the case and that some countries, group A, traditionally import certain commodities from those countries which did not devalue, while

---

[39] See International Monetary Fund, *International Financial Statistics* (December, 1955), pp. 36–37.

[40] In principle, of course, a favorable movement in the terms of trade would be quite consistent with a rise in the import costs of exports. Since the United Kingdom's imports of food constitute a much higher percentage of her total imports than is the case in the other European devaluing countries (36 percent in 1954 compared to 29 percent for Germany and 20 percent or less for the other countries in the group), a decline in food prices and a rise in the prices of raw materials would improve Britain's terms of trade relatively to those of the other countries and would at the same time cause an upward movement in export prices. In fact, however, this was not the case. The index of food prices in world trade was almost constant from 1951 to 1953 and rose in 1954 from 100 to 107. In the same period the prices of nonfood agricultural products fell from 111 in 1952 to 100 in both 1953 and 1954, and prices of minerals fell, in a similar manner, from 108 in 1952 to 100 in 1953 and 99 in 1954. This supports our conclusion that the rise in export prices was not induced by higher costs of imported raw materials. The price indexes are from Table 151, "World Trade: Index Numbers by Commodity Classes," 1953 = 100 in Statistical Office of the United Nations, Department of Economic and Social Affairs, *Statistical Yearbook, 1958* (New York, 1958). The percentages of imports accounted for by food were computed from data in Statistical Office of the United Nations, Department of Economic and Social Affairs, *Yearbook of International Trade Statistics, 1954* (New York, 1955).

other importers, which we shall label B, traditionally import these commodities from those countries which did devalue. Now, if for some reason other than the devaluation the total imports of a particular commodity group decreased in the A countries and increased (or remained the same) in the B countries, this could result in an increased share of the world's total exports of this commodity group being exported by the United Kingdom. (In other words, we may be faced with a situation in which world exports—and imports—are a weighted average of several sectors and that what was changing was the weights.)

We have attempted here a partial investigation of this possibility by examining, for a few of the United Kingdom's largest customers, the import figures of several commodity groups and determining changes in the relative share of purchases from the United Kingdom in their imports of these commodities. The results are summarized in Table XIV.

The three countries whose imports we have examined individually are of three distinct types: Norway, which is a nonsterling, non-Commonwealth, devaluing country; Australia, a sterling, Commonwealth, devaluing country; and Canada, a nonsterling, nondevaluing member of the Commonwealth. We have also computed the ratio of imports of vehicles from the United Kingdom to those from the United States into South American countries as a whole. On the basis of this investigation we reject the hypothesis stated above. This is not to deny that different countries have traditional sources for their imports. The average percentages of imports supplied by the United Kingdom vary widely from country to country and from commodity to commodity. But if the hypothesis were correct, the range of variations over the time period studied would be relatively small. Changes in the United Kingdom's share in world exports would occur because traditional customers of the United Kingdom altered their total imports of, for example, vehicles, not because there was any change in the relative importance of various suppliers to any one country. The share of Britain's exports in total imports into any one country should have remained fairly stable. In most of the cases studied this was, in fact, not true; the British share fluctuated widely. Furthermore, the amplitude of these fluctuations did not seem to depend on the size of the average. Thus, the ratio of British to American cars imported behaved very similarly in Australia and Canada, even though the former fluctuated around a much higher mean than the latter.

Some Tentative Conclusions

We have examined the shares of the United Kingdom in various markets for her exports and have found the results, on the whole, to be "disappointing," particularly in view of the fact that the devaluation was a large one. We have offered a number of possible explanations for the

TABLE XIV
The United Kingdom's Percentage Share of Imports into Australia, Canada, Norway, and South America

	1948	1949	1950	1951	1952	1953	1954
Australia*							
Vehicles	62	77	85	80	78	56	76
Power-generating machinery	45	57	53	53	51	55	58
Iron and steel	47	62	45	39	25	60	65
Textiles	52	73	77	68	65	67	65
Canada							
Vehicles	13	20	30	13	8	10	8
Iron and steel	4	7	15	14	12	14	15
Textiles	57	51	47	45	40	46	44
Norway							
Vehicles	28	31	31	50	33	30	28
Power-generating machinery† .... (a)	31	28	28	23	24	—	—
(b)	—	—	—	20	23	27	19
Iron and steel	24	15	22	12	13	20	18
South America							
Vehicles							
Ratio of imports from the United Kingdom to imports from the United States (percent)† .... (a)	25	45	40	21	25	26	—
(b)	—	—	—	18	19	20	10
(c)	—	—	—	20	20	23	12

* The Australian figures are not based on the calendar year. The entry in the table for 1948 actually applies to 1947–48; the entry for 1949 is the figure for 1948–49, etc.
† More than one series available, no one of which is continuous for the whole period.

behavior of these export shares after devaluation. These are not mutually exclusive, and we feel that they all played a part in the final outcome.

Some of these phenomena, such as the Korean War, were both unpredictable and outside the control of Great Britain. Others were also outside Great Britain's control, but obviously predictable, such as the recovery of Germany and Japan and the devaluation of other currencies. Still others, such as the rise in the British price level, were at least to some extent endogenous and connected with the devaluation.

The fact that other countries devalued quite clearly reduced the benefit accruing to Great Britain from the devaluation. It is fairly obvious a priori that this should be so and the data are entirely consistent with it. Actually, however, Britain's share of exports fell relatively to those of the other devaluing countries. This suggests that perhaps the devaluation may have been more successful than the figures indicate, not in the sense that it actually improved the situation, but in the sense that it prevented a more severe deterioration in Britain's worldwide competitive position than in fact took place.

The Korean War had a large and dramatic effect on the level of world trade, both in value and in volume terms. The impact on the structure of trade and the shares of the several countries in the world markets for their exports is less obvious. It does seem fairly clear, however, that the armament and defense spending in Britain diverted resources away from exports. This, coupled with the shift of spending in favor of American goods in response to increases in the dollar earnings of many countries, served to depress Britain's market shares significantly. It is difficult to say whether, or to what extent, this represented a permanent loss in markets, but there are indications that at least some of the substitutions which importers were forced to find for British goods during the war continued after the hostilities ended and British goods were again readily available.

The economic recovery of Germany and Japan had a clearly adverse effect on the United Kingdom position in world markets. One cannot say, however, that this vitiated the effects of the devaluation. In fact, it is likely that Britain would have been in an even more unfavorable position relative to those two countries if she had not devalued. What the revival of Germany and Japan in this period implied for our study is that the effects of the devaluation are hidden. Since Japan did not devalue and Germany devalued much less than Britain, it is likely that Great Britain would have been in an even more unfavorable position relative to these two countries if she had not devalued.

The effects of quantitative restrictions and direct controls are very difficult to assess. On the whole, they probably did not offset the favorable effects of the devaluation. Where they discriminated against the dollar, of course, they reinforced the effects of the devaluation, since they favored the soft-currency countries, including those which devalued. Where discrimination against the dollar was relaxed, this would clearly operate to the disadvantage of the devaluing countries, and we are left once again with the question of whether and by how much things would have been worse if not for the devaluation. The fact, mentioned above, that Britain's exports declined relative to those of the other devaluing countries, suggests that we should be cautious in attributing the behavior of British export shares to a reduction in antidollar discrimination.

Inelasticity of supply, as manifested by observed shortages and long order books, seems to have affected adversely the export of all products of heavy industry during the Korean War. Supply also seemed to be a factor, though its exact importance is a matter of debate, limiting the export of automobiles before the war. In the years 1953 and 1954, however, there is no indication that supply conditions seriously restricted the expansion of British exports. However, if Britain suffered a permanent loss of customers because she was not able to satisfy their demand during the war, this in a sense constitutes a "supply factor."[41] Another possible effect of inelastic supply would be to raise the prices of export goods relative to the general price level, but we did not observe this in any of the commodity groups we have examined except for machinery, and there we have reason to

---

[41] Such an effect, however, is uninteresting if we are evaluating the wisdom of the decision to devalue in 1949, since it obviously could not have been predicted by the authorities making the decision.

suspect an upward shift in the demand curve or inelasticity of demand on a worldwide basis.

We suspect that Great Britain did not succeed in preventing increases in the domestic price level as much as was necessary in order for her fully to reap the benefits of devaluation.[42] From the data we have examined, comparing British prices with United States prices, the picture emerges of price level increases in Great Britain inadequate to wipe out the effects of devaluation on the relative prices of British and American exports, but big enough to offset much of the advantage. Compared to that of other devaluing countries, British export price behavior was about average in 1950 and 1951, but from 1952 to 1954 British prices fell less than those of the other European devaluing countries. As far as domestic price levels are concerned, it is difficult to make precise comparisons, but it seems quite clear that Britain was one of the more inflationary countries in Europe. (The countries that did not devalue had, not surprisingly, the lowest price level increases.)

Finally, we concluded that we could not attribute the pattern of British exports to shifts in total imports of traditional customers with no shift in the pattern of imports into individual countries. For those countries whose imports we studied, the proportion originating in Britain fluctuated widely, in some instances even more widely than the British share of total world exports of a given commodity group.

In conclusion, we must again emphasize the fact that we are not judging the wisdom of devaluation as a whole on the basis of the experience in exports. Furthermore, we are aware that this was not the only important consideration of the authorities in effecting the devaluation. Nevertheless, it is difficult to avoid the conclusion that from the point of view of actually improving Britain's export position, the devaluation did not accomplish much. Probably its strongest effect was the hidden one of softening the blow of Japanese and German recovery, since Japan remained with the dollar and Germany devalued by less than the United Kingdom. From this point of view however, one could argue that it might have been better to devalue a year or two later, when the competition from these two countries began to make itself strongly felt.

Similarly, a postponement of devaluation may have been preferable to the extent that exports could not have increased much more than they did because of the shortages of supply at the turn of the decade.[43]

To the extent that the result of the devaluation was to make other countries' import controls and regulations more readily enforceable, this is at best a moral victory, since it did not help Britain's balance-of-payments position.

---

[42] By "benefits" we are here referring, of course, to increases in exports, not to the domestic standard of living or to the terms of trade.

[43] *Vide* Roy Harrod, *Policy Against Inflation* (New York: St. Martin's Press, 1958), p. 132 ff.

The weakening of Britain's competitive position vis-à-vis the other devaluing countries indicates that exchange-rate adjustment was not a sufficient condition for improving her foreign trade position, though it may have been necessary and it is at least probable that that position would have deteriorated more if there had been no devaluation. The fact that this weakening continued after the Korean War boom means that it cannot be attributed solely to the armaments expenditures and that further improvement needed to be sought in the direction either of controlling domestic inflation or of stimulating British business to more imaginative selling efforts abroad and to greater response to changes in consumers' needs and tastes. This latter consideration is impalpable and eludes analytical treatment, but it is not therefore the less important. That it has been a real problem is indicated by the constantly recurring exhortations of British business leaders and financial writers to British firms, urging them to engage in more aggressive "salesmanship," to adapt to customers' desires, and to adopt vigorous measures to "capture" markets.[44]

---

[44] *Vide,* e.g., *Board of Trade Journal,* Vol. CLXVI, No. 2988 (March 27, 1954), pp. 626–32; *Economist,* February 11, 1950, pp. 330–32. The problem apparently persists; *Vide Economist,* March 18, 1961, pp. 1042–43.

7. Economic Policy in Eastern Europe from 1950 through 1956*

Edward Ames[1]

Purdue University

Abstract: Growth in East European industrial output, employment, and labor productivity, while rapid, slowed down markedly after 1950, as did agricultural collectivization. These are all explainable by inflationary pressures. At first, governments reacted to inflation only by drastic operations like currency conversions, but in 1952, Stalin's *Economic Problems* presented a more basic price analysis. His successors rejected it in favor of farm price revision and altered investment. By 1955, a controversy over direct controls had obscured interest in pricing and monetary aspects of inflation, and stressed Marxian theories of whether shortages—an inflationary phenomenon—should be met by more investment in raw materials industries or by increased authority to plant managers.

BY THE END of the 1940's, the Soviet satellites of Eastern Europe had virtually (except for East Germany) completed the nationalization of industry. The nationalized plants were operated under the Soviet "Khozraschet" system in which the plant management controlled current output, but could not undertake construction work; credit was used only for inventory and payments purposes (except in agriculture) and could be issued only by the central banks; and construction was financed almost wholly from the state budgets whose revenues came mainly from profits earned in the sale of consumer goods.[2] Output in these countries, while

---

* Reprinted from *The Annals of the American Academy of Political and Social Science*, Vol. 317, May 1958, pp. 22-35.

[1] Limitations of space have made necessary heroic simplifications of a complex subject, and certain statistical liberties have been taken, notably in the area of presenting series pertaining to groups of countries. Statements are therefore made without the conditions which might be made if this treatment were of book length.

[2] The main source of investible funds, the turnover tax, is in form an excise tax. If supply is perfectly inelastic (as is the case of Soviet bloc enterprises, which are governed by production plans), excise taxes are borne wholly by sellers and have the same effect, therefore, as profits taxes. I shall, for convenience, treat the revenue from turnover taxes as part of the profit originating from the sales of consumer goods. This is not the practice of such writers as Abram Bergson and Hans Heyman, *Soviet Na-*

above the low prewar levels (except in East Germany), seems to have been below peak levels of the wartime period, and Poland in particular had probably some underutilized capacity in its newly acquired Silesian territories.

When, therefore, these countries began industrialization, there was good reason to suppose that rapid expansion could take place, given Soviet-type controls over the level and type of investment. Centralized budget financing and the taxation of consumer-goods industry would aid the rapid development of heavy industry; the forced development of cooperative farms would provide a supply of industrial labor; and political and economic controls would force popular compliance with the intent of the government.

In 1949 and 1950 "very high"[3] rates of industrial growth were achieved. This effort to maintain high rates of growth, accompanied by an almost unlimited political power, gradually petered out around 1954–55. If an explanation of this slowing down were possible, it might suggest how far and how fast a new surge of industrialization which appeared to be getting under way in 1956–57 might go.

The data readily available on output of basic industrial materials (Table 1) show that the increase in electric power output was larger in 1950 than in any year until 1955; the largest increase in coal and cement output for the entire period 1950–56 was in 1950; the peak increase in steel output was in 1951. Only in the case of pig iron was the greatest growth as late as 1953. Absolute growths in output indices (Table 2) increased slightly in 1951 over 1950, but *percentage* rates of growth were highest in 1950 and therefore dropped despite continuing growth in the output of producer goods[4] (Table 3) and of imports of Soviet equipment.[5]

Investment programs capable of producing given additions to total

---

tional Income and Product, 1940–1948 (New York: Columbia University Press, 1954) or Franklyn Holzman, *Soviet Taxation* (Cambridge, Mass.: Harvard University Press, 1955). These writers assume, respectively, that the tax is a transfer payment (as the United States Department of Commerce assumes in its treatment of United States excise taxes), and that the tax actually raises retail prices above what they would otherwise be.

[3] The words "very high" are, of course, to be understood with reference to Soviet bloc indices which typically show larger changes than they would if computed by our methods. The writer does not assume more for any output index in Eastern Europe than this: if the Soviet bloc index shows a larger change from Year 1 to Year 2 to Year 3, a properly constructed index would also show this same relationship. Readers are directed to the voluminous United States literature on Soviet output indices.

[4] Since armaments expenditures of these countries began a rapid increase in 1951, the increase in producer goods indices could represent an increase in armaments production rather than capital goods. It is the writer's understanding from American press accounts, however, that the equipment of East European armies was mainly of Soviet manufacture.

[5] It has not been possible to present a continuous series for Soviet machinery exports, which at this period would have been largely to this area.

TABLE 1
OUTPUT OF PRINCIPAL INDUSTRIAL RAW MATERIALS IN SOVIET EASTERN EUROPE, 1950–56
(In Thousand Metric Tons)

Raw Materials	1950	1951	1952	1953	1954	1955	1956
Electric Power*	44.1	49.5	55.4	59.9	65.5	73.3	79.8
Increase over previous year	7.6	5.4	5.9	4.5	5.6	7.8	6.5
Percentage increase	20	12	12	8	9	12	9
Coal and Lignite	295,800	310,300	329,500	359,500	377,800	405,200	417,300
Increase over previous year	33,400	14,500	19,200	30,000	18,300	27,400	12,100
Percentage increase	13	5	6	9	5	7	3
Pig iron	4,551	4,859	5,726	7,380	8,020	9,036	9,685
Increase over previous year	596	308	867	1,654	640	1,016	649
Percentage increase	15	7	18	29	9	13	7
Steel	8,224	9,743	10,997	12,395	12,669	13,801	14,997
Increase over previous year	1,303	1,519	1,254	1,398	274	1,132	1,196
Percentage increase	19	18	13	13	2	9	8
Cement	8,344	9,156	10,188	11,955	12,455	13,704	14,731
Increase over previous year	3,186	812	1,032	1,767	500	1,249	1,027
Percentage increase	62	10	11	17	4	10	7

* Billion kilowatt hours.

SOURCE: For East Germany, 1949, *Economic Survey for Europe*, 1953 (UN Economic Commission for Europe, Geneva, 1954), p. 273. Other countries, 1949: I. Semenov and N. Sokolova, "Construction of a Socialist Economy in the European People's Democracies," *Voprosy Ekonomiki*, No. 3 (1956), p. 163. For 1950–56, tabulations are given in *Voprosy Ekonomiki*, No. 5 (1957), p. 97, except for Rumanian cement production 1949–53, which was obtained from the *Economic Survey for Europe* (1953), *op. cit.*, p. 276, and for 1954, which was interpolated by the writer. Rumanian pig iron production 1951–56 is from the *Anuarul Statistic al RPR 1957* (Bucharest, 1957), p. 86.

TABLE 2
Estimated Combined Official Indices of Industrial Output, Industrial Employment, and Output per Man-Year in Soviet Eastern Europe, 1949–56*

	1949	1950	1951	1952	1953	1954	1955	1956‡
Six Countries, Combined Indices†								
Industrial output (1949 = 100)	100	128	158	188	214	231	252	271
Increase over previous year, points	16	28	30	30	26	17	21	21
Percent	20	28	23	19	14	8	9	8
Industrial employment (thousands)	6,178	6,923	7,472	7,900	8,270	8,513	8,657	n.a.
Increase over previous year, thousands	n.a.	745	549	428	370	243	144	n.a.
Percent	n.a.	12	8	6	5	3	2	n.a.
Output per man-year (1949 = 100)	100	114	131	147	160	168	180	n.a.
Increase over previous year, points	n.a.	14	17	16	13	8	12	n.a.
Percent	n.a.	14	15	12	9	5	7	n.a.
Five Countries, Combined Indices†								
Industrial output (1949 = 100)	100	129	159	192	219	235	258	279
Increase over previous year, points	16	29	30	33	27	16	13	21
Percent	20	29	23	21	14	7	6	8
Industrial employment (thousands)	4,165	4,700	5,062	5,394	5,717	5,883	6,036	6,297
Increase over previous year, thousands	n.a.	535	362	332	323	166	153	261
Percent	n.a.	13	8	7	5	3	3	4
Output per man-year (1949 = 100)	100	114	131	148	160	166	178	185
Increase over previous year, points	n.a.	14	17	16	12	6	12	7
Percent	n.a.	14	15	12	8	4	7	4

n.a.—not available.

* The industrial output indices are obtained from official indices of producer and consumer goods (except for East Germany, where only total output was used). These were weighted by the average industrial employment of the respective countries, 1953–55. Industrial employment data are from direct reports wherever possible; elsewhere they are derived by dividing official indices of output by official indices of labor productivity. Details of the computations are available from the writer on request. The output per man-year are obtained by division of output by employment.

† The *five-country* indices refer to Poland, Czechoslovakia, Hungary, Rumania, and Bulgaria. The *six-country* indices refer to these countries plus East Germany. Albania was *not* included in any index because the writer could find no adequate figures on industrial employment, which in any case must be very small. Hungarian employment includes Hungarian employment only for January–September.

‡ The 1956 index of employment is not affected by the decline in output after the Hungarian uprising in October. The other two indices, however, include Hungarian annual totals and thus include the effects of the uprising.

TABLE 3
OUTPUT OF PRODUCER AND CONSUMER GOODS IN FIVE EASTERN EUROPEAN
COUNTRIES 1949–56, ACCORDING TO OFFICIAL INDICES (1949 = 100)

Outputs	1949	1950	1951	1952	1953	1954	1955	1956
Industrial output, total	100	129	159	192	219	235	258	286†
Producer goods	56	72	91	113	132	141	154*	172
Consumer goods	44	58	69	79	87	94	104	115
Indices of output of	100	128	161	200	234	250	273*	304†
Producer goods								
Increase over previous year								
Points	n.a.	28	33	39	34	16	23	31
Percent	n.a.	28	26	24	17	7	9	11
Consumer goods	100	130	158	181	200	216	239	264†
Increase over previous year								
Points	n.a.	30	28	23	19	16	13	25
Percent	n.a.	30	21	15	10	8	6	10
Increases in the components of industrial output								
Producer goods, in points of total index	n.a.	16	19	22	19	9	13	18
Consumer goods, in points of total index	n.a.	14	11	10	8	7	10	11
Increases in producer goods output, in percent of the total increase in output	n.a.	53	64	69	70	56	56	62

n.a.—not available.
* Assuming no change for Bulgaria, for which no index is available.
† These indices differ from those of Table 2 which use the Hungarian output index of 1956. The writer has been unable to find Hungarian output indices for producer and consumer goods separately for 1956. He therefore omitted Hungary from his 1956 computations. He did this because he wished to determine the extent to which the role of consumer goods in output increases (last item in column) might have changed in 1956.
Method of computation: Indices of producer and consumer goods output for individual countries were used. They were weighted as follows: For 1953 and 1955 the percentage breakdown of output as between the two categories was available for these countries. Assuming labor productivity the same in the two categories, employment data were broken down for two years into "producer goods labor" and "consumer goods labor." These employment figures were used as weights. While this procedure would be very bad if any better method were available, it seems permissible in the absence of anything better; and the results conform largely with what might have been expected on analytical grounds.

output may require varying amounts of capital equipment. If the East European investment programs had scheduled first those objectives requiring small amounts of capital, and only later those requiring larger amounts, larger investment and smaller increases in output would have been observed.[6] This possibility does not explain the slowing down in the rate of growth of industrial employment (Table 2). While in 1950 industrial employment rose by 12 percent, in 1952 it rose only by 6 percent and dropped steadily to 2 percent in 1955.

Industrial Employment and Productivity Indices

Increases in industrial employment come about partly through decreases in the number of dependents in urban families and partly through

[6] One reason for such "decreasing returns" might be a deficiency in better grade mineral reserves. These have been discussed by V. H. Winston in N. J. G. Pounds and N. Spulber, (eds.), *Resources and Planning in Eastern Europe* (Slavic and East European Series, Vol. 4 [Indiana University Publications, 1957]), pp. 36 ff.

movement of peasants into the cities. However, the growth in the acreage of cooperative farms was greatest in 1950 and declined steadily until 1955[7] (Table 4).

Cooperative farm expansion will tend to create migration into the cities partly because some peasants not wishing—or permitted—to join cooperatives will move to the cities, and partly because cooperatives combine small landholdings into units large enough to permit the use of machinery.[8] Thus it is tempting to make a causal connection between the slowdown in the expansion of industrial employment from 1950 through 1955 (and the speedup in 1956) and similar changes in the growth of cooperative farms.

The official indices of output per man-year show the same general tendencies as total output and industrial employment. The largest increases, both absolute and in percent (Table 2), occurred in 1951 and were followed by declines until 1955. If the construction projects completed in later years were more capital-consuming than those completed in earlier years, in order to compensate, they would presumably have to be less labor-requiring than the earlier projects. But then the growth in labor productivity should have continued stable, or even increased.

TABLE 4
AREA OF COOPERATIVE FARMS, IN THOUSAND HECTARES, 1950–56

Countries	1950	1951	1952	1953	1954	1955	1956
Six Countries*							
Area	3,690	4,860	6,460	8,230	8,090	9,150	10,320
Increase over previous year							
in thousand hectares	2,890	2,170	1,600	1,770	—140	1,060	1,170
in percent	361	59	33	27	— 2	13	13
Five Countries†							
Area	3,690	4,860	6,310	7,480	7,310	8,050	8,930
Increase over previous year							
in thousand hectares	2,890	2,170	1,450	1,170	—170	740	880
in percent	361	59	29	19	— 2	10	11

* Bulgaria, Czechoslovakia, Hungary, Poland, Rumania, East Germany.
† Excluding East Germany.

These official productivity indices apply only to industry where productivity increases certainly exceeded those in the rest of the economy. Even if they correctly measured industrial labor productivity, therefore, they would exceed indices of overall productivity. Thus, whenever wages increased as rapidly as, or more rapidly than, official productivity indices, there was almost certainly to be an increase in demand for consumer

---

[7] This statement is not strictly true if East Germany is included. Collectivization started later there than elsewhere, so that the expansion (including that in East Germany) led to somewhat higher levels in 1953 than in 1952. For the other five countries, however, it is true.

[8] If the amount of machinery increases more rapidly than cooperative farm acreage, the movement into cities may be greater. The available information shows, however, that the tractor power available per acre of cooperative land did not change markedly from 1949 to 1955.

TABLE 5

CHANGES IN MONTHLY WAGES AND IN ANNUAL OUTPUT PER WORKER,
IN INDUSTRY, SIX EAST EUROPEAN COUNTRIES, 1950–56

(Percent above previous year)

Countries		1950	1951	1952	1953	1954	1955	1956[a]
Poland	Monthly wage[b]	21	10	9	42	6	4	11
	Output per worker[c]	10	13	1	7	6	6	5
Czechoslovakia ...	Monthly wage[d]	11	7	8	8	7	2	4
	Output per worker[c]	7	7	15	4	3	8	7
Hungary	Monthly wage[e]	8	7	28	4	11	5	5
	Output per worker[c]	20	12	9	4	0	6	
Rumania	Monthly wage[f]	11	10	—15	14	13	21	8
	Output per worker[c]	8	14	13	5	3	11	10
Bulgaria	Monthly wage[g]	6	7			6	2	2
	Output per worker[c]	16	14	12	9	2	8[a]	
East Germany	Monthly wage[h]	13	13	12	9	9	3	3
	Output per worker[i]	14	8	8	10	5	9	10

Pairs of numbers enclosed in square indicate cases where inflationary pressure certainly increased.
[a] Tabulations of output per worker are from *Voprosy Ekonomiki*, No. 5 (1957), p. 96.
[b] *Rocznik Statystyczny 1957* (Warsaw, 1957), p. 267.
[c] Unless otherwise noted, from the tabulations of Semenov and Sokolova, in *Voprosy Ekonomiki*, No. 3 (1956), pp. 159 ff.
[d] For 1949–53, *Rozvoj narodniho hospodarstvi CSR v letech 1948–1953* (Praha, 1955), p. 59. Changes from 1952 to 1953 are net of the 80 percent reduction in all prices at the time of the June 1953 currency conversion. For 1954–56, same source as in [a].
[e] For change from 1949–50, same source as [a]. For later years, UN *Monthly Bulletin of Statistics*, 1957. 1956 figures are for January–September only.
[f] For 1951–56, data on average retail sales per person employed in the economy were calculated from *Anuarul Statistic R.P.R.*: These are value terms; they can change without corresponding changes in money wages *if* (1) taxes or voluntary savings change or if (2) the amount of involuntary savings (currency inflation) changes. With caution, therefore, they may be used as a guide to wage changes, since these are not available. The 1950 figure *is* a wage change, given in *Economic Survey of Europe Since the War* (Geneva, 1953), p. 33.
[g] For 1950–51, *Economic Survey of Europe Since the War*, p. 33; for 1954–56, *Economic Survey of Europe in 1956* (Geneva, 1957), p. 14. Other years not available.
[h] For 1949–50, the 1950 report of the Planning Commission; for 1951–52, speeches by Leuschner (October 2, 1952) and Rau (May 16, 1953); for 1953; Ulbricht speech of March 30, 1954, to SFD Party Congress. The 1953 figure relates to socialist enterprises only; other figures to all industry. Data for 1954–56 are from the source listed in [a].
[i] For 1950, Grigorev, "Rise of Peaceful Economy of the German Democratic Republic," *Voprosy Ekonomiki*, No. 8 (1951), p. 83. For 1951–55, Kohlmey, "The Economy of the German Democratic Republic on the Threshold of the Second Five-Year Plan," *Voprosy Ekonomiki*, No. 11 (1956), p. 45 ff.

goods relative to output; for, as may be seen in Table 3, over most of this period output of consumer goods increased less rapidly than output of industry as a whole. Data on productivity and wages are shown in Table 5. In over half of the total cases for which data are available, wages grew more than industrial productivity. If industrial productivity indices are as little as one point higher per year than the overall indices, two thirds of the cases noted would fall into the "inflationary" category.

To sum up: (1) while industrial output has risen steadily—even, on balance, rapidly—it has failed to maintain its rates of growth; (2) industrial employment and average output per worker have shown the same tendencies; (3) money wages have risen steadily and probably, on balance, more rapidly than output; so that (4) there has been continuing or at least recurrent inflationary pressure. The rest of this paper will explain the interrelation among these phenomena.

Obstacles to Industrial Expansion

The present problem is most readily presented by considering an East European economy as comprising three sectors: the state, the workers, and the peasants. The state owns all manufactured goods (including processed foods), which it sells to workers and peasants; the peasants own farm goods, which they sell to the state or to the workers; and the workers own labor, which they sell to the state. Peasants, moreover, may become workers. The state hopes that many will do so. The state can fix all prices and wages except those which the peasants charge the workers; but it cannot fix—although it can influence—the amounts of labor and farm produce which will be sold it. The state wishes to retain as many manufactured goods for itself as it can. The goods it does retain will be called accumulation.[9]

While certain levels of accumulation may present no particular obstacles, an indefinite expansion of accumulation may present difficulties because of the interrelations between the other two sectors.

Relations between state and workers involve the exchange of labor for consumer goods. To increase accumulation, the state must prevent workers' consumption from rising as much as total industrial output. If workers save there is no problem. However, living standards are apparently so low in Eastern Europe and expectations of inflation so high that voluntary savings cannot be increased much. Semivoluntary savings (subscriptions to government bond issues) have been achieved through high-pressure tactics. Workers' consumption can also be limited by the absence of adequate stocks of goods in stores, an arrangement made more orderly through issuance of ration cards. In this way, the workers are forced to save paper money. Alternatively, the state could raise prices relative to wages and thus reduce consumption and attract investible funds in the form of profits.

Relations between the state and peasants involve the exchange of manufactured goods for farm goods. Since farm goods are relatively nonessential to accumulation,[10] the state's need for them is primarily to ob-

---

[9] An apology is due here to Karl Marx, who presents the term in his *Critique of the Gotha Program*, the cornerstone of modern Communist national income terminology. More precisely, the term should be "accumulation and social consumption funds." The former includes additions to plant, equipment, and state-held inventory; the latter services not paid for directly by their users, and ranging from free schools and hospitals to free armies and secret police services. The two categories are here combined, for simplicity, into the single term "accumulation." For simplicity it is also assumed that only manufactured goods are here involved, services being ignored, although it is well known that "stone walls do not a prison make."

[10] However, to the extent that the satellites export consumer goods to the U.S.S.R.

tain profits from their resale to the city population. The state must, therefore, acquire additional farm goods without corresponding increases in farm consumption so that it may increase profits and thereby accumulation. It can do so either if peasants save—voluntarily or otherwise—or if prices of manufactured goods rise relative to the prices the state pays for farm goods.[11]

Consumption Control

In both sets of transactions, the state has a choice of methods for holding down consumption. It may allow the prices it charges to rise relative to the prices it pays and retain the added profits. It may also force up savings by selling bonds or by putting direct controls over prices and the quantities of goods it buys and sells.

If workers are forced to save more than they wish in cash, they can spend less on goods than they wish, assuming the amount of work they were willing to perform were unaffected by this scarcity of goods. On the other hand, if they are satisfied with given amounts of consumer goods, involuntary savings will be associated with involuntary labor—the state will have to use "persuasion" or "force" to get the labor it wishes. Increases in accumulation will thus tend to be accompanied by willingness of workers (and state enterprises) to pay more than official prices in order to obtain more goods (and labor) than are available, and a second price level (often inexactly termed a "black market price level," although it need not be illegal) will appear. "Progressive" piecework wage systems are instituted in which the pay for any given increment of output exceeds the average piecework rate for output up to that level. The state itself will sell unrationed goods at a "commercial" price higher than it charges for rationed goods, and the connection between commodity and labor shortages is emphasized by having ration cards issued through the personnel departments of plants.

Similarly in agriculture, involuntary savings will be associated with shortages of goods in rural stores and with the failure of government purchasing agencies to buy as many goods from the peasants as they wish to. In this case also, multiple pricing will appear; the state buys a certain quantity of goods (compulsory deliveries) at very low prices, and additional amounts at higher (contract) prices. Peasants will sell to workers at "free-market" prices approximating those the government charges workers in "commercial" (unrationed goods) stores.

Whatever the price system, the state's efforts to increase accumulation

---

in exchange for machinery, the acquisition of farm goods by the state may be a necessary part of the accumulation process.

[11] Soviet bloc governments in their farm policy try to lower the "parity index," whereas the United States tries to raise the index. If the United States is faced with chronic farm overproduction, the Soviet bloc should be faced with chronic farm shortages.

may actually limit the movement of population off the farm. Suppose the state has instituted multiple prices and direct controls. If accumulation is to increase, urban—as well as rural—incomes must be held down. Urban incomes must be kept above rural incomes if movement to the cities is to be encouraged. But if workers have money which they can only spend in the free market, they will bid up free-market prices and raise peasant money incomes. They will simultaneously reduce the sale of farm goods to the state, the differential between urban and rural standards of living, and the profits earned by the state in the processing and distribution of food. Industrial and construction plans assume the movement of peasants into industry so that wages must increase to attract this labor. In attracting it, however, the state increases involuntary savings and the control problem.

Suppose the state wishes to maintain a unified pricing system and to increase accumulation by raising retail prices relative to wages and to the prices it pays peasants. It cannot then raise urban prices and not rural, or vice versa. But when retail prices go up, peasants may sell less farm goods to the state, or workers supply less labor. In both cases, workers' demand—and hence prices—in the free market will rise because of the decrease in goods in other retail channels, or because the smaller supply of labor relative to demand pushes up money wages and spending power. Here, too, movement to the city will slow down.

An Interpretation of Soviet Bloc Economic Policy

It is tempting to ascribe political causes to Soviet bloc economic policy. The orders of the Communist parties to increase accumulation in early 1951 and to slow it down in 1953 can be associated with the beginning and end of the Korean aggression. The decision to begin the Five-Year Plans in the late 1940's can be associated with concern over West European economic recovery and with desire to isolate the satellites from trade with the West; in internal politics, it reflects Soviet concern over "cosmopolitanism" and "Titoism." The decision to slow down the growth in accumulation in 1953 would then reflect the uncertainties of Stalin's heirs. Increased accumulation apparently beginning in 1956–57 would then reflect either the success of the new Soviet leadership in eliminating its competitors or its concern over popular discontent, notably as expressed in the Hungarian uprising of 1956.

Such an approach, however, would be valid if only political factors constrain economic policies in Eastern Europe. But in 1951–52, rates of growth in accumulation dropped off despite efforts to increase it, and in 1953–54, the growth in consumer goods output slowed down despite efforts to increase it. The wishes of governments are thus not always attained. The obstacles are not, in general, political.

Alternatively, economic policy can be defined solely in terms of the objectives listed in the long-run economic plans. Of these, each country now has had two—one published in the late 1940's and the other being approved for 1956–60.[12]

Inferences as to the reasons for deviations of performance from plans, and for changes from one plan to another, must necessarily run in terms of long-run factors such as availability of resources, trends in population growth, and so forth. Such evaluation of the fulfillment of a long-term plan is valid if the plan itself was the basis for economic policy throughout the entire planning period; comparison of two long-run plans is meaningful if transient objectives are embodied in neither and if economic factors such as those suggested in the section Obstacles to Industrial Expansion of this paper may be ignored.[13]

In 1951, the Communist parties of Soviet East Europe prepared goals superseding those of existing plans; in 1953 they prepared other goals, apparently replacing the 1951 objectives; in 1955 they apparently discarded their 1953 objectives. These changes seem as important as the basic long-run plans. Although these appear to cover a relatively long period, they may in fact be revised at any time.

Before October, 1952, Soviet bloc economic policy was most dramatically expressed in "abolition of rationing." These occurred in Poland (January, 1949), Hungary (December, 1951), and Bulgaria (May, 1952). In Bulgaria, the abolition of rationing was a part of a currency conversion operation. Two other countries also had currency conversions: Poland (October, 1950) and Rumania (January, 1952).[14] Abolition of rationing replaces multiple pricing of consumer prices—rationed goods prices, commercial prices and free market prices—by a single price level high enough to restrict consumer demand to the volume of goods available. In cases where the new level could be set *at or below* the former commercial store level, apparently no currency conversion[15] was needed. If the new level would have had to be *above* commercial prices, a currency conversion was ordered so as to reduce the equilibrium level of prices.[16]

---

[12] A thorough appraisal of these plans is given in N. Spulber, *The Economics of Communist Eastern Europe* (Cambridge, Mass., 1957), esp. sec. III.

[13] In accordance with Soviet practice, published satellite long-term plans have been primarily a set of production targets. They contain relatively little explanation of the reasons for the selection of particular objectives and even less examination of the consistency of these objectives.

[14] See my "Soviet Bloc Currency Conversions," *American Economic Review* (June, 1954), for a detailed discussion of the relation between price unification and currency conversions. One conversion (Czechoslovakia, June, 1953) occurred after 1952.

[15] That is, the turning in of several units of old currency for one unit of new, so as to reduce the money holdings of the population. In terms of the discussion in the part Obstacles to Industrial Expansion of this paper, it eliminates accrued involuntary savings, cutting down excess demand for goods and labor.

[16] As a precautionary measure, prices are apparently fixed, at the time of unification, somewhat above the level the authorities expect to be a permanent level. This caution is explainable by the fact that some wages are usually increased, with unpredictable results. In any case, price unification is usually followed, after a period of months, by one or more price reductions.

Explanation of Price Problems

Soviet bloc literature on price problems prior to October, 1952, is almost confined to statements that high free-market prices are due to speculators; that shortages in retail stores are due to inefficiency; that shortages of farm goods are due to kulaks; and that shortages of labor are due to poor party propaganda. The literature is perhaps silent because price unification lowers "real wages"[17] by eliminating the lower (rationed goods) prices.

In October, 1952, Stalin published his *Economic Problems of Socialism in the USSR*. It has the merits of admitting an unpleasant fact; giving a real, though possibly faulty diagnosis of its cause; and prescribing a real, though possibly incorrect remedy. Stalin's most important assertion was that "it would be incorrect . . . to assert that there are no contradictions between our productive forces and productive relations." This in its context is an assertion that Soviet institutions are an obstacle to the development of heavy industry. Until October, 1952, Soviet bloc economists had been hampered by the claim[18] of full correspondence between the two so that no economic policy problems might exist. His diagnosis ran as follows: the state can allocate capital goods and the output of state enterprise, but it cannot allocate the output of collective farms. These are cooperative and are owners of their output, capable, in some degree, of bargaining with the state and of deciding how much to sell on the free market. Stalin's prescription is to "raise collective farm property to the level of national property" by means of "product exchange" in which the state would contract in advance to barter industrial goods for the entire output of collective farms above their own requirements. In this way, farms would receive income only from the state, and workers could spend income only in state stores. The principal criticism of Stalin's view is that even if involuntary cash holding cannot spill over from the workers to the peasants, multiple pricing and controls in either sector singly can have undesirable results.[19] On the other hand, in the absence of such pricing and controls, his solution would make no economic difference.

After Stalin's death, this policy received little mention. Party central committees and government bodies of the satellites, after July, 1953, began to put out resolutions and decrees giving a somewhat different argument:[20] (1) Output of consumer goods has tended to lag behind output

[17] It does not necessarily decrease consumption, and there is no real evidence of changes in consumer goods output as a result of price unification.

[18] Voiced for instance in the tremendously authoritative *Short History of the Communist Party of the Soviet Union*, 1945 Russian edition, p. 118.

[19] I have summarized Soviet bloc views on multiple pricing and controls affecting workers in the article cited; those on multiple pricing and controls affecting peasants are summarized in the *Economic Survey of Europe in 1956, op. cit.*, pp. 21 ff.

[20] Summaries of the actions in individual countries are given in the handbook *Khozyaistvennoe Razvitie Stran Narodnoi Demokratii* (Economic Development of the

of producer goods; (2) it has lagged because agricultural output has failed to increase much, so that there are deficiencies in the raw materials supply for the consumer goods industries; (3) short-term increase in consumer durable goods output can satisfy part of this demand; (4) agricultural output or at least sales by the peasants to the state can be encouraged by raising compulsory delivery and contract prices, by reducing compulsory deliveries and rent on farm machinery, and by tax reductions. Some farm cooperative members may be allowed to return to private agriculture. Even if peasants do not increase output, but merely sell less on the free market and more to the state, an improvement occurs, partly because money in circulation goes down—as a result of state profits on handling farm goods—and partly because the state can better control the distribution process.

Lag in Consumer Goods Output

The statement often appearing in satellite writings of 1953–54 that consumer goods output had lagged behind producer goods output makes the foregoing argument a *non sequitur*, strictly speaking. Suppose, for example, that prices were held constant and wages decreased. Then an increase in accumulation without any increase in consumption would cause no particular difficulties which would justify "lag" in a pejorative sense. Only if wage and price changes have caused a disequilibrium in consumer goods markets is it possible to speak of a lag in consumer goods output.

The decrees of 1953–54 in several countries even proposed increases in investment in consumer goods industries, housing, and agriculture and reductions in total investment. In 1952 output of consumer goods (Table 3) had increased no more than output per worker (Table 2). Since some consumer goods plants were under construction throughout the period, there was presumably idle capacity which could only be used if accumulation declined (there being no urban unemployment, and the movement off the farm having dropped with the better treatment of peasants).

The small growth in producer goods output is explained, in 1954–55, by the slowing of the growth of accumulation. The small growth of consumer goods output through 1955[21] is more puzzling. If consumer goods are mostly processed farm goods, such slowing down would mean that farmers had not sold more to the state despite the more favorable terms

People's Democracies), N. I. Ivanov (ed.), published by the Soviet Ministry of Foreign Trade, 1954. A more theoretical analysis is given by I. Dudinski, "Commodity Production in the European People's Democracies," *Voprosy Ekonomiki* Vol. 5 (1954), p. 59.

[21] Not until 1956 did the growth in consumer goods output regain its 1952 rate. By that time, expanding this output was not a primary government objective. If this is the belated effect of the consumer goods program, then it may be concluded that where Malenkov sowed, Khrushchev reaped.

offered them. Any of a number of explanations would suffice: continued free-market sales, increased peasant food consumption, or lower farm production. Generally lower prices in state stores[22] argue against the first, while some official statements[23] suggest the last two. Given an increase in wages relative to prices (Table 5) in 1954, the diagnosis of a "lag in consumer goods output" is a possible diagnosis.

In 1955, however, a new official analysis replaces the "disproportion" between investment and consumer goods by a disproportion between raw materials and processed goods, leading to shortages of the former (excess capacity of the latter). Two types of raw materials are mentioned: agricultural and industrial, particularly fuel and minerals. Shortages in raw materials are to be remedied by expanded investment in these sectors. In fact, since other investment is not to decline, total investment must rise.

Although "raw materials" are treated as a unit in this literature, agricultural and industrial raw materials are really quite different problems. Investment in agriculture means, to a considerable extent, mechanization.[24] Mechanization does not increase yields, but it does decrease labor requirements. Since increased consumer goods ouput in 1953–54 had reduced the labor available for accumulation, expanded accumulation in 1955–56 must involve more movement off the farm. Hence mechanization —and collectivization—were once again stressed beginning in 1955.[25]

Production of Industrial Raw Material

The disproportion of industrial raw materials production appears as shortages of supplies, interruptions of electric power service and of materials deliveries, hoarding of scarce materials, low quality output, and so on. Table 1 shows continuing decline in the growth of coal and pig iron output through 1956. Beginning in 1950–51, "materials balance" systems were introduced to guarantee supplies of hundreds of individual commodities to priority consumers. The administration of this system causes general dissatisfaction, partly because of its bureaucratic methods, and partly because its operations require an unambiguous relation between requirements for individual material and output of individual plants and between minimal stocks of individual materials and output, which are hard to determine.

---

22 E. C. E., *Economic Survey of Europe in 1956*, p. 14, indicates relatively large price reductions in 1954, smaller reductions in 1955, very small reductions in 1956.

23 Such as that of the Central Committee of the Hungarian Workers Party in March, 1955.

24 Expansion of livestock involves investment to the extent that animals are held off the market for breeding. To some extent this is financed from the proceeds of the higher livestock prices introduced in 1953–54. To some extent, however, it does involve loans by the investment banks of the various countries from budget receipts.

25 It will be interesting to see the effect of the dissolution of Polish cooperative farms in late 1956 on Polish accumulation.

There are two views of this disproportion. The orthodox view is that a shortage occurs because investment in the materials-producing industry has been too small. This is a defect in planning and can be remedied by increased investment. Meanwhile, strengthening of controls over utilization may be useful until materials output rises relative to output of users.

A heterodox view is that the shortages occur because of inherent inefficiencies in allocations (the bureaucracy) or else because plant managers have no incentive to use materials efficiently. Even if output were too low, that would reflect the fact that planners (bureaucrats) and producers alike have no incentive to eliminate shortages. The remedy for a shortage, then, is to reduce centralized controls, increase the scope of plant managers' decisions, and create incentives for producers to make more and consumers to use less.

These views are called "orthodox" and "heterodox" in terms of Stalin's analysis in the *Economic Problems of Socialism.*[26] Stalin said that the "law of value" did not apply in the Soviet Union to capital goods output (and his reasoning would generally apply to industrial materials output) since: all industrial plants belong to the same owner, the state; plant managers are agents of the state, whose function it is to operate a part of the state's property on the basis of the state's plans; prices are fixed by the state and serve only as a unit of measurement of performance and for auditing purposes. As a result the only incentive of plants is to fulfill plans. In contrast, collective farms are somewhat independent economic units with the consequences already discussed.

The heterodox view apparently has considerable appeal throughout the satellites.[27] Even in the U.S.S.R., Khrushchev went partway in meeting objections to "bureaucracy" by replacing centralized control in Moscow with regional controls. It is unclear what will be the outcome of this discussion. The economic leadership of the satellites would clearly prefer to eliminate shortages by expanding output—even if this means some waste —rather than to eliminate them by dismantling the control structure.

Curing Shortages

Neither the orthodox nor the heterodox prescriptions for shortages provide necessary or sufficient conditions for curing them. A shortage may exist because output is too small, or consumption too large, or in-

---

[26] *Loc. cit.*, pp. 8–9, p. 28. See also Venediktov, *Gosudarstvennaya Sotsialisticheskaya Sobstvennost* (State-owned Socialist Property), Moscow, 1948, for an exposition of the legal consequences of this view. Vladimir Gsovski, *Soviet Civil Law* (Ann Arbor, Michigan), has set forth some of the difficulties in the Soviet concepts.

[27] See P. J. D. Wiles, "Changing Economic Thought in Poland," *Oxford Economic Papers* (June, 1957), for expressions by Polish economists. I. Dvorkin, "The Reactionary Essence of Contemporary Reformism," *Voprosy Ekonomiki*, No. 6 (1957), esp. pp. 95–96, attacks Yugoslav views in general, while Grigorev and Kostin, "Against Attempts at Revision of Marxist Political Economy," *Voprosy Ekonomiki*, No. 4 (1957), single out two East German economists as under Yugoslav influence.

ventory increases too great. It should be possible to raise production either by increased budget appropriation for investment or by allowing the producers to finance expansion from higher profits.[28] Likewise, consumption could be held down either by more vigorous bureaucratic intervention[29] or by higher prices of materials, if plant management is forced to show a profit. If the state is prepared to subsidize losses, however, it will be difficult to enforce efficiency.

Even if the state were not willing to cover losses, however, plants could incur losses and hoard inventory if enough credit is available. In fact, there is scattered evidence of a continuous credit expansion throughout this period which had enabled enterprises to obtain funds without making profits or appropriations. It increases effective demand for materials; and since prices are fixed, a shortage must develop. Since the banking systems must refuse drafts which cover transactions at illegal prices, secondary price levels (as in retail trade, labor, and agriculture) cannot create stability in the system. Enterprises, anticipating further shortages, naturally hoard whenever possible so that interruptions in deliveries will not prevent production plan fulfillment.

The heterodox view is thus correct in stressing the difference between the incentives of management and of the state. The orthodox view is correct in linking centralized control with price fixing in its treatment of the law of value. Shortages in Eastern Europe are no different in principle from shortages in Western Europe in the 1940's.[30] This hypothesis is not currently acceptable in Eastern Europe, however, because it bypasses the emotionally charged issue of centralized control and also because it does not fit into generally accepted monetary theory.[31]

---

[28] Stalin points out, however (*loc. cit.*, pp. 12–13), that if the U.S.S.R. invested only in industries where profits were large, it would have to invest mainly in consumer goods industries and not heavy industry. This statement, of course, might not hold if the state were willing to bid up sufficiently the prices of heavy industrial goods.

[29] However, materials-balance literature stresses the practical difficulties in establishing an unambiguous relation between output and materials requirements.

[30] Thus Oskar Lange's article, "For a New Economic Programme" (*Zycie Gospodarcze*, July 16, 1956, available in translation through the Center for International Studies at M.I.T.), reads as an attack on repressed inflation by a former member of the department of economics at the University of Chicago should read; it resembles attacks on the economic policy of the postwar Labor government in England; or attacks on United States price controls in 1946. Instead of attacking inflation, he attacks controls. If the controls were removed without appropriate credit restrictions, price increases would begin. As recent Yugoslav experience shows, the shortages might disappear, but price rises and balance of payments problems would continue.

[31] Before the Communist regimes, "money" and "note circulation" were used almost interchangeably in central bank literature; this was justifiable because of the low level of deposit banking in most countries. Marx had the same practice, which was also justified in Europe of the 1860's. The Communist requirement that payments among enterprises be made by draft has greatly altered the importance of deposits in the total money supply, but has not been fully appreciated; the view is held that increases in notes are inflationary, but increases in deposits are not. It is fortified by a "real bills doctrine" (like that of much United States and other central bank dis-

Thus the change in official policy in 1955–56, increasing investment in agriculture and industrial raw materials, is an attempt to cope with inflationary problems by new means. It differs from the pre-1953 policy by greater emphasis on unified pricing in the consumer and peasant sectors and from the 1953–54 policy by greater emphasis on investment in raw materials industry rather than price policy as a means of maintaining equilibrium. The new policy, however, reflects a desire to maintain a centralized structure of controls which has apparently been challenged in recent years. If the orthodox view triumphs politically, as it apparently has (except in Poland), it must still be seen whether the acceleration in the growth of industrial output in 1955–56 can be maintained, or whether it will slow down, as was the case after 1950. If price policy, as before, retards the movement of population into the cities; and if shortages of materials cannot be resolved by the new investment program, then the slowdown observable after 1950 will probably resume.

---

counting legislation): a loan secured by goods does not push up prices (or create shortages), since output must rise as much as the money supply. East European bank loans have, for practical purposes, commodity collateral.

PART IV

1. The Progressive Division and Specialization of Industries*

Edward Ames and Nathan Rosenberg

Purdue University

I. Introduction

THE TITLE of this paper is an expression used by Allyn Young,[1] who asserts that potential economies from investment "are segregated and achieved by the operations of specialized undertakings which, taken together, constitute a new industry." This segregation process is one of the most notable aspects of industrialization, but one about which rather little has been added in a systematic way since Adam Smith; even he, despite the renown of his remarks, devoted a total of four pages to the specialization of labor. We hope, by using a little formal reasoning, to rescue specialization from its current undeserved neglect. Since a major aspect of economic development is, in fact, embodied in changing patterns of specialization, we hope also to suggest some promising lines for the further study of the development process.

To illustrate the type of problem we are interested in, we offer a simple set of historical facts, which have no simple theoretical explanation. Until the 1820's there was no machine tool industry in either Great Britain or the United States. Machine tools were certainly used, but they were made by the firms which intended to use them. About this time, the machine shops of factories began to separate from the parent plants and become independent firms. Around 1860 there were many such firms, and they tended to produce a wide variety of tools. During the last part of the century, however, there was a strong tendency for these firms to reduce the variety of their output, so that while the assortment of tools made in

* Reprinted from the *Journal of Development Studies*, Vol. I, No. 4 (July, 1965), pp. 363–83.
[1] In "Increasing Returns and Economic Progress," *Economic Journal* (December, 1928), p. 539.

either country grew, the variety produced per firm declined.[2] In the 20th century, by contrast, there has been an opposite tendency. The number of firms has not increased with output, and may even have declined, whereas the number of kinds of tool produced per firm has increased. There is no theoretical economic explanation of why either the 19th-century changes or the opposite 20th-century changes might have occurred.

In contrast to consumer goods industries where mass production techniques prevail, the capital goods industries possess certain unique features. The great bulk of their output consists of construction and machinery and equipment produced to conform to an exacting set of specifications laid down by the buyer of the capital good. As a result of this market constraint, the capital goods industries are characterized by (1) a large number of firms, (2) small average size of firms, (3) a highly heterogeneous output, and (4) small production batches. Economies of scale are not very conspicuous while problems of product mix and process mix are obviously very important.[3] We argue that these features amount to a situation with which economic theory cannot now cope. These industries are very important ones, so the gap in our theory is not to be overlooked.

It is natural to conjecture that in some sense the firm optimizes the number of items in its catalog, as well as its level of output of each item. The number of items, however, is discrete, being a whole number, and does not yield to the charms of the calculus. Thus conventional maximization theory does not help. It is useful to formulate the problem in terms of firms with joint production, if only because such a formulation makes it clear how complicated the theory of specialization is when viewed in this context.

II. The Analytical Framework

Consider a firm producing two outputs, and using for the purpose a certain collection of inputs, which have given prices. Denote by $(x_1, x_2 | N)$ a situation in which outputs are x_1, x_2, and inputs are some given set of quantities, N. This situation is efficient, in the sense that the firm cannot produce more of one output, given N, without producing less of the other.

Let $S(N)$ denote the set $\{(x_1, x_2 | N)\}$ of all combinations of output which can be produced with the given set N of inputs. Let us assume

[2] See Nathan Rosenberg, "Technological Change in the Machine Tool Industry, 1840–1910," *Journal of Economic History* (December, 1963), pp. 414–43; *Twelfth Census of the United States* (1900), Part IV, Vol. X, "Manufactures"; *Special Reports of the Census Office* (1905), Part IV, "Metalworking Machinery"; J. H. Clapham, *An Economic History of Modern Britain* (Cambridge, Eng.: Cambridge University Press, 1959) Vol. I, chap. v.

[3] See, for example, Murray Brown and Nathan Rosenberg, "Patents, Research and Technology in the Machine Tool Industry," *Patent, Trademark and Copyright Journal of Research and Education* (Spring, 1961), pp. 1–15.

that there are pairs $(\bar{x}_1, x_2)$ and $(x_1, \bar{x}_2)$ having the property that for any element of $S(N)$, say $(x_1', x_2'|N)$, $x_1' \leqslant \bar{x}_1$, $x_2' \leqslant \bar{x}_2$; also that $x_1 \geqslant 0$, $x_2 \geqslant 0$. These pairs correspond to "specialization in output 1," and "specialization in output 2," respectively. (Such specialization may not imply that only one product is made; it means that as much of that product as possible is made for any collection of inputs.)

Now consider sets of output which are "between" these two. That is, consider pairs of the form $(\alpha x_1 + (1 - \alpha)\bar{x}_1, (1 - \alpha)x_2 + \alpha\bar{x}_2)$, and denote these by $(x_1(\alpha), x_2(\alpha))$. We inquire whether these are in $S(N)$. Under proper continuity conditions there will certainly be an element of $S(N)$ of the form $(x_1(\alpha), x_2'|N)$, and another of the form $(x_1', x_2(\alpha)|N)$. However, the minimum cost of producing $(x_1(\alpha), x_2(\alpha))$ may well be more or less than the cost associated with N, even though the cost of the pairs $(x_1(0), x_2(0))$ and $(x_1(1), x_2(1))$ is exactly N, by assumption.

Denote by $N(\alpha)$ the minimum cost of producing each particular combination $(x_1(\alpha), x_2(\alpha))$. From the foregoing construction, $N(0) = N(1) = N$, but if $\alpha \neq 0$, 1, $N(\alpha)$ is presumably not N. A tendency to specialize will exist if $N(\alpha) \leqslant N$ for values of α in some neighbourhood of 0 or 1 and $N(\alpha) > N$ for intermediate values of α; a tendency to diversify will exist if the inequalities are reversed.

This result was obtained by starting from a given set of quantities of a given collection of inputs with given prices. If a different set of quantities had been used, a different pair of bounds $(\bar{x}_1', x_2')$ and $(x_1', \bar{x}_2')$ would have been obtained; and if input prices had been different, $N(\alpha)$ would have had different values. Meaningful statements about specialization and diversification can be made in this context only if the properties of $N(\alpha)$ in the preceding paragraph turn out to depend only on α, and not on the actual amounts of inputs used, or the prices of inputs, at least for significant ranges of variation for both these collections of variables.

Assertions about specialization, in this context, are assertions that firms will select extreme values $\alpha = 0$ or $\alpha = 1$ in preference to nonextremal values; or that firms will shun these extremal values. The most general production function is one in which quantities of all the goods made in the economy appear as outputs of each firm, and the firm selects some convex combination $(\Sigma \alpha_i \bar{x}_i)$ of these. It is a familiar fact, of course, that for most firms almost all the α_i will equal zero, since most firms produce none at all of most of the kinds of goods used in the economy. It is also a familiar fact that there is a considerable amount of invariance in the list of goods (and even the proportions) produced by individual firms over moderately long periods of time. It therefore seems natural to investigate the question of specialization more directly, rather than as a limiting case of the difficult problem in joint output just formulated.

A theory of specialization, moreover, would have uses beyond those outlined. In the foregoing analysis, the set $((x_1, x_2|N))$ may be renamed, so that x_1 and x_2 represent quantities of inputs 1 and 2, and N represents a given bill of output. It is then possible to formulate another problem relating to the specialized use of inputs as compared to the combined use of both, given a particular output N. Manifestly, individual firms use a relatively small proportion of the total number of inputs used in the economy.

Rather than consider specialization as a series of limiting cases in the theory of joint production functions, it is natural to approach the problem directly, and to try to see what can be said about the number of outputs or inputs used by firms. Such statements can be directly verified by reference to historical data. Indeed a variety of relevant generalizations have been proposed by economic historians. Some of these may even be relevant outside the context in which they were advanced: although originally formulated about countries which have succeeded in industrializing, they may be useful in outlining feasible courses for countries which are only beginning to industrialize.

We have found it possible to make some headway in the theory of specialization using the definitions given by Leibenstein.[4] He, in turn, is obviously influenced by Stigler.[5]

1. A *commodity* is the entity that is the object of the production process, and has a specific set of attributes or specifications.
2. A *factor* is an entity, units of which can be purchased on the market, that has the capacity to carry out one or more activities.
3. An *activity* is our primitive concept. It refers to those necessary acts carried out by a factor, or functions of a factor, necessary in the productive process. We define a set of related activities as an *operation*.
4. A *process* is a specific set of operations necessary to produce the commodity in question. There may be a number of possible alternative processes.
5. By a *firm*, we refer to the entity that purchases factors, creates commodities, and sells commodities.[6]

An activity we associate with a command, "If X, do Y." On an assembly line, the activity may reduce to "if a gizmo appears, fasten a grommet to it." The associated operation may be sequential: "Drill a hole, insert a rod, fasten the grommet." Or the operation may be branching: "If the hole is less than two inches deep, return the gizmo; if it is two inches deep, pass the gizmo; if it is more than two inches deep, discard the gizmo." The activity, we say, is what is done by a particular agent, in the course of a process. The agent may be a man, or an entire firm. The process yields a commodity.

---

[4] H. Leibenstein, *Economic Backwardness and Economic Growth* (New York: Wiley, 1957), chap. 7, esp. page 80; see also his *Economic Theory and Organizational Analysis* (New York: Harper & Bros., 1960), chaps. 7–8.

[5] George Stigler, "The Division of Labor is Limited by the Extent of the Market," *Journal of Political Economy*, (June, 1951), pp. 185–93.

[6] Leibenstein, *op. cit.*, p. 80.

Since men and machines are not stationed in a 1 to 1 proportion in an industrial process, the "length" of the process depends upon whether it is defined in terms of men or of machines. This fact turns out to be crucial when we consider specialization.

The specification of activities is not unique. From this fact stems a major operational difficulty. If I go to a craftsman and tell him "Make me a watch," I have apparently given a single order. If I must prepare the job specification for an assembly line producing watches (or if I make a time and motion study of the craftsman) I define a more complex sequence of commands. Indeed, a large part of the process of substituting machinery for labor is based on the precise specification of the sequence of commands. But one aspect of this process is the substitution of the command (to labor) "Tend this machine" for the commands "do x_1, x_2, . . . x_n." For machines, the commands (specifications) grow longer. The "simple machine" executes the command "Do x." The more complicated machines execute the command "Do $x_1, x_2, . . . x_n$."

It is convenient to define *specialization* at this point. It is clear that "complete specialization" by X means that X does one activity, and in general the more things X does, the less X specializes. It is also clear that the more things X does, the more skillful X is (the more skills he has).[7] Here X is an individual (man, machine, firm). When X, however, is a group, specialization is an average. We shall define the *skill* of a group as the average number of activities its members perform; and we shall take the reciprocal of this number as an index of specialization.[8]

Specialization is a ratio; it has a number of units of doers in its numerator, and a number of activities performed in its denominator. In this general form, we shall distinguish several types.

The term "vertical" is used here to mean "with reference to a particular

---

[7] According to this definition, then, someone who was completely unspecialized—completely self-sufficient—would also have to be very highly skilled, a consideration which doubtless goes a long way toward explaining the limited number of genuine Walden Pond enthusiasts.

[8] This definition of skill coincides best with the antithesis craftsman-factory worker, in which a worker capable of performing every step in an industrial process is replaced by a group, each member of which performs a single activity. Actually, in a broader sense "skill" may be considered a multidimensional property, combining skill (in this narrow sense) with aptitude for a particular occupation. Thus plumbers and doctors may be equally skilled (in the sense of performing an equal number of activities); but since the two have different aptitudes, which the community values differently, the two command different incomes. This distinction between training and skill must be understood. We do not talk about training, and feel that confusion in the literature occurs in part because training and skill have been wrongly associated. Our definition is in line with *The Wealth of Nations*, which asserts that division of labor gives rise to "differences of talent more important than the natural ones." "The difference between the most dissimilar characters, between a philosopher and a common street porter, for example, seems to arise not so much from nature as from habit, custom, and education. By nature a philosopher is not in genius and disposition half so different from a street porter, as a mastiff is from a greyhound, or a greyhound from a spaniel, or this last from a shepherd's dog." Adam Smith, *The Wealth of Nations* (New York: Random House, 1937), pp. 15–16.

process."[9] A process may involve several firms, as in the case of making finished metal goods from ores. It may be associated with the sequence of activities conducted by a single firm. *Vertical specialization* by a firm will refer to a tendency for a firm to carry on a single activity in a process involving many firms. Vertical specialization by a factor will refer to a tendency for that factor to carry out a single activity within the productive process of a firm.

Horizontal specialization will refer to a collection of markets, which may be considered as a unit. Here a collection of sellers sell a variety of kinds of commodities (services) to a variety of kinds of buyers. The amount of horizontal specialization will be the average number of kinds of buyers to whom the average sellers sell.

We start our discussion with vertical specialization, that is, with a single assembly-line type of operation. Suppose that production may be described in terms of successive appearances of the object on an assembly line. The object, say, passes through n different states in the course of the process. That is, the production process involves the sequence State 1—Activity 1—State 2—Activity 2 . . . Activity $(n-1)$—State n. We view two sets of inputs, called capital and labor, and consider specialization in terms of this sequence.

In *The Wealth of Nations*, the extreme of specialization contemplates associating with the i'th activity one worker and one machine. In the total absence of division of labor, there will be n activities per worker; and no machines are used. This definition is not very satisfactory. An increased specialization of labor increases average productivity of labor and also total output, whence follows the theorem "The division of labor is limited by the extent of the market." Since an increase in specialization is equivalent to a shift in supply (marginal cost) schedules, the cost of a marginal increase in specialization should equal the marginal revenue from the additional output. Suppose (marginal) divisions of labor classified on the basis of decreasing marginal product, that is increasing marginal cost, and there will be an optimal division of labor. Increased division of labor, in Smith, is associated with the increased possibility of introducing machines. A machine does rapidly what a pair of hands does slowly. Furthermore, the probability of invention increases, the more specialized the pair of hands. Therefore, the more specialized is labor, the greater the expected future rate of technological change. This change alters the market equilibrium associated with an optimal division of labor.

This statement, more sophisticated technically than Smith's, seems to summarize the literature on vertical specialization. It fails,[10] however, to consider the fact that labor and machines have different degrees of spe-

---

[9] This usage has been anticipated in P. Sargant Florence's interesting book, *Investment, Location, and Size of Plant* (Cambridge, 1948), especially in chap. 3.

[10] Apart from a failure to distinguish between hand tools and machines, which need not be labored here.

cialization with respect to any one process, such that the more specialized the one, the less specialized the other.

Imagine a portion of the production process representable in the following scheme. In this section

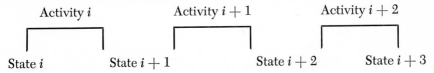

Activity i	Activity $i+1$	Activity $i+2$
State i State $i+1$	State $i+2$	State $i+3$

of the process, the object on the assembly line starts in state i, and after three activities ends in state $i+3$. Imagine a skilled worker who performs all three activities. Each activity involves the use of one machine. For simplicity, we suppose that each machine has two lights. When the green light is on, the worker pulls a green lever, admitting one object into the machine. When the object is processed, a red light flashes on and the worker pulls a red lever, which drops the processed article into the hopper of the next machine.[11] This we will call Technology A. Next suppose this worker replaced by three workers, each of whom performs one operation using one machine. This we call Technology B. It corresponds to "division of labor" as Smith spoke of it (in the classic pin factory example). Finally, we suppose a third situation, Technology C. Here the three machines have been combined into one, tended by a single worker. As before, he has two lights to watch and two levers to pull.

In Technologies A and B each machine performs one activity. In Technologies B and C, each worker performs one activity. In Technology A, however, one worker performs three activities, and in Technology C one machine performs three activities. Thus the following tabulation of specialization may be made:

Technology	*Labor Specialization*	*Machine Specialization*
A	1/3	1
B	1	1
C	1	1/3

Manifestly these three situations are different; vertical specialization is a phenomenon in all cases, but the specialization of labor and of machinery vary in different ways from one case to the next.

One aspect of technological change has indeed been that described by Adam Smith. It is this aspect which Marx and Engels gloomily remark make the workmen "an appendage of the machine, and it is only the most simple, most monotonous, and most easily acquired knack, that is required of him." In contemporary jargon, man becomes "the cheapest non-

---

11 We repeat that we ignore "training." It is not necessary to our argument.

linear servomechanism." It corresponds to the change from *A* to *B*, above.[12]

Even if specialization had increased as much as Smith and Marx suggest, it would not necessarily involve making people into "appendages of the machine." If increased specialization is accompanied by increased training, then the more specialized societies may also be the most educated. Certainly the U.S. experience[13] suggests that the importance of training rises as industrialization advances. In particular, as we will suggest below, "maintenance" workers (who are typically highly trained) increase in importance relative to "production" workers. Moreover, professional and technical personnel grow rapidly in their relative importance, as do clerical and kindred personnel. Thus higher training may more than offset the deleterious effects, if any, of more specialization.[14]

The history of technology deals extensively with what we would call the skill and the training of machines. One aspect of technological change is exemplified by the change from *B* to *C* in our scheme. Here the individual machine becomes more skilled (less specialized) by taking on more activities in the assembly line. This is not the same thing, of course, as the increased "training of machines." The history of servomechanisms discusses the way in which machines have gradually become able to make more decisions. And just as an increase in the "education" of labor can result in increased productivity, given a set of machines, so also an increase in the "education" of machines increases their powers of discriminating, resulting in lower cost, for a given set of workers.[15] If more highly

---

[12] Smith was very much troubled by the conversion of the human input into a servomechanism. "The man whose whole life is spent in performing a few simple operations, of which the effects too are, perhaps, always the same, or very nearly the same, has no occasion to exert his understanding, or to exercise his invention in finding out expedients for removing difficulties which never occur. He naturally loses, therefore, the habit of such exertion, and generally becomes as stupid and ignorant as it it possible for a human creature to become. . . . His dexterity at his own particular trade seems to be acquired at the expense of his intellectual, social, and martial virtues. But in every improved and civilized society this is the state into which the labouring poor, that is, the great body of the people, must necessarily fall, unless government takes some pains to prevent it." Adam Smith, *op. cit.*, pp. 734–35.

[13] Fritz Machlup, *The Production and Distribution of Knowledge in the United States* (Princeton, N.J.: Princeton University Press, 1962), pp. 380–82; and Gladys Palmer and Ann Miller, "The Occupational and Industrial Distribution of Employment, 1910–1950," in W. Haber, F. H. Harbinson, L. R. Klein, and G. L. Palmer (eds.), *Manpower in the United States* (Harper & Bros., 1954), p. 87.

[14] Charles Babbage, *On the Economy of Machinery and Manufactures* (London, 1838) observes (p. 17) that "the higher the (training) required of the workmen in any one (activity) of a manufacture, and the smaller the time during which it is employed, so much the greater will be the advantage of the separating that (activity) from the rest, and devoting one person's attention entirely to it." and (p. 149) "we avoid employing any part of the time of a man who can get eight or ten shillings a day by his skill in tempering needles, in turning a wheel, which can be done for sixpence a day." (Words in parentheses have been changed to conform to the usage in this article.)

[15] It is possible that the eventually decreasing capital/output ratios reported by Leontief, Kuznets, and others are explainable in terms of better educated machines.

trained machines require more highly trained workers, Marx is wrong in saying that increased specialization of labor means reduced training for workers, and consequently their gradual economic and moral deterioration. In fact, greater specialization of labor is offset by greater training.

In the process of technological change, however, the sequence of activities may become irrelevant to the structure of jobs associated with labor and machines. Thus the automatic telephone exchange performs the same functions as the operator of a manual switchboard. However, division of labor has not meant the division of jobs into types corresponding to the individual steps performed by the operator; responding to an outgoing call, recording the address of the call, ascertaining whether the line is busy, etc. These steps are all performed within the machine. A variety of workers' jobs are associated with the machine, but these are not organized in terms of this sequence of steps. The assembly-line metaphor is inadequate, since a single job involves tending the machine with respect to something which influences all stages of the completion of telephone calls.[16]

These two changes in specialization described, respectively, by the classical economists and the technological historians, appear to become nonoperational concepts where machines become so skilled that the job functions of workers no longer are arranged according to the sequence of activities in the process. This situation with respect to labor is an analogue of the situation with respect to tools which existed before the industrial revolution. Then, labor tended to be highly skilled, so that a single worker was associated with an entire process. Tools, however, consisted of hammers, forges, files, saws, etc.; their function was specialized, but it could not be identified with any single position along an assembly-line process, any more than a worker tending an automatic switchboard is associated solely with busy signals. In effect then, 20th-century technology contrasts with earlier technology in this respect; formerly the sequence of activities was associated with a single skilled worker, and tools were specialized, though not ordered with the activities of the worker; today the sequence of activities is associated with a single machine, and workers are specialized, though not ordered with the activities of the machine.[17] Adam Smith's case of division of labor is a special one: workers and machines can be put into a sequence of pairs of which the production line is an example.

---

[16] The American chemical and oil industries possess 50 "maintenance" employees per 100 "production" employees. *Factory Management and Maintenance* (New York: McGraw-Hill, 1958) p. 183.

[17] James Bright, *Automation and Management*, (Boston: Division of Research, Graduate School of Business Administration, Harvard University, 1958). Chapter 12 is concerned in part with this matter, and in part with the question of whether workers of a given degree of specialization require more training (in his terminology *skill*) as technology changes. He also refers to changes in the importance of maintenance workers (i.e., workers not in an ordering with machine activities) and production workers (i.e., workers).

The hypothesis advanced above is a sort of statistical generalization about changes in the vertical specialization of inputs within a firm: technological change, on the average, increases the (vertical) specialization of labor and decreases the (vertical) specialization of machinery.

The citation which gives a title to this paper refers to another, and equally interesting, proposition. Young observes that "Notable as has been the increase in the complexity of the apparatus of living, as shown by the increase in the variety of goods offered in the consumers' markets, the increase in the diversification of intermediate products and of industries manufacturing special products or groups of products has gone even further."[18] That is, technological change leads to decreases in the number of activities performed by the average firm located along an industrial process. It therefore may increase the number of firms. The firm specializes (vertically) and the number of interfirm transactions required to produce a unit of goods for final consumption increases.[19]

Propositions relating to vertical specialization of this sort are frequently related to propositions about the specialization of input factors. In a preindustrial society of unspecialized labor and specialized machines, the boundary between firms in a process was apt to be the boundary between kinds of labor. Stigler cites Allen[20] to the effect that in the 18th century the locks, stocks, and barrels (to name only a few parts) of guns were all made by individual craftsmen, and "gunsmiths" merely ordered the finished parts and had them assembled by special subassembly "firms."

Conversely, in contemporary industry, labor is specialized and machines unspecialized, so that the boundaries between firms in a process are apt to be at the boundaries between the activities of different machines. This principle does not explain why steel mills own their own iron mines, but it may explain why pig iron, steel conversion, and rolling all take place within a single firm.[21] As it became possible to handle hot metal in large quantities, steel conversion and rolling became the function of a single "machine."[22]

---

[18] Young, *op. cit.*, p. 537.

[19] In the context, the common usage for the opposite of vertically specialized would seem to be vertically *integrated*, with *integration* the concept corresponding to *skill*, where the agent is a firm. We have hesitated to use this term here, because it has become associated with issues of competition and monopoly, with which we are not much concerned.

[20] George Stigler, *op. cit.*, p. 193; G. C. Allen, *The Industrial Development of Birmingham and the Black Country, 1860–1927* (London, 1929) pp. 56–57, 116–17. See also the article by John D. Goodman, "The Birmingham Gun Trade," in Samuel Timmins (ed.), *Birmingham and the Midland Hardware District* (London, 1866), pp. 381–431.

[21] S. Fabricant agrees with Stigler that "as an industry grows in size, there is a tendency for it to disintegrate vertically." ("Study of the Size and Efficiency of the American Economy" in E. A. G. Robinson (ed.), *Economic Consequences of the Size of Nations* (London: Macmillan, 1960), p. 49. If so, it might be explainable in terms of gradual branching of assembly lines.

[22] "The Ford Motor Company's engine plant at Cleveland, Ohio, is in a very real

But production processes are not simply linear. They branch. In any linear production process, different inputs converge (as on an assembly line) to make an output. But is also true that if this process is viewed at any particular stage, it may diverge. Thus some coal goes to steel mills, other coal to other users. Some iron is converted into steel, some is not. Some steel is rolled, some is cast; some rolled steel is used for automobiles, other rolled steel is not, and so on.

It is sometimes argued[23] that technological change means decreased vertical specialization of equipment (technological interrelatedness); a firm cannot sell intermediate products because these have only a momentary existence within a multiactivity machine. If the final product of the firm cannot profitably be sold because of a price change, the firm cannot retain a share in a market for the intermediate product. A firm with more specialized equipment would be able to sell such intermediate output. Hence, if industrialization (and technological change) means increased skill (less specialization) of machines, it makes the "more advanced" firms less able to react to price changes, since they cannot salvage a part of their equipment for use in selling intermediate products.

For example, Italy and Flanders, Hicks has suggested,[24] regressed from an industrial to a preindustrial condition in the 16th and 17th centuries, because their textile industries were displaced by foreign competition, and they could use their manufacturing facilities for no other purpose. In contrast, American metalworking plants shifted from guns to sewing machines to bicycles to motorcycles and finally to automobiles in the half century before the first world war.[25] This contrast results from the difference in "flexibility" in the use of machines. Italian and Flemish industry could make only textiles (or semifinished textiles). American industry could use its plant to make a succession of quite different commodities.

Perhaps an even more pertinent case concerns the American producers of textile *machinery* who demonstrated great versatility in adapting their output to changing demand requirements throughout the 19th century. The resourcefulness and ingenuity of the textile machinery producers in fact played a major role not only in the mechanization of textiles but in the application of techniques of "machinofacture" to other industries, including machine tools, locomotives, firearms, and agricultural machinery.[26]

---

sense one enormous specialized machine tool intended to take raw metal, cast it, and machine it into finished engine blocks and heads, by means of fully automatic and automated machinery." Robert Woodbury, *History of the Grinding Machine* (Cambridge, The Technology Press, 1959), p. 121.

[23] Marvin Frankel, "Obsolescence and Technical Change in a Maturing Economy," *American Economic Review* (June, 1955), pp. 296–319; Don Gordon, comment thereon, and Marvin Frankel, "Reply," *American Economic Review* (September, 1956), pp. 646–56.

[24] *Essays in World Economics* (Oxford, 1959), pp. 173–74. The example is also found in Carlo Cipolla, "The Decline of Italy," *Economic History Review*, Second Series, Vol. V, pp. 178 ff.

[25] Rosenberg, *op. cit.*

[26] See John L. Hayes, *American Textile Machinery* (Cambridge, 1879), pp. 55–62.

The contrast between the fate of the handloom weavers and the producers of the machinery which eventually displaced them is, we think, highly instructive.

Ceteris paribus, the closer firms are to the final product stage, the greater their vulnerability to shifts in consumer demand for specific commodities.[27] Resources at "higher order" stages of production, by contrast, are engaged in producing intermediate products which are eventually employed as inputs in a very large number of final products. A striking feature of 19th-century industry is the extent to which resources and facilities devoted to machine production and metal processing more generally became skilled in the production of intermediate products which could be used throughout the economy. They came to possess a pool of skill and knowledge, moreover, which (in spite of the typically limited range of outputs produced at any moment in time) enabled them to shift from the production of one sort of machine to another with comparatively minor modifications. Indeed, we find here one of the most important cases of a single learning process lying at the heart of economic development. What was learned was the capacity to produce and employ machinery over a wide range of productive activity.[28]

By simple extension this analysis may help to explain the greater resiliency of industrial economies to secular changes in demand by comparison with the often-cited less favorable experiences of underdeveloped countries.[29] Industrial economies have a much higher proportion of their resources engaged in the production of intermediate goods. However, all intermediate goods are not equally important. One particular class, machines (including, of course, the machine-producing machines), is of the greatest strategic importance. The facilities, skills, and techniques acquired with this particular range of intermediate products constitute a major determinant of an economy's capacity to adapt to external changes and to undertake technological innovations on its own initiative. An important dimension of the development process can thus be isolated by examining the disproportionate growth of specific intermediate products.

The discussion so far has assumed more or less explicitly that it was possible to arrange all production processes into "assembly lines," within

---

[27] We are disregarding here cyclical phenomena and therefore also the well-known short-run instability of the capital goods sector. Our interest and emphasis here is upon secular shifts.

[28] The suggestive analysis by Edith Penrose of the economics of diversification and, in particular, her treatment of the firm as a "pool of resources," is highly relevant to a further exploration of this subject. See Edith Penrose, *The Theory of the Growth of the Firm* (Oxford: Basil Blackwell, 1959), especially chap. vii.

[29] ". . . once a country has reached a certain stage of development, it does appear to acquire (or to be able to acquire) a kind of resilience against changes in its comparative advantages. One of the great advantages of 'advanced' specialisms is that they carry with them the *capacity* of doing other things; thus, if an 'advanced' country is driven off one specialism, it does not find it insuperably difficult to grow another." J. R. Hicks, *op. cit.*, p. 173.

a firm, or else in some sequence of firms. But it is by no means clear that such orderings are meaningful in a modern economy. Thus fuel oil may be a final consumer good (if it heats a house), an item of fixed cost (if it heats a factory), or an item of marginal cost (if it powers a truck). A board may be used as a consumer good, if it is used as a shelf in a house; as a capital good, if it is used to make a factory partition; as an intermediate good, if it is used for crating a product; as a raw material, if it is used for furniture, and so on. The attempt to sort production processes into a set of assembly lines seems to create extreme difficulties.

On the other hand, the concept of "raw material" or "intermediate product" or "finished goods" may be economically meaningful, used in the context of a particular industry. Thus coal is a collection of different solid fuels, some of which are used by households, some by businesses, and so on. Coal is one of the inputs of power plants, and as such competes with fuel oil, natural gas, and so forth. It is not economic nonsense to consider the market for fuels used by power plants; nor is it nonsense to observe that some plants may be designed to use a single type of coal (are completely specialized) while others may use many types of coal, or may even sometimes use solid fuel, and sometimes liquid fuel or even gas, depending on price. Such plants, with respect to their inputs, are less specialized than power plants which use only one type of coal.

It is in connection with situations of this sort that the concept of "horizontal specialization" becomes useful. A situation involving horizontal specialization exists whenever commodities may be grouped, either because they are all sold by a definable group of sellers, or bought by a definable group of buyers. The concept of "a definable group" frequently overlaps or coincides with some technological considerations. In fact, such groupings are unavoidable if economists are to talk about entities such as "the coal industry," "the steel industry," the "chemicals industry," which sell literally thousands of different commodities differing only "slightly" one from the other. In discussing horizontal specialization, we are really talking about specialization in cases where firms produce a range of products, or buy a range of products which are very much alike with respect to some observable (economic or noneconomic) criterion.[30]

To return to the problem raised at the outset of the paper, it would seem that firms which are less specialized horizontally are more complex; one aspect of complexity, then, relates precisely to the extent of horizontal specialization, so that except as an alternative to the rather barbarous "horizontal skill", it is redundant.

Consider the set of markets for different types of steel. Sellers are steel producers, and buyers steel users. With regard to this set of markets, a group of sellers (say sellers of one country) is specialized if the average number of types of steel sold per firm is small. A set of buyers (say

---

[30] In current usage, a firm whose output is not specialized has diversified. We shall use skill in place of diversification to stress the symmetry of our argument.

buyers of one country) is specialized, if, on the average, its members buy, on the average, a small number of kinds of steel. Speaking of this market, Kindleberger asserts that "great specialization can be achieved only at the cost of flexibility." By this he means that British firms, in particular, bought only Bessemer steel and not Siemens-Martin acid steel. Hence, when the price of the latter dropped, the less specialized (German) firms could substitute cheaper grades, while the more specialized (British) firms could not.[31]

III. Implications for the Development Process

The foregoing argument has been mainly taxonomic, but the purpose has not been taxonomic. We shall therefore suggest several conjectures about problems of major importance to economic history and economic development, to illustrate the kinds of problems to which our theory of specialization applies. Limitations of space and time preclude an extended discussion. We shall discuss only one group of problems in this paper, but we suggest that the others, too, might more readily be solved with the theoretical apparatus presented here than with the more traditional Marshallian techniques. In listing the following assertions, we are not passing judgement upon their validity, but only calling attention to their economic interest.

1. In early stages of a country's industrialization, firms tend to specialize; in later stages they diversify.

2. The more industrialized a country is, the less its dependence upon particular sources of materials (the less specialization with respect to inputs).

3. The more industrialized a country is, the more skilled (the less specialized) its machines become (backward countries use relatively simple machinery).

4. The more industrialized a country is, the more specialized labor becomes within the production process, and the less the horizontal specialization of labor is (on any job, the worker carries out fewer activities, but the larger the number of industries in which this job exists).

5. The more industrialized a country is, the more diversified will be the composition of its exports.[32]

---

[31] C. P. Kindleberger, "Foreign Trade and Economic Growth," *Economic History Review*, Second Series, Vol. XIV (December, 1961), p. 299.

[32] We took from Joseph Coppock, *International Economic Stability* (New York: McGraw-Hill, 1962), Table A–2, figures on 1957 per capita incomes, on the one hand, and the largest, and three largest exports as percent of total exports on the other, for 62 countries. These turned out to have negative correlation of about .25, which is significantly different from zero at about the .03 level. It is thus a fact (as economic facts go) that the more developed a country was, the *less* was its export specialization. It is not a fact of overwhelming importance, since this type of specialization would "explain" only about 6 percent of the variations in real income.

6. Specialized firms are more vulnerable to changes in demand, *ceteris paribus,* the closer their output is to the final product stage in a production process.

We shall introduce our discussion with a classical problem in the theory of probability: the problem of gambler's ruin. In brief, it is shown that if two gamblers have equal probabilities of winning a game, the gambler with the smaller initial capital will, on the average, be ruined before the gambler with the larger initial capital.[33]

Suppose conditions of pure competition in world markets, in which there is a large number of commodities, the prices of which move up or down at random from one date to the next. If inflation or deflation does not exist, the probability of increases and of decreases in individual prices are equal. Suppose exporters face steady domestic costs, and product prices are fixed in world markets. Then at any moment for each good there is a certain price drop which would force an exporter to stop producing. If an exporter produces several commodities, then he will go out of business when all prices reach these shutdown levels. From this point of view, the total amount by which prices must decrease in order to drive the exporter out of business is comparable to the gambler's initial capital. One firm will have a longer expected "duration of game to ruin" than another if it starts with a larger initial capital. This may happen because initially its costs are relatively low. Alternatively, it may have a larger initial capital because (even though its costs are no lower) it has a greater number of exportable commodities for sale. In this case, the reasoning of the gambler's ruin problem will apply with one proviso: that the probabilities of increases or decreases in the individual commodities are independent.

This reasoning, so far, merely suggests that under somewhat restrictive assumptions, skilled (horizontally diversified) firms are more apt to survive a given length of time than specialized firms. It may, however, be turned into a proposition about economic development. Suppose that as a country industrializes, the average skill (diversification) of firms increases. Then at any particular moment, the firms of less industrialized countries stand a greater probability of ruin than those of more industrialized countries. In other words, the earlier a country has started to industrialize, relative to another, the more likely it is to remain at a competitive advantage in the future.[34]

Suppose, moreover, that the probabilities of price changes for different commodities are related in the following way: the more industrialized the country, the less likely that a price change for one commodity will be

---

[33] William Feller. *An Introduction to Probability Theory and its Application* (second ed.; New York: Wiley, 1957), Vol. 1, chap. xiv.

[34] See Edward Ames and Nathan Rosenberg, "Changing Technological Leadership and Economic Growth," *Economic Journal,* March, 1963.

associated with a similar change for another.[35] Then the less industrialized a country is, the more it resembles a one-commodity economy even if it actually produces many commodities; the more industrialized it is, the closer it approaches the conditions of the "gambler's ruin problem." This possibility is known in economic development literature as the "dependence of underdeveloped countries on a few specialized raw materials."

A second problem relates to the decline of the handloom weavers and the Luddite movement. Suppose that as industrialization proceeds, individual job descriptions in plants become more specialized, but individual specialized jobs spread through a wider variety of industries. (Vertical specialization of labor increases while horizontal specialization declines.) Then at an early stage of industrialization, workers belonging to a particular trade are highly skilled, but lack alternative employment; at a later stage they are less skilled, but have alternative employment. Hence, on the gambler's ruin principle, labor, due to its job immobility, actually has more to lose from technological change in a backward than in an industrial economy. Luddites, then, are a phenomenon primarily of early periods of industrialization.[36]

We have suggested above that labor has become more specialized and machinery more skilled. If the skilled workers of early industrialization become "Luddites" when confronted with new technology, we might expect the owners of skilled machinery to become Luddites under modern conditions. There is no obvious way in which they have shown increased "political" objections to technological change. If they have not, we suggest that it would be interesting to know why not. One conjecture would be that for firms, the increased skill is two-dimensional; increased vertical skill makes an industry vulnerable, while increased horizontal skill does not. If the assembly line view of an economy is discarded, most firms will be viewed as producing mixtures of intermediate and finished goods. Then a technological change will not cause an entire industry to perish

---

[35] It will be recalled that the business cycle is being disregarded here.

[36] Our conclusion is here reached on the basis of exploring one dimension only of the process of industrialization. The decline in worker protest movements is also further reinforced by other phenomena associated with industrialization. Thus, industrialization appears to bring with it the growth of organizations and institutional procedures for the orderly settlement of disputes. All highly industrialized societies in the noncommunist world possess procedures for the channelization and resolution of worker grievances, collective bargaining machinery for the determination of wages, hours, promotion, layoffs, fringe benefits, etc., and recourse to specific agencies for the mediation and arbitration of disputes. Therefore, worker protest may be regarded (contrary to Marx) as reaching its peak in the earlier rather than the later stages of industrialization, when workers have not yet adjusted to the discipline and coercions of factory life, when the conflict between the old and new forms of economic organizations creates the greatest psychological stresses, when the worker has not yet acquired the vested interests in the form of rising per capita incomes eventually generated by an industrial society, and when the machinery for the resolution of industrial conflict has not yet been developed. Cf. Clark Kerr *et al.*, *Industrialism and Industrial Man* (Cambridge, Mass.: Harvard University Press, 1960), esp. chaps. 7 and 8.

(as the Italian and Flemish textile industries did), but will only affect some part of its markets or processes. Industrialization, then, appears to increase "flexibility" (for otherwise machine owners would be Luddites). This word, in deliberate quotation marks, is generally meaningless. We suggest that "flexible" may mean "having little horizontal specialization." If so, here is another real problem to be dealt with in terms of specialization.

The foregoing two paragraphs will, we hope, prove annoying to economic theorists and historians alike. To the former we shall answer: There is no adequate explanation of either the equilibrium or the optimal number of commodities[37] used by a firm or an economy, and the theory of specialization has hardly changed since Adam Smith. If these propositions are wrong in theory, we hope theorists will become annoyed enough to correct us.

To the latter we shall say: a variety of assertions are made in the literature about the appearance and disappearance of industries, labor skills, and machine processes. These changes may occur as a result of noneconomic phenomena. (For instance, the Middle East stopped being a farm area when its irrigation was destroyed by war and salinization. Pennsylvania stopped mining iron because Minnesota suddenly turned out to have very large deposits.) But in part they have occurred for economic reasons. It would be helpful to know, as a matter of fact, when the appearance and disappearance of industries was due to economic factors; and how much can actually be known about the extent of specialization at various periods of history. The assertions cited in this paper may not be true, but they are interesting. If they are true they have important consequences.

Conclusions

The conclusions to be drawn from this analysis are in part of a theoretical nature: it is possible to apply a consistent set of terms to problems involving the number of products produced by firms; the number of inputs used by firms; and the amount of vertical integration achieved by firms. This terminology reveals a number of interesting problems which are ordinarily glossed over by theories which assume, in the main, single-product firms producing homogeneous, divisible products for final consumers. On purely theoretical grounds, these problems are interesting enough to warrant further exploration of the concepts advanced here.

In addition, however, the analysis raises certain practical considerations concerning the establishment of new firms in underdeveloped countries. A developing country necessarily recapitulates some of the history of countries which have developed before it. For example, indices of per capita income, percent of population in manufacturing, etc., will neces-

---

[37] Since everything which has a price is a commodity, the optimal number of commodities includes an optimal number of processes.

sarily follow, in some sense, the path of earlier countries. It is natural to consider whether its indices of specialization and skill must repeat the history of predecessors.

Consider the suggestion advanced about labor and machines. It has seemed that the first effect of industrialization in the West was to decrease the skill (increase the specialization) of labor; and only later to increase the training required of labor. In the case of machinery (apart from the use of machines to do heavy work), the tendency has been to increase first the skill and later the "training" of machines. If industrialization follows that pattern generally, it might well be the case that developing countries could postpone the creation of an educated labor force until relatively late in their program. If, on the other hand, it is possible for the developing country to bypass certain stages of the history of predecessors, the date for an intensive educational effort should be advanced. Moreover, "technological policy" might well militate in favor of the adoption of relatively simple industrial processes in the first case, and in favor of "truly modern" plants only in the second.

A second group of problems would bear upon protectionism in developing countries. If, indeed, diversification of output increases with industrialization, and if diversification decreases the risk of failure of firms in a world market, then firms in a developing country face relatively high probabilities of failure in any competition with firms of developed countries, and can succeed only if they are protected—even if comparative advantage may work in their favor in some sense. But we cannot argue that this view is correct. It may be merely another in the long literature of plausible but indefensible claims about development processes.

Finally, we have laid considerable stress upon the importance of firms which make some mixture of intermediate and final goods. The problems of such firms tend to disappear in the literature which deals with national accounts, i.e., final demand. But it may well be that a key to industrialization lies in the development of firms which use a common technology to make both intermediate and final goods: such firms are efficient means of diffusing new techniques through an economy. If it is possible for a developing country to assist in the growth of such firms, it may have a powerful instrument for economic growth. We do not suggest that such assistance can in fact be offered. We do suggest that the kinds and degrees of specialization suitable to an economy may depend upon the level of development of that economy; and that attempts to establish unsuitable specialization patterns may lead to unviable economic organizations.

2. Changing Technological Leadership and Industrial Growth[*]

Edward Ames and Nathan Rosenberg[1]
Purdue University

Although this science contains indeed a number of correct and very excellent precepts, there are nevertheless, so many others, and these either injurious or superfluous, mingled with the former, that it is almost quite as difficult to effect a severance of the true from the false as it is to extract a Diana or a Minerva from a rough block of marble.

—DESCARTES

THIS PAPER EXPLORES afresh the thesis that there is (or has been) a net penalty incurred by countries which have been innovators. A considerable literature explores this "penalty for taking the lead" or "handicap of the early start."[2] Despite several controversies, in which the thesis has never been properly proved, nor even adequately formulated, it continues to be stated as a self-evident truth.[3] Since the thesis deals with important issues,

---

[*] Reprinted from the *Economic Journal*, Vol. LXXIII, (March, 1963), pp. 13–29.
[1] Edited by C. F. Carter and E. A. G. Robinson—assisted by Robert C. O. Matthews. The authors are grateful to two of their colleagues, June Flanders and Jonathan R. T. Hughes, for useful comments on an earlier draft.
[2] The subject has most recently been examined and the earlier literature partially reviewed in C. P. Kindleberger, "Obsolescence and Technical Change," *Oxford University Institute of Statistics Bulletin* (August, 1961), pp. 281–97. The most important earlier references are: Thorstein Veblen, *Imperial Germany and the Industrial Revolution;* F. R. J. Jervis, "The Handicap of Britain's Early Start," *The Manchester School*, Vol. XV, pp. 112–22; Marvin Frankel, "Obsolescence and Technical Change in a Maturing Economy," *American Economic Review* (June, 1955), pp. 296–319; Don Gordon, "Obsolescence and Technological Change: Comment," and Marvin Frankel, "Reply," *American Economic Review* (September, 1956), pp. 646–56; Ingvar Svennilson, *Growth and Stagnation in the European Economy* (Geneva: United Nations Economic Commission for Europe, 1954).
[3] E.g., W. W. Rostow, *The Stages of Economic Growth* (Cambridge, Eng.: Cambridge University Press, 1960), p. 70. On the other hand, K. Mandelbaum, *The Industrialization of Backward Areas* (2d ed., New York: Kelley and Millman, 1955), p. 3, discards the thesis on a rather casual basis. Mandelbaum appears to believe that once a country has been left behind it becomes increasingly difficult even to make a start.

we think it analytically worthwhile to state formally and in rather general terms the conditions under which the several forms of the thesis might be valid. This procedure serves to illuminate several aspects of the growth process, and to pose new questions for examiners.

Writers who have claimed there is a penalty in taking the lead have really only discussed one or two isolated phenomena relevant to this broader question of whether or not such a penalty exists. A simple formalization of the problem will place the entire issue in better perspective and make possible a critical examination of its implications.

We insist at the outset that even if (1) there are *some* penalties for taking the lead, it does not necessarily follow that (2) on balance, late starters are better off than early starters. Writers, however, who start off with the initial (rather innocuous) assertion often slip, unknowingly, into the latter proposition, which, we shall argue, is extremely difficult to defend.

Let us suppose two countries, Eastland and Westland, identically endowed at the time of Noah with population and resources. Suppose that Eastland remains in an agrarian, underdeveloped state until the year 1900; at that time it is in exactly the condition Westland was in 1700. Westland, however, began to industrialize in 1700, so that by 1900 it is an urban, factory society. We propose to discuss the thesis, developed by writers from Veblen through Kindleberger, that Eastland can develop more rapidly and/or to a higher level after 1900 than can Westland. In Kindleberger's words, "there may be a penalty in the early start, if institutions adapt themselves to a given technology, and if static patterns of capital replacement develop as habits."[4]

It is certainly a fact that the countries whose industries have grown fastest in the past 100 years are not those which grew most rapidly in the preceding century. The leading industrial countries of the Middle Ages— Brabant, Lombardy, Venetia—have never regained their former position in the world, any more than Egypt has regained rule over the grain trade. Certain special circumstances have intervened—e.g., the United Kingdom began running out of cheap coal about 1900[5]—but it is an open question whether such factors are exclusively responsible for the facts. It is natural

---

[4] C. P. Kindleberger, *op. cit.,* p. 282. The concluding sentence of H. J. Habakkuk's highly interesting new book, *American and British Technology in the 19th Century* (Cambridge, Eng.: Cambridge University Press, 1962) reads: "Such lags as there were in the adoption of new methods in British industry can be adequately explained by economic circumstances, by the complexity of her industrial structure and the slow growth of her output, and *ultimately by her early and long-sustained start as an industrial power*" (italics added).

[5] Even the adequacy of a country's resource endowment, after all, depends on what industries use it, and hence on world prices and other economic facts. Partly, however, resource endowment depends upon technology; this is a branch of knowledge which increases in a way still largely unknown, but certainly not wholly dependent upon economic events. See Edward Ames, "Research, Invention, Development and Innovation," *American Economic Review* (June, 1961), pp. 370–81.

to inquire whether any economic theory of "leadership" in industry can be formulated. Is the historical fact that a displaced leader does not regain its primacy an accident? Would it be natural to expect leadership to rotate among different countries?

The problem involves two distinct concepts: a country's output and a country's technology. Underdeveloped countries are, as a matter of fact, poor (they have small outputs per capita) and backward (they use technology which others have abandoned). It is perhaps possible for a country with a backward technology to be wealthy, or for a poor country to be technologically advanced, but these possibilities are seldom realized. The connection between the levels of output and of technology must therefore be distinguished conceptually in dealing with real situations in which they are closely related.

With regard to either output or technology, it is necessary to distinguish levels, amounts of change, and rates of change. The fact that a country today is changing rapidly implies nothing, in principle, about its level of development either today or at some date in the future. A failure to distinguish between levels and rates of change may lead to interesting welfare results. If a country has a choice (in some sense) between developing for a century at a slow rate up to a level L_1, or else stagnating for half a century and then developing at a rapid rate to a higher level L_2, then its decision is based upon the familiar balancing of present and future satisfactions, with this peculiarity, that several generations are involved.

The importance of the latecomer theses may be illustrated by what is to us a pair of *reductio ad absurdum* propositions, which are sometimes almost seriously advanced:[6]

1. It is sometimes alleged that the reason industrial output in Germany and

---

[6] In this discussion, as elsewhere in the paper, we assume that all countries have the same resource endowments. Obviously the discussion is completely irrelevant if the differences between pairs of countries are explainable by differences in resource endowment. Thus, to us both the stocks of plant and technology must be variables, rather than resources, although for some purposes they can certainly be treated as resources. Our practice, in this paper, of enclosing resource endowment in the *ceteris paribus* pound does not necessarily reflect our own view of the importance of this factor. We merely find it here a convenient assumption, since we are attempting to meet on its own grounds a form of analysis which relegates resource endowment to an insignificant role. There has been a strong tendency in recent years to downgrade the independent significance of natural resources in the development process. Thus, the papers presented to the Conference on Natural Resources and Economic Growth, held at Ann Arbor, Michigan, April 7–9, 1960 (reprinted in *Natural Resources and Economic Growth*, J. J. Spengler, ed.) approach the subject from a wide variety of interests, but stress two themes: (1) the powerful impact of classical economic theory (particularly the Ricardian–Malthusian variant) has led to a vast exaggeration of the relative importance of natural resources and the constraints which they impose upon an economy's development; (2) the relative importance of natural resources is a declining function of development itself. As Kindleberger puts it, "It may be taken for granted that some minimum of resources is necessary for economic growth, that, other things being equal, more resources are better than fewer, and that the more a country grows the less it needs resources, since it gains capacity to substitute labor and especially capital for them" (p. 172).

Japan has grown more rapidly, and has tended to become cheaper than output in the United States and the United Kingdom is that bombing attacks during World War II destroyed a mass of obsolete equipment in the former countries, giving these "latecomers" an advantage by paving the way for more modern techniques. If this argument were valid, a feasible form of U.S. foreign economic assistance would then be the systematic bombing of the cities of our economically developed allies, in order to further their economic development.[7]

2. If an underdeveloped ally, envious of Japan or fearful of Communist China, should wish to industrialize, the United States should urge upon it the slogan, "mañana!" For the later it begins, and the more backward it is when it begins, the sooner and the farther it can outstrip its competitors. "Industrialize tomorrow, industrialize yesterday, but never industrialize today," is a paraphrase of a Red Queen, but it should perhaps be a U.S. slogan.[8]

We suspect that such policies as these would somehow be unsympathetically received by their intended beneficiaries. On the other hand, the absurdity of a misstated theory should not imply the incorrectness of a properly stated one. It is useful to see under what conditions a "theory of the late starter" might be correct.

Suppose we were able to quantify the concept of a "state of technology" so that we could locate three different states, A, B, and C on a map, in such a way that we could measure the distances $A-B$, $B-C$, and $A-C$. It would be convenient if all these points were on a single line; but if they were, and technological change were thus one-dimensional, all the interesting features of latecomer theses would automatically be disproved, as later discussion will show. For expository purposes we assume a two-dimensional technology which can be represented diagrammatically. Any movement to the north or east in our diagram represents improved technology. An origin is assumed to the southwest. The three states, A, B, and C may then be represented as follows:

---

[7] Not only are people found who argue that economies may benefit from mass destruction; one author appears to argue that even armies do. "The disaster which the British suffered at Dunkirk in 1940 served one useful purpose. It swept the slate clean, for the British Army had lost all its equipment in the evacuation. It taught them what would and what would not do, in attempting to defend their Island against the Luftwaffe and perhaps the Wehrmacht, should actual invasion come. Out of the bitter experience came improved designs for planes and tanks, and enormously stepped-up requirements" (Courtney Robert Hall, *History of American Industrial Science* [New York, 1959], p. 387). Habakkuk has suggested that differences in economic performance in the years after World War II may be explained, in part, by considerations of ideological and emotional reinforcement, which, in turn, are a consequence of the war. "In our own day, the need to restore economies shattered by war has fired Europeans with a fervour for the task—a fervour which, together with the disruption of old routines by the war, goes some way to explain why, since 1945, France and Germany have grown more rapidly than countries like Britain and the U.S.A., which have not had to meet the challenge of rebuilding large parts of their industrial capacity from scratch" (Habakkuk, *op. cit.*, p. 219).

[8] Robert Campbell, *Soviet Economic Growth* (Cambridge, Mass.: The Riverside Press, 1960), in discussing the Soviet attempt at rapid industrialization, states that: "Their task was not complicated by the presence of existing plants and an already familiar technology, and they could build a modern industry from the ground up" (p. 165).

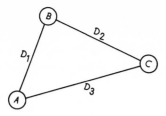

We now say that an economic activity at A is "underdeveloped," one at B is "developed but obsolete," and one at C is "developed and progressive." As an empirical matter, we shall assert that a country at C produces more than one at B, and a country at B produces more than one at A. This assertion is not, however, a logical necessity. Now consider two economic entities, one at A and one at B. When will that at A move to C while that at B will not? Second, assuming that both will eventually get to C, under what conditions (if any) will that starting from A (the underdeveloped entity) reach C before that starting from B (the developed entity)?

Let us provisionally assume that two economies possess the attributes of two firms. This assumption will make it possible to talk about some aspects of the thesis. But a part of the literature on "the late start" associates the problem with factors outside any single firm, so that the comparison of a pair of firms does not exhaust it. It will later become necessary, then, to consider how the corporate structure of two economies (one at A and one at B) may complicate the problem.

An enterprise at an arbitrary point P on the map shown above will move to a point P' if it profits from doing so; that is, we associate with an arbitrary point P a revenue Γ_p and a cost c_p, so that profit $\mathrm{II}_p = \Gamma_p - c_p$ at point P. The selection of a particular technology means that $\mathrm{II}_p > \mathrm{II}_{p'}$, so that technology P is preferred to any other technology P'. If P is optimal, then it is optimal both in respect to "more advanced" and "more backward" technologies in the neighborhood of P.

Now we return to A, the underdeveloped, and B, the developed but obsolete firms, and consider their movement to a developed and progressive point C. Assume the two firms are purely competitive, so that prices may be taken as given. Then we may associate with the three points cost functions $C_A(x)$, $C_B(x)$, and $C_C(x)$, where x represents output. In terms of conventional thinking about technology, we assume that $C_A(x) > C_B(x) > C_C(x)$ for every relevant level of output x. Thus if a firm is confronted with given, perfectly elastic demand curves, it selects among the profit functions $\mathrm{II}_A(x)$, $\mathrm{II}_B(x) = \mathrm{II}_A(x) + (C_A(x) - C_B(x))$, and $\mathrm{II}_C(x) = \mathrm{II}_B(x) + (C_B(x) - C_C(x)) = \mathrm{II}_A(x) + (C_A(x) - C_C(x))$. On this assumption, the cost (and hence the profit) of producing at technology C is the same, regardless of whether the producer has always been at C, whether he is now at C but was formerly at B, or whether he is now at C but was formerly at A. In this case the inequalities $C_A(x) > C_B(x)$

$> C_C(x)$ will ensure that all producers will adopt technology C (unless, of course, there is a technology C' which is superior to C).[9]

A portion of the latecomer literature is based upon propositions about how the movements to C from A and B will take place. They are all based upon advantages which A is alleged to have over B.

A "weak" statement of this sort says: A and B will both move to C. But the time which A takes to reach C will be less than the time which B spent in getting from A's condition to C. (This statement does not imply that A will reach C first, but only that it will travel faster on the "journey" to C than B.)[10]

In part, the weak statement depends on the assertion that the latecomer need not repeat the mistakes of its predecessors. The United States built an extensive canal system, which it replaced by railroads, and it is replacing its railroads by motor roads. The latecomer will certainly avoid the canals, and probably the railroads. It is for this reason that in our diagram we show a route from A to C which does not pass through B. But this formulation as yet does not explain why the latecomer would use only highways, while the United States would retain the (developed but obsolete) railroad. It is necessary to explain why the latecomer may reach an advanced technology which the developed but obsolete firm will not adopt.[11]

---

[9] A. Gerschenkron, "Economic Backwardness in Historical Perspective," in B. F. Hoselitz, (ed.), *The Progress of Underdeveloped Areas* (Chicago, 1952), p. 6, argues that apart from "existing institutions," such as serfdom or political disunification, the more backward is a country, the more it gains from development. A. Nove, *The Soviet Economy* (New York: Frederick A. Praeger, 1961) asserts that "A further very important 'advantage' in the growth race is backwardness itself . . . ." (p. 300).

[10] If a country's welfare depends (at any time) upon the level, rather than the rate of change in its output or consumption, statements of this sort have nothing to do with the welfare implications of particular development patterns.

[11] This weak statement does not explicitly consider the possibility that even false starts can yield some advantage to the early comer; e.g., the *Great Eastern* was a spectacular commercial failure, but British industry may have learned something useful from building her. The latecomer may not have to "produce" new knowledge and new techniques, but he does have to produce the skills required to take advantage of existing technology. Whereas exploration and pioneering generate costs which are avoidable by the latecomer, they also generate many other forces which are essential to further economic growth. Indeed, one may argue that industrialization is, in large measure, a learning process. The capital stock of any economy includes the acquired skills—technical, managerial, professional—in short, the "intangible capital" embodied in its living population. This "stock" of intangible capital was accumulated, in large part, as part of the process of exploration and pioneering in the country taking the lead. (See T. Schultz, "Investment in Man: An Economist's View," *Social Science Review* (June, 1959), pp. 109–17; T. Schultz, "Investment in Human Capital," *American Economic Review* (March, 1961), pp. 1–17; Richard B. Goode, "Adding to the Stock of Physical and Human Capital," *American Economic Review Papers and Proceedings* (May, 1959), pp. 147–55; S. Kuznets, "Problems in Comparison of Economic Trends," in S. Kuznets, *et al.* (eds.), *Economic Growth: Brazil, India and Japan*, pp. 3–28; A. Hirschman, *The Strategy of Economic Development*, esp. chap. 1.) Furthermore, such skills, once acquired, constitute a major portion of an economy's capital stock. Astonishment at the rapid rates of postwar recovery in Germany

The latecomer may well be able to avoid a further cost incurred by the pioneer. An "early starter" may proliferate a wide variety of standards and specifications which later become difficult to change. It is in the nature of pioneering that exploration takes place on many fronts. A diversity of standards and specifications is often created which is, in effect, a "residue" deposited upon the structure of the economy. This unnecessary diversity may in turn hamper the achievement of economies of large-scale production in, for example, industry *B* which produces an intermediate (or capital) good which is an input for industry *A*.

Thus, in the production of railway locomotives in the United States in the mid-19th century, makers of locomotives found themselves producing to a wide range of specifications for different railroad companies, each of which laid down precise standards of workmanship (many of which were determined by historical "accidents") to suit its own needs.[12] The result was a considerable reduction in the economies of large-scale production which a more highly standardized product would have permitted.

One real advantage of the late starter may be the clear perception of the advantages of standardization, and therefore the early adoption of uniform standards. The pioneering country, on the other hand, may be able to adopt uniform standards, but due to technological interrelatedness only at a substantial cost, at later stages of its development.[13]

A "moderate" latecomer statement may also be found: if today *A* and

---

and Japan is due, in part, to persistent failure to give appropriate recognition to the importance of intangible "human capital." A demolished Hamburg in 1945 was in no sense reduced to the equivalent of a Bombay or a Calcutta. (As related miscalculation, even the massive R.A.F. bombing raids upon Hamburg in the summer of 1943 had a much more limited impact in reducing the city's contribution to German wartime production than had been estimated at the time. See the various reports by the U.S. Strategic Bombing Survey, European War, especially the overall report (U.S. Government, 1945).)

[12] Charles H. Fitch in a "Report on the Manufactures of Interchangeable Mechanism," *Tenth Census of the U.S.* (1880), Vol. II, p. 47, points out that the early standardization of equipment by each railroad made it difficult for locomotive manufacturers to standardize their output at a later date, since the adoption of standardization by manufacturers would cause a period of mixed standards among the users of their products, and hence high repair and maintenance costs. See also Kindleberger, *op. cit.*, pp. 284–91. In somewhat analogous fashion, Svennilson attributes the backwardness of the British steel industry and its failure to achieve an optimum size plant in the interwar years, in part, to the failure to achieve more standardization in the steel-using industries. Svennilson argues (*op. cit.*, p. 125) that plants were small and costs were high in the steel industry because sellers were unable to influence buyers, who insisted on very specialized qualities of steel. He admits that mass-produced low-cost steel might have led buyers to revise their policies; but he fails, in our opinion, to ask a reasonable question: Why did new and integrated firms not enter the industry to displace the inefficient plants already existing?

[13] Habakkuk (*op. cit.*, p. 185), in attempting to account for British failure to exploit technological possibilities more rapidly in the 19th century, suggests that "because labour was abundant, the proposals for uniformity in the dimensions and fitting of machinery, put forward by Whitworth, were very slow to be adopted." Cf. Joseph Whitworth, *On a Uniform System of Screw Threads,* communicated to the Institute of Civil Engineers, 1841.

B both start toward C, A (the less developed country) will reach C first. In other words, there will be a change in leadership. This conclusion is apparently reached in one of two ways. One way is to assert that as a country develops, its rate of development slows down. If A is sufficiently backward, its rate of growth can be so great that it can overtake B.

This statement contains a logical weakness. Suppose that there is a decreasing relation between the level of a country's development and its rate of change. Then any country at a given "distance," technologically, from C, will be developing at a given rate. By the time A has reached a level of technology no farther from C than B's starting point, it will have slowed down to B's rate of development. Therefore, B will necessarily reach C first, as it had a shorter distance to travel.[14]

The defect is not *necessarily* fatal. For suppose that a very drastic change in technology occurs in 1900. Then it may be that by 1950 B's technology is completely obsolete with reference to what is needed for the year 2000. Then the distance which B must travel to reach C will be at least as great as that which A must travel to reach C. (In our diagram, $D_2 \geqslant D_3$.)[15]

But this argument depends upon some very special propositions about the nature and sequence of technological change. One must postulate sharp discontinuities and disjunctions, such that the newly emerging technologies at any time are of such a nature that the currently most technologically advanced economies possess no special advantages (either in skills, experience, scientific knowledge, and adaptability) in their development. If, however, as Usher has persuasively argued, technological change must be understood as a continuous process of cumulative synthesis emerging out of a perception of deficiencies in existing techniques and knowledge, then there is at least a strong presumption that the (unknown) technology of the year 2000 will be "closer" to that of the United States in the year 1950 than to that of Ghana in the year 1950. ". . . the history of technology can be much more adequately presented from the point of view of continuously emergent novelty than from the romantic concept of occasional innovation at widely spaced intervals."[16]

---

[14] Soviet literature gets around this difficulty by asserting that if A is socialist and B is capitalist, then B will slow down while A will not. Therefore A can "overtake and surpass" B. Some such *deus ex machina* is needed to meet this difficulty. But even here, a latecomer thesis could exist in an assertion that Communist China will overtake the U.S.S.R.

[15] Imagine that in 2000 technology is based on completely new principles. Then it will be as easy to teach these principles to Ghanaians as to U.S. factory workers of 1950. Moreover, Ghanaian plant and equipment can be as readily converted to the new technology as U.S. plant and equipment. Then this argument holds. If, however, the new technology of 2000 makes both the Ghanaian and U.S. economies of 1950 more obsolete, then the argument does not hold.

[16] A. P. Usher, "Industrialization of Modern Britain," *Technology and Culture* (Spring, 1960), pp. 109–10. The *locus classicus* for Usher's analysis is his *A History of Mechanical Inventions* 2d ed., 1954. Cf. also A. P. Usher, "Technical Change and

In addition to the weak and moderate statements, a "strong" statement is also found. This statement asserts that A will move to C, while B will not move at all.[17] On this view, A will certainly overtake B. It is worth considering this possibility (apart from the fact that it is mentioned in the literature) because it brings into direct discussion a point which is interesting and perhaps important. We return to the three cost functions $C_A(x)$, $C_B(x)$, and $C_C(x)$. All of these are functions of output; and it is natural to associate their respective differences, $d_{AB}(x) = C_A(x) - C_B(x)$, $d_{AC}(x) = C_A(x) - C_B(x)$, and $d_{BC}(x) = C_B(x) - C_C(x)$ with the "distance," or magnitude of the technological changes from A to B, from A to C, and from B to C, respectively. Here, obviously, $d_{AC} = d_{AB} + d_{BC}$.[18] It apparently makes no difference (as the problem has so far been formulated) whether the underdeveloped country (A) retraces the developed-but-obsolete country's route A–B–C, or "takes the shortcut A–C"; both countries will ultimately end up at C.

Suppose, however, that the development process involves both a change in technology and a change in scale. This possibility is suggested by what Samuelson has called the "Generalised LeChatelier Principle."[19] This principle asserts that if the number of restraints on a cost function is reduced the function itself can only remain constant or decrease at any level of output. Thus a firm at B has all the technology available at A, and more besides; one at C has all that available at B and more besides. Marginal cost at each level of output at B is thus not more than at A, and at C not more than at B. Replace "not more than" by "less than" in the foregoing sentences, and assume that the cost of moving from a technology T to another technology T' is an increasing function of output at T, but does not depend on T'.[20] Call this transition cost $M(x)$, then we find that a firm at A selling at price p has a choice between locating at A, producing x_A units with cost function $C_A(x)$; locating at B, paying $M(x_A)$ to move, and then selling at p subject to cost function $C_B(x)$; or locating at C, paying $M(x_A)$ to move, and selling at p, subject to cost function $C_C(x)$. Whatever $M(x)$, if B is sufficiently close to A, the firm may find it profit-

---

Capital Formation," in *Capital Formation and Economic Growth*, pp. 523–50. A recent comparison of Usher and Schumpeter may be found in Vernon Ruttan, "Usher and Schumpeter on Invention, Innovation, and Technological Change," *Quarterly Journal of Economics* (November, 1959), pp. 596–606.

[17] Gerschenkron, *op. cit.*, p. 7, argues that the backward country will adopt techniques at least as modern as the advanced country. He thus adopts a stand between moderate and strong on our scale.

[18] This assertion differs, of course, from the assumed conditions of the weak and moderate statements.

[19] Samuelson, *Foundations of Economic Analysis* (Cambridge, Mass., 1947), pp. 36 ff.

[20] One reason it was hard to introduce steel in Britain was that it competed with iron in many uses, so that considerable and lengthy tests of its physical and economic properties were required throughout all industry. Once innovators had incurred the transition costs of testing, however, imitators could rapidly follow (J. H. Clapham, *An Economic History of Modern Britain* [Cambridge, Eng., 1952], Vol. II, p. 56).

able to move to a more distant technology C, where the savings in cost $(C_A(x) - C_C(x))$ are greater, but not to move to a nearer technology B, where the savings in cost $(C_A(x) - C_B(x))$ are less. In other words, it will make large, but not small, technological changes.[21]

On the other hand, a firm at B may confront a higher transition cost $(M(x_B) > M(x_A)$, since $x_B > x_A)$ than the firm at A, while the cost reduction $(C_C(x) - C_B(x))$ it achieves is less than that achieved by the former. That is, the fact that C is closer to B than to A may offset the greater cost reduction resulting because output at C is greater than that at B. A situation is then possible in which the "underdeveloped" firm at A would move to C, while the "developed but obsolete" firm at B would not.[22]

The concept of transition cost is flexible enough to cover a variety of situations. Consider four agricultural economies: in A there is neither fertilizer nor contour plowing; in B there is fertilizer but no contour plowing; in C there is contour plowing but no fertilizer; and in D there is contour plowing and fertilizer. D is "the economy of the future," and A is an "underdeveloped economy." Assume that a country without contour plowing suffers erosion, and that an investment in terracing must take place before contour plowing can be instituted. In this case, C would move to D without a transition cost, while A would not. Here a developed but obsolete economy has an advantage over the latecomer. However, B has no such advantage over A. In this sense there is a transition cost from A or B to C or D, but no transition cost from C to D. In this sense, transition costs depend upon the entire path of a country's past history, or (to put it another way) the direction from which a particular technology (in this example, contour plowing plus fertilizer)is approached.[23, 24]

---

[21] This statement implicitly assumes that there exists an answer to the following dilemma: granted a sufficiently long period, any transition cost, however large, can be made to pay for itself. This statement, in turn, states that the accumulated income is infinite. The problem of evaluating income streams over an infinite future is common to all growth theory, and is not satisfactorily solved to date. Cf. F. P. Ramsey, "A Mathematical Theory of Saving," *Economic Journal*, 1928, pp. 543–59.

We are indebted to our colleague, Professor Stanley Reiter, for these observations.

[22] M. Cipolla, "The Decline of Italy," *Economic History Review*, 1952, pp. 178 ff., argues that guild restrictions in 17th-century Italy produced what we would call "infinite" transition costs, which prevented the Italian textile industry from adopting the improved methods of its British, Dutch, and French competitors and caused its disappearance.

[23] A former colleague of the authors was employed teaching the Lebanese to grow cedars. The problem was that destruction of the forests at an earlier date had led to erosion, and hence transition costs. The soil-exhausting techniques of tobacco and cotton cultivation in the American south might also be cited.

[24] G. B. Richardson, *Information and Investment* (Oxford University Press, 1960), p. 114, makes essentially this point, in a diffuse reference to Frankel. Habakkuk, *op. cit.*, p. 218, cited Richardson's point in an explanation of the loss of British supremacy in textiles. These various references do not clearly distinguish between cases where individual firms are burdened by the past and cases where the past impedes entry, by making it hard for new firms to fit into the interstices among existing industries.

The transition costs $M(x)$ have been assumed to be an increasing function of output, but independent of technology.[25] On this basis we have argued that a more developed economy will fail to make a change to an advanced technology, while a less developed economy will make the change. But transitional costs may depend on the level of technology from which the change is initiated. If it is true that the more advanced the technology being taught workers, the more expensive the education, then the higher the level to which an economy is moving, the greater the transition costs; if it is true that the more advanced a technology is, the easier it is to retrain the labor force, then the higher the level from which an economy starts, the less the transition costs. If the more advanced the existing technology is, the greater are the retooling and rebuilding costs, then the latecomer thesis is strengthened. If new technology is capital-saving compared to older (for given levels of output) all latecomer theses are weakened.

One part of the "latecomer" thesis is that the economies now developed but obsolete will remain so. This is not necessarily implied by the discussion of transition costs thus far presented. If it is true that a firm at A will move to C, while one at B will not, we can imagine the following sequence of technologies:

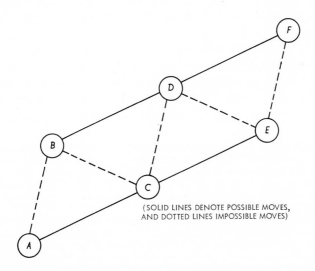

(SOLID LINES DENOTE POSSIBLE MOVES, AND DOTTED LINES IMPOSSIBLE MOVES)

Here a firm at A would move to C and then to E, while a firm at B would move to D and then to F.[26] These moves would imply a "leapfrog" game in

[25] This assumption means, in effect, that if technological change involves retraining labor, it does not matter to what new skill the labor is retrained; if factories must be retooled or demolished, it does not matter what the nature of the new equipment or building is.

[26] The literature on "turnpike theorems" may turn out to be relevant to this discussion (R. Dorfman, P. Samuelson, and R. Solow, *Linear Programming and Eco-*

which first one and then the other would assume technological "leadership." The process would exist because large technological changes are profitable, while smaller ones are not. But there is no necessary reason why this process should come to an end.

If, however, transition costs rise sufficiently fast with output, then at each stage the firm must contemplate a larger leap than it made the last time.[27] If knowledge increases at an even pace, the firm must wait longer at each stage than the last to accumulate the knowledge necessary to make the (larger) next leap. At some point, then, each firm will find itself expecting to have to accumulate knowledge an indefinitely long period before it can afford to make another leap. At this point we would expect technological progress to stop forever—even though at the end of the period an indefinitely large jump would occur. Thus, one firm or the other might establish a permanent lead.

From this point of view, one can draw some of the dubious historical examples so dear to economists. The Russian iron industry of 1750 was the largest in the world.[28] It was based on a charcoal technology. It was displaced in the 1790's by the British, who changed from charcoal to coke as fuel. Now in the 20th century the Soviets, by use of sintering, oxygen blast, and so on, would replace the West by adopting on a larger scale technology which is one step ahead of that in use elsewhere. Likewise the Indians and Chinese, whose technology in 1000 surpassed that of Western Europe, fell behind in the 18th century, and would presumably be in line to regain a lead in the $(20 + x)$th century without in the meanwhile having passed through our own stage of development. If, however, the higher the level of technology, the greater the obstacles to its change, then either the Asiatic countries will never regain the lead or if they do regain it they will never lose it again. Clearly the difficulty with this type of argu-

---

nomic Analysis, chaps. 11 and 12). These theorems are based upon the dual concepts of rates of growth and composition of capital. Formally, they assert that rates of growth may be increased if a nonoptimal capital mix is altered; and it makes no difference if one type is increased, or another destroyed, in the alteration process. This subject is still in an unsatisfactory state, and to elaborate on it would require a separate treatment.

[27] The assumption that transition costs are a rising function of output is consistent with Frankel's "technological interrelatedness," as we understand the concept. Technological interrelatedness means that single components of a productive process cannot be replaced on a "one-at-a-time" basis. "Interrelatedness has the effect of requiring the new method, if it is to be introduced, to earn higher profits than would otherwise be necessary. Let the difference between required profits with interrelatedness and required profits without it be called the 'profit gap.' The size of this gap may be taken, in any particular case, as a measure of the handicap imposed on innovation by interrelatedness" (Marvin Frankel, "Obsolescence and Technological Change," *American Economic Review* (June, 1955), pp. 306–7).

[28] W. Bowden, M. Karpovich, and A. P. Usher, *An Economic History of Europe Since 1750,* p. 301. British *output* in the 18th century (*ibid.,* p. 385) may be compared to Russian *exports,* as given in P. G. Liubomirov, *Studies in the History of Russian Industry* (Ocherki po istorii russkoi promyshlennosti) (Moscow, 1947), pp. 215, 441.

ment is that it is not easy to ascertain which frog leaps last. Whether Western Europe, or the U.S.S.R., or China, or India leaps last makes presumably a great deal of difference, but there is no a priori way of deciding the last (and therefore the best) leap.

Let us now return to the distinction we have made between a firm and an economy. An economy may progress by having new firms replace old firms. Inflexibility of existing firms need be no obstacle to the economy. Thus if cost and revenue functions are not "real," but subjective constructions by enterprises, then as "middle age" advances, any enterprise, however successful it may have been, will see increasing obstacles to further innovations.[29] Here $M(x)$ is an increasing function of time, as well as merely of output.[30] But to the extent that these obstacles are "imaginary" it is natural to ask why new firms are not formed. For these firms, the transition cost would be low, and consequently the economy would adopt new technology by the simple device of forming new firms (or, alternatively, by existing multiple-product firms adding to their product lines). "Freedom of entry," then, is a way to eliminate transition costs due solely to the immobility of older firms.[31] Even where the obstacles are "real"

---

[29] In contrast, Gerschenkron (op. cit., p. 6) treats the beginning of industrialization as if it were in part the removal of a real or imaginary transition cost.

[30] There may exist real impediments to change. Thus, England's alleged "stagnation," supposedly beginning around the turn of the present century, may simply reflect the fact that as coal reserves have been depleted, the cost of producing at a constant rate of output has risen over time. Such a situation would affect firms of all ages in the coal industry. Although output per man-year figures (for all persons employed in mining) are subject to some obvious limitations, they are still of considerable interest. Output per person employed in British mines was reported to be at a yearly average of 319 tons for the period 1879–83, 287 tons for 1894–98, 257 tons for 1909–13, and 221 tons for 1922–25 (Committee on Industry and Trade: Survey of Metal Industries (London: Her Majesty's Stationary Office, 1928), pp. 435, 439). One need not share the somewhat apocalyptic concern of W. S. Jevons in The Coal Question (1865) over the eventual exhaustion of coal resources to point to the rising costs of coal extraction and its importance to the competitive position and rate of growth of the British economy. (Cf. D. Gordon, op. cit., p. 650.) Gordon also points out that "to some extent the 'stagnation' of the British economy is an appearance created by comparisons with Germany and the United States" and that "German per capita output has not as yet surpassed that of Britain despite a resource picture which, if anything, favors the former" (loc. cit.: cf. also A. J. Taylor, "Labour Productivity and Technological Innovation in the British Coal Industry, 1850–1914," Economic History Review [August, 1961], pp. 48–70, and E. H. Phelps Brown with S. J. Handfield-Jones, "The Climacteric of the 1890s," Oxford Economic Papers [October, 1952], pp. 266–307). The "resource exhaustion" argument has no logical connection with the "penalty of taking the lead" argument, since resources are exhausted simply as a function of their rate of utilization. Such exhaustion hardly constitutes a part of the penalty for technological leadership as such. The superior resource position of the late industrializers (with an identical initial endowment of resources, by assumption) at any particular point in time merely reflects their earlier failure to utilize their resource base.

[31] The failure to deal with at least the possibility of new entrants seriously vitiates much of Frankel's interesting discussion of technical interrelatedness (Marvin Frankel, op. cit., pp. 296–319). Frankel deals with situations where it is impossible to replace single components of a productive sequence separately because of specifications im-

rather than imaginary for older firms, i.e., where there are transition costs (due to, say, technological interrelatedness) for firms with existing plants, the freedom of new firms to enter the industry with new plants embodying the new technology will guarantee technological progressiveness for the industry as a whole. Moreover, occupational immobility within a single generation[32] does not imply that younger people must take jobs in their fathers' industries. In this case technologically progressive firms would have young employees and "mature" firms older employees.

If obstacles to entry were the same for an economy in all stages of its development they would be irrelevant to the latecomer thesis. But if they increase as a country develops they contribute to a sluggishness of early starters compared with latecomers. For example, early English automobile manufacturers were newly formed firms, but they found it hard to introduce mass production because of the entrenched position of other machinery firms and of their own employees.[33] Likewise, the "late-coming" continental industry in effect invented investment banking, while "early starting" England never adopted it.[34] It is therefore sometimes argued that early starters develop rigidities which affect not only firms but also freedom of entry. The point is that in certain situations external economies appear to exist, but in fact cannot be utilized by newcomers.[35] These

---

posed by the other machines in the existing productive sequence. "Confronted with this situation, the enterprise would compare the new and old methods not on a component or machine basis but on an entire plant basis since only by replacing existing plant in toto could it utilize the new machine" (p. 302). But one cannot jump from the firm to the industry, since new firms are not subject to the constraints which the past presumably imposes upon the present via technical interrelatedness. To complete the argument it would be necessary to demonstrate why *new* firms do not enter the industry (in Schumpeterian fashion) when superior techniques are available and are not being employed by existing firms. Frankel does not address himself to this highly important aspect of his problem. Indeed, in discussing whether an industry will adopt a new innovation, he inserts in a footnote (p. 304), quite gratuitously, the "assumption" that there is no entry of new firms: "This statement assumes that, for whatever reason, entry of new firms is blocked." But in making this assumption Frankel is, in effect, conceding that the analysis which he developed at the level of the individual firm is not transferable to an entire industry. In attempting to restate the crux of his argument in reply to Gordon's strictures, Frankel appears to us to reduce it to the following propositions: 1. For any particular period of time, all existing capital goods constitute a free gift from the past. 2. However, some capital goods are "freer" gifts than others. It is better to have a capital stock inheritance from the past which is free of interrelatedness ("no strings attached") than to have an inheritance characterized by interrelatedness. Interrelatedness constitutes a constraint upon freedom of choice (D. Gordon and M. Frankel, *op. cit.*, pp. 646–57). We find little with which to disagree in Frankel's "Reply."

[32] In the United States, for instance, it has been difficult to persuade coal miners and railroad workers to change their occupation. This difficulty seems partly due to the fact that these workers often live in small towns, where alternative employment does not exist. To seek a job means also to move to a new community. The children of these workers, however, may be attracted to jobs elsewhere.

[33] Habakkuk, *op. cit.*, pp. 202–3.

[34] Gerschenkron, *op. cit.*, pp. 13 ff.

[35] An example is the Case of Kindleberger's Tunnel. English coal mines own freight cars, and railroads own the tunnels. Railroads would not profit by adopting

situations appear to depend upon alleged complexity and interrelatedness in early starting economies (the authors know nothing about obstacles to entry in Afghanistan, India, Ghana, etc., but suspect they may be at least as great as those in the United Kingdom).

Suppose an economy in which each firm produces a single product, and in which a given set of consumer goods is produced. Development consists in introducing new intermediate goods, including equipment. It is possible that every time a new type of equipment is introduced an old one is removed from the market, but there is no reason why this situation should exist. Indeed, the development process seems to have increased "specialization," in the sense that more names of commodities, occupations, etc., exist in a developed than in an underdeveloped economy. Despite the increased variety of output, costs of finished goods do not rise. In some sense, then, the firm in a developed economy buys a wider variety of inputs, and hence, on the average, a smaller number of units of each kind of input per unit of output.[36]

Specialization in a developed economy is different from that in an underdeveloped economy. The two deserve different names, but do not have them. In the developed economy the specialized firm produces articles which have only a single purpose; the many purposes served in such an economy make it probable that another firm exists which pro-

---

larger sized coal cars (which have less dead weight per unit of capacity), and in fact would have to enlarge the tunnels. The coal mines will not adopt larger cars, since they would not go through the tunnels. Therefore a potential economy is not achieved because it is external to both industries: "wholesale destruction would have helped, and the British economy has been worse off, rather than better, with the free gift of the past. Capital investment may be more readily made good in a developed economy than the blocks to technical change from external economies overcome." But his reasoning is not entirely convincing: "wholesale destruction might have enabled the contry to make a fresh start. And a fresh start was needed. No nation normally has the option of destroying or scrapping existing equipment and starting again, in the same way as a developing country, or one emerging from a destructive war." But why, indeed, not? In the very next sentence Kindleberger states, as if in explanation: "Private owners clinging to their privileges inhibited the railroads from acting as if the old cars, or freight cars without brakes, had no value" (C. P. Kindleberger, *op. cit.*, p. 288). On this basis, it appears that Kindleberger's analysis reduces simply to irrational or nonmaximizing behavior on the part of the capitalists. Kindleberger had earlier (p. 286) cited the fact "that in the United States 15,000 miles of track was converted from broad to narrow gauge in two days in 1886."

[36] If this is a reasonable view, and if (reasoning from general equilibrium theory) each industry buys from each other industry, the number of kinds of interindustry relations in an economy of n industries is $n(n-1)$, which varies with n^2. Thus "complexity" of the economy increased with the square of the number of commodities produced, that is, with the level of development. If the firm has a specialized service concerned with buying inputs, and if the "span of attention" of the individual buyer is such that he cannot keep track of more than some number of different inputs, then the overhead costs of a firm will necessarily rise as the economy develops. These overhead costs are externally induced, and do not vary with output of the firm. In this sense the development of the economy imposes an external diseconomy on each firm. For the treatment of some related issues see Seymour Melman, "The Rise of Administrative Overhead in the Manufacturing Industries of the United States, 1899–1947," *Oxford Economic Papers,* New Series (February, 1951), pp. 62–112.

duces articles which either are similar except in some small detail[37] or which are made using very much the same labor skills and equipment. In contrast, the specialization in an underdeveloped economy takes place in an environment where many fewer kinds of commodity[38] are produced. It is not obvious that specialization in the sense of multiplicity of commodity names or skill names makes for less occupational mobility than specialization in the sense of a small number of rather disparate commodity names or skills.

Suppose, however, that it were the case that the early stages of economic development involve concentration on a relatively small number of industries, and that only in later stages does there occur the proliferation of specialties which characterises the highly developed economy. In this case, if it is also true that the highly differentiated economy tends to have relative immobility of resources, then underdeveloped countries could grow more rapidly than the developed countries. Nothing in this possibility, however, suggests that latecomers would not be as affected by retardation as they reached the stage of increased complexity as early developers, and it is not easy to make even a moderate or strong proposition for this argument.[39]

The foregoing discussion does not touch upon a major aspect of the latecomer thesis: the rate of growth is a fraction, the numerator of which is the change in output and the denominator the total output in a period; and part of the literature states that for any given output increase (resulting, for instance, from a foreign-aid program of given size) the lower the output base is, the higher the growth rate. This preoccupation with the denominator breeds neglect of the numerator: the smaller the base level of output, the harder it is to attain any given numerator. Our discussion has been mainly concerned with the connection between levels and changes of output and technology, but implicitly it makes a further point: a moderate or strong latecomer thesis must assert that the retardation which affected the early starters either will not affect the latecomer at all or will only affect it after it has overtaken the early starters.

Finally, we may examine arguments sometimes advanced from "economic sociology." Economic growth is almost always associated with

---

[37] J. M. Clark has mentioned jurisdictional disputes between the makers of roofing and of siding for Quonset huts.

[38] Oskar Lange has shown that articles whose prices vary proportionately over time may be treated as a single commodity (*Price Flexibility and Employment*, Bloomington, 1944, p. 103).

[39] We do not propose to discuss Habakkuk's view (*op. cit.*, chap. VI, *passim*) that innovation is a result rather than a cause of economic growth. The contrary view is explained adequately in Schumpeter's *Theory of Economic Development*. Sociologically, Habakkuk's attitude on another point, the existence of an industrial plant in Britain, "which in many branches was adequate to the demands made upon it" (p. 212), resembles the comment attributed by Americans to British employers and labor (pp. 198–99) that "the working-man does not need more than so many shillings a week."

changes in the composition of aggregate demand and therefore of total output. (The relative importance within G.N.P. of $C + I + G + E_x$ changes. So also does the composition of each of these categories.) Successful economic growth therefore involves, *inter alia*, the maintenance of a high degree of flexibility of resource use. One measure of success in the operation of market forces is thus the responsiveness of resources to the changes dictated by changes in the composition of aggregate demand. An economy which finds it increasingly difficult to accommodate itself to these changes will necessarily encounter increasing difficulties in sustaining its economic growth. It may be argued, then, that movement along any historical growth path involves the introduction of rigidities and resistances and thereby reduces an economy's capacity to accommodate itself to further change.

This is essentially Svennilson's explanation of European stagnation in the interwar years. Western European countries, in varying degrees, experienced difficulty in bringing about the transformation of domestic resource use required by the drastically altered composition of postwar demand. But Svennilson's analysis states further that a "mature" economy is less viable and more resistant to change than a less developed economy.

> There is no doubt that, in the oldest and most advanced industrial countries, transformation of the economy in accordance with the new trends in technology and demand meets with strong resistance from the accumulated stock of capital, from the traditional special skill of labour—in fact, from the whole organization of society . . . On the other hand, resistance is much weaker in a society which offers a virgin soil for the development of manufacturing industries.[40]

The resistances to resource reallocation in interwar Western Europe were, indeed, real enough. But Svennilson's thesis requires more for its

---

[40] Ingvar Svennilson, *op. cit.*, p. 206. See also *ibid.*, pp. 9–10, 34–40, 44–52. Cf. Schumpeter's brilliant analysis of the atrophy of capitalist institutions in *Capitalism, Socialism and Democracy*, Part II. John Jewkes has argued that advanced capitalist economies develop social and political resistances to change, although they need not succumb to them; nor does he share Svennilson's view on the comparison of the mature with the immature economy: "an advanced industrial country will have created classes and institutions, vested interests each of which, it is arguable, will seek, in the last resort by political action, to maintain its own position. The entrepreneur may be powerful enough to force the State to give him protection, the trade union may seek to maintain the same earnings in the same industry for an undiminished number of workers. Of course, the community as a whole cannot, by staking its claim, determine its economic standing (unless it can find some benefactor in the international field). But the efforts of groups to do so may be successful and, by delaying necessary readjustments, may undermine the position of an advanced industrial country. Some such cause, probably, lay at the root of the British industrial decline between the wars. Of course, industrial retardation of this kind is not inevitable" (John Jewkes, "The Growth of World Industry," *Oxford Economic Papers*, New Series, Vol. 3 [February, 1951], pp. 10–11). Cf. also W. A. Lewis, *Economic Survey, 1919–1939*; W. A. Lewis, "International Competition in Manufactures," *American Economic Review Papers and Proceedings* (May, 1957), pp. 578–87; E. A. G. Robinson, "Changing Structure of the British Economy," *Economic Journal*, September, 1954.

support than the trivial statement that we do not live in a frictionless world. It presumes that the obstacles to resource mobility are an increasing function of an economy's maturity. But this extremely important proposition, when appropriately expressed in a *comparative* sense, is not at all obvious. Even if there was considerable resource immobility in British industry during the interwar years, it is not clear that these immobilities were greater than those encountered in the Brazilian (or Bulgarian or Indian) economies during the same period. On the contrary, we should be inclined to argue that industrial countries, even the "oldest and most advanced," possess, *on balance*, far greater versatility, flexibility, and capacity to accommodate to change than do predominantly agricultural, low-income economies which presumably offer "a virgin soil for the development of manufacturing industries."

Here again it is important to maintain the distinction between factors which are alleged to be responsible for an eventual retardation of growth in industrial economies and factors demonstrating the existence of penalties for taking the lead. For the problems involved are not those resulting from early technological leadership as such, but are, in some sense, an outgrowth of the growth process itself. If retardation is inevitable in a mature economy, it is, presumably, inevitable for the followers as well as for the leaders.

Conclusions

The latecomer thesis can be formulated in three variants. The *weak* thesis asserts that the latecomers will pass through any sequence of development more rapidly than early starters. The *moderate* thesis asserts that latecomers will ultimately reach higher levels of development than early starters, even though the latter do not cease developing. The *strong* thesis states that latecomers will surpass early starters, partly because the latter will cease to develop. Each of these theses implies preceding ones in the list, but not later ones.

The *weak* thesis depends ultimately on the propositions that latecomers can avoid past mistakes of early starters; that latecomers will make no more current mistakes than late starters; and that mistakes do not contain useful experience (in some sense) for those who make them.

The *moderate* thesis is based in part on the assertion that early starters are subject to retardation which does not affect latecomers. This is possible if a continuing technological change affects the economies of early starters more adversely than those of latecomers (in terms of obsolescence of skills and plant).

The *strong* thesis is based upon transition costs: if the cost of moving from a lower to a higher technology is an increasing function of the level of technology already reached the rate of development will slow down as a country develops. This is true because changes sufficiently large to be worthwhile can be made only at increasingly infrequent intervals (and in the limit can never be made). Thus if a latecomer "makes the last change" it attains a permanent leadership.

The validity of these theses depends upon a variety of empirical problems:

1. Granted that latecomers have certain advantages, they also have certain disadvantages. It is moot whether on balance they have an advantage in terms of any of these theses.

2. Granted that latecomers may initially grow at a rapid rate, it is moot whether they will escape the retardation afflicting early starters when they reach comparable states of development.

3. Granted that in fact some latecomers have tended to catch up with the British, it is moot whether their success is due to economic rather than to sociological or "irrational" factors.

4. Many of the arguments used to defend the theses apply only to economies into which new firms may not enter; the moot question of whether obstacles to entry increase as economies develop—for economic or noneconomic reasons— is therefore of major importance.

5. The definition of interrelatedness given in the literature states that a firm has interrelated assets (processes) when it cannot replace one without simultaneously replacing others. But the word interrelatedness is also used in the literature on latecomers in the context of a group of industries. For this concept no adequate definition is given; and it is not clear why (*a*) interrelatedness should increase as a country develops, or (*b*) obstacles to entry should increase as interrelatedness increases. Yet the latecomer theses typically make assertions of this sort.

The results of our argument were in large part reached by the explicit assumption that technologies of different countries could be placed in ordinal, or even cardinal, relationships to each other. This assumption, it is clear, makes it possible to achieve results which are more precise than would otherwise be attained. There exists, of course, no measure of the sort assumed. To this extent, our results lack precision. However, even a cursory examination of the literature reveals constant use of notions of this sort, so that at least we have brought some dirty linen into the open, where it belongs. Those who object to this expository device will, of course, be careful to avoid using similar concepts themselves. We shall be interested to see how they will cope with interesting and important problems such as those raised by the latecomer thesis.

Even though no such measure of technology now exists, we can describe some of its properties, using problems arising in the latecomer thesis. A measure of technology, for instance, cannot be a movement along a single line. If it were, the (real) possibility of shortcuts by latecomers would have to be discounted. We use a two-dimensional technology in our diagrams; if present growth rates are substantially affected by the course of past development a multidimensional measure of technology may be necessary.

Such a concept might provide a bridge between Schumpeter's innovation, which represents discrete change, and Usher's technology, which represents continuous change. Economic discussion of technological change is hampered by the fact that both views can be defended, while no test is available to show how either may be related to real economies. This discussion has been weakened by the absence of such a test; if it existed, many other economic problems could also be handled more readily.

All published latecomer theses have logical defects, but these may often be repaired. What remains is a series of empirical conjectures, the verification of which depends upon the truth of certain hypotheses about the relation between changes in output and changes in technology. Even if no latecomer thesis were a logical necessity (and we feel this is the case), some such thesis might well be true as historical fact. But the available factual discussion goes little beyond tantalizing suggestions, and indeed can hardly do so until the development of adequate theory and measures of technological change.

3. Observing the Effects of Research on Business*

Edward Ames

Purdue University

CURRENT AMERICAN RESEARCH about research suffers from at least two difficulties. First, everyone recognizes that the government's policy is not really to encourage research, but to make new kinds of military hardware; and business's aim is not to encourage research, but to develop new and more profitable goods, services, and production processes. Since it is not now possible to obtain data on the amount of technological change (new goods, services, and processes) in the economy, it is not possible to observe the consequences of research programs on the economy. Second, it is ordinarily held to be impossible to measure research output. In this case, even if technological change were quantifiable, it would be impossible to talk in concrete terms about how research is related to technology.

In what follows, an effort will be made to resolve the first problem. It will be shown that some aspects of technological change are in fact observable and quantifiable, at least at the level of an individual industry. If these findings meet the test of close scrutiny, then half of the larger problem can, in principle, be met. Having seen the possibility of direct measures of technological change, we can, with perhaps a lighter heart, proceed to study the connection between the output of new technology and the input of research.

There will be presented below the results of examining various records maintained by Bell Telephone Laboratories, Inc. These records refer to the adoption, alteration, and abandonment of specifications of "apparatus" and "equipment" used by the American Telephone and Telegraph Company and its subsidiaries. I have nowhere seen similar data published, and I think that they will perhaps suggest avenues for further study.

If technological change is ever to be quantified, and associated with a supporting research operation, then the telephone industry would seem

* The Business History Conference, 1962: "America as a Business Civilization," papers presented at Michigan State University, February 24, 1962. (Bureau of Business and Economic Research; Michigan State University, East Lansing, Michigan, pages 11-37.)

to be a perfect laboratory for starting experiments. The industry is virtually monopolized by American Telephone and Telegraph and its subsidiaries. One of these—Western Electric—makes most of the hardware used in the system and is the buying agent for those subsidiaries which actually sell telephone service. Another—Bell Telephone Laboratories— is one of the largest research organizations (I am tempted to say *research faculties*) in the country and is responsible for all research subcontracting in the system. Moreover, the system has a major (and unique) technical problem, called "compatibility." Since it must be possible to connect each telephone in the country to each other telephone, special control must be exercised to make sure that new types of hardware[1] are compatible with existing types. Bell Laboratories, therefore, must ascertain the compatibility of new hardware with existing hardware, before it can be used by any operating company,[2] or made by Western Electric. All these companies are large, all are regulated by state and federal government, and all have careful records. They represent an almost perfect environment in which to observe the introduction of new technology into an industry.[3]

Western Electric supplies thousands of individual items of hardware to operating companies. A new item in Western Electric's catalog means a technological change in the operating companies, since these can now buy an output which they could not formerly buy. However, a change in Western Electric's own manufacturing processes need not change technology of the operating companies. (In some cases, of course, a change in Western Electric technology necessitates a change in operating company technology.)

Conceptually, the introduction of a new item into the catalog represents an innovation. It represents a discrete change in the set of possibilities open to the operating companies, a change from n to $n + 1$ in the number of inputs on which the operating companies seek to minimize the costs of a given output of telephone messages, and a change which cannot be broken down into arbitrarily small parts.[4] On the other hand the changes themselves are numerous. Taken one at a time most are not very important. In this sense, one can think of innovations as a set of changes, perhaps with "magnitudes" distributed on the basis of a probability law of some sort.

In a recent paper I presented a contribution to the "theory" of the

---

[1] I use the term *hardware* because *equipment* is used in a very special sense in the body of the paper.

[2] "Operating companies" provide regional local telephone service. I use the term here to include also long distance facilities operated by A.T.&T.

[3] The objection is often made that since A.T.&T. is a monopoly, its behavior is perhaps atypical. To this, it may be answered that my remarks apply to the possibility of observation. A competitive industry might indeed be different, but as yet nobody can tell.

[4] See Schumpeter, *Theory of Economic Development* (Cambridge, Mass., 1934), pp. 61–65.

production of innovations.[5] In order to retain some consistency in my own discussion I repeat some simple definitions:

Research is a flow of new statements about the natural world.

Invention is a flow of prototypes of articles which have never been made before, or processes which have never been used before.

Development is a flow of instructions (blueprints, diagrams, etc.) which enable the construction and equipment industries to build fixed plant of kinds never used before, and also enable the personnel of these plants to operate them when finished. It may also make it possible to use existing fixed plant to make articles unlike those they had hitherto made.

If this terminology is to be useful, it should be possible to apply it to the data on new technology which are presented here.

The distinction between research and development exists administratively within Bell Laboratories, but it is clear that there is overlap. Thus "systems development," the unit which plans the most complicated and expensive changes in technology, does draw upon research personnel as well as upon engineers. On the other hand, invention is specially recognized within the Laboratories only where it involves patenting. The patent operation, which will be discussed below, is talked of as a legal problem, and (in connection with licensing agreements) a matter of intercorporate strategy. Patenting is even handled by A.T.&T. rather than the Laboratories. Thus the economic concept of invention, given above, has no organizational recognition in the administrative structure of Bell Laboratories.

The terms *apparatus* and *equipment* are used in the Bell System for internal control purposes. Apparatus is relatively cheap and simple, equipment relatively expensive and complex. In principle equipment has several interdependent functioning parts, while apparatus does not. (A piece of apparatus is often a component of a piece of equipment.)[6] Terminology in the Bell System is in flux, and in the future "equipment" may be considered an old-fashioned term for "system" and "apparatus" an old-fashioned term for "component," corresponding to the systems and components engineering units in the Laboratories. No data are available on systems, the largest and most complex units of hardware; or on components, in the development and design of which a large body of Bell Laboratories personnel is engaged.

The administration of the Bell Laboratories generates data about the rate of technological change. Bell Laboratories assigns a code to new pieces of apparatus consisting of a name (e.g., cord, relay, coin collector,

---

[5] "Research, Invention, Development and Innovation," *American Economic Review*, Vol. LI (June, 1961), p. 370.

[6] The telephone instrument used in pay stations contains various such parts—a voice transmitter, a receiver, a coin-collecting mechanism, a dialing mechanism for activating central office switching equipment, bell, cord, case, etc.—yet (probably because of its size, cost, and quantity of manufacture) it is considered apparatus.

jack mounting plate) and a (sequential) number. When the new apparatus becomes available to operating companies, a descriptive index card is printed. These cards are sent to purchasing departments of the operating companies, and constitute the catalog of purchasable items. When a change in a piece of apparatus occurs, a replacement card is issued. In some cases, Western Electric may discontinue production of an item, while it still has an inventory on hand, or Bell Laboratories for technological reasons may wish to restrict use of an item. Then an entry "A and M only" on a new card restricts future use of the item to "assembly and maintenance," that is, forbids its use in new installations. Finally an entry "M.D." may be made, when manufacture is discontinued and the item is no longer available to operating companies. Here, too, a new card is issued.

Since 1931 Bell Laboratories has kept an annual record of the number of new codes assigned to apparatus, and the number of "M.D." designations issued, and the number of "active" code numbers at the end of each year. The number of codes rated "A and M only" is available since 1938. These data are given in Table I.

These new codes always represent development.[7] They may also involve invention, where codes are issued to apparatus of a kind not previously made. It is not clear what proportion of the new codes issued involve invention (of some degree of importance).

To gain some clues as to the relation between invention and development, a special set of data was devised. Bell Laboratories maintains a historical file of all apparatus cards issued since about 1910.[8] These are arranged chronologically by code number. There is a card issued whenever a new code number is assigned; and a card is issued to record minor design changes, and discontinuation of individual items.

Some changes in apparatus take place on the initiative of Western Electric. These ordinarily do not affect the user, but are attempts to reduce manufacturing costs. (Such changes might include changes in the diameter or length of pins on which small parts move or in the composition of the alloys of which the parts are made. The user would ordinarily be unaware of and uninterested in the fact that they occur.)

Other changes, however, take place on the initiative of Bell Laboratories. In the main these changes do matter to the user, and frequently change the operating characteristics of the apparatus. When these changes

---

[7] The qualification is introduced because some changes represent merely changes in terminology. A large number of codes issued in 1955, for instance, merely brought the nomenclature of the Bell System into line with that elsewhere (e.g., *condensers* were renamed *capicitors*).

[8] Some earlier cards also exist, but an examination of these and similar cards suggests that standardization of apparatus did not actually take place until the Laboratories was created in 1924. Rather, one has the impression from the cards that several administrative units in the system divided the responsibility on a functional basis, and that either the records are incomplete or part of the apparatus in fact escaped standardization.

TABLE I
CHANGES IN APPARATUS CODES IN FORCE 1931–59

Year	Apparatus Coded During Year (1)	Code Nos. Released as Mfr. Disc. (2)	Col. 1 Minus Col. 2 (3)	End of Year Cum Total of Code Nos. Mfr. Disc. (=4−2) (4)	End of Year Cum Total of Code Nos. not Mfr. Disc. (=5−3) (5)	End of Year Cum Total of all Code Nos. (=4−5) (6)	Codes Rated "A and M only" During Year (7)
1931	1781	550	1231	14610	23759	38369	
1932	744	358	386	14968	24145	39113	
1933	602	436	166	15404	24311	39715	
1934	754	273	481	15677	24792	40469	
1935	603	287	316	15964	25108	41072	
1936	2775	321	2454	16285	27562	43847	
1937	2081	815	1266	17100	28828	45928	106
1938	2414	1147	1267	18247	30095	48342	147
1939	1781	1624	157	19871	30252	50123	
1940	1881	2047	(−) 166	21918	30086	52004	150
1941	1473	1054	419	22972	30505	53477	183
1942	716	1057	(−) 341	24029	30164	54193	10
1943	550	259	291	24288	30455	54743	0
1944	315	199	116	24487	30571	55058	13
1945	353	308	45	24795	30616	55411	10
1946	1031	252	779	25047	31395	56442	43
1947	1388	587	801	25634	32196	57830	20
1948	1130	773	357	26407	32553	58960	4
1949	1376	985	391	27392	32944	60336	31
1950	941	1502	(−) 561	(A) 29049	32383	(A) 61432	10

TABLE I (Continued)

Year	Apparatus Coded During Year	Code Nos. Released as Mfr. Disc.	Col. 1 Minus Col. 2	End of Year Cum Total of Code Nos. Mfr. Disc. $(= 4 − 2)$	End of Year Cum Total of Code Nos. not Mfr. Disc. $(= 5 − 3)$	End of Year Cum Total of all Code Nos. $(= 4 − 5)$	Codes Rated "A and M only" During Year
	(1)	(2)	(3)	(4)	(5)	(6)	(7)
1951......	1194	1705	(−) 511	30754	31872	62626	26
1952......	1252	2437	(−) 1185	33191	30687	63878	63
1953......	1263	1518	(−) 255	34709	30432	65141	46
*1953 (Adj)......	1263	1518	(−) 255	(*) 31273	(*) 29273	(*) 61026	46
1954......	1004	1322	(−) 318	33075	28955	62030	27
1955......	2839	973	1866	34048	30821	64869	10
1956......	1760	312	1448	34360	32269	66629	7
1957......	1577	521	1056	34881	33325	68206	11
*1957 (Adj)......	1577	521	1056	(−) 26283	(−) 34450	(−) 70733	11
1958......	1679	1555	124	37838	34574	72412	9
1959......	1002	1284	(−) 282	39122	34292	73414	8

NOTES: (−) Based on a count of catalog cards made at the end of 1957.
(A) Includes 155 codes of old Mounting Plates, not previously listed in catalog added to M.D. Header Cards.
(*) In columns 4, 5, and 6, figures for 1953 and earlier years are cumulative. However, a count of catalog cards was made at the end of 1953. Based on this count the following figures were deducted from the figures given on the 1953 line in order to arrive at the figures given on the "1953 Adjusted" line: 4–3536, 5–1159, 6–4115.
SOURCE: Bell Telephone Laboratories.

take place, cards are issued telling the new specifications of the apparatus. Both old and new revised cards are kept in the historical file.

The cards issued annually by Bell Laboratories thus record some new apparatus—apparatus given new code numbers—and some alterations in old types of apparatus. Both kinds of cards represent development, but only a part of the former would involve invention of apparatus. These cards would not note either development or invention in manufacturing processes.[9] But though Bell Laboratories records how many *code* numbers it issues per year, it does not record how many new *cards* it prints per year.

In order to estimate the annual issue of apparatus cards I took a sample of the historical index. This index consisted of 68 drawers of cards, not all of them full. The sample consisted of 2,741 cards, drawn at a rate of 1 per centimeter of drawer. Of this total, 644 were issued in 1920 or before. The dates of issue of the remaining 2,097 are given in Table II,

TABLE II

A RANDOM SAMPLE OF APPARATUS CARDS BY YEAR OF ISSUE

Year	Original Issue Sample Numbers*	Year	Original Issue Sample Numbers*
1921	56	1941	71
1922	70	1942	62
1923	69	1943	30
1924	72	1944	24
1925	62	1945	24
1926	46	1946	23
1927	72	1947	35
1928	38	1948	50
1929	62	1949	54
1930	61	1950	56
1931	91	1951	70
1932	40	1952	73
1933	21	1953	62
1934	21	1954	57
1935	23	1955	110
1936	31	1956	46
1937	34	1957	49
1938	50	1958	73
1939	72	1959	73
1940	64		

* Collected by Dr. John Carlson and me from the historical card index of Bell Telephone Laboratories (see text for details).

---

[9] The Laboratories maintains a card index of correspondence concerning changes in apparatus, arranged by code. It would be possible, although tedious, to ascertain the numbers of changes instituted by Western Electric, as compared with the Laboratories. Such data would suggest the importance of manufacturing processes themselves, as originators of technological changes of importance to the users of the product; as contrasted with changes originating in the research and development work in the Laboratories.

column 2. It was not practical to determine how many cards were in the index, so that the sample is only an index of the relative numbers issued.

The records on equipment are somewhat different from those on apparatus. When a new type of equipment is approved, a document called a Specification ("Spec") is issued. This consists of a description and a set of circuit diagrams. The specification may contain several "codes"[10] if the equipment has subassemblies, or if some parts are optional or alternatives.[11] Bell Laboratories maintains a library and distribution service, so that the engineers in the operating companies can obtain sets of specifications and diagrams. The card index to these specifications contains a record of all equipment, and the dates of changes made in the individual items. The following discussion of equipment is based on analysis of this catalog. The Spec series devoted to equipment have, since 1929, been the "J-Spec series." Before then, two series, X-61000 and X-63000, were used, the former being used for manual and the latter for dial switching systems. Every piece of equipment has a Spec number—X or J followed by a five-digit number, the first two digits designating the general use of the equipment and the last three a sequential listing. A "small" change involves a new appendix to the Spec; a "larger" change requires a new issue (with retention of number). The designations "A and M only" and "M.D.," which are used as with apparatus, are the subject of special appendices (or occasionally issues) in the case of equipment. The card index records the dates of all issues and appendices for Specs issued since about 1921. Thus the statistics of changes in specifications can be studied much more readily for equipment than for apparatus.

Table III presents three series: the number of new specification numbers (J-Spec) issued annually since 1927, a complete enumeration by the Laboratories; an estimate of the number of Specs issued (new plus alterations) annually since 1921,[12] based on a sample in which I counted every fourth card in the index, including the J, X-61000 and X-63000 series;[13] and estimates of the number of revisions of specification, as the difference between the foregoing series.[14]

---

[10] An apparatus "code" is the code number of a particular piece of apparatus. A "code" for equipment refers to a subassembly. The equipment as a whole is referred to as a "Spec."

[11] Apparatus is here viewed roughly as a subassembly of a code, and a code as a subassembly of equipment.

[12] There is some reason to suppose that the entries for 1921–24 are not complete, for the index contains cross-references to other indices in use before the establishment of the Laboratories. These are not readily available, and may no longer exist.

[13] The equipment which has been superseded by a different type bears a notation in the index of the Spec which displaces it. My count of Specs in the X series does not include a relatively small number of X-Specs which were superseded by X-Specs not in the 61000 or 63000 series. These X series do not refer to equipment, but to other things used by the system, and I concluded that I would not have homogeneous data if I included them.

[14] The very large number of new specification numbers issued in 1928–31 seems

TABLE III

EQUIPMENT SPECIFICATIONS ISSUED ANNUALLY, 1921–59

Year	New Specification Numbers*	Revisions†	Total†
(1)	(2)	(3)	(4)
1921			12
1922			28
1923			24
1924			68
1925			184
1926			168
1927			156
1928	130	90	220
1929	154	118	272
1930	123	149	272
1931	146	162	408
1932	67	157	224
1933	17	83	100
1934	24	40	64
1935	44	88	132
1936	82	82	164
1937	58	206	264
1938	63	153	216
1939	66	150	216
1940	94	194	288
1941	85	191	276
1942	53	151	204
1943	9	31	40
1944	9	51	60
1945	8	44	52
1946	52	80	132
1947	94	98	192
1948	66	134	200
1949	68	184	252
1950	68	164	232
1951	63	113	196
1952	37	111	148
1953	39	157	196
1954	55	177	232
1955	32	156	188
1956	29	171	200
1957	59	157	216
1958	56	192	248
1959	65	131	196

* Full count by Bell Telephone Laboratories.
† Based on 25 percent sample.

These tables suggest that technological change in a large firm involves numerous changes in the list of hardware it uses. The central notion of "changes in a list" bears some relation to the familiar notion of changes in an inventory. Since, however, the change in nomenclature is to be dis-

---

to reflect the renumbering into the J series of equipment formerly listed in the X-61000 and X-63000 series. I base this conclusion upon my examination of the index cards themselves, rather than upon any consideration of the inherent plausibility of these data.

tinguished from changes in the inventory of hardware itself, care is necessary in adapting familiar concepts to the unfamiliar data given here.

The question, "How long does technology of a given type remain in use?" is not the same as the question, "How long does a physical piece of equipment last?" although the two are related. Imagine the following sequence of events:

1. An article is accepted by the Laboratories.
2. Some operating companies use it.
3. It may become widely used.
4. An alternative device is developed.
5. The alternative gradually displaces the original article.
6. The article is purchased only for replacement and repair purposes.
7. It eventually is taken out of production.[15]

Consider a piece of apparatus or equipment given a code number in year T. What is the probability that it will "survive" (i.e., *not* be listed "manufacture discontinued") until the end of years $T + 1$, $T + 2$, etc.?[16] Can one, in short, prepare a survivor table for technology?

For a random sample of 204 apparatus codes, Dr. Carlson obtained the date of issue of the specification number and the date of discontinuation of manufacture. Using ordinary actuarial principles, it was then easy to compute survivor tables (Table IV and Graph 1), and the proportion of apparatus and equipment types surviving after one, two, three years, etc.

Apparatus shows a relatively high "infant mortality." One fifth of the new apparatus codes are designated "manufacture discontinued" within six years. It takes another 14 years for a second fifth, and 14 more years for the third fifth to drop out. Thus if a new type of apparatus survives the relatively sharp mortality during the first few years, it is apt to continue in use with relatively fewer chances of being taken out of use—at least until about age 35, where we begin to lose confidence in our data because of the smallness of the sample.

For the largest equipment changes, the adoption and abandonment of specification numbers, Dr. Carlson took a sample of 474 equipment specifications and prepared Table V. Equipment specifications are subject to lower infant mortality rates than apparatus, but by age 26, about 45 percent of both have been eliminated. Thereafter, equipment goes out of use more rapidly than apparatus.

Two conjectures about this state of affairs are possible. The first is that the simpler and cheaper apparatus is changed more easily, or perhaps

---

15 Laboratories personnel suspect that there is a tendency for apparatus to remain "on the books," even if little used; so that periodically drives must be undertaken to rid the catalog of items which in fact are little used. If this view is correct, the "manufacture discontinued" date given an item is not altogether reliable as a date when the apparatus became obsolete.

16 This data collection was done jointly by Dr. John Carlson of Cornell University and me, in May, 1960. The "survivor tables" were calculated by him. We also collected certain other data of use to him, rather than to this study.

TABLE IV
The Survival of Apparatus Codes

Age	Total Codes Surviving to Beginning of Year	Manufacture Discontinued During Year	Rate of Discontinuation of Manufacture	Rate of Survival to End of Year
0.........	204	3	.015	.985
1.........	199	9	.045	.941
2.........	189	7	.037	.906
3.........	179	6	.034	.875
4.........	172	3	.017	.860
5.........	167	6	.036	.829
6.........	158	5	.032	.802
7.........	152	2	.013	.792
8.........	148	6	.041	.760
9.........	140	4	.029	.738
10.........	136	7	.051	.700
11.........	125	1	.008	.694
12.........	123	1	.008	.688
13.........	121	2	.017	.676
14.........	119	3	.025	.659
15.........	116	1	.009	.653
16.........	115	4	.035	.630
17.........	111	3	.027	.613
18.........	108	1	.009	.607
19.........	108	2	.019	.595
20.........	100	1	.010	.589
21.........	95	0	.000	.589
22.........	94	2	.021	.577
23.........	92	0	.000	.577
24.........	90	2	.002	.564
25.........	86	0	.000	.564
26.........	84	2	.024	.550
27.........	81	0	.000	.550
28.........	81	3	.037	.530
29.........	76	2	.026	.516
30.........	73	1	.014	.509
31.........	71	8	.113	.451
32.........	62	4	.065	.422
33.........	56	5	.089	.384
34.........	51	2	.039	.369
35.........	46	1	.022	.361
36.........	42	2	.049	.343
37.........	38	1	.026	.334
38.........	36	0	.000	.334
39.........	32	0	.000	.334
40.........	31	0	.000	.334

tested less thoroughly than the more expensive equipment. The costs of failure of equipment being greater, equipment is not apt to be adopted (given a code) unless it is relatively foolproof. Therefore, its infant mortality rate is relatively low. Second, since equipment is complicated, it is made up of many components. But many electrical components are relatively standard, so that individual jacks, switches, relays, etc., may serve several technological generations of equipment. Therefore, apparatus has

GRAPH 1

PERCENTAGE OF EQUIPMENT SPECIFICATIONS AND APPARATUS CODES
SURVIVING TO GIVEN AGE

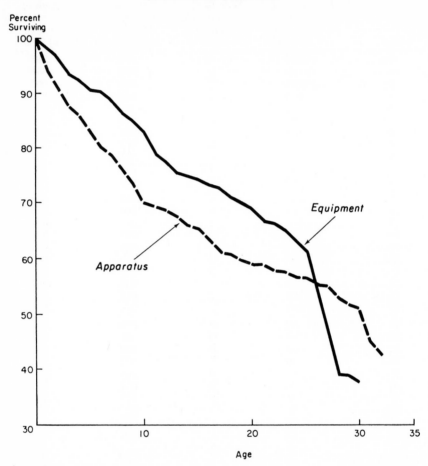

greater technological longevity than equipment, once it has survived in-fancy. No direct test of these possibilities has been found possible.

The Bell Laboratories data give some clues as to the age of distribution of the technology in use in the telephone system. Once again, tests must be made separately for apparatus and equipment. The following data, of course, do *not* represent the age distribution of the physical assets of the telephone system. Some hardware actually in use has a code number now designated "manufacture discontinued." Other newly installed hardware may have a code number issued many years ago and use the original de-sign. Thus the age of physical hardware may be either greater than or less than the age of the technology represented by the data given here, and no attempt is made to compare the two.

Western Electric publishes a periodical check list of apparatus cards

TABLE V
THE SURVIVAL OF EQUIPMENT SPECIFICATIONS

Age	Specifications Surviving to Beginning of Year	Manufacture Discontinued During Year	Survival Rate During Year	Rate of Survival to End of Year
0.........	474	1	.998	.998
1.........	460	8	.983	.981
2.........	438	7	.984	.965
3.........	414	13	.969	.935
4.........	397	6	.985	.921
5.........	384	6	.984	.906
6.........	369	1	.997	.903
7.........	359	8	.978	.883
8.........	346	8	.977	.863
9.........	324	7	.978	.844
10.........	304	7	.977	.825
11.........	286	12	.958	.790
12.........	262	5	.981	.775
13.........	245	7	.974	.755
14.........	221	1	.995	.751
15.........	218	2	.991	.743
16.........	213	3	.986	.733
17.........	208	2	.990	.726
18.........	198	5	.975	.708
19.........	183	2	.989	.700
20.........	162	3	.981	.687
21.........	147	4	.973	.669
22.........	134	1	.993	.664
23.........	128	2	.984	.653
24.........	115	3	.971	.634
25.........	105	4	.962	.610
26.........	100	9	.910	.555
27.........	87	15	.828	.460
28.........	65	10	.846	.389
29.........	42	0	1.000	.389
30.........	30	1	.967	.376
31.........	18	1	.944	.355
32				

in force.[17] This list identifies a card by the apparatus name (e.g., switches), by the card number or apparatus code number, and by date of issue. It thus is possible to determine how many *cards* of various ages were in use on December 31, 1959 (Table VI). There were about 7,500 cards in use on December 31, 1959, and 34,300 code numbers of apparatus being manufactured. Thus there were, on the average, 4.7 code numbers on each card. (Many items, such as relays, are listed in series.) A change in any one item on a card would necessitate a new card. Thus cards would tend to be changed more often than the apparatus designated

---

[17] Checking List of Apparatus Card Catalog, Western Electric Company, New York, December 31, 1959. The purpose of this document is to enable operating companies to make sure their own card catalogs are up to date for purposes of ordering apparatus.

TABLE VI
APPARATUS CARDS OF VARIOUS AGES
IN USE DECEMBER 31, 1959

Year	Cards of Given Year in Use Dec. 31, 1959	Year	Cards of Given Year in Use Dec. 31, 1959
1921	6	1941	123
1922	12	1942	187
1923	22	1943	65
1924	18	1944	54
1925	32	1945	60
1926	29	1946	76
1927	44	1947	48
1928	30	1948	158
1929	60	1949	168
1930	38	1950	293
1931	72	1951	240
1932	34	1952	459
1933	30	1953	488
1934	20	1954	576
1935	42	1955	1000
1936	36	1956	467
1937	46	1957	549
1938	47	1958	488
1939	113	1959	871
1940	141		

SOURCE: Tabulation of *Checking List of Apparatus Card Catalog*, Western Electric Company, New York, December 31, 1959.

by the cards. The numbers of cards of various ages in use at the end of 1959 reflect in part the numbers of new codes issued during these years, and the numbers of changes made in old codes during these years (where these changes needed to be brought to the users' attention).

More distinctions in degrees of technological change are available for equipment than for apparatus. The largest additions to technology occur when new J-Spec numbers are issued. The age distribution of technology at the end of 1959, as measured by the date of issue of the Spec number of equipment, is given in Table VII.

Smaller changes in equipment occur when a new issue of a specification is made; and still smaller ones when an appendix to a specification is issued. Such an appendix may affect several "codes" (subassemblies) or only one. Such smaller changes occur over the "life" of a Spec. The age distribution of technology in May, 1960, as measured by the most recent change in a specification, is given in Table VIII. (In some cases, the most recent change was the original issue of the specification.)

The tabulations already presented indicate that half the apparatus cards in force at the end of 1959 had been published later than the beginning of 1954; half the equipment codes in use at the same date had been issued later than the beginning of 1946; and half of the equipment specifications in force in May, 1960 had either been newly issued, or been altered in some way since the beginning of 1957.

TABLE VII
EQUIPMENT IN USE AT THE END OF 1959
BY DATE OF INTRODUCTION

Date of Introduction	Number of Equipment Specifications	Percent of Total	
		of Given Age	of Given Age or Less
(1)	(2)	(3)	(4)
before 1928..........	1	.37	
1928.............	8	2.96	99.61
1929.............	11	4.07	96.65
1930.............	10	3.70	92.58
1931.............	12	4.44	88.87
1932.............	4	1.48	84.43
1933.............	2	.74	82.95
1934.............	1	.37	82.21
1935.............	7	2.59	81.84
1936.............	11	4.07	79.24
1937.............	5	1.85	75.17
1938.............	6	2.22	73.32
1939.............	12	4.44	71.10
1940.............	17	6.30	66.65
1941.............	11	4.07	60.36
1942.............	7	2.59	56.29
1943.............	2	.74	53.69
1944.............	3	1.11	52.95
1945.............	2	.74	51.84
1946.............	7	2.59	51.10
1947.............	12	4.44	48.51
1948.............	11	4.07	44.07
1949.............	11	4.07	39.99
1950.............	13	4.81	35.92
1951.............	12	4.44	31.11
1952.............	5	1.85	26.66
1953.............	8	2.96	24.81
1954.............	9	3.33	21.85
1955.............	6	2.22	18.52
1956.............	4	1.48	16.29
1957.............	17	6.30	14.81
1958.............	14	5.18	8.52
1959.............	9	3.33	3.33

Let us define technological change as the introduction of new types of apparatus and equipment, and the discarding of old. At any time, the research and development operation in Bell Laboratories may be said to reach into the catalog and select some items for revision or discard. It is natural to inquire which items are actually selected.

Various conjectures might be advanced as to the nature of the selective process. Suppose hardware becomes technologically obsolete with the mere passage of time. Then the longer the interval which has elapsed since something received a code number, the more probable its alteration or demise in the course of the year. This policy will be called a FIFO research policy, to bring terminology into line with inventory practice, and viewing Bell Laboratories as controlling an inventory of technology.

TABLE VIII

EQUIPMENT IN USE, MAY, 1960, BY DATE OF MOST RECENT
ALTERATION IN SPECIFICATIONS

(In Number of Specifications)

| Year of Most Recent Alteration | Number of Specifications | | Survivals, as Percent of Specifications Issued that Year |
	Sample Numbers	Estimated Totals	
(1)	(2)	(3)	(4)
1930.............	4	20	.073
1931.............	5	25	.061
1932.............	1	5	.022
1933.............	0	0	.000
1934.............	1	5	.078
1935.............	1	5	.038
1936.............	1	5	.030
1937.............	1	5	.019
1938.............	1	5	.023
1939.............	2	10	.046
1940.............	4	20	.069
1941.............	4	20	.072
1942.............	5	25	.123
1943.............	3	15	.375
1944.............	2	10	.167
1945.............	0	0	.000
1946.............	4	20	.384
1947.............	7	35	.265
1948.............	4	20	.104
1949.............	10	50	.250
1950.............	3	15	.059
1951.............	6	30	.129
1952.............	11	55	.281
1953.............	8	40	.270
1954.............	12	60	.306
1955.............	19	95	.409
1956.............	20	100	.531
1957.............	39	195	.975
1958.............	38	190	.879
1959.............	49	245	.987
1960.............	25	125	

Suppose, second, research and development work concentrates upon the least satisfactory articles. If a piece of hardware is badly designed, its defects will appear soon after its introduction. If it is well designed, it will have a long, useful life. On this hypothesis, the longer a code number has survived, the less likely it is that it will be replaced in a given year. This policy will be termed a LIFO research policy, on the grounds that the latest items in the technological inventory are the first to leave.

Finally, suppose that alteration or abandonment of a type of hardware is related only to new research and development, and thus is mainly concerned with application of new ideas rather than the displacement of old ideas. On this hypothesis, the probability that a given item will be replaced or altered is independent of the technological age of the item. The third possibility will be called a *random access* research policy, on the grounds that all technology, regardless of acquisition date, is equally likely to be removed in a given period.[18]

The "survivor tables" (Tables IV and V) do not answer the question of research policy satisfactorily. They relate only to the largest changes, in which manufacture of a particular item is discontinued, and ignore smaller changes, in which new apparatus cards, or changes in a Spec, are made. It proved impractical to make survivor tables for the smaller changes, because of the way the data were kept by Bell Laboratories. Instead, a different experiment was designed.

The data on apparatus include (1) the cards in use December 31, 1959, by date of issue (Table VI), and (2) the distribution, by date of issue, of a sample of cards (Table II). If (2) were a complete enumeration, the ratio (1) $\div$ (2) for any year would indicate the proportion of cards still in use to the cards originally issued in that year. If these ratios are considered survival rates, and plotted on semilogarithmic scale, all research policies would yield a curve which declined as the age of the card increased. A FIFO research policy would approximate a curve convex upward; a LIFO policy a curve convex downward, and a random access curve a straight line. Since even a "systematic" research policy could not be expected to operate with complete uniformity, an empirical curve would only approximate a smooth line, with deviations due to lack of uniformity in the workings of research policy.

Since the data on issues are taken from a sample, and not a complete enumeration, the ratio of cards printed in year Y in force at the end of 1959 to the sample number for year Y is a multiple of the percentage actually surviving, with allowance for sampling fluctuations. A chart of the ratios of the two series, on semilogarithmic scale, would provide an estimate of the theoretical relationship described in the preceding paragraph. Despite irregularities the convexity properties associated with the various research policies, in particular, would be unchanged. Table VII reproduces the ratios, and their logarithms, and Graph 2 indicates that, in fact, there seems to be a random access rather than either a LIFO or FIFO policy.* It would appear that a particular unit of apparatus, regardless of its age, had a probability of about .085 of being altered enough in a given year to require issuing a new card. The number .085 is not to be taken as being very precise, since it is the slope of a visually fitted straight line to the chart. I do not know a more sophisticated test that would be appropriate to this calculation.

---

[18] These definitions, of course, do not assert that planning in Bell Laboratories consciously follows the practice described, for there is no reason to suppose it does. They amount to a statement that however research is planned, the effect of the planning is that described above.

* Since this paper was published, this assertion has been challenged by sharp-eyed observers of the graph.—E.A.

The sample sizes for equipment were smaller, and the sampling variation correspondingly larger, than for apparatus. For this reason, annual estimates were replaced by biennial estimates for the period 1930–31 to 1958–59. Two estimates were made. The first reflects the probability that equipment will be designated "manufacture discontinued," and is designated "Spec Number Retention" on Graph 2.[19] The second reflects the

GRAPH 2

APPARATUS AND EQUIPMENT IN USE 1959–60 IN PERCENT OF ORIGINAL ISSUE
OF GIVEN YEAR

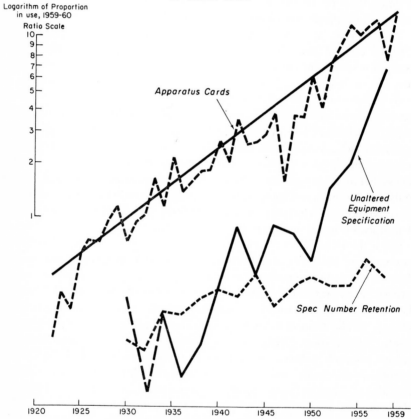

probability that equipment will either be designated "manufacture discontinued" or be altered (by having a new issue or appendix) and is designated "Unaltered Equipment Specifications" in Graph 2.[20]

Since two factors operate to reduce Unaltered Equipment Specifications, and only one to reduce Spec Number Retention over time, the former is naturally steeper than the latter. Spec Number Retention shows

---

[19] It was obtained by dividing column 2, Table VII, by column 2, Table III, for the biennial sums.

[20] It was obtained by dividing column 2, Table VIII, by column 4, Table III, for biennial totals.

marked linearity, except perhaps at the end of the scale where equipment introduced before 1935 is in question. Thus this series, like the Apparatus Cards series on the same graph, seems to support the random access hypothesis of research.

Even using biennial data, the Unaltered Equipment Specification series shows considerable fluctuation. My eye is tempted to see a convex downward curve, corresponding to the LIFO research policy; more elaborate statistical tests would be required to prove the matter conclusively. In view of the sampling fluctuations and the probability of autocorrelation in the data, I am unable to devise a suitable test for this purpose. But in any case, the random access hypothesis is not disproved either.

In any case, the slope of the Unaltered Equipment Specifications curve is greater, on the average, than that of the Apparatus Cards curve. Therefore, there is a greater probability in any year that equipment will be altered than apparatus. This result is consistent with the discussion of the survivor tables, where it was suggested that a piece of apparatus may be used in more than one technological generation of equipment.

We have treated technology as a list of items in a Western Electric catalog. Some balance sheet notions apply to such a list. Technology itself at any moment is an inventory of things which can be used. Over time, new technology is entered into the account, and old technology is discarded. Technological change, in some treatments, is the net change in the total stock; in others, the gross additions; in still others, the turnover in the account, the sum of additions and deletions. Finally, technological change is sometimes identified with invention, and invention with patenting, so that it would be useful to see how these data compare with patent data for the telephone system.

First, consider the additions to the stock. An elaborate time-series correlation analysis is probably premature, given our present understanding of these data. Instead, I have presented indexes of five-year averages in Table IX. With the exception of the patent data, which are new, the other data are taken from the earlier tables. Relegating to footnotes certain special observations,[21] some general conclusions stand out:

1. Since the late 1930's there have been in general greater increases in the alterations of existing apparatus and equipment than in the number of new code or specification numbers. This fact suggests that changes

21 (1) Bell Laboratories was established in 1924, and gradually took over research and development work formerly performed in part by Western Electric. The decline in patenting by Western Electric in 1930–34 as compared with 1925–29 reflects this administrative transfer. (2) During World War II, Bell Laboratories and Western Electric both began to do extensive work on government contract, in contrast to the earlier period. Therefore the new technology available to the telephone system dropped sharply. However, these companies were evidently able to patent some of the results of their work for the government. (3) The input of new technology into the system was thus affected adversely not only by the depression of the 1930's but also by World War II. Some part of the new apparatus cards issued in the 1950's represented only changes in the names of parts. These changes were particularly important in 1955.

TABLE IX
SOME LONG-TERM MOVEMENTS OF PATENTING
AND TECHNOLOGICAL CHANGE

	Patents Issued*			Apparatus		Equipment		
	Bell System Total	Western Electric	Other	New Codes	New Cards	New Specs	Revisions	Total
1925–29...	126	427	54	n.a.	133	n.a.	n.a.	101
1930–34...	123	202	104	50†	111	120	102	108
1935–39...	100	100	100	100	100	100	100	100
1940–44...	114	131	110	51	119	80	91	87
1945–49...	81	116	73	55	89	92	80	83
1950–54...	97	130	89	59	151	84	109	101
1955–59...	87‡	135‡	75‡	92	167	77	119	106

* Source: American Telephone and Telegraph Company.
† 5/4 of the 1931–34 total.
‡ 5/4 of the 1955–58 total.

in production methods and in the operating performance of existing models may have been more important than the design of drastically new models of hardware. To support this view we draw attention to the increase in patenting by Western Electric in the postwar period, compared to the decline in the rest of the system.

2. The series relating to apparatus show greater increases (smaller decreases) than those relating to equipment. This fact suggests an increased complexity of the latter (as measured by, say, the number of components) over time.

3. The trend in patenting tends to resemble the change in new equipment specifications, but not the other measures of technological change. Taken in conjunction with the preceding paragraph, this fact may indicate that for this industry at least, the decline in numbers of patents has taken place because individual items patented have become more complex.

4. These conclusions are based upon a relative measure of additions to new technology, and therefore do not really provide any basis for assigning any absolute measure of importance to the data pertaining to any single year. For this reason, it would be desirable to find some yardstick to describe their meaning more accurately.

For apparatus, the data are sufficiently complete to permit the calculation of some "pure numbers" relating to technological change. It is possible to calculate four indices, each of which has some intuitive meaning. I present all four, at the risk of undue length.

1. A contrast may be made between the *addition* to technology made available during a period, and the *turnover* in technology, represented by the sum of new methods adopted and old methods eliminated. In Table X, columns 1 and 2 refer to the former and columns 3 and 4 to the latter.

2. The importance of either additions or turnover in technology in

TABLE X
SOME ALTERNATIVE MEASURES OF TECHNOLOGICAL
CHANGE IN APPARATUS

	Additions to Technology,* in Percent of		Total Technological Turnover,† in Percent of	
	Initial Technology‡	Total Technology§	Initial Technology‡	Total Technology§
1930–34..........	22	13	31	19
1935–39..........	39	23	56	34
1940–44..........	16	10	32	19
1945–49..........	17	10	27	15
1950–54..........	17	9	43	23
1955–59..........	31	14	47	22

 * The numerators of these ratios are the numbers of new apparatus codes granted during the years in question (Table I, column 1).
 † The numerators of these ratios are sums of new codes plus codes rated "Manufacture Discontinued" during the years in question (Table I, column 1, *plus* column 2).
 ‡ The denominators of these ratios are the numbers of codes for which manufacture had not been discontinued at the beginning of the period (Table I, column 5).
 § The denominators of these ratios are the total numbers of codes which had been issued (including those discontinued) at the beginning of the period (Table I, column 6).

some period must be evaluated in terms of the total stock of technology at the beginning of the period. The stock of technology may be the set of all practices in use at the time the change occurs. On the other hand, the stock of technology should perhaps include, in addition, technology once used, but abandoned prior to the change in question. In Table X, columns 1 and 3 refer to the first concept and columns 2 and 4 to the second.

Whichever of these four definitions is used, technological change (Table X) was greater in the late 1930's than at any time since. Whichever definition is used, a sharp drop occurred during World War II. Whichever definition is used, an increase took place thereafter, and the late 1950's showed greater change than the 1940's or the early 1930's. The four measures do not agree as to when this last increase began, and how great it was, compared to the peak in the late 1930's.

We can only regret that comparable data are not available for equipment, which is bigger and more glamorous.

The measures of technological change which have been given here reflect research and development work of Bell Laboratories. To use an analogy from ordinary production processes, they constitute, in fact (disregarding work on government contract), the Laboratories' output of finished goods. It is well known, however, that a plant may accumulate stocks of goods in process, without completing anything; or it may have considerable amounts of completions, which are basically obtained by a running down of goods in process. The question of the future technological development of the telephone system cannot be decided by examining these data alone. To answer that question, it is also necessary to know whether the goods in process (research results not yet transformed into hardware) are available to replace those results which have been used. If all types of technological change had steadily declined in the postwar period—and not merely new equipment Specs—we might still anticipate accelerated technological change in the future. Such a prediction would be justified if it could be shown that research results had been reached more rapidly than technological change had taken place. If so, a rising backlog of technology in process has been created. To investigate this question would take another paper.

To conclude: Data have been presented on the adoption, alteration and discontinuation of individual types of apparatus and equipment in the telephone industry. These data supplement in important ways the data concerning patents. They cast some light on the research process in this industry, for they suggest that there is no higher probability that an item whose present design was finished in, say, 1940 will be replaced in 1962 than an item finished in, say, 1950. They also give information on the turnover of technology and the age distribution of technology now in the system. These results are difficult to assign meaning to, since nothing comparable is known about other industries. If comparison should become possible, a more complete understanding of the process of technological change in individual industries would result.

4. Technological Change in the Machine Tool Industry, 1840–1910*

Nathan Rosenberg
Purdue University

I

Technological change has come to absorb an increasing share of the attention of the economist in recent years. Several attempts have been made to assess the quantitative importance of technological change, as opposed to increases in factor supplies, in accounting for the secular rise in per capita incomes in the United States. It appears, in all these studies, that technological changes (shifts in the production function) have been far more important than has the mere growth in the supplies of capital and labor inputs, as conventionally measured (movement along an existing production function).[1] In a sense, this should be cause for deep concern, since the comparative neglect of the process of technological change (with the major exceptions until very recent years, of the works of Marx, Schumpeter, and Usher) suggests a serious malallocation of our intellectual resources. If the studies of such people as Abramovitz and Solow are even approximately correct with respect to orders of magnitude, then the contribution of technological change to rising per capita incomes absolutely dwarfs the contribution from a rising but qualitatively unchanging stock of capital. It would appear that we have indeed been playing Hamlet without the Prince.

Even the recent quantitative studies referred to in the previous paragraph provide the beginnings of only a very partial corrective to this

---

* Reprinted from the *Journal of Economic History*, Vol. XXIII, No. 4 (December, 1963), pp. 414–43.
[1] Robert Solow, "Technical Change and the Aggregate Production Function," *Review of Economics and Statistics*, Vol. XXXIX, No. 3 (August, 1957), pp. 312–20; Moses Abramovitz, "Resource and Output Trends in the U.S. Since 1870," *American Economic Review Papers and Proceedings*, Vol. XL, No. 2 (May, 1956), pp. 1–23; Benton Massell, "Capital Formation and Technological Change in U.S. Manufacturing," *Review of Economics and Statistics*, Vol. XLII, No. 2 (May, 1960), pp. 182–88.

neglect. For what they attempt to establish are, essentially, the quantitative *consequences* of technological innovation. From the point of view of our understanding of the process of economic change, the critical, unanswered question is: what are the major causes of technological change? Why do some firms, industries, regions, countries, show an apparently greater readiness and ability to undertake technological innovations than do other firms, industries, regions, countries? The question may be given a further historical dimension if we seek to explain the apparent variations in innovative activity for the same firm (industry, region, country) at different points of time.[2]

The present paper constitutes a modest attempt to examine and to explain the rapidity of technological change in a sector of the American economy which played a strategic role in the industrialization process.

In the past decade or so, the attempt to formulate a theory of the "takeoff" into economic growth has centered upon the process whereby an economy, in a relatively short time period, sharply accelerates the annual rate of net additions to its capital stock.[3] This has been an important and fruitful line of inquiry, if only because it has generated historical research which now reveals the considerable diversity of different economies during the process. Historical data accumulated by Kuznets for 12 countries show no individual case of abrupt increases in net investment of the magnitude implied by the takeoff hypothesis, and cast overwhelming statistical doubt upon any attempt to link precisely the acceleration in the rate of growth of per capita income with rising capital formation proportions.[4]

It seems apparent, then, that changes in rates of investment are only a part of the process by which economic growth is initiated and maintained, and that attention may be usefully directed to other aspects of the transition to growth. Recent work by Gallman and Kuznets makes it clear that growth has been associated with major changes in sector shares of commodity output and with an associated sharp *compositional* shift in the pattern of investment activity.[5] It is with the latter point that we are primarily concerned.

---

[2] The two most important works which should be consulted by anyone interested in this area of research are H. J. Habakkuk, *American and British Technology in the 19th Century* (Cambridge, Eng.: The University Press, 1962), and W. Paul Strassmann, *Risk and Technological Innovation: American Manufacturing Methods During the Nineteenth Century* (Ithaca: Cornell University Press, 1959).

[3] W. W. Rostow, "The Take-Off into Self-Sustained Growth," *Economic Journal*, Vol. LXVI, No. 261 (March, 1956), pp. 25–48, and W. A. Lewis, "Economic Development with Unlimited Supplies of Labour," *The Manchester School*, Vol. XXII, No. 2 (May, 1954), pp. 139–91.

[4] Simon Kuznets, "Quantitative Aspects of the Economic Growth of Nations: VI. Long-Term Trends in Capital Formation Proportions," *Economic Development and Cultural Change*, Vol. IX, No. 4, Part 2 (July, 1961).

[5] Robert E. Gallman, "Commodity Output, 1839–1899," *Trends in the American Economy in the Nineteenth Century* (Studies in Income and Wealth, Vol. 23 [Prince-

The development process in the United States has been characterized by a significant increase in the importance of manufactured producers' durables and a decline in the relative importance of construction goods. This suggests that an important aspect of industrialization may be illuminated by examining the changing historical role of the capital goods industries, and more particularly that growing portion of them which is devoted to the production of producers' durable goods. The role of these industries in introducing and in diffusing technological change is obviously multidimensional, but two aspects at least may be singled out: (1) All innovations—whether they include the introduction of a new product or provide a cheaper way of producing an existing product—require that the capital goods sector shall in turn produce a new product (capital good) according to certain specifications. We may usefully look upon the capital goods sector as one which is, in effect, engaged in custom work. That is, firms in this industry have typically become highly specialized, in the sense that most firms produce a relatively narrow range of output (at least in industrialized economies) in response to technical specifications laid down by a wide range of customers in the consumer goods or other capital goods industries. (2) In addition to this "external" adaptation there is an important "internal" one. Quite simply, members of the producers' durables industry have an internal motivation to improve their own techniques in the production of the durable goods themselves. Their success in accomplishing this improvement in turn affects the price of their machinery output and therefore is an important determinant, first, of investment activity throughout the economy and second, of the rate at which technological innovations, once made, will be diffused—that is, of the speed with which the economy will install and apply new techniques of production once they have been discovered. Moreover, third, cost reduction by the capital goods industries is thus capital-saving for the economy, and cost reduction here also raises the marginal efficiency of capital of other industries. For these reasons it is suggested that a significant—and so far largely unexplored—dimension of the transition to economic growth lies in the ability of the capital goods sector to assimilate and develop proficiency in the new machine technology and thus both to generate, and to adapt itself to, the continually altering technological requirements of an industrializing economy. It will be argued that the machinery-producing industries possess certain unique characteristics which played a major role in accounting for the rapid production and diffusion of technological innovations, which were such a well-known and outstanding feature of the period under consideration.

Machine tools are the most important members of the larger classification of power-driven metalworking machinery. The basic distinction

ton, N.J.: Princeton University Press for National Bureau of Economic Research, 1960]) pp. 13–67; Simon Kuznets, *Capital in the American Economy* (Princeton for National Bureau of Economic Research, 1961), chap. iv.

is that machine tools shape metal through the use of a cutting tool and the progressive cutting away of chips, whereas other metalworking machinery shapes metal without the use of a cutting tool—by pressing (forming, stamping, punching), forging, bending, shearing, etc. There is considerable complementarity and substitution between the two classes of tools, and occasional reference will necessarily be made in what follows to developments outside the category of machine tools as defined here.

II

In 1820 or so, there was no separately identifiable machine tool or machinery-producing sector in the American economy. Although machines of varying degrees of complexity were, of course, being used, the production of the machines had not yet become a specialized function of individual firms.[6] Machines were, by and large, produced by their ultimate users on an *ad hoc* basis. For many years, the most intractable problems associated with the introduction of techniques of "machinofacture" lay in the inability to produce machines which would perform according to the special and exacting requirements and specifications of the machine user.[7] A major episode, then, in the process of industrialization lay in the emergence of a specialized collection of firms devoted to solving the unique technical problems and mastering the specialized skills and knowledge requisite to machine production.

It is useful to examine the growth of the machinery-producing sector from the point of view of the learning process involved. For, as we shall see, most machinery production poses a broadly similar set of problems and involves a broadly similar set of skills and technical knowledge in their solution. Moreover, the pace of industrialization was, in large measure, determined by the speed with which technical knowledge was diffused from its point of origin to other sectors of the economy where such knowledge had useful applications.

The growth of independent machinery-producing firms occurred in a continuing sequence of stages roughly between the years 1840–80.[8] These

---

[6] "There were mules and steam-engines before there were any labourers whose exclusive occupation it was to make mules and steam-engines; just as men wore clothes before there were such people as tailors." Karl Marx, *Capital,* Vol. I (Modern Library Edition [New York: Random House, 1936]), p. 417.

[7] The experiences of Eli Whitney with his government musket contract are by now legendary. See Jeanette Mirsky and Allan Nevins, *The World of Eli Whitney* (New York: Macmillan Co., 1952). Compare H. J. Habakkuk, "The Historical Experience on the Basic Conditions of Economic Progress," *International Social Science Bulletin,* Vol. VI, No. 2 (1954), pp. 189–96.

A skeptical note on Whitney's role in developing the "American system" has recently been struck in Robert S. Woodbury, "The Legend of Eli Whitney and Interchangeable Parts," *Technology and Culture,* Vol. II, No. 2 (Summer, 1960), pp. 235–53.

[8] It is not a historical coincidence that specialized machinery producers began to

stages reflect both the growth in the size of the market for such machines and the accretion of technical skills and knowledge (and growth in the number of individuals possessing them) which eventually created a pattern of product specialization by machine-producing firms which was closely geared to accommodating the requirements of machine users.

In the earliest stages, machinery-producing establishments made their first appearance as adjuncts to factories specializing in the production of a final product. Thus the first machine-producing shops appeared in the textile firms of New England attached directly to such firms as the Amoskeag Manufacturing Company in Manchester, New Hampshire, and the Lowell Mills in Lowell, Massachusetts. As such shops achieved success as producers of textile machinery, they gradually undertook, not only to sell textile machinery to other firms but to produce a diverse range of other types of machinery—steam engines, turbines, mill machinery and (most important) machine tools—as well. In the early stages then, skill acquired in the production of one type of machine was transmitted to the production of other types of machines by this very simple expedient whereby a successful producer of one type of machinery expanded and diversified his operations. Thus, with the introduction of the railroads in the 1830's, the Lowell Machine Shop (which became an independent establishment in 1845) became one of the foremost producers of locomotives.[9] Similarly, locomotives were produced by the Amoskeag Manufacturing Company; and the locomotive works in Paterson, New Jersey, grew out of the early cotton textiles industry in that city. The most successful of all American locomotive builders, the Baldwin Locomotive Works in Philadelphia, grew out of a firm previously devoted, *inter alia*, to textile-printing machinery.[10]

---

emerge on the national scene during precisely the same period as the development of our national railway network. Until roughly 1840, machinery production was not only relatively unspecialized—each producer typically undertaking a wide range of output—but it was also, because of the high cost of transporting machinery, a highly localized operation—each producer typically producing for a very limited geographic radius. The growing specialization in machine production after 1840, characterized by the emergence of large numbers of producers each of whom typically concentrated on a very narrow range of machines, was closely linked with the transportation improvements and consequent reduction in freight costs during the period.

[9] *A Chronicle of Textile Machinery 1824–1924* (Boston: Saco-Lowell Shops, 1924) pp. 16–20.

The number of locomotives built by the Locks and Canals Company and by the Lowell Machine Shop between 1835 and 1861 is given, together with the purchasing railroad companies, in George S. Gibb, *The Saco-Lowell Shops* (Cambridge, Mass.: Harvard University Press, 1950), Appendix 6, p. 641.

[10] John L. Hayes, *American Textile Machinery* (Cambridge, 1879), pp. 57–58; Jonathan T. Lincoln, "Machine Tool Beginnings," *American Machinist*, Vol. LXXVI (August, 3, 1932), pp. 902–3. Although Mattias Baldwin in 1852 described himself as a "Manufacturer of Locomotive, Marine, and Stationary STEAM ENGINES," his advertisements also added: "All kinds of Machinery furnished to order." *Journal of the Franklin Institute*, Vol. L (June, 1852), opposite p. 444. A report of British observers for the same period states, "The practice which prevails of combining

Whereas the production of heavier, general-purpose machine tools—lathes, planers, boring machines—was initially undertaken by the early textile machine shops in response to the internal requirements of their own industry and of the railroad industry, the lighter, more specialized high-speed machine tools—turret lathes, milling machines, precision grinders—grew initially out of the production requirements of arms makers. Somewhat later, the same role was played by the manufacturers of sewing machines and, toward the end of the period under consideration, by the demands of bicycle and automobile manufacturers.[11]

Thus the machine tool industry itself was generated as the result of the specific production requirements of a sequence of industries which adopted techniques of machine production throughout the period. In each case, the introduction of a new process or a new product required an adaptation and adjustment in the capital goods industries to new technical requirements and specifications which did not initially exist. There took place, as it were, a period of technical gestation at the intermediate stages of production, during which time the appropriate accommodations were made to the specific technical needs of the new process or product. As the demand for particular kinds of machines became sufficiently great, reflecting the fact that the same machines came to be employed in a progressively increasing number of industries, the production of that machine itself came to constitute a specialized operation on the part of individual establishments.[12]

---

various branches of manufacture in the same establishment, would . . . render separate descriptions of each somewhat complicated. In some cases the manufacture of locomotives is combined with that of mill-gearing, engine-tools, spinning, and other machinery. In others, marine engines, hydraulic presses, forge-hammers, and large cannon are all made in the same establishments. The policy of thus mixing together the various branches arises, in addition to other causes, from the fact that the demand is not always sufficient to occupy large works in a single manufacture." *The Industry of the United States in Machinery, Manufactures and Useful and Ornamental Arts*, (compiled from the official reports of Messrs. Joseph Whitworth and George Wallis [London, 1854]), p. 3.

[11] Joseph W. Roe, "Machine Tools in America," *Journal of the Franklin Institute* (May, 1938), pp. 499–511.

[12] As early as 1855, a team of British engineers which had traveled to the United States for the purpose of inspecting American methods of arms manufacture felt compelled to make the following observations on the extent to which specialized machinery had been developed in American industry: "As regards the class of machinery usually employed by engineers and machine makers, they are upon the whole behind those of England, but in the adaptation of special apparatus to a single operation in almost all branches of industry, the Americans display an amount of ingenuity, combined with undaunted energy, which as a nation we would do well to imitate, if we mean to hold our present position in the great market of the world." *Report of the Committee on Machinery of U.S.* (H.C., 1855), p. 32. Similar observations and admonitions appear through a succession of reports by British observers to international exhibitions through the subsequent decades of the nineteenth century. See, for instance, the report on machine tools in *Reports on the Paris Universal Exhibition, 1867, Presented to both Houses of Parliament* (1868), Vol. IV, esp. pp. 370–73, and "Machines and Tools for working Metals, Wood and Stone," in *Reports*

The machine tool industry, then, originated out of a response to the machinery requirements of a succession of particular industries; while still attached to their industries of origin, these establishments undertook to produce machines for diverse other industries, because the technical skills acquired in the industry of origin had direct application to production problems in other industries; and finally, with the continued growth in demand for an increasing array of specialized machines, machine tool production emerged as a separate industry consisting of a large number of firms most of which confined their operations to a narrow range of products—frequently to a single type of machine tool, with minor modifications with respect to size, auxiliary attachments, or components.

In late years . . . manufacturers starting in his branch of industry [metalmorking machinery] have very generally limited their operations to the production of a single type of machine, or at the most to one class embracing tools of similar types. For example, there are large establishments in which nothing is manufactured but engine lathes, other works are devoted exclusively to planers, while in others milling machines are the specialty.

This tendency has prevailed in Cincinnati perhaps more than in any other city, and has been one of the characteristic features of the rapid expansion of the machine-tool industry in that city during the past ten years. During the census year there were in Cincinnati 30 establishments devoted to the manufacture of metal-working machinery, almost exclusively of the classes generally designated as machine tools, and their aggregate product amounted to $3,375,436. In 7 shops engine lathes only were made, 2 were devoted exclusively to planers, 2 made milling machines only, drilling machines formed the sole product of 5 establishments, and only shapers were made in 3 shops.[13]

In 1914, there were 409 machine tool establishments in the United States producing an output of $31,446,660.[14] In the same year the *Amer-*

on the Philadelphia International Exhibition of 1876, Presented to both Houses of Parliament (1877), Vol. I, esp. pp. 228–35. In the latter report, Mr. John Anderson, the author, states: "To realize the nature of the competition that awaits us, their [American] factories and workshops have to be inspected, in order to see the variety of special tools that are being introduced, both to insure precision and to economize labour; this system of special tools is extending into almost every branch of industry where articles have to be repeated. This applies to furniture, hardware, clocks, watches, small arms ammunition, and to an endless variety of other things. The articles so made are not only good in quality, but the cost of production is extremely low, notwithstanding that those employed earn high pay" (p. 235). Mr. Anderson closes with a rhapsody on the tool-using and toolmaking abilities of the Americans, and on the urgency of Britain's girding her loins for the coming industrial and engineering competition.

[13] *Twelfth Census of the United States* (1900), Vol. X, Part 4, "Manufacturers," p. 385. This report also refers to the existence of a total of 90 metalworking machinery firms in the five leading centers of Cincinnati, Philadelphia, Providence, Hartford, and Worcester. For a breakdown by value of output of major categories of metalworking machinery in 1900 and 1905, see *Special Reports of the Census Office* (1905), "Metal-working Machinery," p. 227.

[14] *Census of Manufactures* (1914), Vol. II, "Reports for Selected Industries," p. 269. For the same year there were 277 metalworking machinery plants, other than those producing machine tools, with an output valued at $17,419,526.

ican Machinist, in a survey which was admittedly incomplete, published
a map showing the locations of 570 firms engaged in the production of
"machine tools, small tools, machinist's tools and machine tool appurte-
nances. . . ." These firms were all in the northeast quadrant of the country, with Ohio leading with 117 and then Massachusetts with 98, Connecticut with 66, Pennsylvania with 60, New York with 57, and Illinois
with 42.[15]

III

A proper understanding of the "portentously rapid" rate of technological innovation which accompanied American industrialization during
the period under consideration requires that we focus attention upon a
particular aspect of the changing nature of manufacturing activity. For
this purpose it is necessary to discard the familiar Marshallian approach,
involving as it does the definition of an industry as a collection of firms
producing a homogeneous product—or at least products involving some
sufficiently high cross-elasticity of demand. For many analytical purposes
it is necessary to group firms together on the basis of some features of
the commodity as a final product; but we cannot properly appraise important aspects of technological developments in the 19th century until we
give up the Marshallian concept of an industry as the focal point of our
attention and analysis. These developments may be understood more
effectively in terms of certain functional processes which cut entirely
across industrial lines in the Marshallian sense.[16]

It is a common practice to look upon industrialization as involving,
not only growing specialization but also growing complexity and differentiation.[17] While this is certainly true in the sense that there takes place
a proliferation of new skills, facilities, commodities, and services, it also
overlooks some very important facts. The most important for present
purposes is that industrialization was characterized by the introduction
of a relatively small number of broadly similar productive processes to
a large number of industries. This follows from the familiar fact that
industrialization in the 19th century involved the growing adoption of a
metal-using technology employing decentralized sources of power.[18]

If we look at the vertical dimension of productive activity in the sense

---

[15] *American Machinist,* Vol. XL (January 29, 1914), p. 210.

[16] We suggest, only in passing, that such a focus may also provide a more fruitful
approach to a theory of the multiproduct firm.

[17] " . . . industrial differentiation . . . has been and remains the type of change
characteristically associated with the growth of production. Notable as has been the
increase in the complexity of the apparatus of living, as shown by the increase in the
variety of goods offered in consumers' markets, the increase in the diversification of
intermediate products and of industries manufacturing special products or groups of
products has gone even further." Allyn Young, "Increasing Returns and Economic
Progress," *Economic Journal,* Vol. XXXVIII, No. 152 (December, 1928), p. 537.

[18] A. P. Usher, *History of Mechanical Inventions* (Cambridge, Mass.: Harvard
University Press, 1954), esp. chaps. xiii–xv.

of the sequence of stages involved in the production of a final product, it appears that in preindustrial economies, skills and techniques tended to be much more specific and tied down to individual vertical sequences than was the case in industrial economies. The central role, in industrial economies, of the application of decentralized power sources in the working of metals has meant the employment of similar skills, techniques, and facilities at some of the "higher" stages of production for a wide range of final products. Thus, in contrast to sequences of parallel and unrelated activities, we find a phenomenon which we will call "technological convergence." This convergence exists throughout the machinery and metal-using sectors of an industrial economy. Throughout these sectors there are common processes, initially in the refining and smelting of metal ores, subsequently in foundry work whereby the refined metals are cast into preliminary shapes, and then in the various machining processes through which the component metal parts are converted into final form preparatory to their assembly as a finished product. It is with the machinery stages, of course, that we are primarily concerned here.

The use of machinery in the cutting of metal into precise shapes involves, to begin with, a relatively small number of operations (and therefore machine types): turning, boring, drilling, milling, planing, grinding, polishing, etc. Moreover, all machines performing such operations confront a similar collection of technical problems, dealing with such matters as power transmission (gearing, belting, shafting), control devices, feed mechanisms, friction reduction, and a broad array of problems connected with the properties of metals (such as ability to withstand stresses and heat resistance). It is because these processes and problems became common to the production of a wide range of disparate commodities that industries which were apparently unrelated from the point of view of the nature and uses of the final product became very closely related (technologically convergent) on a technological basis—for example, firearms, sewing machines, and bicycles.

This technological convergence had very important consequences for both (1) the development of new techniques and (2) their diffusion, once developed.[19] The intensive degree of specialization which developed

---

[19] On this point it is difficult to avoid the conclusion that we are still suffering, in our understanding of technological innovation, from a Schumpeterian blight. For all his profound understanding of the capitalist process, Schumpeter never quite overcame his preoccupation with the charismatic aspects of leadership and its role in instituting changes in the operation of the economic system. As a result, his own towering intellectual leadership in this area has led to an excessive concern with the more dramatic and discontinuous aspects of innovation, with the circumstances surrounding the initial "breakthrough," and to a neglect of the less spectacular dimensions of innovation. We refer, in particular, to two other aspects: (1) the cumulative impact of relatively small innovations (which were of great importance in the design, development, and adaptation of machines) and (2) the determinants of the rate and the area over which an innovation, once made, is eventually diffused. These points will be treated subsequently in this paper.

in the second half of the 19th century owed its existence to a combination of technological convergence plus what Stigler has called vertical disintegration—that is, a tendency for individual sequences in the production of a final product to be undertaken as separate operations by separate firms. Stigler suggests that vertical disintegration, and therefore increasing process specialization by firm, is likely to be characteristic of growing industries.

If one considers the full life of industries, the dominance of vertical disintegration is surely to be expected. Young industries are often strangers to the established economic system. They require new kinds of qualities of materials and hence make their own; they must overcome technical problems in the use of their products and cannot wait for potential users to overcome them; they must persuade customers to abandon other commodities and find no specialized merchants to undertake this task. These young industries must design their specialized equipment and often manufacture it, and they must undertake to recruit (historically, often to import) skilled labor. When the industry has attained a certain size and prospects, many of these tasks are sufficiently important to be turned over to specialists.[20]

It seems clear that the extraordinary degree of specialization achieved in the machine-producing sector of the American economy is attributable, not only to the growth of individual industries experiencing vertical disintegration in Stigler's sense, but also to the simultaneous growth of several industries which were technologically convergent in our sense. The extent of machinery specialization which was achieved would not have been possible if there were only vertical disintegration *without convergence*. For the degree of specialization achieved owed its existence in large part to the fact that certain technical processes were common to many industries. Individual firms producing nothing but milling machines would not have emerged in an economy where only firearms manufacturers employed milling machines, nor would specialized grinding machine producers have emerged in an economy where only bicycle manufacturers employed grinding machines. With technological convergence, however, milling and grinding became important operations in a large number of metal-using industries, thus permitting a degree of specialization at "higher" stages of production which would not otherwise have been possible. Since, as Adam Smith, Allyn Young, and George Stigler have taught us, "the division of labor is limited by the extent of the market," the unique degree of specialization developed in the American machinery-producing sector owed as much to technological convergence as it did to the expansion in the demand for individual final products.

The importance of this specialization must be conceived, not only in a static sense, but in a dynamic sense as well. For there is an important

---

[20] George Stigler, "The Division of Labor is Limited by the Extent of the Market," *Journal of Political Economy,* Vol. LIX, No. 3 (June, 1951), p. 190.

learning process involved in machinery production, and a high degree of specialization is conducive not only to an effective learning process but to an effective *application* of that which is learned. This highly developed facility in the designing and production of specialized machinery is, perhaps, the most important single characteristic of a well-developed capital goods industry and constitutes an external economy of enormous importance to other sectors of the economy.

Metal-using industries, therefore, were continually being confronted with similar kinds of problems which required solution and which, once solved, took their place in short order in the production of other metal-using products employing similar processes. Using Usher's useful terminology, metal-using industries were continually engaged in a "setting of the stage" for particular problems which, once they were solved, produced free technological inputs to other metal-using industries.

In all of this the machine tool industry, as a result of technological convergence, played a unique role both in the initial solution of technological problems and in the rapid transmission and application of newly learned techniques to other uses. We suggest that the machine tool industry may be regarded as a center for the acquisition and diffusion of new skills and techniques in a machinofacture type of economy. Its chief importance, therefore, lay in its strategic role in the learning process associated with industrialization. This role, as I have asserted and will now elaborate further, is a dual one: (1) new skills and techniques were developed or perfected here in response to the demands of specific customers; and (2) once they were acquired, the machine tool industry was the main transmission center for the transfer of new skills and techniques to the entire machine-using sector of the economy.

IV

In this sector we will examine the nature and the consequences of technological convergence. An exhaustive cataloging of specific instruments is neither possible nor, fortunately, is it necessary for our purposes. The basic pattern which I wish to emphasize with respect to both the origin and diffusion of machine tool innovations will be explored by reference to its historical role in four industries: firearms, sewing machines, bicycles, and automobiles. If time and space permitted, a more comprehensive account would include also a wide spectrum of machine tool-using industries ranging from watches and clocks, scientific instruments, hardware, and typewriters to agricultural implements, locomotives, and naval ordnance.

What is important here is a historical sequence in which the need to solve specific technical problems in the introduction of a new product or process in a single industry led to exploratory activity at a vertically "higher" stage of production; the solution to the problem, once achieved, was conceived to have immediate applications in producing other products to which it was closely related on a technical basis; and this solution was transmitted to such other industries via the machine tool industry. The machine tool industry may be looked upon as constituting a pool or reservoir of skills and technical knowledge which are employed throughout the entire machine-using sectors of the economy. Because it dealt with processes and problems common to an increasing number of industries, it played, during this period, the role of a transmission center in the diffusion of the new technology. The pool of skill and technical knowledge was added to as a result of problems which arose in particular industries. Once the particular problem was solved and added to the pool, the solution became available, with perhaps minor modifications and redesigning, for employment in technologically related industries. Thus, as a result of technological convergence, external economies of enormous importance were rapidly generated.

Throughout the whole of the first half of the 19th century and culminating perhaps with the completion of Samuel Colt's Armory in Hartford in 1855, the making of firearms occupied a position of decisive importance in the development of specialized, precision machinery. The notion that the system of interchangeable parts sprang full-blown from Whitney's genius in musket manufacture has now been accorded a decent burial.[21] What is clear is that the new machinery and technology were the joint product of efforts to overcome the same group of problems, not only by Whitney, but by men employed at such places as Robbins and Lawrence, Ames Manufacturing Company, Colt's Armory, and the government armories at Springfield and Harpers Ferry as well.

The introduction of Thomas Blanchard's stocking lathe for the shaping of gunstocks, in 1818, represents an interesting transitional innovation, inasmuch as it was originally developed for the shaping of wooden materials but involved a principle which eventually found wide applications in other materials for reproducing irregular patterns. Blanchard's lathe, which replaced the tedious and time-consuming hand techniques of shaping the gunstock by whittling, boring, and chiseling, was introduced at the national armories at Springfield and Harpers Ferry during the 1820's.[22] The principle embodied in the machine was quickly applied to such sundry items as hat blocks, handles, spokes of wheels, sculptured busts, oars, and shoe lasts.[23]

---

[21] Woodbury, "Legend of Eli Whitney." (See n. 7.)

[22] Charles Fitch, "Report on the Manufactures of Interchangeable Mechanism," *Tenth Census of the United States* (1880), Vol. II, pp. 13–19. (Hereafter cited as Fitch, *Report.*)

[23] The application to the last item was apparently too quick, for Blanchard was upheld, as late as 1849, in an infringement suit involving the application of his lathe to turning shoemaker's lasts. See *Journal of the Franklin Institute,* Vol. XLVII (1849), pp. 259–62.

The British commission on arms manufacture which visited the United States in

The firearms industry was instrumental in the development of the whole array of tools and accessories upon which the large-scale production of precision metal parts is dependent: jigs (originally employed for drilling and hand filing), fixtures, taps and gauges, and the systematic development of die-forging techniques.[24]

The milling machine, perhaps with the turret lathe one of the two most versatile of all modern machine tools, owed its origin in the United States to the attempt of arms makers to provide an effective machine substitute for highly expensive hand filing and chiseling operations. Although here, as in so many other cases, its exact origins are shrouded in obscurity, it is clear that both Eli Whitney and Simeon North employed crude milling machines in their musket-producing enterprises in the second decade of the nineteenth century, as did John H. Hall at the Harpers Ferry Armory.[25] Its subsequent development was largely the work of the national armories, especially the highly important work of Thomas Warner at the Springfield Armory,[26] and such gun-producing firms as Robbins and Lawrence, of Windsor, Vermont. The design of the plain milling machine was stabilized, in the 1850's, in the form which came to be known as the Lincoln miller, and rapidly assumed a prominent place in all the metal trades. Fitch states that, between 1855 and 1880, ". . . nearly 100,000 of these machines or practical copies of them, have been built for gun, sewing-machine and similar work."[27]

The final major contribution of the arms makers was the role played in the development of the turret lathe which, together with the milling

---

1853 was particularly impressed with the gunstock lathe, at the time apparently still unknown in England. "It is most remarkable that this valuable labour-saving machine should have been so much neglected in England, seeing that it is capable of being applied to so many branches of manufacture, its introduction into the armory will prove a national benefit." *Report of the Committee on Machinery of U.S.* (H.C., 1855), p. 39. The British government subsequently purchased these machines from the Ames Manufacturing Company of Chicopee, Massachusetts.

[24] Fitch reports that die-forming machines were employed at Harpers Ferry as early as 1827. (Fitch, *Report*, p. 20.) The most significant subsequent improvements were achieved at the Colt Armory under the guidance of its ingenious superintendent, Elisha K. Root. Although the sewing-machine industry relied more heavily upon casting than on forging, drop forging with dies was introduced into sewing-machine manufacture as early as 1856. (Fitch, *Report*, p. 37.) Compare also W. F. Durfee, "The History and Modern Development of the Art of Interchangeable Construction in Mechanism," *Transactions, American Society of Mechanical Engineering*, Vol. XIV (1893), esp. pp. 1,250–51.

[25] Fitch, *Report*, pp. 22–26; Joseph W. Roe, "History of the First Milling Machine," *American Machinist*, Vol. XXXVI (June 27, 1912), pp. 1,037–38; Robert S. Woodbury, *History of the Milling Machine* (Cambridge, Mass.: M.I.T. Press, 1960), chaps. i and ii. Woodbury's book, which is part of a series devoted to the history of machine tools, is an invaluable guide to the detailed technical development of the milling machine.

[26] Fitch, *Report*, pp. 3 and 25; Felicia J. Deyrup, *Arms Makers of the Connecticut Valley* (Northampton, Mass.: Smith College Press, 1948), pp. 153–54.

[27] Fitch, *Report*, p. 26. Fitch cites examples for 1880 of arms making plants where milling machines constituted between 25 and 30 percent of the total number of machines in use (p. 22).

machine, was indispensable to the production of all commodities based upon interchangeable parts. The turret lathe, holding a cluster of tools placed on a vertical axis, made it possible to perform a sequence of operations on the workpiece without the need for resetting or removing the piece from the lathe. It therefore revolutionized all manufacturing processes requiring large volumes of small precision components, such as screws—which were, in short order after the development of the turret lathe, produced on turret lathe machines.[28]

The origin of the turret lathe (initially employing a horizontal axis for the turret) has been attributed to Stephen Fitch, of Middlefield, Connecticut, in 1845, while he was engaged on a government contract for the production of percussion locks for an army horse pistol.[29] The turret lathe principle was employed and improved at the Colt Armory (where Root introduced a double-turret machine in 1852) and by Frederick W. Howe while superintendent of the Robbins and Lawrence Company at Windsor, Vermont; and turret lathes were built and sold commercially by that company in 1854. A turret screw machine, designed in 1858 by H. D. Stone, was sold commercially by the Jones and Lamson Company.[30] From this point on, the machine was adapted and modified for innumerable uses in the production of components for such products as sewing machines, watches, typewriters, locomotives, bicycles and, eventually, automobiles. Its most important subsequent improvement was introduced by Christopher Spencer, a former Colt employee and the inventor of the Spencer repeating rifle. As a result of a machine which he invented for turning sewing-machine spools, Spencer went on to explore methods for making metal screws automatically and, in so doing, invented the automatic turret lathe.[31] The importance of this innovation is difficult to exaggerate, since the self-adjusting feature of the cam cylinder with adjustable strips, through which automaticity was achieved, was eventually to make possible all modern automatic lathe operations. Together with the subsequent perfection of multiple spindle techniques, it was instrumental in a major acceleration in the pace of machine tool operations.

From the 1850's through the 1870's, the technical requirements of the sewing-machine industry played a major role as a source of machine tool

[28] *Ibid.,* p. 28.

[29] E. G. Parkhurst, "Origin of the Turret, or Revolving Head," *American Machinist,* Vol. XXIII (May 24, 1900), pp. 489–91. Compare also Guy Hubbard, "Development of Machine Tools in New England," *American Machinist,* Vol. LX (February 21, 1924), pp. 272–74.

[30] Fitch, *Report,* pp. 27–28; Joseph W. Roe, *English and American Tool Builders,* (New Haven: Yale University Press, 1916), p. 143. The successors of the Robbins and Lawrence Company, the Jones and Lamson Machine Company, remained one of the leaders in turret lathe production for many years. See James Hartness, *Machine Building for Profit* (Springfield, Vt.: Jones & Lamson Machinery Co., 1909). Hartness introduced the flat-turret lathe and was a pioneer in the application of hydraulic feeds to machine tools.

[31] Guy Hubbard, "Development of Machine Tools in New England," *American Machinist,* Vol. LXI (August 21, 1924), p. 314; Roe, *Tool Builders,* p. 176.

innovations. Although sewing-machine production was virtually non-existent in 1850, it constituted a flourishing industry in 1860,[32] and grew with remarkably swift strides, nationally and internationally, in the following decade.[33] Out of the innumerable modifications of the sewing machine grew the vast boot-and-shoe and men's and women's ready-to-wear clothing industries; and the machine, by 1890, was used extensively in the production of such items as awnings, tents and sails, pocketbooks, rubber and elastic goods, saddlery and harnesses, etc., and in bookbinding. The rapid diffusion of the sewing machine after 1860 was due to the fact that it provided a highly effective mechanical device for performing an operation common to many industries. It therefore constitutes a major historical example of what we have called technilogical convergence.[34]

The machining requirements and processes of sewing-machine manufacturing were broadly similar to those of firearms production, and sewing-machine manufacturers were quick to adopt these processes.[35] However, just as in the case of firearms, the solution of technical problems in sewing-machine production resulted in major additions to the stock of machine-cutting instruments which, in turn, were applied to the pro-

---

[32] *Manufactures of the United States in 1860* (compiled from the original returns of the Eighth Census), p. clxxxix. The Twelfth Census conveniently collates the basic earlier census data on the sewing machines; *Twelfth Census* (1900), Vol. X, p. 404. An illustration and description of the Singer Sewing Machine, as it appeared when patented in 1851, appears on the front page of *Scientific American,* Vol. VII, No. 7 (November 1, 1851).

[33] "In the Exhibition at London in 1851, only two very imperfect sewing machines were exhibited. In 1855, at Paris, there were 14 varieties of sewing machines, some of which were so perfect that little or no material advance has since been made; and in 1862, in the London Exhibition, about 50 different arrangements of machines were shown. . . . In the 'Exposition Universelle,' now open in Paris, there are no less than 87 exhibitors of sewing machines. Their manufacture is now very general in European countries. France has 27 exhibitors, America 21, and England 12. Even so small a principality as Hesse has two exhibitors of sewing machines; the colony of Canada, five." Captain Hichens on "Apparatus for Sewing and Making up Clothing," in *Reports on the Paris Universal Exhibition, 1867. Presented to both Houses of Parliament* (1868); Vol. V, pp. 131–32.

[34] See the summary of census statistics for 1880 and 1890 for industries in which the sewing machine was employed extensively, in Chauncey M. Depew (ed.), *One Hundred Years of American Commerce* (New York, 1895), Vol. II, p. 538. See also the description of sewing machines for specialized purposes in Frederick A. Paget, "Report on the Machines and Apparatus used in Sewing and Clothing." *Reports on the Philadelphia International Exhibition of 1876. Presented to both Houses of Parliament* (1877), Vol. I, pp. 242–43.

[35] The sewing-machine industry relied much more heavily than did the firearms industry upon cast iron and was instrumental in bring about important improvements in foundry operations. The molding press, for example, was introduced by Albert Eames, who was at the time (around 1873), foreman of the foundry at the Wheeler and Wilson Sewing Machine Company and who was earlier employed in firearms manufacture. The molding press played an important role in the production of sewing-machine parts, in hardware generally, and in other industries dependent on casting. Fitch, *Report,* pp. 36–37; also Fitch, "Report on the Manufacture of Hardware, Cutlery, and Edge-tools," *Tenth Census of the United States* (1880); Vol. II, p. 10.

duction of other metal-using products. The most important innovations in the sewing-machine industry were products of the remarkable Brown and Sharpe Manufacturing Company of Providence, Rhode Island.

The Brown and Sharpe Company was founded in 1833 by David Brown and his son, Joseph R. Brown. Until 1850, the firm was engaged in the production and repairing of clocks, watches, and mathematical instruments. In 1850, the firm introduced a fully automatic linear dividing engine and shortly thereafter a vernier caliper and then, in 1855, a precision gear-cutting machine.[36] In 1858, the firm commenced production of the Willcox and Gibbs sewing machine, which was an immediate success and resulted in a very considerable plant expansion. The unique machine tool contributions of this firm were generated primarily by the necessity to provide the appropriate machinery for their sewing-machine operation. But the results of these efforts were machine tools of a general usefulness far surpassing the industry of origin.[37]

The first of these machines, a turret screw machine, devised for sewing-machine parts, was impressed into other uses upon the outbreak of the Civil War and thereafter became a major tool in machine shop practice generally.[38] The primary purchasers of Brown and Sharpe's screw machine were producers of hardware and tools, sewing machines, shoe machinery, locomotives, rifles and ammunition—and machine tools.[39]

Another machine tool extensively developed by Brown and Sharpe arose out of a major production problem in the building of sewing machines and one which was to assume even greater proportions in the future production of automobiles—that is, the precision grinding, to a fine finish, of hardened steel parts. This problem was encountered by Brown and Sharpe in providing components of the Willcox and Gibbs sewing machine—needle bars, foot bars, and shafts.[40] Brown finally produced a cylindrical grinding machine which was employed within his own firm and was sold to other firms (including foreign firms) beginning in 1865.[41] After several years of extensive modification and redesigning, the firm introduced a universal grinding machine of far greater versatility which was exhibited at the Centennial Exhibition in Philadelphia in 1876.

---

[36] Roe, *Tool Builders*, pp. 202–6; Robert S. Woodbury, *History of the Gear-Cutting Machine* (Cambridge, Mass.: M.I.T. Press, 1958), pp. 80–81. Brown and Sharpe undertook the production of automatic gear cutters in 1877.

[37] Woodbury, *History of the Grinding Machine* (Cambridge, Mass.: M.I.T. Press, 1959), pp. 60–61.

[38] *Ibid.* Compare Luther D. Burlingame, "The Universal Milling Machine," *American Machinist,* Vol. XXXIV (January 5, 1911), p. 9.

[39] I am grateful to Professor Duncan McDougall for kindly placing at my disposal his data on the sale of machinery output of the Brown and Sharpe Company.

[40] Woodbury, *Grinding Machine*, pp. 60–61.

[41] *Ibid.*, pp. 61–62; Guy Hubbard, "100 Years of Progress in American Metalworking Equipment," *Automotive Industries,* Vol. CXIII, No. 5 (September 1, 1955), p. 315.

This machine is the direct ancestor of the modern heavy production grinding machines.[42]

The development of the universal milling machine by Brown and Sharpe is, perhaps, the most outstanding example of a machine which was initially developed as a solution to a narrow and specific range of problems and which eventually had enormous unintended ramifications as the technique was applied to similar productive processes over a wide range of metal-using industries.

The universal milling machine had its immediate stimulus in the production of Springfield muskets by the Providence Tool Company at the outbreak of the Civil War. One of the gun parts (the nipple) required a hole to be drilled in it, and for this purpose the Providence Tool Company employed twist drills, the twist drills in turn being made by a crude process of hand filing the spiral grooves in tool-steel rods or wire. Frederick W. Howe, at the time superintendent of the company, brought the matter to the attention of Joseph Brown, whose appreciation for the problem was heightened by the fact that Brown and Sharpe employed similar drills in the production of the Willcox and Gibbs sewing machine. Brown's solution was the universal milling machine, the first of which was sold to the Providence Tool Company in March, 1862. It was an amazingly useful machine, which would not only cut the grooves of spiral drills but could be employed in all kinds of spiral milling operations and in gear cutting, as well as in the cutting of all sorts of irregular shapes in metal.[43] Within the first 10 years, Brown and Sharpe sold universal milling machines to manufacturers of hardware, tools, cutlery, locks, arms, sewing machines, textile machinery, printing machines, professional and scientific instruments, and locomotives, to machine shops and foundries, and of course to machine tool manufacturers. Later on in the century, with each successive product innovation, universal milling machines were sold to a succession of firms producing cash registers, calculating machines, typewriters, agricultural implements, bicycles, and automobiles. Even this impressive list of users is far from exhaustive. Toward the end of the 19th century, heavy-duty milling machines increasingly undertook machining operations previously performed by planing and shaping machines.

The Brown and Sharpe sales records show, furthermore, that the largest single group of buyers of their universal milling machine was other machine tool producers. Thus, the creation of a new machine tool to solve technical problems in the production of a final product resulted in a significant source of increased productive efficiency in the machine tool industry itself.

---

[42] Woodbury, *Grinding Machine*, pp. 64–71. Brown and Sharpe applied the hydraulic feed technique to the grinding machine in 1902, a technique which makes it easier to operate any machine tool automatically. *Ibid.*, p. 139.

[43] Burlingame, "Milling Machine" (cited in n. 38).

By 1880, the proliferation of new machine tools in American industry had begun to reach torrential proportions.[44] Although there were relatively few dramatically new machines comparable to the milling machine or turret lathe, the period from 1880 to 1910 was characterized by an immense increase in the development of machine tools for highly specialized purposes by a continuous adaptation of established techniques such as automatic operation to new uses, and by a systematic improvement in the properties of materials employed in machine tool processes. The introduction of high-speed steel in machine-cutting tools and the use of superior artificial abrasives such as silicon carbide in grinding processes are the outstanding examples of the last development. In all of this the emergence of the new forms of transportation, most notably the bicycle and automobile, played a vital role.

Although high-wheeled English bicycles were exhibited at the Philadelphia Exposition in 1876 and at that time engaged the interest of Colonel Albert A. Pope, who was to play a pioneering role in their eventual introduction in the United States, they did not achieve large-scale popularity until they assumed their modern "safety" form in the early 1890's.[45] The industry's spectacular growth during the 1890's and its subsequent abrupt decline are indicated by the fact that there were 27 establishments producing bicycles and tricycles in 1890, 312 in 1900, and 101 in 1905. The value of the industry's output was $2,568,326 in 1890, $31,915,908 in 1900, and $5,153,240 in 1905.[46]

Many of the unique problems associated with the production of a satisfactory bicycle—given its source of locomotion—revolved around the need for lightness,[47] hardened precision parts, and efficient power transmission and friction reduction. In solving these problems, bicycle manufacturers and machine tool makers not only introduced novel techniques but redesigned, perfected, and popularized techniques which antedated the bicycle and thus made them available for numerous new uses. The most important direct beneficiaries of the innovations in bicycle pro-

---

[44] An admirable descriptive survey, profusely illustrated, of the "state of the arts" in machine tools in 1880 may be found in *Tenth Census* (1880), Vol. XXII, "Report on Power and Machinery Employed in Manufactures."

[45] It is of more than passing interest as evidence of technological convergence between sewing machines and bicycles to note that, in England as well as in the United States, the earliest bicycles were produced in sewing-machine plants. Colonel Pope in 1878 produced his first "Columbia" in a corner of the Weed Sewing Machine Company plant at Hartford. In England in the late 1860's, the Coventry Sewing Machine Company played a similar role.
   See *Twelfth Census* (1900), Vol. X, p. 331; Albert A. Pope, "The Bicycle Industry," in Depew, *One Hundred Years*, Vol. II, p. 550; G. C. Allen, *The Industrial Development of Birmingham and the Black Country, 1860–1927* (London: G. Allen, 1929), p. 243; J. Clapham, *An Economic History of Great Britain* (Cambridge, Eng.: The University Press, 1952), Vol. II, pp. 96–97.

[46] *Special Reports of the Census Office* (1905), Part 4, "Selected Industries," p. 289. Compare *Thirteenth Census of the United States* (1910), Vol. X, "Manufactures," pp. 825–28.

[47] Some of the earliest bicycles are reported to have weighed over 100 pounds.

duction were the automobile makers. But, in some measure, these innovations were transferred and made an important impact in all forms of manufacturing where friction reduction and power transmission constituted serious problems and wherever the newly designed machine tools had useful applications.

The problems posed by large-scale bicycle production were instrumental in improving and popularizing two highly important machining techniques and applying them to new uses: the forming tool and the oil-tube drill. Although the forming tool was employed previous to 1890, its use was confined to metals of soft composition, such as were used in making caps for salt and pepper boxes. Its much more important application to hardened metals, which made of it a standard machine shop practice, resulted from the transfer of the technique to the production of bicycle-wheel hubs. Similarly, the oil-tube drill, which had an oil channel leading to or near the point, and which made possible the lubrication and cooling of cutting edges as well as the removal of chips, had been employed before 1890 in drilling gun barrels. Its rapid diffusion after 1890 resulted from its extended application, together with the forming tool, in the drilling of holes in bicycle-wheel hubs.[48]

The requirements of bicycle production played a crucial role in the development of effective techniques for making ball bearings which, in turn, had an incalculable impact through reducing the effects of wear and friction on all machine processes. The highly exacting requirements of the ball bearing, as well as of the hardened cup and cone on which the bicycle balls roll, necessitated grinding operations of great precision.[49] In some cases the grinding machines which had been designed by Brown and Sharpe for grinding sewing-machine needle bars were adapted for this new use.[50] The eventual solution to the grinding problems involved, however, as they pertained both to the bicycle and automobile, relied heavily upon the improvements in grinding from the work of men like Charles H. Norton[51] and Edward G. Acheson, who revolutionized grinding operations through the introduction of artificial abrasives on the grinding wheel itself.

The bicycle industry was responsible also for numerous other innovations and modifications whose ultimate use extended far beyond the bi-

---

[48] *Twelfth Census* (1900), "Manufactures," pp. 385–88. See also Fred Colvin, *Sixty Years with Men and Machines* (New York: Whittlesey House, 1947), pp. 88–89.

[49] "The successful ball bearing depends upon having the balls themselves perfectly spherical and all of identical diameter. The ball must run in races perfectly circular, perfectly concentric, and of exact dimensions. Not only must the balls and their races be machined to a fine surface finish, but all these dimensions must be held to close tolerances, and all these parts must be hardened. Only grinding could deal with this problem." Woodbury, *Grinding Machine*, p. 110.

[50] *Ibid.*, p. 111.

[51] A former Brown and Sharpe employee, who had been initiated earlier into the problems of grinding at the Seth Thomas Clock Company.

cycle industry. The flat-link chain, an integral part of the safety bicycle, was applied to numerous other uses as a convenient device for the transmission of power. The chainless bicycle had focused attention on the need for hardened bevel gears, and the resulting improvements in gear-cutting machinery, such as those of Leland and Faulconer Company, were of considerable importance in the automobile.[52] The production possibilities of the turret lathe and of the automatic screw machine in mass production operations were extended by the "demonstration effect" of their application to new uses in the bicycle industry.[53] The need for metals with specific proporties, such as the light tubular steel employed in the frame, and the high-tensile-strength steel wires employed in the wheel spokes, led to metallurgical explorations which were of great benefit in other metal-using industries.[54]

The automobile was in the earliest stages of its phenomenal growth in the first decade of the present century. The value of automobile output in 1900 was less than $5,000,000, and—although there were 57 establishments engaged in automobile manufacturing—their work was still essentially experimental.[55] In 1909, there were 265 establishments manufacturing complete automobiles and 478 manufacturing automobile bodies and parts; the corresponding figures for 1914 were 300 and 971, respectively. The value of automobile output rose from $26,645,064 in 1904 to $193,823,108 in 1909 and to $503,230,137 in 1914. For the same years, the number of automobiles made was 21,692, 126,570 and 568,781.[56]

The massive requirements for heavy, high-speed and increasingly automatic tools generated by this growth in automobile output quickly made of the automobile industry the largest single buyer of machine tools, and in so doing they exerted a profound effect on the industry and on the designing of machine tools.[57] But while it is easy to look upon the automobile industry as something *sui generis*, such an attitude would reflect an immature appreciation of the technological basis underlying auto-

---

[52] Woodbury, *Gear-Cutting Machine*, pp. 78–126.

[53] "The bicycle impinged upon the locomotive through the medium of machine tools when the new turret lathes, which had been developed to form wheel hubs, were applied to the manufacture of locomotive crankpins. . . ." Colvin, *Sixty Years*, p. 89.

[54] In 1894, Pope's bicycle plant in Hartford built ". . . what was then the most up-to-date mill in the country for making cold drawn steel tubing. There was also a research department for testing metals and improving bicycle design." John B. Rae, *American Automobile Manufacturers* (Philadelphia: Temple Press, 1959), p. 9.

[55] *Special Reports of the Census Office* (1905), Part 4, "Manufactures," p. 269. In the 1900 Census Reports, the brief treatment of motor vehicles appears in the chapter on locomotives. Most of the 4,192 motor vehicles mentioned in that report were in fact powered by steam or electricity. *Twelfth Census* (1900), "Manufactures," pp. 255–59.

[56] *Census of Manufactures* (1914), Vol. II, "Reports for Selected Industries," pp. 731–32.

[57] Woodbury states that after 1900 the automobile industry became ". . . the largest single customer of the machine tool industry, taking 25 to 30 percent of the output. . . ." Woodbury, *Grinding Machine*, p. 120.

mobile production. For by 1900, as we have seen, there existed an extensive accumulation of technological and engineering experience in the production of machine tools and a highly developed sophistication in designing and adapting basic types of machine tools for special production purposes.

The problems of large-scale automobile production involved the extension to a new product of skills and machines not fundamentally different from those which had already been developed for such products as bicycles and sewing machines. Underlying the discontinuity of product innovation, then, were significant continuities with respect to productive processes. The transition to automobile production for the American economy after 1900 was therefore *relatively* easy, because the basic skills and knowledge required to produce the automobile did not themselves have to be "produced" but merely transferred from existing uses to new ones. This transfer was readily performed by the machine tool industry.

The transfer process is seen most clearly in the further evolution and adaptation of the grinding machine, which, as we have seen, had been developed to an advanced state before the advent of the automobile. The automobile, however, far surpassed the relatively modest needs of the sewing machine and bicycle in its need for precision-finished, hardened steel parts. Until confronted with the compelling needs of the automobile, the grinder had been used either for relatively light operations or for finishing components which had acquired their basic shapes upon a lathe. In response to the needs of automobile production, the grinding machine was converted into a tool capable of heavy production operations in the course of which it frequently replaced entirely the lathe and other machine tools. Its role here was indispensable in that it provided, for its time, the only way of undertaking the precision machining of the stronger and lighter alloy steels which played such a prominent part in automobile components.

Thus, within a few years after 1900, specialized grinding machines were devised for vital parts of the automobile engine and transmission, including special ones for crankshafts, for camshafts, for piston rings, and for cylinders. Perhaps most far-reaching of all, because of their importance elsewhere, were the contributions to gear cutting. The automobile generated a demand for strong durable gears which was quite unprecedented. Here the technological interrelations between the bicycle and the automobile are particularly clear, since the most important innovator in the grinding of gear teeth was the Leland and Faulconer Company. "Faulconer was, in 1899, the first to design a machine for production grinding of hardened bevel gears for bicycles."[58] This was the same firm which was later to become the Cadillac Automobile Company. The earliest automobile firms drew very heavily upon the business and technical leader-

---

[58] *Ibid.*, p. 99.

ship, plant facilities, and skilled labor of the bicycle industry, the decline in which coincided exactly (in the first decade of the century) with the rapid growth of automobiles.[59]

The requirements of automobile production induced innovations or substantial improvements across the whole range of machine tools, in drilling and tapping, in milling, in lathe work generally, etc. Moreover, it brought about a significant substitution of one machine process for another, most particularly as a result of the development of power presses and dies. Intricate automobile components which would once have been produced by the lathe, drill press, milling machine, or casting or forging, were increasingly stamped directly out of sheet metal—a technique which had been given considerable impetus in the production of bicycles.[60]

The relations between the machine tool builders and the automobile industry also provided compelling evidence of the manner in which technological convergence produces learning experiences which generate diffuse and unanticipated benefits—for the automobile, itself a machine of considerable complexity, encounters many problems in its operation similar to those of the machines which produce it. As a result, not only were existing machine tool techniques adapted to the production of this new product, but important features of the automobile itself were actually transferred and embodied into machine tools.[61] Thus, the transmission for the drive and feed mechanisms of machine tools was considerably improved when machine tool builders adopted the alloy steel sliding gears and integral keyshafts developed by automobile designers. Moreover, the introduction of antifriction bearings into key points of the machine tool resulted from the demonstration of their usefulness in automobiles. Finally, the whole approach to the lubrication of machine tools was radically revised as a result of the automobile. An important problem in the maintenance of machine tools had been the frequent breakdowns when inexperienced or negligent operators failed to attend properly to the numerous separate lubrication points of their machines. The solution, of

---

[59] "When the demand for bicycles decreased some manufacturers turned to the automobile, and many establishments that made only bicycles in 1900 are now [1905] devoted primarily to the manufacture of automobiles, while others make them to a greater or less degree in connection with the manufacture of bicycles. . . ." *Special Reports of the Census Office* (1905), Part 4, "Manufactures," p. 289. See also Rae, *American Automobile Manufacturers*, pp. 8–10. The emergence of early automobile firms out of bicycle firms is a sequence which was reproduced in Great Britain. See S. B. Saul, "The Motor Industry in Britain to 1914," *Business History* Vol. V. No. 1 (December, 1962), pp. 22–44.

[60] H. J. Hinde, "Relation of Power Presses and Dies to the Automobile Industry," *Mechanical Engineering*, Vol. XLIII (August, 1921), p. 531.

[61] Just as, at an earlier date, the working action of the Colt revolver was incorporated into machines used for *producing* the revolver. ". . . the same arrangement of parts characteristic of the Colt revolver seems to have been carried through the principal machines for its manufacture, the horizontal chucking lathes, cone-seating and screw machines, barrel-boring, profiling, and mortising machines, and even the compound crank-drops, exhibiting the same general arrangement of working parts about a center." Fitch, *Report*, pp. 27–28.

course, was the eventual adoption of the centralized, self-acting lubrication system of the automobile, which went into operation automatically as soon as the machine was activated.[62]

V

We have attempted to show how, with the growing volume of manufacturing output, increasing vertical disintegration from the point of view of a single industry was accompanied by technological convergence of larger groups of industries. The result of this convergence was a growth in a relatively small number of process specializations the consequences of which, for the production and diffusion of new technical knowledge, we have examined by focusing attention on a sequence of industries which played a most important role in this development. A few further comments appear to be called for.

An explanation of many of the technological changes in the manufacturing sector of the economy may be fruitfully approached at the purely technological level. This is not to deny, of course, that the ultimate incentives are economic in nature; rather, the point is that complex technologies create internal compulsions and pressures which, in turn, initiate exploratory activity in particular directions. The notion of imbalances in the relation *between machines* is virtually *de rigueur* in any treatment of the English cotton textile industry in the 18th century (Kay's flying shuttle leading to the need for speeding up spinning operations, etc.). We suggest that, *within a single complex machine or operation*, even more important imbalances frequently exist among its component parts. A concept of technological disequilibrium may be helpful here. At any time, the component parts of a machine may vary in their ability to exceed their present level of performance, which is determined by the capacity of some limiting component. Any important improvement in the operation of a component, whether it be the currently limiting one or not, is likely to create new obstacles, in the form of limitations imposed by another component, to the achievement of a higher level of performance. Thus single improve-

---

[62] S. Einstein, "Machine-Tool Milestones, Past and Future," *Mechanical Engineering,* Vol. LII (November, 1930), p. 961; F. K. Hendrickson, "The Influence of the Automobile on the Machine-Tool Industry in General," *Mechanical Engineering,* Vol. XLIII (August, 1921), p. 530. In discussing the relationship between the milling machine and the automobile, Einstein concluded: "The automotive industry asked of the machine-tool designer automatic machines, either through modification of standard designs or machines of entirely special design—quick-acting fixtures, either hand-operated or automatically operated—more powerful and stronger machines occupying a minimum amount of floor space. On the other hand, the automotive industry supplied the machine-tool designer with a vast variety of highly successful mechanisms and constructive details, from which he could draw freely such elements and such ideas as could be adapted to the design of machine tools." "Discussion at the Machine Shop Practice Session," *Mechanical Engineering,* Vol. XLIII (August, 1921), p. 534.

ments tend to *create* their own future problems, which compel further modification and revision.

The interdependence between the forming tool and the oil-tube drill in the machining of bicycle hubs, referred to earlier, is an important case in point. The introduction of the forming tool for the outside of bicycle hubs created a disequilibrium between the operations carried on for the outside and the inside of the hub. Since the forming tool worked more rapidly on the outside of the hub than the old-fashioned drills worked on the inside, the fullest gains from the use of the forming tool required a speeding up of drilling operations. This imbalance was corrected by the oil-tube drill which, in speeding up drilling operations, brought about a closer synchronization between the two operations. Numerous other instances of the role of disequilibrating forces could easily be cited,[63] but the induced improvements in machine tool design following the introduction of high-speed steel around the turn of the century are easily the most important within our period.

When Frederick W. Taylor and his associates introduced high-speed steel (a steel alloy which drastically improved the ability of a cutting tool to maintain its hardness at high temperatures) it became possible at once to remove metal by cutting operations at dramatically higher speeds. But it was impossible to do so on machines designed for the older carbon steel cutting tools, because they could not withstand the stress or provide sufficiently higher speeds in the other components of the machine tool. As a result, the availability of high-speed steel for the cutting tool quickly generated a complete redesign in machine tool components—the structural, transmission, and control elements:

> During the first decade of the 20th century we see high-speed steel revolutionizing the lathe—as it does all production machine tools. Beds and slides rapidly become heavier, feed works stronger, and the driving cones are designed for much wider belts than of old. The legs of big lathes grow shorter and shorter, and finally disappear as the beds grow down to the floor. On these big machines massive tool blocks take the place of tool posts and multiple tooling comes into vogue.[64]

---

[63] For example, the redesigning of milling cutters at the Cincinnati Milling Machine Company, when it was discovered that ". . . the cutters of the time were not as strong as the machines that were driving them and therefore gave out long before the maximum power of the machine was reached." Woodbury, *Milling Machine,* p. 80.

[64] Guy Hubbard, "Metal-Working Plants," *Mechanical Engineering,* Vol. LII (April, 1930), p. 411. See also Frederick W. Taylor, *The Art of Cutting Metals* (New York: American Association of Mechanical Engineers, 1907); *Special Reports of the Census Office* (1905), Part 4, "Metal-working Machinery," pp. 232–33; Ralph Flanders, "The Influence of the Automobile on Lathe Practice," *Mechanical Engineering,* Vol. XLIII (August, 1921), p. 532; Carl J. Oxford, "One Hundred Years of Metal Cutting Tools," *Centennial of Engineering 1852–1952* (Chicago: American Association of Engineers, 1953), pp. 346–50; S. Einstein, "Machine-Tool Milestones, Past and Future," *Mechanical Engineering,* Vol. LII (November, 1930), pp. 959–62.

The final effect, then, of this redesigning which was initiated by the use of high-speed steel in cutting tools was to transform machine tools into much heavier, faster, and more rigid instruments which, in turn, enlarged considerably the scope of their practical operations and facilitated their introduction into new uses.

Many aspects of technological change, in order to be adequately understood, must be examined in terms of particular historical sequences, for in technological change as in other aspects of human ingenuity, one thing often leads to another—not in a strictly deterministic sense, but in the more modest sense that doing some things successfully creates a capacity for doing other things. We have indeed already explored this theme at some length: given what we have called technological convergence, experience in the production of firearms made it a relatively simple matter to produce sewing machines,[65] just as the skills acquired in producing sewing machines and bicycles greatly facilitated the production of the automobile. This is even more apparent, in microcosm, in the chronological history of certain individual firms, some of which, over a period of several decades, ran the entire gamut of the sequence of products—or of the machinery for producing the products—which we have considered here. This was true of the Pratt and Whitney Company. Beginning with the Civil War and over the next fifty years, Pratt and Whitney introduced in succession machinery for the production of firearms, sewing machines, bicycles, and automobiles, as well as numerous other kinds of high-precision specialized machinery.[66] A machinery plant in Hartford which was originally owned by the Robbins and Lawrence Company, and later acquired by the Sharps Rifle Manufacturing Company, ran through a succession of owners (including the showman Phineas T. Barnum) and produced successively machine tools, guns, sewing machines, bicycles, motorcycles, and automobiles.[67] The Leland, Faulconer and Norton Company (later the Cadillac Automobile Company) of Detroit, which was founded in 1890 as a producer of machine tools and special machinery, introduced machinery for producing bicycle gears during the brief heyday of the bicycle, switched to building gasoline engines for motor boats when the bicycle industry began to decline, and by 1902 had undertaken the production of automobile engines.[68]

An examination of these continuities in technology provides a basis for understanding historical events which otherwise appear to be random or

---

[65] Just as it simplified, for example, the development of the typewriter, whose problems remained unsolved until it was placed in the hands of the skilled machinists and technical experts at E. Remington and Sons, gun manufacturers at Ilion, New York, *Twelfth Census* (1900), "Manufactures," p. 442.

[66] *Accuracy for Seventy Years, 1860–1930* (Hartford, Conn.: Pratt & Whitney Co., 1930).

[67] Guy Hubbard, "Development of Machine Tools in New England," *American Machinist,* Vol. LX (January 31, 1924), pp. 171–73.

[68] C. B. Owen, "Organization and Equipment of an Automobile Factory," *Machinery,* Vol. XV (March, 1909), p. 493.

capricious. The interesting thing about the group of industries discussed here is that they were all dependent, in their development, upon technological changes dealing with a limited number of processes and that the solution to problems posed by these processes eventually became the specialized function of a well-organized industry. A question of more contemporary interest is whether similar technological convergences are occurring in 20th-century conditions; whether, for example, the chemicals and electronics industries are playing the same roles of information production and transmittal that machine tools played at an earlier stage in our history.[69] The answer to the question may be very important, even from the point of view of pure theory. For a theory which assumes that most technological change enters the economy "through a particular door," so to speak, might turn out to be much simpler, and therefore more elegant, than one which assumes that technological changes may be initiated, with equal probability, anywhere in the economy.

---

[69] The government's current role in subsidizing research and development activity has an earlier and interesting parallel in the innovations emerging out of firearms production—an industry where, as we have seen, the government played a role as a major producer as well as "consumer."

5. Machine Tool Output, 1861-1910[*]

Duncan M. McDougall[†]

Carleton University

Introduction

A QUANTITATIVE STUDY of the American machine tool industry in the latter half of the 19th century faces a data problem of formidable proportions. This results not only from the lack of statistical information, common to many areas of research of that period, but primarily from the fact that it was not until the end of the period that a distinct machine tool industry emerged in the sense of a group of firms whose principal product was machine tools. Until about 1900, the machine tool industry could not be called a large, independent sector of the economy like many of the other groups of companies that led in American industrialization.

A reading of the classic work by Roe on the early American machine tool manufacturers gives the opposite impression.[1] A whole chapter is devoted to Joseph Brown and the Brown and Sharpe Manufacturing Company of Providence, Rhode Island, as one of the leading New England machine tool companies. Founded on the invention of the universal milling machine and the precision devices invented and produced by Brown, Brown and Sharpe was undoubtedly a leading company. On the other hand, examination of the financial records of the company reveals that the value of its output of sewing machines, manufactured under license from Wilcox and Gibbs, exceeded the value of machine tool shipments until 1885, 25 years after the invention of the universal milling machine. The year 1898 was the first in which the value of machine tool

* Reprinted from *Trends in Output, Employment, and Productivity in the United States after 1800* (Studies in Income and Wealth 30; New York: National Bureau of Economic Research, 1966), pp. 497–517.

† The author wishes to acknowledge financial assistance from the Ford Foundation, the Interuniversity Committee on American Economic History, and Purdue University; the cooperation of many persons in the machine tool industry; and the assistance of George A. Wing and Arvid M. Zarley, all of whom contributed greatly to this paper, but none of whom are responsible for the conclusions, opinions, or statements contained herein. That responsibility remains the author's alone.

1 J. W. Roe, *English and American Tool Builders* (New Haven, 1916).

shipments accounted for more than 50 percent of the total sales of Brown and Sharpe and, although that percentage was approached in subsequent years, it was not reached again before 1904 when the data end (Table A–1).[2]

A further indication of the relatively small and unspecialized nature of the industry is the fact that the National Machine Tool Builders Association was founded by 17 firms as late as 1902, and the Association has published no industry data for the period before 1900. Finally, it was not until the 1914 Census of Manufactures that the federal government published separate data for industrial machinery output, including machine tools, but the report is far from complete. The earlier decennial census reports on manufacturing have a section listed as machinery, but machine tools are not treated separately. The sector as reported includes such things as agricultural implements, sewing machines (including presumably the total output of Brown and Sharpe until at least the census of 1880), pumps, engines, professional and scientific instruments, and an omnibus category of foundry and machine shop products, n.e.s. (not elsewhere specified)—by far the largest category of all.

This paper deals only with metal-cutting machines and includes no information on metal-forming types. A lathe or milling machine would be an example of the first type, a press or hammer would be an example of the second. Furthermore, the paper deals with general-purpose standard machines of the light variety. Neither machines made on special order for a particular job nor industry-specialized machines such as textile or mining machinery are included. The machines considered here are the versatile, primary machines used in the production of other machinery as well as in the production of such goods as sewing machines and typewriters, not generally considered to be machines. It has proved impossible to quantify the size of the special-order output of machine tools in the 19th century. Manufacture of such tools was apparently concentrated in Philadelphia, particularly in the William Sellers Company and in the group of firms eventually combined as the Niles-Bement-Pond Company.[3] All attempts to uncover any records of the early Philadelphia companies met with failure.

The period covered in this paper is 1861–1910. The beginning date was chosen because no reliable quantitative data were found for any earlier years. Hubbard, in a series of articles in the *American Machinist* about the early beginnings of machine tool manufacture in New England, lists an impressive number of persons and companies involved in machine tool design and production before 1860.[4] Yet the impression gained

---

[2] There is, of course, a difference between sales and shipments, but the relative importance of machine tools in total sales is nonetheless represented accurately.

[3] Roe, *English and American*, pp. 249–60.

[4] C. Hubbard, "Development of Machine Tools in New England," *American Machinist*, Vols. 59 and 60, 1923 and 1924.

is of a series of small undertakings to meet specific needs, such as government musket contracts, or construction of special machinery to meet individual industry demands. For example, a mechanic in a textile mill or a small shop might build a lathe for his own use, but there is no evidence in Hubbard's work that there were machine tool companies as such. Roe, although more concerned with technical developments in machine tool design than with quantitative measures of the industry, uses 1850 as the beginning date of the American machine tool industry. As subsidiary evidence, it might be noted that none of the charter companies of the National Machine Tool Builders Association existed in 1860, as far as can be determined from the various regional genealogies of the industry.

The primary source of the data used in the paper is company records. The best records, and the only ones for 1861–81, were obtained from the Brown and Sharpe Company for 1861–1905. The records list a total of 23,658 machine tools shipped by the company from September, 1861, to June, 1905.[5] Each shipment is recorded by type and size of machine, date of shipment, name and location of consignee, and price. Year-end financial statements of the same company were also obtained for 1869–1905. A second shipment series was obtained from the Bullard Company of Bridgeport, Connecticut, covering a total of 6,535 machines shipped between April, 1881 and December, 1912. Those records did not include price, but a separate price record found for 1895–1912 made possible calculation of dollar sales for the shorter period. Sales figures have also been obtained for the G. A. Gray Company, Cincinnati, for 1886–1910, and for the Cincinnati Shaper Company for 1899–1910. A 20 percent sample of the shipment records of the two Cincinnati companies showing region of destination, by various time periods, is also available.[6] Finally, a series of the dollar value of new orders was obtained from the Warner and Swasey Company of Cleveland for 1880–1910, and a series of sales figures from the same company beginning in 1903. A total of 21 existing machine tool companies with roots extending back into the 19th century were communicated with in the study. All requests were met with offers of assistance, but all except the above-mentioned few reported that early records had been destroyed, frequently as a result of consolidation or reorganization of firms.[7]

The subsequent analysis in this paper is based, therefore, on the records of a relatively small number of firms. There is no way of telling how

---

[5] Shipments differ from production by the number of machines produced but retained for the company's use and by the net change in machine inventory. Data for shipments only were available.

[6] The information on the Cincinnati companies was made available to the author through the kindness of George A. Wing.

[7] The greatest disappointment in this project was the discovery that the first volume of the shipment records of the Pratt and Whitney Company of West Hartford, Connecticut, covering the period up to about 1904 had been destroyed 18 months before I wrote to the firm.

representative of the industry the sample is. We do know that Brown and Sharpe was an early technical leader in the machine tool field and one of the leading producers of light machine tools in New England. The Brown and Sharpe Company began in 1853 when Lucien Sharpe, who proved to be the businessman of the combination, was brought into the company formed in 1833 by David and Joseph R. Brown, father and son, to make and repair clocks. In 1850 Joseph Brown developed the first automatic linear dividing engine for graduating rules, a machine Roe mentions as still being in use in the shop in 1916. The next efforts were production of protractors and calipers with the vernier scale attached. Standards and accuracy of measurement continued to be an important concern of the firm—as they still are today—but, from the point of view of this paper, the developments must be considered peripheral to the main subject. The first machine tool produced for sale by the company was a turret screw machine of a general design well known at the time, sold in 1861 to the Providence Tool Company which had a contract to manufacture Springfield muskets for the government. Joseph Brown's significant contribution to machine tool design came in 1861–62, when he invented the universal milling machine. The first of these new machines was shipped in 1862, again to the Providence Tool Company.

Throughout the period covered by the available records, Brown and Sharpe concentrated on the production of light, standard machine tools, screw machines, grinding machines, and the universal milling machine. In this respect, it was apparently similar to Pratt and Whitney, whose product line was much the same in nature although more extensive in both kind and number of machines produced. Brown and Sharpe is therefore probably a good sample of the light machine tool operations in New England as a whole.

The Bridgeport Machine Tool Company, which was to become the Bullard Company, was established in 1880 as a producer of machine tools in Bridgeport, Connecticut, by E. P. Bullard. Bullard was a mechanic who had become a machine tool agent in New York City and, from his experience in selling tools, he recognized the need for a more accurate engine lathe than those currently available. He engaged a mechanic to produce the lathes in Bridgeport but, within a year, had taken full control of the operation. The first shipment of the new company was a total of twenty-five 16-foot by 5-inch engine lathes between April and June, 1881, consigned to the Westinghouse Airbrake Company of Pittsburgh. In 1883, Bullard made a significant contribution to the technical progress of the machine tool art with the invention of a small boring mill capable of accurate production work. The new machine was publicized for the first time in 1883, but no shipments were made until 1885. With the movement into the boring mill and the larger engine lathe, the Bullard Company developed a product line of machines that were larger, as measured by average price per machine, than those developed by Brown and Sharpe.

There is no way of assessing the representativeness of the sample collected. The records of Brown and Sharpe are extremely valuable because it is fairly certain it was quantitatively a large firm and was certainly a leader in the technology of the light machine tool field. Bullard is also a valuable sample because, while not quantitatively so large a firm as Brown and Sharpe, its output encompassed the larger type of production machine tool. The evidence available for the Ohio companies is only meager and, while implications can be drawn from the information available, it will not support much analysis.

Little more can be said beyond affirming that the information gathered for this paper exceeds anything previously available, and that an effort has been made to track down as much relevant material as possible. What follows, therefore, while strictly speaking a quantitative study of selected firms, represents the growth pattern of the American type of production cutting machine tool through the first decade of this century.

Growth of Output

The literature on the history of the American machine tool industry never fails to point to the supreme importance of the machine tool in the development of what came to be called the American system of manufacture. There can be no doubt that the mass production, the standardization of parts, and precision manufacturing all stemmed from advancing technology embodied in machine tools. What seems clear from the record, however, is that these accouterments of an industrial society came at a fairly late stage in the process of development and were associated with a particular change in output mix.

Perhaps the most impressive aspect of the quantitative records available is that the volume of shipments was so small (Table A–2). The first machine tool was shipped by Brown and Sharpe in 1861. It was not, however, until 1875 that the cumulative total of machines shipped passed the 1,000 mark, and not until 1883 that it reached 2,000. Between September, 1861, and June, 1905, the records show that Brown and Sharpe shipped a total of 23,658 machine tools, but 12,447 of the total number, or 52.6 percent, were shipped between January, 1899, and June, 1905. The Bullard Company began shipping machines in April, 1881, but it was not until 1890 that the cumulative number of shipments passed the 1,000 mark. Up to the end of 1910, Bullard shipped a total of 6,162 machines, but 3,229 of the total number, or 52.4 percent, were shipped between January, 1901, and December, 1910.

There is ample evidence that the acceleration in the rate of growth of commodity output which marked the initial period of industrial development in the United States began before the Civil War. Whether or not one wishes to call it the period of "takeoff," following Rostow, it is clear from Gallman's figures that the high decade rates of growth shown for the period just before 1860 must have marked a sharp change from the rates existing in the early decades of the 19th century.[8] Gallman's figures also show evidence of a decline in the growth rates of commodity output, and particularly in the growth rate of value added by manufacturing, in the latter decades of the 19th century. As Gallman pointed out, his results are roughly consistent with the trend-cycle dating determined by Burns from his study of production trends, which shows a period of rapid increase of nonagricultural industrial output between 1875 and 1885 and again between 1895 and 1905.[9]

Table 1 presents rates of change calculated from the available long-term records of machine tool output along with selected rates of change derived from Gallman. The Gallman rates of change are based on single-year figures, while those for the machine tool shipments are three-year averages centered on the years available to Gallman. Presumably, therefore, the Gallman figures would show the influence of business cycles more sharply than the shipment figures do, but the differences are so clear that the conclusions drawn from the table are unlikely to be affected by cyclical variations in the underlying figures.

TABLE 1

RATES OF CHANGE IN MACHINE TOOL PRICES AND OUTPUT,
SELECTED VARIABLES, DECENNIAL OR QUINQUENNIAL, 1864–69
(Percent)

Year	Value Added in 1879 Prices of Manufac- turing (1)	Change in Value in 1879 Prices of Manufactured Producer Durables Output (2)	Change in Number of Brown and Sharpe Shipments of Machines		
			Total (3)	Domestic (4)	Foreign (5)
1864					
1869	26	72			
1874			25	4	
1879	82	67	25	35	—12
1884	90		50	121	67
1889	112	117	376	300	654
1894	71		229	201	400
1899	51	48	221	170	320

SOURCE: Col. 1 from Gallman, "Commodity Output," Table 3, p. 24; col. 2 calculated from *ibid.*, Table A–12, p. 65; cols. 3–5 from company records.

The conclusion derived from the table is that the light production machine tool was not quantitatively important in the period of American industrialization but became important at a later period. This conclusion

---

[8] Robert E. Gallman, "Commodity Output, 1839–1899," *Trends in the American Economy in the Nineteenth Century* (Studies in Income and Wealth 23 [Princeton N.J.: Princeton University Press] for National Bureau of Economic Research, 1960), pp. 15–17.

[9] A. F. Burns, *Production Trends in the United States since 1870* (New York: National Bureau of Economic Research, 1934), pp. 215–20.

could result from the fact that only one company is considered. The explanation of the difference in the aggregate and single-company growth figures could merely reflect a sudden increase in the prominence of Brown and Sharpe, or a technical development that permitted a sharp increase in the output of the firm. Both explanations appear unlikely. Brown and Sharpe had a wide reputation as a machine tool producer, if its exhibition of tools at international expositions as early as 1869 is any indication.[10] Also, the second hypothesis seems unlikely in view of the fact that the company's product line, which represented inputs to its own productive process, shows no apparent marked technical change over time.

The more likely explanation is found in the relation between machine tool output and the industrial destination of the machines, which can be inferred from the major product of the buyer. The name of the buyer does not always appear in the available records showing the consignee of shipments. Where the consignee was an agent and only the agent's name was listed, it was impossible to determine the eventual destination of the machine. In other records, the name of the consignee gave no clue to the industry to which it belonged, although in some such cases the firm could be allocated by reference to other sources. Of a total of 22,478 machines shipped by Brown and Sharpe to December, 1904, 8,499 or 37.8 percent were consigned to domestic and foreign agents or allocated to unknown buyers. Of this number, 4,469 or more than half were consigned to foreign agents. Of the total of 6,162 machines shipped by Bullard to December, 1910, 2,498 or 40.5 percent were consigned to domestic and foreign agents or allocated to unknown buyers. Of this number, 1,284 or more than half were consigned to foreign agents. The problem of the agent comes up again with respect to machine tool companies as consignees. We know, for example, that Pratt and Whitney established agencies in many parts of the United States fairly early in its history, and acted as agents for Brown and Sharpe as well. The very minor number of machines consigned to Pratt and Whitney indicates that, in spite of the affiliation, final consignee was specified on sales through the agent. There is no way of telling, however, how many local machine shops, especially those begun by Brown and Sharpe apprentices, might have acted as agents.

Table 2 presents quinquennial totals of part of the industrial distribution of shipments by Brown and Sharpe and by Bullard. There are two significant points shown by the table. The first is the clear association between the expanding output of machine tools and the growth of industries producing fairly complex and technically sophisticated final products. The bicycle, the cash register, and the electrical equipment industries, and government arsenals all placed substantial orders for ma-

---

[10] Brown and Sharpe published a catalog in French in August, 1867, and one in German in April, 1868.

TABLE 2
Industrial Distribution of Machine Tool Output, Quinquennial, 1861–1909
(Number of Machines)

Purchasing Industry	1861–64*	1865–69	1870–74	1875–79	1880–84†	1885–89	1890–94	1895–99	1900–4	1905–9
A. Sold by Brown and Sharpe										
Machine tools	16	22	16	8	63	90	194	439	649	
Rifles and ammunition	100	11	41	10	5	9	62	85	259	
Sewing and shoe machines	22	62	135	35	120	88	93	140	253	
Calculators and cash registers	0	0	0	0	9	13	101	183	716	
Professional and scientific instruments‡	0	10	6	9	35	30	65	144	282	
Government arsenals	3	14	14	1	6	379	113	409	601	
Electric equipment	0	0	0	3	60	49	157	538	797	
Bicycles	0	0	0	0	0	27	32	267	78	
Automobiles	0	0	0	0	0	0	0	55	268	
Railroads and R.R. equipment	4	9	19	11	69	71	95	117	182	
Sum of cols. as percent of total machines§	95.4	80.0	68.5	61.1	71.3	67.8	58.2	63.3	65.4	
B. Sold by Bullard										
Machine tools					36	87	99	66	101	91
Railroads and R.R. equipment					112	65	104	77	207	212
Iron and steel					3	31	85	81	65	91
Electric equipment					4	53	54	52	192	167
Government arsenals					1	10	49	31	24	17
Bicycles					0	0	0	0	5	2
Automobiles					0	0	0	0	19	88
Sum of cols. as percent of total machines§					76.1	70.3	68.2	74.2	71.9	65.6

* September, 1861, to December, 1864, Brown and Sharpe.
† April, 1881, to December, 1884, Bullard.
‡ Includes companies making watches, clocks, cameras, optical equipment, and dental equipment.
§ These are column totals as a percentage of the total number of machines that could be allocated by user.
SOURCE: Company records.

chines after 1885. Second, the difference in the relative size of the machines in the Brown and Sharpe and Bullard product lines shows up in the table. Bullard shipped no machines to companies producing cash registers between 1881 and 1910, only 18 machines to sewing machine companies, and only 7 machines to bicycle companies. On the other hand, the percentage of total Bullard shipments consigned to iron foundries and iron and steel mills was six times the corresponding percentage for Brown and Sharpe. Sales by the two companies to automobile producers show an interesting difference. Bullard shipped its first machine to an automobile company in 1901 by which time Brown and Sharpe had shipped 101 machines but, as the automobile increased in size and complexity, heavy tools became more important as inputs, and shipments by Bullard increased markedly.

A machine tool of the type considered here is a fairly versatile input. It is true that the machines produced before 1910 were specific in the types of operations they could perform; an engine lathe, for example, was quite limited in the kinds of operations it could be set up to accomplish at one time, but these machines could be used to produce many different products. The reasonable conclusion seems to be that, until after 1884 or more noticeably after 1895, the demand for light machine tools was relatively limited. The large demand for machine tools beginning at the turn of the century can be associated with the development of a new technology, and with the beginnings of what Rostow has called the period of "high mass consumption."

Market for Machine Tools

While the volume of shipments from machine tool companies was apparently quite modest until nearly the end of the 19th century, the market was anything but local. During the Civil War the market was dominated by domestic demands from armament makers. Between September, 1861, and the end of 1864, Brown and Sharpe shipped a total of 201 machines, 100 of them to armament makers in New England. As soon as the war demand ended, the market area expanded considerably. The first shipments by Brown and Sharpe to foreign customers were made in 1865, when two machines were shipped to Canada and two to France. From 1865 on, the foreign market accounted for a significant proportion of Brown and Sharpe shipments, never accounting for less than 10 percent of the total in any one year, and in some years rising to over 50 percent. For the Bullard Company, foreign shipments were not as significant a proportion of the total until after 1896 but, of the 90 machines shipped in the first year, 1881, 2 were consigned to foreign customers. In the 15 years between 1881 and 1895, there were only 5 years when no foreign shipments were made, and a total of 37 machines were shipped abroad. In 1896, 25.9 percent of the machines shipped went to foreign buyers, and in the four years 1897–1900 the proportion was between 50 and 60 percent. In the decade 1901–10 an average of 23 percent of Bullard shipments was consigned to foreign customers (Table A–3).

A sample of the shipments of the two Cincinnati companies shows that the New England toolmakers did not monopolize the foreign trade. A 20 percent sample of the shipments by the G. A. Gray Company between 1884 and 1907 (sample size, 799 machines) shows 165 machines, or 20.8 percent of the total, consigned to foreign customers. The same type of sample taken from the records of the Cincinnati Shaper Company between 1899 and 1907 (sample size, 554 machines) shows that 110 machines, or 19.9 percent of the total, were shipped abroad. Finally the sales records of the Warner and Swasey Company of Cleveland show an average share of foreign in total sales of 18.8 percent between 1903 and 1910.

As one would expect, northwest Europe dominated the foreign market. The number of machines shipped by Brown and Sharpe and by Bullard to foreign regions, by quinquennia, is shown in Table 3. On the reasonable assumption that foreign companies purchasing American machine tools were not tied to particular American producers, this table can be taken as representative of the regional distribution of foreign shipments by the American machine tool industry as a whole. There are differences between the two panels of the table. The Brown and Sharpe figures show a smaller proportion of total foreign shipments to northwest Europe and a larger proportion to Russia (including Eastern Europe) and Asia than the Bullard figures do. The differences are accounted for by relatively large shipments by Brown and Sharpe to government arsenals in Russia between 1895 and 1901 (over 300 machines) and to Japanese government arsenals and shipyards in 1904 (260 machines). Since the Bullard line of products was not suitable for armaments manufacture at that time, the company did not share the market.

That northwest Europe was the major foreign market for shipments is, of course, not surprising. Nor is the distribution by country of destination within Europe. Table 4 presents the distribution of shipments to northwest Europe, by country of destination, for Brown and Sharpe only.[11] The United Kingdom was clearly the largest single purchaser of machines from Brown and Sharpe, not only in total but also in all subperiods except 1865–69 and 1885–89. The large volume of shipments to France in the latter quinquennium is made up primarily of shipments to French government arsenals, which received nearly 200 machines between 1886 and 1888.

In the total number of machines shipped, France was the second largest

---

[11] In Tables 3 and 4, the distribution was derived from records that generally list only one consignee. Thus, a London or Antwerp agent might subsequently ship a machine consigned to him to another region or country. In view of the number of agents scattered throughout Europe, this possibility is unlikely to affect the distribution appreciably.

TABLE 3
FOREIGN SHIPMENTS OF MACHINE TOOLS, BY REGION OF DESTINATION, QUINQUENNIAL, 1861–1909
(Number of Machines)

Period	Northwest Europe	South Europe*	Russia and East Europe†	Canada	Central and South America	Australia	Asia	Africa
A. BROWN AND SHARPE								
1861–64‡	0	0	0	0	0	0	0	0
1865–69	27	3	1	16	0	0	0	0
1870–74	60	10	5	34	0	0	0	0
1875–79	55	0	0	5	3	1	2	0
1880–84	84	0	2	29	7	2	0	0
1885–89	633	0	2	13	5	7	0	7
1890–94	431	6	38	25	8	7	0	7
1895–99	2,560	43	257	39	16	7	16	2
1900–4	2,349	49	127	140	18	2	331	5
Percentage distribution of totals	82.9	1.5	5.8	4.0	0.8	0.2	4.7	0.2
B. BULLARD								
1881–84§	7	0	0	1	1	0	0	0
1885–89	13	0	0	0	0	0	0	0
1890–94	7	0	0	4	0	0	0	0
1895–99	446	0	8	2	1	0	0	0
1900–4	394	3	1	30	1	0	2	0
1905–9	341	20	9	29	4	1	9	0
Percentage distribution of totals	90.6	1.7	1.3	4.9	0.5	0.0	1.2	0.0

* Italy, Spain, Portugal, Greece, Turkey.
† Poland, Rumania, Bulgaria.
‡ September, 1861, to December, 1864.
§ April, 1881, to December, 1884.
SOURCE: Company records.

TABLE 4

SHIPMENTS BY BROWN AND SHARPE TO NORTHWEST EUROPE, QUINQUENNIAL,
1865–1904

(Number of Machines)

Period	United Kingdom	France	Germany	Sweden, Denmark	Belgium, Netherlands	Switzerland, Austria
1865–69....	4	12	4	0	0	0
1870–74....	28	1	17	13	0	1
1875–79....	23	20	11	0	1	0
1880–84....	56	7	20	1	0	0
1885–89....	181	352	67	23	3	7
1890–94....	182	60	92	47	14	36
1895–99....	975	511	621	243	80	130
1900–04....	1,106	587	323	121	77	135

SOURCE: Company records.

customer and Germany the third largest. Most, although not all, of the difference is accounted for by the large shipment to French arsenals noted above. The time distribution of machines to other regions generally coincides with what is known about their periods of industrialization. Expectably, the destination of the machine shipments moved across Europe in general conformity with the eastward progress of the industrial revolution.

The same sort of geographic distribution of machine shipments based on the level of industrial activity in a region is evident in Table 5, where the distribution of shipments to United States regions (census definition) is given for Brown and Sharpe and for Bullard. The dominant position of the Middle Atlantic region is clear from the table. In all but the first subperiod 1861–64, that region received more machines than any other from both companies. The New England and east North Central regions received some machines in all subperiods, and while neither was as quantitatively important as the Middle Atlantic region, the inference certainly is that the domestic market for the tools of these New England companies was widespread. The transportation costs—probably fairly substantial, at least in the early period—did not limit Brown and Sharpe to a local market.

That transportation cost was not a strong deterrent is shown most strikingly by the increase in the volume of shipments to the east North Central region after 1880. As Roe has pointed out, "prior to 1880 practically all of the tool building in the United States was done east of the Alleghenies," but that "good tool building appeared in Ohio in the early eighties, and within the ten years its competition was felt by eastern tool builders."[12] It is clear, however, that growth of manufacturing and of a machine tool industry in the Ohio Valley had only good effects upon the New England companies. Increased industrial activity meant increased

---

[12] Roe, *English and American*, p. 261.

TABLE 5

Shipments to United States Regions, Quinquennial, 1861–1909
(Number of Machines)

Period	New England	Middle Atlantic	East North Central	West North Central	South Atlantic	East South Central	West South Central	Mountain	Pacific
A. Brown and Sharpe									
1861–64*	112	81	3	0	5	0	0	0	0
1865–69	95	122	15	0	5	0	0	0	2
1870–74	161	208	20	2	0	2	1	0	4
1875–79	69	90	35	4	2	0	0	0	8
1880–84	272	419	138	17	24	4	2	0	9
1885–89	396	491	221	26	52	8	6	3	7
1890–94	699	784	373	26	90	18	3	4	10
1895–99	1,252	1,270	853	35	93	23	7	10	23
1900–04	1,840	2,219	1,695	151	250	16	12	19	83
Percentage distribution of totals	32.6	37.9	22.4	1.7	3.5	0.5	0.2	0.2	1.0
B. Bullard									
1881–84†	90	214	20	0	3	0	3	0	0
1885–89	206	276	85	0	14	1	1	0	1
1890–94	173	351	37	0	109‡	0	0	1	3
1895–99	126	296	14	4	49	0	0	0	47
1900–04	188	521	241	20	69	8	11	4	25
1905–09	206	500	421	36	36	19	14	6	31
Percentage distribution of totals	22.1	48.3	18.3	1.3	6.3	0.6	0.4	0.2	2.4

* September, 1861, to December, 1864.
† April, 1881, to December, 1884.
‡ Between 1890 and 1892, 46 machines were shipped to the Navy Department in the District of Columbia.
Source: Company records.

machine tool inputs, and New England production machine tools were among the best available.

The table does indicate that, whereas from the subperiod 1885–89 on Brown and Sharpe shipped machines to all regions, Bullard did not consistently ship to all regions until the period 1900–04. That the difference resulted from the higher transportation costs incurred by the larger and heavier Bullard machines is unlikely. The more likely explanation is that the heavier production machine is not required as an input until a region reaches a certain threshold of industrial sophistication.

The information available from the Cincinnati firms shows that they also enjoyed a wide geographic market for their output. The 20 percent sample of the shipments of G. A. Gray Company for the period 1884–1907 contains 631 domestic shipments. The percentage distribution of the destination of the shipments shows that 8.2 percent went to New England, 26.9 percent to the East,[13] 53.2 percent to the North Central region,[14] 4.6 percent to the South, and 7.0 percent to the West. The percentage distribution of the 444 domestic machine shipments in the 20 percent sample of the Cincinnati Shaper Company between 1899 and 1907 shows that 5.2 percent went to New England, 45.7 percent to the East, 26.8 percent to the North Central region, 10.4 percent to the South, and 11.9 percent to the West. It appears from these figures that Roe's statement that the Ohio companies competed with the New England firms was correct. It is also true that such competition, carried on in a rapidly expanding market, had beneficial effects on the firms in both regions. The relative size of the firms in both regions should be noted. Roe mentions that the Gray Company started in 1883 to build lathes, but soon specialized on planers and "is now [1916] one of the foremost firms in the country specializing in this type of tool."[15] Yet the 20 percent sample taken from Gray's shipment records shows a sample size of only 987 machines shipped between 1884 and 1915, 767 of which were domestic shipments.

Feast or Famine Industry

Discussions of the machine tool industry mention in some form or other the fact that fluctuations in output of the industry tend to be much wider than fluctuations in general industrial output or in the index of economic activity. It might be argued, however, that this characteristic of the machine tool industry is part of a well-known phenomenon of an industrial economy which has acquired and is using a large stock of producer durable equipment. During a period of industrialization, sufficient momentum might be generated by new, rapidly growing industries so that

---

[13] Defined as New York, New Jersey, Pennsylvania, Maryland, Delaware.

[14] Defined as Ohio, Indiana, Illinois, Wisconsin, Michigan, Minnesota.

[15] Roe, *English and American*, p. 273.

the output of machine tools is little affected by fluctuations in general commodity output.

Whatever the theoretical merits of such a hypothesis, it is clear from the available records of machine tool output and sales (Table A–2) that the firms were subject to substantial fluctuations in demand. Unfortunately, the National Bureau reference cycle chronology does not give measures of the severity of cycles for the period under review here, and it is impossible therefore to say whether machine tool demand fluctuated more widely than aggregate demand.

Comparison of the National Bureau reference cycle chronology with the measures of machine tool output shows three periods of nonconformity.[16] The reference cycle peak of 1869 and trough of 1870, the peak of 1887 and trough of 1888, and the peak of 1895 and trough of 1896 are not reflected clearly in the output measures. For the first period, 1869–70, only the output series for Brown and Sharpe is available, and so perhaps no great importance should be attached to the nonconformity. For the second period, 1887–88, four series are available and only the new-orders series of Warner and Swasey shows a contraction. For the third period, 1895–96, four series are available and only the Gray Company sales series shows a contraction. Both 1886–90 and 1895–99 were periods of substantial increase in the level of machine tool output. The nonconformity with reference cycle dating might then serve as evidence that, during periods of vigorous demand associated perhaps with rapid technical change, the output of machine tools is unaffected by cyclical contractions in aggregate demand.

The evidence almost disappears, however, when the output series are separated into domestic and foreign shipments, which is possible with the Brown and Sharpe and the Bullard data (Table A–3). There is no contraction in the Brown and Sharpe domestic shipment series in 1869–70, or in the Bullard domestic shipment series in 1887–88. But there is a clear contraction in the Brown and Sharpe domestic shipment series in 1887–88, and the domestic shipment series of both companies show a contraction after 1895, Bullard in 1897, and Brown and Sharpe in 1896–97.

The differences in the cyclical behavior of the total and domestic shipment series is perhaps to be expected from the differences in the reference cycle dates in the United States, France, Great Britain, and Germany. There is very little evidence of an inverse cycle in domestic and foreign shipments, but the foreign shipments of Brown and Sharpe reached a peak in 1888, and there was a strong foreign demand for both Brown and Sharpe and Bullard output between 1895 and 1901 which submerged the domestic contraction of 1895–96.

---

[16] A. F. Burns and W. C. Mitchell, *Measuring Business Cycles* (New York: National Bureau of Economic Research, 1946), p. 78.

Summary

The data collected for this paper are undoubtedly far from satisfactory as a basis for an analysis of the 19th-century machine tool industry, but company records are the only source from which a quantitative record of the industry can be established.

The data assembled suggest that the demand for light, metal-cutting machine tools was relatively small during the initial period of industrialization, when technical development was embodied in fairly large and crude systems. Sewing machine manufacturers were a steady component of the demand for Brown and Sharpe machines back to 1861. It was not until the 1890's, however, that manufacturers of electrical equipment, calculators, cash registers, and bicycles provided a rapidly expanding market for light tools.

The data also show that the American machine tool industry enjoyed a truly worldwide market during the 19th century. Much has been written about the technical superiority of the American machines during the period, and certainly the records indicate that quality was recognized by expanding export markets in six continents.

For this particular industry, 1910—the end date of the analysis here— is significant because it can serve as a dividing line in the history of machine tools. After 1910, the assembly line called for more specialized and special-order machines than before, and faster cutting speeds and heavier machines were in demand. The automobile industry alone created a revolution in machine tool building.

Appendix

In addition to background data for the text tables, the appendix presents some additional information collected from machine tool companies during the study but not used directly in the earlier pages.

Table A–1 presents information relating to Brown and Sharpe only. The figures on total sales were taken from annual financial statements, while the amount of sewing machine work and "other work done" came from other records. The same basic data must have been used in both records, because the breakdown of the sales figures adds to total sales. Other work done is not further specified, but it must have included machine tool sales and probably also repair work and miscellaneous products. The shipment records mention production of core ovens, foundry rattlers, and soda kettles, which would serve to utilize the foundry facilities of the company. Also noted are grindstones and grindstone troughs which would be the forerunners of the grinding machines, an important part of machinery shipments after the late 1870's. Between 1873 and 1881, the company produced 199 cylindrical sewing machines or seamers with an aggregate value of $26,891 that were shipped to domestic and British print works and bleacheries. No description of this machine was found, but the name suggests that Brown and Sharpe's experience in sewing machine production enabled it to produce the machine as a stopgap measure during the depression following 1873.

The profit series in Table A–1 is taken from a set of financial statements found in the company's files. The statements apparently were put together as a hybrid balance sheet and income statement for the information of the owners of the business to show the position of the firm on January 1 of each year. They were probably used by the owners to determine the total dividends to be paid each year.

To arrive at the profit figure, a figure of capital value on January 1 was first derived. Capital value was computed as the sum of cash, notes, accounts, value of land, plant, and equipment, and what was called "stock," which may or may not include the inventory of finished and unfinished goods. The profit during the year (column 6) was derived by taking the difference between two successive capital values, adding the dividends taken out during the year, and subtracting the amount received from Darling, Brown, and Sharpe, the precision instrument subsidiary until 1893 when Darling's share was purchased by the parent company. Causes of the fluctuations in what is called profits could not be determined by examination of the records. The substantial figures for the period 1869–73 appear to be largely the result of an upward valuation of the land, buildings, and tools owned by the company, and the losses of 1874 and 1875 of a downward revaluation of buildings and fixtures.

The financial statements are clearly unacceptable in terms of good accounting practice. Business decisions probably were made in part on the basis of them, however, and on that ground the profit series is relevant information. That other factors also influenced decisions is clear from the lack of correspondence between the dividend series and the profit series. Dividends do not move in the same direction as profits in as many as half of the years shown.

TABLE A–1
SUMMARY OF FINANCIAL STATEMENTS, BROWN AND SHARPE, 1863–1905
(Dollars, Current Prices)

Year	Total Sales (1)	Sewing Machine Work (2)	Other Work Done (3)	Machine Tool Shipments (4)	Dividends Paid (5)	Profit or Loss (6)
1861°...				3,590		
1862....				17,771		
1863....	89,827	59,728	30,099	15,294		
1864....	168,437	108,130	60,307	37,436		
1865....	159,059	109,649	49,410	29,248		
1866....	254,874	201,607	53,267	33,459		
1867....	231,547	194,387	37,159	28,018		
1868....	210,720	155,940	54,780	40,930	24,000	
1869....	292,571	215,832	76,739	52,410	27,200	165,225
1870....	331,366	261,273	70,092	54,350	32,000	128,348
1871....	393,781	297,863	95,918	74,841	32,000	158,477
1872....	288,138	193,057	95,080	75,094	32,000	70,984
1873....	225,331	131,111	94,219	77,493	16,000	85,647
1874....	156,309	111,823	44,486	23,463	—	—49,472
1875....	188,793	137,910	50,884	20,005	—	— 781
1876....	179,330	134,534	44,977	33,613	—	10,928
1877....	158,676	104,109	54,567	36,450	67,875	14,157
1878....	173,450	124,153	49,297	20,346	27,150	35,167
1879....	243,524	164,867	78,656	40,890	76,925	70,513
1880....	334,866	183,806	151,061	74,504	54,300	78,063
1881....	436,036	190,774	245,262	122,872	—	132,124
1882....	495,993	187,173	308,811	124,010	36,200	150,526
1883....	433,903	162,075	271,827	120,230	76,925	136,470
1884....	440,698	194,847	245,850	95,565	76,925	163,992
1885....	401,001	197,751	203,250	66,949	31,675	78,999
1886....	557,195	160,689	396,506	162,400	72,400	124,176
1887....	592,246	149,261	442,985	189,305	22,625	139,915
1888....	772,439	237,386	535,052	243,843	27,150	199,421
1889....	881,455	183,530	697,925	298,580	45,250	156,254
1890....	960,840	117,176	843,665	312,322	40,725	222,265
1891....	881,055	105,182	775,874	247,236	49,775	174,870
1892....	892,481	140,598	751,883	259,698	63,350	208,525
1893....	836,695	147,696	689,000	239,660	36,200	33,179
1894....	701,395			185,455	27,150	103,824
1895....	1,029,160			378,942	54,300	221,587
1896....	1,098,710			467,997	45,250	174,657
1897....	1,270,082			612,216	36,200	501,272
1898....	1,541,354			799,885	54,300	421,254
1899....	2,070,859			1,015,093	99,550	522,434
1900....	1,963,382			966,341	72,400	492,953
1901....	1,961,215			845,374	72,400	526,888
1902....	2,426,404			1,197,145	90,500	502,461
1903....	2,540,331			1,166,546	181,000	359,256
1904....	2,339,047			1,035,161	181,000	830,022
1905....	3,604,377				208,150	

NOTE: Details may not add to total because of rounding.
° September to December, 1861.
SOURCE: Company records. See text for derivation of col. 6.

TABLE A–2

MEASURES OF OUTPUT OF SELECTED MACHINE TOOL COMPANIES, 1861–1910

Year	Brown and Sharpe Ship- ments (num- ber) (1)	Bullard Ship- ments		G.A. Gray Sales (dollars) (4)	Cincin- nati Shaper, Sales (dollars) (5)	Warner and Swasey New Orders (dollars) (6)	Total Output, Metal- Cutting Tools* (dollars) (7)
		Num- ber (2)	Dollars (3)				
1861.....	17†						
1862.....	64						
1863.....	53						
1864.....	67						
1865.....	45						
1866.....	49						
1867.....	42						
1868.....	63						
1869.....	85						
1870.....	95						
1871.....	124						
1872.....	111						
1873.....	133						
1874.....	44						
1875.....	31						
1876.....	57						
1877.....	63						
1878.....	37						
1879.....	83						
1880.....	184					2,210‡	
1881.....	229	90§				28,403	
1882.....	207	96				36,042	
1883.....	213	89				38,521	
1884.....	177	64				44,712	
1885.....	135	62				40,846	
1886.....	331	107		41,416		53,294	
1887.....	374	123		80,552		118,656	
1888.....	457	135		91,811		59,610	
1889.....	568	170		113,177		111,705	
1890.....	574	192		176,708		118,438	
1891.....	500	155		169,603		163,778	
1892.....	541	169		161,453		85,764	
1893.....	522	113		86,290		122,584	
1894.....	392	56		58,590		73,329	
1895.....	815	96	116,476	123,382		155,120	
1896.....	1,015	135	121,150	111,349		280,488	
1897.....	1,206	155	177,326	134,159		300,544	
1898.....	1,508	273	499,620	185,906		313,813	
1899.....	1,962	334	396,618	288,561	42,000	290,893	
1900.....	1,666	319	422,631	362,510	84,000	334,663	
1901.....	1,476	314	440,760	242,159	84,000	338,469	17,900,000
1902.....	2,126	362	544,826	330,659	137,000	328,413	22,800,000
1903.....	2,152	358	537,359	320,774	152,000	327,044	23,700,000
1904.....	1,885	167	219,140	169,952	97,000	200,804	18,300,000
1905.....	1,180	383	509,408	294,800	158,000	496,110	28,700,000

TABLE A–2 (*Continued*)

Year	Brown and Sharpe Ship- ments (num- ber) (1)	Bullard Ship- ments		G.A. Gray Sales (dollars) (4)	Cincin- nati Shaper, Sales (dollars) (5)	Warner and Swasey New Orders (dollars) (6)	Total Output, Metal- Cutting Tools* (dollars) (7)
		Num- ber (2)	Dollars (3)				
1906.....		469	733,908	266,098	139,000	756,521	36,400,000
1907.....		444	719.082	339,776	182,000	546,879	41,300,000
1908.....		108	185,868	89,044	114,000	309,408	16,800,000
1909.....		278	510,549	168,601	187,000	990,502	33,500,000
1910.....		346	694,337	313,352	240,000	739,429	44,300,000

* These figures are said by the NMTBA to include more than 90 percent of total industry shipments, to exclude repair work, and to include parts shipped with machines.

† September to December, 1861.

‡ August to December, 1880.

§ April to December, 1881.

Source: Cols. 1–6 from company records; col. 7 from National Machine Tool Builders Association, Washington, D.C., release F–A40a, February 21, 1962.

TABLE A–3

DOMESTIC AND FOREIGN DESTINATION OF OUTPUT, BROWN AND SHARPE AND
BULLARD, 1861–1910

Year	Brown and Sharpe Shipments			Bullard Shipments		
	Domestic (number) (1)	Foreign (2)	Foreign as Percent of Total (3)	Domestic (number) (4)	Foreign (5)	Foreign as Percent of Total (6)
1861*....	17	0	0.0			
1862.....	64	0	0.0			
1863.....	53	0	0.0			
1864.....	67	0	0.0			
1865.....	41	4	9.9			
1866.....	43	6	12.2			
1867.....	31	11	26.2			
1868.....	55	8	12.7			
1869.....	67	18	21.2			
1870.....	72	23	24.2			
1871.....	100	24	19.4			
1872.....	87	24	21.6			
1873.....	107	26	19.5			
1874.....	32	12	27.3			
1875.....	28	3	9.7			
1876.....	36	21	36.8			
1877.....	51	12	19.0			
1878.....	22	15	40.5			
1879.....	71	12	14.5			
1880.....	169	15	8.2			
1881.....	208	21	9.2	88†	2†	2.2
1882.....	174	33	15.9	90	6	6.2
1883.....	182	31	14.6	89	0	0
1884.....	152	25	14.1	63	1	1.6
1885.....	115	20	14.8	62	0	0
1886.....	200	131	39.6	106	1	0.9
1887.....	284	90	24.1	113	10	8.1
1888.....	241	216	47.2	135	0	0
1889.....	370	198	34.9	168	2	1.2
1890.....	445	129	22.5	188	4	2.1
1891.....	396	104	20.7	149	6	3.8
1892.....	450	91	16.8	168	1	0.6
1893.....	434	88	16.9	113	0	0
1894.....	282	110	28.1	56	0	0
1895.....	638	177	21.7	92	4	4.2
1896.....	560	455	44.8	100	35	25.9
1897.....	444	762	63.2	64	91	58.7
1898.....	719	789	52.3	129	144	52.7
1899.....	1,205	757	38.6	151	183	54.8
1900.....	928	738	44.3	143	176	55.2
1901.....	1,123	353	23.9	216	98	31.2
1902.....	1,669	457	21.5	330	32	8.8
1903.....	1,593	559	26.0	283	76	21.2
1904.....	972	913	48.4	115	52	31.1
1905.....				307	66	17.7

TABLE A–3 *(Continued)*

Year	Brown and Sharpe Shipments			Bullard Shipments		
	Domestic *(number)* (1)	Foreign (2)	Foreign as Percent of Total (3)	Domestic *(number)* (4)	Foreign (5)	Foreign as Percent of Total (6)
1906.....				332	137	29.2
1907.....				293	152	34.2
1908.....				82	26	24.1
1909.....				245	33	11.9
1910.....				273	73	21.1

° September to December, 1861.
† April to December, 1881.
SOURCE: Cols. 1, 2, 4, and 5—from company records; col. 3—col. 2 as per cent of col. 1, Table A–2; col. 6—col. 5 as percent of col. 2, Table A–2.

6. The First 1,945 British Steamships*

Jonathan R. T. Hughes and Stanley Reiter

Purdue University

This paper presents data showing the main characteristics of all the steamships built in the United Kingdom and placed under permanent British registry from 1814 through 1860. The historical setting in which the British steam merchant fleet developed is discussed and the data are interpreted in relation to that environment. It is argued on the basis of these data that many of the prevailing notions about steam shipping before 1860 need to be revised.

1. Introduction

THIS PAPER PRESENTS data which have not been utilized before, showing the main characteristics of all the steamships built in the United Kingdom and placed under permanent British registry[1] from 1814 through 1860.

* Reprinted from *American Statistical Journal, June 1958*, Vol. III, No. 282, p. 360.

[Shortly after publication of this paper the authors learned that its title is precisely incorrect. These 1,945 ships were those that had been built and still *existed* under British registry at the beginning of 1861; an estimated 58 to 60 percent of all the steamships which had ever been known to have been built in the U.K. However, *none* of the major conclusions depends upon the number of ships, but rather, they are derived from the mean characteristics—the general profiles—of the various categories of ships over time. We therefore are confident of our main conclusions and of the quality of the analysis we made a decade ago when this work was done. We cannot say what differences the missing ships would make. We must simply await improvements of the data. Our transport capacity index should now be used with caution, although there are reasons to suppose that, as a growth index, it is not likely to be improved upon significantly by the data from the missing ships.]

[1] The data presented below are not the same as annual data given in the *Statistical Abstract for the United Kingdom* for ships "built and first registered in the United Kingdom." Such data include ships which, although first built in the U.K., later passed out of British registry by reason of sales to foreigners. As is indicated below, the ships included in the data presented in this paper were entered permanently into U.K. registry during the period covered by these data. Hence in some years sales of British-built steamers to foreigners is reflected in the difference between the first registrations and the permanent registrations indicated by the data below. Similarly, because of British purchases of steamers from abroad (which might originally have been British built but which had temporarily passed out of British regis-

These data should provide scholars the means to gain a clearer perspective of the history of steam navigation prior to the outbreak of the American Civil War.

The only official data on British steamship construction which have been generally available to scholars heretofore have been the "Number and Tonnage" figures given in the *Statistical Abstract for the United Kingdom* from 1840 onward. These *Statistical Abstract* data are aggregates enumerating all steamships built and first registered in the U.K. and contain no information regarding how much of annual construction actually passed into permanent U.K. registry. Nor do these series contain any information regarding the number of wood and iron steamers built, or the types, whether paddle or screw propelled. The new series presented in this paper fill all of these gaps.[2] In addition, measures have been constructed which show carrying capacity of new construction entered into permanent U.K. registry. These measures take into account advances in the technology of shipbuilding.

The present paper presents information which indicates that many of the prevailing notions about steam shipping before 1860 need to be rather sharply revised. It is shown, for example, that the general adoption of iron in steamship construction dates from the 1840's, more than a full decade earlier than the accepted estimates; that by the end of the 1850's most of the British steam merchant fleet was iron rather than wood; that the iron-screw steamer was predominant in new British steamship construction from at least 1851 onward; that the 1853 trade boom together with the stimulus of the Crimean War demand for shipping were decisive in introducing the iron-screw steamer; that the iron-screw steamer very largely supplanted both wood and iron paddle steamers by the end of the Crimean War. On the basis of this evidence including our measure of transport capacity it will be argued that contemporaries were probably correct in their estimates of the extent of the steamship's penetration of the shorter ocean-freight routes in the 1850's and early 1860's—estimates which have been thought to be open to serious doubt. It is argued that Britain's new steam merchant marine was a powerful influence in the development of Britain's exceedingly strong balance-of-payments position in the third quarter of the 19th century.

---

try), additions to the British steam merchant fleet may in some years seem to be slightly larger than was warranted by current U.K. construction. For details of British ship registry practices see: Ernest W. Blocksidge, *Hints on the Register Tonnage of Merchant Ships* (Liverpool, 1942), pp. 9–13.

[2] The authors are indebted to the Cunard Steamship Company, Ltd., for providing data on early Cunard steamers which could be used in checking the accuracy of the transport capacity measures in Table 2 below, and for information on the obsolescence of early steamers.

2. The Data

At the order of the 1861 session of parliament a return was printed containing certain information covering all of the "Steam Vessels" permanently registered in the merchant fleet of the U.K. on or before January 1, 1861.[3] The following information is contained in this Parliamentary Paper: the length, breadth, and depth of hold of each ship is given, together with its gross and net tonnages, and the indicated horsepower of its engines. The type of each ship is given, whether it was wood paddle, wood screw, iron paddle, iron screw or steel. Finally, the date of build, port of registry, and name of the registered builder (or builders) for each ship is stated.

There are 1,945 steam vessels listed in this fashion as "the whole" number of British steamers permanently registered in the U.K. from 1814 through 1860, with a total of 440,999 net and 692,101 gross tons.[4] The data are continuous from 1823 onward and hence the analysis below concentrates on the period 1823–60.

It is not difficult to understand why these data have not been utilized before, considering their organization—or rather, their lack of it. The

---

3 Full title: "A RETURN, 'in a Tabular Form, with Consecutive Numbers, of the whole of the Steam Vessels Registered in the United Kingdom on or before the 1st day of January 1861; stating in separate Columns, the following Particulars:— Official Number of Vessel; Vessel's name; Port of Registry; Date of Registry; Date of Build; Registered Owners; Dimensions of Vessels in Length and Breadth, and Depth of Hold; Tonnage (exclusive of Engine Room); and Gross Tonnage, distinguishing Vessels built of Iron and Vessels having Screw Propellers; also distinguishing Vessels measured under the Merchant Shipping Act of 1854 from those measured under previous Acts; and Estimated Horse Power of their Engines, and giving the Aggregate Number of Vessels and Amount of Tonnage; with an Index for easy reference attached to it, giving the Names of the Vessels in Alphabetical Order, with Numbers to each, corresponding with the Consecutive Numbers in the Return (in continuation of Parliamentary Paper No. 449, of Session 1860)'," *Accounts and Papers*, 1861, LVIII (371).

4 The "net tonnage" figures in Tables 1 and 2 below are the official "gross tonnage" measurements less tonnage assigned to the engine rooms of the ships. Gross tonnage is generally "the measurement of the under-deck tonnage, with the addition of the 'tween-deck spaces situated above the tonnage deck and all 'enclosed' spaces above the upper deck." Blocksidge, *op. cit.*, p. 7. Of the 1,944 ships included in Tables 1 and 2, 94 ships lacked entries in one or more of the categories "net tonnage," "gross tonnage," "indicated horsepower." Estimates of the missing measurements were based on corresponding measurements for other ships built in the same year, or as nearly in the same year as possible (and if possible, ships having the same owners), and having the same dimensions and known tonnages and horsepower as the ships in question. It was felt that this procedure yielded more accurate estimates than would the standard procedure of using linear regressions. The error introduced by these estimates is no doubt an insignificant part of the total. Tables 1 and 2 include river steamers; these are not included in certain *Statistical Abstract* data on steamships. Because these ships were all officially registered, they were of greater than 15 net register tons; ships of less than that tonnage (or 15 tons burden under the older British Registry legislation) need not have been officially registered. Blocksidge, *op. cit.*, pp. 9–10.

ships were given numbers by 95 British ports of registry from London
to Wexford. This serial ordering begins with London, presumably because it had the greatest number of registries, and then proceeds alpha-
betically from Aberystwith to Yarmouth for 63 English and Welsh ports.
The numbers continue from Aberdeen to Wigtown for Scottish ports and
from Ballina to Wexford for Irish ports. A special index follows with the
names of all the ships in alphabetical order. Each ship entry includes the
official British registry number, but one can conveniently find an individual ship only if one knows its name; the registry numbers are not presented serially. No attempt was made to order the ships other than by
port of registry. To use these data for different purposes involved their
complete reorganization at each stage of analysis; 1,945 individual ships
with at least 13 entries per ship—a considerable task if done by hand.
Punch-card calculators were used by the present authors for the thousands of computations involved in organizing these data.[5]

3. Growth of the British Steam Merchant Fleet 1823–60

In Table 1 the data are organized in continuous annual series running
from 1823[6] through 1860. By the end of 1860 a total of 1,945 steam vessels
had been entered into permanent British registry with 692,101 gross tons.[7]
It is seen that the growth of the steam merchant fleet was slow until the
early 1840's, a peak was reached in 1841, another in 1847 and in 1850
there began a strong upward surge in additions to the fleet which reached
its peak in 1855, the final year of the Crimean War boom in shipbuilding.
A substantial recovery became apparent only in 1860.

These movements in additions to the steam merchant fleet roughly correspond to changes in the data for total ships (both sail and steam) built
and first registered in the United Kingdom. This may be seen in Chart 1
where data for the volume of foreign trade are compared to data for ships

---

[5] The authors are indebted to the Computing Laboratory of Purdue University for
assistance with the computations. We would be glad to provide at cost a set of
punched cards containing the original data to any scholar interested in making further
use of these data.

[6] According to these returns a single steamer, the "Industry" was entered permanently into British registry in 1814. The port of registry was Glasgow; the owner was
A. McGeorge. This ship was 68 feet long, 17 feet wide, 8 feet deep, net tonnage was
43, gross tonnage 69, and indicated horsepower was 14. No other steamers appear
until 1823 when four were put under permanent registry.

[7] Including the adjustments in the data noted above. In 1860 the *Statistical Abstract* lists 2,000 as being the number of steam vessels "registered as belonging" to
the United Kingdom and the register tonnage is given as 454,327. The differences
between these figures and those in Table 1 are easily accounted for. The *Statistical
Abstract* data include vessels registered in the channel islands, whereas the data in
Table 1 include only registry ports on the main islands (i.e., Great Britain and Ireland) and the *Statistical Abstract* data are *register tonnages*. The latter are significantly lower than *gross tonnage* estimates. See Blocksidge, *op. cit.*, pp. 5–9 on
tonnage measurements.

TABLE 1

Year of Build	Wood Steamships								
	Paddle			Screw			Total		
	No.	Net Tons	Gross Tons	No.	Net Tons	Gross Tons	No.	Net Tons	Gross Tons
1823..	4	427	817	—	—	—	4	427	817
1824..	4	341	682	—	—	—	4	341	682
1825..	5	419	894	—	—	—	5	419	894
1826..	11	964	1,831	—	—	—	11	964	1,831
1827..	3	451	662	—	—	—	3	451	662
1828..	3	63	141	—	—	—	3	63	141
1829..	4	301	613	—	—	—	4	301	613
1830..	5	443	752	—	—	—	5	443	752
1831..	4	447	725	—	—	—	4	447	725
1832..	8	910	1,491	—	—	—	8	910	1,491
1833..	8	503	1,222	—	—	—	8	503	1,222
1834..	17	2,350	4,042	—	—	—	17	2,350	4,042
1835..	20	2,273	4,187	—	—	—	20	2,273	4,187
1836..	18	2,468	4,440	—	—	—	18	2,468	4,440
1837..	29	3,632	6,285	—	—	—	29	3,632	6,285
1838..	31	1,789	3,547	—	—	—	31	1,789	3,547
1839..	16	1,473	2,732	—	—	—	16	1,473	2,732
1840..	23	2,936	5,572	1	292	355	24	3,228	5,927
1841..	27	9,265	14,644	—	—	—	27	9,265	14,644
1842..	22	4,734	8,465	—	—	—	22	4,734	8,465
1843..	27	1,547	3,223	—	—	—	27	1,547	3,233
1844..	23	2,481	4,631	—	—	—	23	2,481	4,631
1845..	15	927	1,806	—	—	—	15	927	1,806
1846..	26	2,027	3,719	1	163	240	27	2,190	3,959
1847..	47	4,396	8,735	—	—	—	47	4,396	8,735
1848..	46	2,506	5,399	—	—	—	46	2,506	5,399
1849..	22	2,177	3,815	—	—	—	22	2,177	3,815
1850..	12	3,525	6,268	2	549	698	14	4,074	6,966
1851..	20	5,179	8,758	1	103	151	21	5,282	8,909
1852..	35	2,669	5,319	2	180	265	37	2,849	5,584
1853..	31	3,571	6,239	3	221	321	34	3,792	6,560
1854..	26	2,326	4,206	3	1,527	2,189	29	3,853	6,395
1855..	28	3,235	5,328	2	162	185	30	3,397	5,513
1856..	43	2,768	5,719	2	163	232	45	2,931	5,951
1857..	55	1,066	4,057	5	163	313	60	1,229	4,370
1858..	33	2,245	4,710	2	64	112	35	2,309	4,822
1859..	39	771	2,619	5	858	1,182	44	1,629	3,801
1860..	35	1,096	2,769	5	195	275	40	1,291	3,044

TABLE 1 (*Continued*)

| Year of Build | Iron Steamships | | | | | | | | |
| | Paddle | | | Screw | | | Total | | |
	No.	Net Tons	Gross Tons	No.	Net Tons	Gross Tons	No.	Net Tons	Gross Tons
1823..	—	—	—	—	—	—	—	—	—
1824..	—	—	—	—	—	—	—	—	—
1825..	—	—	—	—	—	—	—	—	—
1826..	—	—	—	—	—	—	—	—	—
1827..	—	—	—	—	—	—	—	—	—
1828..	—	—	—	—	—	—	—	—	—
1829..	—	—	—	—	—	—	—	—	—
1830..	—	—	—	—	—	—	—	—	—
1831..	—	—	—	—	—	—	—	—	—
1832..	—	—	—	—	—	—	—	—	—
1833..	—	—	—	—	—	—	—	—	—
1834..	—	—	—	—	—	—	—	—	—
1835..	—	—	—	1	368	473	1	368	473
1836..	2	194	284	—	—	—	2	194	284
1837..	4	390	677	—	—	—	4	390	677
1838..	5	174	298	—	—	—	5	174	298
1839..	5	295	559	—	—	—	5	295	559
1840..	7	576	947	1	1,734	3,509	8	2,310	4,456
1841..	7	971	1,548	—	—	—	7	971	1,548
1842..	10	818	1,319	1	116	171	11	934	1,490
1843..	6	669	1,105	—	—	—	6	669	1,105
1844..	29	4,025	6,947	3	255	400	32	4,280	7,347
1845..	26	3,126	5,483	3	424	651	29	3,550	6,134
1846..	17	4,589	7,233	10	2,716	3,803	27	7,305	11,036
1847..	31	7,919	12,270	6	1,777	2,458	37	9,696	14,728
1848..	19	3,518	5,853	6	1,667	2,999	25	5,185	8,852
1849..	20	4,285	6,763	8	2,715	3,919	28	7,000	10,682
1850..	18	3,673	5,871	12	2,393	3,547	30	6,066	9,418
1851..	18	3,902	5,850	15	6,824	10,180	33	10,726	16,030
1852..	15	2,707	4,038	20	12,695	18,984	35	15,402	23,022
1853..	20	4,599	7,538	43	21,321	31,455	63	25,920	38,993
1854..	25	5,479	9,143	82	39,274	56,310	107	44,753	65,453
1855..	35	4,633	8,066	84	42,541	64,261	119	47,174	72,327
1856..	32	6,350	10,273	71	27,355	38,567	103	33,705	48,840
1857..	42	4,061	8,521	68	27,045	38,432	110	31,106	46,953
1858..	34	4,956	8,081	41*	29,263*	41,344*	73*	34,219*	49,425*
1859..	30	8,319	13,734	48†	15,546†	21,663†R	78†	23,865†	35,397†
1860..	30	6,434	13,462	75R	32,924R	45,461R	105R	39,358R	58,923R

TABLE 1 (*Continued*)

				Total Wood and Iron Steamships					
Year		*Paddle*			*Screw*			*Total*	
of		*Net*	*Gross*		*Net*	*Gross*		*Net*	*Gross*
Build	*No.*	*Tons*	*Tons*	*No.*	*Tons*	*Tons*	*No.*	*Tons*	*Tons*
1823..	4	427	817	—	—	—	4	427	817
1824..	4	341	682	—	—	—	4	341	682
1825..	5	419	894	—	—	—	5	419	894
1826..	11	964	1,831	—	—	—	11	964	1,831
1827..	3	451	662	—	—	—	3	451	662
1828..	3	63	141	—	—	—	3	63	141
1829..	4	301	613	—	—	—	4	301	613
1830..	5	443	752	—	—	—	5	443	752
1831..	4	447	725	—	—	—	4	447	725
1832..	8	910	1,491	—	—	—	8	910	1,491
1833..	8	503	1,222	—	—	—	8	503	1,222
1834..	17	2,350	4,042	—	—	—	17	2,350	4,042
1835..	20	2,273	4,187	1	368	473	21	2,641	4,660
1836..	20	2,667	4,724	—	—	—	20	2,662	4,724
1837..	33	4,022	6,962	—	—	—	33	4,022	6,962
1838..	36	1,963	3,845	—	—	—	36	1,963	3,845
1839..	21	1,768	3,291	—	—	—	21	1,768	3,291
1840..	30	3,512	6,519	2	2,026	3,864	32	5,538	10,383
1841..	34	10,236	16,192	—	—	—	34	10,236	16,192
1842..	32	5,552	9,784	1	116	171	33	5,668	9,955
1843..	33	2,216	4,328	—	—	—	33	2,216	4,328
1844..	52	6,506	11,578	3	255	400	55	6,761	11,978
1845..	41	4,053	7,289	3	424	651	44	4,477	7,940
1846..	43	6,616	10,952	11	2,879	4,043	54	9,495	14,995
1847..	78	12,315	21,005	6	1,777	2,458	84	14,092	23,463
1848..	65	6,024	11,252	6	1,667	2,999	71	7,691	14,251
1849..	42	6,462	10,578	8	2,715	3,919	50	9,177	14,497
1850..	30	7,198	12,139	14	2,942	4,245	44	10,140	16,384
1851..	38	9,081	14,608	16	6,927	10,331	54	16,008	24,939
1852..	50	5,376	9,357	22	12,875	19,249	72	18,251	28,606
1853..	51	8,170	13,777	46	21,542	31,776	97	29,712	45,553
1854..	51	7,805	13,349	85	40,801	58,499	136	48,606	71,848
1855..	63	7,868	13,394	86	42,703	64,446	149	50,571	77,840
1856..	75	9,118	15,992	73	27,518	38,799	148	36,636	54,791
1857..	97	5,127	12,578	73	27,208	38,745	170	32,335	51,323
1858..	67	7,201	12,791	43	29,327	41,456	110*	36,528*	54,247*
1859..	69	9,090	16,353	53†	16,404†	22,845*	122†	25,494†	39,198†
1860..	65	7,530	16,231	80R	33,119R	45,736R	145R	40,649R	61,967R

* Includes the "Great Eastern," 13,344 net tons and 18,915 gross tons; and one steel ship, 79 net tons and 111 gross tons.
† Inclues one steel ship, 129 net tons and 204 gross tons.
R Includes three steel ships, 265 net tons and 398 gross tons.
SOURCE: *Accounts and Papers*, 1861 LVIII (371).

CHART 1

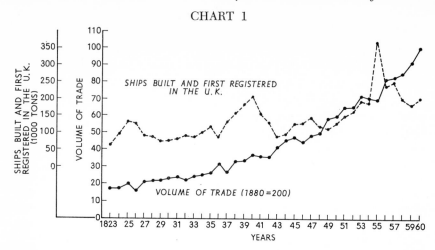

built and first registered in the U.K. The upward trend in foreign trade (and, *ceteris paribus,* in total freight revenues) no doubt accounts in large part for the accompanying upward trend in the tonnage of ships built and first registered in Britain. The rise in the trade data accelerates appreciably in the late 1840's and in the 1850's and is accompanied by a sharp upturn in shipbuilding. We will turn to this in detail below, since it was in this trade upswing that the iron steamer came into its own. The boom in shipbuilding centering upon 1840–41 is evident in both the data for total ships built and registered and in those for steamers entered into permanent British registry (cf. Chart 1 and Table 1) except that the peak in total ships built and first registered comes in 1840 while the peak for steamers added to the British merchant fleet comes in 1841. Whereas the peaks in ship construction in 1847 and 1855 are easily accounted for (below), the 1840(41) peak in shipbuilding in Britain is not adequately accounted for in the literature and remains largely unexplained. It certainly does not conform to movements in other data of economic activity.[8]

The information contained in Table 1 alone is sufficient to justify a rather sharp revision of accepted interpretations of the growth of the British steam merchant marine up to 1861. It is seen in Table 1 that some 60 percent of all the gross tonnage of steamships added to the fleet in 1823–60 were added in the seven years 1854–60. Moreover, about 85 percent of this gross tonnage consisted of iron ships and roughly 70 percent of iron-screw steamers. As early as 1844 the gross tonnage of iron steamers exceeded that of wood[9] and by 1851 the tonnage of iron-screw steamers alone exceeded total wood steamers (both paddle and screw).[10] Hence

---

[8] See A. D. Gayer, W. W. Rostow, and A. J. Schwartz, *The Growth and Development of the British Economy 1790–1850* (Oxford, 1952), Vol. I, pp. 276–303, for other economic data in the period.

[9] 7,347 gross tons of iron steamers compared to 4,631 gross tons of wood. Table 1.

[10] 10,180 gross tons of iron-screw steamers, 5,850 gross tons of iron paddle, and 8,909 gross tons of wood steamers of both kinds.

the well-known view that "iron had not been generally adopted for steamers before the decade 1855–65"[11] is rather far from the mark. From 1851 onward, the additions of iron-screw steamers to the fleet led all other types and by 1853 iron-screw steamers clearly dominated all others combined in the growth of the steam merchant marine. Considering the data in Tables 1 and 2 it ought to be noted that G. S. Graham's recent statement

> . . . iron proved to be a stubborn and uncertain medium, especially in the hands of craftsmen trained to handle timber, and by the mid-1850's had superseded wood only in the construction of steam passenger or small experimental war vessels . . . .[12]

should not be accepted without considerable reservation. Not only did the tonnage of iron steamers make up the great bulk of all steam tonnage added to the fleet "by the mid-1850's," but the average size (reflected in average transport capacity in Table 2 below) of wood-paddle steamers in the 1850's was but a fraction of the average size of iron-screw steamers that comprised 70 percent of all the steamers added to the merchant fleet. Unless one argues that there are no ships except "steam passenger" ships in Tables 1 and 2 (no war ships are in the data) Graham's statement needs revision.

Rapid obsolescence was a characteristic of these early steamers, so that by 1860 only 929 steam vessels (excluding river steamers) were employed in the coastal and foreign trade.[13] The reasons for rapid obsolescence are obvious. As is usually the case[14] in major transport innovations, changes in design, engines, and construction came rapidly once the adoption of the basic innovation became widespread; i.e., once the shift to iron-screw steamers accelerated, and competition insured that the shift would in fact continue. The transport advantages of iron-screw compared to other types of steamships are clearly seen in Table 2 where the average transport capacity[15] of iron-screw steamers was in general much greater by the mid-1850's than that of any other type of steamer.

Of course the rate of obsolescence varied from ship to ship, but it appears that few of the steam ships built before the 1850's remained in service for much longer than a decade at most. The *Britannia* of 1840,

---

[11] J. H. Clapham, *Economic History of Modern Britain* (Cambridge, 1942), Vol. II, p. 63. Clapham's discussion also suggests rather strongly, p. 64, that most of the steam fleet in the 1850's was still with wood. L. C. A. Knowles places the beginnings of success for the iron steamship in the transport of passengers and cargo only "Between 1850 and 1860." *The Industrial and Commercial Revolutions in Great Britain during the Nineteenth Century* (London, 1926), p. 298.

[12] G. S. Graham, "The Ascendency of the Sailing Ship 1850–85," *Economic History Review* (Second Series), Vol. IX, No. 1 (August, 1956), pp. 75–76.

[13] *Statistical Abstract.*

[14] Consider the experience of air and highway transportation, as well as the early history of rail transportation.

[15] See next section for a discussion of this measurement.

TABLE 2
Ratio of Total Net to Total Gross Tonnage, Transport Capacity per Ship and Total Transport Capacity for Each Year from 1823 to 1860

Wood Steamships

Year of Build	Paddle			Screw			Total		
	Ratio of Net to Gross Tonnage	Transport Capacity per Ship	Total Transport Capacity	Ratio of Net to Gross Tonnage	Transport Capacity per Ship	Total Transport Capacity	Ratio of Net to Gross Tonnage	Transport Capacity per Ship	Total Transport Capacity
1823....	.523	990.5	3,990.4	—	—	—	.523	990.5	3,990.4
1824....	.500	793.2	3,172.8	—	—	—	.500	793.2	3,172.8
1825....	.469	802.6	4,013.2	—	—	—	.469	802.6	4,013.2
1826....	.526	795.8	8,754.2	—	—	—	.525	795.8	8,754.2
1827....	.681	1,331.0	3,993.0	—	—	—	.681	1,331.0	3,993.0
1828....	.447	1,780.0	534.0	—	—	—	.447	1,780.0	534.0
1829....	.491	798.5	3,193.9	—	—	—	.491	798.5	3,193.9
1830....	.589	781.5	3,907.6	—	—	—	.589	781.5	3,907.6
1831....	.616	1,041.9	4,167.7	—	—	—	.616	1,041.9	4,167.7
1832....	.610	1,031.2	8,249.7	—	—	—	.610	1,031.2	8,249.7
1833....	.412	583.9	4,670.9	—	—	—	.412	583.9	4,670.9
1834....	.581	1,374.1	23,359.8	—	—	—	.581	1,374.1	23,359.8
1835....	.543	1,008.7	22,192.0	—	—	—	.543	1,008.7	22,192.0
1836....	.556	1,298.4	23,371.8	—	—	—	.556	1,298.4	23,371.8
1837....	.578	1,252.5	36,321.1	—	—	—	.578	1,252.5	36,321.1
1838....	.504	565.8	17,540.0	—	—	—	.504	565.8	17,540.0
1839....	.539	923.4	14,774.1	—	—	—	.539	923.4	14,774.1
1840....	.527	1,239.0	28,497.8	.822	1,839.6	1,839.6	.545	1,264.1	30,337.4

TABLE 2 (Continued)

Year of Build	Paddle			Screw			Total		
	Ratio of Net to Gross Tonnage	Transport Capacity per Ship	Total Transport Capacity	Ratio of Net to Gross Tonnage	Transport Capacity per Ship	Total Transport Capacity	Ratio of Net to Gross Tonnage	Transport Capacity per Ship	Total Transport Capacity
1841	.633	3,418.8	92,306.9	—	—	—	.633	3,418.8	92,306.9
1842	.559	2,157.5	47,464.7	—	—	—	.559	2,157.5	47,464.7
1843	.480	545.1	14,718.4	—	—	—	.480	545.1	14,718.4
1844	.536	1,124.8	25,871.2	—	—	—	.536	1,124.8	25,871.2
1845	.513	551.2	8,267.9	—	—	—	.513	551.2	8,267.9
1846	.545	732.6	19,047.2	.679	1,173.6	1,173.6	.553	748.9	20,220.8
1847	.503	967.2	45,457.3	—	—	—	.503	967.2	45,457.3
1848	.464	542.5	24,956.6	—	—	—	.464	542.5	24,956.6
1849	.571	1,176.5	25,883.8	—	—	—	.571	1,176.5	25,883.8
1850	.562	3,957.8	47,493.2	.786	2,377.2	4,754.5	.585	3,732.0	52,247.7
1851	.591	3,551.7	71,033.7	.682	916.7	916.7	.593	3,426.2	71,950.4
1852	.502	1,040.7	36,423.1	.679	902.7	1,805.5	.510	1,033.2	38,228.6
1853	.572	1,368.0	42,408.1	.688	719.0	2,156.9	.578	1,310.7	44,565.0
1854	.553	958.0	24,908.7	.698	5,106.0	15,319.7	.602	1,387.2	40,228.4
1855	.607	1,192.9	33,400.4	.876	501.7	1,013.4	.616	1,177.7	34,413.8
1856	.484	783.7	33,697.8	.702	815.9	1,631.7	.493	785.1	35,329.5
1857	.263	205.0	11,275.4	.521	284.8	1,424.1	.281	211.7	12,699.5
1858	.477	855.9	28,243.3	.571	261.6	523.1	.478	821.9	28,766.4
1859	.294	203.8	7,950.1	.726	1,494.7	7,473.5	.428	350.5	15,423.6
1860	.396	300.0	10,499.1	.709	334.9	1,674.5	.424	304.3	12,173.6

Wood Steamships

TABLE 2 (Continued)

| Year of Build | Paddle | | | Iron Steamships | | | Total | | |
| | | | | Screw | | | | | |
	Ratio of Net to Gross Tonnage	Transport Capacity per Ship	Total Transport Capacity	Ratio of Net to Gross Tonnage	Transport Capacity per Ship	Total Transport Capacity	Ratio of Net to Gross Tonnage	Transport Capacity per Ship	Total Transport Capacity
1823.....	—	—	—	—	—	—	—	—	—
1824.....	—	—	—	—	—	—	—	—	—
1825.....	—	—	—	—	—	—	—	—	—
1826.....	—	—	—	—	—	—	—	—	—
1827.....	—	—	—	—	—	—	—	—	—
1828.....	—	—	—	—	—	—	—	—	—
1829.....	—	—	—	—	—	—	—	—	—
1830.....	—	—	—	—	—	—	—	—	—
1831.....	—	—	—	—	—	—	—	—	—
1832.....	—	—	—	—	—	—	—	—	—
1833.....	—	—	—	—	—	—	—	—	—
1834.....	—	—	—	—	—	—	—	—	—
1835.....	—	—	—	.778	3,275.2	3,275.2	.778	3,275.2	3,275.2
1836.....	.683	893.4	1,786.8	—	—	—	.683	893.4	1,786.8
1837.....	.576	889.5	3,558.1	—	—	—	.576	889.5	3,558.1
1838.....	.584	287.5	1,437.6	—	—	—	.584	287.5	1,437.6
1839.....	.528	487.4	2,437.0	—	—	—	.528	487.4	2,437.0
1840.....	.608	727.4	5,092.1	.494	15,779.4	15,779.4	.518	2,609.0	20,871.5
1841.....	.627	1,277.3	8,940.9	—	—	—	.627	1,277.3	8,940.9

TABLE 2 (Continued)

Year of Build	Paddle			Iron Steamships Screw			Total		
	Ratio of Net to Gross Tonnage	Transport Capacity per Ship	Total Transport Capacity	Ratio of Net to Gross Tonnage	Transport Capacity per Ship	Total Transport Capacity	Ratio of Net to Gross Tonnage	Transport Capacity per Ship	Total Transport Capacity
1842......	.620	730.5	7,304.8	.678	626.4	626.4	.627	721.1	7,931.2
1843......	.605	992.6	5,955.6	—	—	—	.605	992.6	5,955.6
1844......	.579	1,350.3	39,158.3	.637	604.4	1,813.3	.582	1,280.4	40,971.6
1845......	.570	1,170.3	30,428.0	.651	1,090.2	3,270.7	.579	1,162.0	33,698.7
1846......	.634	2,618.4	44,512.8	.714	2,356.4	23,564.1	.662	2,521.4	68,076.9
1847......	.645	2,611.7	80,961.8	.723	2,253.5	13,520.8	.658	2,553.6	94,482.6
1848......	.601	1,939.2	36,844.5	.556	2,382.1	14,292.5	.586	2,045.5	51,137.0
1849......	.633	2,549.6	50,992.8	.692	3,610.4	28,882.8	.655	2,852.7	79,875.6
1850......	.623	2,544.2	45,796.2	.675	2,053.8	24,645.4	.644	2,348.1	70,441.6
1851......	.667	2,521.9	45,393.4	.670	4,799.4	71,990.9	.669	3,557.1	117,384.3
1852......	.670	2,062.5	30,938.2	.669	6,679.7	133,594.2	.669	4,700.9	164,532.4
1853......	.610	2,466.7	49,334.3	.678	5,112.1	219,821.0	.665	4,273.3	269,155.3
1854......	.599	2,474.5	61,863.6	.697	4,639.4	380,428.2	.684	4,133.6	442,291.8
1855......	.574	1,476.3	51,671.6	.662	5,083.5	427,013.3	.652	4,022.6	478,684.9
1856......	.618	2,385.4	76,331.4	.709	3,694.7	262,321.7	.690	3,287.9	338,653.1
1857......	.477	1,228.5	51,598.2	.703	3,886.3	264,267.0	.662	2,871.5	315,865.2
1858......	.613	1,746.4	59,376.2	.709	4,130.0	161,069.1	.684	3,019.8	220,445.3
1859......	.606	3,364.7	100,942.3	.718	3,251.0	152,776.1	.674	3,295.0	253,718.4
1860......	.478	2,547.7	76,431.7	.725	4,342.1	312,634.3	.668	3,814.4	389,066.0

TABLE 2 (Continued)

	Total Iron and Wood Steamships								
	Paddle			Screw			Total		
Year of Build	Ratio of Net to Gross Tonnage	Transport Capacity per Ship	Total Transport Capacity	Ratio of Net to Gross Tonnage	Transport Capacity per Ship	Total Transport Capacity	Ratio of Net to Gross Tonnage	Transport Capacity per Ship	Total Transport Capacity
1823......	.523	990.5	3,990.4	—	—	—	.523	990.5	3,990.4
1824......	.500	793.2	3,172.8	—	—	—	.500	793.2	3,172.8
1825......	.469	802.6	4,013.2	—	—	—	.469	802.6	4,013.2
1826......	.526	795.8	8,754.2	—	—	—	.526	795.8	8,754.2
1827......	.681	1,331.0	3,993.0	—	—	—	.681	1,331.0	3,993.0
1828......	.447	1,780.0	534.0	—	—	—	.447	1,780.0	534.0
1829......	.491	798.5	3,193.9	—	—	—	.491	798.5	3,193.9
1830......	.589	781.5	3,907.6	—	—	—	.589	781.5	3,907.6
1831......	.616	1,041.9	4,167.7	—	—	—	.616	1,041.9	4,167.7
1832......	.610	1,031.2	8,249.7	—	—	—	.610	1,031.2	8,249.7
1833......	.412	583.9	4,670.9	—	—	—	.412	583.9	4,670.9
1834......	.581	1,374.1	23,359.8	—	—	—	.581	1,374.1	23,359.8
1835......	.543	1,008.7	22,192.0	.778	3,275.2	3,275.2	.567	1,212.7	25,467.2
1836......	.565	1,257.9	25,158.6	—	—	—	.564	1,257.8	25,158.6
1837......	.578	1,208.5	39,879.2	—	—	—	.578	1,208.5	39,879.2
1838......	.511	507.7	18,277.6	—	—	—	.511	527.2	18,977.6
1839......	.537	819.6	17,211.1	—	—	—	.537	819.6	17,211.1
1840......	.539	1,119.7	33,589.9	.524	8,809.5	17,619.0	.533	1,600.3	51,208.9

TABLE 2 (Continued)

Year of Build	Total Iron and Wood Steamships								
	Paddle			Screw			Total		
	Ratio of Net to Gross Tonnage	Transport Capacity per Ship	Total Transport Capacity	Ratio of Net to Gross Tonnage	Transport Capacity per Ship	Total Transport Capacity	Ratio of Net to Gross Tonnage	Transport Capacity per Ship	Total Transport Capacity
1841	.632	2,977.9	101,247.8	—	—	—	.632	2,977.9	101,247.8
1842	.567	1,711.5	54,769.5	.678	626.4	626.4	.569	1,678.7	55,395.9
1843	.512	626.5	20,674.0	—	—	—	.512	626.5	20,674.0
1844	.562	1,250.6	65,029.5	.637	604.4	1,813.3	.564	1,215.3	66,842.8
1845	.556	943.8	38,695.9	.651	1,090.2	3,270.7	.564	953.8	41,966.6
1846	.604	1,478.1	63,560.0	.712	2,248.9	24,737.7	.633	1,635.1	88,297.7
1847	.586	1,620.8	126,419.1	.723	2,253.5	13,520.8	.601	1,666.0	139,939.9
1848	.535	950.8	61,801.1	.556	2,382.1	14,292.5	.540	1,071.7	76,093.6
1849	.611	1,830.4	76,876.6	.692	3,610.4	28,882.8	.633	2,115.2	105,759.4
1850	.593	3,109.6	93,289.4	.693	2,100.0	29,399.9	.619	2,788.4	122,689.3
1851	.622	3,063.9	116,427.1	.671	4,556.7	72,907.6	.642	3,506.2	189,334.7
1852	.575	1,347.2	67,361.3	.669	6,154.5	135,399.7	.638	2,816.1	202,761.0
1853	.593	1,798.9	91,742.4	.678	4,825.6	221,977.9	.652	3,234.2	313,720.3
1854	.585	1,701.4	86,772.3	.697	4,655.9	395,747.9	.677	3,547.9	482,520.2
1855	.587	1,350.3	85,072.0	.663	4,977.1	428,026.7	.650	3,443.6	513,098.7
1856	.570	1,467.1	110,029.2	.709	3,615.8	263,953.4	.669	2,526.9	373,982.6
1857	.408	648.2	62,873.6	.702	3,639.6	265,691.1	.630	1,932.7	328,564.7
1858	.563	1,307.8	87,619.5	.707	3,758.0	161,592.2	.656	3,886.9	427,563.8
1859	.556	1,578.2	108,892.5	.718	3,023.6	160,249.6	.650	2,217.1	270,483.6
1860	.464	1,337.4	86,930.8	.724	3,928.9	314,308.8	.656	2,799.1	403,063.9

the first steam Cunarder in regular transatlantic service, was retired from that service in 1849; and Cunard's famous iron-paddle steamer *Persia*, launched in 1856, was retired from the Atlantic service in 1868, after a scant 12 years of service.[16]

Given the high rate of obsolescence and the fact that most of the British steam merchant fleet of 1860 had been built within a decade of that date, it is clear that by 1860 the British steam merchant marine was iron, and moreover, iron screw.[17] The implications of this fact can be appreciated by inspection of the measures of transport capacity in Table 2 below—the earning capacity of this steam fleet was growing prodigiously. In fact, even though by 1860 steamers accounted for only 10 percent of total British register tonnage, the total freight earnings accruing to these steamers must have been much greater. By 1865 steamships accounted for some 20 percent of the total register tonnage, but Sir John Clapham thought it possible that the steamers did more transport work than all the sailing ships combined.[18] The argument applied (although to a lesser degree) to the late 1850's as well; the transport superiority of Britain's new steam fleet no doubt made important contributions to Britain's balance of payments.[19] To the extent that this was so, the rising trade deficit incurred from the 1850's onward was offset more easily year by year because of freight earnings, especially since the proximity of coal and iron to the sea, together with British shipbuilding skills, brought a decisive shift in comparative advantage in shipping to Britain.[20]

---

[16] Private communication to the authors from the Cunard Steamship Company, Ltd. It should be emphasized that some steamers in less competitive routes might enjoy a comparatively long service. By the end of the 19th century the rate of obsolescence slowed down significantly as designs and engines had passed through many experimental stages.

[17] There were in fact already five steel ships in the registry by 1860 (Table 1). Clapham, *op. cit.*, pp. 56, 62 found his first steel steamships in the merchant fleet only in 1863–65. The data in Table 1 make it possible to avoid repetition of earlier errors concerning the size of Britain's early steam merchant fleet. For example, Gayer, Rostow, and Schwartz, *op. cit.*, p. 286, cite G. R. Porter's *Progress of the Nation* to the effect that by 1842 some 4 percent of registered British shipping was steam. This is obviously an overstatement. Total tonnage under British registry in 1842 was 2,991,000, 4 percent of which would be 119,640 register tons; according to the data in Table 1 only about 70,000 *gross* tons of steam shipping had been added to the British merchant fleet by 1842, and much of that must by 1842 have been rendered obsolete and taken out of service.

[18] *Op. cit.*, p. 72.

[19] Although the data in Table 2 do not include a breakdown between ships employed in river or coastal trade, and those employed in ocean trade, it should be borne in mind that many of the smaller steamers were used only in river or coastal trade. Again, it is also possible that many of these steamers were used mainly for passenger service. It would be unwise, therefore, to *overemphasize* the contribution made by the steamers to the balance of payments.

[20] Largely at the expense of the American merchant fleet. Note the failure of American construction of steam and motor ships to continue to grow, in terms of tonnage, from 1853 to the 1880's. *Historical Statistics of the United States* (Washington, D.C., 1949), p. 211. Also the sharp decline after the 1850's (beginning then) in the growth of American tonnage employed in foreign trade leading to absolute decline beginning in 1862. *Ibid.*, pp. 207–8.

Data exist which tend to support this view. It can be seen in A. H. Imlah's estimates of the current account shown in his pioneering work[21] on the British balance of payments. They show that the current account was especially strong (almost continuously in surplus from 1856 to 1874) in the third quarter of the 19th century, and that one of the main elements of this strength came from the sharp increase in net shipping earnings. If Clapham was correct, then the rapidly growing steam fleet (and its capacity to transport cargo, below) was no doubt an important contributor to Britain's commercial strength in the period.

By the late 1850's the development of the iron-screw steamer had made it already clear that Britain would gain greatly in her share of ocean freight earnings in the last half of the 19th century. The growth of the tonnage of iron-screw steamers in the British steam fleet shown in Table 1 underlines this point graphically. In terms of transport capacity, Britain's new steam fleet was even more impressive by 1860.

4. The Measurement of Transport Capacity

The customary measure of the cargo transporting capacity of a ship is its gross tonnage; the customary measure of the amount of shipping capacity built (or existing) in any year is the sum of the gross tonnages of the ships in question.

The adequacy of this measure of the amount of shipping is vitiated in the present case by the fact that important and rapid changes in design and construction of ships and engines took place during the period covered. Comparisons of the data for individual ships early and late in the period indicate that changes were made in hull design, evidenced by changes in the magnitudes and ratios of the linear dimensions of ships and in the changing composition of the fleet as between wood and iron hulls. Changes were made in engine design,[22] evidenced by systematic differences in the portion of gross tonnage occupied by engines and fuel for ships of given horsepower; changes were made in propulsion equipment, evidenced by the changing composition of the fleet constructed year by year in favor of screw propulsion at the expense of the paddle. In these circumstances a gross ton does not denote the same cargo transporting capacity for every ship. Thus, the changing composition from year to year of the fleet constructed means that an aggregate gross ton does not signify the same cargo transporting capacity in different years. In view of the rapid rate of technological advance in this period we are

---

21 "British Balance of Payments and Export of Capital 1816–1913," *Economic History Review* (Second Series), Vol. V, No. 2, 1952.

22 See Graham's account, *passim;* of changes in steam engines employed in ocean shipping. For an excellent account of the technical improvement of shipping during this period see Edgar C. Smith, *A Short History of Naval and Marine Engineering* (Cambridge, 1937), esp. pp. 94–186.

led to seek a more satisfactory measure of the amount of shipping constructed, where we view shipping as transportation capacity.

The transportation capacity of a ship may be considered its ability to move cargo a given distance in a given time. More specifically, we can consider the cargo transporting capacity of a ship to be:

Number of cargo ton — miles per hour =

$$\left(\begin{array}{c}\text{net tonnage}\\ \text{of the ship}\end{array}\right) \times \left(\begin{array}{c}\text{cruising speed}\\ \text{of the ship}\end{array}\right).$$

We shall call this quantity the *cargo transporting capacity,* or more briefly, the *transport capacity* of the ship.[23] By summing the transport capacities of the ships built in any year we obtain a measure of the transport capacity of the fleet built in that year, which we may call the aggregate transport capacity. The validity of this measure of shipping capacity is not affected by changes in the composition of the fleet from year to year or by changes in the design of ships, because the significant consequences for cargo carrying capacities of such changes are measured directly by this quantity. Thus, changes in hull design of ships produce changes in the space available for cargo, and in their speed; changes in engine design similarly produce changes in the space available for cargo and in speed; changes in design of propulsion equipment similarly affect cargo space and speed (e.g., more efficient propulsion equipment makes it possible to reduce the size of engines and hence the space taken by engines and fuel without sacrifice of speed; or to increase speed without reducing cargo space).

Computation of the transport capacity in the present case was impeded

---

[23] A fully satisfactory measure of transport capacity would include a measure of that portion of port time (time spent in docking, loading, and unloading) attributable to the ship. Our presumption is that port time, like sailing time, decreased as the technology of the steamship developed and spread into use. To the extent that this was so the transport capacities shown in Table 2 tend to understate the levels and the rate of increase over time of the actual capacity of the fleet to transport cargo. The presumption that port time would be shorter for steamers than for sail is supported by the following considerations.

Steamers represented substantial commitments of capital. Taylor estimates that "a steamship ordinarily cost three or four times as much as a sailing packet of comparable size." George R. Taylor, *The Transportation Revolution 1815–1860* (New York: Rinehart and Co., Inc., 1951), p. 119.

The large commitment of capital, the relatively smaller cargo space, and the substantially larger proportion of port time to total time of transport for steamers would in the presence of the spur of competition provide substantial inducements to reduce port time. Moreover, the relatively rapid deterioration of iron steamers from rusting would provide an additional inducement in the same direction.

We have only isolated pieces of information on port time, and none of it separates that part due to port facilities from that part due to the ship. However, what data we have tends to support the view that port time was less for steamers than for sail. This is clear in the case of the coal trade, where the introduction of steam colliers encouraged the introduction of power equipment at docks to facilitate loading and unloading (see pp. 479, 480 below).

by the fact that the official data do not include the speeds of ships. They do, however, include the indicated horsepower of the engines and the linear dimensions of each ship. Because the speed of a ship of moderate speed depends to a first approximation on the power available to drive it and on the resistance due to skin friction with the water, it was possible on the basis of this information to estimate the speed of each ship by means of certain conventional formulas to be found in standard reference works on naval architecture and marine engineering. The speed of each ship was estimated by means of the following formulas:[24]

$$V = C \cdot \sqrt{25,000 \, \frac{P}{S}} \tag{1}$$

$$S = L\{1.5H + .73B\} \tag{2}$$

In these formulas, P denotes horsepower, S the wetted surface of the ship in square feet, V the speed, in nautical miles per hour, L the length of the ship in feet, H the mean molded draft (depth of hold) in feet, B the width in feet, and C a constant determined from data.

The transport capacity of the fleet could then be determined from the estimates made of the transport capacities of the individual ships using their estimated speeds.

Those considering using this measure of cargo-carrying capacity must settle for themselves the question whether it is preferable to use a measure correct in principle, but subject to an error of unknown magnitude analogous to an error of measurement, or to use an alternative measure, which is in principle unsatisfactory, but whose value is perhaps known more precisely.[25]

The Cunard Steamship Company was generous in making available the speeds of some 20 ships built during the period 1845–61.

Trial computations for these ships led to the decision to divide the

---

[24] The formulas are taken from D. W. Taylor, *The Speed and Power of Ships; a Manual of Marine Propulsion* (1938), pp. 171, 20–21 respectively.

Formula (1) is obtained from Kirk's Formula by taking the constant $k = 4$, the figure suggested by Kirk for ships with a high coefficient of fineness.

Formula (2) is obtained from Normand's formula by taking the block coefficient equal to .65 the value given by Charles H. Hughes, *Handbook of Ship Calculations Construction and Operations* (3d ed.: New York and London, 1942), p. 170. See also Clement Machrow, and Lloyd Woollard, *The Naval Architect's and Shipbuilder's Pocket-book of Formulae, Rules and Tables and Marine Engineer's and Surveyor's Handy Book of Reference* (14th ed. [revised]), pp. 175, 176.

Judgments involving the shapes of ships, based on examination of these data, on their linear dimensions and on such illustrations of early steamships as were available to the authors, were used as a basis for selecting the values of the two constants, k, and the block coefficient, used in these formulas. The arbitrary nature of this method of choice was partly offset by the introduction of the constant C, which was estimated from numerical data, see below.

[25] These hard alternatives may be softened by the fact that there is some information about the errors due to estimating speed. See Table 3 below.

ships into two groups, those built prior to 1848, and those built after 1848. For those prior to 1848 the value $C = 1.11$ was used, for those after 1848, the value $C = 1.39$ was used. The following table shows the estimated and actual speeds and the error for the ships for which the speed is available.

The measures of transport capacity obtained with the aid of these formulas are given in Table 2. This table also shows the ratio of net to gross tonnage in each year (in effect a weighted average of the ratio of net to gross tonnage of each ship weighted by gross tonnage), and the transport capacity per ship in each year. These data enable us to compare the fleet measured by transport capacity with the fleet measured by gross tonnage.

TABLE 3

ACTUAL SPEED, ESTIMATED SPEED, AND ERROR FOR VARIOUS SHIPS
BY YEAR OF BUILD

Ship	Year of Build	Actual Speed in Miles Per Hour	Estimated Speed	Error
Cambria	1845	9.25	10.9	+1.65
America	1848	10.5	10.9	+ .40
Canada	1848	10.5	11.4	+ .90
Niagara	1848	10.5	11.3	+ .80
Asia	1850	12.25	11.5	− .75
Africa	1850	12.25	10.7	−1.55
British Queen	1851	10.0	10.8	+ .80
Delta	1853	9.0	9.1	+ .10
Melita	1853	9.5	9.1	− .40
Karnak	1853	9.5	10.8	+1.20
Emeu	1854	9.5	10.6	+1.00
Jura	1856	9.5	11.7	+2.10
Etna	1856	9.5	12.4	+2.80
Persia	1856	13.8	12.8	−1.00
Australasian	1857	12.5	9.5	−3.00
Olympus	1860	10.5	9.5	−1.00
Atlas	1860	10.5	9.6	− .90
Marathon	1860	10.5	9.6	− .90
Hecla	1860	10.5	9.6	− .90
Kedar	1861	10.5	9.5	−1.00

SOURCE: Private communications to the authors from Cunard Steamship Company, Ltd.

In Chart 2 we plot the logarithms of gross tonnage and transport capacity, respectively, against time. These series move closely together, except perhaps for the period 1848 to 1854.

Linear regressions of these series on time yield the least squares trend lines shown in Chart 2. It is seen from these that the original series have exponential trends, and that transport capacity increased during this period at a faster rate than did gross tonnage. The method of estimating the speeds of the ships affords grounds for the belief that the computed transport capacity may overstate the capacity of ships built early in the period and understate the capacity of those built late in the period; so that the rate of increase of transport capacity is lower than it should be.

The equations of the trend lines are:[26]

$$\text{estimated gross tonnage} = 2.63 + .061 \times (\text{time})$$
$$\text{estimated transport capacity} = 3.26 + .067 \times (\text{time})$$

The data in Table 2 sharply amplify the preponderence of iron steamers in the total fleet; and also indicate some advantages of screw propulsion over paddle. By the 1850's iron steamers had outstripped wood both in total and in average transport capacity. Wood-screw ships did not consistently exceed wood-paddle steamers in transport capacity, but did

CHART 2

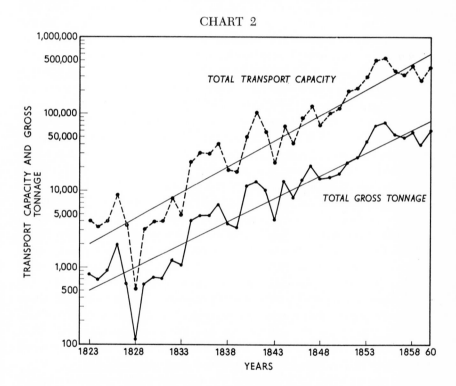

in terms of the ratio of net to gross tonnage—indicating the larger amount of free cargo space which screw propulsion made available compared to paddle. It is notable that, in this respect, wood-screw ships were superior to iron paddle ships and even compared favorably to iron-screw steamers. Nevertheless, as is seen in Table 2, very few wood-screw steamers were placed under permanent registry in this period. This evidence supports the view that wood had disadvantages for ocean transport for which the

---

[26] The squares of the standard errors of estimate for these regression lines are .06 and .07 respectively.

compensation of screw propulsion and the advantages of long familiarity in construction were insufficient.

By the 1850's the highest total *and* average transport capacities had clearly passed over to iron-screw steamers. The sharp decline in both the total and average transport capacities of the wood ships after the mid-1850's probably indicates that the wood steamer was increasingly used only for river transport, and new wood steamers were no longer being purchased for employment in the ocean shipping routes even though a considerable number of wood-paddle steamers were still being placed under permanent registry (Table 1).

The transport capacity measures in Table 2 together with the data in Table 1 suggest some significant points about the role of the steam fleet compared to the sailing ships that still comprised the bulk of British merchant ships under British registry in the mid-19th century. As was argued above, the freight earnings from the new steam fleet doubtlessly added considerably to Britain's ability to reverse the pattern of her balance of payments and to run almost persistent current-account surpluses from the mid-1850's until the mid-1870's. These earnings no doubt came mainly from the shorter trade routes. The actual conquest of the shorter trade routes by British steamers has not yet been measured in quantitative terms (or dated), but on the basis of known historical evidence it is thought that the conquest was extensive by the late 1850's.[27] Even so, there has not been general agreement on the actual degree to which steamers supplanted sail in the mid-19th century. Sir John Clapham, for example, thought it a "great exaggeration" when C. M. Palmer stated in 1864 that "iron steamers [did] most of the carrying trade of the Baltic and Mediterranean."[28] But the data adduced in this paper clearly show that this need not have been an exaggeration at all. Indeed, the shoe would seem to be on the other foot. We have seen that by the end of the 1850's the carrying trade, if it were being done by steamer (and Clapham never argued that it was still dependent upon sail) must have been done by iron steamers, and indeed, by iron-screw steamers—all other kinds of steam ships taken together having been reduced to very small proportions of the British steam merchant fleet in the 1850's.

In a similar vein, G. S. Graham has recently argued against what he considers to have been the undue emphasis placed by historians upon the role of the steamship in the 19th-century development of the British empire.[29] The point may be well taken, but it needs quantitative support. If by "imperial development" one means British overseas investment in

---

[27] E.g., Graham, *op. cit.*, p. 74. Throughout this account there is scattered evidence on this problem. G. R. Taylor states that ". . . steamships had, during the fifties, been able to take over the best-paying part of the ocean trade." He believes that in total world trade, by 1860, the sailing ship still prevailed "very largely." *The Transportation Revolution* (New York, 1951), p. 119.

[28] *Op. cit.*, p. 71.

[29] *Op. cit.*, pp. 74–75.

the colonies, then the steamer, by its freight earnings in the North Sea, Baltic, Mediterranean, and North Atlantic routes, was without doubt an important contributor to the strong balance-of-payments position which sustained British overseas investment in the last half of the century. Graham makes much of the inability of the steamers to compete with sail on the long routes to India, China, and Australia. But considering that more than half of British overseas trade was conducted within the possible steamer routes (Europe accounted for between 30 and 45 percent, North America for another 10–30 percent[30] and this cargo trade data does not include the very profitable emigrant passenger trade in which steamships participated), and considering that the carrying trade of Europe was within the sphere of British steamers, it would seem that it must be shown in quantitative terms that freight earnings from the long-haul cargos of sail were greater than steamer earnings if Graham's point is to be substantiated.[31] Until such evidence is forthcoming it would not be wise to write off the "traditional" emphasis on the role of steam. The data in Tables 1 and 2 above show that by the end of the 1850's Britain's steam merchant fleet was not the wooden assortment of paddle wheelers that many have envisaged (above), but that it was mostly iron-screw, of recent build and growing with increasingly greater transport capacity. It was a commercial weapon worthy of the importance assigned to it by its contemporaries.

5. The Historical Setting

New techniques have only rarely effected major changes in economic activity with what might be called startling rapidity. The case of the iron-screw steamship was no exception. Indeed, by the mid-1850's when the triumph of this kind of ocean transport in the steamship routes was obvious to contemporaries (and visible on the ways of British shipyards) the steamship already had a history stretching back half a century. The iron-screw steamer had been in use for at least two decades, and a great and colorful age of commercial sail on the longest ocean routes still lay in the future.[32] Yet, given the history of experimentation and growth in earlier decades, the rapid increase in the number and tonnage of iron-screw steamers in the British merchant marine in the 1850's together with the resulting displacement of other forms of ocean transport, constitute a striking development; and was certainly an outstanding example

---

[30] See Werner Schlote, *British Overseas Trade from 1700 to the 1930's* (Oxford, 1952), Tables 18, 19, pp. 156–59.

[31] And this may be conceivable if data for freight earnings can be uncovered, since bulk cargos of the kind carried by sail may well have earned more freights (in aggregate) than manufactured goods and passengers. The authors are indebted to Douglass C. North for this observation based upon his as yet unpublished investigation of 19th-century ocean freight rates.

[32] Gerald S. Graham, *op. cit.*, p. 75.

of the force of innovation in the record of British economic growth in the period.

The accelerated introduction of the iron-screw steamer in the 1850's can best be understood in its own historical context. The demand for iron-screw steamers depended mainly upon the needs of overseas trade. A major innovation such as this one might successfully make inroads upon the markets of older and less efficient kinds of shipping because of cost advantages, but a rapid expansion of the *total* market would considerably ease the problem of entry, especially if existing shipping capacity were very nearly utilized. This would presuppose a strong growth of foreign trade, which in turn would, *ceteris paribus,* be related to a sharp rise in domestic and foreign economic activity. Such conditions prevailed in the decade of the 1850's. Moreover, the rise of a competing form of transportation, the railway, threatened the coastal trade in coal and virtually forced the quick adoption of the iron-screw steamer in the coastal transport of coal. Here was a process familiar in economic history —innovation giving rise to innovation on a grand scale.[33]

The British economy evolved slowly from its mainly agricultural base toward an "industry state" in the half century following the end of the French wars in 1815. The growth of industry and trade was uneven, but with the steady increase in population, internal improvements in industrial techniques, transportation, and communications together with the increasing movement of laborers from the countryside into the industrial towns,[34] the transformation became ever more perceptible. The outflow of British people (and other Europeans) to America and to the colonies[35] insured a growth of British overseas trade in industrial products. This growth was augmented by commercial development elsewhere and by the ever-growing interdependence of commercial and financial activity on a world scale. In a very real sense, trade engendered more trade. At the center of this complex of markets the growing British industrial economy became increasingly dependent upon overseas supplies of raw materials, and (by the mid-19th century) of food.

The effects upon Britain's overseas trade are to be seen in Chart 1. Even before the great upsurge of economic activity that characterized the decade of the 1850's, the movement of British foreign trade was

---

[33] For an extensive discussion see, for example, Paul Mantoux's discussion of the effects of Kay's flying shuttle on the textile industry, *The Industrial Revolution in the Eighteenth Century* (London, 1949), pp. 211–13; and Karl Marx, *Capital,* Vol. I (Glaisher, ed.) (London, 1918), pp. 379–82, on the effects upon invention of disparate increases in productivity in related industries caused by innovations; *e.g.,* . . . it was only during the decade preceding 1866, that the construction of railways and ocean steamers on a stupendous scale called into existence the cyclopean machines now employed in the construction of prime movers." p. 380.

[34] This movement was at its height in the 1840's; see A. K. Cairncross, "Internal Migration in Victorian England," *Manchester School* (1949), Vol. XVII, p. 70.

[35] From 1845 to 1850 alone roughly 1.3 million people emigrated from the United Kingdom. *Statistical Abstract.*

strongly upward in volume terms. This no doubt provided enough of a growth element in the ocean-freight market to buoy up the expectations of investors in steamers. Thus in the late 1830's and twice in the 1840's there were fairly marked increases in the construction of steamships, either wood paddle or iron paddle, to be added to the British merchant fleet. But as can be seen in Table 1 it was in the years immediately after the Californian and Australian gold discoveries and during the Crimean War that the character of steamship construction changed radically and the iron-screw steamer clearly displaced wood and iron paddle steamships in United Kingdom shipyards.[36]

While the rapid growth of iron-screw steamer construction is evident as early as 1849, the years 1850 to 1855 saw a spectacular increase in their construction and the introduction of the iron-screw steamer was decisive. The boom in overseas trade (especially raw-material imports and also exports of British commodities to America and Australia up to 1854, together with a sharp rise in exports to the Continent and to the Middle East in 1855) followed by military transport requirements while trade remained at very high levels, led to a strong demand for new shipping capacity, and during the war, especially for steamers.[37]

The rise in ocean freights even before the outbreak of war with Russia in 1854 was very marked and spurred the efforts of shipbuilders and ship speculators. From the first quarter of 1852 to the third quarter of 1853 average cargo freight rates from British ports to New York rose from 15s. to 28s. per ton. During the same period, freights on (measurement) goods to Calcutta rose from 22s. to 42s. per ton, and to Melbourne, from 42s. to 85s. per ton.[38] Such increases of as much as 100 percent reflect the shortage of shipping capacity that existed in the wake of the trade expansion of the early 1850's. But when war came early in 1854 freights

---

[36] The change to iron was marked in sailing vessels as well. "As regards iron-built sailing vessels, the most remarkable feature of our trade is the very increasing favor they are now growing into, and which are now occupying the builders both here [Liverpool], on the Clyde, Newcastle and elsewhere to an unprecedented extent." *Circular to Bankers,* January 8, 1853. By the middle 1850's shrewd and observant contemporary, Thomas Tooke, without distinguishing between kinds of iron ships, saw clearly the change that had taken place. "The number of Iron Vessels now owned by this country is very great, and it is rapidly on the increase. On the Clyde it is a rare sight to see a ship built of wood. The Tyne-built are, also, almost all of iron. At Liverpool also, iron is becoming much used; and even at Sunderland, where they have been so long accustomed to wooden vessels, some of the leading builders are directing their attention to iron." *History of Prices* (London, 1857), Vol. V, p. 331.

[37] The striking rapidity and magnitude of the response of the shipbuilders to the stimulus of increased demand was partly made possible by the flexibility of the British financial system of the period. Ships were financed on the basis of long-dated bills of exchange which were accepted and discounted like ordinary trade bills in the London discount market. The system was largely discredited in 1866 when the great discount house of Overend and Gurney failed and their underwriting, by this means, of the notorious ship speculator, Stephanos Xenos, became known. In *Accounts and Papers,* 1861, LVIII (371) Xenos appears prominently from the mid-1850's onward in the London registrations.

[38] Tooke, *op. cit.,* p. 319.

rose even higher in response to government demand for troop transports to the Black Sea.

Immediately following the outbreak of war government transport demand had been mainly for sail, but several large steamers were chartered from the principal steamship companies and these ships soon proved their superiority. They were mostly of large size[39] and made the voyage from Portsmouth to Constantinople in from 12 to 15 days. The same trip for sail was an estimated 40 to 50 days.[40] Accordingly government charter demand swung over to steamers: there were 31,900 tons of steam under government charter by June, 1855, compared to only 15,800 tons of sail; a year earlier these figures had been virtually the reverse, 14,000 tons of steam and 39,800 tons of sail.[41] By the end of 1854 the government was paying 55s. to 60s. per register ton for steamers; 25s. to 30s. had been the charter price at the beginning of the war.[42]

There developed a shortage of steamers in almost every route when government demand was met.

. . . though every line of the trade has been drained, even to the derangement of our postal services, sufficient steamers cannot be found.[43]

By late 1854 it appeared that British shipping capacity was strained virtually to the limit. Wages of shipbuilders and seamen by 1854 had risen 50 percent or more compared to 1850.[44] The rise in shipbuilders' wages reflected both private and government demand for newly constructed ships. Of the 354 steamships added to the British Navy from 1848 to 1859, 284 were purchased in the three years 1854–56.[45] As can be seen in Table 1 the increased tonnage of steamer construction (and especially of iron-screw steamers) in the early 1850's reached boom proportions during the Crimean War years. During that period the market seemed to warrant a great expansion of steamship construction—and especially of iron-screw steamers.[46] But the Crimean War shipbuilding

---

[39] Averaging well over 1,000 gross tons, the largest, the "Himalaya," chartered from the Penninsular and Oriental Steam Navigation Company, had a gross tonnage of 3,550. *Ibid.*, p. 320.

[40] *Ibid.*

[41] *Ibid.*

[42] *Ibid.*, p. 321.

[43] *Times,* January 4, 1855.

[44] The peak of wage rates reached during the Crimean War represented the highest levels of the whole period 1848–60; wages declined from 1855–56 onward. See Bowley, A. L. and Wood, G. S., "Statistics of Wages in the United Kingdom . . . Engineering and Shipbuilding," *Journal of the Royal Statistical Society,* Vol. LXIX, (1906), p. 518; for wages of seamen, see *Accounts and Papers,* 1867, LXIV (158).

[45] Accounts and Papers, 1859 (sess. 1), XV (180). For total vessels ordered by the Navy and launched in this period see *Accounts and Papers,* 1860, VIII (545), *Report of the Select Committee on Navy Guns and Mortar Boats,* Appendix 3.

[46] Moreover, the steamers constructed were mostly of large size suitable for overseas trade, while the coastal trade was neglected. Steam tonnage employed in coastal trade fell from 85,500 in 1853 to 54,000 in 1854, and was only 57,400 in 1855. *Times,*

boom largely accounted for the depression in shipbuilding after 1855; excess capacity had been created, and especially was this the case when the war ended.

As can be seen in Table 1, the decline in shipbuilding in the years immediately following 1855 was sharp—and this in spite of the unprecedented levels of trade ruling in 1856–60. Here the yards specializing in the construction of iron-screw steamers were evidently not protected by the technological superiority of their product; they were hit as badly by the excess shipping capacity built during the Crimean War as were those shipyards still specializing in sailing ships.[47] However, even though new construction of iron-screw steamers was drastically reduced, the superiority of these ships over sail was becoming increasingly evident and the war-built steamers were evidently capturing the shorter trade routes as early as 1856.

Surplus steamers are now finding their way, to the advantage of all concerned, into trades formerly carried on by sailing vessels.[48]

The Baltic routes especially felt the impact of the Crimean War iron-screw tonnage. On these routes the fuel problem was less of a handicap than on other routes and by 1856 the intrusion of steamers was a notable feature of the Baltic trade. In 1853, 26 steamers had reportedly made 79 voyages from British to Baltic ports; in 1856 the number of steamers in that trade had risen to 136 and the number of voyages to 334.[49] Even as early as the beginning of 1857 some shipowners realized that steam was about to overtake sail in the shorter routes.[50] By the end of 1858 it was noted that steamers had succeeded in the Mediterranean trade.[51] In the coastal trade railway competition had already assured the introduction of steam.

The construction of trunk lines associated with the railway "mania" of the 1840's together with the proliferation of branch lines during the 1850's provided Britain with a vastly improved land transportation base for industrial expansion. But the new railways also broke the bottleneck in coal transport, a field that had formerly been the preserve of the coastal-shipping companies, and provided strong competition for the freight earnings of coal haulage. Development of a rapid internal transportation system capable of handling coal meant that the old wind-driven

---

January 4, 1955; *Statistical Abstract*. This no doubt helped to shift the transport of coal to the railways during the war years and especially in 1855. See below pp. 378–80, esp. Table 4.

[47] The shipowners were well aware of their predicament. "In estimating the prospects for the current year, we cannot hide from ourselves that we have far too much tonnage afloat for the purposes of our legitimate trade." *Times*, January 3, 1857.

[48] Tooke, *op. cit.*, Vol. V, p. 331.

[49] *Times*, January 3, 1857.

[50] "In our opinion the time is rapidly approaching when for short voyages steam will be as a general rule substituted for wind." *Ibid.*

[51] *Ibid.*, January 3, 1859.

colliers faced a kind of competition they had never known before. Moreover, coal-producing areas not served by direct rail connections with London were faced with potential losses of a good part of their market in the metropolis and were forced to find a means of retaliation. Iron-screw colliers provided the means of competing.

From 1850 to 1860 coal transported into metropolitan London rose from 3,639,000 tons to 5,070,000 tons, an increase of 1,431,000 tons. During the same period, coal brought into the London district by inland navigation and railways rose from a mere 85,000 tons to 1,497,000 tons, or by 1,412,000 tons, almost the whole of the increase in the total.[52] By 1860 coal brought into London by coastal shipping stood at 3,573,000 tons, a mere 20,000 tons above the 1850 figure, but in 1855 coal brought into London by coastal shipping had fallen to just above 3,000,000 tons; at the same time inland transport had risen by over one million tons to 1,161,000 tons.[53] From 1855 to 1860, as is apparent from these figures, the coastal trade regained some of its earlier losses to the railways; coal brought in by coastal shipping increased more than that brought in by inland transportation. This change in the fortunes of the coastal trade was due almost entirely to the introduction of iron-screw colliers.

The northern shippers and coal owners had been fairly quick to perceive the advantages of iron-screw colliers in spite of a suggestion to the contrary implicit in the volume data shown above. As early as 1844 interest was aroused in London on the arrival of a Newcastle collier ". . . a fine looking vessel built of iron and fitted with a screw propeller, working an engine of 20 horse power."[54] By the 1850's the beginning of the shift of the English iron industry's center to the North Riding of Yorkshire, following the successful processing of the Cleveland "yellow band" iron ores, produced a powerful group of new industrialists who quickly adopted the iron-screw steamer. One of these men, C. M. Palmer, a northern coal and iron owner as well as a shipbuilder, launched the *John Bowes* in 1852. This ship was an iron-screw collier built to carry 650 tons of coal at 9 miles per hour. On its initial voyage, the *John Bowes* went from Newcastle to the Thames in 48 hours, unloaded in 24 hours, and was back in Newcastle in another 48 hours, having done a job in five days that ". . . would have taken two average sized sailing colliers upwards of a month to accomplish."[55] As can be seen in Table 4, these results were not lost on northern shipowners.

The hundredfold increase in coal shipments by iron-screw collier in a matter of a decade was not only a consequence of increased production

---

[52] *Report of the Commissioners Appointed to Inquire into the Several Matters Relating to Coal in the United Kingdom, Accounts and Papers,* 1871, XVIII (C. 435-II), Appendix to Report of Committee E., p. 975.

[53] *Ibid.*

[54] Harry Scrivenor, *History of the Iron Trade* (London, 1854), p. 311.

[55] J. S. Jeans, *Notes on Northern Industries* (London, 1879), pp. 74–75.

TABLE 4

NUMBER OF CARGOES AND TONS OF COAL CARRIED BY IRON-SCREW
COLLIER, NEWCASTLE TO LONDON BY YEARS FROM 1852 TO 1862

Year	Number of Cargoes	Tons of Coal
1852	17	9,483
1853	123	69,934
1854	345	199,974
1855	174	85,584
1856	413	238,597
1857	977	547,099
1858	1,127	599,527
1859	899	544,614
1860	1,069	672,476
1861	1,299	851,991
1862	1,427	929,825

SOURCE: J. S. Jeans, *op. cit.*, p. 75.

and use of these steamers, but was also a result of rapid technical improvements in such ships. In 1857 an announcement appeared that the *William Cory* was ready for service between Cardiff and London. The explicitly stated purpose for building this ship was to compete with railway transportation. The *William Cory* was designed to carry 1,500 tons of coal—more than twice the capacity of the *John Bowes*. The *William Cory* was also fitted out to take on water as ballast for its homeward voyage and the Victoria Docks had been supplied with hydraulic equipment that would take off the entire cargo in 16 hours.[56] Given the pace of technological advance implied by these two illustrations,[57] the data in Table 4 are easily enough understood. Although the iron-screw collier might have developed rapidly enough on its own, the vigorous railway competition of the 1850's accelerated the introduction of this new form of ocean transport.

The growth of the new iron-steam fleet in this period had broad economic implications. The construction of the new iron-steam fleet (and also the adoption of iron for sailing ships) provided an additional source of demand for iron and underpinned expanded investment and output in the iron industry and in the closely connected coal industry in the 1850's.[58] In this respect the demand effects of iron-ship construction on the iron industry were similar to those observed by Clapham in the period 1873–83.[59] The shift of iron production toward the Northeast during the 1850's was thus no doubt given an additional stimulus by ship-

[56] *Times*, July 16, 1857.

[57] A further discussion about the rate of obsolescence in these early steamships is given above.

[58] A brief discussion of iron and coal output and investment in the 1850's will be found in Jonathan R. T. Hughes, "The Commercial Crisis of 1857," *Oxford Economic Papers* (New Series), Vol. 8, No. 2 (June, 1956), pp. 196–97, 204–5. For Scotland alone, R. H. Campbell, "Fluctuations in Stocks," *Oxford Economic Papers*, (New Series), Vol. 9, No. 1 (February, 1957), p. 43.

[59] *Op. cit.*, p. 61.

building booms in the shipyards of the Tyne and Tees, and in Glasgow and other iron ports in the area. The number of steamer registrations in the Northeast ports in fact rose rapidly from 1851 onward.[60]

The trends in transport capacity and gross tonnage added to the British steam fleet 1823–60 (above p. 748 and Chart 2) are of interest in connection with certain theories of economic development. From the time of Malthus theorists have speculated on the possibilities of exponential growth, and recently attention has again turned to growth models characterized by exponential growth.[61] If these models can be regarded as referring to average behavior of output, then the observed growth of transport capacity (Chart 2) is consistent with the hypothesis of exponential growth for the period 1823–60.

Converting the regression equation for transport capacity into the form of an exponential to the base "*e*" we have:

$$\text{Estimated transport capacity in year } t = e^{(.15t + 7.5)}$$

Transport capacity thus grew on the average at the rate of 15 percent per year during the period observed. It is beyond the scope of the present paper to determine to what extent the growth of transport capacity is representative of overall economic growth in the period. But the transport capacity data certainly help to raise the possibility of exponential growth out of the realm of pure hypothesis; and a cursory examination made by the present authors of aggregate data for the British economy in the first half of the 19th century suggests that further research in this area will yield high returns to interested scholars.

The historical background of the boom in investment in steamers in the late 1840's and in the 1850's can add considerably to our understanding of the rapid expansion of this means of ocean transport in the period and contributes to our understanding of British economic growth in the period. But there remain many unanswered questions; certainly until adequate quantitative evidence on the actual competitive performance of these ships in the ocean-freight markets is forthcoming, the development of the oceangoing steamer in this early period will not be fully understood. What were the actual cost incentives of iron-screw steamers compared to other types in this period? How much longer than wood ships did the iron steamers remain in service? How long did the growth patterns indicated in Tables 1 and 2 above continue after 1860? When did the new steel ships begin to displace iron in the new steam fleet? These are questions which ought to be profitable areas for further investigation.

---

[60] With the exception of Sunderland.

[61] See for example; J. von Neuman, "A Model of General Economic Equilibrium," *Review of Economic Studies*, Vol. 13, No. 1 (1945–46), pp. 1–9; R. M. Solow and P. A. Samuelson, "Balanced Growth under Constant Returns to Scale," *Econometrica*, Vol. 21, No. 3 (July, 1953), pp. 412–24.

6. Summary

Beginning in the late 1840's the growth of the British steam fleet began to accelerate markedly and this fleet was mainly built of iron. As early as 1844 the gross tonnage of iron steamers added to the fleet exceeded wood. By 1851 the gross tonnage of iron-screw steamers alone exceeded all wood steamers. Hence the "general" adoption of iron for steamships certainly began in the early 1840's, or from 10 to 20 years earlier than has customarily been believed. Some 60 percent of the gross tonnage of all steamers added to the fleet in 1823–60 was added in 1854–60, 85 percent of this gross tonnage was iron, and about 70 percent was iron-screw. Given the high rate of obsolescence of these early steamers, it has been argued that by 1860 the British steam merchant fleet was mostly iron-screw and less than a decade old. It was shown that due to technological improvements the rate of growth of the transport capacity of this fleet was even faster than the gross tonnage, and that iron-screw ships were predominant by these measures, and were the most efficient in terms of net cargo-carrying capacity. It has been argued that, in the light of these findings, historians have probably underrated the strength of the British steam fleet which existed by the early 1860's, and that the claims of contemporaries, thought by recent historians to have been exaggerated, were probably justified. At least there is little quantitative evidence to the contrary. Finally, it has been shown that the rapid development of the steam merchant fleet in the 1850's was associated with strong economic expansion both within Britain and in her overseas trade. The growth of the steam fleet was further buttressed by the Crimean War transport demand and was given an additional stimulus by the growth of railway competition for the coastal trade in coal. Hence a favorable economic environment prevailed in Britain for the accelerated introduction of this radical innovation in ocean transport.

7. An Interpretation of the German Risk Fleet Concept, 1899-1914

James H. McRandle
Purdue University
James P. Quirk
University of Kansas

1. Introduction

THE DECADE prior to the outbreak of World War I was marked by various tensions and fears but perhaps no conflict seemed at the time more dangerous than the naval building race between Great Britain and Germany. Under the dynamic leadership of Admirals Fisher and Tirpitz the navies of these two states developed their strength rapidly during this period, and by 1914 each state had imposing collections of the most awesome war machine of the time, the dreadnought battleship. Popular fear in each country of surprise attack by the other power heightened the tensions that existed at the official level. In Great Britain such books as Childers' *Riddle of the Sands* dealt with the subject of surprise attack, while in Germany the term "Copenhagen," appearing frequently in the popular press, reflected the fear that the British fleet might fall upon the German fleet and destroy it at its anchorages as the British had done to the Danish fleet in 1807. Newspapers of both countries, with their calls for "a place in the sun" or "two keels for one," did little to contribute to rational discussion of the relations between the two powers.

It was the popular assumption of the British at the time (and the idea has been carried on to the present by many historians) that the Germans in their naval building program were attempting to match the Royal Navy in strength. In fact, a number of historians have echoed Winston Churchill's thought that for England the fleet was a necessity, for others it was a luxury. This estimate of the situation has not only given particular prominence to the "Anglo-German Naval Arms Race" as a major contributory factor to the outbreak of World War I but it has also placed special onus upon the Germans for directly challenging the British in the one area where they could not afford to be challenged. It has also obscured the fact that a naval arms race had been in progress for years before the Germans began to build a fleet worthy of the name.

The traditional method of studying the naval arms race between Great Britain and Germany has made use of the diplomatic papers and memoirs of the period in order to study the reactions of statesmen to the events in question. Such studies as Marder's *From the Dreadnought to Scapa Flow* or Steinberg's *Yesterday's Deterrent: Tirpitz and the Birth of the German Battle Fleet* have added greatly to our understanding of the sense of bewilderment which seized the German and English public and leaders during the period 1904–14. One can feel again the sense of urgency and suspicion which gripped the chancellories and war rooms of the powers and one can also feel again the sense of awe and terror inspired by the proud silhouettes of the *Colossus*, the *Kaiser*, and all their terrible sisters.

This paper does not propose to review again the diplomacy of the period but rather attempts to analyze the naval arms race in terms of the data available at the time and to interpret this data in terms of a probabilistic model. It is hoped that the paper will thus serve not only to throw further light upon the naval arms race but also to demonstrate something of the scope and limitations of the statistical and mathematical approaches to historical analysis.

While it may be argued that a study of the naval arms race should concentrate on the years 1904–12 (the period from the decision to build the *Dreadnought* to the failure of the negotiations connected with the Haldane mission) there are a number of reasons for beginning a study of the race at an earlier date and continuing it beyond 1912. The most important reason for favoring a span of years from, let us say, 1880 to 1914 is that this enables us to take under consideration the situations which existed in the years when the three most important decisions connected with the naval race were made. However, limitations of time and data have led us to deal in detail only with the period 1899 to 1914.

The first of the three decisions mentioned above was that of the British as embodied in the Naval Defense Act of 1889, which established the "two-power" standard of British sea power, the principle that British security depended upon the maintenance of a fleet as large as the combined fleets of the next two largest naval powers. First Sea Lord Sir John Fisher at a later date would amend this to include an added 10 percent for further safety. The decision of 1889 was made, it should be noted, because of the ominous increase of the French fleet during the 1880's.

The second major decision—the one with which we shall deal most extensively in this paper—was the decision of the German government under Tirpitz to build a "risk fleet," a decision stated in the memorandum appended to the Navy Law of 1900. This memorandum envisioned the building of a navy of such size that, without actually outnumbering the

British fleet, it could become strong enough to make the cost of attacking the German fleet prohibitive. That is, the cost to the Royal Navy of destroying the German fleet would be the loss of her two-power standard of naval supremacy. The goal of this policy was to encourage an English alliance with Germany.

The third of the major decisions was taken by the British navy in 1904 under the leadership of First Sea Lord Fisher with the introduction of the "all big-gun battleship," popularly known as the "dreadnought" (after the first of this type to be commissioned). Fisher argued that the dreadnought would obsolete all existing battleship types. If this argument is accepted, the maintenance of British security no doubt required the introduction of the new model, at least if other navies were actually thinking of building such ships. In reality, opinion in favor of the dreadnought type was by no means universal in 1904 and most other fleets (including the German) hesitated for some time before building their own. Whatever the validity of Fisher's estimate of the situation, the introduction of this ship type helped to precipitate the crisis of 1904–12 and focused world attention on this one type of vessel. We will, of course, never know whether Fisher was correct because, for a variety of reasons, no action of a decisive nature ever took place between dreadnoughts of that era.

A consideration of the implications of these programs indicates that they were mutually contradictory. The optimal size of the German risk fleet was incompatible with the maintenance of the two-power standard by the British. The introduction of the dreadnought tended to destroy the effectiveness of the previously existing ships of the Royal Navy and thus made a successful German challenge of the two-power standard possible.

A second major reason for extending the period of observation backward to 1889 or even earlier is that it enables us to see the impact of the new technology on naval construction and thus to obtain at least a rough estimate of the extent to which the construction data represent not, properly speaking, an arms race but rather a transition to new forms of armament. Steam power and iron or steel construction opened up new possibilities to naval tacticians and cast doubt on all accepted practices. Though boarding pikes and highly polished brass work would linger on into the 20th century and certain ancient weapons such as the ram would temporarily reappear, there was a marked change in the latter part of the 19th century to new weapons of war. Some of the developments would be simply bizarre but other innovations, such as the torpedo and later the submarine, would have a paralyzing effect upon the thinking of senior naval commanders.

The rapid introduction of new weaponry tended to increase the rate of obsolescence. Where ships of the Napoleonic period had life expectancy of 50 or 60 years, those of 1914 were normally considered to be obsolete 15 or 20 years after launching. This fact alone helps to explain the supersensitivity of naval powers to *any* new launching by other powers, since an appearance of ominous instability was engendered by the rapidity of change.

Actually, one of the curiosities of the Anglo-German naval arms race is that it involved a declining number of ships. Figure 1 shows the effect

FIGURE 1

Total Number of Ships in Eight Fleets

(British, French, Russian, German, Austro-Hungarian, Italian, Japanese, American.)

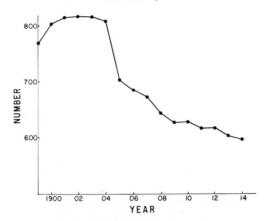

upon size of major navies between 1899 and 1914 of rapid obsolescence and concentration upon the building of a few powerful ship types.[1] This change is perhaps even more dramatic when restricted to those most powerful types comprising the line of battle (see Figure 2). On the other

FIGURE 2

Total Number of Battleships and Armored Cruisers in the Eight Fleets

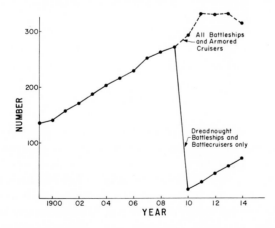

---

[1] Data underlying the figures is given in Appendix A and is discussed in more detail in sec. 3.

hand, the tonnage and horsepower of these fleets increased tremendously
during these same years (see Figures 3 and 4). It should be noted, how-

FIGURE 3
TOTAL DISPLACEMENT TONNAGE OF THE EIGHT FLEETS
(In Thousands of Tons)

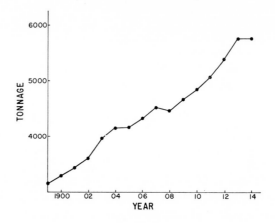

FIGURE 4
TOTAL HORSEPOWER OF THE EIGHT FLEETS
(In Millions of Horsepower)

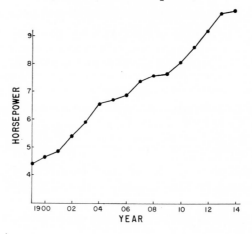

ever, that the growth of horsepower and tonnage is steady through the
whole period and does not show any dramatic rise during the years of
most intense rivalry. One may hazard the guess that were tonnage and
horsepower figures of comparable accuracy available back to the 1870's,
the same line of steady progress would have been indicated.

This change in the direction of fewer, heavier vessels was the result
of the tendency of navies, especially after Fisher's reforms of 1904, to
abandon the concept of the "balanced fleet" for that of the "battle fleet."

The former type was intended to fulfill a number of tasks, many of which were diplomatic or administrative in character, while the latter was intended to fight general engagements in "line of battle." This change marked a victory for the school of thought led by Captain Mahan over that, especially strong in the French and German navies, which favored concentration upon commerce raiding activities. It may well be that the German decision to abandon this latter position was a grave error from the point of view of the war which they actually fought. The change from balanced to battle fleets did not occur with equal rapidity for all states, and France, in particular, continued for some time to cling to the commerce raiding concept, with the consequence that the French fleet declined in quality as measured in terms of heavy ships.

Thus it came to be believed that the nation's security—at least at sea—rested upon a relatively small number of heavy ships which modern technology made quickly obsolete. One of the results of this condition was that each state became acutely aware of the building plans of the other powers. While such an attitude is understandable it did lead to the anomalous situation in which nations saw immediate war dangers not on the basis of what was on the water but on what was on the ways or in the budget. In the spring of 1909, Britain experienced a crisis growing out of a suspected German acceleration of her naval building program. The opposition party in parliament predicted that by 1912 the British would have 16 dreadnoughts while the Germans would have 21. The prime minister, though not quite as pessimistic, thought that the figures would be 20 British to 17 German. The crisis led to a demand for the doubling of the building program ("We want eight and we won't wait"), and popular hatred of Germany rose to unprecedented levels. Ironically, at the moment when the crisis was at its peak, the British had five dreadnought battleships and battle cruisers, the Germans none. By June, 1912, the Germans had only 11 of the heavy ships but would add 3 more before the end of the year. The British would have 18 in June and 22 by the end of the year.

The British had arrived at the inflated figures of 1909 by hypothesizing an increased German building capacity (which was true) and by further assuming that the Germans would continue to work their shipyards at full capacity and ahead of the established program. By imputing to the Germans the worst of motives and by paying no attention to the stated purpose of the German naval law, the British quickly came to the conclusion that the German navy was attempting to become more powerful than the Royal Navy. Similar war scares would be experienced in Germany and numbers of German naval officers and government officials would suffer from what Steinberg[2] calls the "Copenhagen complex."

Yet, despite the suspicion with which each side viewed the other,

---

[2] Jonathan Steinberg, "The Copenhagen Complex," *Journal of Contemporary History*, Vol. 1, No. 3 (1966), pp. 23–46.

there were certain signs in the years after 1912 that the British had tacitly accepted the breach in their two-power standard which would allow the Germans to build up to 60 percent of British strength. There was never any formal agreement on this point between Great Britain and Germany but both Churchill and Tirpitz mentioned such a figure. Suspicions remained, but it may perhaps be suggested that the naval arms race had passed its acute stage by 1912.

While the various crises are an important part of the history of the era in which the naval race occurred, the heart of that race involves the three decisions which we have mentioned and the programs which implemented these decisions. The Tirpitz decision to build a risk fleet, which is the primary concern of this paper, may be analyzed in terms of two separate but related issues. The first consideration, to be dealt with in more detail in the next section, is the question of whether it was ever possible for the Germans to build a fleet which would be too "risky" for the British fleet to attack and whether in fact the Tirpitz building program accomplished this objective. This problem cannot be solved with certainty because the type of battle envisioned by this plan never actually occurred. It may be that the tendency of the Germans and the British to settle many of their outstanding differences after 1912 as well as the acceptance by the British of the loss of two-power superiority indicates that for the British, attacking the German fleet was too risky an undertaking. If this were the case, then this aspect of the Tirpitz policy could be considered a success (we have to assume that other factors which did lead to the outbreak of war can, for the moment, be isolated from the naval program).

The second consideration concerning the naval race, and one which is the main subject of previous studies, is the impact that the German naval program had upon the English political mentality. The ultimate objective of the Tirpitz policy was to bring about agreements between the British and the Germans, not simply to stave off an attack by the Royal Navy; hence the impact of the building program on the thinking of British politicians was crucial to the plan. During the years 1904–12 this impact was largely negative in that the British leadership was convinced that the German plans were warlike and that Great Britain was in imminent danger of attack. To some extent this reaction on the part of the British was the normal reaction which they showed to any building program by any country; partially it was due to the rigidity with which the Germans held to the program of 1900 coupled with the British suspicion that they were exceeding this program.

The British were apparently genuinely surprised that the Germans felt they needed a fleet, and especially one which was, from the British point of view, so inordinately large. This perhaps should not have been quite so surprising in view of the fact that the Germans did have a considerable colonial empire. They possessed the second largest merchant marine in the world, and they depended heavily upon overseas commerce for their well-being. Furthermore, in the recent past their commerce had been interfered with by the British (stopping of mail steamers in the Boer War) and in the not so distant past the north coast of Germany had been blockaded by the Danish navy.

Because of the reaction of the British to the building program, the question has been raised by one of the students of the subject[3] that if the purpose of Germany was to build a fleet which would force the British to seek an alliance with the Germans, why did they continue to build a fleet after 1904, when the British concluded the Entente Cordiale with the French? This argument is somewhat peculiar since it assumes, on the one hand, that the alliance of 1904 had a permanent character, an assumption which neither German nor British statesmen of the period were willing to make. On the other hand, if the alliance between these two strong naval powers was permanent, did Germany have any choice but to build a navy?

As alarming to the British as the fact of the enlarged German fleet was the rigidity with which the Germans held to the building program outlined in the naval law. It seemed as though no changes in the diplomatic scene, no considerations of easing tension could sway the Germans from the building of their fleet according to a certain prearranged schedule. This problem of rigidity is one which must be considered in the light of German internal politics. It must be remembered that the *Marine Amt* had only with difficulty gotten the Reichstag to accept the naval program and that because of suspected reservations on the part of the representatives it was considered much better to continue the program at a regular and predetermined pace rather than to allow it to fluctuate in the face of changing foreign relations. Also, because of the relatively youthful state of the German shipyards it was felt necessary to keep them in business with the assurance of regular orders. At times other considerations such as the need to complete a battleship squadron or the hope of forestalling a price increase by the placing of early orders led the Germans to deviate from the program by beginning some of the work ahead of schedule. Given the rigidity of the whole program, such deviations—which from hindsight apparently did occur for the stated reasons—could only cause the deepest suspicions on the part of the British that the program itself was simply a cover for a truly massive and aggressive buildup of German power.

Finally it should be noted that in the years after 1890 the power position of both Germany and Great Britain had been deteriorating and neither state was accepting the situation gracefully. British troubles in Africa and the reduction of her commitments in the Pacific were paralleled by the problems which Germany faced with the rise of the Franco-

---

3 Ernest L. Woodward, *Great Britain and the German Navy* (Oxford: The Clarendon Press, 1935).

Russian alliance in Europe. By 1900 the United States had replaced Great Britain as the holder of the balance of power, while the center of power on the Continent had passed from Germany. It was unfortunate but perhaps understandable that these two states, with so many ties of commerce and common political interests, should fix upon each other as the principal authors of their troubles. Both sides would act irrationally in the period, allowing concerns of internal politics to imperil their relations with each other. In spite of these grievances, as has already been mentioned, there were signs that the Germans and the British were drawing closer together after 1912 and that the risk fleet was being accepted as a permanent part of the European political landscape.

2. A Suggested Measurement of Risk

The objective of the Tirpitz program was to construct an effective deterrent to an attack on Germany by the British fleet, with the ultimate goal of bringing about an alliance, on equal footing, between Germany and Great Britain. For the deterrent power of the German fleet to be effective, it was required that there exist a substantial risk to the British of losing their position of naval supremacy relative to the rest of the world in the event of an attack by the British on the German fleet. The most casual examination of the data on fleet strengths at the turn of the century, when the Tirpitz program was inaugurated, indicates the utter weakness of the German navy at that time and the consequent lack of an effective deterrent. As the building program advances through the next decade and a half, however, it becomes more difficult to analyze the meaning of the data in terms of deterrent power. In this section we outline one possible measure of the "riskiness" of the German fleet and present some data that gives some indication of the success enjoyed by the Tirpitz program in increasing the deterrent power or riskiness of the fleet over time.

The approach that we adopt differs considerably from that adopted by most other investigators of the naval arms race. Because, in decision making situations, the notion of risk is a subjective concept; it might well be argued that any attempt to assess the success or failure of the Tirpitz program to increase the riskiness of the German fleet should rely primarily upon the letters, documents, memoirs, and public and private statements of the political leaders involved in the race. Woodward's study of the race[4] utilizes this approach and indicates clearly the frictions that Germany's naval buildup created both for English and German leaders and within the German diplomatic group itself. The drawbacks to this kind of analysis, however, are first, if Tirpitz was correct, frictions (and perhaps war) between England and Germany were to be expected in

---

[4] *Ibid.*

any case, whatever the fleet policy pursued by Germany, because of the competition for world markets engendered by Germany's economic growth; if it had not been the fleet, Germany's actions in other ways would have been seized upon as grounds for dissatisfaction on the part of the British. Second, it is difficult to isolate the effects of the Tirpitz policy from the many essentially extraneous factors that affected the British attitudes during the period, including internal political squabbles, the sometimes ill-advised comments of the Kaiser (or of Fisher, Churchill, King Edward VII, *et al.*), "yellow" journalism, and other such factors. In effect, what we are asking is not whether the period of the naval arms race witnessed a disintegration of goodwill between Germany and Great Britain (at least until 1912–14), because such a disintegration certainly did occur—instead, we ask whether the German fleet buildup, by itself, should have been regarded as important a source of such disintegration as other commentators allege.

The method suggested in this paper to measure the riskiness of the German risk fleet at any point in time is that of calculating the probability that in a battle of annihilation between the German and British fleets, the German fleet would be able to sink enough British ships to imperil Britain's command of the seas. This view of the German fleet as a sort of "kamikaze" force is no doubt subject to some criticism as an extreme idealization of Tirpitz' position, but it does not appear to conflict with the naval traditions espoused by all navies of the world at this time. The surrender of the Russian admirals at Tsushima in the face of overwhelming odds was severely criticized not only in Russia but throughout the world. The extreme conservatism of both British and German naval leaders in World War I was a definite break with past traditions.

The basic point of the approach we are adopting is that statistics have meaning only within the context of some interpretive scheme; in historical studies, typically the interpretive scheme is specified in such general and ambiguous terms that it is difficult to assess the value of the scheme. Here we use a model that is simple enough for concrete results to be obtained and the applicability of the model to be criticized on specific and unambiguous grounds. Even within the context of this extremely simplified approach, however, a number of problems arise in the calculation of measures of riskiness derived from battles of annihilation. Among the problems are the following: (1) what model of naval warfare should be employed to calculate probabilities; (2) what ships should be included in the British and German fleets; (3) what weights should be attached to individual ships; (4) how is the level of losses necessary to insure England's loss of command of the seas to be calculated?

At best, the model employed in this paper can only be described as being extremely crude, but even this crude model has created some rather difficult computational problems which still defy solution even with modern high-speed computers. Since the choice of the model has influenced the expedients adopted to solve the other problems that arise in the calculation of the risk measure to attach to Germany's fleet, the model itself will first be described.

Most probabilistic models of warfare ultimately derive from an early attempt to describe combat in terms of expected losses by F. W. Lanchester.[5] While numerous refinements of his original model have been developed, we employ here the simplest of the Lanchester equation models, that which results in "Lanchester's square law," as modified by probability analysis. The derivation of the law and the underlying probability distribution over losses in combat is as follows:[6]

Assume two forces meeting in combat, where each force consists of homogeneous fighting units. The symbol E will be used to denote the "relative fighting efficiency" of a member of the Red force as compared to a member of the Blue force, where E may be interpreted as the ratio of average number of Blue units put out of action (killed) per unit of combat time divided by the average number of Red units killed per unit of combat time, in a fight between one Red and one Blue unit. Each member of the Red force is assumed to be able to fire at any member of the Blue force, and vice versa. Let τ denote the length of combat time, $G(\tau)$ the "intensity of combat" at time τ as measured, say, by the rate of fire of the opposing sides. m and n denote the number of survivors on the Red and Blue forces at any point in time, and $\bar{m}$ and $\bar{n}$ will denote the expected number of survivors. The symbols m_o and n_o are used to denote the initial number of units on the Red and Blue sides before combat begins. Then the Lanchester equations describing losses in combat may be given as follows:

$$\frac{d\bar{m}}{d\tau} = -\bar{n} \quad \frac{1}{1+E} \quad G(\tau)$$

$$\frac{d\bar{n}}{d\tau} = -\bar{m} \quad \frac{E}{1+E} \quad G(\tau)$$

Solving these equations, we obtain Lanchester's square law:

$$E(\bar{m}^2 - m_o{}^2) = \bar{n}^2 - n_o{}^2$$

It should be noted that the differential equation system above only applies to battles in which annihilation of neither force occurs, since in the case of annihilation, either $\dfrac{dm}{d\tau} = 0$ or $\dfrac{dn}{d\tau} = 0$. This difficulty may

[5] F. W. Lanchester, *Aircraft in Warfare: The Dawn of the Fourth Arm* (London: Constable and Co., 1916).

[6] See Phillip M. Morse and George E. Kimball, *Methods of Operations Research* (Washington, D.C.: Operations Evaluations Group, Office of the Chief of Naval Operations, Navy Department, 1964), pp. 63–80.

be resolved by investigating the properties of the probability distribution underlying the Lanchester model. Following Koopman[7] we define the following transformation:

$$t = \frac{\sqrt{E}}{1+E} \qquad \int G(\tau)\, d\tau$$

Then, since in an interval of combat time $d\tau$, the number of Blue units hit by a Red unit (on the average) is given by $\dfrac{d\tau}{n}\dfrac{E}{1+E} G(\tau)$, while the number of Red units hit by a Blue unit (on the average) is given by $\dfrac{d\tau}{m}\left(\dfrac{1}{1+E}\right) G(\tau)$, these expressions may be rewritten as:

$$\frac{dt\sqrt{E}}{n} \quad \text{and} \quad \frac{dt}{m\sqrt{E}}$$

it being assumed that the interval of combat time has been chosen short enough so that no loss of firepower occurs on either side during this interval.

Koopman's derivation of the underlying distribution proceeds by defining the expression $P(m, n, t)$ as the probability that at time t (measured in units that take into account the intensity of combat), the Red side has m survivors and the Blue side has n survivors. $P(m, n, t)$ satisfies the following set of differential equations:

$$\frac{d P(m, n, t)}{dt} = m\sqrt{E}\,[P(m, n+1, t) - P(m, n, t)]$$

$$+ \frac{n}{\sqrt{E}}\,[P(m+1, n, t) - P(m, n, t)] \quad \text{for } m > 0, n > 0.$$

$$\frac{d P(m, 0, t)}{dt} = m\sqrt{E}\,P(m, 1, t); \qquad \frac{d P(0, n, t)}{dt} = \frac{n}{\sqrt{E}}\,P(1, n, t),$$

subject to: $P(m_o, n_o, 0) = 1$; $P(m, n, 0) = 0$ for $m \neq m_o$, $n \neq n_o$, $P(m, n, t) = 0$ for $m > m_o$, $n > n_o$, all t. For the special case where $E = 1$, the differential equation system may be solved iteratively to obtain the expression:

$$P(m, n, t) = c(m, n)\, e^{-(m+n)t} (1 - e^{-t})^{m_o + n_o - m - n} \quad \text{for } m > 0,$$

$n > 0$, where $c(m, n) = \dfrac{mc(m, n+1) + nc(m+1, n)}{m_o + n_o - m - n}$; $c(m_o, n_o) = 1$,

$c(m, n) = 0$ for $m > m_o$ or $n > n_o$.

$$\therefore P(0, n, t) = n\left[\frac{c(1, n+1) + nc(2, n)}{m_o + n_o - 1 - n}\right]\sum_{r=0}^{m_o + n_o - 1 - n}\binom{m_o + n_o - 1 - n}{r}$$

[7] B. O. Koopman, *A Quantitative Aspect of Combat*, OEM sr—1007, Applied Mathematics Panel, Note 6, A.M.G.—Columbia, August, 1943.

$$(-1)^r \left(\frac{1}{n+1+r} \right) [1 - e^{-(n+r+1)t}] \text{ and}$$

$$P(m,0,t) = m \left[\frac{mc(m,2) + c(m+1,1)}{m_o + n_{\bar{o}} - 1 - m} \right] \sum_{r=o}^{m_o + n_o - 1 - m} \binom{m_{\bar{o}} + n_o - 1 - m}{r}$$

$$(-1)^r \left(\frac{1}{m+1+r} \right) [1 - e^{-(m+1+r)t}]$$

(See Appendix B for the derivation of these expressions.)

It has not been our concern here to investigate the progress of battles of annihilation as a function of time but rather to consider the limiting probability distributions over losses as a consequence of such battles. Consequently, we have restricted our interest to $P(0, n, \infty)$ and $P(m, 0, \infty)$ where the exponential terms shown in the final two expressions above vanish. Even in these cases, computational difficulties have precluded the calculation of the probability distribution so that a proxy variable has been used in the measurement of risk presented below.

The choice of the Lanchester model as a method of interpreting the risk fleet concept was governed partly by the basic simplicity of the model, but also because of the remarkable closeness of fit of the model to actual results in land combat. In Engel's study[8] the actual losses of American troops in the battle for Iwo Jima were plotted against expected losses as a function of time using the Lanchester model and the resulting fit was extraordinarily close. While Lanchester's original formulation of his model was intended as a description of air combat, he believed that, with appropriate modifications, the model could be applied to land and sea combat as well. It now appears that the model does not apply to air combat, and no study utilizing the Lanchester approach in analyzing sea battles has come to the attention of the writers, despite its apparent value as a tool in describing land operations.

The reasons for the lack of empirical verification of the Lanchester model in sea combat include the relative scarcity of large-scale sea actions (at least in the present century), the small numbers of units involved in the actions that did take place, the diversity of ship types involved, and the difficulty of assigning weights (values of E) to opposing units on *a priori* grounds, as well as the importance of factors such as weather, information, etc., in determining the results of battles, factors that are not explicitly taken into account in the Lanchester model. In the absence of empirical verification, the applicability of Lanchester's model remains conjectural in attempting to assess the possible results of theoretical battles of annihilation between the English and German fleets.

The Lanchester model applies only to battles between forces com-

---

[8] J. H. Engel, "A Verification of Lanchester's Law," *Journal of the Operations Research Society of America*, Vol. 2, No. 2 (May, 1954).

posed of homogeneous units, and, as Appendix A to this paper clearly indicates, each ship is essentially a unique fighting unit with peculiarities of its own. This is due not only to the leadership qualities and personnel factors associated with particular ships, a characteristic that attaches to ground forces as well, but in addition is due to the differing physical characteristics of individual ships. Even within the same class of ships, it is extremely rare to find two ships with identical fighting characteristics, such as speed, range, armor protection, armament, gun bearings, etc. While models of battles of annihilation between nonhomogeneous forces have been discussed in the literature[9] none of these appear to offer any possibility of application in the near future, due to computational problems. Thus, in the present paper, we have ignored the diversity of ship types and have dealt with theoretical battles involving, for a certain range of time, "traditional battleships," and, later, dreadnoughts, despite the known dissimilarities of ships even within these two general classifications due to the vintage of ships and the differences within vintage classes. In addition, we have assumed E, the ratio of expected German losses to expected British losses, to be 1, that is, German and British capital ships have been treated as equivalent. As Appendix A indicates, German ships, in general, were more heavily armored, slower, and less heavily armed than their English counterparts, so that it is difficult to state on *a priori* grounds which side had the advantage in terms of ship architecture. The evidence provided by the few naval battles that took place during World War I is inconclusive, since the battleship fleets never actually came into contact with one another, the only battles between comparable capital ships being the battle cruiser action at Dogger Bank, and the similar action in the early stages of Jutland. Further, in a study of the present type, where the relevant probability distributions to calculate are subjective in nature, it would hardly be legitimate to use evidence from battles fought after the period under study.

Other than the obvious fact that the assumption of homogeneous fleets (and a value of E of 1) makes computations much simpler, there is another justification for restricting our attention to battleships and dreadnoughts and ignoring the other units of both fleets. This is because the political and naval leaders in both countries invariably used numbers of battleships (and later dreadnoughts) as the measure of relative strengths of the two fleets. As contrasted with the naval disarmament conferences held after the war, in which limitations were placed upon sizes of capital ships, the tacit acceptance of the 3 to 2 (or, more accurately, 32 to 20) ratio between English and German ships in 1913–14 was based purely on numbers of dreadnoughts. Of course, both Fisher and Tirpitz were convinced of the superior fighting qualities of the ships that they had helped launch, but independent sources (such as *Brassey's*) regarded the corre-

---

[9] See R. D. Luce and H. Raiffa, *Games and Decisions* (New York: John Wiley and Sons, Inc., 1957), esp. pp. 467–78.

sponding squadrons of the home fleet and the high seas fleet as roughly equivalent.

Under this set of assumptions, it is, in theory at least, possible to calculate the entire probability distribution over British and German losses in theoretical battles of annihilation for each year between 1899 and 1914. Until 1910, the first year in which an almost complete squadron of dreadnoughts exists in the British navy, the battles considered are battles between traditional (predreadnought) battleships; after this time, only dreadnoughts have been taken into account. This roughly corresponds to the attitudes of the leaders of the two countries, although the dreadnought ratio becomes important (in terms of numbers of ships launched and building) as early as 1908. Between 1906 and 1910, dreadnoughts have been included as traditional battleships, except that Fisher's evaluation of their worth relative to the traditional battleship (1 dreadnought $= 2\frac{1}{2}$ traditional battleships) has been used as a weight.

The risk to the British from the German fleet is the probability that the Germans will sink enough British ships to imperil British command of the seas. The measure used to determine the number of British ships required to maintain command of the seas follows from Lanchester's square law that expected losses are inversely proportionate to the squares of sizes of fighting forces. In order to maintain command of the seas, Britain must possess a number of battleships, m_o, such that

$$m_o{}^2 = (n_{1_o})^2 + (n_{2_o})^2$$

where n_{1_o} and n_{2_o} are the numbers of French and Russian battleships (or dreadnoughts) respectively. In each year, the probability that the number of British battleships remaining after a battle of annihilation with the German fleet will equal or exceed that number required to maintain command of the seas can in principle be calculated. Since, after 1904, the French, and, after 1907, the Russians, reached agreements with the British, it might be argued that the danger of coalition wars against England is either nonexistent or at least is improbable after either of these dates, so that the only consideration is whether or not the British will defeat the Germans in battle. (Even more strongly, it might be argued that the Germans would have to face the combined fleets of all three naval powers after 1907 rather than just the British.) Certainly Woodward[10] adopts this position in his argument that the entire risk fleet concept is invalid after 1904 or 1905. As was mentioned above, the fact that the Triple Entente did emerge from the agreements with France and Russia by the British as a permanent bloc is, of course, not a conclusive argument that such had to be the case. After all, there were war scares in Great Britain concerning France in 1898 and concerning Russia in 1904, and a number of convolutions in the alliance systems of Europe had occurred

---

[10] Woodward, *op. cit.*

between the Franco-Prussian War and the outbreak of World War I. That the British did not regard themselves as wedded to the Entente in the way that Germany, for example, had linked her interests with Austria-Hungary is indicated by the reluctance of the British to enter World War I until Belgian neutrality had been violated, the secrecy with which "discussions" between naval and army leaders in England and France were conducted, and the fact that, by 1914, the British were once again beginning to re-assert their sea supremacy in the Mediterranean.

The numbers required in a calculation of the riskiness of Germany's fleet are given in the table below, and for each year, the probability of a German victory (actually defeating the British) is also given. This probability would correspond to the proposed measure of riskiness if it were assumed that the French and Russians were no longer considered a threat to Britain's command of the seas. It has not been possible to calculate the proposed measure of risk due to computational problems. The nontrivial nature of the computations required is indicated by the fact that for 1899, numbers of the order of 46! must be computed, stored, and manipulated through addition and multiplication operations, while other years covered by the study require similar computations involving numbers of the order of over 80! Unfortunately, we are not aware of any approximations to the area of the appropriate tail of the probability distribution; hence we are forced to use the less satisfactory measure given by the probability of a German victory.

The method used to calculate the probability of a German victory at sea is that derived by Dr. R. H. Brown:[11]

Let the probability that the Red force annihilates the Blue force be denoted by $P(m_o, n_o)$ where m_o and n_o are as defined earlier. Then, as

$$m_o + n_o \longrightarrow \infty$$

$$P(m_o, n_o) - \frac{1}{\sqrt{2\pi}} \int_{-\infty}^{T} e^{\frac{-t^2}{2}} \, dt \longrightarrow 0$$

where $T = \sqrt{\dfrac{3}{m_o + n_o}} \, (m_o - n_o)$, it being assumed that $E = 1$.

While Brown's approximation applies strictly speaking only to the limiting case, the rate of convergence of $P(m_o, n_o)$ to the limiting normal distribution is extremely fast. For example, if $m_o = 5$, $n_o = 3$, the exact probability of winning the battle for the Red forces is .8874, while the normal approximation gives a value of .8898. Thus the probabilities of a

---

11 This result is cited from a letter from Professor Brown. A detailed discussion of his general results is given in Richard H. Brown, *A Stochastic Analysis of Lanchester's Theory of Combat*, Technical memorandum ORO—T—323, Operations Research Office, Johns Hopkins University, December, 1955.

German victory at each point in time may be assumed to be accurate to several significant places, given the set of assumptions listed above.

It might also be pointed out that the rapid convergence of $P(m_o, n_o)$ to its limiting form offers some grounds for believing that the fact that only relatively small numbers of units are involved in naval actions should in itself be insufficient reason for discarding the Lanchester model, which relies upon average rates of killing.

TABLE 1

PROBABILITY OF GERMAN NAVAL VICTORY, 1899–1914
(German Navy vs. British Navy)

Year	No. of British Battleships	No. of German Battleships	British Losses Required	Probability of German Victory
1899......	37	9	11	.0000
1900......	35	11	8	.0000
1901......	35	15	5	.0000
1902......	36	20	6	.0000
1903......	42	19	12	.0000
1904......	45	18	17	.0000
1905......	45	22	16	.0000
1906......	52	19	28	.0000
1907......	52	22	29	.0000
1908......	56	24	32	.0000
1909......	64	24	40	.0000
1910......	9	4	9	.0070
1911......	14	10	14	.0707
1912......	21	11	21	.0011
1913......	24	17	22	.0292
1914......	31	21	29	.0082

In the table above, British and German battleships are those under 20 years of age; after 1909, only dreadnoughts are listed. The British Losses Required column was calculated by use of the square law formula, taking the square root of the sum of the squares of French and Russian battleships under 20 years of age and deducting this from the total for the British fleet. The numbers appearing in this column thus represent the number of ships that the Germans had to sink in any given year in a battle of annihilation in order to transfer command of the seas to a coalition of French and Russian ships, under the assumption that all ships (British, German, French, and Russian) were of equal fighting efficiency. The final column represents the Brown approximation to the probability of a German victory over the British fleet rather than the proposed measure of risk. For the years 1910, 1911, 1912, the probability of a German victory corresponds to the measure of risk since no fleets other than the British and German possess dreadnoughts at this time. If the Woodward argument that the Triple Entente is from the beginning a permanent alliance is accepted, then the figures in the final column measure the riskiness of the German fleet from at least 1907 onward. The risk measure is always at least as great as the probability of victory shown, with substantially higher values in the early years of the race (1899–1902).

It is immediately clear from the table that the Tirpitz policy increased the strength of the German navy relative to the British slightly if at all in the predreadnought era 1899–1909. The 15 conventional battleships built by Germany over this time span were more than matched by the equivalent of 27 additional British battleships together with the relative decline in strength of the French and, particularly, the Russian navies. As was mentioned earlier, the introduction of the dreadnought type by the British offered the possibility to the Germans of the building of an effective deterrent, as the data for 1910–14 indicates; in effect, the British threw away an enormous advantage (in conventional battleships) when the *Dreadnought* was built. However, even in this latter period, the threat posed by the Germans was "large" only in 1911, immediately before the expanded British building program began to overwhelm the German efforts.

These conclusions are reinforced where the disposition of the British navy is taken into account as in the table below.

TABLE 2

PROBABILITY OF GERMAN NAVAL VICTORY, 1899–1914
(German Navy vs. British Home Fleet)

Year	No. of British Battleships	No. of German Battleships	Probability of German Victory
1899.........	21	9	.0001
1900.........	19	11	.0007
1901.........	18	15	.1828
1902.........	19	20	.6091
1903.........	24	19	.0932
1904.........	28	18	.0054
1905.........	32	22	.0092
1906.........	40	19	.0000
1907.........	46	22	.0000
1908.........	50	24	.0000
1909.........	58	24	.0000
1910.........	9	4	.0070
1911.........	14	10	.0707
1912.........	21	11	.0011
1913.........	23	17	.0502
1914.........	26	21	.1033

As contrasted with the German navy, which was concentrated entirely in the North and Baltic Seas (with the minor exception of several older ships in the Pacific), the British traditionally maintained substantial fleets in the Mediterranean, in the Pacific, and in American waters. The table indicates clearly the fact that in the early period of the naval arms race, the German fleet did pose a substantial threat to the British fleet *in home waters*. The reaction of the British was twofold: (1) agreements were reached with the Japanese and later with the French and the Russians leading to the Triple Entente, which permitted the British to recall to home waters many of the ships previously assigned to other fleets and (2) the construction program of the British navy was expanded. The results are striking; whereas roughly 50 percent of the battleships of the British navy were assigned to home waters in 1900–1902, this had risen to 90 percent by 1909. In addition, the quality of the home fleet increased over the period as the newer ships were assigned to that fleet. These changes more than offset the growth in German sea power, until the advent of the dreadnought type. Finally, it should be noted that the increase in probability of a German victory in 1914 is entirely accounted for by the decision to assign ships to a strengthened Mediterranean fleet, which affords some evidence that the German fleet was regarded by the Admiralty as less dangerous than in the earlier years.

That the British regarded the growth in the German navy from 1899 onward as a threat to their security is well known; the above data suggest, however, that the threat was in fact slight except very early in the race (1901–2–3). The British purchased security by the Triple Entente agreements which permitted a transference of ships from abroad to the home fleet. However Britain's main allies, France and Russia, changed from first- to second-class sea powers over the period of the race. From the point of view of Britain's selfish interests, one can hardly help but conjecture that the original advantages gained from the alliances with France and Russia (to the extent that they were offsets to Germany's growing power) were largely dissipated by 1910–14 by England's own growth in naval power, so that she actually had little to gain and much to lose from the Entente after this point.

As we have noted above, the problem of computing the probability of German success in destroying the British two-power standard of naval supremacy has thus far proved insoluble. Because of this, we have resorted to the less satisfactory but still informative calculation of the probability of a German victory. The fact that this probability was close to zero in most years of the race affords considerable support for the belief that the chance of Germany destroying the two-power superiority was also quite small; in addition, there is no pronounced growth over time in this probability. Thus, within the framework of the assumptions set out in this paper, it can be concluded that the Tirpitz risk fleet was in fact a failure.

3. Data on Fleet Strengths, 1899–1914

The tables presented in Appendix A following this paper were derived by the authors from *Brassey's Naval Annuals* 1899–1914, and summarize data for some 1,450 "fighting ships" that were listed in *Brassey's* during this period. The powers chosen to be represented in this series consist of the members of the Triple Entente—Great Britain, France, and Russia; the major members of the Triple Alliance—Germany, Austria-Hungary, and Italy; and two independent powers, Japan and the United States. In summary, the statistics show quite clearly the relative decline of the Russian and French navies over the period, the emergence as first-class powers of the United States, Japan, and Germany, and the continued supremacy of Great Britain in the face of various threats to her two-power standard.

Some rather interesting features of the naval arms race are indicated by Table I. The U.S. Navy, which was sixth ranked in terms of tonnage in 1899 was the fifth in 1905, and stands in second position in 1908. Furthermore, the German navy does not reach second position until 1912, and in fact does not equal French tonnage until 1910. The effect of the Fisher reforms is clearly shown in the drastic decline in number of British ships after 1905 (some 160 "useless" fighting ships were retired at that time). Later tables illustrate the shift in all navies from balanced fleets intended to guard against commerce raiding to battle fleets intended for action against major units of opposing forces. The tendency to build larger, faster, more heavily armed and armored ships can also be noted. These facts have, of course, been known for many years, but the compilations presented here have been arranged to show more clearly these trends and the comparative speed with which these trends made themselves felt in the various navies.

There are a number of sources for statistics on fleet strengths in the pre–World War I period, among which might be mentioned *Nauticus*, *Jane's Fighting Ships* (*All the World's Fighting Ships* in earlier years), and government publications of the various leading powers. The choice of any one or a combination of these sources results in certain kinds of problems of interpretation of results which cannot be completely avoided. The reliance of the writers on *Brassey's* was governed by a number of considerations, the most important of which were: (1) *Brassey's* was generally recognized throughout the world as the leading source of statistics on naval strength during this period; (2) the data collection and classification system had been standardized for some years prior to 1899; (3) a complete set of volumes for the period was available. In addition, the accompanying articles appearing in *Brassey's* during this period proved to be extremely useful in interpreting the data presented, and certain data are available only in *Brassey's* (for example, fleet concentrations). It might be pointed out that *Jane's*, which the writers had originally considered a primary source, was still in its infancy at the beginning of the arms race, and, until 1904–6, was mainly useful as a recognition manual for officers, as well as being an adjunct to a navy game that Jane had constructed. Only a very limited amount of information is, in fact, available in the early volumes of *Jane's*. It is only after *Jane's* support of Fisher's reforms that *Jane's Fighting Ships* begins to approach *Brassey's* in world prestige.

The method employed for recording and summarizing the data presented in *Brassey's* was that of transferring to IBM cards the figures as shown for each ship listed in *Brassey's* for each of the eight countries in the 16 years covered by the study. During the 1899–1914 period, approximately 1,450 fighting ships for these countries were listed as provisional, building, or launched (and not yet completed) or completed in one or more of the 16 volumes of *Brassey's* examined. In many cases, of course, a ship appears in each of these categories at various points in time. For each ship, data were collected with respect to some 25 characteristics, ranging from construction site, launch date, cost and type, to armor protection (belt, turrets, protection to vitals, secondary guns, deck), and number, type and bearing of guns, speed, coal capacity, and other aspects of ship construction. (It might be noted that *Jane's* was used to supplement *Brassey's* as a source when data were not available in the latter publication.) In many cases, data changes occurred over time due to errors made by the editors of *Brassey's* in estimating characteristics, changes in ship design between the provisional and completion dates, and reevaluation of the ship's proper classification by the government involved. These changes have been incorporated into the data shown so that, for example, an increase in displacement for a given navy might be due simply to a revision of previous estimates by the editors of *Brassey's* rather than the launching of a new ship. For this reason, the data should properly be regarded not so much as a set of time series with respect to characteristics of fleets but rather as a statement, at each point in time, of the current beliefs (of the editors of *Brassey's*) as to the characteristics of fleets.

As might be expected, the number and size of errors vary from country to country and from year to year. The data are generally much more reliable (in the sense that fewer corrections occur later) before 1906; following the introduction of the *Dreadnought* and the secrecy provisions imposed with respect to construction details by Fisher, the reliability of figures given for all navies (with the possible exception of the U.S.) decline drastically. Prior to 1906, governments apparently were quite willing to publish details of ship construction, and the U.S. seems to have followed this policy throughout the entire period. The data for Russia is particularly unreliable for the 1899–1914 period; one ship, for example, being listed as launched but not yet completed for 10 years, following which it disappears from the list of ships. At each point in time, however, the data shown represent the best assessment of relative naval strengths of countries by the acknowledged experts of *Brassey's* and hence have particular relevance in terms of the study of the decision problems of the naval arms race. Nonetheless, the existence of these errors should be borne in mind in using the data.

It was clearly impossible to present all of the data obtained in the study in comprehensible form in tables, although the authors can supply the IBM cards and tabulations to interested students of the naval arms race. As gross measures of fleet strengths, it was decided to use numbers of fighting ships in commission, displacement, horsepower, complements, and numbers of guns (by type) (Table I). It must be pointed out that because of the rapid technological changes that occurred in the naval arm of warfare during this period, these indicators are measures of fleet strengths only in a crude manner. Armor, speed, and gun caliber should also be included in these summaries, but the problem of aggregating these characteristics precluded their presentation in Table I. For example, some 200 different armor codes were required with respect to both belt and turret armor, and nearly 100 different bore-caliber types were listed in the sources consulted. (In Table VI, speed, belt armor, and turret armor is listed for British and German battleships, battle cruisers, and armored cruisers.) In general, caliber increased throughout the period for all types of guns, so that a 12″ gun in 1899 was much less effective than a 12″ gun on a newly constructed 1914 ship. The grouping of guns into classes '14″ and over,' '12″ and under 14″,' etc., probably results in an understatement of German firepower relative to British, since the British guns in the '12″ and under 14″' group are usually 12″ guns, while the German guns in the '10″ and under 12″' group are usually 11″ guns. Tonnage in all tables was rounded to thousands (the figures given represent the displacement of the ships), complement to hundreds, and horsepower to thousands. While data were obtained on guns of sizes less than 5.9″, limitations of space as well as the relative lack of importance of such armament argued against inclusion of the data in the tables. (In early years, given naval beliefs current in the period, it might have been desirable to list guns of smaller bore.) On similar grounds, obsolete guns (muzzle loaders, etc.) were excluded from the tabulations. When information was completely lacking with respect to a certain characteristic, it is shown as "n.a." (not available) or footnoted.

Table II presents a comparison of battle fleets for the eight leading naval powers, showing numbers of dreadnought battleships, dreadnought battle cruisers, conventional battleships, and armored cruisers. The table is further broken down by listing separately those ships less than 20 years of age (from launch date). The term dreadnought refers to ships mounting more than four large bore guns of a single type, with the exception of Japan, where three dreadnought battle cruisers had only four main guns. Dreadnought (following the first of its type, the British battleship *Dreadnought*) was not an official term, but the immense popularity of the term argues for its usage here. The difficulty with being precise concerning the meaning of the term dreadnought is illustrated by the fact that some members of the British navy considered the *Lord Nelson* and *Agamemnon* (both launched in 1906) to be dreadnoughts, although they carried only the traditional four big guns. In the tables, these ships are listed as conventional battleships.

Because the rate of technological progress in naval construction accelerated so rapidly during this period, a particularly difficult problem to solve is that of obsolescence. Under the German Naval Law of 1900,

battleships were to be obsoleted after 25 years of service; however, as a
practical matter, the British only employed battleships 20 years of
age or less in any of their active fleets, and Fisher's decision to obsolete
(and, originally, to sell) battleships older than this in 1905 and later was
simply a tacit recognition of a practice that had been adopted years
before. Thus, in the tables on comparative battle fleet strengths, data are
given both for total number of ships and for ships aged less than 20 years.
Official designation by governments of various ships as being obsolete
(usually by conversion of ships to "training" categories, or, in some cases,
through sale to a lesser power) are, of course, taken into account in the
statistics. As Table VI indicates, the classifications dreadnought, battleship,
etc., include a diversity of ships within given classifications; for example,
the early dreadnoughts are obsolete by the beginning of World War I.

In Table III, a breakdown of ships for Germany and Great Britain into
types labeled "Battle," "Cruiser," and "Other" is given, and in addition,
data is shown for ships "provisional and building," "launched" (but not
yet completed), and "completed" in each year. Ships included in the
battle category are ships that are relatively heavily armored and carry
fairly large guns—battleships, "turret" ships (such as the early classes of
U.S. battleships), armored cruisers, and battle cruisers. The cruiser class
consists largely of "unprotected" (lightly armored) ships of the cruiser
variety, while the "other" category includes a wide variety of craft, ranging from coast defense ships (usually slow, obsolete battleships or
monitors) to gunboats, scouts, sloops, and ramming ships. Among the
strange types that occur in navies throughout the world during the
period might be mentioned the U.S. dynamite gunship *Vesuvius*
(mounting a 15″ smooth bore dynamite gun), and the two Russian circular coast defense ships (length 100 ft., beam 100 ft.)!

Table III indicates clearly the decline in availability of information
concerning ships either under construction or provisional (included in the
estimates presented to the Reichstag or the parliament), following 1905.
The consequences of the secrecy provisions adopted both by Great Britain
and, later, by Germany, in precipitating the naval crisis of 1908–9 are
well known. *Brassey's* appeared in the spring of each year, so that the data
shown relate to the naval situation as of (approximately) the end of the
previous year. In a few cases, ships are listed as launched (or completed)
when the editors assumed that such would occur early in the year of
publication. The most notable instance of a discrepancy due to the time
lag in publication is seen in the effects of Tsushima on the Russian and
Japanese navies, which effects do not appear in the tables until 1906.

Table IV shows the disposition of the British fleet for each year of the
period. Fleet designations are those used in 1914, so that the confusing
changes in the names of fleets that occurred between 1905 and 1914 are
suppressed. These data were obtained directly from *Brassey's* but require
some interpretation. Until 1905, the Mediterranean fleet was the "elite"

fleet of the British navy, in that battleships in the fleet were always of the latest vintage, with the older ships being assigned to home waters or elsewhere in the world. Later, when the home fleet becomes the important element, newer ships are assigned to it, while the older ones go to the Mediterranean. The Far East posed special problems, in that an extremely large coal capacity was required for ships in this area, so that specialized types of ships were constructed for this fleet. Prior to 1905, the Mediterranean is thus a stronger fleet relative to the others than is indicated by the pure number of ships, while the opposite is true after that date. It might be noted that the ships listed in the Mediterranean fleet in 1913 were only assigned "temporarily" to that area, but the 1914 assignment is to a "permanent" fleet (in 1913, the ships listed in the Mediterranean were actually a separate squadron of the home fleet). Fisher's policy of concentrating strength in home waters after 1904 is clearly apparent from the summary statistics given in this table. Included in the "inactive" group of ships are those under repair (if detached from their regular fleet assignment), older ships considered of limited usefulness, and newly commissioned ships not yet assigned to a particular station. All such ships are included in the totals "in home waters," together with the various elements of the home fleet.

Table V lists elements of the German fleet assigned to the high seas fleet and to the reserve fleet, both of which are assumed to be home waters fleets. No attempt has been made to distinguish between the Baltic and North Seas fleets, although the importance of providing for rapid and unimpeded transference of ships from one sea to the other was the underlying motive for the widening and deepening of the Kiel Canal, an undertaking that cost the Germans the equivalent of nine dreadnought battleships (approximately 18 million pounds). The canal was not completed in a state that permitted the largest dreadnoughts to move from the Baltic to the North Sea until July, 1914. The (relatively minor) elements of the Far East fleet have been excluded from the totals of ships in home waters.

The comparison between German and British fleet strengths in home waters gives some indication of the extent to which Admiral von Tirpitz was successful in achieving his goal of increasing the riskiness of the German fleet; as the figures indicate, the concentration of power by the British in home waters largely offset any gains that the Germans accomplished by their massive building program.

Table VI presents a detailed summary of characteristics of ships built for the battle fleets by both Germany and Great Britain between 1899 and 1914. As contrasted with the other tables included in this paper, Table VI is based on the information appearing in the 1914 volume of *Brassey's Naval Annual*, so that data on ships already completed is relatively reliable. (Note, however, the erroneous figures given for number of guns 14″ and over for German ships listed as completed in 1914. No German ships launched prior to World War I had guns larger than 13.5″, but the lack of information on this score was apparent in Jellicoe's reports to the Admiralty in 1914 and 1915.) In general, German ships were slower, more heavily armored, and carried smaller guns than their British counterparts, although exceptions occur between 1911 and 1913. The bulk of the construction effort of the Germans was expended upon battleships rather than upon armored cruisers and battle cruisers, a fact that, in light of the changing tactics of the period which rapidly obsoleted the armored cruisers, must have caused the English some regrets when the war broke out. As the data show, the Germans followed the lead of the British in battleship and battle cruiser construction, their first dreadnought battleship being completed in 1909, three years after the appearance of the *Dreadnought* while the first German battle cruiser was placed in commission only in 1913. The general rise in displacement, armor protection, speed, size of guns, and cost is apparent from the data, as is the decline in number of ships launched. In addition, the shift away from Fisher's position that the capital ships should carry only the "largest of the large guns, and the smallest of the small guns" is apparent in the ships under construction in the last years of the period. (It might be noted that only Germany and Great Britain ever constructed Fisher's "favorite," the fast, lightly armored battle cruiser of the *Invincible* type; Japan's excursion into battle cruiser design was closer to the tradition of heavily armored capital ships rather than speedy lightly armored ships.) The coal capacities shown for German versus British ships do not seem to bear out the often quoted contention that the German fleet was built only for operation in North Sea waters (and thus was aimed solely at the British). The structural superiority of German over British ships, as indicated by the actions at Dogger Bank and Jutland, is not apparent in the data; in fact, the deficiencies of British capital ships (particularly battle cruisers) were not known at the time. There is no positive indication given in the table that the paradoxical British proposition that (1) Britain could build ships faster than any other country on earth and (2), in fact, Germany was proceeding at a (*sub rosa*) rate of construction far faster than the British, was justified.

At best the development of measures of fleet strengths as among powers is beset with extraordinary difficulties; not only are there intangible factors, such as leadership and seamanship, to contend with, but even the tangible factors, such as numbers and types of ships, are difficult to assess. Each ship is essentially a unique entity, as the data given in Table VI clearly shows. This is particularly true during a time of rapid technological and tactical change such as the pre–World War I period. The writers believe that it is necessary to develop much more comprehensive and detailed statistics covering the period of the arms race than have been presented in the past to arrive at an understanding of the forces at work. The data presented here are a first attempt in that direction.

Appendix A

TABLE I
SUMMARY DATA
FLEETS IN BEING (SHIPS IN COMMISSION)
1899–1914

Code: A–Number
B–Tonnage   F–Guns 12 and under 14"
C–Complement   G–Guns 10 and under 12"
D–Horsepower   H–Guns 8 and under 10"
E–Guns 14" and over   I–Guns 5.9 and under 8"

Year	Country	A	B	C	D	E	F	G	H	I
1899	Great Britain	260	1,309	794	1,711	4	114	17	70	893
	Austria-Hungary	44	111	98	192		5	8	68	140
	France	140	565	419	799	4	52	63	41	238
	Germany	78	255	200	336		11	64	44	148
	Italy	63	237	167	374			5	12	199
	Japan	40	147	122	268		17	10	18	124
	Russia	76	309	221	378		25	12	104	297
	U.S.	66	210	159	317		24	18	66	126
1900	Great Britain	292	1,368	946	1,870	4	116	17	70	1,008
	Austria-Hungary	41	110	101	185		5	8	58	111
	France	141	573	416	897	4	53	66	51	193
	Germany	81	298	203	363		11	72	56	200
	Italy	63	221	164	366			5	12	185
	Japan	39	172	132	294		25	19	20	150
	Russia	80	344	227	416		25	6	116	341
	U.S.	68	235	171	335		30	18	60	154
1901	Great Britain	288	1,367	927	1,973	4	132	17	72	1,088
	Austria-Hungary	42	112	109	208		5	8	58	101
	France	136	546	404	992	4	57	44	34	207
	Germany	87	338	234	447		11	72	68	252
	Italy	66	257	185	425			10	14	229
	Japan	45	214	166	367		25	19	36	196
	Russia	84	387	278	479		25	18	116	388
	U.S.	67	244	175	357		36	18	66	168
1902	Great Britain	298	1,393	979	2,136	4	156	17	84	1,200
	Austria-Hungary	43	120	116	203		5	8	61	109
	France	126	563	408	874	4	61	45	34	208
	Germany	85	375	255	490		11	71	83	284
	Italy	63	261	187	430			14	14	229
	Japan	45	233	171	392		29	19	38	200
	Russia	93	445	329	595		33	18	116	458
	U.S.	64	268	184	325		50	18	66	212
1903	Great Britain	302	1,588	1,037	2,396	4	224	17	70	1,376
	Austria-Hungary	39	119	n.a.	207		5	8	64	85
	France	132	639	428	1,020	4	63	46	30	275
	Germany	88	403	271	551		11	64	97	330
	Italy	58	250	177	420			14	14	219
	Japan	45	233	n.a.	392		29	19	38	200
	Russia	87	431	n.a.	515		37	16	78	431
	U.S.	67	288	193	418		60	18	66	244

TABLE I (*Continued*)

Year	Country	A	B	C	D	E	F	G	H	I
1904	Great Britain	290	1,682	1,088	2,708	4	251	26	75	1,515
	Austria-Hungary	39	127	n.a.	218		5	8	67	97
	France	131	659	429	1,096	4	61	38	28	312
	Germany	94	435	287	615		11	56	97	337
	Italy	58	276	188	468			15	36	243
	Japan	43	227	n.a.	391		25	19	42	213
	Russia	82	443	n.a.	668		41	16	71	428
	U.S.	72	312	213	422		64	18	76	238
1905	Great Britain	182	1,535	940	2,373	2	284	24	66	1,313
	Austria-Hungary	35	104	n.a.	203		5		43	97
	France	124	670	422	1,124	4	61	38	28	345
	Germany	99	498	331	746		11	74	104	387
	Italy	58	276	n.a.	468			15	36	243
	Japan	45	223	n.a.	401		25	23	42	218
	Russia	80	458	n.a.	682		45	16	68	459
	U.S.	80	402	262	696		72	14	98	328
1906	Great Britain	187	1,640	1,003	2,530		290	24	98	1,349
	Austria-Hungary	36	122	n.a.	235		5		47	121
	France	112	635	412	1,089	4	65	31	18	360
	Germany	99	501	341	758		11	74	104	387
	Italy	57	272	n.a.	465			15	24	243
	Japan	54	342	n.a.	532		51	47	45	311
	Russia	56	296	n.a.	466		17	4	49	303
	U.S.	89	558	343	824		100	22	154	464
1907	Great Britain	190	1,671	1,013	2,591		292	24	122	1,359
	Austria-Hungary	34	118	n.a.	228				51	126
	France	109	660	419	1,121	4	73	31	12	381
	Germany	91	520	344	800		1	82	96	407
	Italy	57	304	n.a.	519		6	15	60	243
	Japan	54	368	n.a.	574		53	47	45	333
	Russia	53	321	n.a.	645		17	16	57	289
	U.S.	86	580	368	866		98	10	170	508
1908	Great Britain	180	1,647	996	2,613		290	16	136	1,319
	Austria-Hungary	29	117	n.a.	228				51	126
	France	94	619	386	1,099		79	23	2	364
	Germany	94	557	358	911		1	72	120	455
	Italy	47	253	n.a.	476		14	19	88	203
	Japan	49	330	n.a.	542		44	29	45	321
	Russia	54	304	n.a.	686		17	16	61	269
	U.S.	95	664	423	1,005		114	18	194	562
1909	Great Britain	171	1,711	1,015	2,721		318	16	138	1,339
	Austria-Hungary	32	113	n.a.	215				43	126
	France	90	614	384	1,115		79	22	75	380
	Germany	96	606	365	1,011			75	57	539
	Italy	44	257	n.a.	469		14	23	94	197
	Japan	52	366	n.a.	573		56	41	53	321
	Russia	54	304	199	486		17	16	65	286
	U.S.	86	693	421	1,012		138	18	186	526

TABLE I (*Continued*)

Year	Country	A	B	C	D	E	F	G	H	I
1910	Great Britain	177	1,760	1,042	2,820		358	8	138	1,303
	Austria-Hungary	35	145	n.a.	284		8		59	126
	France	76	538	322	986		69	12	4	348
	Germany	100	675	409	1,159		1	120	123	523
	Italy	42	259	n.a.	486		14	27	108	178
	Japan	53	385	n.a.	596		56	53	53	319
	Russia	58	365	n.a.	577		25	4	35	300
	U.S.	87	718	422	1,146		150	18	188	502
1911	Great Britain	176	1,706	1,032	2,931		338	8	132	1,217
	Austria-Hungary	35	157	n.a.	298		12		67	126
	France	83	684	389	1,193		95	14	78	326
	Germany	92	684	380	1,240		45	106	100	565
	Italy	38	287	n.a.	484		33	27	59	168
	Japan	50	398	n.a.	620		60	44	60	331
	Russia	54	467	n.a.	739		77	16	78	279
	U.S.	89	762	425	1,138		170	18	193	534
1912	Great Britain	184	1,835	1,059	3,227		418	8	136	1,233
	Austria-Hungary	33	157	n.a.	298		12		67	126
	France	75	683	377	1,164		105	16	78	352
	Germany	99	814	462	1,497		57	132	100	637
	Italy	42	280	n.a.	546		26	27	106	174
	Japan	54	482	n.a.	799		90	44	59	372
	Russia	45	345	n.a.	568		77	15	82	245
	U.S.	82	789	425	1,102		194	18	183	520
1913	Great Britain	188	1,971	1,007	3,527		466	8	136	1,210
	Austria-Hungary	33	196	n.a.	327		36		67	148
	France	74	701	384	1,183		113	16	78	360
	Germany	104	915	528	1,686	42	99	147	100	677
	Italy	41	298	n.a.	553		39	27	106	208
	Japan	34	480	n.a.	799		92	44	59	370
	Russia	46	354	n.a.	567		29	16	82	263
	U.S.	82	808	444	1,120	10	194	18	179	520
1914	Great Britain	184	1,985	1,128	3,536		498	8	134	1,164
	Austria-Hungary	33	198	n.a.	345		36		67	150
	France	73	690	352	1,063		89	14	78	336
	Germany	100	987	540	1,890	16	145	134	94	705
	Italy	42	281	n.a.	601		52	27	106	180
	Japan	53	478	n.a.	790		93	43	59	360
	Russia	38	319	n.a.	483		25	16	82	231
	U.S.	72	794	430	1,121	20	176	16	159	500

n.a.—Data not available.

TABLE II
FLEET COMPARISONS, 1899–1914

Country	Ship Types	1899/1900	1901/2	1903/4	1905/6	1907/8	1909/10	1911/12	1913/14
Austria-Hungary	Dreadnought Btlshps.								2
	Dreadnought B. Cr.								
All	Battleships	5	7	8	5	4	4	9	9
	Armored Cruisers	1	2	2	2	3	3	3	3
Under 20 Years	Dr. Btlshps.								2
	Dr. B. Cr.								
	Battleships	3	2	3	3	3	4	9	9
	Armored Cruisers	1	2	2	2	3	3	3	2
France	Dr. Btlshps.								2
All	Dr. B. Cr.								
	Battleships	28	29	30	28	30	26	29	27
	Armored Cruisers	11	10	15	21	21	21	22	20
Under 20 Years	Dr. Btlshps.								2
	Dr. B. Cr.								
	Battleships	23	22	22	18	21	22	28	23
	Armored Cruisers	10	8	14	20	21	20	22	18
Italy	Dr. Btlshps.							1	3
All	Dr. B. Cr.								
	Battleships	12	13	13	15	17	14	13	15
	Armored Cruisers	6	7	6	7	7	8	10	10
Under 20 Years	Dr. Btlshps.							1	3
	Dr. B. Cr.								
	Battleships	10	10	9	8	11	12	10	12
	Armored Cruisers	3	5	5	6	6	7	8	8

TABLE II (Continued)

Country	Ship Types	1899/1900	1901/2	1903/4	1905/6	1907/8	1909/10	1911/12	1913/14
Japan									
All	Dr. Btlshps.						1*	2*	2
	Dr. B. Cr.								4†
	Battleships	4	6	7	5	13	14	15	14
	Armored Cruisers	6	9	8	10	12	10	10	9
Under 20 Years	Dr. Btlshps.						1*	2*	2
	Dr. B. Cr.								4*
	Battleships	4	6	6	4	12	14	14	13
	Armored Cruisers	4	7	8	10	12	9	9	8
Russia									
All	Dr. Btlshps.								
	Dr. B. Cr.								
	Battleships	15	20	22	24	13	11	12	13
	Armored Cruisers	7	12	9	8	7	7	9	9
Under 20 Years	Dr. Btlshps.								
	Dr. B. Cr.								
	Battleships	13	18	21	23	9	9	9	8
	Armored Cruisers	4	9	5	3	7	7	9	9
U.S.									
All	Dr. Btlshps.						2	4	7
	Dr. B. Cr.								
	Battleships	4	7	11	13	25	28	28	28
	Armored Cruisers	3	3	3	6	15	15	15	14
Under 20 Years	Dr. Btlshps.						2	4	6
	Dr. B. Cr.								
	Battleships	4	7	11	13	22	28	27	24
	Armored Cruisers	3	3	3	6	13	15	14	14

TABLE II (Continued)

Country	Ship Types	1899/1900	1901/2	1903/4	1905/6	1907/8	1909/10	1911/12	1913/14
Germany									
All	Dr. Btlshps.						4	8	16
	Dr. B. Cr.							3	5
	Battleships	15	19	22	25	26	28	23	21
	Armored Cruisers		1	4	6	7	10	11	10
Under 20 Years	Dr. Btlshps.						4	8	16
	Dr. B. Cr.							3	5
	Battleships	9	15	18	22	24	26	20	20
	Armored Cruisers		1	4	6	7	10	11	10
Great Britain									
All	Dr. Btlshps.				1	1	6	14	22
	Dr. B. Cr.					2	3	7	9
	Battleships	52	49	50	53	56	50	39	38
	Armored Cruisers	9	8	16	26	31	36	35	35
Under 20 Years	Dr. Btlshps.				1	1	6	14	22
	Dr. B. Cr.					2	3	7	9
	Battleships	37	35	42	45	45	49	37	36
	Armored Cruisers	7	8	15	26	31	34	35	35

SOURCE: *Brassey's Naval Annuals* 1899–1914.
* Four main guns only.
† One ship with eight main guns.

TABLE III
Summary Statistics—Great Britain and Germany, 1899–1914

Year	Country	Fleet	Status	Number	Tonnage	Complement	Horsepower	Number of Guns				
								14 in. and over	12 in. to 14 in.	10 in. to 12 in.	8 in. to 10 in.	5.9 in. to 8 in.
1889	Great Britain	Battle	Completed	62	680	320	581	4	114	17	38	365
			Launched	15	206	111	234		42		4	180
			Pro & Bldg	12	156	78	280		12		16	162
		Cruiser	Completed	117	472	381	894				30	518
			Launched	14	89	63	161					117
			Pro & Bldg	1	2	2	7					
		Other	Completed	81	157	93	236				2	10
			Launched	4	4	4	4					
			Pro & Bldg	5	5	5	5					
		Totals	Completed	260	1309	794	1711	4	114	17	70	893
			Launched	33	299	178	399		42		4	297
			Pro & Bldg	18	163	85	292		12		16	162
	Germany	Battle	Completed	15	123	83	107			64	8	28
			Launched	4	44	27	52			8	20	88
			Pro & Bldg	5	55	34	66				20	84
		Cruiser	Completed	31	89	76	151				10	120
			Launched	2	6	4	12					
		Other	Completed	32	36	41	78		11		26	
			Launched	1	1	1	1					
		Totals	Completed	78	255	200	336		11	64	44	148
			Launched	6	70	31	64			8	20	88
			Pro & Bldg	6	56	35	67				20	84
1900	Great Britain	Battle	Completed	68	715	405	620	4	116	17	38	401
			Launched	16	214	117	270		43		8	194
			Pro & Bldg	14	182	99	317		20		14	188
		Cruiser	Completed	121	529	414	1011				30	599
			Launched	5	23	17	47					27
		Other	Completed	103	124	127	239				2	8
			Launched	3	3	3	3					
			Pro & Bldg	6	6	8	6					

TABLE III (Continued)

Year	Country	Fleet	Status	Number	Tonnage	Comple-ment	Horse-power	Number of Guns				
								14 in. and over	12 in. to 14 in.	10 in. to 12 in.	8 in. to 10 in.	5.9 in. to 8 in.
		Totals	Completed	292	1368	946	1870	4	116	17	70	1008
			Launched	24	240	137	320		43		8	221
			Pro & Bldg	20	188	107	323		20		14	188
	Germany	Battle	Completed	17	145	96	133			72	20	80
			Launched	4	42	26	54				14	64
			Pro & Bldg	6	69	41	90				22	100
		Cruiser	Completed	31	89	68	151				10	120
			Launched	6	18	12	48					
			Pro & Bldg									
		Other	Completed	33	64	39	79		11		26	
			Launched	2	2		2					
			Pro & Bldg									
		Totals	Completed	81	298	203	363		11	72	56	200
			Launched	10	60	38	102				14	64
			Pro & Bldg	8	71	41	92				22	100
1901	Great Britain	Battle	Completed	61	691	393	707	4	132	17	40	502
			Launched	24	306	157	429		48		16	270
			Pro & Bldg	7	72	54	153				2	96
		Cruiser	Completed	122	530	411	1035				30	580
			Launched	1	11	6	16					16
			Pro & Bldg	1	6	4	12					
		Other	Completed	105	146	123	231				2	6
			Launched	4	4	6	4					
			Pro & Bldg	2	2	4	2					
		Totals	Completed	288	1367	927	1973	4	132	17	72	1088
			Launched	29	321	170	449		48		16	286
			Pro & Bldg	10	80	62	167				2	96
	Germany	Battle	Completed	20	178	117	172			72	32	134
			Launched	6	69	40	86				22	100
			Pro & Bldg	2	22	13	31			4	2	22
		Cruiser	Completed	36	104	78	196				10	118
			Launched	3	9	6	24					
			Pro & Bldg									

TABLE III (Continued)

Year	Country	Fleet	Status	Number	Tonnage	Complement	Horse-power	14 in. and over	12 in. to 14 in.	10 in. to 12 in.	8 in. to 10 in.	5.9 in. to 8 in.
		Other	Completed	31	56	39	79		11		26	
			Launched	1	1		1					
			Pro & Bldg	1	1		1					
		Totals	Completed	87	338	234	447		11	72	68	252
			Launched	7	70	40	87			4	22	100
			Pro & Bldg	6	32	19	56				2	22
1902	Great Britain	Battle	Completed	71	718	450	862	4	156	17	52	610
			Launched	18	324	124	373		32		6	248
			Pro & Bldg	15	172	89	316		12		16	182
		Cruiser	Completed	122	537	412	1045				30	586
			Launched	1	6	5	12					11
			Pro & Bldg	1	3	5	10					
		Other	Completed	105	138	117	233				2	4
			Launched	1	1	2	1					
			Pro & Bldg	3	5	7	18					
		Totals	Completed	298	1393	979	2136	4	156	17	84	1200
			Launched	20	331	131	386		32		6	259
			Pro & Bldg	19	180	101	344		12		16	182
	Germany	Battle	Completed	23	216	138	226			71	48	196
			Launched	5	55	31	76			1	16	68
			Pro & Bldg	5	57	58	79			12	8	56
		Cruiser	Completed	29	93	75	181				10	88
			Launched	3	9	6	24					
			Pro & Bldg	2	6	4	16					
		Other	Completed	33	66	42	83				25	
			Launched									
			Pro & Bldg				1					
		Totals	Completed	85	375	255	490		11	71	83	284
			Launched	8	64	37	100			1	16	68
			Pro & Bldg	8	64	62	96			12	8	56
1903	Great Britain	Battle	Completed	79	932	517	1138	4	224	17	40	786
			Launched	15	193	112	272		60		18	216
			Pro & Bldg	8	107	59	171		8		26	86

TABLE III (Continued)

Year	Country	Fleet	Status	Number	Tonnage	Complement	Horsepower	Number of Guns				
								14 in. and over	12 in. to 14 in.	10 in. to 12 in.	8 in. to 10 in.	5.9 in. to 8 in.
		Cruiser	Completed	122	537	412	1046				30	586
			Launched	3	12	9	32					11
			Pro & Bldg	2	6	4	20					
		Other	Completed	101	119	108	208					4
			Launched	2	2	4	2					
			Pro & Bldg	4	11	12	66					
		Totals	Completed	302	1588	1037	2396	4	224	17	70	1376
			Launched	20	207	125	307		60		18	227
			Pro & Bldg	14	124	75	257		8		26	86
	Germany	Battle	Completed	26	251	157	281			64	62	250
			Launched	5	62	33	80			16	4	66
			Pro & Bldg	3	35	20	49			8	4	38
		Cruiser	Completed	29	94	76	187				10	80
			Launched	5	15	10	34					
			Pro & Bldg	2	6	4	10					
		Other	Completed	33	58	38	83		11		25	
			Launched	1	1	—	1					
			Pro & Bldg									
		Totals	Completed	88	403	271	551		11	64	97	330
			Launched	11	78	43	115			16	4	66
			Pro & Bldg	5	41	24	59			8	4	38
1904	Great Britain	Battle	Completed	87	1032	581	1454	4	251	26	42	948
			Launched	15	200	112	135		32		36	172
			Pro & Bldg	6	88	48	132		8		31	42
		Cruiser	Completed	117	530	404	1043				30	561
			Launched	5	15	15	50					
			Pro & Bldg									
		Other	Completed	86	122	103	211				3	16
			Launched	7	19	21	114					
			Pro & Bldg	1	3	3	17					
		Totals	Completed	290	1682	1088	2708	4	251	26	75	1515
			Launched	27	234	148	299		32		36	172
			Pro & Bldg	7	91	51	149		8		31	42

TABLE III (Continued)

Year	Country	Fleet	Status	Number	Tonnage	Comple-ment	Horse-power	14 in. and over	12 in. to 14 in.	10 in. to 12 in.	8 in. to 10 in.	5.9 in. to 8 in.
	Germany	Battle	Completed	26	257	157	292			56	62	257
			Launched	7	83	47	114			20	8	90
			Pro & Bldg	3	35	18	49			8	4	38
		Cruiser	Completed	35	112	86	241				10	80
			Launched	2	6	4	18					
			Pro & Bldg	3	9	6	30					
		Other	Completed	33	64	21	82		11		25	
			Launched									
			Pro & Bldg									
		Totals	Completed	94	435	287	615		11	56	97	337
			Launched	9	89	51	132			20	8	90
			Pro & Bldg	6	44	24	79			8	4	38
1905	Great Britain	Battle	Completed	85	1084	600	1388	2	284	24	40	924
			Launched	10	143	79	219		8		48	54
			Pro & Bldg	6	92	50	127				36	40°
		Cruiser	Completed	73	407	298	898				26	409
			Launched									
			Pro & Bldg									
		Other	Completed	24	44	42	87					
			Launched	1	3	3	16					
			Pro & Bldg									
		Totals	Completed	182	1535	940	2373	2	284	24	66	1313
			Launched	11	146	82	235		8		48	54
			Pro & Bldg	6	92	50	127				36	40
	Germany	Battle	Completed	31	323	192	393			74	70	327
			Launched	2	26	14	32			8		28
			Pro & Bldg	4	48	30	84			8		28
		Cruiser	Completed	37	119	97	277				10	60
			Launched									
			Pro & Bldg									
		Other	Completed	4	9	9	36					
			Launched	31	56	42	76		11		24	
			Pro & Bldg	1	1	†	†					†

TABLE III (Continued)

Year	Country	Fleet	Status	Number	Tonnage	Complement	Horse-power	14 in. and over	12 in. to 14 in.	10 in. to 12 in.	8 in. to 10 in.	5.9 in. to 8 in.
1906	Great Britain	Totals	Completed	99	498	331	746		11	74	104	387
			Launched	2	26	14	32			8		28
			Pro & Bldg	5	49	30	84			8		28
		Battle	Completed	92	1187	661	1554		290	24	76	950
			Launched	6	90	50	131		8		40	28
			Pro & Bldg	2	n.a.	n.a.	n.a.		n.a.		n.a.	n.a.
		Cruiser	Completed	70	392	297	767				22	399
			Launched									
			Pro & Bldg									
		Other	Completed	25	61	45	209					
			Launched									
			Pro & Bldg									
	Germany	Totals	Completed	187	1640	1003	2530		290	24	98	1349
			Launched	6	90	50	131		8		40	28
			Pro & Bldg	2	n.a.	n.a.	n.a.		n.a.	n.a.	n.a.	n.a.
		Battle	Completed	37	351	210	431			74	91	327
			Launched	6	76	40	116			16	16	68
			Pro & Bldg	3	51	n.a.	n.a.		n.a.	n.a.	n.a.	n.a.
		Cruiser	Completed	38	122	106	285				10	60
			Launched	3	9	6	36					
			Pro & Bldg	3	10	6	45					
		Other	Completed	24	28	25	42		11		3	
			Launched									
			Pro & Bldg									
1907	Great Britain	Totals	Completed	99	501	341	758		11	74	104	387
			Launched	9	85	46	152			16	16	68
			Pro & Bldg	6	61	n.a.	n.a.		n.a.	n.a.	n.a.	n.a.
		Battle	Completed	94	1222	674	1610		292	24	98	958
			Launched	11	185	92	298		50		52	30
			Pro & Bldg									
		Cruiser	Completed	71	402	292	787				24	401
			Launched	1	3	n.a.	n.a.		n.a.	n.a.	n.a.	n.a.
			Pro & Bldg									

TABLE III (Continued)

Year	Country	Fleet	Status	Number	Tonnage	Comple-ment	Horse-power	Number of Guns				
								14 in. and over	12 in. to 14 in.	10 in. to 12 in.	8 in. to 10 in.	5.9 in. to 8 in.
		Other	Completed	25	47	47	194					
			Launched	1	2		30					
			Pro & Bldg									
		Totals	Completed	190	1671	1013	2591		292	24	122	1359
			Launched	12	187	92	328		50		52	30
			Pro & Bldg	1	3	n.a.	n.a.		n.a.	n.a.	n.a.	n.a.
	Germany	Battle	Completed	33	349	206	421			82	62	347
			Launched	4	50	26	86			8	24	48
			Pro & Bldg	6	n.a.	n.a.	n.a.				n.a.	
		Cruiser	Completed	38	126	106	304				10	60
			Launched	3	10	9	39					
			Pro & Bldg	3	n.a.	n.a.	n.a.				n.a.	
		Other	Completed	20	45	32	75		1		24	n.a.
			Launched									
			Pro & Bldg									
		Totals	Completed	91	520	344	800		1	82	96	407
			Launched	7	60	35	125			8	24	48
			Pro & Bldg	9	n.a.	n.a.	n.a.		n.a.	n.a.	n.a.	n.a.
1908	Great Britain	Battle	Completed	92	1240	682	1704		290	16	116	944
			Launched	7	127	56	185		58		4	10
			Pro & Bldg	3	n.a.	n.a.	n.a.		n.a.	n.a.	n.a.	n.a.
		Cruiser	Completed	66	369	273	720				20	375
			Launched	1	3	2	18					
			Pro & Bldg	6	n.a.	n.a.	n.a.					
		Other	Completed	22	38	41	189					
			Launched	1	2		30					
			Pro & Bldg									
		Totals	Completed	180	1647	996	2613		290	16	136	1319
			Launched	9	132	58	233		58		4	10
			Pro & Bldg	9	n.a.	n.a.	n.a.		n.a.	n.a.	n.a.	n.a.
	Germany	Battle	Completed	34	378	220	501			72	86	395
			Launched	5	87	48	135			56		24
			Pro & Bldg	5‡	95	40	n.a.			45		

TABLE III (Continued)

Year	Country	Fleet	Status	Number	Tonnage	Comple-ment	Horse-power	14 in. and over	12 in. to 14 in.	10 in. to 12 in.	8 in. to 10 in.	5.9 in. to 8 in.
		Cruiser	Completed	40	134	106	345				10	60
			Launched	2	8	6	28					
			Pro & Bldg	3§	12	n.a.	40					n.a.
		Other	Completed	20	45	32	55		n.a.		24	
			Launched									
			Pro & Bldg						1			
		Totals	Completed	94	557	358	911		1	72	120	455
			Launched	7	95	54	163			56		24
			Pro & Bldg	8	107	n.a.	n.a.		n.a.	n.a.	n.a.	n.a.
1909	Great Britain	Battle	Completed	95	1328	727	1943		318	16	120	954
			Launched	5	95	43	141		58			
			Pro & Bldg	4	n.a.	n.a.	n.a.		n.a.	n.a.	n.a.	n.a.
		Cruiser	Completed	63	345	261	715		n.a.	n.a.	n.a.	n.a.
			Launched	5	20	20	88					
			Pro & Bldg	7	n.a.	n.a.	n.a.		n.a.	n.a.	n.a.	n.a.
		Other	Completed	13	40	27	63		n.a.	n.a.	n.a.	n.a.
			Launched									
			Pro & Bldg									
		Totals	Completed	171	1711	1015	2721		318	16	138	1339
			Launched	10	115	63	229		58			
			Pro & Bldg	11	n.a.	n.a.	n.a.		n.a.	n.a.	n.a.	n.a.
	Germany	Battle	Completed	36	421	237	562		36	74	26	479
			Launched	7	120	62	186			48	72	
			Pro & Bldg	5	n.a.	n.a.	n.a.		n.a.	n.a.	n.a.	n.a.
		Cruiser	Completed	43	146	102	393				10	60
			Launched	2	8	n.a.	n.a.					
			Pro & Bldg	2	n.a.	n.a.	n.a.		n.a.	n.a.	n.a.	n.a.
		Other	Completed	17	39	26	56		n.a.	1	21	n.a.
			Launched									
			Pro & Bldg									
		Totals	Completed	96	606	365	1011		36	75	57	539
			Launched	9	128	62	186			48	72	
			Pro & Bldg	7	n.a.	n.a.	n.a.		n.a.	n.a.	n.a.	n.a.

TABLE III (Continued)

Year	Country	Fleet	Status	Number	Tonnage	Complement	Horse-power	Number of Guns				
								14 in. and over	12 in. to 14 in.	10 in. to 12 in.	8 in. to 10 in.	5.9 in. to 8 in.
1910	Great Britain	Battle	Completed	98	1363	739	1880		358	8	120	954
			Launched	5	105	43	188		46			
			Pro & Bldg	11	n.a.	n.a.	n.a.		n.a.	n.a.	n.a.	n.a.
		Cruiser	Completed	67	368	275	773				18	349
			Launched	6	28	23	128					18
			Pro & Bldg	7	n.a.	n.a.	n.a.					
		Other	Completed	12	29	28	167					
			Launched									
			Pro & Bldg									
		Totals	Completed	177	1760	1042	2820		358	8	138	1303
			Launched	11	133	66	316		46			18
			Pro & Bldg	18	n.a.	n.a.	n.a.		n.a.	n.a.	n.a.	n.a.
	Germany	Battle	Completed	40	482	276	685		48	120	98	463
			Launched	4	88	40	94		1			42
			Pro & Bldg	8	n.a.	n.a.	n.a.		n.a.	n.a.	n.a.	n.a.
		Cruiser	Completed	45	154	119	427				10	60
			Launched									
			Pro & Bldg	4	n.a.	n.a.	n.a.				n.a.	n.a.
		Other	Completed	15	39	14	47				15	
			Launched									
			Pro & Bldg									
		Totals	Completed	100	675	409	1159		48	120	123	523
			Launched	4	88	40	94		1			42
			Pro & Bldg	12	n.a.	n.a.	n.a.		n.a.	n.a.	n.a.	n.a.
1911	Great Britain	Battle	Completed	91	1296	716	1867		338	8	116	852
			Launched	9	205	69	353		84			n.a.
			Pro & Bldg	8	n.a.	n.a.	n.a.		n.a.	n.a.	n.a.	n.a.
		Cruiser	Completed	73	384	288	897		n.a.		16	365
			Launched	3	13	11	65					16
			Pro & Bldg	6	n.a.	n.a.	n.a.					n.a.
		Other	Completed	12	26	28	167					
			Launched									
			Pro & Bldg									

TABLE III (Continued)

Year	Country	Fleet	Status	Number	Tonnage	Comple-ment	Horse-power	14 in. and over	12 in. to 14 in.	10 in. to 12 in.	8 in. to 10 in.	5.9 in. to 8 in.
		Totals	Completed	176	1706	1032	2391		338	8	132	1217
			Launched	12	218	80	418		84			16
			Pro & Bldg	14	n.a.	n.a.	n.a.		n.a.	n.a.	n.a.	n.a.
	Germany	Battle	Completed	41	525	269	803		44	106	90	495
			Launched	6	143	59	204		56	10		70
			Pro & Bldg	7	n.a.	n.a.	n.a.					
		Cruiser	Completed	43	150	105	421				10	68
			Launched	4	16	12	80					
			Pro & Bldg	2	n.a.	n.a.	n.a.		n.a.	n.a.	n.a.	n.a.
		Other	Completed	8	9	6	16		1			
			Launched									
			Pro & Bldg									
		Totals	Completed	92	684	380	1240		45	106	100	565
			Launched	10	159	71	284		56	10		70
			Pro & Bldg	9	n.a.	n.a.	n.a.		n.a.	n.a.	n.a.	n.a.
1912	Great Britain	Battle	Completed	98	1425	739	2155		418	8	120	854
			Launched	7	194	49	237		68			
			Pro & Bldg	7	n.a.	n.a.	n.a.		n.a.	n.a.	n.a.	n.a.
		Cruiser	Completed	74	381	292	905					379
			Launched	5	21	18	131				16	16
			Pro & Bldg	10	n.a.	n.a.	n.a.		n.a.	n.a.	n.a.	n.a.
		Other	Completed	12	29	28	167					
			Launched									
			Pro & Bldg									
		Totals	Completed	184	1835	1059	3227		418	8	136	1233
			Launched	12	215	67	368		68			16
			Pro & Bldg	17	n.a.	n.a.	n.a.		n.a.	n.a.	n.a.	n.a.
	Germany	Battle	Completed	45	642	350	988		56	132	90	569
			Launched	4	95	40	143		42	10		54
			Pro & Bldg	5	n.a.	n.a.	n.a.		n.a.	n.a.	n.a.	n.a.
		Cruiser	Completed	46	164	107	498				10	68
			Launched	3	15	12	60				4	
			Pro & Bldg	1	n.a.	n.a.	n.a.		n.a.	n.a.	n.a.	n.a.

TABLE III (Continued)

Year	Country	Fleet	Status	Number	Tonnage	Complement	Horsepower	Number of Guns				
								14 in. and over	12 in. to 14 in.	10 in. to 12 in.	8 in. to 10 in.	5.9 in. to 8 in.
				8	8	5	11		1			
		Other	Completed	8	8	5	11		1			
			Launched									
			Pro & Bldg									
		Totals	Completed	99	814	462	1497		57	132	100	637
			Launched	7	110	52	203		42	10	4	54
			Pro & Bldg	6	n.a.	n.a.	n.a.		n.a.	n.a.	n.a.	n.a.
1913	Great Britain	Battle	Completed	102	1563	701	2362	=	466	8	120	856
			Launched	5	126	46	192		48			48
			Pro & Bldg	10	n.a.	n.a.	n.a.		n.a.	n.a.	n.a.	n.a.
		Cruiser	Completed	74	379	278	998				16	354
			Launched	4	26	20	105					27
			Pro & Bldg	6	n.a.	n.a.	n.a.		n.a.			n.a.
		Other	Completed	12	29	28	167					
			Launched									
			Pro & Bldg									
		Totals	Completed	188	1971	1007	3527		466	8	136	1210
			Launched	9	152	66	297		48			75
			Pro & Bldg	16	n.a.	n.a.	n.a.		n.a.	n.a.	n.a.	n.a.
	Germany	Battle	Completed	49	738	390	1132	42	98	147	90	617
			Launched	4	108	43	205			10		60
			Pro & Bldg	4	n.a.	n.a.	n.a.		n.a.	n.a.	n.a.	n.a.
		Cruiser	Completed	47	169	133	543				10	60
			Launched	1	5	4	25					
			Pro & Bldg	4	n.a.	n.a.	n.a.					
		Other	Completed	8	8	5	11		1			
			Launched									
			Pro & Bldg									
		Totals	Completed	104	915	528	1686	42	99	147	100	677
			Launched	5	113	47	230			10		60
			Pro & Bldg	8	n.a.	n.a.	n.a.		n.a.	n.a.	n.a.	n.a.
1914	Great Britain	Battle	Completed	105	1619	848	2383	18	498	8	120	844
			Launched	4	110	40	272		16			40
			Pro & Bldg	13‡	n.a.	n.a.	n.a.		n.a.	n.a.	n.a.	n.a.

TABLE III (Continued)

Year	Country	Fleet	Status	Number	Tonnage	Complement	Horse-power	14 in. and over	12 in. to 14 in.	10 in. to 12 in.	8 in. to 10 in.	5.9 in. to 8 in.
		Cruiser	Completed	67	341	252	986				14	320
			Launched	4	16	10	120					8
			Pro & Bldg	14	n.a.	n.a.	n.a.		n.a.		n.a.	n.a.
		Other	Completed	12	25	28	167					
			Pro & Bldg									
		Totals	Completed	184	1985	1128	3536	18	498	8	134	1164
			Launched	8	126	50	392		16			48
			Pro & Bldg	27‡	n.a.	n.a.	n.a.		n.a.	n.a.	n.a.	n.a.
	Germany	Battle	Completed	51	825	400	1332	16	144	134	92	677
			Launched	4	114	46	204	32	10			58
			Pro & Bldg	3	n.a.	n.a.	n.a.		n.a.			
		Cruiser	Completed	41	144	135	543				2	28
			Launched	2	10	8	90					
			Pro & Bldg	2	n.a.	n.a.	n.a.		n.a.			
		Other	Completed	8	18	5	15		1			
			Launched									
			Pro & Bldg									
		Totals	Completed	100	987	540	1890	16	145	134	94	705
			Launched	6	124	54	294	32	10			58
			Pro & Bldg	5	n.a.	n.a.	n.a.		n.a.			

* Dreadnought characteristics unknown; included as other provisional and building armored cruisers.
† Details missing on German ships.
‡ All data except tonnage refer to four ships launched 1909; data on fifth ship not available.
§ All data except tonnage refer to two ships launched 1909; data on third ship not available.
‖ Ten battleships listed as carrying eight 15" guns each.
Four ships not listed by type; nine battleships listed with eight 15" guns each.

TABLE IV

Disposition of British Fleet, 1899–1914

Location	Fleet	Ship Types	1899/1900	1901/2	1903/4	1905/6	1907/8	1909/10	1911/12	1913/14
Far East	East Asia	Dreadnought Btshp								1
		Dreadnought Bt. Crs.								1
		Battleships	3	5	4	5	4	4		
		Armored cruisers	4	3	2	2	4	4	5	2
		Cruisers	23	31	20	19	14	16	17	11
Mediterranean	Med.	Dreadnought Btshp								4
		Dreadnought Bt. Crs.								4
		Battleships	11	12	14	12	8	6	6	
		Armored cruisers					3	3	3	3
		Cruisers	10	14	13	11	10	5	5	4
America & Africa		Dreadnought Btshp								
		Dreadnought Bt. Crs.								
		Battleships	2	1	1	1				
		Armored cruisers	1	1	1		No longer a separate fleet			
		Cruisers	15	20	18	13	13	11	token forces only	
England	Home	Dreadnought Btshp	1	1	2	6	8	13	15	18
		Dreadnought Bt. Crs.			3	3	4	5	5	4

TABLE IV (Continued)

Location	Fleet	Ship Types	1899/1900	1901/2	1903/4	1905/6	1907/8	1909/10	1911/12	1913/14
		Battleships	20	18	19	24	16	11	10	23
		Armored cruisers	2	2	2	12	14	10	17	17
		Cruisers	7	8	6	6	10	7	10	12
	Inactive*	Dreadnought Btshp								4
		Dreadnought Bt. Crs.								
		Battleships	16	14	13	19	8	16	18	14
		Armored cruisers	3	4	5	7	10	19	10	12
		Cruisers	62	49	68	49	38	37	33	28
	Total Home Waters	Dreadnought Btshp					1	3	10	22
		Dreadnought Bt. Crs.						3	4	4
		Battleships	36	32	32	43	24	27	28	37
		Armored cruisers	5	6	7	19	24	29	27	29
		Cruisers	69	57	74	55	48	44	43	40
	Total Completed	Dreadnought Btshp					2	6	14	22
		Dreadnought Bt. Crs.						3	7	9
		Battleships	52	49	49	56	31	34	34	38
		Armored cruisers	9	9	11	26	31	36	35	35
		Cruisers	118	118	122	70	67	63	65	65

* Includes ships completed during year but not assigned to a particular fleet.

SOURCE: *Brassey's Naval Annuals*, 1899–1914.

TABLE V

Battle Fleet Comparisons, Germany and Great Britain, 1899–1914

Country	Fleet	Ship Types	1899/1900	1901/2	1903/4	1905/6	1907/8	1909/10	1911/12	1913/14
Germany	High Seas	Dreadnought Btshps.						2	7	9
		Dreadnought Bt. Crs.						1	1	3
		Battleships				14	16	14	12	8
		Armored Cruisers				2	4	4	3	1
	Reserve	Dreadnought Btshps.								
		Dreadnought Bt. Crs.								
		Battleships							8	6
		Armored Cruisers								3
	Inactive*	Dreadnought Btshps.						1	1	3
		Dreadnought Bt. Crs.							1	2
		Battleships				8	10	10	17	10
		Armored Cruisers				4	2	5	4	5
	Home Waters	Dreadnought Btshps.						4	8	16
		Dreadnought Bt. Crs.						4	3	5
		Battleships	15	19	22	22	26	28	23	21
		Armored Cruisers	16					9	9	8
Ship Under 20 Years in Home Waters*										
	Great Britain	Dreadnought Btshps.				1	1	6	14	22
		Dreadnought Bt. Crs.					2	3	7	4
		Battleships	21	32	37	44	43	41	31	35
		Armored Cruisers	3	21	19	24	24	29	27	29
	Germany	Dreadnought Btshps.						4	8	16
		Dreadnought Bt. Crs.							3	5
		Battleships	9	11	15	19	22	24	27	20
		Armored Cruisers	3	3	4	6	6	9	9	8

* Includes ships completed but not assigned to a particular fleet.

NOTE: German ships in the Far East include 1 armored cruiser from 1907–1910 and 2 for the 1911–1914 period.

SOURCE: Brassey's Naval Annuals, 1899–1914. (Data are not available on fleet distributions for Germany prior to 1906.)

TABLE VI

Battleship, Armored Cruiser, and Battle Cruiser Characteristics by Launch Date, 1899–1914, Great Britain and Germany

Ship Type/Year/Country	Number launched	Tonnage per ship (000)	Complement per ship (000)	Horsepower per ship (000)	Speed	Over 14 in.	12 in. to 14 in.	10 in. to 12 in.	8 in. to 10 in.	5.9 in. to 8 in.	Coal Normal (000)	Coal Maximum (000)	Belt (in inches)*	Turrets (in inches)*	Cost per ship (Thousands of £)	Completion Date
Battleship																
1899 Great Britain	7	14	8	15	18		4			12	9	20	9HS 7KS	12HS 11KS	1018	1901–2 1902–3
Germany	2	11	7	13	18				4	18	6	10	6HS 11.75HS	12HS 9.75HNS	962	1904–2 1901–2
1900 Great Britain																
Germany	1	11	7	13	18				4	18	6	10	11.75HS	9.75HNS	962	1901–1
1901 Great Britain	4	14	7	18	19		4			12	9	20	7KS	11KS	1098	1903–4
Germany	5	12	7	14	18				4	18	7	14	7KS 9KS	11ST 10KS	1060	1902–3 1903–2
1902 6 Great Britain	2	15	8	15	18		4			12	9	20	9HS	12HS	1095	1904–2
Germany	1	13	7	16	18			4		14	7	16	9KS	10KS	1158	1904–1
1903 Great Britain	4	16	8	18	19		4			10	10	22	9HS	12HS	1400	1905–4
Germany	2 3	12 13	7 7	12 16	20 18			4 4		14 14	8 7	20 16	7ST 9KS	7KS 10KS	959 1158	1904–2 1905–3
1904 Great Britain	2	16	8	18	19		4			10	10	22	9HS	12HS	1437	1906–1
Germany	2	13	7	16	18			4		14	7	16	9KS	10KS	1186	1906–2
1905 Great Britain	2	16	8	18	19		4			10	10	22	9HS	12HS	1453	1906–2
Germany	2	13	7	17	18			4		14	7	16	9KS 9.5KS	10KS 10KS	1186	1907–2
1906 3 Great Britain	2 1	16 18	9 8	17 28	19 22		4 10		10		9 9	25 27	12KS 11KS	12ST 11ST	1643 1813	1908–2 1906–1
Germany	2	13	7	17	18			4		14	7	16	9.5KS	10KS	1214	1908–2

Number of guns per ship | Coal capacity | Armor (columns as noted below)

Ship Type / Year / Country	Number launched	Tonnage per ship (000)	Complement per ship (000)	Horsepower per ship (000)	Speed	Over 14 in.	12 in. to 14 in.	10 in. to 12 in.	8 in. to 10 in.	5.9 in. to 8 in.	Coal Normal (000)	Coal Maximum (000)	Belt* (in inches)	Turrets* (in inches)	Cost per ship (Thousands of £)	Completion date
1907																
Great Britain	3	19	9	23	22		10				9	n.a.	11KS	11KS	1702	1909–3
Germany																
1908																
Great Britain	2	19	7	24	22		10				9	n.a.	7HS / 10ST	9ST / 9ST	1744 / 1825	1910–2 / 1909–1
Germany	4	18	10	25	21			12		12	10	27	12KS	11KS		1910–3
1909																
Great Britain	1 / 1	20 / 19	8 / 8	28 / 24	22 / 22		10 / 10				9 / 9		10ST / 7HS	9ST / 9ST	1662 / n.a.	1910–1 / 1911–1
Germany	3	22	11	28	20		12			14	9	30	10.5KS	11KS		1910–1 / 1911–2
1910																
Great Britain	1 / 1	20 / 20	8 / 8	25 / 29	22 / 22		8 / 10				9 / 9		11ST	10ST	1665	1911–2
Germany	1	22	11	28	20					14	9	30	10.5KS	11KS	n.a.	1912–1
1911																
Great Britain	4 / 2	22 / 23	7 / 9	27 / 27	21 / 21		10 / 10				9		12ST	10ST	1910	1912–1 / 1913–2
Germany	2	24	11	28	24					14	10	36	13.75KS	12KS	n.a.	1912–2
1912																
Great Britain	2 / 2	23 / 25	9 / 9	28 / 30	22 / 21		10 / 10				9 / 9		12ST / 12ST	10ST / 6ST	1951 / 2062	1913–2 / 1912–2
Germany	2	24	11	28	24					14	10	36	13.75KS	12KS	n.a.	1913–1
1913																
Great Britain	2 / 1	25 / 28	10 / 10	29 / 37	21 / 23	10	10			16 / 14	9 / 12	n.a.	12ST	n.a.	2023 / n.a.	1913–2 / 1914–2
Germany	2	26	12	35	23	16	10			14	15	30	14KS	14KS	2023	1915–1
1914																
Great Britain	1 / 1	28 / 26	10 / 12	60 / 35	25 / 23	8 / 16	10			12 / 14	n.a. / 15	n.a. / 30	13ST / 14KS	10ST / 14KS	n.a. / 2023	1914–2 / 1914–3
Germany	2	n.a.	n.a.	n.a.	n.a.	8				16	n.a.		n.a.	n.a.	n.a.	

Totals:

	Great Britain	Germany
Battleships	48	37
Pre-Dreadnoughts	24	18
Dreadnoughts	24	19

* Code for these columns:
HS = Harvey Steel
KS = Krupp Steel
HNS = Harvey Nickel Steel
ST = Steel (probably Krupp Steel)

TABLE VI (Continued)

Ship Type/Year/Country	Number launched	Tonnage per ship (000)	Complement per ship (000)	Horsepower per ship (000)	Speed	Over 14 in.	12 in. to 14 in.	10 in. to 12 in.	8 in. to 10 in.	5.9 in. to 8 in.	Coal Normal (000)	Coal Maximum (000)	Belt (in inches)*	Turrets (in inches)*	Cost per ship (Thousands of £)	Completion date
Armored Cruiser																
1899																
Great Britain	2	12	8	21	21				2	12	8	16	6ST	6ST	770	1901–1
Germany																1902–1
1900																
Great Britain (4)	2	12	8	21	21				2	12	8	16	6ST	6ST	788	1902–1
	2	10	7	22	23					14	8	16	4ST	4KS	n.a.	1903–1
Germany	1	9	5	15	20				2	10	10	n.a.	4KS	6KS	n.a.	1902–1
1901																
Great Britain (9)	4	10	7	22	23		8			14	7	18	4ST	4KS	757	1902–2
	4	14	8	31	23				2	16	12	25	6KS	7KS	1035	1903–6
	1	12	8	21	21				2	12	8	16	6ST	6ST	818	1904–1
Germany	1	9	5	16	21				4	10	10	15	3KS	6KS	885	1903–1
1902																
Great Britain (3)	2	10	7	22	24		8			14	7	18	4ST	4KS	766	1902–1
	1	12	8	21	21					10	2	12	6ST	6KS	750	1903–1
Germany	1	9	5	18	21				4	10	10	15	4KS	8ST	875	1905–1
																1903–1
1903																
Great Britain (5)	3	11	7	21	22		8			10	8	20	6HNS	6HNS	862	1904–2
	2	10	7	22	23					14	7	18	4ST	4KS	743	1905–3
Germany	1	9	6	19	21				4	10	8	18	4KS	4KS	875	1905–1
1904																
Great Britain (5)	3	11	7	21	22				6	10	8	20	6HNS	6HNS	860	1905–2
	2	14	8	24	23				4	4	10	n.a.	6KS	6ST	1170	1906–3
Germany	1	9	6	19	21					10	8	16	4KS	4KS	875	1905–1
1905																
Great Britain (4)	4	14	8	24	23				6	4	10	n.a.	6KS	6ST	1200	1906–2
Germany																1907–2
1906																
Great Britain	2	15	8	28	23				4	10	10	n.a.	6ST	8ST	1430	1908–2
Germany	2	12	6	26	24				8	6	8	20	6KS	6.75KS	n.a.	1908–2

Ship Type/Year/Country	Number launched	Tonnage per ship (000)	Complement per ship (000)	Horsepower per ship (000)	Speed	Over 14 in.	12 in. to 14 in.	10 in. to 12 in.	8 in. to 10 in.	5.9 in. to 8 in.	Normal (000)	Maximum (000)	Belt (in inches)*	Turrets (in inches)*	Cost per ship (Thousands of £)	Completion date
1907																
Great Britain	1	15	8	27	23				4	10	10	n.a.	6ST	8ST	1384	1909–1
Germany																
1908																
Great Britain	1	16	8	40	25				12	8	9	23	6KS	6KS	1250	1909–1
Germany																
Totals	Great Britain 35; Germany 8															
Battle Cruiser																
1907																
Great Britain	3	17	7	41	25		8				10	n.a.	7ST	4ST	1750	1908–2
Germany																1909–1
1908																
Great Britain																
Germany																
1909																
Great Britain	1	19	8	43	25		8				10	n.a.	6ST	4ST	1537	1911–1
Germany	1	19	10	71	28			8		10	10	28	6KS	8KS	1832	1910–1
1910																
Great Britain	1	26	10	76	28		8				10	n.a.	9ST	9ST	2086	1912–1
Germany																
1911																
Great Britain	2 { 1 / 1	19 / 26	8 / 10	44 / 76	25 / 28		8 / 8				10 / 10	n.a. / n.a.	6ST / 9ST	4ST / 9ST	n.a. / 2089	1912–2
Germany	2 { 1 / 1	23 / 23	10 / 10	70 / 87	29 / 28			10 / 10		12 / 12	10 / 10	31 / 31	7.5KS / 7.5KS	8KS / 8KS	n.a. / n.a.	1911–1 / 1912–1
1912																
Great Britain	1	26	10	76	28		8			12	10	n.a.	9ST	9ST	2078	1914–1
Germany	1	25	10	50	29			10			11	36	11KS	11KS	n.a.	1913–1
1913																
Great Britain	1	28	10	99	28		8			12	30	n.a.	9ST	9ST	n.a.	1914–1
Germany	2	28	11	99	27		8 / 8			12 / 12	n.a.	n.a.	7KS	10KS	n.a.	1914–1 / 1915–1
1914																
Great Britain																
Germany																
Totals	Great Britain 9; Germany 6															

Appendix B

Derivation of the Koopman Probability Distribution

Given:

$$\frac{dP(m, n, t)}{dt} = m[P(m, n+1, t) - P(m, n, t)] + n[P(m+1, n, t) -$$

$$P(m, n, t)] = mP(m, n+1, t) + nP(m+1, n, t) - (m+n) P(m, n, t)$$

$$\tag{1}$$

$$\text{for } m > 0, n > 0 \text{ subject to } P(m_o, n_{\bar{o}}, 0) = 1$$
$$P(m, n, t) = 0 \text{ for } m > m_o \text{ or } n > n_{\bar{o}}.$$

To show:

$$P(m, n, t) = c(m, n) \, e^{-(m+n)t} \, (1 - e^{-t})^{m_o + n_o - m - n}$$

$$\text{where } c(m, n) = \frac{mc(m, n+1) + nc(m+1, n)}{m_o + n_o - m - n} \text{ for } m > 0, n > 0.$$

$$\tag{2}$$

$$\text{given that } c(m_o, n_o) = 1, c(m, n) = 0 \text{ for } m > m_o \text{ or } n > n_o.$$

If (2) holds, then

$$\frac{dP(m, n, t)}{dt} = mc(m, n+1) \, e^{-(m+n+1)t} \, (1 - e^{-t})^{m_o + n_o - m - n - 1}$$

$$+ nc(m+1, n) \, e^{-(m+n+1)t} \, (1 - e^{-t})^{m_o + n_o - m - n - 1} -$$
$$(m+n) \, c(m, n) \, e^{-(n+m)t} \, (1 - e^{-t})^{m+n-m-n} =$$
$$[e^{-(m+n)t} \, (1 - e^{-t})^{m_o + n_o - m - n^{-1}}]$$
$$\{[mc(m, n+1) + nc(m+1, n)] \, e^{-t} - (m+n) \, c(m, n) \, (1 - e^{-t})\}$$

Thus:

$$\frac{dP(m, n, t)}{dt} = [\, c(m, n) \, e^{-(m+n)t} \, (1 - e^{-t})^{m_o + n_o - m - n - 1}]$$

$$\{(m_o + n_{\bar{o}} - m - n) \, e^{-t} - (m+n) \, (1 - e^{-t})\}$$

$$\tag{3}$$

Similarly, differentiating (2) we obtain

$$\frac{dP(m, n, t)}{dt} = c(m, n) \, \{e^{-(m+n)t} \, (m_o + n_{\bar{o}} - m - n)$$

$$(1 - e^{-t})^{m_o + n_o - m - n - 1} \, e^{-t} + (1 - e^{-t})^{m_o + n_o - m - n}$$
$$(-(m+n)) \, e^{-(m+n)t}\}$$

Therefore:

$$\tag{4}$$

$$\frac{dP(m, n, t)}{dt} = [\, c(m, n) \, e^{-(m+n)t} \, (1 - e^{-t})^{m_o + n_o - m - n - 1}]$$

$$\{(m_o + n_o - m - n) \, e^{-t} - (1 - e^{-t}) \, (m+n)\}$$

which is identical to the expression (3).

Further note that $P(m, n, 0) = 0$ for $m \neq m_o, n \neq n_{\bar{o}}$, and $P(m_o, n_o, 0) = 1, P(m, n, t) = 0$ for $m > m_o$ or $n > n_o$.

Since

$$\frac{dP(m, 0, t)}{dt} = mP(m, 1, t)$$

$$\frac{dP(0, n, t)}{dt} = nP(1, m, t)$$

we have $\dfrac{dP(m, 0, t)}{dt} = mc(m, 1)\ e^{-(m + 1)t}\ (1 - e^{-t})^{m_o + n_o - m - 1}$

$$\therefore P(m, 0, t) = mc(m, 1)\ \int e^{-(m + 1)t}\ (1 - e^{-t})^{m_o + n_o - m - 1}\ dt$$

$$= mc(m, 1)\ \int e^{-(m + 1)t} \sum_{r = 0}^{m_o + n_o - m - 1} (-1)^r \binom{m_o + n_{\bar{o}} - m - 1}{r}\ e^{-rt}\ dt$$

Therefore

$$P(m, 0, t) = mc(m, 1) \sum_{r = 0}^{m_o + n_o - m - 1} (-1)^r \binom{m_o + n_{\bar{o}} - m - 1}{r}\ \cdot$$

$$\int e^{-(m + 1 + r)t}\ dt = mc(m, 1) \sum_{r = 0}^{m_o + n_o - m - 1} (-1)^r \binom{m_o + n_o - m - 1}{r}$$

$$\left(\dfrac{-e^{-(m + 1 + r)t}}{(m + 1 + r)}\right) + c(m, 0)$$

Since $P(m, 0, 0) = 0$

$$P(m, 0, t) = mc(m, 1) \sum_{r = 0}^{m_o + n_o - m - 1} (-1)^r \binom{m_o + n_{\bar{o}} - m - 1}{r}$$

$$\left(\dfrac{1}{m + 1 + r}\right)(1 - e^{-(m + 1 + r)t})$$ and similarly for $P(0, n, t)$.

PART V

1. The New England Textile Industry, 1825-60: Trends and Fluctuations[*]

Lance E. Davis
Purdue University

H. Louis Stettler III
Johns Hopkins University

I. Introduction

MANY STUDIES of the growth of the American economy during the first three quarters of the 19th century have suffered both from the diffusion of their focus and from the weakness of their statistical foundations. Reliance on the federal census returns necessitates estimating the underreportings that plague those volumes and, perhaps more important, limits the study to bench-mark years—a limitation that excludes any discussion of fluctuations between those years. Moreover, these studies have frequently attempted to draw economywide conclusions from data indicative of conditions in only a local area or, conversely, to describe each area in terms of a national average. Thus, there have been frequent attempts to apply technical coefficients or economic relations derived from one area to another region characterized by an entirely different technology or subject to very different market forces.

For most of the period before 1870, no national market existed for many industries. In this period it appears almost useless to study the economy as an integrated whole rather than as a sum of various quite heterogeneous parts. Any national figures, almost by definition, blur the local characteristics; and, all too frequently, marginal changes (changes that are small, but possibly of crucial importance for growth) in local figures get lost in the national totals. Ideally, it would be best to study every industry in every region; however, because of the scarcity of source material, it is improbable that this goal can be achieved. What is more

[*] Reprinted from *Output, Employment, and Productivity in the United States after 1800,* (1966), pp. 213–38.

possible, however, is a study of the important industries in each region during those periods when the industry was changing rapidly (either expanding or contracting). Since almost all industries that play a significant role in the process of economic growth could be included in this more restrictive study, such an approach seems fruitful despite the narrowing of focus. At the same time, insofar as it is possible to estimate output from all industries in all regions, studies of aggregate income will not be hampered. In fact, even these broader studies may be improved, since a comparison of local firm records with census reports may provide a better measure of underreporting than anything previously available.[1]

Furthermore, from the point of view of economic theory, a certain economy is achieved in studying those sectors that are undergoing rapid change. Moreover, since rapidly changing industries or those heavily concentrated (geographically) tend to leave business records and other economic artifacts which may substitute for the census as a source of statistical data, there is an additional incentive to adopt this regional methodology.

II. The Estimates

The Data

The cotton textile industry provides a fine example of what can be done with a regional approach (in fact, the example may be too good). The industry was heavily concentrated in New England and, within New England, the growth of the industry after 1820 was associated with the rise of a particular group of firms. Fortunately there exist today, at various museums and libraries on the East Coast, the original business records of a significant proportion of these firms.[2]

---

[1] The records of some of the textile mills, for example, include copies of the census enumerators' reports as well as their mill records—which show quite different totals. The following table shows the discrepancies for six mills reporting to the 1859 Census (in millions of yards).

	Total	Merri- mack	Hamil- ton	Suffolk	Tremont	Law- rence	Massa- chusetts Cotton
Reported..........	96.0	20.8	12.2	8.0	11.9	18.7	24.4
Actual............	96.4	22.1	11.6	8.5	11.0	18.6	24.6

These six firms are a sample; all errors exceed 5 percent, but they appear random with mean equal to zero. There is, of course, no guarantee of the randomness of the errors. More important objections to use of the federal census after 1820 for the textile industry flow from (1) constantly changing definitions (e.g., establishment); (2) the paucity of information gathered and reported vis-à-vis the Massachusetts census (especially the failure to report yards of output in 1839); (3) the lack of a local breakdown in 1850; and (4) the number of different "official" versions.

[2] The materials for this paper were gathered from various textile collections deposited at the Baker Library, Harvard, the Merrimack Valley Textile Museum, and the Manchester Historical Society Museum. There are to the knowledge of the authors other collections in the possession of local historical and academic units; in fact,

There were two principal types of textile firms in New England.[3] The firms of the Massachusetts type, modeled after the Boston Manufacturing Company, were located on the major rivers of northern New England. They were typically multifacility operations (sometimes with bleacheries or printworks) and generally capitalized in excess of $500,000. From the beginning, these firms were integrated producing units heavily concentrated in the low-count goods. Existing alongside the Massachusetts-type operations were a much larger number of small proprietary single-mill firms located on the streams of lower New England. These so-called Rhode Island-type mills were small, often specialized, and tended to produce medium grades of cloth (particularly printing cloths).[4] During the mid-1840's the structure of the industry in lower New England changed, and thereafter the Rhode Island mills began to resemble their northern counterparts more closely.

Table 1 lists the firms whose records were used in this study. The distribution of firms is not wholly geographical. Firms of the Rhode Island type were located in Massachusetts as well as in Rhode Island and Connecticut. Moreover, although Metacomet was located in New Bedford and resembled the larger firms, it was really representative of the post-1845 mills springing up in lower New England, and was therefore included as a Rhode Island-type mill.

The company records for at least 16 of the Massachusetts-type mills exist for at least some part of the period prior to the Civil War. The journals, semiannual accounts, and treasurer's reports give sufficient information to ascertain the amount of cloth produced by each firm.[5] Generally, the output by six-month periods is available, but for certain years the output of Nashua and Jackson was only given on a yearly basis. For the Rhode Island-type firms, output could be estimated from either weaving ledgers or consignment books.[6] Typically, these data were available on a monthly basis.

---

the problem of data is not its insufficiency but rather its overabundance. In choosing the particular data used in this paper, preference was given to those records that were complete and continuous for long periods, and reasonably intelligible.

[3] The relative contributions of the two families of firms to the growth of the New England textile industry might be seen from the county returns in Massachusetts. Middlesex and Hampden counties included the large mill centers of Chicopee and Lowell; Bristol and Worcester counties were always centers of the smaller enterprises. The number of spindles (in thousands) follows:

	1820	1837	1855
Middlesex-Hampden..............	10	233	635
Bristol-Worcester	18	240	508

[4] The best discussion of the two types of enterprise is found in Caroline Ware's *The Early New England Cotton Manufacture* (Cambridge, Mass., 1931).

[5] In some cases it was necessary to add yards sold to the change in inventory for a period, since output figures were not always present whereas sales and inventory values were more common.

[6] The use of the consignment books introduces a sequence of lags, since there is no way of dating consignments in terms of the time elapsed between production and

TABLE 1
SAMPLE MILLS, 1815–60

Firm Name	Years for Which Records Were Examined
MASSACHUSETTS TYPE	
Boston	1815–60
Merrimack	1824–60
Hamilton	1828–60
Suffolk	1832–60
Tremont	1832–60
Lawrence	1833–60
Massachusetts Cotton	1840–60
Naumkeag	1848–60
Lancaster	1847–60
Dwight*	1834–60†
Lyman*	1850–60
Nashua	1826–60
Jackson	1832–60
Amoskeag*	1837–60
Laconia	1845–60
Pepperill	1851–60
RHODE ISLAND TYPE	
Rampo	1821–33
Slater	1826–34
Slater and Tiffany	1827–37
Sutton	1830–59
Metacomet	1848–60

* Records are available for different groups of mills operated by these companies.
† Includes the records of the Cabot and Perkins Companies which were merged into Dwight in 1856.

Adjustments to a Uniform Accounting Period

Reporting techniques differed greatly from mill to mill. Every month represented the closing of at least one company's accounts. Moreover, companies changed their final closing date from time to time. To make the data comparable, each mill's output was allocated uniformly over the months covered by the accounting period. Uniform allocation was selected for a number of reasons. First, it has been generally inferred that the short-run marginal cost curves were steep about some "capacity" level.[7] Second, the data required to construct a monthly deflating index were not available. What data exist are generally of poor quality because they represent only the history of the Rhode Island-type mills, whose output was often curtailed in response to a freshet or to install new equipment. These conditions were not characteristic of the rest of the industry. Third, a monthly index constructed from Rhode Island data,

shipment. In the case of Slater and Tiffany, pounds of cloth produced were known but not yards.

[7] See R. C. O. Mathews, *A Study in Trade-Cycle History* (Cambridge, Eng.), p. 130.

Nashua reports, and consumption of cotton in Cabot mill number 1 (where monthly data were available), with adjustments made for floods, replacement of equipment, and other local events, is not significantly different from the results achieved by uniform allocation. The monthly figures were summed to standard quarters and calendar years. Annual

TABLE 2

QUARTERLY OUTPUT OF SELECTED FIRMS OF THE
MASSACHUSETTS TYPE, 1821–60
(Thousand Yards)

Year	Jan. 1– Mar. 31	April 1– June 30	July 1– Sept. 30	Oct. 1– Dec. 31
1821........	337	363	370	384
1822........	403	439	420	380
1823........	408	465	454	433
1824........	451	487	483	865
1825........	1,044	886	813	774
1826........	783	988	1,138	1,168
1827........	1,193	1,442	1,659	1,658
1828........	2,414	2,688	2,858	2,746
1829........	2,569	2,681	2,702	2,711
1830........	2,711	3,032	3,354	3,282
1831........	3,701	3,899	4,036	3,956
1832........	4,094	4,604	5,799	6,091
1833........	6,956	7,481	7,975	8,052
1834........	8,570	9,050	9,001	9,038
1835........	9,971	10,920	11,282	11,196
1836........	11,534	12,328	12,642	12,186
1837........	12,690	12,620	12,063	11,746
1838........	12,610	13,884	14,241	14,028
1839........	14,461	15,080	14,961	14,540
1840........	14,471	13,877	13,406	14,083
1841........	14,734	15,088	16,020	16,234
1842........	16,888	16,913	16,404	16,047
1843........	15,727	15,868	16,697	16,958
1844........	17,878	17,916	18,783	18,596
1845........	19,622	19,994	21,163	21,296
1846........	21,747	21,863	21,718	21,882
1847........	22,271	22,474	22,593	22,923
1848........	24,073	25,680	27,260	26,786
1849........	28,030	28,229	28,994	29,827
1850........	27,782	27,604	29,129	28,022
1851........	28,249	28,799	31,452	32,832
1852........	34,427	35,246	37,102	37,272
1853........	34,580	31,172	35,938	36,509
1854........	35,198	35,241	35,993	36,446
1855........	35,976	36,018	35,396	35,956
1856........	37,316	37,258	38,132	38,570
1857........	34,638	33,929	31,451	29,474
1858........	33,561	35,984	39,373	40,840
1859........	40,962	41,350	42,889	43,430
1860........	43,084	43,229	40,881	40,447

SOURCE: Company records of Boston, Merrimack, Hamilton, Suffolk, Tremont, Lawrence, Naumkeag, Lancaster, Dwight, Lyman, Nashua, Jackson, Amoskeag, Laconia, and Pepperill.

output by firm may be found in Table A–1, while the quarterly output of selected Massachusetts firms will be found summed in Table 2.

Choice of Output Measure

The output reported in these tables is in terms of yards. The company books described output variously—in pieces, pounds, and yards. Yards were, however, the most common; they were available in all but a single case. Pieces, a widely varying metric, were the least common. Pounds of output, when not reported, could usually be estimated from the weight of cotton inputs corrected for the mill's waste factor or from the yards of output, if the weight per yard ratios were available for the full range of product. Yards were used as the measure for this study, because they represented a more meaningful unit of demand, because they were more generally available, and because they appear to be a more useful tool in comparing input and output ratios.[8] Despite these advantages, yards are not a perfect measure. Because of the lack of homogeneity arising from changing width and count patterns, they too may be criticized. However, tests suggest that for this sample at least the bias injected by nonhomogeneity may not be too significant.[9]

Adjustment to Regional Levels

Table 3 shows the relationship between sample output and the output of various regions as they appeared in the census. The relationships are rather stable except for the initial change in the thirties. This jump may

---

[8] Robert Layer (in *Earnings of Cotton Mill Operatives, 1825–1914* [Cambridge, Mass., 1955]) feels that pounds are a superior measure. Nominally, pounds ignore width differentials but not count differences. Since yards and standard yards appear to have a relatively stable relationship on the aggregate level, the question of unit recedes in significance. Output in yards or pounds would differ by a scale factor. There are, however, certain marginal considerations which make yards preferable. In estimating production functions, the marginal products of labor, cotton, and capital can be ascertained by using yards as a measure of output; if, on the other hand, pounds were used, the rather constant proportion between cotton input and cloth output (regardless of the quality of output) does not allow the other parameters to have significant coefficients.

[9] For those mills that reported both yardage and pounds, it was possible to compensate for quality and width differences by converting their output into standard yards. Therefore, the 39 mills with data on both yardage and pounds were divided into two classes, those producing mostly low-count (under 16) goods and those producing finer quality (over 18) cottons. The output of the former class were then converted into standard 14s × 14s, 48 × 48, 36″ wide brown sheeting; and the latter's output into 22s × 22s, 40, 36″ wide sheeting. Apart from the late twenties, when the sample size was small (only 13 mills), the relations between standard and recorded yards was extremely stable (see Table A–2); and both series tend to move together. In the thirties, for example, there was first a movement toward heavier goods and then a movement toward lighter ones. If, however, total standard yards (the sum of the standard columns) is compared with total recorded yards, a slight trend toward the coarser cloth is evident.

be explained in terms of the development of Lowell and the later textile centers in Manchester and Springfield. In Massachusetts, the sample shows a gain of 3 firms between 1832 and 1834 (Suffolk, Tremont, and Lawrence), while 18 were actually incorporated. During the period 1828–30, however, only Hamilton enters the sample while 24 firms were incorporated. A portion of the fall in relative output recorded in 1860 is a result of firms leaving the sample in that year.

TABLE 3

RATIO OF OUTPUTS OF SAMPLE FIRMS TO CENSUS OUTPUT TOTALS
SELECTED YEARS, 1831–59

Year	Rhode Island, Connecticut	Massachusetts	Maine, New Hampshire	New England
1831........	.04	.16	.10	.11
1837........		.29		
1839*......	.01	.30	.40	.22
1845........		.28		
1849........	.04	.23	.32	.19
1855........		.29		
1859........	.03	.26	.29	.20

* Ratio based on estimate of textile output.
SOURCE: 1840, 1850, 1860 federal censuses; 1831, from Survey of Friends of Domestic Industry; 1837, 1845, 1855 Massachusetts censuses.

The movements in the sample output series may be used to provide an index of cyclical movements in textile output. Moreover, when inflated to approximate total production they furnish a measure of total output between bench-mark years. Their usefulness, however, depends on the validity of two assumptions: that the sample of firms is representative of the entire industry, and that the census provides adequate estimates of total output in the bench-mark years. As to the first, the evidence suggests that the sample of Massachusetts-type firms was quite representative of the entire universe, but that the sample of Rhode Island firms was probably less so. As to the second, the Massachusetts inflations based on the state census probably provide a more trustworthy measure of activity in the bench-mark years than the New Hampshire-Maine and New England inflations based on the federal census do.[10]

The results of such inflations are presented in Table 4. The Massachusetts mills were inflated on a straight-line basis between the census years 1831, 1837, 1845, and 1855. The series was extrapolated to 1860 according to the 1845–55 increments; and backward extrapolation from 1831 to 1825 was based on an incremental change of zero. This latter extrapolation probably overstates output in the earlier years (since it appears that the sample size increased relative to the universe in the

---

[10] Because of omissions in the 1840 census, it was necessary to estimate textile output and this procedure injects another element of bias into the inflation based on the federal census.

period) but, in the absence of any bench-mark, it remains the best alternative.

The Maine and New Hampshire inflation was based on the federal census and the survey of 1831. The same basic procedure used in the Massachusetts inflation was followed, but the 1825–31 period was treated in the same manner as the 1831–39 interval. Rhode Island and Connecticut were treated in the same manner as Maine and New Hampshire; however, the changing sample size during the intercensual period created additional problems. Even if these could be solved, however, the smallness of the Rhode Island and Connecticut sample, particularly in the

TABLE 4
Output by Region, 1826–60
(Thousand Yards)

	Sample			Inflated			
Year	Rhode Island, Connecticut	Massachusetts	Maine, New Hampshire	Rhode Island, Connecticut	Massachusetts	Maine, New Hampshire	New England
1826....	770	3,757	321	27,018	23,475	3,211	37,072
1827....	1,337	4,920	1,031	37,100	30,753	10,313	54,107
1828....	1,427	8,768	1,939	35,731	54,797	19,386	97,327
1829....	1,050	8,313	2,350	32,194	51,957	23,501	96,937
1830....	1,536	9,895	2,484	42,715	61,845	24,838	112,536
1831....	2,035	12,637	2,955	47,212	79,231	30,810	141,727
1832....	1,813	14,730	5,858	44,167	81,832	41,841	175,961
1833....	1,605	22,434	8,029	45,650	106,828	50,183	245,672
1834....	1,240	27,558	8,092	47,391	111,482	44,954	272,129
1835....	1,125	35,262	8,107	44,642	130,598	40,533	314,262
1836....	1,489	38,531	10,159	58,421	132,866	46,178	335,797
1837....	1,014	35,453	13,667	69,926	118,175	56,944	323,151
1838....	1,190	39,675	15,088	99,083	134,449	58,030	359,868
1839....	893	42,714	16,328	85,769	147,288	58,316	369,014
1840....	372	40,900	14,938	80,870	143,509	53,349	371,012
1841....	710	44,876	17,201	151,064	160,272	61,431	432,476
1842....	235	45,526	20,726	48,750	165,548	74,023	437,005
1843....	993	44,936	20,520	198,400	175,756	73,303	426,125
1844....	741	48,332	24,842	145,098	179,000	88,721	465,593
1845....	778	48,434	33,643	149,231	179,958	120,152	497,640
1846....	711	51,752	35,461	133,962	190,097	126,649	527,120
1847....	834	54,849	35,417	151,455	203,150	126,487	532,422
1848....	5,157	65,790	38,642	117,740	240,988	138,007	589,217
1849....	6,346	68,233	46,848	148,271	242,902	145,989	600,318
1850....	6,143	72,210	40,320	146,962	262,583	127,032	585,179
1851....	4,245	73,513	48,741	103,790	266,350	155,276	634,098
1852....	5,612	86,440	57,609	140,652	312,058	185,596	745,210
1853....	6,168	85,195	55,417	158,154	306,452	180,570	725,552
1854....	5,989	88,627	54,255	157,605	316,521	178,823	735,368
1855....	5,731	91,647	51,603	154,474	328,482	172,067	735,370
1856....	6,142	97,437	53,840	170,139	347,990	181,769	774,588
1857....	5,812	86,445	43,048	165,114	308,732	147,072	661,353
1858....	7,464	93,840	56,510	218,246	347,555	195,401	765,920
1859....	7,456	105,192	63,440	225,939	404,580	222,051	856,362
1860....	6,130	104,570	63,172	245,200	402,192	224,332	850,188

1839–47 period, argues against attaching great significance to the inflated series.

Two different estimates of total New England output suggest themselves. First, it is possible to sum up the inflated series for the three state groups; second, one could inflate, in a manner similar to the treatment of New Hampshire and Maine, the output figures from all mills for which the data were of good quality. The difference between the two series is much greater than can be explained by the exclusion of Vermont from the first variant. Unfortunately, the former series is also subject to wide fluctuations induced by the inclusion of the poor quality series from Rhode Island. As a result, the second technique is almost certainly a better indicator of textile activity in New England, and it is a series so constructed that is included in Table 4.

III. Analysis of Fluctuations in Textile Outputs

Recently there has been some controversy over business fluctuations in the antebellum decades, and the textile series cast some light on the dating of the so-called cycles.[11]

Specific Cycles

The strong trend element and the discrete entry of firms into the sample somewhat complicate the analysis of the fluctuations of textile activity; however, Table 5 presents two series that throw some light on the subject; and Table 6 contrasts the textile series with the National Bureau turning points. Column 1 of Table 5 shows changes in the output of the sample firms of the Massachusetts type after correction for lumpiness of entry. To correct for lumpiness, change in output for any pair of years was calculated by summing the differences in production for only those firms which operated throughout both years. This corrected series indicates four years (1825, 1832, 1842, and 1850) when total sample output increased, but the level of production by established firms contracted. Column 2 presents the first differences for the inflated New England series previously presented in Table 4.

The first cycle apparently reached its peak during the last quarter of 1824 and the first quarter of 1825. Output increased until that date for both sample firms and fell for the next three quarters. Inventories were accumulated during the second half of 1824 and remained at substantial levels until mid-1826. Real sales fell during 1824, recovered during the

---

11 The question of specific cycles was recently raised by Jonathan R. T. Hughes and Nathan Rosenberg in "The United States Business Cycle before 1860: Some Problems of Interpretation," *Economic History Review,* 1963; and some questions of long swings were discussed by Lance E. Davis in "The New England Textile Mills and the Capital Markets: A Study of Industrial Borrowing, 1840–1860," *Journal of Economic History* (March, 1960).

first three quarters of 1825, subsided again until the fourth period of 1826 and the first of 1827. These fluctuations are somewhat at variance with the standard cycle that shows contraction to 1824, recovery during 1824, and contraction again in 1825–26.

All indexes show an increase in textile activity until 1828; however, output increases stopped in the third quarter of that year and did not reach the same level until mid-1830. Inventories increased in the first quarter of 1829 and fell only in the second half of 1830, but real sales fell after mid-1828 and rose again in late 1829. These movements seem to be in accord with measures of general business activity.

The recovery continued until mid-1831, and at that time output peaked for each of the operating companies. Large inventories were, however, accumulated during the next year, and sales fell for the entire sample in 1832. Complete recovery was evident in 1833. It is an open question whether this dip was a product of the smoothing process (since it is not noticeable in the second series) or actually represented a decrease in industry activity. However, additional evidence appears to support the latter conclusions. The standard works on business fluctuations show a general contraction during 1831–34; the Cole and Smith volume-of-trade index shows a drop in 1832; and, perhaps most important, the Rhode Island sample (containing a constant number of firms during this period) shows a decrease in output and a substantial fall in profits.[12]

Textile output increased from 1833 to 1836; however, the rate of growth of output and sales fell substantially during middle and late 1834. After the peak of the third quarter of 1836, output stagnated at a lower level for a year. In the last half of 1837, sales fell sharply, output less rapidly, and inventories accumulated. The severity of the contraction was limited to the third and fourth quarters of 1837. Recovery was immediate and continued sporadically through 1838 and 1839, but the rate of increase was lower in the latter year. Late 1839 and 1840 witnessed a fall in output and sales, and inventories tended to accumulate during the first and third quarters of 1840. The year 1841 marked a moderate recovery in sales and output but only a slight reduction in inventories. The peak of this moderate recovery was reached in the second quarter of 1842, and was followed by three quarters of contracting output. Sales fell during the same period but not as rapidly as production, and as a result inventories were reduced. The trough was reached by the second quarter of 1843. These movements do not coincide precisely with the accepted series. The National Bureau marks 1838 as the trough, but textile activity increased throughout most of that year. Similarly, the N.B.E.R. figures do not show the recovery of 1841 and fall in 1842. The troughs of 1843, however, do coincide. The Cole and Smith series also

---

[12] Arthur H. Cole and Walter B. Smith, *Fluctuations in American Business, 1790–1860* (Cambridge, Mass., 1935).

shows no recovery in 1838, but it does reflect the contraction-expansion-contraction phases of 1840, 1841, and 1842.

The middle and late 1840's witnessed a period of sustained increase in both output and sales of cotton cloth. Inventories were reduced to virtually nothing in 1846, but accumulated during the later forties. The industry's growth rate accelerated rapidly during this period through

TABLE 5

ANNUAL CHANGES IN TEXTILE OUTPUT, 1821–60

Year	Massachusetts, Corrected (Thous. Yards) (1)	New England (Mill. Yards) (2)
1821	194	
1822	187	
1823	119	
1824	137	
1825	—188	
1826	236	
1827	1,164	17
1828	1,037	43
1829	—454	0
1830	1,582	16
1831	2,742	29
1832	—305	34
1833	1,439	70
1834	55	27
1835	7,704	42
1836	3,270	21
1837	—3,079	—13
1838	4,223	37
1839	3,038	9
1840	—1,813	2
1841	3,524	61
1842	—3,039	5
1843	—589	—11
1844	3,396	39
1845	102	32
1846	3,317	29
1847	2,961	5
1848	4,957	57
1849	2,544	11
1850	—855	—15
1851	977	49
1852	10,292	11
1853	—1,247	—20
1854	3,433	10
1855	3,020	0
1856	5,791	39
1857	—10,992	—113
1858	7,394	105
1859	11,353	90
1860	—723	—6

SOURCE: Col. 1 from Table A–1; col. 2 from Table 4.

TABLE 6

OUTPUT TURNING POINTS, TEXTILE SERIES AND
N.B.E.R. ESTIMATES, 1825–58

Trough		Peak	
Textile	*N.B.E.R.*	*Textile*	*N.B.E.R.*
1825	1826	1828	1828
1829	1829	1831	
1832		1833	1833
1834	1834	1836	1836
1837	1838	1839	1839
1840		1842	
1843	1843	1844	1845
1845		1846	
1847	1846	1848	1847
1850	1848	1852	1853
1853	1855	1856	1856
1857	1858	1858	1860

SOURCE: Textile series from Table 5; National Bureau of Economic Research series from W. C. Mitchell, *Business Cycles, The Problem and Its Setting* (New York, 1927), pp. 425–27.

the expansion of existing mills, the entry of new firms at existing sites (the sample added nine new mills built by the old firms and four by new firms), and the development of new sites (for example, Lawrence and New Bedford). The expansion slackened after mid-1848 and ended in the first quarter of 1850, when sales and output fell. Inventories peaked in the fourth quarter, and the trough was reached by the first quarter of 1851. After that date all indexes showed continued improvement until 1853 when output in the first half fell but immediately recovered. This brief drop in production and the concomitant fall in sales were borne entirely by the firms producing finer goods. Output continued to grow during the years 1854, 1855, and 1856. This pattern differs substantially from the general cycle pattern of the National Bureau. Although the Massachusetts data suggest a mild contraction in 1845 and the New Hampshire mills cut back production in late 1847, the Bureau's dates are noticeably out of phase with the fluctuations of textile activity during the 1845–48 period. The textile depression of 1850 seemingly occurred at a time of relative prosperity. Thereafter, however, throughout the mid-1850's textiles appear to have led the economy.

The dominating economic event of the late 1850's was the panic of 1857. Sales and output began to erode early in that year but dropped swiftly during the last half. The year-end inventories were almost twice the level of 1856. Recovery was evident with the new year; predepression levels of sales and output were attained in the third quarter of 1858. Inventories were pared by over 35 percent but were still substantially above the 1856 level. Output and sales reached a prewar peak in 1859; inventories dropped below the 1856 levels; and profits attained their highest level since 1846. Again, the textile industry apparently led the economy.

Long Swings

The data also appear to cast some light on the existence of long swings in the American economy during the antebellum decades. Cole has observed an apparent long swing during the 1840's and 1850's. In his examination of the period, he found a trough in 1843 and another in 1858 and concluded "there evidently were forces which, acting slowly, gave decade-long sustaining power to values."[13] A similar swing was found in

TABLE 7

THREE-YEAR MOVING AVERAGES OF CHANGE IN TEXTILE
OUTPUT, 1822–59

Year	Massachusetts (Thous. Yards) (1)	New England (Mill. Yards) (2)
1822	167	
1823	148	
1824	23	
1825	62	
1826	404	
1827	812	
1828	582	20
1829	722	20
1830	1,292	15
1831	1,341	26
1832	1,294	44
1833	398	44
1834	3,068	46
1835	3,678	30
1836	2,633	17
1837	1,473	15
1838	1,396	11
1839	1,818	16
1840	1,585	24
1841	441	23
1842	33	18
1843	76	11
1844	971	20
1845	2,273	33
1846	2,128	22
1847	3,747	30
1848	3,489	24
1849	2,217	18
1850	890	15
1851	3,473	15
1852	3,342	13
1853	4,161	0
1854	1,737	—3
1855	4,083	16
1856	725	—28
1857	733	10
1858	2,587	27
1859	6,010	—66

SOURCE: Table 5.

[13] Cole and Smith, *Fluctuations,* pp. 126–127.

interest rates of the period.[14] The textile series also show such a swing and, in addition, suggest that the 1843–58 swing was not unique. Table 7 presents three-year moving averages of the changes in textile output. These series indicate a trough in 1843–44, an intervening peak in 1847–49, and a trough in 1856–57. Moreover, they show an earlier swing with an apparent trough in 1824–25 and a peak in 1834–35.

IV. Productivity Change

Table 8, constructed from the spindleage, payroll, and output records of the Tremont, Suffolk, Hamilton, Lawrence, Boston, and Nashua mills, provides some measure of the increase in productivity realized by the Massachusetts-type firms during the antebellum period.[15] Column 1 shows average output per man-day and column 4 average output per spindle in the six mills. Columns 2 and 5 present a three-year moving average of the raw data, and columns 3 and 6, five-year moving averages chosen to smooth the effect of short-term fluctuations.

The series presented in columns 4, 5, and 6 show an increase in output per spindle of almost 50 percent during the 1830's. Thereafter, the series decline slightly, but the fall is merely a reflection of a reduction in the hours of work and implies no decrease in productivity. (When the series are adjusted to a common workday, they display no significant change after 1840.) The labor figures (columns 1, 2, and 3) also indicate a substantial increase in productivity during a part of the period. These latter series display a monotonic increase until about 1850; thereafter, however, output per worker remained relatively constant.

A comparison of the two series with each other and with the usual indexes of business activity produces only tenuous results. Despite what one might think a priori, the two do not move together in the short run. In the long run, the upward trend of labor productivity and the change in the direction of the capital index about 1840 might suggest that innovation before 1840 was capital-saving as well as laborsaving, while thereafter the laborsaving, capital-using innovations appear to have been more prevalent. The short-cycle behavior also displays no consistent patterns, although, as Layer has indicated, the labor productivity fell during the boom of 1846 and increased significantly during the depression of the early 1840's. Moreover, the long swings in productivity usually noted in studies of the long cycles of the post-Civil War economy are notably absent from the textile data.[16]

It has been frequently argued that the American textile industry un-

---

[14] Davis, "The New England Textile Mills," p. 13.

[15] The hourly and daily data for the last four mills was originally gathered by Robert Layer. He generously allowed us to use his worksheets.

[16] The relationships between output and wages are discussed in Robert Layer, *Earnings*, pp. 24–27.

derwent a revolutionary transformation in the decade between 1814 and 1824, but that thereafter technical progress was relatively slow. Certainly the industry during the decade following the War of 1812 was marked by many obvious changes. In terms of industrial organization, the integrated mill, so successfully pioneered by the Boston Manufacturing Company, was widely introduced. Moreover, there were also important

TABLE 8

OUTPUT PER MAN-DAY AND OUTPUT PER SPINDLE-YEAR, 1821–60

Year	Yards Per Man-Day			Yards Per Spindle-Year		
	Raw (1)	3-Year Moving Average (2)	5-Year Moving Average (3)	Raw (4)	3-Year Moving Average (5)	5-Year Moving Average (6)
1821						
1822						
1823						
1824						
1825						
1826						
1827				130		
1828				161	166	
1829				206	195	191
1830				219	222	213
1831	40.07			241	229	243
1832	35.56	35.15		228	264	249
1833	30.02	34.66	37.23	323	262	254
1834	38.59	36.93	37.25	235	267	258
1835	42.19	40.62	39.45	244	246	262
1836	40.07	42.88	42.64	260	251	255
1837	46.39	44.13	44.40	249	265	273
1838	45.94	46.91	45.13	287	287	287
1839	48.39	46.77	46.39	326	309	294
1840	45.88	46.88	47.26	314	311	301
1841	46.38	47.66	48.18	294	297	299
1842	50.72	50.04	50.52	283	285	292
1843	53.03	53.46	52.32	277	284	285
1844	56.62	54.82	53.14	293	283	284
1845	54.82	53.97	53.22	278	287	287
1846	50.47	52.13	54.48	290	288	293
1847	51.09	53.63	55.39	295	298	291
1848	59.33	57.20	57.61	309	296	293
1849	61.19	62.17	60.73	284	294	286
1850	66.00	64.41	63.94	289	276	280
1851	66.05	66.22	65.48	255	269	270
1852	66.62	66.40	66.20	263	260	279
1853	66.53	65.98	65.78	261	280	274
1854	64.80	65.07	64.79	316	285	276
1855	63.88	63.27	62.78	277	285	272
1856	61.14	63.28	65.69	262	261	270
1857	63.83	66.60	67.74	245	252	265
1858	74.82	71.22	66.98	250	262	272
1859	75.01	69.97		292	285	
1860	60.12			313		

SOURCE: Company records of Tremont, Suffolk, Hamilton, Lawrence, Boston, and Nashua.

developments in machine technology. The decade saw the invention and widespread innovation of the power loom, the Waltham dresser, the double speeder and filling frame, the self-acting loom temple, and a number of pickers and openers.[17]

These developments, admittedly of an almost revolutionary character, antedate this study. The study does, however, cast some light on the developments after 1824. The case for relative stagnation in the latter period rests, not on any quantitative evidence, but only on the observation that the changes that did occur do not appear particularly important when contrasted with the developments in the previous period.[18] Gibb, working from the records of the textile machinery firm, has argued that techniques continued to improve rapidly after 1824, and the productivity figures from the Massachusetts mills bear out his conclusions. True, there were no revolutionary changes in industrial organization, but there were developments in textile machinery. The 20 years after 1824 saw the development of the cap spinner and an imperfect ring spinner, the self-acting mule, and improvements in the roving frames. These developments almost certainly contributed to a steady increase in per worker productivity during the 1830's and 1840's. Moreover, new machines do not tell the entire story. More important, throughout the period new refinements were worked out in the machine shop and then were incorporated in the latest models of the old machine.

Also contributing to the rise in per worker productivity and certainly the prime cause of the increasing output per spindle, reflected in the figures in Table 7, was the great rise in spindle speed associated with the innovation of the belt drive. Even if machine technology had not changed, the output of the existing capital stock would have risen significantly because of the much higher operating speeds which could be attained with the new drive system. Before 1828 mechanical problems inherent in the English gear drive (problems that multiplied rapidly in the imperfect American copies of the drive) severely limited operating speed. In that year, however, Paul Moody in building the Appleton mills introduced the belt drive principle to textile production. Thereafter, the new principle was widely imitated and American mills greatly increased their speed of operation.[19]

---

[17] For a detailed account of these developments, see George S. Gibb, *The Saco-Lowell Shops* (Cambridge, Mass., 1950).

[18] In discussing the technology, most works on American history describe the early contributions of Slater and the Waltham system, but fail to emphasize the long-run revolutionary impact of the succession of gradual changes which characterized the period between 1825 and 1850.

At times the authors emphasize innovations which were not widely adopted before the 1860's. (See, for example, H. Faulkner, *American Economic History* [New York, 1960], p. 248.) In other cases, they single out the period after 1850 and gloss over the middle period. (See R. Russel, *A History of the American Economic System* [New York, 1964], p. 179).

[19] Gibb, *Saco-Lowell Shops*, pp. 76–80.

The increase in speed meant that output per spindle rose by almost 50 percent. The number of spindles has been used typically as an index of textile capital, but the increase in output per spindle implies that such a measure cannot be reliably employed in any study spanning the period before and after the innovation of the belt drive.[20]

Finally, Table 9 compares the productivity of the six firms with the average productivity of the entire industry. The United States figures are drawn from the federal censuses and, therefore, may be distorted. However, since even the Massachusetts figures based on the fairly reliable

TABLE 9

MEASURES OF TECHNICAL EFFICIENCY IN COTTON TEXTILE PRODUCTION
FOR SAMPLE, UNITED STATES, AND MASSACHUSETTS
(Yards)

Year	Output Per Spindle Per Year			Output Per Man Per Year		
	U.S.	Massa-chusetts	Sample	U.S.	Massa-chusetts	Sample
1820*	142		234	2,000		
1831	185	233	241	3,707	5,938	10,618
1837		224	260		6,395	12,823
1845		215	278		8,483	14,437
1849	217	232	284	7,796	10,399	16,215
1855		207	277		9,055	16,928
1859	219	248	292	9,410	10,800	19,878

* Based on a sample of firms which reported yardage produced.
SOURCE: 1820, 1850, and 1860 for Massachusetts and U.S., from censuses; 1831, from survey of that year; 1837, 1845, and 1855 Massachusetts figures, from state censuses.

state census show lower productivity, it seems unlikely that the weakness of the census fully explains the difference. The sample firms, although not on the average producing a coarser cloth, show remarkedly higher output-to-labor and output-to-spindle ratios even though the figures on output per man-year for the sample firms have been deliberately underestimated (the data in Table 9 are based on an average 265-day work year).[21] An examination of the six sample firms indicates that they were

---

[20] This is also true in the period after the introduction of belt drive, even though Taussig claims that spindles are "the best single indication of the extent and growth of such an industry as cotton manufacture" (Taussig, *Some Aspects of the Tariff Question* [Cambridge, Mass., 1915], p. 265).

It is easy to cite examples in which the use of the number of spindles as a measure of output leads to error:

Example 1. With use of the spindle figures, the estimated output for the U.S. in 1839 would be 412 million. If the value of outputs in 1839 were deflated by a price index and then converted into yards (on the basis of 1840), the estimate would be 357.

Example 2. Between 1890 and 1910, spindle speed increased by 11 percent, spindles by 93 percent, and consequently expected output by 112 percent. Actual output increased by 108 percent.

[21] A further bias may be introduced against the tentative conclusion by assuming that the proportion of inputs used in the production of intermediate products (batting, thread, yarn, etc.) was the same as the proportion of cotton used in each. Also

substantially larger than the average.[22] Therefore, insofar as economies of scale exist, they probably account for part of the differences between the sample and the average.

Moreover, as Anne Grosse has shown, there are usually significant differences between the technically "best practice" and the normal mill practices in the textile industry. Management is not omnipotent and even if it were, it must utilize both old and new equipment.[23] Since the sample mills were the industry leaders or large mills with machine shops, which actually developed new machines and improved existing ones, it seems reasonable to assume that their technology was closer to "best practice" than was that of the average mill. The histories of the mills seem to indicate that the equipment of the leading firms was continually modified by their shop crews, while firms without shop connections had to buy complete new machines. These latter purchases could not be made until the entire new machine was available and, under any conditions, would not have been made until the total cost of the new machines' output was below the variable cost of the old machines' product. In fact, the average of 21 percent, by which spindle productivity in the sample mills exceeded productivity in all Massachusetts during 1831–55, is not very far from Mrs. Grosse's 25 percent estimate for the excess of best over average practice in the United States in 1941–46.[24]

A comparison of the figures presented in Table 9 and Mrs. Grosse's work shows at least one marked difference. In the more recent period, Mrs. Grosse has shown that average practice tends to approach best practice (i.e., the divergence between average output per spindle and best practice output tends to fall over time). No such convergence is ap-

---

it may be assumed that at least 10 percent of the employees were not in the four major departments. The census data ratios would then be increased by 14 percent for the U.S. and 12 percent for Massachusetts. The only case in which the relative values would be changed is 1831 for which the Massachusetts capital ratio would exceed the sample ratio.

[22] The number of spindles per mill was as follows:

	Sample	Mass.	U.S.
1831..............	6,073	1,359	1,567
1837..............	7,164	2,011	
1839..............	6,794	2,145	1,842
1845..............	6,842	2,707	
1849..............	8,370	6,048*	3,284*
1855..............	8,403	5,168	
1859..............	9,912	7,711*	4,799*

* The census reported only firms. Many firms were multimill operations.

[23] Anne Grosse, "The Technological Structure of the Cotton Textile Industry," in W. Leontief (ed.), *Studies in the Structure of the American Economy* (New York, 1953), pp. 360–420.

One should also mention T. Y. Shen's thesis, "Technological Change in the Cotton Textile Industry," a best-practice study. This work has been reported in T. Y. Shen, "Job Analysis and Historical Productivities in the American Cotton Textile Industry," *Review of Economics and Statistics*, May, 1958.

[24] Grosse, "Technological Structure," p. 410.

parent in Table 9. Although it is not possible to explain this difference with certainty, one partial answer suggests itself. In the period covered by the Grosse study, best-practice techniques were fairly constant. (Her best-practice estimates were constant from 1926 to 1935 and from 1936 to 1949.) In the earlier period, on the other hand, there was a continual improvement in best-practice techniques until the late 1840's. During this period, therefore, it is possible that average mills continually adopted newer practices but were still unable to close the gap between themselves and the leading firms. Even this answer, however, fails to explain the lack of convergence in the 1850's, when best-practice techniques showed little improvement. As for best practice relative to spindles (as opposed to labor), however, the early textile data do show the Massachusetts figures closing on the sample data.

V. Summary

The records of business firms represent a relatively untouched resource for studies of the American economy in the 19th century. In this study, based on the records of a number of cotton textile firms, we have attempted to provide some information on the fluctuations in industrial output between the census bench-mark years. Firm records can also serve as a basis for studies of fluctuations in inventories, sales, costs, profits, and other variables for which we have only bench-mark data. If studied regionally, firm records may be able to yield quantitative evidence regarding interregional differences in relative costs and techniques. In addition, an analysis based on firm records can yield some estimates of productivity changes and their causes and can, perhaps, suggest some ways by which these changes are transmitted through the economy.

TABLE A-1

ACTUAL OUTPUT STANDARDIZED WITH TABLE 3 TREATMENT, BY MILLS, 1815–60

(Thousand Yards)

Date	Boston	Merri- mack	Hamil- ton	Suffolk	Tre- mont	Law- rence
1815	76					
1816	189					
1817	261					
1818	530					
1819	996					
1820	1,262					
1821	1,456					
1822	1,643					
1823	1,762					
1824	1,899	389				
1825	1,711	1,807				
1826	1,785	1,971				
1827	1,862	3,057				
1828	1,967	3,988	2,810			
1829	1,813	4,357	2,141			
1830	1,879	5,778	2,236			
1831	2,003	6,358	4,275			
1832	1,982	6,244	3,490	2,396	615	
1833	1,674	6,673	3,526	4,294	5,161	1,104
1834	2,090	6,948	3,926	3,839	4,578	6,173
1835	2,420	9,026	4,171	4,329	6,182	9,130
1836	2,450	9,961	4,612	4,579	6,661	10,265
1837	2,703	9,047	4,061	3,566	6,848	9,224
1838	2,820	9,998	5,104	4,520	6,713	10,518
1839	2,862	11,711	5,528	4,857	6,735	11,018
1840	2,580	9,922	5,606	5,118	7,123	10,549
1841	2,705	12,488	5,447	5,132	7,089	11,561
1842	2,488	12,625	5,212	4,807	6,314	10,858
1843	2,190	12,612	5,215	4,532	6,083	10,339
1844	2,683	13,299	5,828	5,061	6,624	10,480
1845	2,559	13,320	5,445	5,553	6,642	10,604
1846	2,477	13,052	6,343	5,689	6,584	12,816
1847	2,936	13,193	7,074	5,843	6,748	13,476
1848	3,172	14,729	8,953	5,732	7,401	14,199
1849	3,416	14,635	9,024	6,155	7,515	13,607
1850	3,472	17,663	10,208	4,656	5,666	11,128
1851	2,788	19,602	10,338	4,695	4,235	10,859
1852	2,724	19,989	11,696	6,420	7,715	13,696
1853	2,968	17,862	12,058	6,935	8,706	14,743
1854	3,154	17,354	11,658	6,709	10,021	13,726
1855	3,310	18,553	11,724	7,109	8,755	14,187
1856	3,698	19,765	11,218	8,049	10,797	15,927
1857	3,538	19,029	10,508	6,523	9,602	14,696
1858	3,497	19,680	10,336	7,361	8,552	16,371
1859	4,166	22,103	11,592	8,507	11,003	18,627
1860	4,573	22,447	12,917	8,455	11,169	19,183

TABLE A–1 (*Continued*)

Date	Naum-keag	Lan-caster	Dwight I	Dwight II	Dwight III	Lyman I
1815						
1816						
1817						
1818						
1819						
1820						
1821						
1822						
1823						
1824						
1825						
1826						
1827						
1828						
1829						
1830						
1831						
1832						
1833						
1834						
1835						
1836						
1837						
1838						
1839						
1840						
1841			407	44		
1842			1,654	1,565		
1843			1,403	2,558		
1844			1,563	2,791		
1845			1,555	2,515	236	
1846			1,445	2,386	956	
1847		327	1,553	2,607	1,087	
1848	4,877	1,422	1,510	2,558	1,231	
1849	5,394	3,192	1,523	2,373	1,393	
1850	5,458	4,058	1,461	2,185	1,418	4,831
1851	5,614	4,102	1,528	1,787	1,384	6,574
1852	5,701	4,369	1,543	2,356	1,306	8,595
1853	5,294	4,026	1,572	2,444	1,440	4,172
1854	5,112	3,869	1,486	2,521	1,361	8,202
1855	5,460	4,678	1,679	2,486	1,403	8,289
1856	5,392	5,039	1,447	2,546	1,519	8,110
1857	4,925	4,612	1,284	2,885	1,154	4,240
1858	4,868	4,636	1,789	2,139	1,204	8,955
1859	5,366	5,340	1,930	2,485	1,342	8,553
1860	5,539	5,309	1,776	3,503	1,449	4,309

TABLE A-1 (*Continued*)

Date	Lyman II	Nashua	Jackson	Laconia	Pepperill	Amoskeag I
1815						
1816						
1817						
1818						
1819						
1820						
1821						
1822						
1823						
1824						
1825						
1826		321				
1827		1,031				
1828		1,938				
1829		2,350				
1830		2,483				
1831		2,954				
1832		3,347	2,510			
1833		3,721	4,308			
1834		3,706	4,385			
1835		3,646	4,460			
1836		5,591	4,567			
1837		6,560	4,975			1,272
1838		7,755	4,997			1,407
1839		9,033	4,980			1,453
1840		7,690	5,173			1,126
1841		8,203	5,321			1,077
1842		7,582	4,803			1,102
1843		7,814	4,867			1,148
1844		8,485	5,368			1,160
1845		11,041	5,473	1,974		1,189
1846		11,133	5,250	3,093		1,190
1847		10,479	4,980	5,509		540
1848		11,767	5,219	8,355		
1849		12,445	5,115	10,787		
1850		12,548	4,339	8,111	755	
1851		9,535	3,713	10,937	7,174	
1852	324	10,529	4,162	12,296	10,624	
1853	2,969	11,005	4,818	10,569	9,919	
1854	3,446	11,975	5,000	9,571	9,794	
1855	4,006	12,840	5,098	3,811	10,707	
1856	3,923	11,689	6,474		13,291	
1857	3,440	10,430	6,103		10,946	
1858	4,446	11,834	6,843		14,768	
1859	4,172	13,881	8,441		14,976	
1860	3,834	15,265	8,568		15,792	

TABLE A–1 (Continued)

Date	Amos-keag II	Amos-keag III	Rampo	Slater	Slater and Tiffany	Sut-ton	Meta-comet
1815							
1816							
1817							
1818							
1819							
1820							
1821			149				
1822			181				
1823			317				
1824			350				
1825			245				
1826			281	488			
1827			320	678	338		
1828			261	643	604		
1829			305	458	546		
1830			336	608	589		
1831			271	696	662	405	
1832			247	619	610	335	
1833			119	461	572	452	
1834				393	365	479	
1835				247	374	503	
1836				415	600	473	
1837	857			620	61	331	
1838	927			506		683	
1839	860			509		383	
1840	946					372	
1841	884	1,714				710	
1842	914	6,322				234	
1843	507	6,182				992	
1844	1,050	8,777				740	
1845	1,242	12,719				776	
1846	1,549	13,242				710	
1847	1,537	12,369				833	
1848		13,299				403	5,020
1849	498	17,999				845	5,500
1850	1,568	12,996				842	5,303
1851	1,564	15,816				875	3,370
1852	1,700	18,295				955	4,656
1853	1,458	17,646				998	5,170
1854	1,452	16,460				757	5,232
1855	1,423	17,721				1,286	4,445
1856	1,411	20,972				1,000	5,141
1857	544	15,024				511	5,300
1858	504	22,559				1,645	5,820
1859	1,900	24,240				1,800	5,656
1860	1,681	21,863					6,130

TABLE A–2

COMPARISON OF STANDARD AND RECORDED YARDS, BY COUNT, 1825–60

(Thousand Yards)

Year	Producers of Low-Count Goods*			Producers of Medium-Count Goods†		
	Number of Mills	Estimated Standard Output	Recorded Output	Number of Mills	Estimated Standard Output	Recorded Output
1825...	3	1,586	1,711	3	2,349	1,801
1826...	5	1,629	2,106	3	2,562	1,971
1827...	5	2,669	2,893	3	3,975	3,057
1828...	7	6,787	6,717	3	5,185	3,988
1829...	7	6,282	6,305	3	5,664	4,357
1830...	8	6,588	6,600	5	7,512	5,778
1831...	8	9,492	9,233	6	8,266	6,358
1832...	11	14,361	14,343	6	8,117	6,244
1833...	15	24,224	23,790	6	8,674	6,673
1834...	15	31,127	28,700	6	9,032	6,948
1835...	17	36,094	34,341	7	12,118	9,323
1836...	17	39,271	38,729	7	14,980	11,657
1837...	17	37,759	37,940	7	12,554	9,944
1838...	18	42,823	42,429	8	16,050	12,350
1839...	18	45,921	45,016	8	18,713	14,393
1840...	18	45,022	43,842	8	19,504	13,016
1841...	18	47,218	45,460	9	20,218	15,952
1842...	18	43,948	42,066	9	21,645	18,264
1843...	18	42,782	41,043	9	20,240	17,227
1844...	18	47,263	44,531	9	23,094	19,205
1845...	21	52,362	49,295	10	25,249	19,435
1846...	22	57,126	53,388	10	26,936	20,598
1847...	24	60,901	57,048	10	25,797	19,937
1848...	24	73,018	69,679	10	27,755	21,757
1849...	24	77,505	73,463	10	27,008	21,755
1850...	24	68,311	66,346	10	31,373	24,829
1851...	24	73,055	69,893	10	32,481	26,245
1852...	24	91,907	85,568	10	34,105	27,555
1853...	24	90,909	87,019	9	30,330	24,317
1854...	24	88,982	86,725	9	26,567	23,824
1855...	24	87,353	83,006	9	31,573	25,411
1856...	24	91,798	86,540	9	34,671	26,428
1857...	24	81,018	77,276	9	31,372	24,896
1858...	24	89,255	84,433	9	32,168	26,914
1859...	24	102,670	96,562	9	37,801	30,119
1860...	24	107,829	101,466	9	36,060	29,604

* Boston, Hamilton, Suffolk, Tremont, Lawrence, Naumkeag, Jackson, Nashua, Pepperill.
† Merrimack, Dwight.

2. Stock Ownership in the Early New England Textile Industry[*]

Lance E. Davis[†]

Purdue University

The unique features of ownership patterns in the early New England textile industry have long been recognized. Hitherto it has been the interlocking or horizontal relationships that have been studied. This article deals, instead, with the vertical pattern—describing ownership in terms of occupational groupings of all the investors rather than the kinship of the dominant owners. Conclusions are drawn in respect to such important points as the principal sources of textile capital, the rate of mercantile capital reinvestment in manufacturing, the relationship between investment and industry integration, and the increasing importance of nonbusiness and institutional vested interests.

STUDENTS OF AMERICAN ECONOMIC DEVELOPMENT have generally agreed that the New England cotton textile industry, and particularly that portion characterized by the large Massachusetts-type mills, was the first branch of American industry to feel the full impact of the industrial revolution.[1] In 1800 few American firms produced textiles; but by 1860 cotton manufacturing represented a capital investment of over $65 million in the six New England states alone.[2] Since capital was far from abundant

---

[*] Reprinted from *Business History Review,* Vol. XXXII, No. 2 (Summer, 1958), pp. 204–22.

[†] The author wishes to express his thanks to his colleagues at Purdue University—and in particular Professors Irving Morrissett, Jared Sparks, and Duncan McDougall—for their help and advice on matters of both content and grammar. Moreover, the author wishes to acknowledge the aid of the department of political economy of Johns Hopkins University and the Purdue Research Foundation that together financed the research on which this paper is based.

[1] Students of the period divide textile producers into two categories. The small single-operation mills that were the American heirs to the English development are termed Rhode Island-type mills. These firms are typified by the Slater enterprises near Providence, Rhode Island, and by the development at Fall River in Massachusetts. The Massachusetts type is the name given to the large integrated mill that grew out of the development of the Boston Manufacturing Company at Waltham, Massachusetts.

[2] The Census of Manufactures in 1860 reported that total capital in cotton textile

in antebellum America, the process by which this relatively large sum was accumulated and mobilized is an interesting subject for analysis.

A recent study of the large "Massachusetts" mills has shown that the sale of equity was the most important single source of finance. This examination of firm records indicates that sale of stock provided the mills with almost all of their original finance; and, even after the firms had been in existence for a quarter century, the study shows that contributed equity still represented over one half of their total capital.[3] Still unanswered, however, are two basic questions: who were the stockholders, and from what sources did they garner the funds that they invested in the textile industry? This study attempts to provide at least partial answers to these questions.

The answers are based on the records of eleven cotton textile mills of the Massachusetts type: the Amoskeag, Boston, Dwight, Cabot, Perkins, Hamilton, Nashua, Lyman, Lawrence, Lancaster, and Massachusetts Cotton mills. Analyses were made of the stockholder records of these firms for the date of the original stock subscription and for the fourth and ninth years of each decade in the period 1829–59. The fourth and ninth years were chosen because more stockholder records were available for these years than for any other five-year intervals; but even so, the records are incomplete. However, the records for every selected year are complete for at least two firms up to 1839, and for at least six firms thereafter. Table 1 shows the firms and years for which information is available, together with the total value of their outstanding stock.[4] Although the survey was limited to stockholders who, at some time during the period, had investments of $2,500 or more in the industry, this restriction resulted

---

production in the United States amounted to $93,143,759. Of this amount more than two thirds ($65,947,819) was invested in the six New England states. The total estimated capital in all industry in the entire U.S. was $1,009,855,715. Thus New England textiles represented about 7 percent of the total. These official figures probably underestimate the total actual investment. United States Secretary of the Interior, *Manufactures in the United States in 1860* (Washington, D.C., 1865), pp. 679, 735, and 742.

[3] Lance E. Davis, "Sources of Industrial Finance: The American Textile Industry, A Case Study," *Explorations in Entrepreneurial History*, Vol. IX (April, 1957), pp. 190–92.

[4] The figures displayed in Table 1 represent the par value of *all* outstanding stock, and no allowance has been made for purchases at prices above or below the par value nor has any attempt been made to deduct the shares received as stock dividends. The paucity of data on stock prices as well as the complexity of stock transactions make it all but impossible to adjust the figures for price changes. At the same time, without stretching the facts very far, stock dividends can be looked at as voluntary reinvestment in the business, since the typical stockholder then had much more to say about dividend policy than does the average stockholder today. The mill records, from which these figures and other data in this article come, are on deposit in the manuscript collection of the Baker Library, Graduate School of Business Administration, Harvard University.

TABLE 1

TOTAL VALUE OF STOCK OUTSTANDING*

(In Thousands of Dollars of Par Value)

	First Year	1829	1834	1839	1844	1849	1854	1859
Amoskeag	$ 965			$ 988	—	$3,000	$3,000	$3,000
Boston	100	$600	$ 600	600	$ 600	540	450	450
Dwight	—				—	—	700	1,700
Cabot	400			—	—	—	†	
Perkins	360			—	—	—	1,000	‡
Hamilton	—	—	—	—	1,200	1,200	1,200	1,200
Nashua	—	600	—	750	800	1,000	1,000	1,000
Lyman	1,470						1,470	1,470
Lawrence	1,200		1,200	1,500	1,500	1,500	1,500	1,500
Lancaster	100				117	—	—	—
Mass. Cotton	1,200			—	1,200	1,800	1,800	1,800

* Blank spaces indicate firms were not in operation; dash (−) indicates no stockholders' lists were available.

† Cabot merged with Perkins, 1852.

‡ Perkins merger with Dwight, 1856.

in the exclusion of less than one fifth of the total value of the equity (see Table 2).[5]

The company records listed the stockholders only by name and city of residence, and it was necessary to obtain further identification from city directories, university alumni records, local histories, and other similar sources. These chronicles provided information about the occupation and business connections of most stockholders, but they seldom identified the sources of their invested wealth. Lacking better information, it was assumed for the purposes of this analysis that the invested capital originated in the occupation in which the buyer was engaged at the time of his purchase, or, in the case of retired persons, in the last occupation in which he was engaged prior to his retirement. In a few instances in which the actual sources of capital were known, this arbitrary assumption proved to be reasonably realistic.[6]

---

[5] If the occupational composition of the small stockholders differed greatly from that of the large purchasers the conclusions may be subject to some revision; however, a spot check on the small investors in particular mills does not seem to show any marked departure from the pattern established by the large investors.

[6] Throughout this article, major dependence is placed on four measures of contribution. First, the relative proportion of the total equity that was held by the members of each occupational group included in the survey. Second, the relative proportion of the total number of stockholders represented by each group included in the survey. Third, the average investment *per stockholder per firm* for each occupational group. And fourth, the average *total* investment of the individual members of each occupational group in the eleven firms. Some reliance is also placed on the estimates of total absolute contribution as displayed in Table 3; the reader should bear in mind that the latter are estimates only.

TABLE 2
VALUE OF CAPITAL STOCK OWNED BY STOCKHOLDERS
INCLUDED IN THE STUDY
(In Thousands of Dollars of Par Value)

	First Year	1829	1834	1839	1844	1849	1854	1859
Amoskeag	$ 895			$ 950		$2,292	$1,862	$1,947
Boston	100	$474	$ 448	428	$ 390	381	343	308
Dwight	390						627	1,662
Cabot	354							
Perkins	348						937	
Hamilton					1,008	840	856	773
Nashua		600		692	755	776	861	862
Lyman	1,408						1,012	1,227
Lawrence	1,240		1,095	1,169	1,091	994	1,022	1,027
Lancaster	85				111			
Mass. Cotton	1,040				994	1,413	1,366	1,306
Percent of total included in the sample	.946	.896	.857	.844	.803	.741	.733	.752

TABLE 3
ESTIMATED VALUE OF TOTAL EQUITY CONTRIBUTED BY VARIOUS
OCCUPATIONAL GROUPS TO EIGHT COTTON TEXTILE FIRMS
(In Thousands of Dollars)

	1829	1834	1839	1844	1849	1854	1859
Merchants & merc. firms (excl. textile)	$637	$1,237	$1,443	$2,315	$2,921	$2,744	$3,006
Textile merchants & tex. merc. firms	108	411	979	1,192	1,124	872	837
Manufacturers, artisans & mfg. firms	180	112	237	249	347	483	648
Professional persons	326	349	575	764	813	791	876
Misc. persons & firms	1	20	28	103	80	181	222
Financial institutions	308	203	537	270	742	902	854
Financiers	99	183	572	756	657	629	976
Foreign persons & firms*	0	6	24	76	146	322	265
Women	49	93	94	292	436	588	742
Trustees	30	140	314	704	1,219	1,676	2,003
No occupation	77	223	236	273	316	449	520
No information	221	203	475	581	933	932	1,170

* Includes all non-Massachusetts residents.

TABLE 4

Average Investment per Stockholder per Firm, by Occupation of Stockholders

(In Thousands of Dollars)

	First Year	1829	1834	1839	1844	1849	1854	1859
Merchants & merc. firms (excl. textile)	$11.6	$10.9	$12.8	$11.5	$11.3	$17.2	$12.2	$12.8
Textile merchants & tex. merc. firms	20.0	10.7	22.1	23.2	20.2	19.7	17.1	15.5
Manufacturers, artisans & mfg. firms	7.9	14.5	16.0	11.8	6.9	9.4	11.2	10.5
Professional persons	8.9	10.8	10.4	9.7	9.1	9.4	7.5	8.8
Misc. persons & firms	6.1	0	9.0	7.0	5.2	4.8	8.2	8.4
Financial institutions	7.4	21.4	25.5	24.1	9.2	14.6	12.7	15.8
Financiers	11.0	12.0	8.4	14.9	7.2	11.2	13.0	16.5
Foreign persons & firms*	5.5	0	0	5.3	7.3	5.6	7.0	6.9
Women	6.1	7.5	9.5	4.5	8.4	6.8	7.9	7.2
Trustees	9.4	7.7	5.9	12.5	6.8	10.1	9.6	9.0
No occupation	9.1	7.8	11.4	9.9	6.4	9.0	9.5	11.6
No information	7.1	8.2	10.1	8.8	6.8	7.5	6.6	7.4

* Includes all non-Massachusetts residents.

TABLE 5

Average Total Investment per Individual Included in the Study, by Occupation

(In Thousands of Dollars)

	First Year	1829	1834	1839	1844	1849	1854	1859
Merchants & merc. firms (excl. textile)	$16.3	$10.9	$13.3	$14.6	$14.7	$17.6	$16.7	$17.4
Textile merchants & tex. merc. firms	35.7	12.8	31.6	36.8	32.1	28.9	24.5	20.5
Manufacturers, artisans & mfg. firms	8.3	14.5	16.0	12.2	6.9	9.4	11.2	10.5
Professional persons	12.1	10.8	12.0	12.3	13.5	12.9	10.6	12.3
Misc. persons & firms	12.2	0	9.0	7.0	6.3	7.7	15.4	16.9
Financial institutions	7.4	34.2	25.5	30.7	11.6	21.3	24.6	28.2
Financiers	16.1	12.0	10.1	23.8	25.4	17.2	17.6	23.9
Foreign persons & firms*	5.5	0	0	5.3	7.3	5.6	7.0	6.9
Women	8.1	7.5	9.5	4.5	9.6	7.8	8.4	7.9
Trustees	9.4	7.7	5.9	12.3	6.8	10.3	9.6	9.0
No occupation	11.0	7.8	11.4	19.9	8.1	9.0	10.2	11.6
No information	7.1	7.2	10.1	8.8	6.8	7.6	6.6	7.7

* Includes all non-Massachusetts residents.

TABLE 6

PERCENTAGE DISTRIBUTION OF EQUITY HOLDINGS
BY OCCUPATIONAL GROUPS

	First Year	1829	1834	1839	1844	1849	1854	1859
Merchants & merc. firms (excl. textile)	.360	.299	.393	.347	.300	.299	.276	.248
Textile merchants & tex. merc. firms	.166	.062	.142	.185	.163	.120	.080	.068
Manufacturers, artisans & mfg. firms	.051	.085	.021	.055	.025	.032	.050	.054
Professional persons	.105	.121	.100	.103	.111	.085	.076	.072
Misc. persons & firms	.009	.000	.017	.004	.014	.008	.014	.018
Financial institutions	.020	.167	.066	.095	.041	.076	.077	.070
Financiers	.089	.059	.064	.107	.100	.066	.059	.080
Foreign persons & firms*	.003	.000	.000	.004	.010	.015	.027	.022
Women	.008	.015	.024	.012	.047	.043	.055	.061
Trustees	.045	.022	.041	.055	.089	.123	.155	.166
No occupation	.031	.038	.072	.044	.029	.031	.043	.043
No information	.112	.130	.059	.088	.070	.099	.088	.096

* Includes all non-Massachusetts residents.

TABLE 7

PERCENTAGE DISTRIBUTION OF THE NUMBER OF
SHAREHOLDERS BY OCCUPATIONAL GROUPS

	First Year	1829	1834	1839	1844	1849	1854	1859
Merchants & merc firms (excl. textile)	.322	.298	.379	.285	.258	.198	.227	.203
Textile merchants & tex. merc. firms	.085	.064	.079	.104	.074	.071	.047	.047
Manufacturers, artisans & mfg. firms	.066	.064	.016	.044	.034	.034	.045	.053
Professional persons	.137	.181	.118	.129	.120	.104	.102	.086
Misc. persons & firms	.015	.000	.008	.007	.025	.019	.018	.023
Financial institutions	.028	.085	.032	.052	.080	.060	.061	.047
Financiers	.083	.053	.095	.092	.069	.068	.046	.051
Foreign persons & firms*	.006	.000	.000	.011	.014	.031	.040	.033
Women	.012	.000	.032	.033	.053	.073	.071	.089
Trustees	.049	.032	.087	.059	.126	.141	.163	.193
No occupation	.035	.053	.079	.059	.044	.042	.046	.039
No information	.160	.170	.071	.133	.099	.151	.134	.137

* Includes all non-Massachusetts residents.

TABLE 8
NUMBER OF PERSONS INCLUDED IN THE SAMPLE
BY OCCUPATION

	First Year	1829	1834	1839	1844	1849	1854	1859
Merchants & merc. firms (excl. textile)	147	28	46	60	89	114	153	131
Textile merchants & tex. merc. firms	31	5	7	18	22	28	30	31
Manufacturers, artisans & mfg. firms	41	6	2	12	20	23	41	47
Professional persons	58	17	13	29	35	44	67	54
Misc. persons & firms	5	0	1	2	9	7	9	10
Financial institutions	18	5	4	11	15	24	29	23
Financiers	37	5	10	16	17	26	31	31
Foreign persons & firms*	4	0	0	3	6	18	37	29
Women	8	2	4	9	21	37	61	71
Trustees	32	3	11	16	57	80	150	170
No occupation	19	5	10	8	15	24	39	34
No information	104	16	9	36	45	87	123	115

* Includes all non-Massachusetts residents.

The Stockholders

The Mercantile Groups

The most important and numerous group of stockholders were non-textile merchants purchasing shares in their own names, or, less commonly, in the names of their firms. In all, some 234 nontextile merchants and 17 nontextile mercantile firms owned shares in one or more of the 11 firms; however, the importance of the individual contributions within this group varied greatly. Its membership ranged from individuals whose holdings totaled a bare $2,500 on the one hand to persons whose personal investments ran as high as $200,000.

Over the period studied, the average investment per nontextile merchant per firm remained remarkably constant while the average total investment per merchant in the eleven firms rose slowly from $11,000 to $17,000.[7] However, the *proportion* of equity held by this group has a very different pattern. This ratio rose between 1829 and 1834, from about 30 to almost 40 percent, then declined steadily throughout the remainder of the period. By 1859, these merchants owned less than one quarter of the equity included in the sample. The relative distribution of shares owned by these merchants and by other occupational groups is shown in Table 6.[8]

---

[7] See Tables 4 and 5.

[8] Estimates of the *absolute* amounts of equity owned by each of the occupational groups are shown in Table 3; they are less reliable than the estimates of proportionate shares shown in the text, because of the problems created by the changing number

Not only do the nontextile merchants bulk large among stockholders in each of the cross-section years, but also they appear to have made a substantial contribution to new equity. The group subscribed to over one third of all new issues; and, although their average investment per firm was only $11,600, the average individual investment was in excess of $16,000. Nor did their contribution to new issues diminish perceptibly over time. As late as 1854 this mercantile group contributed 32 percent of the equity capital of the newly organized Lyman Company.

In many ways the textile merchants represent the most interesting single group.[9] They are set apart from the other merchants not only by the size of their investments but also by their investment motives. While other merchants could look at textile stock as only one more of a series of investment alternatives, the textile merchants must also have seen such investment as a method of securing their raw material sources.

During the entire period, only 45 textile merchants and 7 textile firms were identified among the stockholders included on the sample; however, their contribution to textile finance was far out of proportion to their numbers. Only once during the entire period did this group represent more than 8 percent of the total number of investors; but during the middle years of the survey their holdings represented about 16 percent of the total equity.[10] During the 1830's their holdings rose from 6 to 18.5 percent of the total stock surveyed; but after 1840 their importance gradually diminished; and in 1859 they owned only 7 percent. Although the records show an increase in the number of textile merchant owners during the 1830's, this increase was small; and the group's increasing importance among occupational groups can be traced almost entirely to the increasing size of the individual merchant's investments. In 1829 the average investment of textile merchants in each firm was less than $11,000; 10 years later, however, this figure had more than doubled (see Table 4). Even more striking is the rise in the average investment per individual. In the same period this figure increased by almost 200 percent,

---

of firms and incomplete data. Most of the discussion of capital contributions has, therefore, been limited to the proportions of equity contributed. The estimates in Table 3 are based on the eight firms for which there are records for more than one half the selected years. Data missing for these firms were estimated by a method based on Yates' "missing plots" technique. See F. W. Yates, "The Analysis of Replicated Experiments Where Field Results are Incomplete," *Empire Journal of Experimental Agriculture*, Vol. I. (1933), pp. 129–42. From the information displayed in Table 3, it appears that the decline in mercantile holding referred to above was only a *relative* decline caused by the industries' equity issue increasing more rapidly than the merchants' holdings. (Possibly for no other reason than that the number of merchants was increasing less rapidly than the population in general.) The estimates of absolute contribution show that the mercantile holdings increased in every year (except 1854) from 1829 to 1859.

[9] Since only those merchants who could positively be identified as trading primarily in textiles are included, the category probably underestimates the actual contribution of this group.

[10] See Tables 6 and 7.

$12,800 to $36,800 (see Table 5). Similarly, the post-1844 decline in the importance of the textile merchants' investments can in large part be attributed to a fall in the average investment per individual. By 1859 the average textile merchant held equities totaling only about $20,500, and in each mill he had less than $16,000.[11]

In new issues, too, the textile merchants made a contribution far out of proportion to their small numbers. Although the group represented only a little more than 8 percent of the new stock purchasers, they purchased about 17 percent of the new equity issues. Moreover, the average investment of each purchaser in the new issues of the mills was in excess of $35,000.

If the eleven firms studied here are typical of the large Massachusetts-type mills, this analysis tends to substantiate the belief that a large portion of the equity capital of the early American textile industry was drawn from mercantile sources. However, the same evidence casts some doubt on several corollary assumptions that are often made about the causes and nature of this transfer from mercantile to industrial investment.

An examination of the contribution of the entire mercantile sector attests to the importance of trade-born capital in the financing of American textiles. The mercantile groups together contributed over one half of the original equity and represented over one third of the total holdings in almost every cross-section year.[12]

Most writers have recognized the importance of mercantile capital, but many have attributed the transfer of capital from trade to industry almost entirely to the declining returns in commerce that followed the post-Napoleonic depression.[13] Although such a decline may have triggered the first capital emigration, the evidence suggests that such a decline is not a satisfactory explanation of the continued transfer. While the stock holdings of the nontextile mercantile groups declined in relative importance over the period, the estimates of their total contributions to equity capital (Table 3) indicate that the absolute size of these holdings continued to increase, at least until 1860. Moreover, similar steady increases in the number of investors and in the average size of the individual's investment also seem to indicate that the transfer was not a short-run phenomenon induced by a sudden sharp decline in commercial profits, but, instead, a long-run process lasting at least until the Civil War.

Undoubtedly, declining profits provided some impetus to *push* capital

---

11 If the estimates in Table 3 are correct, the reduction in the importance of textile merchants after 1839 represents not only a relative but also an absolute decline in their holdings. The table shows an increase in the holdings until 1844, but after that date there appears to have been an absolute withdrawal of capital amounting to $355,000 by 1859.

12 The total contribution of the two groups fell below one third of the total surveyed only in 1859.

13 See, for example, Victor S. Clark, *History of Manufactures in the United States 1607–1860* (New York, 1929), Vol. VI, p. 367; or Caroline Ware, *The Early New England Cotton Manufacture* (Boston, 1931), p. 141.

from trade, but it is difficult to ignore the *pull* supplied by the high expected profits and the supposed safety of textile investment. If the decline
of the returns to investment in trade had been the only cause of the
transfer to industrial capital, it is reasonable to assume that an increase
in commercial profits would have caused a withdrawal of merchants' investments in industry and a reinvestment in trade, or at least a cessation
of new transfers from trade to industry. But it appears that mercantile
capital continued to flow into textile production even during periods of
commercial prosperity.[14]

Although high expected profits may be largely responsible for the
transfers of mercantile capital to the textile industry during the 1830's,
some other factor must be adduced to explain the continued flow during
the fifties when textile profits were low and the expectation of future
prospects dim.[15] It appears likely that this flow can, in part, be explained
by the merchants' search for a reasonably safe investment that did not
require their personal attention rather than an investment chosen to
maximize their short-run monetary profits. Except for the issues of railroads (never known for their safety), private bonds were largely unknown; and, aside from the flotations of railroads, commercial banks and
textiles, there were few available equity issues. Thus, since men of wealth
were usually prohibited from investing in Savings Banks and Trust Companies, the only investment alternatives aside from textiles that combined
safety and impersonality were the bond issues of government bodies—
and these were often rather unrewarding and at times not even safe.

Finally, the evidence indicates that the transfer process cannot be
correctly described as a flight of capital from trade to industry. No doubt
some merchants withdrew completely from trade and invested large portions of their fortunes in industry; however, the evidence suggests that
this was not the usual case. Instead, it appears that the merchants only
gradually withdrew their funds from trade and transferred them to industry. Table 5 shows that the merchants' average investment increased
gradually through the period, and an examination of the accounts of individual stockholders also confirms the gradual nature of their investment.

The investments of the textile merchants appear to have rested on the
three legs of profits, wealth, and economic control. Before 1820 textile
merchants were largely engaged in the import and sale of foreign cloth,
and, as a result, the merchants were not particularly concerned with the

---

[14] Although no precise estimates of the returns from trade do exist, such returns
are probably loosely correlated with the volume of trade, for which some evidence
does exist. See, for example, Walter Buckingham Smith and Arthur Harrison Cole,
Fluctuations in American Business 1790–1860 (Cambridge, 1935), pp. 73 and 104.

[15] An examination of the records of the nine firms possessing adequate financial
data (Amoskeag, Dwight, Cabot, Perkins, Hamilton, Lancaster, Lawrence, Lyman,
and Mass. Cotton) show that profits (as a percent of total capital stock) average
10.3 percent from 1830 to 1834; 9.4 percent from 1835 to 1839; 6.8 percent from
1840 to 1844; 12 percent from 1845 to 1849; 6.1 percent from 1850 to 1854; and
6.0 percent from 1855 to 1859.

infant textile industry. As the industry grew, however, established merchants shifted from foreign to domestic goods and new merchants entered the domestic field. Profits were frequently large and capital began to accumulate in the hands of those merchants specializing in the sale of American goods. At the same time, two forces combined to draw the group's capital into the manufacture of textiles. In the industry's early years the large mills were highly profitable. Because of their close association with textile manufacture, the textile merchants must have been able to recognize this profitability and have been in a position to subscribe to the new equity issues.[16] Moreover, the merchants must have realized that their own prosperity depended on a continued supply of finished cotton. Although no direct evidence can be marshaled to support the belief that textile merchants attempted to cement their sources of supply by investment in textile production, indirect evidence makes this conclusion seem reasonable. The records show that members of textile mercantile firms invested much more heavily in those mills served by their firms than they did in the remainder of the 11 mills. Moreover, studies of the structure of the early textile industry have shown that most of the original Massachusetts-type mills were established as noncompetitive operations with each mill specializing in one particular textile product.[17] Since the textile merchants were faced with an almost monopolistic group of mill suppliers, it seems reasonable to assume that the necessity of maintaining a source of supply must have dictated their investment in textiles.

The high profits of the mid-forties brought many new firms into the industry; and entry apparently did much to reduce the strength of the forces that had combined to draw the capital of textile merchants into the mills. The influx of new firms drove profits below the returns in alternative investments. The textile merchants, because of their position, should have been among the first to sense the effects of increased competition. At the same time, entry caused increased sales competition among the mills and reduced the merchants' need for ties of ownership to maintain their sources of supply. The result was a withdrawal of capital by the textile merchants.

Financial Institutions

Among the records of stockholders appear the names of 35 commercial banks, 7 savings banks, 5 fire and marine insurance companies, 5 broker-

---

[16] The stock subscriptions were usually first opened to the friends and associates of the original promoters and public sale was atypical.

[17] Other evidence of the noncompetitive market structure is found in the continual exchange of cost, price, and labor information that passed between the mills. For a full discussion of the industry's organizational structure see Vera Shlakman, *Economic History of a Factory Town; A Study of Chicopee, Massachusetts* (Northampton, Mass., 1935).

age firms, 2 private banks, 1 life insurance company, and 1 trust company. Two conditions set these financial intermediaries apart from the other occupational classes. First, since these institutions often served only as intermediaries, the true capital source remains partly obscured; and second, the intermediaries apparently acquired their holdings for a wide variety of reasons. Although no exhaustive study of motivation is possible, it appears that the insurance companies purchased equity as a permanent part of their investment portfolio; that at least some of the commercial and savings banks acquired their holdings in the process of loan creation (i.e., the shares were signed over to them as collateral or they were received in partial payment of the forfeited loans); and that the brokers frequently purchased their shares for resale.[18] Despite this variety of motives, these financial institutions did provide capital, either directly (through the deliberate investment of their own or their customers' funds) or indirectly (by permitting individuals to hypothecate stock and thus invest in the industry without forfeiting their other enterprises).[19] In its ultimate effect there is little difference between direct and indirect investment. In the former case, the intermediaries make a direct capital grant to the recipient firm. In the latter, the institution interposes an added guarantor (the borrower) between itself and the capital recipient. Thus potential investors who otherwise would be forced to hold surplus funds in liquid reserves are allowed to invest in industrial equity. For these investors know that the intermediaries would be willing to convert equity shares into liquid reserves by substituting their capital for the funds of the investor if the need should arise. The history of the Massachusetts Hospital Life Insurance Company provides evidence of the importance of indirect lending. While the Mass. Hospital never purchased textile equity as a permanent earning asset, the company did, as a result of its loan policy, become the registered owner of a large quantity of the issues of the 11 firms. In no cross-section year did that institution hold less than $80,000 in stock in the 11 companies, and in 1854 the holdings totaled $390,500.

Just as the motives for shareholding of these financial intermediaries differed from those of the merchants, so the pattern of their investment also differed markedly from that of the mercantile investors. Although these intermediaries accounted for a sizable share of the equity in every cross-section year, the group made only a small (2 percent) contribution

18 The records of the New England Mutual Life Insurance Company make it very clear that stock was purchased as a part of the investment portfolio. Conversely, the records of the Provident Institution for Savings and the Massachusetts Hospital Life Insurance Company (a trust company) show that almost all of their holdings arose out of loan creation.

19 In the period under consideration, the hypothecation of stock resulted in ownership passing temporarily into the hands of the lender. The firm records, then, show the lending firm as the registered stock owner until the loan has been repaid and title again passed to the original owner.

to original sales. Moreover, despite the evidence of substantial fluctuation, there appears to have been no significant trend in their relative contribution, their relative importance among the total number of stockholders, the average investment per firm, or in the average size of the individual institution's investment.[20]

That the relative holdings of the financial intermediaries did not increase despite the rapid increases in the size and numbers of these institutions, can probably be traced to two related circumstances. First, only the insurance companies purchased textile stock as a permanent part of their portfolio; and, although their rate of growth was high in the two decades before Lincoln's election, their absolute size was never large. Thus, the majority of the textile shares held by the group reposed in the hands of the trust companies and the commercial and savings banks— institutions that acquired their holdings in the course of their loan activities. And, although these latter institutions were rapidly increasing their loans during the forties and fifties, this expansion was occurring in real estate and personal security loans and not in loans on intangible securities.[21]

Although the five-year cross-sections do not permit a complete analysis of cyclical fluctuations, some evidence suggests that the intermediaries' holdings may have been affected by fluctuations in business activity. In 1834 (a year of panic) and in 1844 (after a prolonged depression) the relative contribution of the financial institutions fell precipitously (see Table 6).[22] Since these fluctuations are more pronounced in the holdings of the commercial and savings banks than they are in the portfolios of the other financial institutions, they probably reflect shifts in loan policy induced by deteriorating business conditions.

Financiers

Persons engaged in financial enterprises appear on the textile companies' books as stockholders almost as frequently as financial institutions. The sample yields the names of 59 persons who could be termed financiers; these include 19 commercial bank officers, 17 officers of insurance companies, 15 brokers, 4 trust officers, and 4 private bankers.

Although the proportion of stock held by these financiers was only about two thirds that held by the textile merchants, over time the two

---

20 See Tables 4, 5, 6, and 7.

21 See, for example, the balance sheets of the Provident Institution for Savings and the Massachusetts Hospital Life Insurance Company. In the case of the Provident Institution, security loans declined from $472,445 in December, 1840, to $37,500 in December, 1858.

22 The estimates of absolute holdings (see Table 3) also seem to bear out the contention that there is some relationship between the holdings of this group and the state of business activity. Both 1834 and 1844 show a sharp drop in the absolute holdings of the financial institutions.

series appear to have moved closely together. The relative contribution of the financiers rose from 6 percent in 1829 to almost 11 percent 10 years later. After that date, the trend was reversed, and the ratio displays a gradual decline reaching 6 percent again in 1854.[23] Unlike the movements of the textile merchants' holdings, the fluctuations in the relative importance of financiers can be attributed both to changes in the relative number of investors and to changes in the average investment of each individual.[24]

The contribution of the financial group to new equity issues did not diverge far from the pattern of their holdings in a typical cross-section year. They purchased about 9 percent of the new equity included in the survey, and their individual investments in these new issues averaged slightly over $16,000.

These figures seem to indicate that the financiers were as aware of the actual levels of profit as were the textile merchants. The financiers' entry coincides closely with the years of high profits, and their exit follows swiftly on the heels of declining profits.[25] It is not difficult to believe that the "men of money" would be acutely aware of the industry's true profit prospects, and that these men would not be bound to textiles by any nonprofit considerations. However, their apparent reentry in the late fifties is more difficult to rationalize. It may have reflected some astute guesses about the proximity of hostilities coupled with an awareness of the profit potential of the textile industry in wartime.

Out-of-State Contributions to Equity

In the entire study, no characteristic stands out more plainly than the almost total absence of foreign capital. Even if the category "foreign capital" is used to include all non-Massachusetts investors, the contribution is insignificant.

Among the stockholders included in the survey were 59 persons who did not live in Massachusetts and 2 firms whose offices were outside the Commonwealth. Of the 59 out-of-state stockholders, 7 were residents of foreign countries, 29 were Nashua and Amoskeag owners residing in New Hampshire, and 27 did not live in either Massachusetts or the state in which their mills were located.[26] The two out-of-state businesses were Paddleford and Far, the Savannah cotton house, and Baring Bros., the English private bankers.

---

[23] See Table 6. The estimates of absolute contribution also show a pattern similar to that established by the textile merchants. Table 3 shows an increase until 1844 followed by a reduction in the succeeding years (except for an increase in 1859).

[24] See Tables 5 and 7. Interestingly enough, however, there appear to have been no regular movements in the average size of the investment per firm (Table 4).

[25] See footnote 15.

[26] The Nashua and Amoskeag were located in New Hampshire, while the other nine firms were located in Massachusetts.

Until 1839 no out-of-state owners can be identified on the list of stock-holders; and, although their importance gradually increases during the ensuing 20 years, by 1859 they owned only slightly more than 2 percent of the total equity surveyed. The individuals in the group seldom held stock in more than a single firm and their average investment ($5,500 to $7,300) was lower than that of any other class.

Nor was the out-of-state group important in the financing of new firms. Of the nine new issues included in the survey the out-of-state group sub-scribed to only .3 percent (.003).

Although foreign capital made significant contributions to other sectors of the American economy, the textile industry appears to have drawn little direct benefit from this source. The seven alien holders (three Englishmen, three Germans, and one Canadian) subscribed to no new stock issues, and holdings of the largest investor never exceeded $16,000.

Today the corporate form of business is often thought of as an instru-ment designed to depersonalize capital and thus free it of its geographic ties; however, there is nothing in the pattern of equity ownership of these early mills that would attest to the importance of that feature.[27] The de-pendence upon local capital is so strong that it seems to suggest that the location of the early textile industry in New England might be traced not only to immobile labor and power sources but also to the existence of a substantial quantity of immobile capital.

Women and Trustees

Although accounts held in the name of women or trustees were rare in the industry's formative years, maturity brought with it increased par-ticipation by these two groups.[28] Their individual investments remained small; but each succeeding survey included a greater number of their accounts; and, by 1859, women and trustees together held almost one fourth of the total shares surveyed (and, of course, this is one quarter of a much larger total).[29]

A comparison of the records of the individual firms shows that the increase in the importance of women and trustees was linked not only with the passage of time, but also with the age of the firm. The two groups ap-pear earlier and become important sooner in the three older firms (the

---

[27] Nor for that matter does the corporate form even appear to have freed capital from personal ties in the Boston area. The records show that most stockholders regu-larly attended meetings and took an active part in the direction of the firm's activities. Their comments make it clear that many felt that their companies were as much their personal property as their own partnerships and sole proprietorships.

[28] The estimates of absolute contribution show a steady increase throughout the period (see Table 3).

[29] There is no way of estimating the number of estates that are represented by the trustee figures. The stockholder records most frequently list the trust account under the name of the trustee (followed by the note "trustee"), and the same persons often served as trustees for several estates.

Boston, Hamilton, and Nashua) than they do in the remaining eight mills. Moreover, the contribution of the women and trustees was important in the original financing of only one mill—the Lyman—and here the new issue did not represent a voluntary purchase of shares, but merely a substitution of shares in the new mill for those in an already established enterprise (the Hadley Falls Company).

In her excellent monograph on the New England textile industry, Miss Ware has attributed the rising proportion of holdings of women and trustees to the industry's high profits and increasing stability that made investment appear both safe and lucrative.[30] While there is no certain method of verifying this hypothesis, some evidence indicates that at least a part of the increase can be attributed not to voluntary investment by widows and orphans but to the deaths of the original investors and the distribution of their estates, including textile shares, to their heirs.[31] An examination of the women listed on the individual stockholder accounts indicates that well over two thirds of the new women holders had the same surname as men who had previously held shares but whose names had ceased to be listed. Furthermore, the notation "widow of . . . ." not infrequently followed the name of the new shareholder. In a few cases, the trustee accounts carried the notation "Josiah Quincy trustee for Paschal Pope." In these cases, investigation usually showed that Paschal Pope had held stock in the company in an earlier year. Finally, the fact that the size of the women's and trustees' holdings were related to the age of the firm (as well as the historical year) also supports the view that inheritance helped determine ownership. If safety and profitability had been the cause of the increased investment, the investments should have moved into all firms in the same chronological period. If, however, the stock was acquired by inheritance, the women and trustees could be expected to appear first in the oldest firms, since the owners of older firms could be expected to die earlier than the owners of newer companies, on the average. An examination of the holdings by firms does in fact show a marked positive partial correlation between firm age and women and trustee holdings.

Other Groups

Little industrial capital found its way to the textile industry through investment by persons earning a living in nontextile manufacturing. In the 30-year span, 71 such person (31 artisans, 27 managers and officers in manufacturing companies, and 13 owners of manufacturing companies)

---

[30] Caroline Ware, *The Early New England Cotton Manufacture,* pp. 122 and 148.

[31] Even if the original stock had been acquired through inheritance, it would still be possible to argue that continued ownership implied a belief in the safety and profitability of the investment. However, in the absence of a well-defined equity market, it is safe to infer that often the legatees could dispose of their shares only at a substantial loss.

and 1 manufacturing company held stock in one or more of the 11 mills. However, their holdings represented only about 5 percent of the total. They typically invested only a small amount and in only a single concern, and they did not increase their relative contribution over the period.

The failure of the nontextile industrial group to increase its relative share appears as something of a surprise. Given the industrial development that marked the first half of the century, it appears reasonable to expect manufacturing capital to have become more important as the period progressed. That this did not occur, indicates, perhaps, that manufacturing wealth did not increase more rapidly than the accumulation of capital in the economy as a whole; or, perhaps, in the later years falling profits caused a withdrawal of capital from textiles that offset the increase that otherwise would have occurred; or, perhaps most likely, almost all industrial capital was reinvested in the business in which it originated.[32]

The 100 professional persons who owned stock in the 11 firms made a greater contribution than the nontextile industrialists, but their proportionate share of holdings declined over the period, from 12 to 7 percent.[33] However, if the estimates of absolute capital are reliable, the decline does not indicate a withdrawal of capital, but merely a rate of increase lower than the rate of the industry's expansion.

Summary and Conclusions

Recent studies have indicated that the sale of equity shares provided the American textile industry with most of its original capital. This study utilizes the records of 11 Massachusetts-type textile mills to trace the source of the equity capital. These records, supplemented by local histories, city directories, and university alumni records, served to identify the majority of the stockholders by occupation. A comparison of the holdings of the occupational groups at five-year intervals permitted an estimate of the trends in the relative importance of each group to be made; and, in addition, it provided some insights into the investment behavior of the members of each group.

If the 11 firms were typical of the early cotton manufacture, mercantile wealth appears to have been the most important single source of textile finance—at least one third of the total in every year except 1859. The evidence also suggests that the shift from mercantile to industrial capital was a slow process, with merchants only gradually withdrawing their funds from trade and investing them in industry. Moreover, although the first movement of capital from trade to industry may have been insti-

---

[32] If the equity figures had been disaggregated and those shares representing stock dividends assumed to represent reinvestment in textiles, the figures would show a substantial increase in industrial capital during the 1840's.

[33] The 100 included 60 lawyers, 19 doctors, and 21 judges, ministers, dentists, and teachers.

gated by a decline in trading profits, the transfer process appears to have continued even during periods of mercantile prosperity.

During the 1830's, textile merchants were by far the heaviest investors in the textile industry. This propensity to invest can probably be attributed to their knowledge of, and close contact with, the textile manufacturing firms, and to their need to assure a source of domestic supply in a market that was not yet very competitive. During the 1840's textile merchants withdrew their capital from textile production. The withdrawal apparently resulted from falling profits in textile manufacture coupled with increasing competition among manufacturers.

Even in the industry's formative years, a significant portion of its equity shares was held by financial intermediaries; but despite the rapid growth in the resources of these financial institutions, there appears to have been no sustained increase in the proportion of equity supplied by them.

Unlike some other young industries of the antebellum period, New England textiles received only a negligible amount of capital from abroad and very little from other parts of the country. Although the equity holdings of non-Massachusetts owners increased with time, even at the end of the period they represented only 2 percent of the industry's capital. In the entire period only seven aliens held stock in one or more of the firms; and the total holdings of the largest investor among the seven never exceeded $16,000.

Over the period, the most significant increases in ownership are recorded for women and trustees. Although these two groups held almost no shares in 1830, by 1859 they accounted for almost one fourth of the total. The evidence suggests, however, that the increases can be attributed not to the positive attractions of textile investment but to the natural processes of death and inheritance.

3. Capital Immobilities and Finance Capitalism: A Study of Economic Evolution in the United States, 1820-1920*

Lance E. Davis
Purdue University

I. Introduction

THE CLASSICAL MODEL of resource allocation assumes that within any economy capital is perfectly mobile; and implies, therefore, that once allowance for uncertainty and risk is made, returns on investment are equal in all industries in all regions. This model is logically perfect but it does not provide much help in understanding the process of development and the concomitant decline in uncertainty discounts. With such a model it is difficult to explain the evolution of financial capitalism as a by-product of the economic process, and the rise of the great financial fortunes has been explained in terms of artificial monopolies, the "laws of capitalist development," and outright theft.[1] This paper will argue that a model based on the existence of certain interregional and interindustry capital immobilities provides a better explanation for American development, and that the rise and decline of financial capitalism can be analyzed within the framework of such a model. Within this context, the fortunes

* Reprinted from *Explorations in Entrepreneurial History / Second Series*, Vol. 1, No. 1 (Fall, 1963), pp. 88–105.
[1] For examples of these different interpretations see V. Lenin, "Imperialism, the Highest Stage of Capitalism," in *V. I. Lenin Collected Works*, Vol. XIX (New York, 1942); G. Edwards, *The Evolution of Finance Capitalism* (New York, 1938); M. Josephson, *The Robber Barons* (New York, 1934); and T. Lawson, *Frenzied Finance* (New York, 1905).

accumulated by Rockefeller, Morgan, et al., represent payments of economic rent attached to a scarce talent (the ability to mobilize capital),
and the decline in the economic importance of the "men of money" a
reflection of the increase in the availability of mobile capital.

Capital can be said to be immobile if savers are unwilling or unable
to make their accumulations available to capital users whose activities
yield the highest economic return.[2] Such a failure can occur if there are
no effective capital markets, if savers value safety above all else, if they
are unwilling to invest their savings in enterprises divorced from their
personal experience, or if there are substantial noneconomic rewards to
investments whose economic yields are very low. If immobilities exist,
savings tend to take the form of hoards, near-hoards, or investment in
assets within the saver's immediate knowledge. Immobile capital appears
to be characteristic of most newly developing economies, and only gradually as development proceeds is capital made truly mobile.[3] Successful
capital mobilization involves both the education of the saver and the
evolution of a series of financial markets able to smooth the flow of funds
from savers to investors. Until capital does become mobile, it is the rare
individual who possesses the talent to move capital across geographic and
industrial boundaries.

In the United States, such immobilities distorted the pattern of growth
throughout the entire 19th century; but they became much more important in postbellum decades. It was during these later years that the
financial capitalists gained national prominence. The increasing impact

---

[2] Much of the literature on the role of capital in economic development has centered on problems of capital accumulation (that is, on problems inherent in attempts
to increase the rate of savings to a level sufficient to permit enough capital formation
to underwrite industrialization). Certainly insufficient savings can seriously retard
growth; however, there is little evidence to indicate that it acted as an important
brake on the development of the Western world. The evidence that does exist
strongly suggests that the rates of savings in these countries was always fairly high,
and recently Dean and Cole have shown that England industrialized with a savings
ratio of only 9 percent. In the case of the United States, Kuznets has found some
slight inverse correlation between investment in producers durables and investment
in housing before 1920; however, this correlation, although suggestive of some slight
savings restraint, is hardly compatible with a belief in serious industrial retardation
engendered by a shortage of capital. See R. Goldsmith, "The Growth of Reproducible
Wealth in the United States of America 1805–1950" in International Association for
Research in Income and Wealth, *Income and Wealth of the United States, Trends
and Structure*, Income and Wealth, Series II (Baltimore, 1952); S. Kuznets, *Capital
in the American Economy: Its Formation and Financing* (Princeton, 1961); and P.
Dean and W. Cole, *British Economic Growth 1688–1959* (London, 1962).

[3] Professor Poston has shown that such immobilities plagued the economic growth
of the nations of Western Europe. In the case of England, for example, several 15th-
century fortunes were sufficient to finance the entire 19th-century textile industry,
but textiles were continually capital-starved despite high economic returns while
funds flowed freely into landed investments in the face of zero or near zero earnings.
In the case of France, French industry was unable to secure funds while the nation
was willing to finance the Russian army and court. M. M. Poston, an unpublished
series of lectures given to the graduate economic history seminar at Johns Hopkins
University during the academic year 1954–55.

of these immobilities can be traced to the rapid rise in the demand for external finance. This rise can, in turn, be attributed to the shift of industry from the East to the West, to a series of technological innovations in manufacturing that increased both total capital requirements and the minimum size of initial investment, and to new developments in agriculture that required greater amounts of capital equipment.[4]

II. Changes in the Demand for and the Supply of Capital

A. The East

Eastern savers were historically the nation's most sophisticated, but even in the East savings were not easily mobilized. The first two decades of the 19th century saw a rapid decline in the profitability of foreign trade, and a few years later, the Erie Canal triggered a similar fall in the returns to eastern agriculture. At first glance, it appears that capital was quite mobile and moved rapidly out of these declining industries and into more rewarding ventures. A more careful examination of the evidence, however, suggests that, although the transfers were fairly effortless, capital did not become geographically mobile and to a large extent was mobile between industries only when the savers themselves moved with their capital.

The cotton and woolen textile industries received the bulk of the new capital. In the case of cotton, the beneficiaries were all eastern firms; and, despite the obvious locational advantages, no capital moved into the South. Moreover, it appears there was also little personal divorcement in the capital transfer; a list of the officers of the new mills closely resembles a list of the successful merchants of a decade earlier.[5] A similar financial pattern is found in the history of the woolen industry. Original capital came in large measure from individuals who had accumulated savings in trade and agriculture, but these savers transferred themselves

---

[4] The demand for external finance (funds in excess of those generated by the business itself) is a function not only of the total capital requirement but also of the timing of those requirements. In the case of American agriculture, for example, the total capital requirements of a corn farm in the Old Northwest during the 1830's and forties were probably greater than the requirements of a wheat farm in the prairies two or three decades later. However, the timing of their requirements was quite different; and, as a result, the demand for external finance by the wheat farmer was greater than that of his predecessor. In the case of corn, the largest capital requirements were for land clearing, but these could be met gradually out of the income generated by the enterprise. For the wheat farm, however, machinery was needed before the farm could become an economical unit.

[5] An examination of the ownership of the large New England cotton textile mills indicates that the stockholders were almost all Massachusetts residents, and, although the firms' securities were listed on the Boston exchange, few shares were ever traded. Instead, the firms depended almost entirely on personal subscription for both initial and additional finance. Lance E. Davis, "Stock Ownership in the Early New England Textile Industry," *Business History Review*, Vol. 32, (1958), pp. 204–22, and J. Martin, *Century of Finance* (Boston, 1898).

with their capital to the new industry. Again, this transfer implied little geographic mobility. As woolen manufacture began to move west toward its source of supply, the worsted mills (requiring heavy capital investment) remained concentrated in the East because "capital was more plentiful in that area."[6]

Aside from textiles, even within the East, capital was not very mobile. In the case of the boot and shoe industry, for example, the shift from shop to factory was financed almost entirely with internal funds and outside capital was not enlisted until late in the century.[7] A similar inability to acquire impersonal finance marked the early history of the steel industry. Capital requirements in iron manufacture had been small and were usually met by the ironmaster himself with occasional (in the case of the largest enterprises) recourse to a few partners. The development of the Kelly and Bessemer processes created the possibility of economical steel production but also intensified the industry's need for external finance. The first Bessemer mill was finished only because the Pennsylvania Railroad (a prospective customer) was willing to advance $600,000 when the owner's personal finances were exhausted.[8] Similarly when Ward and Durgen began to build the first "Kelly" plant, financial demands greatly exceeded their personal accumulations, and it was only by appealing to "other iron men, some in England and some in the United States" that they were able to acquire the necessary capital.[9] Only gradually during the last decades of the 19th century were funds made available to eastern industry through "normal" channels.

B. The West

Despite the evidences of immobilities in the East, that area was probably affected less than either the South or West. The bulk of the nation's savings appear to have accrued in the East, but an ever-increasing proportion of economic activity was located outside the area. Thus, the inability to mobilize capital most likely caused greater dislocations in the South and West than in the East. The West provides an intermediate example of these distortions. The region's history is replete with examples of the effects of these barriers, but since the area developed relatively late, it benefited both from the gradual evolution of mobile capital and from the mobilizing activities of the financial capitalists.

Early in its history the West needed external capital to finance its transport system. In response to this demand, finance moved westward in the 1830's and 1850's; however, while some of the funds came from

---

[6] A. Cole, *The American Wool Manufacture* (Cambridge, Mass., 1926), pp. 226–31, 274.

[7] B. Hazard, *The Organization of the Boot and Shoe Industry in Massachusetts Before 1875* (Cambridge, Mass., 1921).

[8] A. Carnegie, *Autobiography* (Boston, 1924).

[9] J. Boucher, *William Kelly* (Greenburg, Pa., 1924).

eastern savers, the bulk were drawn from abroad.[10] Significant barriers to domestic East-West capital flows continued to exist, and firms unable to draw on the talents of the financial capitalists were largely forced to depend on local savings.

In the case of western agriculture, the opening of the trans-Mississippi West coupled with a series of important technological developments in wheat production greatly increased the industry's demand for external finance. Threshers, first innovated in the West in the 1840's, were replaced in the 1850's and 1860's with more productive and much more capital intensive machines, and by the Civil War reapers too were needed if a farm was to be profitable.[11] Moreover, as planters and shellers were developed, corn farming began to demand some investment in machinery. Local banks were unable to supply these additional requirements, and in the absence of normal alternatives, the farmers turned to the equipment manufacturers for credit.[12] Since the manufacturers were also limited to local personal capital, this informal credit arrangement, while increasing intraregional mobility, did nothing to promote mobility between regions.

An examination of four of the West's most important manufacturing industries (milling, meat packing, oil refining, and agricultural machinery) indicates that the effects of imperfect capital mobility were not limited to agriculture. Although some short-term requirements were met from sources outside the region, local capital provided almost all the initial long-term finance; and most growth was financed through retained earnings. Moreover, in those rare instances when outside capital did play an important role, it appears to have been almost entirely mobilized through personal contacts.[13]

In the case of meat packing, a movement from farm to factory revolutionized the industry in the mid-thirties. Even after that date, despite some infusions of bank credit and short-term eastern risk capital to finance inventories, most firms were organized on the basis of the proprietor's personal capital (or the pooled resources of two or three partners), relying on their suppliers' willingness to defer payment to finance their inventories and upon retained earnings for growth.[14] Although there was

---

[10] L. Jenks, *The Migration of British Capital* (New York, 1927), and R. McCrane, *Foreign Bondholders and American State Debt* (Chapel Hill, N.C., 1935).

[11] L. Rogin, *The Introduction of Farm Machinery in its Relation to the Productivity of Labor in Agriculture of the United States during the Nineteenth Century* (Berkeley, Calif., 1931).

[12] Both McCormick, the nation's largest producer of reapers, and the J. I. Case Company, one of the largest thresher manufactures, sold machinery to customers on a long-term blasis. See C. McCormick, *The Century of the Reaper* (Boston, 1931), and S. Holbrook, *Machines of Plenty* (New York, 1955).

[13] The evidence, in fact, suggests that in the cases of agricultural machinery, oil refining, and meat packing, industrial concentration can be traced in large part to differences in businessmen's ability to command capital through personal connections.

[14] Local banks very early helped the industry finance its inventories and by the

some increase in the local banks' contributions to short-term requirements, in essence this pattern of finance continued until the 1880's. At this time, the changes wrought by the advent of refrigeration greatly increased the packers' demand for long-term external finance.[15] The typical packer, without large personal resources or entrée to the eastern capital markets, found himself unable to innovate the new technology and, as a result, was frequently forced out of business. On the other hand, the few business-men capable of commanding finance were able to profit and expand.[16]

Between the end of the 18th century and the 1870's technology in flour milling changed but little, and since the old technology offered no im-portant economies of scale, average firm size remained small.[17] Initial capital requirements seldom exceeded an amount that the miller himself could accumulate (although there are evidences of occasional loans from local farmers who expected to use the facilities), and growth depended largely upon plowbacks. In the 1870's, however, the innovation of Hun-garian reduction milling greatly increased minimum efficient mill size and, therefore, the industry's demand for external finance.[18] Businessmen, however, found it extremely difficult to attract depersonalized capital (either from inside or outside the region), and well into the 1880's even the largest firms were still family enterprises.[19]

Meat packing attracted some short-term eastern capital, and milling ultimately some British; but the agricultural machinery industry, although

---

1840's eastern capitalists were regularly placing short-term funds in western centers. Farmers frequently waited a year for payment for pigs sold the industry. R. Clemen, *The American Livestock and Meat Industry* (New York, 1923).

[15] Before the Civil War meat packing had meant pork packing, but shortly there-after consumer tastes began to shift toward beef. In the mid-eighties (after the wide-spread innovation of refrigerator cars) it was found most profitable to slaughter and dress the beeves in the West and ship the carcasses to market in the East. The process was, however, more capital-intensive than the older one, and the financial demands of the industry increased concomitantly. Clemen, *Livestock.*

[16] Both the Swift and the Armour packing empires were based at least in part on mobilization talents of their owners. While most western packers could find no out-side sources of capital, Armour was able to utilize the financial resources of his brother's New York commercial house, and Swift, after earning a fortune in the East, migrated West with his accumulation. Clemen, *Livestock.*

[17] There were, of course, some large milling enterprises, but they appear to have been no more economical than much smaller mills. C. Kuhlmann, *The Development of the Flour Milling Industry in the United States* (Boston, 1929).

[18] Without the new mills it was impossible to utilize the spring wheat of the upper Great Plains. J. Gray, *Business Without Boundary* (Minneapolis, Minn., 1954).

[19] In the 1880's the first outside capital began to flow into the Minneapolis mills, but even then it was British rather than American. Of the largest mills, Pillsbury had been purchased by British capital by the end of the eighties, but the Washburn mills remained a local enterprise until the formation of General Mills in the 1920's. Both of these concerns date from the 1870's. Because of the difficulties of mobilizing capital it was not unusual for a person of some wealth to build a mill and bring in a skilled operator as a partner. This latter transaction did little to depersonalize capi-tal as the experience of the Washburn mills (the nation's largest) indicates. W. D. Washburn built the original mills and brought in George Christian as an operating partner; however, several years later when the pair broke up it was Washburn who assumed operating control. Gray, *Business.*

its large scale capital requirements antedate both, appears to have remained almost entirely self-financed until the end of the century. The manufacture of plows and scythes had typically been carried on in small firms, but the development of mechanized reapers and threshers moved the industry out of the shop and into the factory. This move, however, was largely financed from personal investments and retained earnings. McCormick, the nation's largest producer of reapers, for example, brought together a series of partners to finance his Chicago factory and then used the firm's profits to buy them out.[20] The J. I. Case Company (a major producer of threshers) was entirely self-financed.[21] In neither case did depersonalized capital become important until much later. Case attracted some outside finance after the death of the founder in 1891, but McCormick remained a family enterprise until J. P. Morgan organized the International Harvester combine in 1902.

Like the meat-packing industry, the industrial structure of the oil refining industry was shaped in part by the immobilities of capital. Refining, based on the discoveries of "Colonel" Drake in the late 'fifties, remained an industry of small producers until the end of the next decade. In the early stage, firms tended to be financed by the personal accumulations of their owners, and occasionally when more capital was needed additional partners were enlisted. Rockefeller's first experience in oil refining, for example, was as a member of such a partnership.[22] The 'seventies were marked by a series of new technological developments in refining; and, although the new technology greatly reduced costs, it also increased capital requirements.[23] As in meat packing, the new technology placed a great premium on a firm's ability to mobilize capital. Firms with access to outside finance were able to expand at the expense of those unable to afford the new technology, and Rockefeller with his close ties to the Cleveland banking community was able to take the first steps toward ultimate domination of the industry.[24]

---

[20] McCormick entered into two partnerships to meet the capital requirements of his Chicago plant. In both cases (first with Gray and then with Ogden and Jones) he used his profits to buy out the partners. It is interesting to note that so little was capital depersonalized that it appears as if its owners insisted on a partnership arrangement even though their investments were essentially short term. McCormick, *Century.*

[21] Holbrook, *Machines.*

[22] A. Nevins, *John D. Rockefeller* (New York, 1940).

[23] The new developments were concentrated in distilling and in techniques of integrating operations. H. Williamson and A. Daum, *The American Petroleum Industry: The Age of Illumination* (Evanston, Ill., 1959). Although quantitative data for the seventies is lacking, some indication of the increase in the demand for capital may be found in the industry's capitalization trends in the two succeeding decades. In the years from 1880 to 1899, although the number of firms declined by 20 percent, the industry's capitalization almost tripled. *Ibid.*, p. 616.

[24] When other firms were unable to adopt the new techniques because of lack of capital, Rockefeller with his carefully preserved banking connections was able to acquire sufficient loan finance to first build the most efficient firm in the Cleveland

C. The South

In many respects the South represents the most puzzling of the three regions. As in the West, outside capital flowed but slowly into the region, but in the South even local capital was not effectively mobilized. In the West, mobilization of long-term capital was first achieved through the efforts of a few financial capitalists and by personal transfers from savers to capital-using firms. In the South even these crude methods were late developing. Much of the region's original accumulations had been in agriculture; but, despite declining returns in the "Old South" after the 1830's, capital did not flow into more lucrative activities. Some agricultural capital did move into the "West" (Alabama, Mississippi, and east Texas) but usually only when it was accompanied by its owners. Moreover, within the "Old South" there was practically no transfer from agriculture to industry. Despite locational advantages, textiles were unable to attract external finance; instead funds continued to be reinvested in agriculture.[25] Not until well after the Civil War did the textile industry become firmly established in the South, and then it was local capital and the accumulations of the mill owners and their friends that provided the finance. When in the 1880's some external capital did enter the industry, it came from the East, not the South. It was well into the 20th century before the South made any significant contribution of depersonalized capital to its industry.[26]

III. The Emergence of Financial Capitalism

During the last decades of the 19th century, in the East and West at least, the demand for long-term external finance was largely met through the offices of a group of financial capitalists. These men possessed personal contacts that allowed them to move capital across industry and geographic boundaries. Their numbers and activities are too numerous to detail, but the histories of three (Rockefeller, Carnegie, and Morgan) provide considerable insight into the role of these financiers in the mobilization process.

---

area and to then buy out many of his less efficient competitors. It was his Cleveland refineries that were the basis for Standard Oil. A. Nevins, *Rockefeller,* and P. Trescott, *Financing American Enterprise* (New York, 1963).

[25] William Gregg, a successful southern textile mill owner, continually complained about his inability to attract external capital. Nor was capital shortage a cause of his problems. Gregg said, "Charleston has ample capital if she could be brought to use it for improvements within the state." During the 1850's while returns in agriculture were near zero and textiles were earning in excess of 10 percent, Gregg found it impossible to attract external funds, but investment in farm acreage and farm equipment were increasing significantly. B. Mitchell, *William Gregg, Factory Master of the Old South* (Chapel Hill, N.C., 1928); J. D. B. De Bow, *Statistical View of the United States: Compendium of the Seventh Census* (Washington, D.C., 1854); and *Eighth Census of the United States,* Vol. III, *Manufactures.*

[26] B. Mitchell, *The Rise of Cotton Mills in the South* (Baltimore, 1921).

Rockefeller possessed the ability to mobilize the capital of the commercial banking system. Early in his life he built a close personal relationship with the Cleveland banking community, and it was this connection that permitted him to parlay a small fortune earned in the wholesale trade into the Standard Oil Company. Later, as the extent of his operations increased, he developed equally strong ties with the New York bankers. Because of this ability, Standard had finances when others did not. In fact, at times Standard, because it possessed excess funds, was called on to act as a financial intermediary. In the 1880's when the company's rate of expansion had begun to decline, for example, Rockefeller was deluged with requests to make capital available for a myriad of other enterprises.[27]

Carnegie's talents, on the other hand, lay in his ability to bring together savers and businessmen in search of additional capital. Beginning on a small scale in the iron industry, he organized the Keystone Bridge Company in 1863, and culminated his activities a decade later with the Carnegie Steel Company. In the case of Keystone, for example, he brought together the bridge designer and three officers of the Pennsylvania Railroad and for additional finance he called on his friends in the iron industry. In Carnegie's own words: "my letters to iron manufacturers in Pittsburgh were sufficient to insure the new company credit."[28]

Morgan, the most successful mobilizer of capital in American history, brought together the accumulations of financial institutions, of domestic savers, and of foreign capitalists. Although Morgan earned his original reputation in international finance, he soon began to apply his talents to domestic mobilization.[29] In the early 1870's his first syndicate (based largely on foreign capital) broke Jay Cooke's monopoly in the govern-

[27] Nevins, *Rockefeller,* and Trescott, *Enterprise.* It might be added that Rockefeller honored few of the requests outside the oil industry; however, the requests themselves are strong evidence of an imperfect capital market. Rockefeller himself commented implicitly on the state of the capital market at the time of his entry into the mining enterprises of the Mesabi. "We had invested many millions, and no one seemed to want to go in with us to buy stocks. On the contrary, everybody seemed to want to sell. The stock was offered to us in alarming quantities—substantially all the stock of the companies came without any solicitation on our part—quite the contrary—and we paid for it in cash." Nevins, *Rockefeller,* Vol. II, pp. 395–96.

[28] A. Carnegie, *Autobiography,* p. 114. Nor were Carnegie's mobilization activities always restricted to ventures in which he had an operational interest. One of his most revealing ventures resulted in the sale of 4½ million dollars of Allegheny Valley Railroad bonds. In the early seventies the Allegheny Valley Railroad, unable to sell its bonds through formal channels, appealed to Carnegie for help. Carnegie in a series of negotiations (negotiations that included convincing the management of the Pennsylvania Railroad to advance funds to the Allegheny and to exchange the Allegheny bonds for bonds of the Erie and Pennsylvania Railroad held, and involving marketing arrangements with both Baring Brothers and Junias Morgan) managed to sell the bonds and earn himself a substantial commission. *Ibid.,* pp. 167–69.

[29] It is interesting to note that even late in his career, long after he had begun to delegate most of his firm's operation to his "men," Morgan continued to handle foreign exchange transactions himself. Jonathan R. T. Hughes, *The Good Land* (in preparation).

ment bond market and, in the latter half of the decade, he managed to sell a large block of the Vanderbilts' New York Central holdings in London without seriously affecting security prices. These successes were, however, based largely on Morgan's foreign connections. In 1877 in a small but significant operation Morgan demonstrated an ability to move capital within the United States. In that year, as Congress dawdled over an army appropriations bill, Morgan, able to move finance across regional barriers, offered to advance funds for western army payrolls at a 1 percent discount when the best local offer was 25 percent.[30] From that point on, Morgan's domestic interests increased. His bank developed an extensive list of savers who trusted Morgan's judgment and were willing to put funds into Morgan-backed enterprises even though they were unwilling to trust the normal markets.[31] In addition, he gained access to the accumulations of a number of financial institutions.[32] By 1912, it is estimated that, although his bank had deposits of only 162 million, he was able to command an additional 2 billion dollars belonging to his clients and to other financial intermediaries.[33] It is not, therefore, surprising that it was Morgan who first mobilized the external finance for the steel, agricultural machinery, and a host of other rapidly expanding industries. Nor is it surprising that his few failures (the New England railroad network, for example) were concentrated in areas and industries that had already achieved a relatively high degree of capital mobility.

IV. The Evolution of Mobile Capital and the Decline of Financial Capitalism

As the economy became more developed, barriers to capital movements began to break down. Movements of regional interest rates clearly reflect these improvements in the capital markets. At the end of the Civil War rates in the East were relatively low while those in the West and South were much higher. By the outbreak of World War I, however, rates in the West had fallen almost to eastern levels, and rates in the South, although still relatively high, were nearer those of the other regions.[34]

---

[30] C. Hovey, *The Life Story of J. Pierpont Morgan* (New York, 1911).

[31] The practice of utilizing lists of clients survived into the 1930's when it came under fire as evidence of favoritism. See F. Pecora, *Wall Street Under Oath* (New York, 1939).

[32] Morgan himself became vice president and director of the National Bank of Commerce and with his ally, George Baker, president of the First National Bank, dominated banks and trust companies controlling assets of about 1.9 billion dollars. Morgan also became interested in a number of insurance companies, and his widely discussed purchase of the Equitable can probably be best viewed as an attempt to add to his pool of finance. L. Brandeis, *Other People's Money* (New York, 1932), and T. Lawson, *Frenzied Finance* (New York, 1905).

[33] G. Edwards, *Evolution*.

[34] See U.S. Department of the Interior, *Report on Real Estate Mortgages*, Eleventh Census: 1890 (Washington, D.C., 1895); U.S. Department of Agriculture, *Bulletin 384*, "Costs and Sources of Farm-Mortgage Loans in the United States"; L. Zartman, *The Investments of Life Insurance Companies* (New York, 1906).

Moreover, the rapidly growing competition among investment banking firms is also strongly suggestive of an increase in the mobility of capital. In the 19th century, the number of firms capable of effectively marketing national securities could be counted on the fingers of two hands. Between 1912 and 1929, however, the number of member firms in the Investment Bankers Association (some indication of the size of the industry) almost tripled.[35] As capital became more mobile, competition increased; and monopoly rents almost certainly declined. Thus it is not surprising that in 1934, when the members of J. P. Morgan and Company were forced to choose between investment and commercial banking, all but one of the senior partners chose to leave the investment field.[36]

The transformation from immobile to mobile capital can be attributed to two developments. First, through a process of education, savers became more willing to place their accumulations in investments far removed from their immediate knowledge. Second, the formal capital markets had matured and financial intermediaries capable of smoothing the transfer of funds from saver to investors had evolved.

The process of investor education was everywhere slow, but it proceeded more rapidly in some regions than others. In the East, the original transfer from commerce and agriculture to textiles was a personal one and involved little education. The heirs of the original investors did, however, become acquainted with paper securities. The tempo of education increased as the eastern saver began to buy the securities of railroad and canal companies and later (during the Civil War) the bonds of the federal government.[37] Finally, in the decades after the war, the sales campaigns of the investment houses made stocks and bonds common words in the saver's vocabulary, and convinced even the most skeptical that a piece of paper could be as safe an investment as a house, farm, oi factory. In a sense, Morgan's very success contributed to the end of his monopoly.

Barring the early experience with textiles, the western investor's experience roughly paralleled the easterner's. However, because development came later to the West, the entire process was delayed several decades. Most frequently, the westerner's first contact with paper securities came from his investments in local transport projects; and, although direct evidence is lacking, it appears logical to assume that his experience with these issues opened a wider range of depersonalized investments for him. Certainly by the early 20th century the process had proceeded far enough to lead an important New York banker to say: "The whole great Mississippi Valley gives promise that in some day distant perhaps

---

[35] From 257 to 751. Edwards, *Evolution*, p. 229.

[36] P. Sweezy, "The Decline of the Investment Banker," *Antioch Review*, Vol. 1, (1941), pp. 63–68.

[37] Most usually, savers first invested in the issues of local companies whose works they could see but then gradually their investment horizons widened.

it will be another New England for investments. There is developing a bond market there which is of constant astonishment to eastern dealers."[38]

The Washburn Flour mills provide an interesting example of western capital mobilization. When the original owners died, their heirs were anxious to sell and, in addition, the mills needed additional new capital for growth. However, no outsiders were yet willing to invest. In 1898 an eastern promoter, realizing the potential profits, attempted to bring in outside capital; but even at that late date he was unable to mobilize the necessary funds. Because of the firm's failure to acquire external finance through "normal" markets, growth was financed through the personal connections maintained by an officer (William Dunwoody) with the banking community. Ownership ultimately passed into the hands of the managers, but to finance the sale a 2½-million-dollar loan was negotiated through the Philadelphia commercial banks in 1914. For the first time "foreign" capital had been mobilized through normal channels. Finally, with the organization of General Mills in 1928, the company's stock was listed on a national exchange; and the process of mobilization completed.[39]

In the South, however, saver education did not proceed as rapidly as it had in the other two regions. In fact, by the end of the century the process had hardly begun. Although it is impossible to determine the exact causes of this delay, it almost certainly in part reflects the close ties that existed between land ownership and social position. Moreover, since the area possessed a fine natural transportation network, there were few paper securities to act as educational vehicles.[40] Finally, while federal bonds convinced many savers in the North and West of the safety of paper securities, the Southerner's experience with Confederate bonds could hardly have led him to the same conclusion.

Mobilization was also greatly aided by the evolution of financial intermediaries designed to speed the flow of funds from savers to investors. In both the East and the West short-term mobility was achieved before long-term, and to a large extent this development is a reflection of the willingness of the commercial banks to make finance available to the new enterprises. In its first year of operation the Boston Manufacturing Company, the first of the new Massachusetts textile mills, drew on the state's banks for short-term finance; and well before the Civil War interest differentials caused short-term funds to flow from New York banks to New England industry.[41] Moreover, although the practice may not have

---

[38] Frank A. Vanderlip, vice president of the National City Bank in 1905, quoted in Edwards, *Evolution*, p. 185.

[39] Gray, *Business*.

[40] It has been argued that the existence of a natural transport system may have actually retarded southern development, and in this peculiar secondary sense at least the argument may have some validity. For a statement of the more usual argument see D. North, *Economic Growth of the United States, 1790–1860* (New York, 1961).

[41] It appears that over one half the capital requirements of the textile industry were met by the commercial banks. While short-term funds did flow between eastern

been widespread, the banks promoted some interregional mobility. As early as the 1840's the western meat-packing industry drew on short-term eastern funds, and at times eastern bankers employed agents to search for short-term investment opportunities in the West.[42]

Western bankers too provided short-term finance for enterprise in their region. The banks of Chillicothe, Circleville, Columbus, and Xenia advanced funds to cover livestock inventories, and in Cincinnati, Alton, and Chicago local bankers provided short-term finance for the cities' meat packers.[43] Similar support was received by the milling and agricultural machinery industries, and Rockefeller's story has indicated the role played by Cleveland bankers in the petroleum industry.

In the South, however, the commercial banks contributed much less to the mobilization of capital. During the 1850's Gregg continually complained of the unwillingness of the local banks to provide short-term capital to industry, and 40 years later the managers of the South's new textile firms echoed the same laments.[44] The explanation of this failure probably lies in the structure of the region's banks. Before the war most southern states, unlike those in the North and West, did not adopt free banking laws; and the banks that were chartered tended to be dominated by the local landed gentry. Given the directors' personal biases and the absence of effective competition, it is not surprising that they tended to discriminate against industrial loans. Nor did passage of the National Banking Act end discrimination. The act required larger initial capitalization than the area could typically afford, and in practice the law also appears to have discriminated against the South in the allocation of bank-note quotas. Thus in 1870 the 11 southern states had 24 percent of the nation's population but only 9 percent of its national banks.[45]

Even in the North and West the commercial banks usually limited their contributions to short-term finance, and gradually other intermediaries began to meet the long-term demands of industry. In the first half of the century, savings banks promoted some long-term mobility, and during the latter decades life insurance companies made major contributions to the process. Originally, however, these institutions had tended to be almost as provincial as the savers themselves, and only gradually did they overcome the legal and cultural restrictions that

cities, there is no evidence of any significant long-term movements. L. Davis, "The New England Textile Mills and the Capital Markets: A Study of Industrial Borrowing 1840–1860," *Journal of Economic History*, Vol. 20 (1960), pp. 1–30; Vol. 21 (1961), pp. 222–26.

[42] Clemen, *Livestock*.

[43] Clemen, *Livestock*. At times even banks appear to have supplied some long-term finance. " . . . the firm of Newberry and Dale of Chicago had been furnished funds to the extent of $80,000 for a business carried on under their own name, although in reality, they were merely packing on commission for the president and directors of the bank." *Ibid.*, p. 139–40.

[44] Mitchell, *Gregg*, and Mitchell, *Rise of Cotton Mills*.

[45] P. Trescott, *American Enterprise*.

limited the score of their investment portfolios. In Massachusetts, for example, laws prohibiting savings banks from making loans to out-of-state firms almost antedated the banks themselves; and similar restrictions tended to be placed on both savings banks and life insurance companies by other states. Even in states without such legal regulation (Maryland, for example) there were strong cultural biases against distant investments.[46] Despite these restrictions, the intermediaries did make long-term capital available to local enterprises. In Massachusetts the savings banks made important contributions to the textile industry; in New York they were early investors in the Erie Canal; and in Maryland they transferred capital from savers to a host of new industries.[47]

Later, as life insurance companies began to assume significant size, they also increased the scope of their portfolios. In part, this broadening reflected a reduction in legal barriers; in part, the evolution of supporting intermediaries that made distant investment easier; and in part, a growing sophistication of the companies' managers. Almost every state had laws prohibiting loans on out-of-state property, but as time passed these laws were usually relaxed. In New York, for example, insurance companies had been prohibited from making mortgage loans on out-of-state property, but in 1868 they were permitted to lend on property within 50 miles, in 1872 on property in any adjoining state, and a few years later on property anywhere.[48] At the same time, it became simpler to make distant loans. The last half of the century saw the organization of firms (Wells-Dickey, for example) specializing in the interregional placement of mortgages and of investment houses (like Vermilyea and Company) specializing in placing intermediaries' funds in the formal securities of distant corporations.[49] Finally, the evolution of professional management brought an increasing awareness of the profitability of distant investments. The Northwestern Mutual, for example, at first invested only in Wisconsin enterprises, but its directors soon became aware of the potential profits from investment in areas less well served by the capital markets. As a result, the company became one of the chief sources of finance for the growing economies of Chicago and Indianapolis.[50]

---

[46] As late as 1849 the directors of the Savings Bank of Baltimore (one of the nation's largest financial institutions) refused to grant a loan to a mill in Baltimore county (some 11 miles from the bank) because of "the board's lack of knowledge about property in the county." P. L. Payne and L. Davis, *The Savings Bank of Baltimore, 1818–1866* (Baltimore, 1956).

[47] See L. Davis, "United States Financial Intermediaries in the Early Nineteenth Century: Four Case Studies" (Ph.D. dissertation, Johns Hopkins University, 1956); and N. Miller, *Enterprise of a Free People* (Ithaca, N.Y., 1962).

[48] L. Zartman, *The Investments of Life Insurance Companies*, (New York, 1906).

[49] C. Popple, *Development of Two Bank Groups in the Central Northwest*, (Cambridge, Mass., 1944); M. James, *The Metropolitan Life, A Study in Business Growth* (New York, 1947).

[50] M. Williamson and O. Smalley, *Northwestern Mutual Life* (Evanston, Ill., 1957).

In terms of nonbank intermediaries, the South again represents a case of retarded development. No mutual savings banks were chartered south of Maryland, and the 1890 census lists only six southern Class A life insurance companies operating during the eighties.[51] In part, the slow growth of southern insurance companies probably reflects the volatility of the region's death rates, a volatility that for years caused northern companies to restrict their sales of policies to Southerners.[52] More important, however, it almost certainly reflects the distribution of income in the area. Both savings bonds and life insurance companies have their greatest appeal to low and middle income groups, and in the South (where income distribution was highly skewed) these two classes must have contributed less to the savings stream than they did in other areas.

Outside the South, by the early 20th century, intermediaries had become efficient capital mobilizers. This development, coupled with the increasing willingness of savers to make direct investment in enterprises removed from their immediate knowledge, greatly reduced the monopoly of mobile capital previously held by the financial capitalists. (The financiers had, in a sense, joined the handloom weavers and the glass blowers among the ranks of the technologically unemployed.) This conclusion does not, of course, deny that some immobilities still existed; it suggests only that the opportunities for huge monopoly profits had been largely removed.[53]

---

[51] Of these, three had gone out of business by 1890. U.S. Department of the Interior, *Report on Insurance Business in the United States at the Eleventh Census* (Washington, D.C., 1895).

[52] In 1847 the New England Mutual Life had broken with tradition and agreed to insure Southerners as long as they did not remain in the South during the summer. Lance E. Davis, *Early Intermediaries*.

[53] A recent study indicates that it is still difficult to mobilize credit for new enterprises and for firms located away from the formal markets. In these cases, entrepreneurs profiting from their ability to mobilize capital are still prevalent. Lance E. Davis, *Financing New Enterprises* (in preparation).

4. The New England Textile Mills and the Capital Markets: A Study of Industrial Borrowing, 1840-60[*]

Lance E. Davis[†]

Purdue University

STUDY OF ANTEBELLUM economic development of the United States has been hampered by an acute shortage of reliable statistical data. Studies of the early capital markets are no exception to this general rule. For the years after 1856, Frederick Macaulay's excellent study provides sufficient quantitative basis for general research; but, in the earlier years, only Bigelow's single unsupported interest series provides the economic historian with statistical information on the condition of the credit market.[1]

I

This paper presents a body of hitherto unanalyzed financial data, and these new series, although limited in their scope and coverage, appear to cast some additional light on the conditions and structure of the Boston credit market in the two decades preceding Lincoln's election. Section

[*] *Reprinted from Journal of Economic History*, Vol. XX, No. 1 (March, 1960), pp. 1–30.

[†] The author wishes to express his thanks to his colleagues at Purdue University, and in particular to Irving Morrissett and Jonathan R. T. Hughes, for their help and advice on matters of both content and grammar. Moreover, the author wishes to acknowledge the aid of the department of political economy of Johns Hopkins University and of the Purdue Research Foundation that together financed the research on which this paper was based.

[1] Frederick R. Macaulay, *Some Theoretical Problems Suggested by the Movements of Interest Rates, Bond Yields and Stock Prices in the United States Since 1856* (New York: National Bureau of Economic Research, 1938); Erastus A. Bigelow, *Tariff Questions in the United States* (1862).

II of the paper presents some new information about the suppliers of finance. Section III provides a monthly interest series that is independent of Bigelow's estimates. Although in general the new figures support the earlier findings, at several points the two series are in marked conflict. Finally, Section IV is devoted to a discussion of the term structure of interest rates. Here the investigation indicates that the assumption of a sectored credit market better explains the interest structure than does an analysis based on the more traditional expectational theory of the term structure.

In the mid-19th century loanable funds were supplied by a wide range of lenders: commercial banks, savings banks, trust companies, insurance companies, private individuals, and business concerns. The heterogeneity of this group makes it extremely difficult to obtain a satisfactory quantitative description of the market from an investigation of the suppliers.[2] However, the existence of a considerable body of business records suggests the possibility of achieving this end through an analysis of the records of the borrowing institutions. For this study the loan records of eight Massachusetts type cotton textile mills (the Amoskeag, Boston, Dwight, Cabot, Perkins, Lawrence, Lyman, and Massachusetts Cotton) were used.[3]

These textile records appear to provide a fairly adequate basis for a study of the Boston credit market. The eight firms were all large integrated producers of cotton textiles, all were located close to the Boston credit market and maintained offices in that city, and all belonged to the complex of mills that was associated with the early Boston mercantile capitalists. Thus the mills appear to have been a nearly homogeneous group of first-class industrial borrowers; and, therefore, without stretching credulity too far, it is possible to assume that the eight were all identical in respect to risk. In addition, the firms were all voracious borrowers, consuming almost every available penny of credit, and borrowing from almost every existing type of lender. Therefore, the 2,385 loans in the study cut across the credit market and provide a cross section of antebellum industrial finance in New England.[4] Moreover, although the mills were growing, their productive processes, their organization, their capital structure, and their channels of distribution had been established before 1840 and changed relatively little thereafter. (Those firms that were organized after 1840 simply adopted the structure and techniques of the

---

[2] In addition, the fact that there have been few attempts to analyze the financial records that do exist—in particular commercial bank records—further complicates any description drawn from the supply side.

[3] These records are on deposit in the Baker Library, Graduate School of Business Administration, Harvard University, Boston, Mass.

[4] The 2,385 loans represent about 80 percent of the original cash loans of the eight firms. The remaining 20 percent were excluded because of lack of adequate information. Trade credit was not included in the study. Finally, because borrowers frequently were permitted to renew loans at the rate prevailing at the time of the initial loan, renewals were also excluded.

older firms.) Thus, there should have been no shifts in the structure of the firms that would have affected their borrowing habits.

The study does not purport to describe "the" American money market, but the evidence indicates that for short-term credit its implications may be broader than the Boston market alone. Ordinarily most textile credit was obtained from institutional sources in Boston; however, when it became difficult to obtain funds in that city, the mill owners did not hesitate to turn to other areas and to noninstitutional sources. Since the Massachusetts market operated under the terms of a 6 percent usury law,[5] (a law that appears to have been fairly well observed, at least by the major institutional lenders, until the mid-1850's) and since during most of the period the rate charged by unregulated lenders appears to have been very close to or in excess of 6 percent, the textile firms frequently found it advantageous to tap the New York money market where less stringent interest limitations existed.

Despite the arbitrary limit imposed by the usury laws, the interest figures still provide considerable information about the conditions of the credit market. From the point of view of finance, these limited rates were, after all, the cost of credit. From the more general point of view, the condition of the economy, the existence of uncontrolled (out-of-state) and extralegal lenders permitted a significant proportion of the loans to be contracted at "free-market" rates. Loans made by these two groups served to "pull" the average above the legal limit in times of credit stringency, although the fluctuations were undoubtedly less and the normal rates undoubtedly lower than they would have been in an uncontrolled market.[6]

However, if, because of the effects of the usury law, the actual rate was below the free market equilibrium rate for the period that seems

---

[5] *General Statutes of Massachusetts,* chap. 53, sec. 3, Laws of 1860.

[6] It might be noted that the Boston experience with usury laws appears to have differed markedly from the English and, to some extent, other American experience. In England the usury laws forced the actual rate above what it would otherwise have been. There, the controlled institutions ceased making loans altogether whenever the free market rate rose above the legal limit. Instead these institutions moved into other assets yielding more competitive returns. In the western United States a similar situation appears to have prevailed. Thomas Berry reports that in Ohio the usury laws resulted in a withdrawal from loan investment and a channeling of capital into inland bills on which the rate was not controlled. Thus increases in the rate of interest reduced the volume of credit. In Boston, however, the controlled institutions continued to lend during such periods, and these low interest loans tended to hold the average interest rate below what it otherwise would have been. The explanation of this difference probably lies in the difference in legal investment opportunities. In Boston, the large institutional lenders and, to lesser extent, the commercial banks were legally and culturally limited in their investment alternatives. Thus an equilibrium rate in excess of the legal limit did not force them into other investments. For a discussion of the British experience, see Jacob Viner, *Studies in the Theory of International Trade* (New York: Harper & Bros., 1937), pp. 119–289, and particularly pp. 149, 219, and 257. On experience in Ohio, see Thomas S. Berry, *Western Prices Before 1861* (Cambridge, Mass.: Harvard University Press, 1943), pp. 494–95.

indicated (the actual rate hugs the 6 percent limit in 10 of the 14 years between 1840 and 1853), nonprice rationing must have played an important role in finance.[7] This conclusion suggests that industries less well connected than textiles—and new industries in particular—may well have found loan finance almost impossible to obtain through traditional channels in times of credit stringency.[8]

Although the short-term market appears to have encompassed the entire Northeast, that same area included several almost independent long-term markets. The willingness of the New York bankers to contract short-term out-of-state loans, and the mercantile custom of investing liquid funds in commercial drafts on other cities when rates there exceeded those at home, probably worked to equalize short-term rates (as far as the laws would permit) in the northeastern cities. Equally strong evidence, however, indicates that the Boston long-term credit market was divorced from the long-term markets in other areas. In Massachusetts the greatest suppliers of long-term credit were the institutional lenders—particularly the savings banks and the trust companies—and these institutions were prohibited by law from lending to persons or corporations residing outside the Commonwealth.[9] Moreover, similar restrictions against "foreign" lending were imposed by law or custom on institutional lenders in other states.[10]

II

The lenders were grouped into eight categories: commercial banks, savings banks, trust companies, insurance companies, individuals (including trust accounts personally held), cotton mercantile firms, manu-

---

[7] See Chart I and Table A–1.

[8] Even the textile firms occasionally had to turn to nonregulated lenders to fill their credit needs. For example, in December, 1851, the treasurer of the Lancaster Mills reported: "It is owing to the heavy charge of interest and diminishing production that our business has not been more profitable. It will be recollected that in the month of July money became suddenly very scarce indeed. Just at the time we had the dividend to provide for and our payments were unusually heavy. It was impossible to obtain all that was wanted from the bank, and on the balance it was necessary to pay a high rate of interest." Lancaster Mills, "Treasurer's Report (Statement of Profit and Loss)," December 23, 1851. This manuscript is on deposit in the Baker Library, Graduate School of Business Administration, Harvard University, Boston, Mass.

[9] A certain amount of circumvention did take place through the use of intermediate in-state borrowers; however, an examination of the records of several institutional lenders indicates that this practice was rare and restricted to very reliable firms with close in-state connections (for example, firms whose majority ownership was lodged in the hands of Boston residents). For a complete description of such circumvention, see Lance E. Davis, "United States Financial Intermediaries in the Early Nineteenth Century: Four Case Studies" (Ph.D. dissertation, Johns Hopkins University, 1956).

[10] Extreme provincialism appears to have marked the portfolios of savings banks (the leading institutional lenders) throughout the antebellum period. Such provincialism certainly characterized the investment policies of the banks in New York, Pennsylvania, and Maryland. Peter L. Payne and Lance E. Davis, *The Savings Bank of Baltimore 1818–1866* (Baltimore: The Johns Hopkins Press, 1956), pp. 110–13.

facturing companies, and miscellaneous institutions.[11] Of the eight, insurance companies and miscellaneous institutions were relatively unimportant.[12] For analysis, the loans were divided into four groups. Type I includes demand loans and those with original maturities of less than 30 days. To a large extent these loans represented emergency credit; and, as a result, they were concentrated in periods of credit stringency. Type II includes loans of from 30 days to six months; these loans were primarily normal short-term commercial credit. Type III includes loans of from 6 months' to 12 months' maturity; and Type IV includes all loans of one year or longer.

A study of the composition of lenders suggests that the formal credit market was not a single market but a group of markets, each with its own suppliers. Some lenders loaned almost exclusively on short term, some exclusively on long term, and only a few appeared willing to lend on any desired maturity.[13] Formal loans of Types II and III (1 to 6 and 6 to 12 months) were generally supplied by the commercial banks; over the entire period, the commercial banks made 87 percent of the new Type II and 63 percent of the new Type III loans.[14] There were only two exceptions to this rule. Between 1844 and 1846, the banks withdrew almost completely from the industrial loan market; and, from 1854 to 1860, because of their inability to take advantage of the higher rates engendered by the business boom, they reduced their maturities to increase the margin over risk. In the latter period, their contribution to new Type III loans declined from 79 percent in 1854 to 34 percent in 1857.[15]

The long-term market (Type IV) was, to a large extent, dominated by the savings banks and trust companies. These institutions seldom con-

---

[11] The relative importance of the eight groups is shown, by types of loans and by years, in Table A–1. A summary for the entire period is presented in Table 1.

[12] Prior to 1850, the fire insurance companies provided some loan finance, but the quantity was never significant. During the 1850's life insurance companies supplied an ever-increasing volume of credit, but even as late as 1860, their total contribution was small. Their loans do, however, indicate a willingness to supply industrial finance. Although Harvard University, The Boston Athenaeum, and the Church of The Redeemer are numbered among the miscellaneous institutions, this category is included only as a residual group. At no time did its members supply any significant volume of credit.

[13] The reader should bear in mind that only formal new loans are included in this study and the addition of renewal or trade credit might alter the conclusions markedly. In particular the inclusion of renewals would have increased the proportion of savings banks and trust companies in the long-term totals and trade credit would have increased the representation of mercantile houses, individual and miscellaneous institutions in the 30-day to 6-month category. Renewals were not included because of the difficulty in determining what was a renewal and what was really only a part of the actual loan. Trade credit was excluded because such loans can not be readily increased independently of the scale of operations and, in addition, the terms of such offering did not change significantly during the period.

[14] See Table 1.

[15] See Table A–1.

tracted loans of less than one year duration and not uncommonly made loans for as much as seven years. Moreover, since automatic renewal was apparently a *de facto* condition of the loans, and since such renewals often increased the actual length of the loan to well over 10 years, the institutional lender supplied truly long-term credit.

TABLE 1

20 Years' Summary of Relative Contributions of
Eight Lender Groups to New Formal Loans by Length of Loan
(Renewals and Trade Credit not Treated)
(In Percent)

Lender	Demand and Up To 30 Days	30 Days To Six Months	Six Months To One Year	One Year And Over	Total Of 2,385 Loans
Commercial banks	22.7	86.9	63.0	3.5	58.1
Savings banks	2.0	1.4	4.3	39.7	10.1
Trust companies	5.5	0.6	6.0	29.1	8.2
Insurance companies	1.2	0.3	1.7	1.5	0.9
Individuals	19.5	2.5	10.8	22.0	9.9
Mercantile houses	20.5	4.1	13.2	2.8	7.3
Manufacturing firms	26.2	3.9	1.0	0.6	4.9
Miscellaneous institutions	2.4	0.3	0.0	0.8	0.6
TOTAL	100.0	100.0	100.0	100.0	100.0

An examination of the composition of the "individual" category indicates that its members were drawn from two quite distinct groups. First, there were a number of lenders who supplied the long-term credit on an almost permanent basis. Although a large percentage were retired merchants, a surprisingly large number were persons actively engaged in some nontextile business and more than a few were trustees lending for widows and orphans. The size of the loans (the largest $50,000; the smallest, $68) as well as collateral secondary evidence suggest that these permanent lenders were drawn from all income groups. Second, there was a group of lenders who extended credit only on very short term, who usually loaned only in times of business crises, and who almost always loaned at rates well above the legal limit. Although many of these lenders were wealthy persons who individually supplied large blocks of loan finance, some were lower-middle class tradesmen and professional people who could afford to lend only very small amounts. However, even the less well-to-do demanded and received substantial interest payments. For example, the highest rate charged on any of the 2,385 loans—36 percent—was on a 30-day loan of $320. Moreover, each borrowing firm tended to rely on the same lenders. Although the same individual's name seldom appeared on the books of more than one firm, in any given firm the same names were likely to reappear in each period of credit stringency. It appears that each firm had a list of standby creditors on whom they could draw if need arose.

Emergency funds were also drawn from cotton textile houses. In many ways these cotton mercantile houses (firms that marketed the mill's output) constitute the most interesting single group of lenders. These firms supplied a significant portion of textile credit in all years; but their lending activities were concentrated most heavily in periods when the mills experienced difficulties in borrowing elsewhere; and, equally significant, their loans were usually concentrated in those maturities that were most difficult to obtain from alternative sources. Although the cotton houses usually supplied very short-term credit, at times they moved into the longer term markets. For example, in 1854–57, when the commercial banks shortened their maturities, the mercantile houses absorbed intermediate-term paper. Again following the panic of 1857 the mills found it difficult to obtain long-term credit, and again the mercantile houses obliged. Although over the entire period the mercantile firms provided only 13 percent of the new Type III credit, in 1856 and 1857 they provided 32 and 35 percent respectively; and although over the whole period they provided only 3 percent of new Type IV credit, in 1858 they supplied 6 percent and in 1859, 24 percent.[16] The willingness of the textile houses to supply the mills' needs is not overly surprising. The merchants' profits depended on a continued supply of textiles. Moreover, the interest charged by the merchants was, at times, well in excess of the legal limit. Since other mercantile establishments must also have been tied to their suppliers and had liquid funds to invest, it seems possible that the period was marked by a regular flow of loanable funds from the mercantile to the industrial sectors of the economy—a flow that was particularly significant in periods of credit stringency.

The manufacturing firms, with few exceptions, lent almost entirely on very short term (their loans usually matured in 3 to 20 days). Apparently these loans represented a recognition by the mill managers that it was desirable to keep liquid funds at interest. Thus, it appears reasonable to conclude that the 19th-century firms entered the short-term loan market for the same reasons that today induce firms to enter the treasury bills market.

Compared to modern credit markets, one of the most interesting features of the antebellum markets was the diversity of persons and institutions making significant contributions to the supply of credit. Although, then as now, the commercial banks and the nonbank intermediaries were the dominant lenders, the eight textile firms treated in this paper also seemed willing to borrow from other manufacturing companies, mercantile wholesale houses, and *any* other institution or person showing a willingness to advance *any* amount of money. Throughout the two decades the activities of these "abnormal" lenders was very significant on the margin, and in some markets (particularly the very short term)

---

[16] See Table A–1.

and in some periods, they actually came to dominate lending activities. The activities of the "abnormal" lenders usually paralleled those of the commercial banks; and like the commercial banks they were usually restricted to the short end of the market.

With a few exceptions, the long-term market was dominated by the nonbank intermediaries. Over the 20-year span, the Massachusetts Hospital Life Insurance Company (a trust company) was the largest single lender, but taken together, the savings banks constituted a more important credit source. Although the rates charged by these nonbank intermediaries were usually below the rates prevailing in the shorter term markets, political and legal barriers prevented their entry into the short end of the market. Conversely, the low rates charged by these institutions usually kept other lenders out of the long end.

A study of the lender structure of interest rates indicates that there were certain sustained differentials in the rates charged by lender groups (see Table 2); however, differences in the degree to which the usury laws were observed appear to explain these differentials satisfactorily. Over the entire period, the rates charged by the savings banks and trust companies were below those charged by the other major suppliers. These institutions were semibenevolent in character, and, since their directors

TABLE 2
SUMMARY OF AVERAGE INTEREST RATES CHARGED BY
EIGHT LENDER GROUPS FOR ALL YEARS 1840–60
(In Percent)

Lender Type	Average Interest Charge
Commercial banks	6.6
Savings banks	5.8
Trust companies	5.9
Insurance companies	6.2
Individuals	6.3
Mercantile houses	6.9
Manufacturing firms	5.7
Miscellaneous institutions	5.3

received no profits from their operations, they could afford to obey the letter of the law. The legal interpretation of the usury law permitted commercial banks to charge 6 percent discount (6.3 percent interest); and, in the early years, the limitation was usually obeyed. Later on, however, the average rate rose slowly as the usury law fell into disuse. The remaining lender types appear to have been little affected by the law, and their rates fluctuated widely in response to changes in economic conditions.

One fact stands out clearly from a comparison of the rates charged by the various lenders. In times of "normal" business activity all eight rates tended to bunch together (usually somewhere between 6 and 7 percent); but in times of abnormal business conditions, the dispersion of the rates increased tremendously. Dispersion increased both in the 1840's when the average rates fell rapidly, and in the mid-1850's when the rates rose. The bunching of rates in the "normal" periods seems to indicate that the free market equilibrium rate was not far from the legal limit; however, the increased dispersion during the periods of credit stringency in the 1850's seems to indicate that the rate that would have prevailed in the absence of the usury laws was well in excess of the legal limit. Moreover, the increased dispersion during periods of the 1840's and, in particular, the "stickiness" of the trust companies' charges, seem to indicate that the institutional lenders (the savings banks, trust companies, and insurance companies) frequently refused to make loans at less than the customary rates, and at times preferred to hold cash rather than to make loans at less than 6 percent.

III

Chart I and Table A–2 display the average rate of interest paid by the textile firms in each month from January, 1840, to December, 1860. The averages are weighted by the dollar value of the loans.[17]

The seasonal adjustments show only a very small seasonal component in the average interest rate figures (Table 3). The volume of loans, however, was heavily concentrated in the fall when textile firms borrowed to finance their raw cotton inventories. If the cotton mills had been a dominant force in the credit market, interest rates should have tended to increase during the fourth quarter. The absence of such a seasonal increase indicates that the mills were apparently competitive borrowers in a credit market much broader than the textile industry alone.

Bigelow's series does, however, show a marked seasonal upturn for the months between October and January (the indices are 104.4, 106.9, 113.3, and 105.3 respectively), an upturn that is almost entirely absent in the textile series.[18] The textile figures do show that rates in October, Novem-

---

[17] The average used was the weighted average $\overline{X} = \dfrac{\Sigma(X_i V_i)}{\Sigma V_i}$ where the X_i represents the interest rate charged on individual loans and the V_i represents the dollar value of these individual loans.

[18] The source of Bigelow's series remains unknown. Bigelow himself refers to them as figures on the Boston and New York markets. Arthur H. Cole thinks they refer to the New York market; however, F. R. Macaulay feels equally certain that they refer to the Boston market. Both authorities agree that they are the rates for short-term commercial paper. During the pre–Civil War period such commercial paper was probably more speculative than the industrial loans contained in the textile series. Risk differentials may explain the difference in levels between Bigelow's and the textile series (the former series average about 2 percent higher than the latter); however, the two should be expected to move together. If Bigelow's series refers to New York, then noncoordinate movements may be explained by the conditions peculiar to one market; however, if his figures are for Boston, the discrepancies are more difficult to explain. See Arthur H. Cole and Walter Buckingham Smith, *Fluctuation in*

CHART I

INTEREST RATES TEXTILE SERIES AND BIGELOW'S SERIES BY MONTH 1840–60

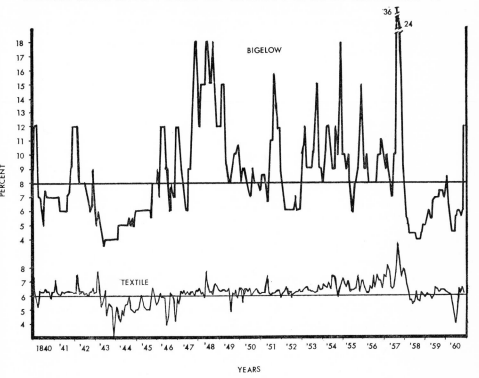

ber, and January were slightly higher than the annual average (100.7, 101.5, and 101.0) but, on the other hand, December is slightly below that average—(98.2)—and in every case the movement is much less than the movement in Bigelow's series.[19] Whether this difference reflects a basic conflict between these data and Bigelow's series or merely a difference between the Boston and New York money markets is difficult to ascertain. There is some evidence that indicates that the high year-end rates may well have been a local New York phenomenon. Miss Myers has shown that an active call loan market coupled with a pyramiding of country bank reserves in the New York banks characterized the New York market as early as the 1830's.[20] Since call loans coupled with reserve pyramiding

---

American Business, 1790–1860 (Cambridge, Mass.: Harvard University Press, 1935), p. 125; and Macaulay, *Interest Rates,* p. A335. For purposes of comparison, Bigelow's series is presented in Chart I and Table A–3.

[19] A rough test of significance shows that the November, December, and January figures are significantly different from 100 at the 95 percent level. However, although November and January figures support Bigelow's conclusion, the December figure is in definite conflict. The same test applied to Bigelow's indices indicates that all four months are significantly different from 100.

[20] Margaret G. Myers, *The New York Money Market, Origins and Developments* (2 vols.; New York: Columbia University Press, 1931), Vol. I, pp. 135–48.

TABLE 3*

SEASONAL INDEX FOR WEIGHTED TEXTILE RATES AND BIGELOW'S
INTEREST RATES FOR THE PERIOD 1840–60

Month	Textile Series	Bigelow's Series
January	101.0	105.3
February	101.0	100.7
March	100.1	102.9
April	99.7	97.6
May	98.8	91.3
June	98.1	91.8
July	99.5	91.2
August	97.5	94.0
September	102.1	100.5
October	100.7	104.4
November	101.5	106.9
December	98.2	113.3

* The seasonal adjustment is based on the method outlined in Arthur F. Burns
and Wesley C. Mitchell, *Measuring Business Cycles* (New York: National Bureau
of Economic Research, 1947), pp. 43–55.

did account for seasonal increases in rates throughout the latter portion
of the 19th century, and since New York alone had an important call loan
market and was alone an important recipient of country bank reserves, the
year-end upturn could have been peculiar to the New York market.

Over the 20-year period the average interest figures display a complete
absence of trend. Although Bigelow's series indicate no trend, the
rapid growth of banks and other financial institutions during the two prewar decades and the existence of a marked downward trend in Macaulay's
figures for the years 1856 to 1900 make the absence rather surprising.[21]
This secular stability of the interest rates may well have been one manifestation of the well-enforced usury laws. The data suggest that until the
mid-1850's the local usury law placed an effective upper limit on the
interest rates charged by financial institutions, damping any tendency
for the rate to swing above 6 percent for a lengthy period. With few
exceptions, the average monthly rate approximated the legal limit in 10 of
the 14 years between 1840 and 1853; such stability suggests that, had a
free market existed, the trend value of the free market rate would have
been above 6 percent in 1840 and declined gradually over the period.
Moreover, an examination of the loans made by out-of-state lenders
(subject to less restrictive legislation) and by noninstitutional lenders
(who paid less attention to legal restrictions) shows a gradual reduction
toward 6 percent in the rates charged over the period. Thus, although
the period may be too short to establish definite trends, it appears likely
that the usury law masked the effects of the improvements in the capital
markets that occurred in the two decades before the war.

The existence of the legal interest limit may well have reduced the
magnitude of the upward movements in interest rates that would normally

---

[21] Macaulay, *Interest Rates*, p. 230.

have been expected to accompany changes in business activity. Rates fell markedly during the period 1843 to 1846; but on only a few occasions before 1853 did the textile firms borrow enough from noninstitutional lenders and from commercial banks outside of Massachusetts to force the monthly average rate significantly above the legal limit.[22] During the first decade of this study, the borrowing firms responded to credit tightening by increasing their borrowing from out-of-state banks and from individuals, manufacturing concerns, and mercantile houses. However, with increasing frequency after 1853 the borrowing firms began to report among the costs of bank loans, such items as *"6 percent interest plus ¾ percent commission."* By 1857 the average rate paid to Massachusetts banks (interest plus commissions was above 7 percent.[23] Collateral evidence indicating the extent of the breakdown of the usury laws is found scattered through the contemporary journals; for example, in 1857 the Boston Board of Trade reporting on antirecession measures recommended "that the usury laws, which are so generally disregarded as to be almost a dead letter, should be abolished entirely."[24]

From the analysis of Bigelow's series and from his study of the fluctuations in other economic magnitudes during the antebellum decade, Arthur Cole has concluded that the period was marked by a long swing in economic activity, a swing with its troughs in 1843 and 1858.[25] An examination of the textile series appears to offer some additional substantiation of the existence of such a long swing. Interest rates were lower in 1843 than at any other time during the period and they were higher in 1857 than in any year since 1840.

There is no doubt, moreover, that from 1843 to 1846 credit was much easier to obtain than it had been during the previous two decades.[26] Nor is there any doubt that the low rates affected the entire eastern seaboard and not just the Massachusetts market. Contemporary journals report sharp declines in interest rates in almost every eastern center during 1843, and this condition of excess supply appears to have continued to characterize local markets until 1846. In August, 1843, the *New York Express* reported:

Money is as abundant as ever. Our banks are discounting favorite paper at four per cent and regular offering at five per cent. At no period within forty years

---

22 The monthly rates exceeded 7 percent in January, 1840, February, 1841, March, 1842, June, 1848, and May, 1851.

23 The interest rates cited in the textile series include both interest and commission payments.

24 *Bankers' Magazine*, Vol. VII, n.s. (December, 1857), p. 500.

25 Cole and Smith, *Fluctuations*, p. 127.

26 In England, too, the market was characterized by very low rates. The Bank of England deliberately held its rates low and by May, 1844, the market rate had fallen below 2 percent. R. G. Hawtrey, *A Century of Bank Rate* (London: Longmans, Green & Co., 1938), p. 19.

have our banks found it so difficult to loan money as at the present time, nor have they ever discounted notes at so low a rate of interest.[27]

Similar reports emanated from Boston, Philadelphia, and Baltimore throughout 1843; and, although the bottom appears to have been reached in December, the rate only slowly and haltingly edged its way back toward the legal maximum.[28] Although the following three years were marked by some short periods of credit stringency, the rate did not reach "normal" levels premanently until March, 1847.[29]

Traditional cycle theory concludes that interest rates fall in the later stages of a depression and remain low through the period of recovery.[30] During the years in question, business was recovering from one of the most serious depressions that the young economy had yet experienced and as in traditional theory, the explanation of the decline and slow recovery of the interest rates appears to lie in the psychological reaction of the worried borrowers to such a period of extended depression. The years 1840 through 1842 had been marked by severe depression and, in the absence of a central bank capable of acting as a lender of last resort, interest rates had remained close to the legal limit throughout most of the depression.[31] Recovery began early in 1843 and continued with only a slight interruption in 1846.[32] Borrowers, however, remembering the strain placed on them during the depression by their credit position and the banks' loan policies, refused to borrow despite the banks' attempts to increase loans by lowering interest rates. In the words of a contemporary:

[27] *Niles' Weekly Register,* Vol. LXIV (August 13, 1845), p. 384.

[28] The textile series show a low of 3 percent in December, 1843, (See Chart I) and in January *Niles'* reports: "New York money is more in demand this week." *Niles' Weekly Register,* Vol. LXIV (January 13, 1844), p. 320.

[29] Evidence from the textile series (Chart I) and from contemporary chronicles indicates that interest rates rose sharply during the early fall of 1844 and again in the spring and late fall of 1845. *Niles' Weekly Register,* Vol. LXVII (September 21, 1844), p. 48; Vol. LXVII (February 8, 1845), p. 386; Vol. LXIX (December 13, 1845), p. 250.

[30] For example, in Hawtrey's analysis of business-cycle behavior, the interest rates are supposed to remain low almost until the end of the upswing. The National Bureau findings for more recent periods are not this extreme, but they also indicate a lag between their reference cycle and the interest rates on commercial paper. Alvin Hanson, *Business Cycles and National Income* (New York: Norton, 1951), pp. 377–84. Wesley C. Mitchell, *What Happens During Business Cycles, A Progress Report* (New York: National Bureau of Economic Research, 1951), p. 167. For the early 19th century the English experience appears marked by a pattern similar to the American. Interest rates tended to rise during phases III–VII of the National Business reference cycle and to have declined during phases VII–III. Arthur D. Gayer, W. W. Rostow, and Anna J. Schwartz, *The Growth and Fluctuations of the British Economy 1750–1850* (2 vols.; Oxford: Clarendon Press, 1953), Vol. II, p. 676.

[31] In earlier periods of financial stringency, the Second Bank of the United States had acted as a lender of last resort. See, for example, Payne and Davis, *The Savings Bank of Baltimore,* p. 85.

[32] Willard Thorp, *Business Annals* (New York: National Bureau of Economic Research, 1926), pp. 132–34; Leonard P. Ayers, *Turning Points in Business Cycles* (New York: Macmillan Co., 1939), p. 6 and pp. 177–78.

The public voice united with a rather irresistably controlled legislation, and compelled the country into an actual *hard money* attitude. . . . The whole people are learning to do a close business, buy only what is actually wanting and what they have the means at hand to pay for.[33]

Almost three years passed before borrowers were willing once more to absorb the total supply of credit at what had been considered "normal" rates.

A comparison of the textile rates with Bigelow's series shows a sharp divergence between the two during 1848. The latter series characterizes 1848 as a year of extreme credit stringency and indicates that in no month did the rate fall below 13½ percent. Over the entire year it averaged 15 percent. As Arthur Cole has pointed out, it does not appear that there were any nationwide disturbances that could have accounted for such high rates; and even within the city of New York, it is difficult to find an explanation for such abnormally high levels.[34] The textile series, on the other hand, suggests that normal rates prevailed for 10 of the 12 months of 1848 and that abnormally high rates characterized only the months of June and July. For this shorter period, collateral evidence does seem to provide an explanation for the rate increases. *Hunt's Merchants' Magazine* reports that the New York money market experienced a considerable tightening of credit in June and July due to a foreign specie drain—a consequence of the French Revolution of 1848 and other unsettled conditions in Europe—together with a movement of funds from the city to the country banks.[35] Moreover, that same journal reports a general easing of credit during the month of August.[36]

During the second and last "abnormal" period, 1853 to 1857, there is general agreement between the textile series and Bigelow's figures; and both, in turn, appear to be substantiated by contemporary evidence. The textile series shows a gradual increase in the level of rates beginning in 1853 and continuing (although not without interruption) until mid-1857. In the late spring and early summer of that year, the average level dropped sharply; however, this drop was followed, in August and September, by a very rapid rise in interest rates—a rise that pushed rates to their highest level in the 20 years covered by this study.[37] A similar story unfolds in the financial periodicals of the period. For example, in July, 1857, the *Banker's Magazine* reported "There has been increasing ease in

---

[33] *Niles',* Vol. LXIV (August 26, 1843), p. 416.

[34] Smith and Cole, *Fluctuations,* pp. 125–26. Nor can foreign difficulties account for the year-long increase. In Britain, for example, 1848 was a year of progressive easing of the credit market. The bond rate, the market rate, and the rates on bills of exchange all declined significantly over the year. Gayer, Rostow and Schwartz, *Fluctuations,* Vol. I, p. 331.

[35] *Hunt's Merchants' Magazine,* Vol. XIX (July, 1848), pp. 81–82.

[36] *Ibid.,* Vol. XIX (September, 1848), p. 201.

[37] Precisely the same pattern of events was observed in England during the spring, summer, and fall of 1857. See Jonathan R. T. Hughes, "The Commercial Crisis of 1857," *Oxford Economic Papers,* Vol. VIII–2, n.s. (June, 1956), pp. 194–227.

CHART II
TERM STRUCTURE OF INTEREST RATES FOR FOUR LENGTH TYPES
BY QUARTERS 1840–60

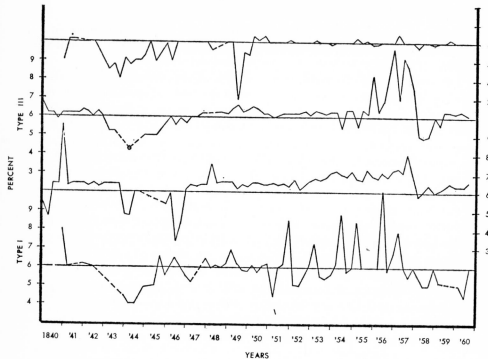

the Money Market since March last." Two months later the situation had changed drastically, and the editor wrote:

This has been the most eventful month in financial circles that we have had occasion to comment on since the commencement of our work in July 1846. Those whose recollections go back to the spring of 1837 when the banks and merchants almost universally suspended payment, cannot bring to mind any period in the interim when such a sudden and severe revulsion has occurred as we have witnessed since the 24th of last month.[38]

Bigelow's figures show a similar pattern of fluctuations; as usual, however, his rates average considerably higher than the textile series.

IV

Chart II and Table A–4 show weighted interest rates by quarter for textile loans of four maturities. A comparison of the four series plotted on Chart II indicates that the markets for funds of different lengths were, to

---

[38] *Bankers' Magazine*, Vol. VII, n.s. (July, 1857), p. 88, and Vol. VII, n.s. (October, 1857), p. 334.

some extent, independent. Through most of the period, the shorter term rates (Types I, II, and III) were above the long-term rates. Over the whole period, rates on Type IV loans averaged 5.8 percent while rates on Types I, II, and III loans averaged 6.2 percent (6.0, 6.4, and 6.3 respectively). it is difficult to see how, given the greater liquidity of the shorter maturities, an analysis based on the assumption that the long-term rate tends to equal the average of expected short-term rates, could adequately explain these persistent differentials.[39] On the other hand, if one assumes a number of markets each with its own buyers and sellers (admitting some overlap between the markets), the explanation of the relationship between the long- and short-term rates can be directly deduced from the characteristics of these markets in the antebellum period.[40] The suppliers of long-term credit form a class quite distinct from the persons and institutions that loaned on short term. The long-term market was dominated by institutional lenders (particularly savings banks and trust companies); and these lenders, because of their quasi-public position, tended to be more observant of the usury laws. Moreover, because of cost consideration, their deposit contracts, and certain legal restrictions, these institutions often found it impossible to move into the shorter term markets. Thus, the institutional lenders, unwilling to disobey the law and unable to lend on short maturities, acted in a way that tended to keep the long rate below the short rate. On the other hand, a significant proportion of the short-term lenders (persons, mercantile houses, and, at a later date, even the commercial banks) were much less bound by the usury laws.

In general, the four series presented in Chart II support the belief that the short-term rates tend to fluctuate more violently than the longer term rates. The standard deviations for the four series are .011 for Type I, .008 for Types II and III, and .005 for Type IV.[41] An expectational theory of

---

[39] The more widely accepted expectational explanation of the term structure has been developed by J. R. Hicks, *Value and Capital* (2d ed.; Oxford: University Press, 1946) chap. xi, and Friedrich A. Lutz, "The Structure of Interest Rates," *Quarterly Journal of Economics*, Vol. LV (November, 1940), pp. 36–63. Recently John M. Culbertson has cast some doubts on the usefulness of the theory and has shown that for recent American developments, at least, an explanation based on the existence of semi-independent markets for each maturity seems to accord better with the facts. "The Term Structure of Interest Rates," *Quarterly Journal of Economics*, Vol. LXXI (November, 1947), pp. 485–517. Culbertson's concept of segregated credit markets was anticipated by the work of G. Heberton Evans (See, for example, his *Basic Economics* [New York: Alfred A. Knopf, 1950], pp. 226–34), and Winfield Riefler (See *Money Rates and Money Markets in the United States* [New York: Harper & Bros., 1930]).

[40] There appears to have been enough marginal movement between the markets to cause rates in the separate markets to move together, but not sufficient movement to equalize the rates. This situation probably reflects the willingness of individuals to move between markets combined with the unwillingness and inability of the commercial banks to extend long-term credit and of the other financial institutions to move into the short end of the market.

[41] Although for the whole period the standard deviation of Type III is slightly greater than that of Type II (.0084 vs. .0079), if the years 1856 and 1857 are excluded as abnormal the four conform perfectly to traditional theory.

the interest structure could explain this phenomenon, but the evidence strongly suggests that an explanation based on a sectoring of the credit market better fits the facts. As John M. Culbertson has pointed out, the demand for long-term funds to be more stable than the demand for short-term funds because the planning period is longer in the case of long-term investment and thus the decisions are less susceptible to spur-of-the-moment changes in administrative thinking.[42] A study of the minutes and executive memoranda of the textile mills indicates that Culbertson's thesis provides a valid description of the investment decisions of these firms in the antebellum period.

Moreover, in the years 1840 to 1860, there also appears to have been a greater stability in the *supply* of long-term funds relative to the supply of short-term credit. The institutional lenders of long-term finance (the trust companies and savings banks) were far less likely to be met with a sudden depositor run than were the leading short-term institutional lenders—the commercial banks. Thus, the long-term lending institutions were not faced with the same necessity to adjust their loans in response to the short-term economic fluctuations that dictated the commercial banks' investment policy.

In most respects, except for the tendency of the short-term rate to remain above the long-term rate, the behavior of the rate structure in the two antebellum decades appears to conform closely to the behavior of the structure in the 20th century.[43] From his study of the behavior of the American money market between 1920 and 1957, John M. Culbertson concludes: (1) that movements in the short- and long-term rates have been simultaneous and in the same direction; (2) that there have been wider fluctuations in the short-term rate than in the long-term rate; and (3) that there is no evidence of a lead or lag relationship between the long- and short-term rates.[44] As an examination of Chart II indicates, these same terms could be used to describe the behavior of the term structure of interest rates in the earlier period.

Whether one subscribes to an expectational or to a sectoring theory of the term structure, the movements of the rates during the third quarter of 1849 and the first and third quarter of 1857 are irregular enough to require explanation. In the third quarter of 1849, the long-term rate (Type IV) dropped precipitously (from 6 to 3 percent) while the shorter rates showed little change. In 1857, the intermediate rate (Type III) rose much more sharply than either the shorter or longer rates. In both cases,

---

[42] Culbertson, "The Term Structure of Interest Rates," p. 509.

[43] In the recent period the short rate has usually been below the long rate. Since 1920 the short rate has exceeded the long rate during only two relatively short periods, 1920 and 1928–29. Culbertson, "The Term Structure of Interest Rates," p. 504; and *Federal Reserve Chart Book: Financial and Business Statistics, Historical Supplement* (Washington, D.C.: Board of Governors, 1957), pp. 37–39.

[44] Culbertson, "The Term Structure of Interest Rates," p. 504.

an analysis based upon the assumption of several quasi-independent credit markets can provide an explanation of the irregularities.

The 1849 drop in the long-term rate was coincident with a flood of new long-term loans made by several Massachusetts savings banks and by the Provident Institution for Savings in the Town of Boston in particular. Within the space of a few weeks these banks placed several hundred thousand dollars in additional funds into the long-term loan market, and the decline in interest rates appears to represent the market adjustment to this sudden increase in supply. The explanation of the banks' behavior is more difficult to understand; however, the sudden "dumping" may have been the result of the personal ties that linked the banks' directors with the managers of the mills. The directors of the textile firms frequently served on the boards of trustees of the large savings banks, and the low interest loans could have been the result of this connection. On the other hand, the banks acting competitively simply may not have realized the effect of their collective activities on the rate of interest.

The irregular movement of the term structure during 1857 appears to reflect the final vestiges of the usury law coupled with the strained business conditions of that year. Although by 1857 the usury law was ignored by many lenders, some banks (particularly in Boston) still chose to obey. Thus, as credit began to tighten in response to the deteriorating business conditions, these banks, unable to increase their interest charges, began to reduce the maturities of their loans and, in several cases, to cease making loans altogether.[45] To fill the gap in the intermediate-term credit market left by the withdrawal of the commercial banks, the mills turned to Boston mercantile houses for additional loan finance. These merchants, however, appear to have ignored the usury law; and their loans were made at rates considerably in excess of the rates that had been charged by the commercial banks. As a result, the interest charges on intermediate-term loans rose not only because of the general rise in interest rates but also because of the substitution of higher for lower cost suppliers of intermediate-term credit. The shorter term rates, on the other hand, rose only because of the changes in general market conditions.

V

Studies of the development of the early American capital markets have been handicapped by insufficient knowledge of actual financial conditions. This paper—based on the records of eight textile firms—attempts to provide additional information on the Boston credit market for the 21 years from January, 1840, to December, 1860.

The paper presents a new series of monthly average interests rates that

---

[45] An examination of the average maturities indicates that the commercial bank tended to reduce maturities in periods of credit stringency and increase them in periods of easy money.

is independent of Bigelow's estimates, the only series previously available. The two series are in general agreement (Bigelow's tends to average about 2 percent higher but this difference can probably be explained by risk differentials) but they conflict in their description of money market conditions during much of 1848. Collateral evidence seems to support the new series rather than Bigelow's earlier estimates. Differences are also found in the seasonality of the two series. Bigelow's figures show a marked increase in rates during the late fall and early winter, but the new series displays no such strong pattern.

The new interest figures tend to support Arthur H. Cole's thesis that the economy was subject to a long swing in economic activity during the two antebellum decades. The interest figures show a long cycle in rates with troughs in 1843 and 1858; the same swing found by Arthur H. Cole in time series of other economic magnitudes.

Although the evidence on the term structure of interest rates indicates that, in most respects, the pre-Civil War markets behaved much like the markets in more recent times, in one important respect the description of the older interest structure differs markedly from the new. Since 1920 the long-term rate has been below the short-term for only two brief periods; but from 1840 to 1860, the short rate was almost continuously above the long. The evidence suggests that these phenomena, as well as some other peculiar movements in the term structure, can be explained better by a theory that assumes the existence of several quasi-independent money markets than they can by the more widely held expectational theory.

Finally, the fact that this study has been based on the records of eight firms suggests that similar records could provide the basis for other general studies of American development. Although firm records are far from a perfect source, they are superior to other available evidence and they can open the door to work in areas that have long been neglected because of the lack of any quantitative data.

TABLE A–1
Relative Importance of Lenders by Year and Loan Length, 1840–60
(Percent of Total Dollar Value)

Lender	Year	Type I	Type II	Type III	Type IV	Year	Type I	Type II	Type III	Type IV
	1840					*1841*				
Commercial banks			100	100				91	92	
Savings banks										
Trust companies										78
Insurance companies								3	5	
Persons (including trustee accounts)							35	6	3	22
Mercantile firms							60			
Manufacturing firms							5			
Misc. institutions										
	1842					*1843*				
Commercial banks			91	84	2			62	100	60
Savings banks				9	23					
Trust companies		91			70					
Insurance companies										
Persons (including trustee accounts)		9		4	2					19
Mercantile firms			9	1						
Manufacturing firms				2				38		21
Misc. institutions										
	1844					*1845*				
Commercial banks		10	10	4						19
Savings banks					6					48
Trust companies										
Insurance companies										
Persons (including trustee accounts)		25	30	85	78		2		100	33
Mercantile firms		38			6					
Manufacturing firms		27	61	12	10		98			
Misc. institutions								100		
	1846					*1847*				
Commercial banks		14	10	18			40	97	79	
Savings banks									21	40
Trust companies										56
Insurance companies										
Persons (including trustee accounts)		16	3	19			15	1		4
Mercantile firms			20	23						
Manufacturing firms		69	68	41			38	2		
Misc. institutions					100		6			
	1848					*1849*				
Commercial banks		39	90	77			21	89	85	10
Savings banks		7	4	23	85			6	11	45
Trust companies									5	23
Insurance companies		7	1							
Persons (including trustee accounts)		20	2		15		4			22
Mercantile firms		14						5		
Manufacturing firms		13	3				49			
Misc. institutions							25			

TABLE A–1 (*Continued*)

Lender	Year	Type I	Type II	Type III	Type IV	Year	Type I	Type II	Type III	Type IV
	1850					*1851*				
Commercial banks		10	82	79	10		14	95	62	
Savings banks			0		33				18	39
Trust companies		12	1	8	43				3	23
Insurance companies				2						4
Persons (including trustee accounts)		3	4	1	13		19		17	34
Mercantile firms		53	13	11	1		46	4		
Manufacturing firms		21					21	1		
Misc. institutions										
	1852					*1853*				
Commercial banks			88	100	1		41	92	76	
Savings banks					31			3	8	23
Trust companies			3		37			3	14	17
Insurance companies										
Persons (including trustee accounts)		10	4		31		11		2	52
Mercantile firms			3				28	3		
Manufacturing firms		90	1				17			
Misc. institutions							3		8	
	1854					*1855*				
Commercial banks		32	97	79			19	84	59	
Savings banks			1	9	39				3	47
Trust companies		8		9	43		11	2	16	30
Insurance companies			1		4		2		3	5
Persons (including trustee accounts)		20		3	3		51	5	18	10
Mercantile firms		25						8	2	9
Manufacturing firms		11	1				1			
Misc. institutions		5			11					
	1856					*1857*				
Commercial banks		33	96	40			34	92	34	
Savings banks				3	61		10	2	3	57
Trust companies		27		6	26				10	10
Insurance companies				5	5		3	1	5	1
Persons (including trustee accounts)		27	3	15	8		39	3	13	33
Mercantile firms		11	1	32			6	2	35	
Manufacturing firms		2					8			
Misc. institutions							0			
	1858					*1859*				
Commercial banks			90	47				92	51	21
Savings banks					27					42
Trust companies				8	49					
Insurance companies				2	0					4
Persons (including trustee accounts)		52		15	17		21	1	25	11
Mercantile firms			8	29	6			4	24	22
Manufacturing firms		49	2				79	3		
Misc. institutions										

TABLE A–1 (*Continued*)

Lender	Year	Type I	Type II	Type III	Type IV	Year	Type I	Type II	Type III	Type IV
	1860									
Commercial banks			90	62						
Savings banks			9		24					
Trust companies					52					
Insurance companies										
Persons (including trustee accounts)				21	20					
Mercantile firms				17	4					
Manufacturing firms		93								
Misc. institutions		7								

TABLE A–2
WEIGHTED AVERAGE INTEREST RATES BY MONTH 1840–60
(Per Cent)

Year and Month	Rates*	Rates†	Year and Month	Rates*	Rates†	Year and Month	Rates*	Rates†
1840								
Jan.	7.1	6.7	May	6.3	6.4	Sept.	6.2	6.1
Feb.	6.2	6.1	June	6.2	6.3	Oct.	6.3	6.2
Mar.	5.6	5.6	July	6.2	6.2	Nov.	5.8	5.7
Apr.	5.3	5.6	Aug.	6.4	6.5	Dec.	6.3	6.4
1841								
Jan.	6.3	6.2	May	6.1	6.2	Sept.	6.3	6.1
Feb.	7.1	7.1	June	6.3	6.4	Oct.	6.3	6.3
Mar.	6.3	6.3	July	6.2	6.2	Nov.	6.3	6.2
Apr.	6.1	6.1	Aug.	6.3	6.4	Dec.	6.3	6.4
1842								
Jan.	6.2	6.1	May	6.3	6.4	Sept.	6.0	5.9
Feb.	6.3	6.2	June	6.3	6.4	Oct.	6.3	6.2
Mar.	7.5	7.5	July	6.1	6.1	Nov.	6.3	6.2
Apr.	6.1	6.1	Aug.	6.2	6.4	Dec.	6.6	6.7
1843								
Jan.	6.2	6.1	May	5.3	5.4	Sept.	5.4	5.3
Feb.	6.3	6.3	June	5.8	5.4	Oct.	5.3	5.3
Mar.	5.7	5.7	July	6.4	6.4	Nov.	5.2	5.2
Apr.	6.4	6.4	Aug.	4.7	4.9	Dec.	3.0	3.1
1844								
Jan.	4.6	4.5	May	5.0	5.1	Sept.	5.9	5.8
Feb.	5.2	5.1	June	4.7	4.7	Oct.	5.0	5.0
Mar.	4.5	4.5	July	5.4	5.5	Nov.	4.9	4.8
Apr.	4.2	4.2	Aug.	5.5	5.7	Dec.	4.8	4.9
1845								
Jan.	5.0	5.0	May	5.5	5.5	Sept.	5.0	4.9
Feb.	5.0	4.9	June	5.2	5.3	Oct.	5.8	5.8
Mar.	5.3	5.3	July	5.0	5.0	Nov.	6.6	6.5
Apr.	6.0	6.0	Aug.	5.0	5.1	Dec.	6.0	6.1
1846								
Jan.	5.4	5.3	May	5.9	6.0	Sept.	6.2	6.0
Feb.	5.7	5.6	June	5.8	5.9	Oct.	6.0	6.0
Mar.	6.1	6.1	July	3.9	3.9	Nov.	5.8	5.7
Apr.	5.9	5.9	Aug.	4.7	4.8	Dec.	4.2	4.3
1847								
Jan.	5.9	5.8	May	6.4	6.5	Sept.	6.3	6.2
Feb.	5.5	5.5	June	6.1	6.2	Oct.	6.3	6.3
Mar.	6.3	6.3	July	6.3	6.3	Nov.	6.0	6.0
Apr.	6.1	6.2	Aug.	6.1	6.2	Dec.	6.4	6.5
1848								
Jan.	6.3	6.2	May	5.8	5.8	Sept.	6.3	6.2
Feb.	6.6	6.5	June	7.7	7.9	Oct.	6.1	6.1
Mar.	6.2	6.2	July	6.7	6.7	Nov.	6.8	6.7
Apr.	6.3	6.3	Aug.	6.3	6.4	Dec.	6.7	6.8

* Weighted interest rates.
† Seasonally adjusted rates.

TABLE A–2 (*Continued*)

Year and Month	Rates*	Rates†	Year and Month	Rates*	Rates†	Year and Month	Rates*	Rates†
1849								
Jan.	6.5	6.4	May	6.3	6.4	Sept.	6.2	6.1
Feb.	6.3	6.2	June	6.3	6.4	Oct.	6.1	6.1
Mar.	6.5	6.5	July	6.6	6.7	Nov.	6.4	6.3
Apr.	6.5	6.5	Aug.	4.8	4.9	Dec.	5.8	5.9
1850								
Jan.	6.6	6.5	May	6.5	6.6	Sept.	6.2	6.1
Feb.	6.4	6.3	June	6.3	6.4	Oct.	6.3	6.3
Mar.	5.6	5.5	July	6.5	6.5	Nov.	6.5	6.4
Apr.	6.5	6.5	Aug.	6.0	6.1	Dec.	6.2	6.3
1851								
Jan.	6.1	6.1	May	7.2	7.3	Sept.	6.2	6.0
Feb.	6.2	6.2	June	6.2	6.3	Oct.	6.3	6.3
Mar.	6.2	6.2	July	6.1	6.1	Nov.	6.4	6.3
Apr.	6.2	6.2	Aug.	6.2	6.3	Dec.	6.4	6.5
1852								
Jan.	5.9	5.8	May	6.1	6.2	Sept.	6.2	6.1
Feb.	6.2	6.2	June	6.3	6.5	Oct.	6.3	6.3
Mar.	6.3	6.3	July	5.9	5.9	Nov.	6.3	6.2
Apr.	6.5	6.6	Aug.	6.1	6.2	Dec.	6.4	6.5
1853								
Jan.	6.3	6.2	May	6.4	6.5	Sept.	6.2	6.1
Feb.	6.3	6.3	June	6.4	6.5	Oct.	6.3	6.3
Mar.	6.5	6.5	July	6.3	6.3	Nov.	6.7	6.6
Apr.	6.7	6.7	Aug.	6.3	6.4	Dec.	6.5	6.7
1854								
Jan.	6.5	6.5	May	6.9	7.0	Sept.	6.8	6.6
Feb.	6.8	6.7	June	6.5	6.7	Oct.	5.9	5.9
Mar.	6.7	6.7	July	7.4	7.4	Nov.	6.6	6.5
Apr.	6.6	6.6	Aug.	7.4	7.6	Dec.	7.0	7.1
1855								
Jan.	7.2	7.1	May	6.3	6.4	Sept.	6.5	6.4
Feb.	6.8	6.7	June	6.4	6.6	Oct.	7.3	7.2
Mar.	6.6	6.6	July	6.4	6.4	Nov.	6.3	6.2
Apr.	7.0	7.1	Aug.	6.5	6.7	Dec.	7.0	7.2
1856								
Jan.	7.0	7.0	May	6.7	6.8	Sept.	7.4	7.2
Feb.	6.5	6.4	June	6.5	6.6	Oct.	7.0	7.0
Mar.	6.2	6.2	July	7.4	7.5	Nov.	7.0	6.9
Apr.	6.2	6.2	Aug.	6.6	6.8	Dec.	6.6	6.8
1857								
Jan.	7.5	7.4	May	6.6	6.7	Sept.	9.7	9.5
Feb.	7.3	7.3	June	6.5	6.6	Oct.	7.9	7.8
Mar.	7.1	8.1	July	6.6	6.6	Nov.	7.3	7.2
Apr.	7.7	7.8	Aug.	7.7	7.9	Dec.	7.9	8.1

TABLE A–2 (*Continued*)

Year and Month	Rates*	Rates†	Year and Month	Rates*	Rates†	Year and Month	Rates*	Rates†
1858								
Jan.	7.8	7.7	May	5.7	5.8	Sept.	5.7	5.6
Feb.	6.8	6.7	June	5.5	5.6	Oct.	5.6	5.6
Mar.	6.3	6.3	July	5.6	5.6	Nov.	6.2	6.1
Apr.	5.7	5.7	Aug.	6.2	6.3	Dec.	6.1	6.2
1859								
Jan.	5.9	5.8	May	5.8	5.9	Sept.	6.3	6.2
Feb.	6.1	6.1	June	6.0	6.2	Oct.	6.4	6.4
Mar.	6.0	6.0	July	6.6	6.7	Nov.	6.4	6.3
Apr.	6.0	6.0	Aug.	6.5	6.6	Dec.	6.4	6.5
1860								
Jan.	6.3	6.2	May	5.4	5.5	Sept.	6.4	6.3
Feb.	6.2	6.1	June	4.7	4.8	Oct.	6.2	6.2
Mar.	6.1	6.1	July	4.0	4.0	Nov.	6.6	6.5
Apr.	6.0	6.0	Aug.	5.6	5.8	Dec.	6.2	6.3

SHORT-TERM INTEREST RATES IN THE NEW YORK AND BOSTON MARKETS: BIGELOW'S ESTIMATES BY MONTH
1840–60 (Percent)

Month	1840	1841	1842	1843	1844	1845	1846	1847	1848	1849	1850	1951	1852	1853
Jan.	9	7	12	6	4	6	8	12	18	12	10½	7½	8½	8
Feb.	12	7	12	5	4	6	9	12	12	12	8	8½	7½	10
Mar.	12	7	12	6	5	6	7	10	15	15	9	8½	6	12
Apr.	7	7	8	5	5	6	12	9	15	15	9	8	6	10
May	7	6	8	4½	5	6	12	8	15	11	8½	6½	6	9
June	8	6	8	3½	5	6	12	6	18	9	8	9	6	9
July	5	6	8	4	5	6	9	6	18	8	7	11	6	9
Aug.	7½	6	7¼	4	5	6	9	9	15	8½	8	11	6	10
Sept.	7	7	7	4	5½	6	6	9	15	9	9	15	7	12
Oct.	7	7½	6	4	5	5½	8	12	18	10	8	16	6	15
Nov.	7	9	6½	4	5½	8	7	15	15	10	8	12	6	12
Dec.	7	12	9	4	5	8	7	18	12	10½	8	12	6	9

TABLE A–3 (Continued)

Year and Month	End of Month	Year and Month	End of Month	Year and Month	End of Month	Year and Month	End of Month	Year and Month	End of Month	Year and Month	End of Month	Year and Month	End of Month
1854		1855		1856		1857		1858		1859		1860	
Jan.	8	J.	10	J.	12	J.	10	J.	7½	J.	5½	J.	8½
Feb.	9	F.	10	F.	9	F.	9	F.	5½	F.	6	F.	6½
Mar.	10	M.	9	M.	10	M.	10	M.	5	M.	5½	M.	5
Apr.	12	A.	10	A.	8	A.	9	A.	4½	A.	5½	A.	4½
May	12	M.	8	M.	8	M.	7	M.	4½	M.	6¾	M.	4½
June	11	J.	6	J.	8	J.	8	J.	4½	J.	7	J.	5½
July	9	J.	7	J.	8	J.	10	J.	4	J.	7	J.	6
Aug.	9	A.	8	A.	8	A.	10	A.	4	A.	7	A.	6
Sept.	12	S.	8	S.	9	S.	36	S	4	S.	7½	S.	5½
Oct.	10	O.	9	O.	10	O.	24	O.	4½	O.	7½	O.	6
Nov.	12	N.	12	N.	10	N.	15	N.	5	N.	7	N.	12
Dec.	18	D.	15	D.	11	D.	9	D.	5	D.	8	D.	12

TABLE A-4*†

Term Structure of Interest Rates by Quarters 1840–60
(Percent)

Year and Qtr.	Type I‡	Type IIs	Type IIIᵐ	Type IV#
1840				
1		5.5	6.8	
2		4.7	6.2	
3		6.4	6.2	
4		6.4	5.9	
1841				
1	8.0	9.6	6.2	5.0
2	6.0	6.3	6.2	6.1
3		6.4	6.2	6.1
4		6.4	6.2	
1842				
1	6.1	6.4	6.4	
2		6.3	6.3	6.0
3	6.0	6.4	6.0	6.0
4		6.3	6.3	
1843				
1		6.4	6.0	4.5
2		6.4	5.2	4.8
3		6.4	5.2	4.1
4		4.9		
1844				
1	4.4	4.8		5.1
2	4.0	4.7	4.3	4.8
3	4.0	6.0		5.0
4	4.5	6.0		5.0
1845				
1	4.9		5.0	5.3
2				6.0
3	5.0		5.0	5.0
4	6.6			
1846				
1	5.6	5.3	5.7	5.9
2		5.9	6.0	5.0
3	6.4	3.3	5.6	6.0
4		4.3	5.9	
1847				
1	5.6	6.1	5.7	6.0
2	5.2	6.4	6.0	6.0
3		6.3	6.0	
4		6.4	6.2	6.0
1848				
1	6.4	6.4		
2	6.0	7.5		
3	6.1	6.5	6.3	6.0
4	6.0	6.6	6.3	5.6
1849				
1	6.2	6.6	6.2	6.0
2	6.9	6.6	6.5	6.0
3	6.2	6.2	6.7	3.0
4	5.9	6.4	6.3	5.4
1850				
1	5.8	6.3	6.4	5.3
2	6.1	6.5	6.6	6.3
3	5.8	6.5	6.5	6.1
4	6.1	6.4	6.2	6.3
1851				
1	6.2	6.4	6.2	6.0
2	4.4	6.5	6.0	6.0
3	6.0	6.4	6.1	6.0
4	6.2	6.5	6.3	6.0
1852				
1	8.6	6.3	6.3	6.1
2	5.1	6.7	6.3	6.0
3	5.0	6.2	6.3	6.0
4		6.4	6.4	6.0
1853				
1	6.1	6.7	6.2	6.0
2	7.2	6.8	6.4	6.1
3	5.6	6.7	6.3	6.0
4	5.5	6.8	6.2	6.0
1854				
1	5.7	7.1	6.3	5.9
2	6.2	7.2	6.3	6.0
3	8.8	7.0	5.4	
4	5.8	6.9	6.4	6.0

TABLE A-4*† (Continued)

Year and Qtr.	Type I‡	Type II§	Type III‖	Type IV#
1855				
1	6.0	7.2	6.4	6.0
2	8.4	6.8	5.6	6.3
3	6.0	6.7	6.4	6.0
4	6.0	7.3	6.2	6.1
1856				
1	6.0	6.9	8.2	5.9
2	6.0	6.8	6.3	5.9
3	10.2	7.1	6.8	6.0
4	5.9	6.9	8.2	6.0
1857				
1	6.7	7.3	9.6	6.0
2	7.9	7.4	7.0	6.5
3	6.0	7.2	9.2	6.0
4	5.4	8.0	8.7	6.0
1858				
1	6.0	7.0	7.5	6.0
2		5.8	5.0	5.7
3	5.0	6.0	4.9	6.0
4	5.0	6.4	5.0	6.0
1859				
1	6.0	6.0	6.0	5.9
2	5.2	6.1	5.6	5.0
3		6.3	6.3	6.0
4		6.5	6.3	6.2
1860				
1	5.0	6.3	6.2	6.0
2	4.5	6.3	6.3	6.0
3				
4	6.0	6.6	6.1	6.0

* Blanks indicate less than five loans.
† Demand loans from savings banks which in fact were made for a specified number of years were excluded from Group I and placed in Group IV.
‡ Demand and less than 30 days.
§ 30 days to six months.
‖ Six months to one year.
One year and over.

5. Sources of Industrial Finance: The American Textile Industry—A Case Study[*]

Lance E. Davis
Purdue University

Introduction

IT IS A GENERALLY RECOGNIZED FACT that capital accumulation is a necessary prerequisite for economic progress. However, the accumulation of real capital is a dual process; it requires both savings and the mobilization of these savings under the control of entrepreneurs. In the last few years the first of these two aspects has come under the close scrutiny of many economists, but the latter process has been largely ignored.

This paper is a case study of one of the first and most important American industries to adopt capital-intensive techniques—the cotton textile industry.[1] The study is based on the data provided by the records of nine textile mills. These records have been deposited in the business history collection of the Baker Library of the Graduate School of Business Administration, Harvard University.

The records describe the financial structure of nine Massachusetts-type textile firms.[2] The individual firm series range from 7 to 33 years. They

[*] The author wishes to express his thanks to Professor Irving Morrissett for his help and advice on matters both statistical and editorial. Further, the author wishes to acknowledge the aid of the department of political economy of John Hopkins University that financed the research on which this paper is based.

[1] The industry began to innovate a mass-producing technology as early as 1813; and, if value added is taken as a measure of importance, it had by 1860 become the most important industry in the United States. U.S. Department of the Interior, *Manufactures of the United States in 1860: Compiled from the Original Returns of the Eighth Census* (Washington, D.C.: Government Printing Office, 1865), pp. 733–42.

[2] Students of the period divide textile producers into two categories. The small single operation mills that were the American heirs to the English developments are termed Rhode Island-type mills. These firms are typified by the Slater enterprises near Providence, Rhode Island, and by the development at Fall River in Massachusetts. The Massachusetts type is the name given to the large integrated mills that grew out of the development of the Boston Manufacturing Company at Waltham, Massachusetts.

begin in the year 1827 with the records of the Hamilton Manufacturing Company. Other records are added so that the post-1845 years are represented by the data of from six to eight firms. The nine firms that appear for seven or more years are, in addition to the Hamilton, the Amoskeag, Dwight, Cabot, Perkins, Lancaster, Lawrence, Lyman, and Massachusetts Cotton mills. Together they constituted about one sixth of the number of Massachusetts-type mills that were producing in the 1840's and 1850's. The nine are not, of course, a random sample of all textile mills or even of all Massachusetts-type mills; but they are the only records available for a detailed study of this type. On the basis of this study we shall attempt to present some cautious generalizations about how capital was mobilized in the early American textile industry.

The Model

Examination of the records suggest that the sources of capital utilized by a firm at any point in time depend, at least in part, upon two distinct factors—the historical date and the age of the firm. The state of business activity and the institutional environment within which a firm operates (the stage of development of the capital market, the willingness of investors to hold equity shares, etc.) affect the availability of capital. In these terms availability is a function of historical date. At the same time, capital structure depends upon the age of the firm. For example, it is obviously impossible for retained earnings to become an important source of capital until some profits have been earned.

More complex techniques are necessary if the investigation of the importance of firm age and historical date is to be pushed beyond the "first glance" stage. A multiple-regression model permits an evaluation of the importance of each variable and also describes the firms' responses to changes in each of the variables. In the model chosen, the dependent variables are the percentage of each firm's assets represented by equity (y_1), loans (y_2), and retained earnings (y_3). The independent variables were year (x_1), and firm age (x_2), including the quadratic terms (year)^2, (age)^2, and (year $\times$ age). The estimating equation then is:

$$y_i = a_1x_1 + a_2x_2 + a_3x_1{}^2 + a_4x_2{}^2 + a_5x_1x_2$$

In all, there were 173 observations (firm years) for each of the dependent variables.

The model allows for the secular changes in the financial structure of the nine firms, but not for cyclic fluctuations. The cyclic effects are considered in a later section of the paper where residuals from a set of regressions are presented and discussed.[3] The data seem to show that both firm

---

[3] Because of the presence of these cyclic elements, the independent variables should not be expected to explain all of the variation in the dependent variables.

age and chronological year are important to an explanation of the firms' financial structure. For each source of capital (equity, loans, and retained earnings) the independent variables accounted for almost one half of the total variance. The coefficients of determination were .487 for equity, .452 for loans, and .505 for retained earnings.

The model describes only the changes in financial structure of the nine firms. As has been said, the nine do not represent a random sample of all Massachusetts-type firms producing in the antebellum period; instead they were chosen because they were the only firms that yielded comparable records for any significant number of years. Examination shows that the nine were not even representative of a homogeneous industry unless one is willing to lump them together under the very broad heading of cotton textiles. (Actually, the mills did not produce a homogeneous product. For example, although several mills produced drillings, at least one produced ginghams and another produced fancy dress goods). Moreover, all nine came from that segment of the industry that depended upon water power (there were no steam mills); and none was so unsuccessful that it actually failed during the period of study.[4] Despite these deficiencies, the sample is the best available, and it does not appear unwarranted to use the experience of the nine as the basis for broader generalizations. Therefore, let us assume that the nine represent a random sample of all moderately successful Massachusetts-type textile mills employing water as their prime source of power and operating in the years between 1831 and 1860. For the purpose of generalization, the usual large-sample tests of significance were used and these tests show that the three coefficients of determination are significant at the 1 percent level.[5]

Trends in Financial Structure

Since the data seem to show a significant relationship between a firm's financial structure and its age and the date, it appears useful to investigate the nature of this relationship as specified by the shape of the regression lines. For the nine firms in the sample, the regression equations are:[6]

---

[4] However, two of the firms (Cabot and Perkins) could hardly have been termed successful, and these two might well have failed had they not merged with a more successful firm.

[5] The nine yielded 173 firm-year observations. Since the 173 are obviously not independent, the relevant number of degrees of freedom is, no doubt, considerably smaller; however, there is good reason to believe that the number of independent observations is great enough to permit large sample tests to be used. If the number of degrees of freedom is as few as 19 the coefficients are significant at the 5 percent level; and if the number is as many as 26, they are significant at the 2 percent level.

[6] In the regression equations, the coefficients with a double underline (═══) are significant at the 1 percent level, those with a single underline (————) at the 5 percent level, and those with a dotted underline (——————) at the 10 percent level. For these computations large sample tests were used.

$$Y_1 = 85.53 - .1149X_1 - .5372x_2 + .0001X_1{}^2 + .0010X_2{}^2 - .0173X_1X_2 \quad E$$

$$Y_2 = 10.98 - .6041X_1 - .1734x_2 + .0274X_1{}^2 - .0267X_2{}^2 + .0322X_1X_2 \quad L$$

$$Y_3 = 4.76 + .0712X_1 + 1.601 \ X_2 + .0016X_1{}^2 + .0491X_2{}^2 - .0750X_1X_2 \quad R$$

Charts 1a, 2a, and 3a depict the relationship between the dependent variables and the chronological date when firm age is held constant, and Charts 1b, 2b, and 3b show the effects of age upon the utilization of capital sources when the chronological date is held constant.

Chart 1 shows the effect of the independent variables on the firms' equity issues. Throughout the historical period covered by this study (1827–60), equity represented the most important source of capital. An examination of the regression curves shows, however, that the relative importance of this source declined both over the life of the firm and over historical time. (These are independent effects, insofar as the model could separate them.) Since the nine firms financed almost all their original plant and equipment through the sale of equities, and since in general they did not increase their equity issues after the first few years of their existence, the declining importance of the equity contribution is not surprising. Among the nine firms in the sample, four sold no new equities after the 5th year of their life, and none sold new shares after the 11th. The substantial growth which did occur is attributable to retained earnings and loans.

That the textile firms were hesitant to issue additional equities is apparent; the reasons for this action are less obvious. The growth of an organized equity and bond market was an important feature of American economic development in the period 1810–60. Although the formal market for industrial equity was still small in 1860, the Boston and the New York stock markets did handle such shares, and the 30 years prior to the outbreak of the Civil War had seen an increasing volume of these "industrials" traded on both markets.[7] The apparent development of a formal market should have made equity capital more available to the textile industry, but the textile firms seldom drew on this potential source of capital to finance their growth.

Many factors may account for the apparent refusal to issue new equity, but three are outstanding: the lack of a real market, the original stockholders' fear of capital dilution, and the peculiar conditions sometimes attached by the law to particular equity issues.

In the case of the nine firms, the original shares were closely held and an examination of the nature of the newly developing capital market suggests that the ability of that market to mobilize capital was more apparent than real. The shares in the Massachusetts-type firms were seldom

[7] See, for example, Joseph G. Martin, *Seventy-Three Years History of the Boston Stock Market* (Boston: Privately printed, 1871) pp. 64–73, and Margaret G. Myers, *The New York Money Market, Vol. I, Origins and Development* (New York: Columbia University Press, 1931), pp. 14–15.

CHART 1
RELATION BETWEEN EQUITY, YEAR, AND AGE OF FIRM

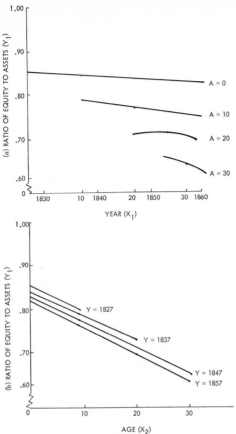

traded, and when ownership changed it was frequently within the family. In fact, the chronicler of the Boston Security Exchange warns his readers not to rely on his industrial quotations because the market was so extremely thin. In addition, the owners were undoubtedly aware of the threat of dilution. For example, the Boston Manufacturing Company in 1820 was able to issue new equity only after the stockholders had forced the company to divide the surplus and thus prevent dilution.[8] Such a fear would not prevent the sale of new equity shares to the original stockholders, but, if dilution was to be prevented, the available capital was limited to the assets of these original investors.

Legal bars also seem to have prevented the full utilization of equity as a source of capital. During the 1840's several firms attempted to secure new financing by issuing additional shares in periods of depressed stock

---

[8] Records of the Boston Manufacturing Company, Vol. 1, Directors' Records (February 25, 1820).

CHART 2
RELATION BETWEEN LOANS, YEAR, AND AGE OF FIRM

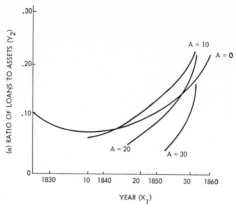

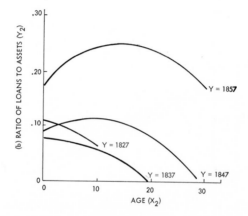

prices, when sales could be consummated only at prices below the original par value of the stock. Such sales did bring net capital into the firm, but they favored the new stockholder at the expense of the old. To protect the original investors the Massachusetts legislature began to restrict the terms on which textile firms could sell additional equity. After 1849 firms often were permitted to increase their capital only

Provided that no sales of capital stock hereby authorized shall be issued for a sum or amount to be actually paid in on each less than the average par value of the shares of the present capital stock of the said corporation . . . .[9]

Chart 1 seems to show that the later the historical date the less dependence firms of the same age placed upon equity capital; and further, that in the same historical year the older firms were less dependent on equity capital than were the younger mills. These conclusions lend proof to what students of the period, familiar with the firms and environment,

[9] Special Acts of the Legislature of the Commonwealth of Massachusetts, 1849, 238.

CHART 3

<small>RELATION BETWEEN RETAINED EARNINGS, YEAR, AND AGE OF FIRM</small>

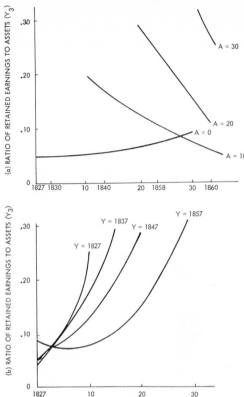

might have suspected. Not only was an organized market for stocks and bonds developing in the period; but also long-term loan capital from credit intermediaries—savings banks, trust companies, and life insurance companies—was becoming more available. This increase in availability, coupled with the particularly favored loan position enjoyed by the textile industry, could have been expected to lead to an increase over time in the amount of loan capital employed by the firms, and thus to reduction in the relative importance of equity in firms of the same age at later dates. The reduced importance of equity over the firms' lives (independent of the effect of historical time) also lends proof to what might otherwise have been suspected. As a firm ages, if it is successful, it appears reasonable to expect an increase in the amount of capital realized from retained earnings and as a result a reduction in the importance of equity.

The effect of the development of the long-term credit market upon the firms' financial structure can be seen clearly in the relationship between loan capital and historical time shown in Chart 2a. Over time, loans appear to have increased at an increasing rate; and, in most instances, for any given year new firms borrowed more than old. Since all nine firms were well connected with the Boston financial institutions, this latter result is most likely a reflection of falling demand for loan finance as retained earnings and trade credit increased. The negative time term is, perhaps, more surprising; but it was apparently due to the repercussions of the depression of the 1840's—a depression that caused all firms to drastically reduce their borrowings. If those years are dropped both the time and the (time)^2 terms are positive and significant. The most important aspect of the equation is the strong (time)^2 term, a reflection of the rapid increase in borrowing over historical time.[10] A large part of this increase can be attributed to the entry of certain credit intermediaries into the long-term industrial loan market. The records of the textile firms show that prior to 1840 most loans were of less than a year's duration and were seldom renewed. Beginning in the early 1840's, however, the mills began receiving long-term loans from a number of financial intermediaries. Typically, these loans were originally made for periods of two years or longer and renewed almost as a matter of course.[11] The commercial banks apparently did not increase the length of their loans, although some inconclusive evidence suggests that the effective duration of commercial bank loans may have increased by a more liberal renewal policy in the years after 1840.

The entry of the nonbank financial intermediaries into the industrial loan market was probably precipitated by the increase in the size and number of these institutions. Before 1840 they had invested most of their funds in government securities and mortgages. The influx of new intermediaries (and the growth of the established concerns) brought a flood of new funds to the investment market and reduced the returns of the "customary" investments. To prevent their earnings from falling, the credit intermediaries were forced to seek out new investment opportunities.[12] In the years before 1840, these intermediaries had been willing to lend to industry on the hypothecation of mortgages or stocks, but their search for new investment outlets led to the innovation of the less stringent three-signature loan, and this device became the major instrument of industrial borrowing.[13] As the supply of long-term credit increased

---

[10] Only the curve for 10-year-old firms has been plotted, since other ages are characterized by almost identical curves.

[11] The Massachusetts Hospital Life Insurance Company, for example, made several loans during the 1840's and 1850's that were not repaid until after World War I. Records of the Massachusetts Hospital Life Insurance Company, Loan Book. These records are deposited in the offices of the firm, 50 State Street, Boston, Mass.

[12] Though the number and size of all types of noncredit-creating intermediaries were rapidly increasing during the years 1840–60, this rapid increase is nowhere better demonstrated than in the case of savings banks. In Massachusetts the number of savings banks increased from 31 in 1839 to 86 in 1859. During the same period deposits in these banks increased from $5,608,158 to $39,424,418. *Legislative Documents of the Commonwealth of Massachusetts, House 1839* (Boston: State Printers, 1839). Sec'y of the Commonwealth of Mass., *Abstract Exhibiting the Condition of the Institutions for Savings in Mass., 1859.*

[13] The three-signature loan required no tangible collateral. Instead it amounted to

after 1840, the textile industry's demand for loan capital also increased. The industry's increasing demand was in part a function of the growth of the industry, but it was also a function of the peculiar political and legal rules that governed the Boston loan market. During much of the 19th century, Massachusetts intermediaries were forbidden by law to charge more than 6 percent interest on their loans.[14] Because interest rates were generally below 6 percent before 1840, the limit probably had little effect in these early years. From 1840 to 1860, however, bank and firm records show that almost all loans were made at 6 percent. The existence of so constant a rate for so long a period seems to imply that the rate of interest would have been above 6 percent had the free market been allowed to operate. In the absence of a free market those firms that could obtain 6 percent loans must have found them a cheap source of capital and a welcome supplement to retained earnings and equity capital.

No New England industry maintained better connections with the loan market than did the textile firms. Because of its favored position in the loan market, the industry benefited greatly from the limitation on interest. The ability of the industry to maintain such close connections with the credit intermediaries can probably be attributed both to the dominant position of the textile industry in Massachusetts economic development and to the close personal connection between the stockholders in that industry and the directors of the institutions of deposit. Whatever the cause, there can be no doubt that the textile industry did receive the lion's share of the industrial loans made by these institutions. Take, for example, the case of the Provident Institution for Savings in the Town of Boston, the largest savings bank in New England. Between 1839 and 1859 the Provident made 231 loans, exclusive of renewals, to 41 firms in the textile industry.[15]

The changes in the structure of the credit market that has just been discussed account in large part for the increase in the proportion of loans to total assets of the textile companies over historical time. Changes in the proportion of loans over the life of the firm independent of historical time remain to be explained. The fact that loans increased in importance during the first few years of firm life, then declined (see Chart 2b),

---

no more than a personal loan backed by the credit of three endorsers. In practice the endorsers were almost invariably drawn from among the wealthiest men of the business community and the risk involved was extremely slight. The Provident Institution and the Massachusetts Hospital Life Insurance Company both leaned heavily on this type of instrument, and their records show not a single loss in the period 1840–60.

14 The Massachusetts Usury Laws are summarized in *General Statutes of Massachusetts*, chap. 53, ss. 3–5, p. 292 (1860 ed.). This law is based on a series of early legislation: *General Statutes of Massachusetts* 1825-143 and 1826-27; *Revised Statutes of Massachusetts*, 1836, chap. 35, secs. 1–4; *General Statutes of Massachusetts*, 1846-199 and 1855-194.

15 Records of the Provident Institution for Savings in the Town of Boston Record book of the Board of Investment 1839–59. These records are preserved in the offices of the Provident Institution in Boston.

appears to have a simple explanation. In its early years a firm has some trouble getting loans. As it becomes established loans become more available. Ultimately, a successful firm may be able to finance an increasing proportion of its capital expansion and replacement out of retained earnings, and thus need less loan capital.[16] This last conclusion seems to be borne out by the relationship between retained earnings and firm age. Chart 3b shows that the proportion of total assets represented by retained earnings increased very rapidly as the firm grew older.

For the nine firms the relationship between retained earnings and historical year is described by Chart 3a. Apparently older firms (even though they possessed greater retained earnings) were better able to take advantage of the loosening loan market than were younger firms. As a result, the proportion of their retained earnings to total assets fell more rapidly than did that of younger firms. If the nine firms are to be used as the basis for generalization, it should be borne in mind that neither the year nor the (year)^2 coefficients are significant at even the 10 percent level.

Cyclic Variations

The regression lines show only the trends in the data, but it appears reasonable to expect some regular short-term fluctuations in the firm's capital structure. Although the nature of the data preclude vigorous statistical inquiry, an examination of the residuals—the differences between the observed and the predicted regression surface values—suggests something about the nature of these fluctuations.[17] Since the proportions must, by their very nature, sum to one, great care must be taken in interpreting the results. A change in any one can be the result of forces working on the source in question, or merely a response to some change in a difference source. Despite this weakness, the movements of the residuals do suggest something about the nature of business fluctuations in antebellum New England.

Though the cyclic fluctuations may have been the product of many outside forces, this paper will examine only the relationship between financial structure and the state of business activity. Because changes in business conditions should affect all firms in the same direction and at the same time, it seems more reasonable to examine the effects of changing business conditions on the "industry" rather than on the individual firms. Residuals averaged for the nine firms are displayed in Charts 4, 5, and 6.

---

[16] At no age, however, is the rise and fall in the proportion of loans large, and if the reader wishes to use the nine firms as a basis for generalizations, he should bear in mind that these changes may not be significant. The tests of significance show that the (age)^2 and the age times year terms are significant only at the 10 percent level.

[17] Although the results are difficult to interpret, a single run test on the residuals indicates that for all the sources the number of runs above and below the medium are significantly below the number expected on a random basis at the .05 level.

CHART 4

NINE TEXTILE FIRMS AVERAGE EQUITY RESIDUALS BY YEARS (1832–60)

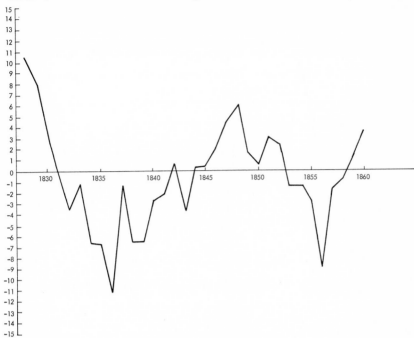

A comparison of the fluctuations in the residuals with changes in more general measures of business activity seems to show that firm financial structure was affected by these changes, but affected in a manner that is not altogether obvious.[18] To anticipate the conclusions of this section, it appears first that the relative importance of retained earnings was affected by the state of general business activity (movements in output and employment) but was not affected by financial conditions; second, that while the condition of the money market was of great importance in determining the proportion of loans, the state of general business affected the loan-to-asset ratio only slightly; and finally, that the absolute volume of equity was affected by neither financial nor more general business conditions (though the relative importance reflected the changes in loans and retained earnings).

Although the equity residuals display a pattern that appears more cyclic than either the loans or retained earnings, equity was less closely connected with the state of business activity than were either of the other elements of capital structure. Because the textile firms seldom issued new equity, and because on the rare occasions that such new issues were made

---

[18] For measures of business activity see Leonard P. Ayres, *Turning Points in Business Cycles* (New York: Macmillan Co., 1939), pp. 174–81; Willard Thorp, *Business Annals* (New York: National Bureau of Economic Research, 1926), pp. 120–27.

CHART 5
Nine Textile Firms Average Loan Residuals by Year (1832–60)

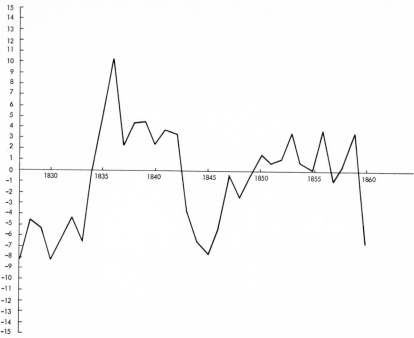

they were more often correlated with the firm's long-term growth prospects than with the state of business activity, the fluctuations in the equity
residuals represent in large measure merely the responses to changes in
the absolute amount of finance derived from loans and retained earnings.
When general economic or financial conditions improved, the volume of
finance derived from loans and/or retained earnings increased. As a result, the ratio of equity to total capital fell. In times of business recession
or financial crisis, the ratio rose as the absolute volume of loans and retained earnings fell. For these reasons, the equity residuals reflect in
reverse both the conditions of the financial market and the more deep-
rooted movements in business activity.

Though the retained earning residuals appear to have been little
affected by the current state of the money market, they do seem to reflect
the more basic changes in business activity. The ratio of retained earnings
to capital appears to have been hardly disturbed by the panics of 1837
and 1854; and, though the year 1857 is marked both by financial crisis
and by a reduction in the share of retained earnings, that year was also
marked by a general downturn in business activity. On the other hand,
fluctuations in output and employment (as opposed to financial panics)
seem to be reflected in the portion of capital represented by retained
earnings. The earning residuals closely mirror the prosperity of the

CHART 6

NINE TEXTILE FIRMS AVERAGE RETAINED EARNINGS RESIDUALS BY YEAR

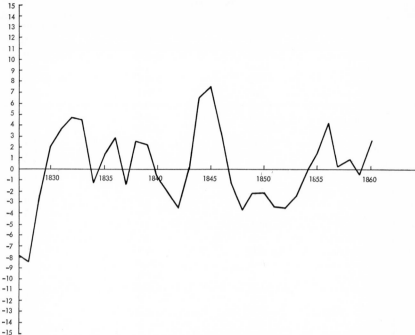

thirties, the 1840–43 depression, and the prosperous period of the mid-forties. Only during the last decade is there a serious discrepancy between movements in the retained earning-to-capital ratio and the changes in business activity. Both Ayres and Thorp describe the period 1849–53 as one of rising business activity; in contrast, the earning residuals display a trough in this same period.

The discrepancy can probably be explained by the existence of certain conditions peculiar to the textile industry. The very high profits of the mid-forties had attracted many new firms to the industry and had encouraged the expansion of the firms already producing textiles.[19] While the remainder of the economy may have been experiencing a period of general prosperity, for the textile industry the early years of the fifties were a period of readjustment—a readjustment marked by falling profits.[20] It appears, therefore, that the state of general business activity did affect the ratio of retained earnings to total assets, but at times this relationship

---

[19] Between 1840 and 1850 the number of active cotton spindles increased from 2,284,631 to 3,998,022 (an increase of about 62 percent). U.S. Department of Commerce, *Historical Statistics of the United States* (Washington, D.C.: Government Printing Office, 1949), p. 187.

[20] From 1844 to 1848 the total profits of the nine firms averaged 16.76 percent (as a percent of total capital stock). From 1848 through 1853 the profits averaged only 5.75 percent.

TABLE 1
Average Residuals for Nine Massachusetts-Type Textile Mills
1827–60*

Year	Equity	Loans	Retained Earnings
1827...............	14.0	—8.4	—8.0
1828...............	10.6	—4.6	—8.6
1829...............	8.2	—5.3	—2.8
1830...............	3.0	—8.1	2.0
1831...............	— .2	—6.3	3.3
1832...............	— 3.5	—4.4	4.6
1833...............	— 1.1	—6.8	4.5
1834...............	— 6.6	.4	—1.4
1835...............	— 6.9	5.5	1.1
1836...............	—11.2	10.4	2.7
1837...............	— 1.3	2.3	—1.3
1838...............	— 6.5	4.3	2.4
1839...............	— 6.5	4.5	2.0
1840...............	— 2.9	2.6	— .5
1841...............	— 2.1	3.7	—2.1
1842...............	.6	3.3	—3.8
1843...............	— 3.6	—4.0	.0
1844...............	.2	—6.6	6.4
1845...............	.2	—7.8	7.5
1846...............	1.9	—5.4	3.5
1847...............	4.3	— .5	—1.3
1848...............	5.9	—2.3	—3.7
1849...............	1.6	— .5	—2.2
1850...............	.7	1.4	—2.2
1851...............	3.0	.7	—3.4
1852...............	2.5	1.0	—3.6
1853...............	— 1.5	3.5	—2.5
1854...............	— 1.4	.7	— .1
1855...............	— 3.0	.1	1.5
1856...............	— 9.1	3.9	4.1
1857...............	— 1.8	—1.0	.1
1858...............	— .9	.5	.9
1859...............	1.1	3.3	— .3
1860...............	3.6	—6.6	2.2

* Values are computed from regression equations. Averages are unweighted, although initial year values far out of line have been dropped. For 1831 average of Hamilton in 1830 and 1832 was used.

was obscured by conditions peculiar to the textile industry. Moreover, the residuals indicate that purely financial phenomena had but little effect on this element of capital structure.

The loan residuals, on the contrary, seem more closely related to the condition of the financial market than to the more basic fluctuations in income and employment. During the last decade of the period, however, this relationship is largely obscured by the "explosion" of the loan residuals. In that decade the sample contains 74 firm years, and among these 74 there is but one negative loan residual. This condition strongly suggests that the quadratic regression curve does not accurately depict the increase in the importance of loans during the fifties, and that some other functional form might better describe these changes. If the trend in the residuals over the last 10 years is ignored, the loan/capital ratio appears to have responded closely to changes in the condition of the financial market. The financial panics of 1834, 1837, 1840, and 1842, and to a lesser extent those of 1854 and 1857, are reflected by a rapid contraction of loans relative to other capital sources. Conversely, "cheap money" seems to have resulted in an increased proportion of loans. Though financial conditions were apparently very important in determining the volume of loan capital utilized, there seems to have been no definite relation between the loans/asset ratio and the more basic movements in business activity. The ratio was high during the prosperous thirties, and it remained fairly high during the ensuing depression. It was low during the prosperity of the mid-forties, but high during the prosperous mid-fifties. Those industries that were less closely connected with the money market may well have discovered that the availability of credit was affected by changes in income and employment, but apparently the textile industry was able to retain its financial ties during these periods of general depression. However, the textile industry (like all others) seems to have found its loans cut off in periods of severe financial crisis.

Summary and Conclusions

The regression curves show the trends in the nine firms' capital structure over both historical time and firm life. Equity was the most important source of capital, but of declining importance over both age and historical time. Loans appear to have been increasingly important over historical time and over the first few years of firm life, but less important as the firm entered middle age. Finally, the ratio of retained earnings to total assets increased as the firms grew older, but it decreased over historical time.

The use of regression analysis has uncovered no revolutionary facts (though perhaps it has shown that loans were a more important source of capital than has been generally realized). What it has done is to make some measure of the importance of each source of capital. Henceforth, it is hoped, historians will be able to speak with greater precision about the relative importance of the three elements of capital structure.

The firms' financial structure responded not only to long-term trends but also to shorter term cyclical changes. The loan element in financial structure was most seriously affected by the state of the financial market. The ratio of loans to total assets fell in times of financial panic and increased in periods of easy money. The state of the financial market apparently had little effect on the portion of assets represented by retained earnings, but this element of capital structure was strongly affected by fluctuating in general business conditions (i.e., by movements in output and employment).

In conclusion, it appears that the historians of New England textile industry have correctly assessed the importance of equity capital in industrial finance. At the same time they may have overemphasized the role of retained earnings (at least as far as the Massachusetts-type mills are concerned) and have failed to acknowledge the contribution that was made by loan capital—particularly the long-term credit granted by the nonbank intermediaries.

APPENDIX: TABLE 1

NINE TEXTILE FIRMS

RELATIVE PROPORTION OF TOTAL ASSETS REPRESENTED BY EQUITY

BY YEARS AND FIRMS

Year	Amoskeag	Dwight	Cabot	Perkins	Hamil-ton	Lan-caster	Law-rence	Lyman	Mass. Cotton
1827					98.3				
1828					94.2				
1829					91.1				
1830					85.1				
1832					76.9				
1833					78.4				
1834					72.0		89.5		
1835			75.4		68.4		79.4		
1836			70.4		65.6		71.8		
1837	86.2		71.9		73.8		82.8		
1838	75.9		73.7	77.0	63.3		76.9		
1839	76.6		70.9	85.2	58.1		71.4		
1840	74.8		82.3	79.2	60.0		78.9		96.9
1841	79.6		80.3	82.7	62.9		79.3		73.6
1842	80.8	83.6	83.1	86.7	61.2		85.2		67.0
1843	80.8	85.1	83.0	87.7	59.2		85.7		80.0
1844	69.6	75.0	79.2	81.3	59.6		85.2		80.0
1845	52.6	82.3	79.8	85.7	58.4		83.3		80.0
1846	60.2	86.8	77.0	86.9	64.7		80.2		69.7
1847	60.5	91.8	79.3	84.4	54.9	82.6	75.0		70.3
1848	62.0	96.6	80.8	89.1	58.1	87.2	78.9		69.2
1849	55.1	88.2	82.6	89.2	57.0	75.7	70.7		59.2
1850	50.8	82.2	80.6	80.7	56.3	73.8	70.7		65.6
1851	47.7	85.5	87.3	84.4	55.2	69.6	74.2		64.2
1852	48.9	82.9	85.3	80.9	54.9	67.0	72.1		61.8
1853	46.1	70.2			58.4	69.1	76.9		63.8
1854	45.7	71.4			58.1	71.9	68.1	80.3	60.6
1855	43.2	70.2			45.4	68.0	70.0	79.0	58.8
1856	39.0				42.9	64.0	57.9	67.7	53.0
1857	43.0				58.8	71.3	54.3	70.3	62.2
1858	41.4				47.1	73.1	72.1	64.1	58.2
1859	42.6				46.6	76.9	61.4	70.0	61.4
1860	40.5				49.2	78.2	61.4	71.0	64.2

SOURCE: Records of the nine firms.

APPENDIX: TABLE 2

NINE TEXTILE FIRMS

RELATIVE PROPORTION OF TOTAL ASSETS REPRESENTED BY LOANS

BY YEARS AND FIRMS

Year	Amoskeag	Dwight	Cabot	Perkins	Hamilton	Lancaster	Lawrence	Lyman	Mass. Cotton
1827					1.6				
1828					4.7				
1829					3.4				
1830					.0				
1832					2.8				
1833					.0				
1834					5.8		9.5		
1835			18.3		5.0		15.3		
1836			19.8		12.1		21.1		
1837	3.9		18.3		7.7		8.9		
1838	3.2		12.1	13.9	12.7		17.7		
1839	7.7		16.4	6.4	13.8		17.0		
1840	8.5		12.0	9.0	6.9		13.9		3.1
1841	13.2		11.2	7.8	6.4		12.0		21.7
1842	16.7	7.2	9.9	5.8	9.7		8.5		27.9
1843	14.2	.0	4.7	.0	10.1		7.6		4.0
1844	11.6	.0	2.8	.0	4.1		0.7		3.2
1845	6.9	.0	6.8	.0	3.7		1.2		.0
1846	14.4	.0	8.7	4.3	2.1		2.0		8.4
1847	7.3	2.2	10.1	7.0	16.5	14.4	14.2		18.8
1848	8.3	.0	9.6	4.4	13.8	12.8	16.2		18.2
1849	9.2	6.3	8.4	4.5	16.0	19.8	20.3		28.1
1850	16.9	14.1	11.0	13.7	16.2	19.1	16.7		19.2
1851	15.5	13.6	11.0	10.9	15.7	26.3	14.5		22.6
1852	18.2	13.9	12.9	11.5	11.6	27.3	17.6		28.2
1853	21.9	25.1			12.7	23.5	16.8		26.5
1854	21.0	24.7			11.0	22.3	14.4		31.4
1855	22.8	25.3			12.7	25.2	11.2	13.7	31.7
1856	28.8				16.4	29.3	8.0	24.7	41.4
1857	19.5				14.0	22.2	27.5	25.7	29.1
1858	20.8				16.7	21.1	25.6	30.8	31.3
1859	20.7				25.4	16.2	31.0	23.5	26.0
1860	19.3				21.4	12.1	29.8	16.8	24.2

SOURCE: Records of the nine firms.

APPENDIX: TABLE 3
NINE TEXTILE FIRMS
RELATIVE PROPORTION OF TOTAL ASSETS REPRESENTED BY RETAINED EARNINGS
BY YEARS AND FIRMS

Year	Amoskeag	Dwight	Cabot	Perkins	Hamil-ton	Lan-caster	Law-rence	Lyman	Mass. Cotton
1827					.1				
1828					1.1				
1829					8.5				
1830					14.9				
1832					20.3				
1833					21.6				
1834					22.2		1.0		
1835			6.3		26.6		5.3		
1836			16.1		22.3		7.1		
1837	9.9		9.8		18.5		8.3		
1838	20.9		14.2	9.1	24.0		5.4		
1839	15.7		12.7	8.4	28.1		11.6		
1840	16.7		5.7	11.8	33.1		7.2		.0
1841	7.2		8.5	9.5	30.7		8.9		4.7
1842	2.5	9.2	7.0	7.5	29.1		6.3		5.1
1843	5.0	14.9	12.3	12.3	30.7		6.7		16.0
1844	18.8	25.0	18.0	18.7	36.3		14.1		16.8
1845	40.5	17.7	13.4	14.3	37.9		15.5		20.0
1846	25.4	13.2	14.3	8.8	33.2		17.8		21.9
1847	32.2	6.0	10.6	8.6	28.6	3.0	10.8		10.9
1848	29.7	3.4	9.6	6.5	28.1	.0	4.9		12.6
1849	35.7	5.5	9.4	6.3	27.0	4.5	9.0		12.7
1850	32.3	3.7	8.4	5.6	27.5	7.1	12.6		15.2
1851	36.8	.9	1.7	4.7	29.1	4.1	11.3		13.2
1852	32.9	3.2	1.8	7.6	33.5	5.7	10.3		10.0
1853	32.0	4.7			28.9	7.4	6.3		9.7
1854	33.3	3.9			30.9	5.8	17.5	10.2	8.0
1855	34.0	4.5			41.9	6.8	18.8	7.3	9.5
1856	32.2				40.7	6.7	34.1	7.6	5.6
1857	37.5				27.2	6.5	18.2	4.0	8.7
1858	37.8				42.2	5.8	2.3	5.1	10.5
1859	36.7				28.0	6.9	7.6	6.5	12.6
1860	40.2				29.4	9.7	8.8	12.2	11.6

SOURCE: Records of the nine firms.

6. From Benevolence to Business: The Story of Two Savings Banks*

Lance E. Davis
Purdue University

Peter L. Payne
The Johns Hopkins University

This comparative study deals with objectives, administration, and portfolio policies of two banks that were among the earliest institutional lenders in America. Founded to assist the "frugal poor," both banks faced the handicaps of provincialism, capital immobility and regulation in their efforts to enlarge their services to the community. Both contributed much to a growing public understanding of banks and banking.

THOSE ECONOMIC HISTORIANS and economists who seek to utilize business histories to formulate generalizations are frequently confronted with the problem of not knowing how representative the subjects of the business histories really are. The primary aim of this essay is to attempt to provide a firmer basis for generalizations concerning the role of mutual savings banks in the development of antebellum America; a period when—it is easily forgotten—the mutuals were almost the only institutional lenders.[1]

In our study of the Savings Bank of Baltimore, we concluded that the early history of this institution appeared "to have been typical of savings banks founded in large cities in the second decade of the nineteenth century."[2] This conclusion was based on a comparison of our findings with the records of the Comptroller of the Currency and existing studies

---

* Reprinted from the *Business History Review*, Vol. XXXII, No. 4 (Winter, 1958), pp. 386–404. The authors wish to acknowledge the aid given by Mr. S. Page Nelson, president of the Savings Bank of Baltimore, and Mr. G. L. Wrenn II, president of the Provident Institution for Savings in the Town of Boston. Without their help and interest this article could not have been written.

[1] Emerson W. Keyes, *A History of Savings Banks in the United States* (2 vols.; New York, 1876), Vol. I, pp. 114–15. (Hereafter cited as Keyes, *Savings Banks.*)

[2] P. L. Payne and Lance E. Davis, *The Savings Bank of Baltimore, 1818–1866: A Historical and Analytical Study* (Baltimore, 1956), p. 21.

of other savings banks.[3] Subsequent research into the records of the Provident Institution for Savings in the Town of Boston has strengthened our belief in the representative nature of the Savings Bank of Baltimore.[4] This article contrasts the development of the two savings banks and deals, in particular, with the evolutionary changes in the two banks' philosophies, their administrative machineries, and their portfolio policies.

The cities in which these two banks were located possessed excellent harbor facilities and were consequently largely oriented toward trade and and commerce.[5] Apart from this, however, they were quite dissimilar. Boston has long been considered the birthplace of "Yankee" Americanism, but Baltimore, though situated north of the nation's capital, is culturally a southern city. Furthermore, in the first half of the 19th century, Boston became the hub of a growing industrial complex that included Massachusetts, southern Maine, and New Hampshire, while Baltimore remained primarily a commercial entrepôt serving the agricultural hinterlands of Pennsylvania and the middle South.

The Philosophy and Customers of the Banks

There were no savings banks in the United States before 1816, but in the following years mutuals were opened in most of the major cities of the Northeast. Both the Provident Institution for Savings in the Town of Boston (1816) and the Savings Bank of Baltimore (1818) were established during this formative period. The founders of these two banks, like their counterparts in other northeastern cities, believed that savings banks would enable the less fortunate classes of society to better themselves in a manner which would avoid the dangers of moral corruption traditionally associated with outright charitable institutions.[6] As a result, the leading

---

[3] For example, F. P. Bennett, Jr., *The Story of Mutual Savings Banks* (Boston, 1924); Charles E. Knowles, *History of the Bank for Savings in the City of New York, 1819–1929* (New York, 1929), hereafter cited as Knowles, *New York*; R. W. Thon, *Mutual Savings Banks in Baltimore* (Baltimore, 1935); Weldon Welfling, *Savings Banks in New York State* (Princeton, N.J., 1938); J. M. Willcox, *A History of the Philadelphia Savings Fund Society, 1816–1916* (Philadelphia [c. 1916]). (Hereafter cited as Willcox, *Philadelphia*.)

[4] Lance E. Davis, "United States Financial Intermediaries in the Early Nineteenth Century: Four Case Studies" (Ph.D. thesis, John Hopkins University, 1956).

[5] Both the 1820 and the 1860 censuses rank Baltimore third and Boston fourth among American cities. In 1820 Baltimore had 62,700 residents and Boston 43,300. Forty years later, the populations were 212,400 and 177,800 respectively. J. D. B. DeBow, *Statistical View of the United States: A Compendium of the Seventh Census* (Washington, D.C.: Beverly Tucker, 1854), p. 192; U.S. Department of the Interior, *Eighth Census of the United States: Miscellaneous Statistics* (Washington, D.C.: Government Printing Office), p. xviii.

[6] Compare, for example, the following typical statements by directors of the two institutions:

There are on the books of the Institution some pleasing instances of the rapid increase in small sums regularly deposited by persons who, persevering in economy and sobri-

citizens of Boston and Baltimore felt that participation in the administration of the savings banks in their cities was an integral part of their civic duties.

The founders of the banks, wishing to inspire confidence, first opened their doors to all, rich and poor alike, but from the start the intention was ultimately to restrict the depositors to the "frugal poor."[7] As both banks were almost instantaneous successes (deposits flowing in from all classes of the community), they soon moved to restrict their depositors. The methods used, however, differed in some respects. As a first step, both banks placed a limit on the size of an individual's weekly deposit. Such action, it was felt, would not only prevent the wealthy classes from using the banks as a depository for their funds but would also reduce the danger of panic withdrawals.[8] Nevertheless, these restrictions failed to prevent some depositors from accruing large sums in their savings accounts. Both banks were therefore forced to adopt other techniques to overcome this problem.

In Boston the directors decided that a depositor whose account exceeded $500 was to be paid no extra dividends on the balance in excess of that amount and his regular interest payments were not to be compounded.[9] It was thought that these measures would effectively dis-

---

ety, are enabled weekly to save a part of their earnings, and thus secure for themselves and their families a resource in sickness and old age. How different must be the hopes and future prospects of the poor wretches who spend a like proportion of their earnings in grog shops to the utter ruin of themselves, and the misery of their families; besides forfeiting all claims to the mercy of an offended Diety.

Savings Bank of Baltimore, "Minutes and Proceedings of the Board of Directors," January 14, 1819.

. . . it was the original and sole design of the institution to foster and encourage among those classes of society whose education and actual situation exposes them to the dangers of improvidence and loss of the earnings of their industry, habits of economy and a spirit of frugality and savings; and to take care to preserve, and put at reasonable interest the savings of this description of persons. . . .

Provident Institution for Savings, "Records of the Board of Trustees," December 26, 1821.

[7] Both the Savings Fund Society (Philadelphia) and the Bank for Savings (New York) also set off by soliciting deposits from all, but they too soon began to discourage wealthy depositors. Willcox, *Philadelphia*, pp. 45–46; Knowles, *New York*, p. 91.

[8] In Boston the directors limited weekly deposits to $100 throughout the antebellum period, though an exception was made in the case of merchant seamen who, because of the irregularity with which they were paid, were permitted to deposit their entire wage. In Baltimore, although the limit was subject to wide fluctuations, it was always at a much lower level. The limit was originally set at $20 a week and it remained at that level until 1831, when it was raised to $30, but within a year it was reduced to $10. After only a few months the limit was again raised to $50 where it remained until 1839. In that year the limit was reduced to $20, no further changes being made before 1860. Similar limits were also adopted by the Philadelphia Savings Fund Society. There the limit was in the form of an annual limitation ($500 before February, 1828, and $200 thereafter). Willcox, *Philadelphia*, pp. 49–50.

[9] Originally, the limit had been set at $100, but soon this figure was increased to

courage the wealthy depositor. In Baltimore the directors of the Savings Bank first considered placing a limit on total deposits, but they abandoned the idea (for fear of penalizing the depositor who had really learned the lessons of thrift) in favor of the more direct method of depositor restriction. This scheme involved a periodic examination of all depositor accounts to ascertain whether the depositors could still be considered members of the "industrious poor." Five times in the years before 1860 the directors ordered such an examination; and, as a consequence of these inspections, a substantial number of depositors who were not of the "laboring poor" were asked to close their accounts.[10]

That the Savings Bank did not adopt the cheaper "deposit limit" method employed by the Provident can probably be explained by reference to the investment alternatives open to savers in the two cities. In Boston a legitimate depositor whose account had reached the limit of $500 could have placed any further savings in "The Big Savings Bank," as the Massachusetts Hospital Life Insurance Company was called.[11] The Massachusetts Hospital Life was a semibenevolent institution that, from 1823, undertook to manage the investment of deposits (of not less than $500) in trust. Moreover, this institution was as safe as the Provident and paid a substantial return to its depositors. In Baltimore no such investment alternative existed; and, had a limit been imposed, the more thrifty depositor would have had no option but to make risky investments himself or consume or hoard the amount he had saved over and above the limit. Because the directors of the Savings Bank of Baltimore did not want to penalize the thrifty person, they were forced to adopt the more expensive —although more flexible—depositor restriction scheme.[12] It is perhaps noteworthy that in every year after 1827 the average balance per account in the Savings Bank of Baltimore was at least one-third greater than the comparable figure for the Provident Institution.[13] An examination of the individual accounts indicates that this difference is a reflection of the absence of large accounts on the Provident's books.

$500 and then in February, 1819, to $1,000. However, the higher limit induced many wealthy persons to open accounts, and, as a result, in December, 1821, the limit was again reduced to $500, at which level it remained throughout the rest of the period.

[10] In 1828 the deposits returned amounted to about 8 percent of the total deposits; in 1839, to about 12 percent; and in 1854 to about 2 percent.

[11] The first actuary of the Hospital Life, Dr. N. Bowditch, "on one occasion [1824] referred to the company as 'a species of Savings Bank for the rich and middle class of Society.'" Gerald White, *The Massachusetts Hospital Life Insurance Company* (Cambridge, 1955), p. 34.

[12] The New York Bank for Savings appears to have adopted the same policy as the Savings Bank of Baltimore. A letter from the bank's directors to Senator Van Schank (February, 1836) says: "the general instructions given to the Accountant and Attending Committee [are] not to receive deposits from any persons who in their judgment are capable of investing for themselves. This fact becomes apparent from the annual reports in which the description and occupations of the depositors are set forth." Knowles, *New York*, p. 91.

[13] See Table I.

TABLE I

TOTAL AMOUNT ON DEPOSIT, NUMBER OF ACCOUNTS, AND AVERAGE
BALANCE PER ACCOUNT, PROVIDENT INSTITUTION AND THE
SAVINGS BANK OF BALTIMORE, 1818–61

January 1*	Number of Accounts		Total Amount on Deposit† (dollars)		Average Balance per Account (dollars)	
	P.I.	S.B. of B.	P.I.	S.B. of B.	P.I.	S.B. of B.
1818....	n.d.‡	—	61,897	—	n.d.	—
1819....	1,188	n.d.	150,383	11,900	127	n.d.
1820....	2,080	256§	296,292	19,999§	142	78§
1821....	3,294	450	391,605	45,169‖	119	100
1822....	4,661	n.d.	593,316	n.d.	127	n.d.
1823....	5,502	n.d.	502,896	n.d.	91	n.d.
1824....	4,273	n.d.	527,330	n.d.	123	n.d.
1825....	4,895	466	625,334	n.d.	128	n.d.
1826....	5,415	734	715,673	n.d.	132	n.d.
1827....	5,734	891	736,972	n.d.	129	n.d.
1828....	6,278	1,079	855,631	199,047	136	184
1829....	6,763	1,280	924,659	237,431	137	185
1830....	7,381	1,526	986,959	285,109	134	187
1831....	8,199	1,724	1,118,618	348,629	136	202
1832....	9,243	2,029	1,333,821	422,512	144	208
1833....	10,153	1,941	1,552,221	445,300	153	229
1834....	11,579	2,224	1,720,940	526,375	149	237
1835....	12,104	2,050	1,804,093	518,110	149	253
1836....	13,324	2,500	2,020,389	664,149	152	266
1837....	13,442	2,902	2,037,514	807,214	152	278
1838....	13,214	3,030	2,035,425	859,541	154	284
1839....	13,199	3,507	2,006,821	1,020,991	152	291
1840....	13,642	3,942	2,071,095	1,085,254	152	275
1841....	14,027	4,143	2,194,784	1,166,372	156	282
1842....	15,273	4,141	2,427,081	1,142,903	159	276
1843....	15,123	3,936	2,356,016	992,900	156	252
1844....	16,248	4,226	2,542,302	1,099,521	156	260
1845....	18,524	5,056	2,904,903	1,284,999	157	254
1846....	19,470	5,628	3,115,584	1,332,018	160	237
1847....	19,938	6,207	3,203,201	1,459,946	161	235
1848....	20,426	6,970	3,453,574	1,608,859	169	231
1849....	20,351	7,686	3,295,350	1,761,371	162	229
1850....	20,386	8,392	3,300,689	1,988,334	162	237
1851....	22,245	9,404	3,654,689	2,237,618	164	238
1852....	23,791	10,742	4,079,646	2,567,623	171	239
1853....	25,626	11,914	4,729,383	2,887,899	185	242
1854....	28,246	12,966	5,251,850	3,236,466	186	250
1855....	27,870	15,170	5,207,188	3,754,824	187	248
1856....	27,927	16,209	5,298,713	4,021,150	190	248
1857....	28,835	17,860	5,714,491	4,519,738	198	253
1858....	28,163	17,821	5,816,674	4,609,206	207	259
1859....	29,035	18,834	6,601,707	4,939,198	227	262
1860....	30,631	20,276	6,501,950	5,518,116	212	272
1861....	32,075	20,956	6,984,056	5,985,734	218	286

* The Savings Bank of Baltimore figures are those for December 31 of the previous year.
† "Total Amount on Deposit" represents the total balances due depositors including interest credited to their accounts.
‡ n.d. signifies that no data are available.
§ January 17, 1820.
‖ January 1, 1821.
SOURCE: Provident Institution for Savings in the Town of Boston, "Deposit Abstract Book"; Savings Banks of Baltimore, "Minutes and Proceedings of the Board of Directors."

Since the banks' founders wished to prove that thrift was rewarding, it was necessary that the depositor earn a "goodly" return. For both moral and economic reasons the directors of both banks chose a rather complex method of paying interest on depositors' savings. First, all depositors were entitled to a set rate of 4 percent interest on their accounts—a rate that the directors thought could be maintained even in years of adverse economic conditions—and, second, the banks' earnings not distributed in this manner were paid as extra dividends to those depositors who kept their savings in the bank for periods over one year, the extra dividend rate being calculated to discriminate in favor of long-standing deposits.[14] The Savings Bank of Baltimore paid a regular dividend of 4 percent per year (compounded semiannually) and, except for three years (1818–21) when the regular dividend was set at 5 percent, the Provident paid a like interest. In Baltimore extra dividends were declared every third year but in Boston distribution was made at five-year intervals.

In both cities the rate of the extra dividend fluctuated with economic conditions and the banks' earnings. Until 1842 the Savings Bank of Baltimore paid, on the average, slightly higher total dividends than did the Provident; after this date, however, the Provident's payments were considerably higher than those of the Savings Bank.[15] The average annual interest rate paid by both banks on a (hypothetical) deposit made in 1818 and still outstanding in 1860 was about 6 percent (no allowance being made for compound interest).[16] Since neither bank accumulated large reserves of undistributed earnings and since the cost of operating both banks was very low, it appears that the explanation of the differences in dividend payments lies in the relative earning power of the assets of the two banks and in the techniques of dividend payment.

An examination of the Savings Bank's portfolio shows that the bank realized a gradual increase in the returns on its assets over the period. This increase was not associated with the introduction of new assets, but merely reflected an overall increase in earning power. Moreover, the increase in earnings was almost entirely offset by an increase in the proportion of depositors qualifying for extra dividends.[17] With the exception of the years 1840–43, dividends were thus fairly constant over the period.

The Provident's earnings, however, increased very rapidly in the years

---

[14] For example, in 1827, the Savings Bank of Baltimore declared three extra dividend rates: one applicable to deposits which had been on the books for over 12 months but under two years (3 percent), one to deposits on the books for over two but under three years (4 percent), and one to deposits that had been on the books for three years and longer (6 percent).

[15] The actual averages are 6.4 percent for the Provident Institution and 5.9 percent for the Savings Bank of Baltimore.

[16] See Table II.

[17] Both banks paid extra dividends only on those deposits on the books at the date of declaration. Thus any sum withdrawn prior to the dividend date did not qualify for any payment.

TABLE II

EXTRA DIVIDENDS PAID BY THE PROVIDENT INSTITUTION AND THE
SAVINGS BANK OF BALTIMORE, 1818–62*

| Year | Provident Institution | | Savings Bank of Baltimore | |
	Rate	Rate per Year of Deposit (1) ÷ 5	Rate	Rate per Year of Deposit (3) ÷ 3
	(1)	(2)	(3)	(4)
1821.........	—	—	.035	.012
1822.........	.040	.008	—	—
1824.........	—	—	.060	.020
1827.........	.0921	.0182	.060	.020
1830.........	—	—	.045	.015
1832.........	.090	.018	—	—
1833.........	—	—	.060	.020
1836.........	—	—	.075	.025
1837.........	.095	.019	—	—
1839.........	—	—	.060	.020
1842	No Extra Dividend Declared			
1845.........	—	—	.030	.010
1847.........	.193	.039	—	—
1848.........	—	—	.060	.020
1851.........	—	—	.070	.023
1852.........	.200	.040	—	—
1854.........	—	—	.090	.030
1857.........	.200	.040	.070	.023
1860.........	—	—	.060	.020
1862.........	.150	.030	—	—

* The rates shown for the Provident Institution are those paid on deposits outstanding for five years or over, and those for the Savings Bank of Baltimore are those on deposits outstanding for three years or over.
SOURCE: Provident Institution, "Deposit Abstract Book"; Savings Bank of Baltimore, "Minutes and Proceedings of the Board of Directors."

after 1842. This increase was due both to a general rise in the earning power of assets and to the increased returns that followed the shift in the bank's portfolio from low-earning short-term commercial bank loans to more profitable long-term loans backed by personal security (in particular, personal security loans to industry).

Throughout the period, the Savings Bank's dividends would have appeared relatively higher, in relation to those of the Provident, had it not been for certain technical factors in dividend computation. Both banks paid dividends only on balances on the books at the date of declaration; but, whereas the Savings Bank declared extra dividends every third year, the Provident took such action only every fifth year. Thus, it was easier for the Savings Bank's depositors to qualify for the extra dividends than it was for the Provident's depositors; and in every year a greater proportion of the former bank's depositors received extra payments.

Once adopted, the extra dividend became a regular part of depositor payment. Although the two banks faced several depositor panics and numerous periods of economic depression without altering their dividend policy, only once, in 1842, was the value of their investments so seriously impaired that the directors felt impelled to use the accrued earnings to write down the depreciated assets.[18]

Administration

The administrative organization that was first adopted by the two institutions reflected the charitable intent of their founders, but the problems that accompanied success and growth could not be met with this early structure. Instead, professional managements—operating the institutions as businesses rather than charitable enterprises—were needed, and the administrations of both banks gradually evolved in this way.

1. The Directors

The original charters placed the decision-making powers in the hands of boards of directors. These boards were elected annually by the body of corporators, and, to make the organization permanent, the directors were empowered to elect new members to this body.[19] Despite the differences in size, the duties of the two boards (as outlined in the charters) were almost identical. Both initiated policy and administered the affairs of the bank, and, although both boards gradually relinquished these powers to the management group, they continued to choose the managers.

2. Administrative Committees

The two boards of directors were, at best, unwieldy decision-making units. Efficiency, therefore, dictated that subcommittees should be established to treat particular problems of a recurring nature. Although there is no evidence of any direct communications, the organizational structure chosen by the Baltimore Bank was almost identical with that selected by the Provident.

The original bylaws of both banks established a subcommittee to supervise the banks' day-to-day operations. In Boston this group, entitled the "Committee of the Week," had three members (two trustees and one vice president) and membership rotated monthly among the trustees and vice presidents, each one of whom was required to serve one month a

---

[18] Instead of declaring extra dividends, the directors of the New York Bank for Savings originally allowed undistributed earnings to accumulate in a surplus account. It was not until 1852, when the state legislature limited surplus accounts to 5 percent of deposits, that the directors, faced with confiscation, declared their first extra dividend. Once begun, the practice was continued and additional dividends were declared in 1855, 1856, and 1858. Knowles, *New York*, pp. 113 and 121.

[19] The only differences were in the names and size of the governing bodies. In Baltimore the board of directors was made up of 25 members (24 directors and a president elected by the directors) and in Boston the board of trustees was made up of 24 trustees, 12 vice presidents, and a president elected by the trustees and vice presidents.

year in this capacity. In Baltimore the committee was called the "Committee of the Month" and had only two members. There, too, membership rotated monthly and all directors were required to spend one month a year supervising the Bank's operations. During the banks' formative years, the committees opened the banks, served the public, kept the books, advised the boards on the investment of deposited funds, and administered the policies laid down by the boards. Under the original bylaws, the committees were the institutions' sole administrative organs and in this role they performed ably for a number of years. As the administrative tasks grew, however, the committees gradually ceded their functions to other groups, and, by 1860, they had retained for themselves only the task of preparing the banks' operating statements. In both banks the decline in the importance of the administrative committees was one manifestation of the change from amateur to professional management.[20]

In Baltimore investment decisions had originally been made by the board of directors, and in Boston the function had been performed by the administrative committee in consultation with the president. The success of the banks, however, brought a flood of deposits, deposits that had to be wisely and quickly invested. Experience proved that the Savings Bank's board of directors was too unwieldy a body to make flexible investment decisions; and in Boston, the rotating membership of the administrative committee—a body already overburdened with other tasks—made implementation of a long-term investment policy very difficult.

In 1820, therefore, both banks established subcommittees to supervise the banks' investments in accordance with the broad investment policy outlined by the boards.[21] It was originally intended that these committees would be elected annually, but, because so many of the members were repeatedly reelected—frequently as many as 10 times—the banks were able to achieve a considerable degree of continuity in their investment policies.

The investment committee of the Savings Bank of Baltimore consisted of three directors, the president, and the secretary (replaced in 1832 by the treasurer). During the first years of its operation the committee seldom made any investment decision without first obtaining the approval of the full board. After 1824, however, the committee operated almost independently, normally turning to the board only for periodic routine approval.[22] In Boston the board of investment was slightly larger—three trustees, one vice president, and the president and secretary (enlarged

---

[20] A similar shift can be seen in the history of the New York Bank for Savings, although in that institution the evolution proceeded much more slowly. In New York the "Committee of the Month" did not cede all of its administrative functions until the bank's administrative reorganization in 1877. Knowles, *New York*, pp. 131–32.

[21] It is interesting to note that the New York Bank for Savings also established an investment committee in 1820. Knowles, *New York*, p. 66.

[22] Only once between 1826 and 1860 did the committee seek the board's approval before making a loan and this was on property outside the city.

in 1834 to include six trustees)—and, although in its first years the scope of its operations was similar to that of the Baltimore bank, it evolved in a quite different direction. Unlike the Baltimore committee, the board of investment ceded its powers in investment matters to the paid officers. By 1840, for example, the officers had become so accustomed to making investment decisions that the board found it necessary to issue a special order to limit new loans and renewals to those they had specifically approved.[23] Furthermore, an increasing number of policy decisions (decisions far divorced from investment) were made by the investment subcommittee and fewer and fewer by the trustees. In 1832, for example, the plan to erect a new bank building was first discussed by the investment committee, and only after their approval was it ratified (without debate) by the full board.[24]

Although by 1830 the entrepreneurial function had shifted to the board of investment, the evolutionary process was not yet complete. The increasing complexity of problems that accompanied the growth of the Provident caused the investment committee members to rely more and more upon the president and treasurer for leadership in decision making; and, except in a few cases in the years after 1840, the ordinary board members merely approved the action of the paid managers.

3. The Officers

Although both banks had opened for business with but a single paid officer, a secretary, rapid growth soon forced the directors to delegate some of the administrative tasks to salaried employees. Thus the early development of both banks was marked by the transfer of routine operations to paid clerks and the transfer of entrepreneurial decisions to salaried professionals, among whom the president emerged as the dominant figure. The evolution from benevolent to professional management was made necessary by the decisions of the institutions to accommodate *all* qualified depositors. Such a choice inevitably entailed growth, and growth necessitated managerial changes. Not all of the directors concurred in this decision; for example, the Provident charter had placed a limit on aggregate deposits, and although this restriction was lifted in December, 1820, a significant minority of the board of trustees voted against its removal.[25] Moreover, two subsequent attempts to reimpose an aggregate limit were defeated only after heated debate.[26] In each case the minority argued that growing business militated against the philanthropic princi-

---

[23] Provident Institution, "Records of the Board of Investment," February 8, 1840.

[24] Provident Institution, "Records of the Board of Investment," August 24, 1832, and "Trustees Records," August 24, 1832.

[25] The limit was first set at $200,000, then raised to $400,000, and finally removed altogether. Provident Institution, "Trustees Records," November 10, 1818; July 18, 1820; December 20, 1820.

[26] Provident Institution, "Trustees Records," March 25, 1829, and July 16, 1859.

ples animating the bank; but in each case the minority was forced to give way to a majority, led by the bank's officers, who realized that a benevolent institution could not function successfully as a financial intermediary.

By the outbreak of the Civil War, business leadership had replaced benevolence in both banks, but, although paid employees had taken over the day-to-day bank administration by 1830, the evolution in policy-making proceeded at a much slower rate.[27] In Baltimore this evolution took place within the board of directors. The minutes of that body indicate that, although the board continued to act on matters of fundamental policy, more and more frequently their actions constituted nothing but post facto approval of management decisions. In Boston, on the other hand, the evolution of policymaking was associated with the growth in stature of the board of investment, and it was through dominance of that committee that the professional management assumed its policymaking function.

The Banks' Investments

As long as the aggregate volume of deposits was small, the banks could depend upon commercial banks to hold their funds; but as deposits grew, the risks entailed in this policy increased both for the mutuals and for the commercial banks of deposit. Thus, before many years had passed, both savings banks were forced to seek alternative investment outlets. Guided by safety rather than yield, both banks acquired bank stock and government bonds, and made private loans.[28] Nevertheless, the portfolios of the two banks displayed considerable differences in the relative importance and the internal composition of each classification of assets.[29]

1. Bank Stock

Stock in local commercial banks was among the first assets acquired by both banks, but over the entire period the Provident's portfolio contained a larger proportion of these assets than did that of the Savings Bank of Baltimore. The first purchases of bank shares probably reflected the banks' needs for assets that were both liquid and divisible.[30] The

---

[27] A similar evolution marks the early history of the New York Bank for Savings. In that institution the directors continued to play an important role both in policy-making and administration until 1877. Knowles, *New York*, pp. 131–32.

[28] The evidence indicates that most other savings banks also aimed at safety rather than yield in their investment policies. In their report of 1861, the Massachusetts Bank Commissioners reported that the investment goals of savings banks should be (1) safety, (2) convertibility, and, only then, (3) yield. Keyes, *Savings Banks*, Vol. 1, pp. 78–83.

[29] See Table III.

[30] The savings banks received their deposits in relatively small blocks and needed investments that could absorb these small amounts. At the same time bank shares were highly liquid since a fairly well-organized equity market existed in both cities.

TABLE III

SELECTED ASSETS EXPRESSED AS A PERCENTAGE OF TOTAL ASSETS, PROVIDENT INSTITUTION AND SAVINGS BANK OF BALTIMORE, 1820–58

End of Year	Bank Stock P.I.	Bank Stock S.B.	Public Funds P.I.	Public Funds S.B.	Total Loans P.I. (7)+(9)+(11)+(12)+(13)	Total Loans S.B. (8)+(10)	Loans on Formal Security P.I.	Loans on Formal Security S.B.	Loans on Real Estate P.I.	Loans on Real Estate S.B.	Loans on Personal Security P.I.	Loans on Short-term loans P.I.	Loans on Discounts P.I.
	(1)	(2)	(3)	(4)	(5)	(6)	(7)	(8)	(9)	(10)	(11)	(12)	(13)
1820	—	17	—	76	48	—	48	—	—	—	—	—	—
1821	—	18	23	74	50	—	50	—	—	—	—	—	—
1822	—	14	34	35	47	51	47	51	—	—	—	—	—
1823	—	13	35	33	60	53	60	53	—	—	—	—	—
1824	10	10	19	28	67	62	44	62	—	—	—	23	—
1825*	16	7	16	20	63	73	49	73	—	—	—	14	—
1826*	16	6	35	16	45	72	35	72	—	—	—	10	—
1827*	24	5	33	12	33	83	24	83	—	—	—	9	—
1828*	27	4	22	20	46	74	32	n.d.	—	n.d.	—	14	—
1829*	25	3	22	28	48	68	32	n.d.	—	n.d.	—	16	—
1830*	24	3	23	24	47	74	35	n.d.	—	n.d.	—	11	—
1831*	32	2	23	5	37	92	21	n.d.	—	n.d.	—	16	—
1832*	34	2	16	10	42	86	16	46	—	39	—	26	—
1833	34	2	18	9	48	89	20	47	—	42	—	28	—
1834	33	2	12	12	51	85	31	44	—	41	—	20	—
1835	30	3	11	15	54	78	22	38	—	40	—	32	—
1836	33	5	12	16	52	73	21	38	—	35	—	32	—
1837	29	7	11	18	54	67	22	35	8	32	—	24	—
1838	30	6	16	22	47	66	19	35	12	31	—	15	—
1839	30	5	14	26	50	62	17	30	20	32	3	10	—

TABLE III (Continued)

End of Year	Bank Stock		Public Funds		Total Loans		Loans on						
	P.I.	S.B.	P.I.	S.B.	P.I. $(7)+(9)$ $+(11)$ $+(12)$ $+(13)$	S.B. (8) $+(10)$	Formal Security		Real Estate		Personal Security	Short-term loans	Discounts
							P.I.	S.B.	P.I.	S.B.	P.I.	P.I.	P.I.
	(1)	(2)	(3)	(4)	(5)	(6)	(7)	(8)	(9)	(10)	(11)	(12)	(13)
1840	29	5	13	24	52	63	22	26	23	37	4	5	—
1841	26	5	13	26	58†	63	2	24	20	38	7	—	—
1842	26	4	40	27	29	58	2	17	17	41	10	—	—
1843	24	5	39	34	33	52	1	18	26	35	5	—	—
1844	21	6	32	34	43	50	1	17	28	33	14	—	—
1845	19	6	27	34	50	51	1	12	31	38	18	—	—
1846	17	5	27	31	53	54	1	20	32	34	14	—	7
1847	18	5	25	34	54	54	—	20	30	33	20	—	4
1848	18	4	15	37	64	53	1	22	29	32	20	—	14
1849	18	4	14	34	65	53	1	20	26	32	29	—	10
1850	17	3	12	30	66	55	1	26	22	30	21	—	23
1851	15	3	12	29	69	59	2	28	23	30	18	—	26
1852	14	3	12	28	68	57	1	29	28	29	27	—	9
1853	28	2	12	19	57	61	2	34	32	27	22	—	—
1854	26	3	11	24	59	64	2	38	37	26	19	—	—
1855	25	2	12	31	56	58	1	32	34	26	21	—	—
1856	19	2	11	30	67	60	1	35	31	25	30	—	—
1857	17	3	11	30	67	58	1	34	32	24	27	—	—
1858	17	2	14	43	61	49	1	24	35	25	22	—	—

* For 1825 through 1832 the figures for the Provident Institution are those for June 30.

† Includes railroad loan of $700,000—29 percent of total assets.

Note: Table may not be internally consistent due to rounding.

Source: Provident Institution, computed from "Records of the Board of Investment"; Savings Bank of Baltimore, computed from "The Minutes and Proceedings of the Board of Directors."

long-term differences between the stock holdings of the two banks appear to have been a reflection of the quality of commercial banking in the two cities. In Boston the commercial banks had long enjoyed a reputation of conservatism and stability, and, among the larger banks, there was little danger of failure. This was not so in Baltimore. It had been the Baltimore branch of the Second Bank of the United States that had been most heavily involved in the embezzlement scandals, and the panic of 1834 had forced the Bank of Maryland, the city's oldest, largest, and supposedly strongest institution to close its doors. Moreover, the value of Boston bank stock appears to have suffered far less from the effects of general economic fluctuations than did the issues of Baltimore's commercial banks.[31]

2. *Public Funds*

As public funds also combine the qualities of divisibility and liquidity, it is not surprising that they too were among the first assets acquired by the two banks. At first the banks limited their purchases to issues of the federal government, but by 1830 the Provident had included the bonds of Boston and Massachusetts, and the Savings Bank had added the bonds of Baltimore and Maryland.

Both banks appear to have looked upon their holdings of United States bonds as secondary reserves: federal issues were added in times of depression, when alternative investments were particularly risky, and were sold both to meet the "panic" demands of depositors and to free funds for other investment in times of prosperity. Until the 1840's the banks held about the same proportion of public funds. Both maintained a fairly constant proportion of local issues (about 10 percent for the Provident and slightly more for the Savings Bank of Baltimore) and both adjusted their holdings of federal bonds to the prevailing economic conditions. After that date, however, the banks' policies diverge considerably. The Provident, to take advantage of new profit opportunities, invested its new deposits in manufacturing loans. The Savings Bank, on the other hand, increased the earning capacity of its portfolio by adding the funds of

---

[31] For example, between April, 1839, and March, 1842, the prices of the bank shares that the Savings Bank of Baltimore held as assets fell by the following percentages: Bank of Baltimore, 20.5; Mechanics Bank, 13.3; Merchants Bank, 15; Western Bank, 25; Farmers and Planters Bank, 25; Union Bank, 25; and Franklin Bank, 70 (Savings Bank of Baltimore, "Minutes of the Investment Committee," April, 1839, through March, 1842); and it may be presumed that the Savings Bank invested only in the stock of the soundest banks. It is impossible to discover the average prices of the stocks of the 25 Boston banks in existence from 1839 to 1842, but even if the most unfavorable situation is taken, and an average of the highest 1839 prices of those stocks is compared with an average of the lowest 1842 prices, a fall of only 14 percent took place. (Joseph Martin, *Seventy-Three Years History of the Boston Stock Market* [Boston: published by the author, 1871], p. 43.) The stocks of Boston banks appear, therefore, to have maintained their values far better than did those of the Baltimore banks.

governmental bodies geographically far removed from Baltimore. Thus, while the Provident made no investment in "foreign" government issues, by 1860 the Savings Bank's portfolio had been expanded to include the issues of North Carolina, Kentucky, and Brooklyn.[32]

3. Private Loans

Marked differences in private loan policies—both in respect of the type of loans made and the terms on which they were granted—make any comparison of the aggregate volume of the private loans made by the two institutions misleading. The Savings Bank of Baltimore loaned both on long term (more than one year) and short term (less than a year); but the Provident made almost no loans for periods of less than one year.[33] In Baltimore the only acceptable collateral was formal securities (e.g., commercial bank stock, public funds, etc.) and mortgages on real estate. In Boston, however, loans were also made to commercial banks on no security, to business firms on the signatures of the officers and two guarantors, and, for a short time, to mercantile and manufacturing concerns on commercial paper. Rational banking policy dictated diversification in both banks' portfolios. The officers of the Savings Bank achieved this by shifting from loans to other investments; the Provident's managers by shifts within the broad area of private loans.

Chronologically, both banks granted loans on formal security several years before they accepted any other kind of collateral, and until in the late 1830's both portfolios display similar trends in this asset componet. As security values fell in the Panic of 1837 and in the subsequent depression of 1840–42, both banks reduced their security loans. The Savings Bank of Baltimore (lending only on short term) reversed its policy when securities again rose in value, but the Provident's management, influenced by the losses experienced in the foregoing period, decided that formal securities were unsuitable collateral for long-term loans. Subsequently, the Provident granted very few long-term loans on the hypothecation of formal securities. Indeed, such loans never again exceeded 2 percent of the bank's total assets.

Throughout the period, the two banks' holdings of mortgage loans display quite different trends. In Baltimore, loans on real estate were first made as early as 1828, but after an initial rise to about 40 percent of total assets, they declined slowly through the remainder of the period, reaching 25 percent in 1858. In Boston, on the other hand, although the

---

[32] In acquiring such assets the Baltimore Bank had adopted a policy that was at variance with the investment policy of most conservative savings banks. The behavior of state governments during the crisis of 1840–42 had caused general concern over the safety of their bond issues. In Philadelphia, for example, the Savings Fund Society did not invest in non-Pennsylvanian issues until 1870, Willcox, *Philadelphia*, p. 167.

[33] The exceptions to this were confined to loans to commercial banks and a short-lived discount business.

bank's managers did not enter the real estate market until 1838, thereafter the proportion of real estate loans slowly rose to reach about 35 percent of the Provident's total assets in 1858.

In Baltimore, the downward trend in mortgages was one manifestation of the more sophisticated investment policy that followed the shift to professional management. Sound portfolio policy required diversification, and this in time meant a reduction in private loans, as no less than 90 percent of the bank's assets were in this category in the early thirties. The falling security prices and rising real estate values during the thirties and early forties resulted in the reduction taking place in security loans, but when the prosperity of the mid-forties reversed the trend in security prices and increased the demand for short-term mercantile credit, the managers began slowly to reduce the volume of mortgage loans, and to build up security loans again.

The Provident's delay in granting mortgage loans may probably be explained by the relative unattractiveness of this type of investment. During the late twenties and early thirties, it would appear (if one may generalize from the experience of the Massachusetts Hospital Life Insurance Company) that the returns on Boston real estate loans were somewhat below the 6 percent that was currently being earned by security loans and other investments.[34] Similarly, the yield on alternative investments provides an explanation for the upward trend in the proportion of mortgage loans after 1840. Real estate values were not too adversely affected by the depression of 1840–42, and, after 1840, real estate loans were yielding close to 6 percent.[35] At the same time, loans on formal securities looked much less profitable; and rational investment policy dictated that further investment in commercial bank stocks be postponed until the damage inflicted by the panic and subsequent recession had

---

[34] For the 10 years 1828 through 1837 Boston commercial bank stock yielded on the average 5.7 percent. Martin, *Boston Stock Market,* pp. 45–56. Although the Massachusetts Hospital Life invested heavily in real estate mortgages throughout the twenties and thirties, it is significant that until the late thirties almost all of these investments were in mortgages on farms in western Massachusetts yielding 6 percent (the legal maximum). If 6 percent mortgages had been available in Boston it appears likely that the Massachusetts directors would have preferred the closer investments.

[35] Although Huse's figures on Boston real estate prices are not strictly comparable between years, they do indicate that Boston real estate values were not seriously depressed by the depression of 1840–42.

Year	Price per foot
1837	$0.30
1838	.26
1839	.49
1840	.35
1841	1.35
1842	.61
1843	1.08
1844	.49

Charles Philip Huse, *The Financial History of Boston* (Cambridge, 1916), p. 380.

been fully evaluated. It is not surprising, therefore, that during the 1840's a shift took place from loans on formal securities and bank shares to mortgage loans.

Among the Provident's loans were some that were made on the hypothecation of collateral that was unacceptable in Baltimore, and among these the most important were loans on personal security. Although few of these personal security loans were contracted before 1840, by the 1850's they constituted about one quarter of the Provident's assets. These loans were usually made to the large "Massachusetts-type" textile mills, but occasionally the larger mercantile partnerships were permitted to borrow in this manner. In all cases, however, the loans were made without the pledge of formal collateral. Instead the bank required only the signatures of the borrowing firm's chief officer and two "guarantors." Thus the borrowing firms were able to acquire long-term finance without tying up their real assets; and, as the borrowing firms were always financially sound and the guarantors were drawn from among the city's most prosperous businessmen, the bank considered that there was little risk attached to these loans.[36]

That the Savings Bank of Baltimore did not invest in personal loans is not surprising. Outside of Massachusetts such loans were considered extremely risky investment. The Philadelphia Savings Fund Society made no personal security loans; in New York they were specifically prohibited; and not even the European savings banks sanctioned them.[37] Given the general bias against such loans, their acceptability in Massachusetts is, at first glance, rather surprising. Closer examination, however, indicates that acceptability is associated with that state's textile industry. This industry continually demanded long-term credit; its liability to asset ratio was very low; and a large proportion of its stock was owned by highly respectable Boston merchants. Massachusetts banks could, therefore, afford to make special concessions to the textile industry, concessions which banks in other states could make only with great risk.

The Provident entered the short-term commercial bank loan market because the directors thought such loans profitable (short-term money returned from 3½ to 5 percent), safe, and instrumental in providing an additional tie between the savings bank and the commercial banking system. The events of the years 1837–42 did much to convince the Provident's managers that these reasons were no longer sufficiently strong to warrant continued investment in this market, while the Provident's actions during that period convinced the commercial bankers that it was not always safe to borrow on the savings bank's terms. By the late 1830's the Provident was large enough, and its portfolio was well enough diversified,

---

[36] Only once was a borrowing firm (the Bay State Mills) unable to repay a loan, and, even in this case, the Provident was able to avoid having to call on the guarantors by waiting for reorganization to be carried out.

[37] Keyes, *Savings Banks*, Vol. I, pp. 78–83; Willcox, *Philadelphia, passim.*

no longer to require support from the commercial banks in time of economic crisis; the panic and subsequent depression had severely strained the commercial banks and forced a reappraisal of the safety of the commercial banking system; and the entry of textile firms into the loan market had provided a new high-yield investment alternative. Conversely, the Provident's refusal to extend the duration of outstanding loans during the crisis convinced the commercial bankers that as long as they depended on short-term credit they always stood liable to redeem their pledges during the periods when they could least afford to lose reserves. Consequently, after 1842, the only new loans that were extended to the banking system were long-term loans at rates comparable to those paid by other borrowers (i.e., about 6 percent).

For a few years in the late forties and early fifties the Provident engaged in an active discount business, and by 1851 these discounts represented more than one quarter of the bank's assets. The Provident's entry into the discount market brought complaints from the commercial banks, and the Bank Commissioners opined that discounting was not a legitimate function of savings banks. Although the Provident defended its discount business, an adverse court decision and continual pressure from the Commissioners forced the mutual to withdraw from this field by 1854. The refusal of the Savings Bank's officers to engage in discounting was probably due to a feeling that such activity was improper for savings banks; a feeling shared by the large savings banks in New York and Pennsylvania as well as by the Massachusetts Bank Commissioners.

4. Semi-Industrial Securities

Although both banks had small holdings of a wide variety of miscellaneous assets, neither invested heavily in industrial, railroad, or public utility stock.[38] In the case of the Provident, legal restrictions long prohibited such investment; but even after such restrictions were removed the bank—with only one exception—never directly invested in these semi-industrial securities, for the Provident's manager found it safer and more profitable to make loans to railroad and public utility companies than to purchase theire equities.[39] The experience of the Savings Bank suggests that the Provident had adopted a wise policy. The Baltimore bank's relatively small holdings of Baltimore and Ohio, New York Central, Baltimore Gas Light Company, and Baltimore Water Company stock yielded no more than alternative investments and since they were subject to wide fluctuations in value they were much less safe. In fact, the only

---

[38] At one time the Provident even purchased an annuity with the Massachusetts Hospital Life Insurance Company.

[39] Railroad companies that received loans from the Provident were the Boston and Lowell, the Boston and Worcester, the Old Colony, the Webster, and the Western. Of the five, the Western received by far the most. Its outstanding loans between 1840 and 1860 were never less than $250,000 and at one time reached $700,000.

loss suffered by the bank during the entire period was in its holding of stock of the Baltimore Water Company.

Portfolio Policy

To conclude, an overall survey of the portfolios of the two banks reveals the influence of provincialism and legal regulation furthermore, both portfolios reflect different investment opportunities and, to some extent, the composition of the boards of directors.

The investment policy of both banks was marked by a considerable degree of provincialism. It is almost as if the managers refused to invest in any asset that they could not touch. The bank shares that they held were the shares of local banks; their loans were almost entirely loans to local residents; and, until the mid-fifties, the state and local bonds that they held were limited to the issues of their own states.[40] Because of their provincialism the banks failed to take advantage of a great range of investment opportunities. For example, during the twenties the Provident was making the bulk of its loans at a rate of interest well below the 6 percent received by the Savings Bank. The provincialism in investment policy strongly suggests that in this early period long-term capital was relatively immobile, and that the geographic concentration of industry may well have been one manifestation of this immobility.

Because of legal restrictions neither bank could charge more than 6 percent on its loans, and their reluctance to aid new business may, in part, be a product of this interest limit. Indeed, many of the differences between the two portfolios can be traced to differences in banking regulations. In Baltimore the Savings Bank was free from regulation but the Provident's managers were (after 1834) prohibited from making some types of investments. They were permitted neither to loan directly to railroads nor to invest in their securities until the early forties, and, even after that date, they were prohibited from investing in non-Massachusetts roads. They could not legally acquire stock in a manufacturing concern until the mid-fifties and at no time were they allowed to acquire the public funds of non-New England bodies.

Within this legal framework, the investment alternatives that faced the two banks were very similar. There was, however, one important exception. In Massachusetts the cotton textile industry was willing to borrow large sums at the maximum legal interest rate. This demand strongly

---

[40] The Savings Bank of Baltimore loaned only to residents of Baltimore City until the mid-fifties when the area was extended to include Baltimore County. The Provident restricted its real estate loans to Boston property; its formal security and bank loans to residents of the Boston metropolitan area; and its personal security loans (with only a few exceptions) to Massachusetts firms. Even in the case of the exceptions (to New Hampshire firms) the loans were made through officers of the firms who were Massachusetts residents. Even after the mid-fifties the Provident did not hold non-New England funds.

influenced the composition of the Provident's portfolio, and it was an important factor in the Provident's ability to maintain earnings at nearly as high a level as the Savings Bank of Baltimore, despite the more rigorous legal restrictions under which it operated. Yet the fact that the Provident provided much more industrial capital than the Baltimore Savings Bank cannot be completely explained by the demands of the textile industry. In part it was also a reflection of the differences in the makeup of the boards of directors. Although merchants dominated both boards, the Boston merchants had been associated with industry since the early 1820's while the Baltimore merchants remained primarily devoted to mercantile pursuits throughout the period. It is reasonable to assume, therefore, that the Boston directors, since they were more familiar with industry, looked with more sympathy on requests for loans from industrial concerns.

Conclusions

If the Savings Bank of Baltimore and the Provident Institution for Savings in the Town of Boston were typical of the early mutuals (and the evidence suggests that they were), it appears that savings banks made an important contribution to early American capital accumulation and mobilization.

The semibenevolent philosophy that gave rise to the mutuals did much to remove the small savers' fear of banks and bankers, and, by providing a safe and profitable depository for savings, the mutuals probably increased the propensity to save among the working classes. Moreover, the mutuals certainly made small savings available for productive investment, especially after the founders had given way to a business-oriented management in the conduct of the operations of the banks.[41] Although it appears that almost all of the banks' direct investment in industry and trade took the form of private loans, their willingness to absorb public issues must also have freed funds for investment in manufacturing concerns.

---

[41] For a detailed study of the role of the Savings Bank of Baltimore in providing capital for the early industrial development of this city, see Payne and Davis, *op. cit.*, pp. 114–37.

7. The Capital Markets and Industrial Concentration: The U.S. and U.K., a Comparative Study [*]

Lance E. Davis
Purdue University

I

ECONOMISTS have tended to place a great deal of importance on the process of capital accumulation. While problems of accumulation have retarded development in many places and times, they seem to have engendered few problems for the U.S. and the U.K. in the 19th century. In both countries the propensity to save appears to have been fairly high as far back as there is evidence. In fact, Postan has argued that any one of a number of British 15th-century "millionaires" could have financed the entire 19th-century textile industry.[1]

To say, however, that accumulation was no problem is not to argue that there were no problems associated with the acquisition of capital. In both countries difficulty was experienced in mobilizing capital (that is, in transferring accumulations from the savers to those who wanted to use these accumulations). The argument advanced in this paper runs in the following terms: Although mobilization problems were experienced in both the U.S. and U.K. in the latter half of the 19th century, differences in the industrial history, the course of economic change, and the geography of the two nations led to significant differences in their ability to mobilize capital resources. These differences, in turn, led in the first instance to marked contrasts in the characteristics of their entrepreneurs and ultimately to important differences in their industrial structures.

---

[*] Reprinted from *Economic History Review*, Second Series, Vol. XIX, No. 2 (1966).

[1] M. Postan, an unpublished series of Lectures given at Johns Hopkins University, 1954–55.

II. Strains on the Financial Network: the Demand for Finance

Over time an economy develops certain methods of mobilizing resources and while these are usually adequate for "normal" transfers, the
system can be strained by extranormal pressures. For any given rate of
growth, we are specifically concerned with three types of shocks.

First, if growth involves a geographic shift in the location of industry,
capital is forced to move across regional boundaries, and traditional capital markets, tied to a particular place, tend to be inadequate. Second,
a similar strain on established institutions is engendered by a pattern of
growth that markedly shifts the industrial composition of output. In this
instance, the barriers are not geographic but industrial. Capital market
institutions tend to be related to historic trade relations and these are
damaged by such a shift. Thirdly, if technological developments involve
substantial economies of scale, finance is required immediately, and firms
cannot grow slowly and create their own savings over time. In this context, it is interesting to note that it is not the total amount of capital, but
the time structure of those demands, that place the strains on an economy's financial network.[2] Let us examine the history of the U.S. and
U.K. with respect to these sources of strain.

There can be little doubt that American geographic expansion strained
the financial network more than did British. In the case of the U.S. the
New England and Middle Atlantic states had been the traditional centers
of development, and in 1850 they still contained the majority of the
capital stock and generated the bulk of new domestic savings.[3] Although
there were continued demands for additional investment in this area, new
demands were opening up west of the Appalachian mountains as well.
Discoveries of resources induced a shift in iron (and later steel) production into trans-Appalachia and underwrote the growth of the petroleum industry in the same area. Links in the production process in turn
engendered further growth in related industries (e.g., machinery). At
the same time, as agriculture moved westward (a movement that gen-

---

[2] This is an interesting but frequently overlooked point. In the case of American
agriculture, for example, the 19th century saw a steady decline in the industry's
capital/output ratio but also a steady increase in its financial requirements (and it
is the latter that strains the financial network). The explanation of this apparent
paradox is quite simple. The largest item in the early farms' capital requirements
was the investment in land clearing, but this requirement could be met over a
period of years (i.e., the farmer himself could squeeze out the necessary savings
from consumption or leisure). As the agricultural frontier moved across the forests
and into the prairies the amount of capital needed to clear the land was substantially
reduced. At the same time, because of technical change, a prairie farmer needed a
substantial amount of capital equipment if he was to compete effectively. Thus, while
total capital requirements were falling, the demand for finance was rising.

[3] Together these facts meant that the majority of free finance (representing the
command over resources available for new investment), the sum of new savings plus
funds freed by depreciation, was located in the East.

erated an increased demand for finance directly), market and material requirements induced a corollary movement of supplying industries (for example, agricultural machinery) and processing industries (meat packing and milling) into the area. (Nor was the strain on the economy limited to the movement itself. Technical developments were making each of these industries more capital-intensive.) Taken together these developments necessitated a geographic transfer of finance on a scale unprecedented in American history.

In Britain, on the other hand, geographic movement put considerably less strain on the economy's financial network. Although the U.K. had experienced major shifts in the location of its industry before 1800, the 19th century saw few further relocations. This is not to argue that industry did not grow, but merely to say that growth was largely concentrated in the already developed centers. With the major exception of the colliery areas (as coal became a more important fuel) and a rare industrial city in the South (Southampton, for example), development was concentrated in London and the northern textile and industrial cities.[4] These could hardly qualify as "new" territory.

An interesting example of the contrasting effects of geographic relocation in the two countries is found in the experience of the textile industry in the postbellum decades. In the case of the U.K. the industry remained centered in the northern textile cities, while in the U.S. the most rapid development was in a new area—the South. In both countries the industry was one of the oldest and most respected, and, in the case of the U.S., it could be argued that it was the only industry that was "industrialized" by the middle of the century. In Great Britain the local capital markets continued to meet the external financial demands of the industry. In the words of one student: "The (cotton) securities are rarely sold by means of a prospectus and they are not underwritten; they are placed by private negotiation among local people who understand the cotton trade."[5] In the United States the problem was much different. Although there are substantial advantages in the South, the shortage of finance in that area prevented major development until the 1870's.[6] Even then it was impossible to raise local capital, and the funds on which the industry grew came from the North (where people were more familiar with textile investment). As a result, throughout the entire period the southern textile industry had to pay a premium price for their finance. Nor was this dis-

---

[4] A. K. Cairncross, *Home and Foreign Investment, 1870–1913* (Cambridge, 1953), pp. 65–83. This is not to say that the center of production of certain industries did not change, but merely that the shifts in general were not into new areas. Thus during the 19th century the locus of iron production shifted from South Wales into the Cleveland and Birmingham areas. However, neither of these new centers can be thought of as new (i.e., without existing financial institutions) areas.

[5] F. Lavington, *The English Capital Market* (London, 1921), pp. 208–9.

[6] B. Mitchell, *William Gregg, Factory Master of the Old South* (Chapel Hill, N.C., 1928).

crimination limited to stock and bondholders. Southern banks also discriminated against the new industry, and textile firms had to appeal to northern sources for even their short-term accommodation.[7] The result was, of course, retarded growth; and it was the second decade of the 20th century before southern textiles clearly dominated the American market: a domination they would almost certainly have achieved a hundred years earlier had capital been more mobile.

Similarly, Britain appears to have experienced less shift in the industrial composition of its output. If development takes the form of the expansion of existing industries, old firms can provide the basis for the new or, if not that, at least there will be people and institutions who are acquainted with the industry and more willing to make funds available for new developments.

In the United States some development certainly took the form of the expansion of already existing industries, but much of the growth after 1850 took place in new industries or industries so different from their antecedents as to be almost unrecognizable. Among new industries, for example, petroleum, unknown at the middle of the century, grew by 1880 to supply the bulk of lubricants for the economy and the source of light for most of rural America (to say nothing of commanding large export markets abroad). In the second group among many others were steel, meat packing, agricultural machinery, and flour milling (to say nothing of agriculture itself). There had never been a substantial iron industry; and, as a result, growth in steel could not be based on established iron firms.[8] Meat packing was revolutionized by the innovation of the refrigerator car in the 1880's, and the economies realized from production in the capital intensive "disassembly" plants were quickly realized. But the new industry would hardly have been recognized by the packer of a decade before.[9] Similarly, agricultural machinery before the 1850's meant blacksmiths and a few plows. Thereafter it meant complicated threshers and reapers, large-scale factories, and complicated problems of financing and servicing.[10] In the same vein, milling before the 1870's was as efficiently conducted by a small local miller as by one of the few large plants in Baltimore or Rochester. The opening of the upper plains, however, brought hard wheat onto the market, and this strain could only be processed by Hungarian reduction milling. The new technique was capital intensive and subject to economies of scale over large ranges of output.

---

[7] B. Mitchell, *The Rise of Cotton Mills in the South* (Baltimore, 1921).

[8] There is one important exception. The first Kelly steel mill at Wyandotte, Michigan, was financed by the iron fraternity. However, the mill was capital-short and much of the finance came from British ironmakers. J. Boucher, *William Kelly* (Greensburg, Pa., 1928).

[9] R. Clemen, *The American Livestock and Meat Industry* (New York, 1928).

[10] C. McCormick, *The Century of the Reaper* (Boston, 1931), and S. Holbrook, *Machines of Plenty* (New York, 1955).

The local miller could no longer compete, and the industry changed completely.[11]

In Britain, on the other hand, a significant proportion of growth took the form of the expansion of already existing industries. In part this pattern on growth reflected conditions endogenous to the U.K. in the 19th century, but in part it merely reflected the fact that in the early years the United States was an almost entirely agricultural nation, and any change, therefore, was likely to alter the industrial structure drastically.[12] There were, of course, new industries in Britain; chemicals, brewing, and engineering were all new in the sense we have used the term, but even these industries antedated their American counterparts. More important, however, British industry continued to be dominated by the "staple" commodities far more than the U.S. Thus in the 1880's iron and steel and textiles still ranked first and second among British industries, and even in 1907 textiles were still the second largest manufacturing industry.[13] Moreover, mining, a staple if not a manufacturing one, was one of the leading growth sectors in the economy throughout the century.[14]

Nor does it appear that British industry was more subject to new technologies involving increasing returns to scale. By the middle of the 19th century technical information flowed easily across the Atlantic, and it is unlikely that techniques known in one country were unknown in the other.[15] At the same time, if one takes into account the fact that the trans-Mississippi West was only gradually being integrated into the national market, it appears that the size of the market in the two countries must have been more or less comparable, with the American, if anything, being slightly larger.[16] It would be useful to compare each industry in each country on this point, but the information is not available. What can be said is that many of the new growth industries in the U.S. apparently were subject to increasing returns (petroleum, steel, milling, and meat packing), while at least a portion of British growth was channeled into industries, like textile, where scale was much less important. Moreover, in the case of the steel industry, British demand and technical considera-

---

[11] C. Kuhlman, *The Development of the Flour Milling Industry in the United States* (Boston, 1929).

[12] In 1800, for example, 90 percent of the American labor force was engaged in agriculture. In the U.K. the figure was only slightly over 35 percent, *Historical Statistics of the United States* (Washington, D.C., 1960). P. Deane and W. Cole, *British Economic Growth, 1688–1959* (Cambridge, 1962), p. 142.

[13] Dean and Cole, *British Growth*, pp. 182–92 and 221–24.

[14] *Ibid.* pp. 214–20.

[15] H. J. Habakkuk, *American and British Technology in the Nineteenth Century: The Search for Labour-Saving Inventions* (Cambridge, 1962).

[16] In 1890 there were about 63 million people in the U.S. and about 38 million in Great Britain. In 1860 the figures were 32 million in the U.S. and 29 million in Britain, but of the U.S. number about 4 million were living west of the Mississippi river. Nor did incomes vary much. In 1890 *per capita* income was £50 (in 1913 prices) in the U.S. and about four fifths that amount in the U.K.

tions forced the industry more heavily into Siemens (i.e., open hearth) steel than its American counterpart, and economies of scale were certainly less in that process.[17] Overall, therefore, it appears that technical conditions in the two countries were probably similar and if anything new techniques with important returns to scale and their concomitant strains on the financial network were likely more important in the U.S.

But it is not just the existence of the economies, but the timing of their innovation that strains the network. Here again the evidence suggests that Great Britain suffered less. The longer a firm exists before it is forced to obtain additional capital, the more likely it is that it can generate the necessary finance internally. Other things being equal, therefore, the longer and more continuous industrial history of Britain should have made is easier for British firms to acquire finance without resorting to the capital markets. Although the evidence is sketchy, what there is does suggest that this was in fact the case. A comparison of the rates of net savings in the two countries indicates that while the U.S. experienced a rate of about 12 percent throughout the second half of the century (indeed that figure has been suggested as a minimum rate for industrialization), the rate in the U.K. reached that magic figure only during the period 1865–79. Moreover, throughout the century a significant proportion of British savings flowed abroad and were unavailable for domestic investment.[18] At the same time, the histories of individual English firms show a much more marked dependence upon internal finance than their American counterparts. Critics have frequently chided British industry for their reluctance to borrow, but that reluctance almost certainly attests to their ability to acquire internal finance.[19]

III. The Financial Network: the Supply of Finance

Not only were the British financial networks less subject to strain during the latter 19th century, but also the networks themselves appear to have been better constructed.

Although commercial banking grew rapidly in the United States, the legal prohibitions against branch banking and the distance between economic centers produced as late as 1870 a pattern of relatively small, not very closely connected, short-term markets. A comparison of interest rates in various regions indicates that there were wide differences in the price of short-term capital. In 1870, for example, there was almost a 10

---

[17] D. L. Burn, *The Economic History of Steelmaking, 1867–1934* (Cambridge, 1910), p. 239.

[18] S. Kuznets, "Long-Term Changes in the National Income of the United States of America since 1890," in *Income and Wealth of the United States, Income and Wealth Series*, Vol. II, pp. 156–57; Dean and Cole, *British Growth*, pp. 266–67.

[19] F. Lavington, *Capital Market*.

percent difference between rates in New York City and those prevailing in the smaller cities on the West Coast.[20]

Because of the prohibition on interstate branching, a national market had to await the development of a national market for commercial paper. In the U.S. the commercial paper market grew only slowly until the latter decades of the 19th century, and it was the first decade of the present century before substantial equality of short-term regional rates was realized.[21]

In England the short-term market developed much earlier. Pressnell has shown that the London balances held by provincial bankers helped mobilize capital in the 18th century. Although this practice may have declined in the first decades of the 19th century, the rise of the commercial paper market after 1825 provided the vehicle for the creation of a national short-term market, and in the 1840's and 1850's it appears that the London rate penetrated the countryside.[22] Although the quantitative evidence on this point is scarce, an index of bank earnings suggests that while differentials existed in the 1840's, by 1860 these differentials had largely disappeared.[23] Thus it appears by the 1860's *at the latest* Britain possessed an operating national short-term capital market.

In the long-term mortgage market, too, there is evidence that the British markets were capable of transferring funds across regional boundaries much before their American counterparts. In the U.S. the westward movement of the frontier engendered a continual demand for agricultural credit across the Appalachians; however, experience with long-term loans in the 1830's and 1840's convinced most commercial bankers (and the legislatures that regulated them) that long-term loans were bad business.[24] As a result, there was no ready institutional framework to handle long-term credit, and new ones had to be devised. At first private parties acting through brokers provided some mortgage credit, but this was a

---

[20] L. Davis, "The Investment Market, 1870–1918; the Evolution of a National Market," *Journal of Economic History*, September, 1965.

[21] The commercial paper market was organized in the eastern cities in the 1840's; however, it does not reach even the largest cities of the Old Northwest Territory until the 1870's, and it is after 1900 before it penetrates the smaller cities of the Pacific Coast.

[22] L. S. Pressnell, *County Banking in the Industrial Revolution* (Oxford, 1956), pp. 75–125 and 405–40; W. T. C. King, *History of the London Discount Market* (London, 1936), p. 42.

[23] The index is constructed from the reports of joint-stock banks 1834–75. It shows in the early 1840's high rates in the Midlands and the North, much lower rates in London and the South. See L. Davis, "Capital Immobilities and Economic Growth: a Study of the Evolution of Two National Capital Markets," Paper presented to the first International Econometrics Conference, Rome, 1965, pp. 14–43.

[24] Many states passed laws prohibiting mortgage loans, and, in those that did not, moral pressure from the banking community tended to prevent their execution. This experience influenced federal legislation and the National Banking Act prohibited national banks from making mortgage loans. This prohibition was not repealed until 1914.

difficult and expensive operation. Gradually more credit passed through institutional investors and in the 1880's a number of mortgage houses (intermediaries that issued bonds against a portfolio of mortgages) began to spring up.[25] However, falling farm prices and crop failures combined to bankrupt many of these houses in the 1890's, and as late as World War I mortgage credit was still not being effectively mobilized in the United States.

In England, on the other hand, the situation was much different. While one is always hesitant to attempt to justify British social structure, there can be no doubt that it did aid the process of capital mobilization. Since large landowners tended to make their homes in London but held agricultural lands in all parts of the country, they were able to negotiate loans in the capital and make these funds available for agricultural development in other regions. Until railways and industry began to compete for finance, loans of this type constituted the bulk of the investments of early nonbank intermediaries. In 1830, for example, The Sun Fire Company had over half a million pounds on mortgage loan to titled landholders.[26] Thus the intimate connection between land and social position, although it may have retarded industrial capital mobilization, made a mortgage market in 19th-century England.

Similarly, the U.K. benefited from much less stringent commercial banking legislation. Commercial banks regularly made mortgage loans, and at times even made such funds available to manufacturing and trade. Although information on the investment of commercial banks is scanty, the records of the bankrupt institutions suggests that they frequently had advanced funds to industrial enterprises.[27] Nor did such loans always lead to insolvency. In 1859, for example, Stephen Moulton was able to nego-

---

[25] On mortgage houses see D. Frederiksen, "Mortgage Banking in the United States," *Journal of Political Economy*, March, 1894, and A. Bogue, *Money at Interest* (Ithaca, 1955). As for the attitude of the traditional intermediaries, the Savings Bank of Baltimore in 1849 refused to lend on property in Ellicott City (11 miles away) because of the "board's lack of knowledge about property in the country." Peter L. Payne and Lance E. Davis, *The Savings Bank of Baltimore* (Baltimore, 1956). However, as institutions grew they became more aware of opportunities and, although late, they were still several decades ahead of the rest of the market. They were not, however, large enough by themselves to arbitrage out the market.

[26] Sun Fire Office *Minute Books*. At that time the list included Lady Delavel, Sir E. V. Mansell, Lord Crewe, Sir John Sawbridge, Sir John F. Leicester, the Duke of Bedford, the Duke and Marquess of Tavistock, the Duke of Devonshire, Lord Kensington, the Duke of Marlborough, and Lord Straw. The fact that they borrowed does not, of course, ensure that they used the funds productively, but it at least gave them access to funds.

[27] The Royal British Bank, for example, had advanced "100,000 against the security of certain iron and coal works in Glamorganshire," S. E. Thomas, *The Rise and Growth of Joint Stock Banking* (London, 1934), pp. 484–85. Again in 1849 the shareholders of the Aberdeen Bank were angry with the directors because "with the knowledge of the extent to which the bank was involved with manufacturing concerns, they should have given off extra stock at a premium some years ago," *Bankers Magazine*, April 30, 1849.

tiate a £6,000 mortgage loan for his new rubber enterprise from the Wilts and Dorset Bank.[28]

Similar conclusions emerge from a comparison of the formal market for securities in the two countries. Despite the facts that the New York stock exchange can trace its origins into the 18th century and corporation laws were much more permissive than in England, there was almost no market for industrial securities until the last five years of the 19th century. In fact, as late as the 1880's an investor interested in industrial issues would more likely turn to the Boston than to the New York market, but even that market was probably more apparent than real. The historian of the Boston exchange warns his reader not to put too much reliance in his industrial price quotations because the market was very thin.[29] In New York it was only in the late 1880's that the growth of large firms and the innovation of preference shares to manufacturing made it possible to market important issues, and it was yet another decade before J. P. Morgan's endorsement made industrials appear really safe.[30] Nor was the disinclination to hold industrials limited to investors alone. It was 1919 before the New York banks gave industrial securities equal treatment with other securities as collateral for call loans.[31] Moreover, the thinness that characterized the equity market also appears to have existed in the industrial bond market. In 1893 the Sun Fire and Life insisted that its American subsidiary sell its newly acquired Proctor and Gamble bonds because the lack of a ready market adversely affected their liquidity.[32]

In Great Britain the market appears to have been very much better developed. Although a general incorporation act was not passed until 1862, by 1877 a single firm (Messrs. Chadwick and Co.) had promoted and sold over £40 million worth of joint-stock shares (mostly industrials).[33] Moreover, although there were complaints about the thinness of the industrial market in the 1870's, there was no question that such a market existed.[34]

---

[28] Moulton had originally taken the loan against his personal estate, but in 1859 converted it to a business loan. W. Woodruff, *The Rise of the British Rubber Industry during the 19th Century* (Liverpool, 1958), pp. 29–33.

[29] J. G. Martin, *Seventy-Three Year History of the Boston Stock Market* (Boston, 1871), pp. 64–73.

[30] See T. Navin and M. Sears, "The Rise of a Market for Industrial Securities 1887–1902," *Business History Review*, Vol. 29 (1955), pp. 105–38.

[31] M. Myers, *The New York Money Market*, Vol. I: *Origins and Development* (New York, 1931), pp. 280–81.

[32] "The Committee prefer in general to hold securities which are regularly quoted and dealt in, which very few of the best industrial bonds appear to be," *Minutes of the Joint Finance Committee, Sun Fire and Life Companies*, March 6, 1893.

[33] See the testimony of Mr. David Chadwick, M.P. before the Select Committee on the Operation of the Companies Act of 1862 and 1867, *Parliamentary Papers, England*, 1877, VIII, QQ. 1936–2081. Chadwick claimed that he had a list of 5,000 potential subscribers who were willing to invest in companies promoted by his firm. The list is almost as long as those maintained by J. P. Morgan a quarter century later.

[34] E. Morgan and W. Thomas, *The Stock Exchange: Its History and Functions* (London, 1962), p. 146.

During the next decade the market became even more active. In 1882 (when there was still no American market for industrials) stocks of manufacturing firms with capital total £54 million were listed on the exchange, and two decades later the total reached £872 million.[35] In the years between 1865 and 1890 major flotations of steel, electricity, chemicals, and brewing were made and the securities easily absorbed by the market.

The case of nonbank intermediaries is less clear, but even here the evidence appears to indicate greater development in the U.K. In the 19th century there were two major types of nonbank intermediaries: savings banks and insurance (fire and life) companies. In the U.K. savings banks were prohibited by law from any investments aside from government deposits.[36] Thus they could play no direct role in the mobilization of capital. Without question, therefore, the American banks (despite a multitude of legal restrictions seriously circumscribing their investment choice) were better able to move capital from savers to investors than were their British counterparts. Although they made little contribution to the interregional movement of funds and were never important outside the Northeast, they made major contributions to the finance of industry in that area (the New England textile industry was a particular beneficiary).[37]

In the insurance field, however, it appears that British firms had a substantial lead over their American counterparts. Not only were they an effective mobilizing force 50 years earlier, but also they continued to hold this advantage throughout the century (and insurance companies were growing much more rapidly than savings banks in the latter period). This difference can probably be traced to the greater size, the longer history, and less restrictive legal regulation that marked the British firms.[38] Although a precise measure of the differentials would involve a close comparison of a representative sample of firms in the two countries (and this information does not exist), some evidence can be adduced by a comparison of the Alliance in Britain with the Northwestern Mutual in the U.S.[39] Both companies invested heavily in mortgages, but while the Sun's were scattered over the length of the British Isles as early as the 1820's, the Northwestern's only gradually spread beyond the Wisconsin-Chicago

---

[35] *Ibid.*, p. 132.

[36] H. O. Horne, *A History of Saving Banks* (London, 1947).

[37] Lance E. Davis, *Nineteenth-Century Financial Intermediaries: Four Case Studies* Thesis, (Johns Hopkins University, 1956).

[38] The longer history gave more time to develop national investment policies by professional management. British firms, since they were usually stock companies, were not affected by legal regulations. American mutuals, on the other hand, were closely regulated, they were frequently prohibited from investing outside their own state and from purchasing certain types of securities (e.g., common stock).

[39] The information on the Alliance comes from the company's financial ledger and minute books. That on the Northwestern Mutual from H. Williamson and O. Smalley, *The Northwestern Mutual Life* (Evanston, Ill., 1947).

complex.[40] Moreover, while the Alliance had begun to invest in railroad shares in the 1840's, the Northwestern does not begin until 40 years later. Similarly, while the Alliance began to absorb industrial securities (particularly from the brewing industry) in the 1880's there are none in the Northwestern's portfolio before World War I. Finally, after 1880 the Alliance began to add common stock to its holdings of formal securities. The Northwestern still holds no common shares.

IV. Finance and Concentration: English and American Case Studies

Although final answers await a detailed comparison, the examination of the case histories of a few selected industries appears to provide some useful insights into the relationship between finance and concentration. For the United States it appears useful to examine steel, meat packing, and petroleum; and for England steel, brewing, and chemicals suggest themselves.

In each of the three American industries, technical change produced a new technology subject to substantial economies of scale, and the search for the finance required to achieve these economies led the firms outside the normal capital markets. Some firms were more successful than others in their search for "informal finance," and the successful firms grew at the expense of their less fortunate competitors. As a result, industrial concentration increased in the affected industries.

The innovation of the capital-intensive Bessemer and Kelly processes was the basis for the development of the American steel industry. Until then iron manufacture was conducted by a number of very small firms (since there were no scale economies) and none of these could command the financial support necessary for the innovation of the new process. As a result, the growth of the steel industry was delayed, and the first two experiments achieved even modest success only because of "informal" arrangements: arrangements that left neither firm with sufficient finance to achieve a significant breakthrough.[41] It was not until Andrew Carnegie turned his financial talents toward steel that the first really successful venture was launched. Although Carnegie knew nothing of steel, he did

---

[40] The Northwestern was one of the more active U.S. companies in interstate mortgage placements. The Metropolitan Life, for example, restricted its mortgages to eastern urban lands until 1918. M. James, *The Metropolitan Life, A Study of Business Growth*, pp. 232–33.

[41] In the case of the Kelly mill at Wyandotte, Michigan, the normal markets failed to produce adequate finance, and it was brought into production only by an appeal to members of the "iron fraternity" in the U.S. and Great Britain. The first Bessemer mill (in Harrisburg, Penn.) was near bankruptcy until the Pennsylvania railroad (needing steel) advanced it some funds. Both were limited in further expansion by the inelasticity of their capital sources. See J. Boucher, *William Kelly*, and A. Carnegie, *Autobiography* (Boston, 1924).

know how to bring together men with finance (he had done this before in a number of iron enterprises and more recently in the Keystone Bridge Company). As a result, he was able to put together a steel complex that was the largest in the industry.[42] So successful was he, in fact, that even in the 1890's he bragged of his ability to acquire finance during depressions when others could not, and it was well known throughout the industry that Carnegie and (later) Jones and Laughlin could acquire finance much more cheaply than their competitors.[43] At no time, however, did Carnegie manage to acquire large blocks of finance through the formal markets. It was not until J. P. Morgan (a master at financial mobilization) put together U.S. Steel and convinced the American investor that industrials were good investments that large blocks of capital were raised in this manner. In the process, of course, almost two thirds of the industry's output was concentrated in a single firm. The process is not, however, reversible; and it is interesting to note that once U.S. Steel managed to attain this type of finance, other firms could copy them. After 1902 there were no longer compelling financial benefits to be derived from huge steel, and concentration has steadily declined throughout the present century.[44]

While steel technology changed in the 1870's, it was in the next decade that the widespread innovation of the refrigerator car changed the structure of the packing industry. As long as markets were small, it did not pay to innovate assembly-line slaughter houses, and packing remained an industry of small firms producing for largely local markets. With broader markets, however, there were substantial profits to be made by firms capable of acquiring the new capital-intensive technology.[45] Since the formal markets could not provide the needed finance, the rewards were concentrated into the hands of the few firms who had access to the informal markets. Armour, for example, had established a New York commercial house operated by his brother and he attracted eastern funds through that institution. He also recognized the need for close informal ties with the commercial banking system, and placed his men on the boards of most of Chicago's major banks. Even before the refrigerator car he had displayed his grasp of the need for adequate finance and his ingenuity at obtaining it. In 1869 he had established a packing house in Kansas City, and when, in 1870, he found it in need of finance, he set up his own bank (Armour Brothers' Banking Company).[46]

Similarly Swift was able to acquire finance when others could not. Basing his original establishment on his own savings earned in the East,

---

[42] Carnegie, *Autobiography*.

[43] D. Burn, *The Economic History of Steelmaking, 1867–1939* (Cambridge, 1940), pp. 248, 261.

[44] Today U.S. Steel produces only about one fourth of American output.

[45] R. Clemen, *The American Livestock and Meat Industry* (New York, 1923).

[46] H. Leech and J. Armour, *Armour and His Times* (New York, 1923), p. 29; P. Trescott, *Financing American Enterprise. The Story of Commercial Banking* (New York, 1963), p. 95; A. Bogue, *Money at Interest* (Cornell, 1955).

he grew by bringing together a closely knit group of financial backers drawn from among his personal friends. Moreover (even more than Armour), he appeared to be able to draw on the resources of the commercial banking system. Thus, in 1893 at the height of the panic, although he owed over $10 million to a number of midwestern commercial banks, he was still able to get additional funds from the Chicago banks.[47] These two and the others that had access to finance (e.g., Morris, Cudahy, etc.) grew rapidly at the expense of the rest of the industry, and within a few years the industry was dominated by half a dozen large firms.

In the case of petroleum, the story is repeated once again. In the 1850's and early 1860's the minimum capital necessary to begin refining was only a few hundred dollars, and small refineries were not significantly less profitable than large ones. In the late 1860's and early 1870's, however, technical developments produced substantial economies of scale, and, as a result, a premium was placed on the ability to acquire finance.[48] Refiners faced by these needs usually turned to the commercial banks for help, but they were most often rebuffed because of the riskiness of the refining industry. Rockefeller,, however, had carefully built up personal contacts with the Cleveland banking community, and they were willing to loan to their friend. Thus Rockefeller was able to build the first "efficient" firm, and as competition from the new refinery squeezed the rest of the industry, he was able to buy out his competitors. It was, of course, the Cleveland refining empire that became the basis for Standard Oil.[49] As his firm grew, Rockefeller enlarged his circle of banking "friends" to include representatives from the large New York banks, and by the 1880's Standard Oil with its almost monopolistic access to the formal capital markets became something of a financial institution itself. Although in general it limited its investments to enterprises more or less related to oil, the firm was swamped with proposals from all sectors of the economy, and at times their investments did run farther afield (the Mesabi iron range is a good case in point).[50]

In England because the capital markets were better, the firms more securely financially based, and the strains on the financial network less, the pattern of development was quite different. Merger, when it did occur, tended to be of the textbook variety (that is, a defensive maneuver in the face of declining markets).

The steel industry was subject to many of the same technological strains as its American counterpart, but there was never a British equivalent of U.S. Steel (or even of Carnegie). The iron industry was well estab-

---

[47] P. Trescott, *Enterprise*, pp. 101–2; B. Pierce, *History of Chicago*, Vol. III, pp. 113–14; L. Swift, *The Yankee of the Yards. The Biography of Gustavus Franklin Swift* (Chicago, 1927), pp. 25–27.

[48] H. Williamson and A. Daum, *The American Petroleum Industry. The Age of Illumination* (Evanston, Ill., 1959).

[49] P. Trescott, *Enterprise;* A. Nevins, *John D. Rockefeller* (New York, 1940).

[50] Nevins, *Rockefeller*, Vol. II, pp. 395–96.

lished long before the discovery of the Bessemer process, and for the most part expansion was based on old, well-established firms. In the 1860's a number of private firms became joint-stock companies, and were able to use the formal capital markets to acquire additional finance. Thus by 1870 Bolckow Vaughn, Ebbw Vale, and Consett could all number their stock-holders in the hundreds. The second wave of steel flotations in the 1870's was equally well subscribed, and the fact that thereafter the industry may have had some difficulty raising equity capital is almost certainly the result of not a poor but a very impersonal market (the investors feeling once duped stayed away in droves).[51] Moreover, there is little evidence that the industry suffered from any shortages of finance in the last quarter of the century. There were only scattered complaints from within the industry, and the authoritative British Iron Trade Report on Germany and Belgium, although enumerating a long list of reasons for the declining position of the British steel industry, does not mention difficulties in acquiring finance.[52]

Nor does the history of amalgamations in the industry suggest any pressure. Although there were occasional mergers and amalgamations, the dominant form of monopolistic organization was the association—a form that offers no financial benefits. The mergers that did occur appear to have been largely defensive, and as late as 1907 there were still over 100 blast-furnace companies and 95 steel firms in the U.K.[53] Thereafter there does appear to have been some increase in merger activity (Dorman Long is a particular example), but how much of this was financially induced is hard to determine.[54] Certainly the history on many of these later combinations appear far more defensive than financially acquisitive.[55]

Although meat packing had no British counterpart, in terms of timing, its growth coincided with the reorganization of the brewing industry in England. At the same time that the refrigerator car altered the structure of the American industry, the change of attitude toward the licensing of public houses in Britain (a product of the prohibition strain in British evangelism) altered the structure of the brewing industry in the U.K. The development of scientific quality control had made large-scale brewing economic, but the changes had been gradual and they had not placed any severe strains on the financial network. In the mid 1880's, however, the more alert brewers realized that, given the increasingly more severe

---

[51] Burn, *Steel*, pp. 252–57. In fact one of the complaints of Burn is that the market was so good it was unnecessary to have expert boards of directors to satisfy stock-holders, and as a result management suffered.

[52] Burn, *Steel*, p. 252; J. Carr and W. Taplin, *A History of the British Steel Industry* (Oxford, 1962), p. 175. In fact Burn's entire argument that industry suffered because there were no financial pressures for amalgamation suggests that there was little restraint.

[53] H. Macrosty, *The Trust Movement in British Industry* (London, 1907), p. 25.

[54] Macrosty, *Trust*, p. 31, and Burn, *Steel*, pp. 249, 271.

[55] H. Levy, *Monopolies, Cartels and Trusts in British Industry* (London, 1927), pp. 194–99.

restrictions on licensing, it would be profitable to invest in tied houses to assure themselves adequate markets. Since the number of potential houses was limited, speed was necessary; and this decision greatly increased the capital requirements of every firm.

In the U.S. similar pressures in meat packing had resulted in the very rapid growth of those few firms able to attract finance. In Britain, ready access to an already developed market made it possible for a larger number of firms to acquire the necessary financial capital. Certainly the more alert firms (particularly Guinness) benefited most, since they were able to buy the most desirable properties, but even the late comers (like Allsopp's) were able to raise the necessary finance (although the best locations were gone). Between 1886, when Guinness marketed its first issue, and 1888 more than £25 million of brewery shares were floated on the London market, and by 1890 there were 200 brewing companies whose shares were actively traded.[56] Although the rapid expansion of the "tied house" had reduced the number of firms in the industry, the reductions were trivial compared to the concentration that had occurred in packing.[57]

Finally, the British chemical industry displays some of the same characteristics as the American petroleum industry. Although it was not a "new" industry in the sense that oil was new, chemicals, like oil, did experience a period of rapid growth in the 1850's and 1860's and important technical changes in the 1870's. The growth in the first decades was the result of increases in the production of soda, increases that were, in turn, based on improvements in the Le Blanc process.[58] Like oil, the industry was characterized by a fairly large number of firms, and, since growth and progress went hand in hand, the firms faced no particular financial stresses. In the 1870's, however, the situation changed. Important improvements were made in the Le Blanc technique, and the established firms began to come under increasing competitive pressure from firms using the Solvay process. Both developments involved the introduction of techniques that were substantially more capital-intensive than those the industry had previously known.[59] Unlike their American counterparts, however, the British capital markets were adequate.

In the Le Blanc portion of the industry, firms that had been partnerships tended to incorporate and acquire the needed finance by the sale of

---

[56] J. Vaizey, *The Brewing Industry, 1896–1951* (Pitman, 1960), pp. 9–12.

[57] At least 125 firms were absorbed between 1888 and 1902, but there were still substantial numbers remaining, *ibid.*, p. 12.

[58] Production of soda ash doubled between 1852 and 1866 and increased by another 30 percent over the next 12 years. Production of other products, although quantitatively less important, grew at even more spectacular rates. The output of bleaching powder, for example, doubled between 1852 and 1866 and then rose by 400 percent over the next 12 years. L. Haber, *The Chemical Industry during the Nineteenth Century* (Oxford, 1958), p. 59.

[59] "The industry's fresh lease on life was purchased at heavy cost for much expensive plant was required and overheads rose steeply," Haber, *Chemicals*, p. 100.

securities or by loans from financial institutions. Allhusen and Company, for example, was first organized as a partnership in the 1840's, and grew to become one of the largest firms in the Tyne area by the 1850's. In 1872 it was incorporated (as the Newcastle Chemical Company Ltd.) and an examination of their capital structure shows equity of over £400,000 and loans and mortgages of an additional £175,000.[60] Thus, despite the fact that there were serious doubts about the long-run prospects of the industry (the Newcastle Chemical Company, for example, experienced continued losses through the 1870's), sufficient funds to finance the new techniques were easily available.

Nor did the new Solvay firms fare much worse. The new electrolytic process, although substantially cheaper than the old one, required about 30 percent more capital than even the newest modifications of the Le Blanc process.[61] But even these new firms were able to acquire finance. For example, one of the most dynamic of the new Solvay firms was the partnership of Ludwig Mond and John Brunner. Although they did experience some early financial difficulties, they managed to acquire sufficient finance to start operations. In fact a part of their initial capital came from Parr's bank.[62] Thereafter, they had no trouble raising sufficient additional finance to underwrite a 2,000 percent increase in business in the 1870's. In 1881 they went public with a capital of £360,000, a figure that was increased to £1,500,000 in 1884 and to £3,000,000 eight years later.[63]

Mergers did occur in the industry, but they were almost always defensive and usually aimed at stabilizing the declining Le Blanc sector. Moreover, when they did occur they experienced little trouble marketing their securities despite the fact that the industry's future must have appeared quite bleak. In 1888, after several decades of discussion, 64 salt firms merged into Salt Union Ltd. Despite the economic pressures and the water written into the capital structure the market easily absorbed the £4,000,000 issue. The merged firm did manage to stabilize the market for a time, and two years later the Le Blanc producers adopted a similar model in an attempt to duplicate the earlier success. The United Alkali Company, a merger of 48 firms in the alkali trade, was formed at the time of the Baring Crisis. Pressure on the money market prevented further issues at that time; however, within a few months the £7,165,000 firm appealed for additional capital, and the required £1,335,000 was quickly subscribed. All this in an industry that had been declining for 20 years and for a firm that, though it paid dividends averaging 3 percent for the first six years of its life, never managed another dividend before 1905.[64]

---

60 *Ibid.*, pp. 18, 20, 57, 156.
61 *Ibid.*, pp. 100–101.
62 *Ibid.*, p. 157.
63 *Ibid.*, p. 158.
64 *Ibid.*, pp. 181–84.

V. Morgan and O'Hagen

In many ways the differences between the financial networks in the U.S. and the U.K. and their effect on the character of entrepreneurship in the two countries are neatly summarized in the contrasting careers of these nation's greatest promoters: J. P. Morgan and H. Osborne O'Hagen. Although Morgan was slightly older, their careers were in many ways parallel during the era of "high finance capitalism." Both first became famous for their role in promoting railroad mergers, and both turned to industrial finance. Both were extremely astute and touched with a financial genius, but there the similarity ends. While both earned substantial profits (in terms of both money and power) from their endeavors, Morgan's rewards were much higher; and a comparison of their operations suggests some reasons for this difference.

In general one would expect that, other things being equal, the better the capital market the smaller would be the monopoly profits associated with an ability to mobilize capital. Moreover, while in the poorer market opportunities for such profits might be found in all areas (including the servicing of well-known firms and established industries), in the better market they would tend to be concentrated in the areas that are most poorly served (i.e., small firms and new industries).

O'Hagen's most profitable ventures were those involving the public flotation of relatively small domestic companies or relatively large American companies. Kayser-Ellison (the special steel manufacturers) and Webely Revolver are typical of the domestic firms that benefited from his services and from which he realized substantial profits. Since the most fruitful domestic venture involved relatively small unknown firms, O'Hagen was forced to rely on scouts who, for a commission, would introduce him to potential customers. He also earned some profits from large-scale ventures, but these were almost invariably foreign companies. Thus his profits from American breweries and the Chicago stockyards were substantial, but they attest to the lack of development of the American market, not the British.

On the other hand, his activities on behalf of large domestic firms were almost invariably much less profitable. In the 1880's he was active in brewery flotations, but competition from other promoters quickly squeezed out any abnormal profits. In the case of the Portland Cement combine, the merger itself was essentially defensive and O'Hagen made very little out of the promotion (in fact, he devoted almost the rest of his active life to its management in hopes of recouping something from his activities).[65]

Morgan, on the other hand, found that in the more poorly organized

---

[65] See H. Osborne O'Hagen, *Leaves from My Life* (London, 1929) Vol. I, pp. 259–91, 280–91, 295–302, 306–14, 446–48, and Vol. II, p. 71.

capital markets of the United States there were substantial profits to be earned by securing finance for large well-known domestic companies. Among his most successful promotions were United States Steel and International Harvester. Both combined firms that were already household words throughout the country (for example, Carnegie in the first instance and McCormick in the second). Morgan also had his failures (i.e., promotions that earned relatively little), and, like O'Hagen's, they were concentrated in areas already adequately served by the financial network. Thus, by the end of the 19th century there was little profit to be made from finding finance for eastern railroads (the New Haven) or for international steamship lines (the International Marine Company).[66] Others were also capable of providing the needed finance.

VI. The Capital Markets and Concentration

This study makes no attempt to account for all trends in concentration in the U.S. and Great Britain. There were many other factors aside from the capital markets. For example, antitrust legislation may have had some effect on concentration in the U.S. after 1911, and free trade may have been partly responsible for the relative inefficiency of monopolistic agglomerations in the U.K. In particular, while this paper attempts to explain certain tendencies toward concentration in the U.S., it explains nothing about actual concentration in the U.K. Instead, it merely argues the negative hypothesis, i.e., why some types of concentrations were less prevalent. It does, however, attempt to supply a partial explanation for certain peculiar differences between the two countries.

Traditionally, monopolistic arrangements have been most common in stable or declining industries where firms join in an attempt to prevent price competition that would threaten profit margins. Rapid growth and technological change, on the other hand, are traditionally considered anathema to monopoly. In England the pattern appears to have confirmed more closely to the traditional model, but in the U.S. it was quite different. In the U.K. there were some tendencies toward concentration in expanding industries, but it neither went so far or bulked so large in the total as it did in the U.S.[67] Thus a student of economic concentration was moved to say, "But while in England the movement toward monopolies only begins when the number of producers has shrunk to 40, 30, 20 or even less, foreign monopolies have often been formed at much more elementary stages of concentration and in some cases when production . . . is increasing."[68] In the case of the United States, while there were cer-

---

[66] C. Hovey, *The Life of J. Pierpont Morgan* (London, 1922). It is interesting to note that O'Hagen had found international shipping unprofitable 10 years before Morgan, O'Hagen; *Leaves*, pp. 385–86.

[67] Nelson, *Merger Movements*, pp. 130–32.

[68] Levy, *Monopolies*, p. 288.

tainly monopolistic concentrations in declining sectors (distilling and sugar refining to cite only two), the apparent rapid increase in concentration in the last half of the decade was marked by growing concentration in rapidly expanding industries.[69]

Case by case the emergence of noncompetitive market structures in expanding industries appears to have been related to those industries' needs for capital. In England, industry faced with similar demands, but also faced with more easily accessible supplies of capital, did not become unduly concentrated. Nelson, for example, has shown that in the U.S. mergers were closely related to the state of the financial markets, but that in the U.K. the relation (if it existed at all) was much less strong.[70] Other evidence, although not complete tends to support the financial thesis.[71]

In the United States it appears that the capital markets were improving over the last quarter of the 19th century, and by the second decade of the present century they were probably as good as the English. If the financial thesis is correct, one would expect that the rate of concentration would decline when a viable national market emerges. In fact, the years since 1906 have been characterized by no significant increase in the extent of concentration, and the best evidence suggests there may have been some decline.[72]

Moreover, over the same period the character of American mergers changed. If one were to argue that the decline in mergers was the result of antitrust legislation, then it would follow that giant mergers (mergers of already large firms) should have declined relative to mergers of a number of small firms (such giant mergers would be more susceptible to justice

---

[69] E.g., petroleum in the nineties, packing and milling in the nineties and steel at the turn of the century. A quantitative study of mergers at the end of the period shows that mergers were concentrated in growth industries and closely correlated with finance. R. Nelson, *Merger Movements in American Industry, 1895–1956* (Princeton, 1959), pp. 104, 129–31. In the case of the U.S. Nelson concludes that merger movements tended to occur when the growth of the general economy, especially the growth industries of high merger activity was characterized by acceleration rather than retardation.

[70] *Ibid.* pp. 133–34.

[71] It would be interesting to investigate the relationship between the capital markets and industrial concentration in the rest of the world. In the case of Germany, for example, it appears that the connection was even more direct. With few established financial institutions, the "D" banks were responsible for a large proportion of the total capital mobilized for industry. This central control of finance soon produced central control of pricing and output decisions and the cartelized market structure that we know today. Given the much shorter industrial history and more primitive financial institution it was impossible to compete without external finance. However, as some firms grew and began to generate their own finance, their dependence on the banks diminished and they occasionally defied bank-engendered policies. See J. H. Clapham, *Economic Development of France and Germany* (Cambridge, 1921). pp. 389–95 and 309–15.

[72] See G. W. Nutter, *The Extent of Enterprise Monopoly in the United States, 1899–1939: a Quantitative Study of Some Aspects of Monopoly*, Chicago, 1951, and M. Adelman, "The Measurement of Industrial Concentration," *Review of Economics and Statistics*, November, 1951.

department prosecution). On the other hand, if one subscribed to the financial thesis one would expect the opposite (since with the improvement of the capital markets the financial incentive—strongest among small firms—would be reduced). The evidence indicates that, since World War I, the proportion of small mergers has declined while that of giant mergers has increased.[73]

In the U.K. the work on the more recent period, while not directly providing evidence on the financial thesis, does nothing to refute that hypothesis. Preis and Hart have shown that concentration in Great Britain increased over the period 1885–1939, but, since their data are derived from firms listed on the stock exchange, it is obvious that financial considerations were not of paramount importance for the firms studied.[74] Evesley and Little, in their analysis of increasing concentration in 14 industries, 1935–51, mention finances as a cause of concentration in only 5, and they give it first importance in only one (wrought iron and steel tubes). (As a comment on the relative development of the capital markets in the 20th century, it is interesting to note that, in two of the five cases, the mergers provided access to American finance.)[75] Moreover, better finances do not appear to have been the explanation for the decline in concentration in any of the industries that were studied.[76]

Conclusions

It appears, therefore, that the difficulties inherent in acquiring external finance in the United States in the 19th century provide an explanation for the basis of the fortunes of certain American entrepreneurs and suggest at least one reason why that economy was characterized by increasing concentration in the growth sectors. In the case of the U.K., on the other hand, adequate financial markets appear to have yielded much smaller returns to financial manipulation, and firms without good financial contacts were much less heavily penalized in the search for funds for expansion. As a result, concentration when it did occur tended more to reflect product rather than financial market considerations.

---

[73] Nelson, *Merger Movement,* pp. 53–64.

[74] P. Hart and S. Preis, "The Analysis of Business Concentration: A Statistical Approach," *Journal of the Royal Statistical Society,* Vol. 119 (1956), pp. 150–81.

[75] R. Evesley and I. Little, *Concentration in British Industry* (Cambridge, 1960), pp. 193–264.

[76] *Ibid.,* pp. 265–92.

INDEX

Index

This book has been set in 10 and 9 point Caledonia, leaded 2 points. Part and reading numbers and titles are set in 18 point Craw Clarendon Book. The size of the type page is 27 x 46 1/2 picas.

DATE DUE